Norway

written and researched by

Phil Lee

with additional research by

Jules Brown, Anette Slettbakk and

Emma Rose Rees

ROUGH
GUIDES

www.roughguides.com

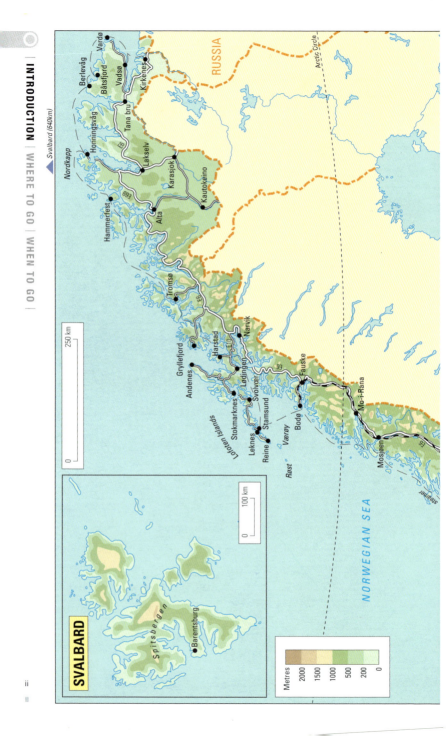

SVALBARD

Spitsbergen

Barentsburg

Metres
2000
1500
1000
500
200
0

RUSSIA

Arctic Circle

Nordkapp

Svalbard (640km)

Vardø
Berlevåg
Båtsfjord
Vadsø
Kirkenes
Honningsvåg
Tana bru
Lakselv
Karasjok
Alta
Kautokeino
Hammerfest

Tromsø

Gryllefjord
Harstad
Narvik
Andenes
Lødingen
Stokmarknes
Svolvær
Lofoten Islands
Leknes
Stamsund
Reine
Bodø
Værøy
Røst
Fauske
Mo-i-Rana
Mosjøen

NORWEGIAN SEA

250 km
0

100 km
0

ii

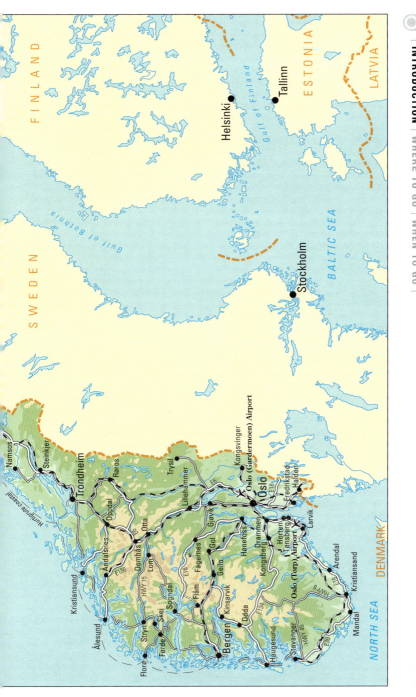

Introduction to

Norway

In a tamed and heavily populated continent, Norway remains a wilderness outpost. Everything here is on a grand scale, with some of Europe's finest and wildest land- and seascapes. From the Skagerrak – the choppy channel that separates the country from Denmark – Norway stretches north in a long, slender band along the Atlantic seaboard, up across the Arctic Circle to the Barents Sea and the Russian border. Behind this rough and rocky coast are great mountain ranges, harsh upland plateaux, plunging river valleys, rippling glaciers, deep forests and, most famously, the mighty fjords which gash deep inland.

The **fjords** are the apple of the tourist industry's eye, and they are indeed magnificent, but except for the lively capital, Oslo, and perhaps historic Bergen, the rest of the country might as well be blank for all that many visitors know. Few seem aware of the sheer variety of the landscape or the lovely little towns that are sprinkled over it. Neither are the Norwegians given nearly enough credit for their careful construction of one of the most civilized, educated and **tolerant societies** in the world – one whose even-handed internationalism has set standards that few other European nations can approach.

Fact file

● Norway is one of the five **Nordic nations**, along with Denmark, Sweden, Finland and Iceland. It is bordered to the east by Sweden, Finland and Russia, but otherwise is flanked by the sea – the Atlantic to the west, the Barents Sea to the north and the Skagerrak, which leads off the North Sea, to the south. Extremely long and thin, Norway has a surface area of 386,000 square kilometres, of which half is mountain and a further third forest, lake and river.

● The country's **population** numbers about 4.5 million, of which more than ten percent (half a million) live in the capital, Oslo. Norway's second city, Bergen, clocks up about 240,000 residents, while around 30,000 indigenous Sami (Lapps) live mostly in the north of the country.

● Norway is a **constitutional monarchy** and the present king, Harald V, came to the throne in 1991. The parliament – the *Storting* – sits in Oslo, but many functions are devolved to a complex network of local authorities. The Lutheran **Church of Norway** is the official state church and over eighty percent of the population belong to it, however nominally. Norway is not a member of the EU, but has signed up to the EEA (European Economic Agreement) free-trade deal.

● The **economy** of Norway is highly dependent on the oil industry, with crude oil accounting for forty percent of the country's total exports. Natural gas, metals and fish products come a distant second, at about eight percent each.

With every justification, the bulk of the population have a deep loyalty for – and pride in – their country, partly at least because independence was so long in coming: after the heady days of the Vikings, Norway was governed by the Danes for four centuries and was then passed to the Swedes, who only left in 1905.

It is the **Vikings** who continue to grab the historical headlines, prompting book after book and film upon (foreign) film. These formidable warriors burst upon an unsuspecting Europe from the remoteness of Scandinavia in the ninth century. The Norwegian Vikings sailed west, raiding every seaboard from the Shetlands to Sicily, even venturing as far as Greenland and Newfoundland. Wherever they settled, the speed of their assimilation into the indigenous population was extraordinary – William the Conqueror, the archetypal Norman baron, was only a few generations removed from his Viking ancestors – and in the unpopulated Faroes and Iceland, the settlers could begin from scratch, creating societies which then developed in a similar fashion to that of their original homeland.

Norway's so-called "period of greatness" came to an abrupt end: in 1349, an English ship unwittingly brought the **Black Death** to the country, and in the next two years somewhere between half and two-thirds of the population was wiped out. The enfeebled country was easy meat for the **Danes**, who took control at the end of the fourteenth century and remained in command until 1814. As colonial powers go, the Danes were comparatively benign, but everything specifically "Norwegian" – from language to dress – became associated

The Puffin (Fratercula arctica)

Some 30cm tall, with a triangular, red, blue and yellow striped bill, the puffin is perhaps the most distinctive of the many seabirds that congregate along the Norwegian coast. It feeds on small fish, and breeds in holes it excavates in turf on cliffs or grassy flatlands, sometimes even adapting former rabbit burrows. Hunting, puffins use their wings to propel themselves underwater and, indeed, are much better at swimming than flying, finding it difficult both to get airborne and to land – collisions of one sort or another are commonplace. Their nesting habits and repetitive flight paths make them easy to catch, and puffin has long been a West Coast delicacy, though hunting them is now severely restricted. In the summer, puffins nest along the whole of the Atlantic coast from Stavanger to Nordkapp, with Værøy (see p.311) and Runde (see p.246) being the most likely places for a sighting. In the autumn the puffins move south, though residual winter populations remain on the southerly part of the west coast between Stavanger and Ålesund.

Roald Amundsen

One of Norway's best known sons, Roald Amundsen (1872–1928) had been intent on becoming a polar explorer since his early teens. He read everything there was to read on the subject, even training as a sea captain in preparation and, in 1897, embarked upon his first trip to Antarctica, with a Belgian expedition. Undeterred by a winter on the ice after the ship broke up, he was soon planning his own expedition, the first ever crossing of the Northwest Passage, from the Atlantic to the Pacific round the north of the American continent. He left in the *Gjøa* in June 1903 and finally reached Alaskan waters three years later.

His next target was the North Pole, but during his preparations, in 1909, the American Robert Peary got there first. Amundsen immediately switched his attention to the South Pole, which he reached on December 14, 1911, famously beating the British expedition of Captain Scott. Amundsen kept going, keen to become the first man to fly over the North Pole. He succeeded in 1926 in the airship of the Italian Umberto Nobile, but two years later he flew north out of Tromsø in a bid to rescue a stranded Nobile and was never seen again.

with the primitive and uncouth. To redress this state of affairs, Norway's bourgeois nationalists of the mid- to late nineteenth century sought to rediscover – and sometimes to reinvent – a national identity. This ambitious enterprise, enthusiastically undertaken, fuelled a cultural renaissance which formed the backdrop to the work of acclaimed painters, writers and musicians, most notably Munch, Ibsen and Grieg, and the endeavours of explorers like Amundsen and Nansen. Its reverberations can be felt to this day, for example in Norway's "No" vote on EU membership.

Where to go

Norway is one of Europe's most sparsely inhabited countries, and for the most part its people live in small towns and villages. Almost inevitably, the country's five largest cities are the obvious initial targets for a visit, beginning with urbane, vivacious **Oslo**, one of the world's most prettily sited capitals, with a flourishing café scene and a clutch of outstanding museums. Beyond Oslo, in roughly descending order of interest, are **Trondheim**, with its superb cathedral and charming, antique centre; the beguiling port of **Bergen**, gateway to the western fjords; gritty, bustling **Stavanger** in the southwest; and northern **Tromsø**. All are likeable, walkable cities worthy of your time in themselves, as well as being within comfortable reach of

some startlingly handsome scenery. Indeed, each can serve as either a base or a starting point for further explorations: the trains, buses and ferries of Norway's finely tuned public transport system will take you almost anywhere you want to go, although services are curtailed in winter.

Outside of the cities, the perennial draw remains the **western fjords** – a must, and every bit as scenically stunning as the publicity suggests. Dip into the region from Bergen or Åndalsnes, both accessible by direct train from Oslo, or take more time to appreciate the subtle charms of the tiny, fjordside villages, among which **Balestrand** and **Mundal** are especially appealing. This is great hiking country too, with a network of cairned trails and lodges (maintained by the nationwide hiking association DNT) threading along the valleys and over the hills. However, many of the country's finest hikes are to be had further inland, within the confines of a

trio of marvellous **national parks**: the **Hardangervidda**, a vast mountain plateau of lunar-like appearance; the **Rondane**, with its bulging mountains; and the **Jotunheimen**, famous for its jagged peaks. Of these three, the first is most easily approached from Finse, Rjukan or Kinsarvik, the others from the comely town of Otta. Nudging the Skagerrak, the south coast is different again. This island-strewn shoreline is best appreciated from the sea, though its pretty, old white-washed ports are popular with holidaying Norwegians; the pick of these towns are **Arendal** and **Mandal**, the proud possessor of the country's finest sandy beach.

Away to the **north**, beyond Trondheim, Norway grows increasingly wild and inhospitable as it sprawls across the Arctic Circle on the way to the modern, workaday port of **Bodø**. From here, ferries shuttle over to the rugged **Lofoten** islands, which boast some of the most ravishing scenery in the whole of Europe – tiny fishing villages of ochre- and

Outside of the cities, the perennial draw remains the western fjords – every bit as scenically stunning as the publicity suggests

red-painted houses tucked in between the swell of the deep blue sea and the severest of grey-green mountains. Back on the mainland, it's a long haul north from Bodø to the iron-ore town of **Narvik**, and on to **Tromsø**. These towns are, however, mere urban pinpricks in a vast wilderness that extends up to **Nordkapp** (North Cape), the northernmost accessible point of mainland Europe, and the spot where the tourist trail peters out. But Norway continues east for several hundred kilometres, round to remote **Kirkenes** near the Russian border, while inland stretches an immense and hostile upland plateau, the **Finnmarksvidda**, one of the last haunts of the Sami (formerly Lapp) reindeer-herders.

When to go

Choosing when to go to Norway is more complicated than you might expect. The **summer season** – when the midnight sun is visible north of the Arctic Circle – is relatively short,

Stokfisk and klippfisk

The Vikings were able to sail long distances without starving because they had learnt how to dry white fish, mostly cod, in the open air. This dried fish, stokfisk, remained edible for years and was eaten either raw or after soaking in water – chewy and smelly no doubt, but very nutritious. In time, stokfisk became the staple diet of western Norway and remained so until the early twentieth century, with every fishing port festooned with wooden A-frames carrying hundreds of drying white fish, headless and paired for size.

It wasn't until the 1690s that the Dutch introduced to Norway the idea of salting and drying white fish, again usually cod. The fish was decapitated, cleaned and split before being heavily salted and left for several weeks. Then it was dried for a further four to six weeks, by being left outside on rocky drying grounds, klipper in Norwegian, hence klippfisk. The Norwegians never really took to eating klippfisk, but they (or rather their merchants) made fortunes by exporting it to Spain, Portugal, Africa and the Caribbean, where salted cod remains extremely popular to this day.

stretching roughly from the beginning of June to the end of August. Visit out of season, and you'll find that tourist offices, museums and other sights have reduced hours, hotels withdraw their generous summer discounts, and buses, ferries and trains run on less frequent schedules. Nevertheless, late May does have its attractions, especially if your visit coincides with the brief Norwegian **spring**, though this is difficult to gauge. Springtime is especially beguiling in the fjords, with myriad cascading waterfalls fed by the melting snow, and wildflowers in abundance. Come before that – from late March to early May – and you're likely to encounter the unprepossessing residue of winter, when the last snow and ice lies soiled on the ground, asphalt dust from studded tyres pollutes the city air and the landscape is blankly colourless. **Autumn** is a much better bet, with September often bathed in the soft sunshine of an Indian summer. There are also advantages to travelling during the **winter**, providing you steer

Between November and February there's an above average chance of seeing the phenomenal northern lights (Aurora Borealis) beyond the Arctic Circle

NORWAY: DISTANCE CHART (Distance in kilometres)

	Bergen	Bodø	Hamar	Hammerfest	Kirkenes	Kristiansand	Lillehammer	Narvik	Nordkapp	Oslo	Røros	Stavanger	Tromsø	Trondheim	Ålesund
Bergen	0	1380	471	2214	2588	492	439	1561	2283	478	637	170	1844	657	378
Bodø	1380	0	1108	956	1331	1534	1065	304	1025	1217	936	1560	562	723	1010
Hamar	471	1108	0	1942	2316	443	59	1279	2011	123	289	575	1606	385	441
Hammerfest	2214	956	1942	0	494	2368	1899	652	181	2051	1810	2394	549	1567	1844
Kirkenes	2588	1331	2316	494	0	2742	2273	1027	517	2425	2185	2768	944	1931	2218
Kristiansand	492	1534	443	2368	2742	0	471	1715	2437	320	753	245	2054	811	811
Lillehammer	439	1065	59	1899	2273	471	0	1246	1968	167	282	587	1562	342	382
Narvik	1561	304	1279	652	1027	1715	1246	0	721	1398	1123	1741	251	904	1191
Nordkapp	2283	1025	2011	181	517	2437	1968	721	0	2120	1869	2463	609	1626	1913
Oslo	478	1217	123	2051	2425	320	167	1398	2120	0	423	452	1733	494	533
Røros	637	936	289	1810	2185	753	282	1123	1869	423	0	740	1352	166	430
Stavanger	170	1560	575	2394	2768	245	587	1741	2463	452	740	0	1852	837	621
Tromsø	1844	562	1606	549	944	2054	1562	251	609	1733	1352	1852	0	1205	1519
Trondheim	657	723	385	1567	1931	811	342	904	1626	494	166	837	1205	0	287
Ålesund	378	1010	441	1844	2218	811	382	1191	1913	533	430	621	1519	287	0

Ferry crossings not included in distances quoted.

xiii

Average daytime temperatures (°C) and rainfall

	Oslo		Bergen		Trondheim		Tromsø	
	°C	mm	°C	mm	°C	mm	°C	mm
January	-3.7	49	1.5	190	-3.3	63	-4.7	95
February	-2.8	36	1.6	152	-1.8	52	-4.1	87
March	1.3	47	3.3	170	1.9	54	-1.9	72
April	6.3	41	5.9	114	5.4	49	1.1	64
May	12.6	53	10.5	106	10.9	53	5.6	48
June	17.0	65	13.5	132	13.8	68	10.1	59
July	18.2	81	14.5	148	15.1	84	12.7	77
August	17.2	89	14.4	190	14.8	87	11.8	82
September	12.8	90	11.5	283	11.2	113	7.7	102
October	7.5	84	8.7	271	7.0	104	2.9	131
November	1.5	73	4.6	259	1.1	71	-1.5	108
December	-2.6	55	1.6	235	-1.8	84	-3.7	106

well clear of the winter solstice, when the lack of light depresses even the Norwegians, and aim instead for early February up to mid-March. The big incentive to visit at this time of year is the range of **winter sports** – from ice-fishing to dog-sledging and, most popular of all, cross-country and alpine skiing. There are skiing packages to Norway from abroad, but perhaps more appealing – and certainly cheaper – is the ease with which you can arrange a few days' skiing wherever you happen to be.

Furthermore, if you are equipped and hardy enough to reach the far north, between November and February there's an above average chance of seeing the phenomenal **northern lights** (Aurora Borealis) beyond the Arctic Circle, and a possibility of glimpsing them as far south as Oslo, too.

As regards **climate**, the Gulf Stream keeps all of coastal Norway temperate throughout the year, with the warmest months being July and August. Inland, the climate is more extreme – bitterly cold in winter and hot in summer, when temperatures can soar to surprising heights. January and February are normally the coldest months in all regions. Rain is a regular occurrence throughout the year, particularly on the west coast, though there are significant local variations in precipitation.

things not to miss

It's not possible to see everything that Norway has to offer in one trip – and we don't suggest you try. What follows is a selective taste of the country's highlights: outstanding scenery, picturesque villages and dramatic wildlife. They're arranged in five colour-coded categories, which you can browse through to find the very best things to see and experience. All highlights have a page reference to take you straight into the guide, where you can find out more.

 Wildlife safaris Page **352** • The bearded seal is just one of the many species of wildlife that live in the icy wastes of Svalbard.

02 **The Flåmsbana** Page **216** • A trip on the Flåm railway is one of the most dramatic train rides in the world.

03 **The Scream** Page **99**
Munch's most famous painting is on display at the Munch Museum in Oslo.

04 **The Oseberg ship**
Page **92** • This superbly preserved Viking longboat can be seen at Oslo's Vikingskipshuset (Viking Ships Museum).

05 **Bergen** Page **187** • The best views of this handsome city are from the Ulriksbanen cable car.

06 **Mandal** Page **137** • This pretty south coast resort boasts the country's finest sandy beach.

07 **Svalbard archipelago** Page **350** • Glaciers cover two-thirds of the surface of Norway's wild and remote Svalbard archipelago, which enjoys continuous daylight from April to August.

08 **Kjerringøy** Page **283** • A tour round this well-preserved trading station gives an insight into the hardships of nineteenth-century life in a remote Arctic outpost.

09 **Ålesund** Page **243** • The small west coast fishing port boasts a host of Art Nouveau buildings with peculiarly Norwegian flourishes.

10 **Henningsvær** Page **306** One of the Lofotens' most picturesque fishing villages, whose traditional wooden houses line a picture-postcard harbour.

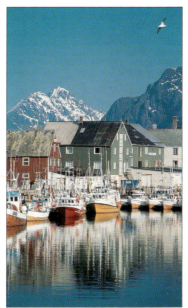

11 **Hørundfjord** Page **237** • A wild and remote fjord, whose deep, dark waters make one of Norway's most dramatic sights.

12 **Union Hotel, Øye** Page **237** Splash out on a stay in one of the fjordland's most original hotels. Sited in the remote village of Øye, it offers charming views over the Norangsfjord.

13 **The Oslofjord** Page **115** The islands of the Oslofjord – Hovedøya and Langøyene – are great for swimming, sunbathing and walking, and lie just a short ferry ride from the city centre.

14 **Vigelandsparken** Page **95**
This beautiful park near Oslo is
home to a huge collection of Gustav
Vigeland's fantastical sculptures.

15 **The Norsk Fiskevaersmuseum**
Page **310** • Much of the attractive nineteenth-century fishing village of Å has been
preserved as the Norwegian Fishing Village
Museum.

16 **Geirangerfjord** Page **235** • Tiny Geirangerfjord is one of the region's most
beautiful fjords.

17 **Walking in the Jotunheimen mountains** Page **166** • Norway's most celebrated hiking area, the Jotunheimen national park is criss-crossed with trails and includes Northern Europe's two highest peaks.

18 **Whalewatching** Page **296** Take a whale-watching safari from Andenes between late May and mid-September, and you're virtually assured of a sighting.

19 **Trondheim cathedral** Page **262** • Scandinavia's largest medieval building.

21 Urnes stave church
Page **226** • Norway's oldest stave church boasts some exquisite examples of Viking carving.

20 The Josteldalsbreen glacier
Page **227** • Take a guided walk out onto this mighty 500-square-kilometre ice plateau.

22 Troldhaugen
Page **199** • The lakeside home of Norway's most famous composer, Edvard Grieg, has been preserved pretty much as he left it.

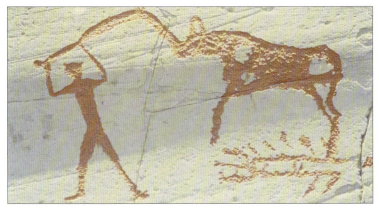

23 **Alta rock carvings** Page **328** • Take a stroll round northern Europe's most extensive collection of prehistoric rock carvings.

24 **The midnight sun at Nordkapp** Page **342** • At this northerly outpost daylight lasts without interruption from early May to the end of July.

25 **Seabird colonies on Værøy** Page **311** • This remote Lofoten island is renowned for its birdlife, including puffins, cormorants, kittiwakes, guillemots and rare sea eagles.

Contents

Using this Rough Guide

We've tried to make this Rough Guide a good read and easy to use. The book is divided into five main sections, and you should be able to find whatever you want in one of them.

Colour section

The front colour section offers a quick tour of Norway. The **introduction** aims to give you a feel for the place, with suggestions on where to go. We also tell you what the weather is like and include a basic country fact file. Next, our authors round up their favourite aspects of Norway in the **things not to miss** section – whether it's great food, amazing sights or a special hotel. Right after this comes a full **contents** list.

Basics

The Basics section covers all the **pre-departure** nitty-gritty to help you plan your trip. This is where to find out which airlines fly to your destination, what paperwork you'll need, what to do about money and insurance, about Internet access, food, security, public transport, car rental – just about every piece of **general practical information** you'll need.

Guide

This is the heart of the Rough Guide, divided into user-friendly chapters, each of which covers a specific region. Every chapter starts with a list of **highlights** and an **introduction** that helps you to decide where to go, depending on your time and budget. Likewise, introductions to the various towns and smaller regions within each chapter should help you plan your itinerary. We start most town accounts with information on arrival and accommodation, followed by a tour of the sights, and finally reviews of places to eat and drink, and details of nightlife. Longer accounts also have a directory of practical listings. Each chapter concludes with **public transport** details for that region.

Contexts

Read Contexts to get a deeper understanding of what makes Norway tick. We include a brief **history** of the country, as well as articles on everything from **Norse mythology** to **flora and fauna**, and Norwegian **cinema**. In addition, there are three extracts of seminal Norwegian **literature**, and a detailed further reading section.

Language

The **language** section gives useful guidance for speaking Norwegian and pulls together all the vocabulary you might need on your trip, including a comprehensive menu reader. Here you'll also find a glossary of words and terms peculiar to the country.

Index + small print

Apart from a **full index**, which includes maps as well as places, this section covers publishing information, credits and acknowledgements, and also has our contact details in case you want to send in updates and corrections to the book.

Map and chapter list

3

Contents

Contexts

355–415

Language

417–425

CONTENTS

map symbols

maps are listed in the full index using coloured text

Major highways	▲	Mountain peak
Major road	♜	Castle
Minor road	♙	Lodge
Tunnel	⊙	Statue
Pedestrianized streets	ⓘ	Tourist office
Path	⊠	Post office
Railway	©	Telephone
Cable car	@	Internet access
Ferry route	◉	Accommodation
Waterway	▣	Restaurant
Chapter division boundary	🅿	Parking
International boundary	★	Bus stop
County boundary		Building
General point of interest	➕	Church (town maps)
Ruins	✝+✝	Cemetery
Airport		Park
Tram line		Forest
T-Bane (underground)		Sand/beach
Church (regional maps)		Glacier

7

Basics

Basics

✈ Getting there

From the UK and Ireland, the most convenient way of getting to Norway is to fly – there's a good selection of flights and the cheapest fares are often less expensive than the long and arduous journey by train or coach. There are a couple of ferries from Newcastle in England to Norway, but these can be pretty costly in high season and are really only worth considering if you're taking your car. Although only SAS flies direct from North America, a handful of airlines fly to the other Scandinavian capitals, though it may be cheaper to route via London, picking up a budget flight onwards from there. There are no direct flights from Canada, Australia or New Zealand.

Airfares depend on the season, with the highest from (roughly) early June to mid-September, when the weather is best; fares drop during the "shoulder" seasons – mid-September to early November and mid-April to early June – and you'll get the best prices during the low season, November through to April (excluding Christmas and New Year, when prices are hiked up and seats are at a premium). Bear in mind, though, that ticket prices from the UK are not subject to seasonal changes to the extent that they are in North America. Note also that flying on weekends is generally more expensive; price ranges quoted below assume midweek travel.

You can often cut costs by going through a **specialist flight agent** – either a consolidator, who buys up blocks of tickets from the airlines and sells them at a reduced price, or a **discount agent**, who in addition to dealing with discounted flights may also offer special student and youth fares and a range of other travel-related services such as insurance, rail passes, car rentals, tours and the like. Note, however, that penalties for changing your plans on discounted tickets can be stiff. Some agents specialize in **charter flights**, which may be cheaper than scheduled services, but again departure dates are fixed and withdrawal penalties are high. Don't automatically assume that tickets purchased through a travel specialist will be cheapest – once you get a quote, check with the airlines and you may turn up an even better deal.

Students might be able to find cheaper flights through the major student travel agencies, such as Council Travel, STA Travel or,

for Canadian students, Travel CUTS (see relevant sections for details).

If you are travelling to Norway as part of a longer trip, consider buying a **round-the-world** (RTW) ticket. However, since Scandinavia is not one of the more obvious destinations for round-the-world travellers, you'll probably have to have a custom-made RTW ticket assembled for you by an agent, which is more expensive than an off-the-shelf RTW ticket.

Buying an **air pass** in conjunction with your air ticket can also reduce costs, if you are planning to travel a lot around Scandinavia. For full details on the different types of air pass available, see p.36.

Booking flights online

Many airlines and travel websites offer you the opportunity to **book tickets online**, cutting out the costs of agents and middlemen. Good deals can often be found through discount or auction sites, as well as through the airlines' own websites.

Online booking agents and general travel sites

ⓦ **www.cheapflights.com** Bookings from the UK and Ireland only. Flight deals, travel agents, plus links to other travel sites.

ⓦ **www.cheaptickets.com** Discount flight specialists.

ⓦ **www.etn.nl/discount.htm** A hub of consolidator and discount agent web links, maintained by the nonprofit European Travel Network.

Ⓦ **www.expedia.com** Discount airfares, all-airline search engine and daily deals.

Ⓦ **www.flyaow.com** Online air travel information and reservations site.

Ⓦ **www.gaytravel.com** Gay online travel agent, concentrating mostly on accommodation.

Ⓦ **www.hotwire.com** Bookings from the US only. Last-minute savings of up to forty percent on regular published fares. Travellers must be at least 18 and there are no refunds, transfers or changes allowed. Log-in required.

Ⓦ **www.lastminute.com** Offers good last-minute holiday package and flight-only deals.

Ⓦ **www.priceline.com** Name-your-own-price website that offers deals at around forty percent off standard fares. You cannot specify flight times (although you do specify dates) and the tickets are non-refundable, non-transferable and non-changeable.

Ⓦ **www.skyauction.com** Bookings from the US only. Auctions tickets and travel packages using a "second bid" scheme. The best strategy is to bid the maximum you're willing to pay, since if you win you'll pay just enough to beat the runner-up regardless of your maximum bid.

Ⓦ **www.skydeals.co.uk** Discount flight-only specialists for worldwide destinations.

Ⓦ **www.smilinjack.com/airlines.htm** Lists an up-to-date compilation of airline website addresses.

Ⓦ **www.travelocity.com** Destination guides, hot web fares and best deals for car hire, accommodation and lodging as well as fares. Provides access to the travel agent system SABRE, the most comprehensive central reservations system in the US.

Ⓦ **www.travel.com.au** Comprehensive online travel company for travel from Australia and New Zealand.

Ⓦ **www.travelshop.com.au** Australian website offering discounted flights, packages, insurance, online bookings.

Ⓦ **travel.yahoo.com** Incorporates a lot of Rough Guide material in its coverage of destination countries and cities across the world, with information about places to eat, sleep etc.

Flights from Britain

There's a good choice of direct flights **from London to Oslo**'s Gardermoen airport with SAS, British Airways and British Midland. SAS also flies from Heathrow to **Stavanger** and **Bergen**, whilst the Danish airline Maersk has six flights a week from London Gatwick to **Kristiansand**, via Copenhagen. There's a reasonable selection of flights from **regional** airports too. Ryanair flies from **Stansted** and **Glasgow** (Prestwick) to Oslo (Torp) airport, an inconvenient 110km from Oslo; SAS flies to Stavanger from **Aberdeen** and **Newcastle**; British Airways operates daily direct flights from Manchester to Oslo; and SAS flies between **Manchester** and Oslo via Copenhagen. When no direct flights are available, SAS, British Midland and BA can often get you to Oslo via another European city, usually Copenhagen and sometimes Amsterdam, at surprisingly reasonable prices.

Provoked by the popularity of the budget airlines, such as Ryanair, the likes of SAS and BA are offering all sorts of special deals at bargain prices. SAS, for instance, have "Rock Bottom" and (slightly more expensive) "Super Saver" tickets, which can sometimes bring their fares low enough to compete with the budget airlines. In addition, SAS offers discounted fares for under-26s and over-65s, though these do tend to carry restrictions: they usually have to be booked at least seven days in advance, you must stay abroad at least one Saturday night, and you can't change your return flight date.

The best starting point to find what is on offer is the **internet**. Airline websites give up-to-the-minute information about timetables, fares and special offers, while various other travel sites will signpost you to the booking agent or airline offering the lowest current prices (see p.13). Failing that, go straight to a **discount flight agent** such as STA Travel (see p.13), who specializes in youth flights, and generally has good deals if you're under 26 or a student, as well as ordinary discounted tickets if you're not.

Special offers and discounted tickets apart, the **scheduled fares** of the three main carriers, SAS, British Midland and BA, are pretty well matched and as such budget airline Ryanair usually manages to undercut them all. The cheapest **fares** at present start at around £70 return from Stansted to Oslo (Torp) with Ryanair. Expect to spend around £130 inclusive of taxes from London to Oslo on most other carriers, and to pay a few pounds more if flying from regional airports. As ever, you'll often need to book well in advance and have flexible arrangements to take advantage of the cheapest fares.

Flight times range from one hour on the Aberdeen–Stavanger flight to about two hours fifteen minutes from London to Oslo.

Airlines in Britain

Braathens ⓦ www.braathens.no. A subsidiary of SAS with a wide network of domestic Norwegian destinations, but currently, no international flights.

British Airways ☎ 0845/773 3377, ⓦ www.ba.com. London Heathrow and Gatwick to Copenhagen, Oslo, Stavanger; Manchester to Oslo; Newcastle to Copenhagen.

British Midland ☎ 0870/607 0555, ⓦ www.flybmi.com. London Heathrow to Oslo, Stavanger and Copenhagen; Glasgow to Copenhagen.

easyJet ☎ 0870/600 0000, ⓦ www.easyjet.com. Online and telephone booking only. Two to three flights daily from London Stansted to Copenhagen.

KLM ☎ 0870/507 4074, ⓦ www.klmuk.com. London Heathrow, London City or Aberdeen to Copenhagen and Oslo, all via Amsterdam.

Maersk Air ☎ 020/7333 0066, ⓦ www .maersk-air.com. London Gatwick to Copenhagen and Kristiansand (via Copenhagen). Sister company, Maersk Air Ltd (☎ 0121/743 9090), flies from Birmingham to Copenhagen.

Ryanair ☎ 0871/246 0000, ⓦ www.ryanair.com. Daily flights from London Stansted to Oslo (Torp), 110km south of Oslo. Also Glasgow (Prestwick) to Oslo (Torp).

SAS Scandinavian Airlines ☎ 0845/607 2772, ⓦ www.scandinavian.net. London Heathrow direct to Copenhagen, Oslo, Stavanger and Bergen, with connections on to several other Scandinavian cities. Also Manchester to Copenhagen and Oslo (the latter via Copenhagen); Birmingham to Copenhagen; Aberdeen to Stavanger; Newcastle to Stavanger.

Flight and travel agents in Britain

Bridge the World ☎ 0870/444 7474, ⓦ www.bridgetheworld.com. Specializing in round-the-world tickets, with good deals aimed at the backpacker market.

Destination Group ☎ 020/7400 7045, ⓦ www.destination-group.com. Good discount airfares.

Flightbookers ☎ 0870/010 7000, ⓦ www.ebookers.com. Low fares on an extensive selection of scheduled flights.

North South Travel ☎ 01245/608 291, ⓦ www.northsouthtravel.co.uk. Friendly, competitive travel agency, offering discounted fares worldwide – profits are used to support projects in the developing world, especially the promotion of sustainable tourism.

STA Travel ☎ 0870/160 0599, ⓦ www

.statravel.co.uk. Worldwide specialists in low-cost flights and tours for students and under-26s, though other customers welcome.

Top Deck ☎ 020/7244 8000, ⓦ www.topdecktravel.co.uk. Long-established agent dealing in discount flights.

Trailfinders ☎ 020/7628 7628, ⓦ www.trailfinders.com. One of the best-informed and most efficient agents for independent travellers.

Travel Cuts ☎ 020/7255 2082 or 7255 1944, ⓦ www.travelcuts.co.uk. Canadian company specializing in budget, student and youth travel and round-the-world tickets.

Organized tours from Britain

As Norway is such an expensive part of Europe, an **inclusive package** can often be the cheapest way to do things, and may also be the only way to reach the remoter parts of the country at inhospitable times of year. If you just want to see one city and its environs, then **city breaks** invariably work out cheaper than arranging the same trip independently. Prices include return travel, usually by plane, and a range of accommodation (with breakfast) from hostel to luxury-class hotel. As a broad guide, two-night hotel stays in Oslo cost around £250–300 per person out of season. If you stay for a week, rates per night fall considerably.

There are also an increasing number of operators offering **special-interest holidays**, ranging from bird-watching and fjord camping trips to Arctic cruises and both midnight sun and northern lights viewing expeditions. Inevitably, prices vary enormously, largely depending on the quality of the accommodation and the type of activity.

Finally, the staggering beauty of the Norwegian coastline attracts **cruise ships** by the shoal. These holidays aren't cheap, starting at around £1800 per person on sailings from the UK, but in terms of comfort and luxury, you almost always get what you pay for. Routes vary considerably, some concentrating on the fjord coastline, others trawling up to the North Cape (Nordkapp), and yet more including Norway on a wider Baltic itinerary. Frequency also varies, with some cruises leaving weekly, but the more exotic weighing anchor only once or twice a year. We've detailed four cruise companies below, but any good travel agent will have the details of many more. The most celebrated Norwegian sea voyage is, however, the journey up the coast from Bergen to Kirkenes on the **Hurtigrute** coastal boast (see p.33).

Specialist agents and tour operators in Britain

Arctic Experience/Discover the World
℗01737/218 800, ⓦwww.discover-the-world.co.uk. Highly respected adventure tour operator. Specializes in cruises to the Arctic in ice-strengthened vessels, which are (quite) far removed from the luxury liners that patrol the fjords. Offers several different sorts of cruise to Svalbard. Every expedition has its own naturalist on board and the emphasis is firmly on nature and wildlife. Shore excursions are by zodiac boats.

Bridge Travel Service ℗ 0870/727 5786,
ⓦwww.scan-travel.co.uk. Large-scale tour operator offering a good range of holidays to Scandinavia and Norway in particular. Options include city breaks to Bergen, fjord fly-drives and escorted tours plus holidays to Tromsø for the northern lights and midnight sun.

Crystal Holidays ℗0870/160 6040,
ⓦwww.crystalholidays.co.uk. Self-drive and skiing holidays, plus city breaks in Bergen and Voss.

DA Study Tours ℗01383/882 200,
ⓦwww.datours.co.uk. Coach tours for culture vultures to Denmark, Norway and Sweden.

DFDS Seaways ℗0870/533 3000,
ⓦwww.dfdsseaways.co.uk. DFDS ferries sail from Newcastle to Kristiansand (see p.134) and offer a good range of holiday tie-ins at reasonable prices. They arrange accommodation in both hut/chalets and independently owned hotels across southern Norway and the western fjords. They also do camping holidays and city breaks to Kristiansand.

Headwater Holidays ℗01606/720 033,
ⓦwww.headwater-holidays.co.uk. Guided walking holidays in the Rondane national park in the summer, cross-country skiing on the Hardangervidda and in the Gudbrandsdal in winter. Canoeing and cycling holidays too.

Inntravel ℗01653/629 010,
ⓦwww.inntravel.co.uk. Outdoor holidays in Norway including skiing, walking, fjord cruises, and whale- and reindeer-watching.

Saddle Skedaddle ℗0191/265 1110,
ⓦwww.skedaddle.co.uk. Highly recommended company organizing a couple of cycling tours of Norway each year, usually one to the Lofoten islands and another round the western fjords.

Scantours ℗020/7839 2927,
ⓦwww.scantoursuk.com. Scandinavia specialists with a wide range of packages and tailor-made holidays. Options include tours of Lofoten, Svalbard and the fjords, plus a two-city break in Oslo and Bergen, along with the train ride in between. There are also a number of weekend and overnight trips to Tromsø to view either the midnight sun or the northern lights.

Specialised Tours ℗01342/712 785,
ⓦwww.specialisedtours.com. Specialists in Scandinavia offering independent, tailormade or group holidays mainly in the fjords and the far north, including Svalbard. Also city breaks in Tromsø, Bergen and Oslo.

Taber Holidays/Norway Only ℗01274/594 642, ⓦwww.taberhols.co.uk. Norwegian specialists with dozens of options, including self-catering holidays, fjord cruises, motoring tours and guided coach trips.

Thomson ℗0870/606 1470,
ⓦwww.thomsonlakesandmountains.co.uk. Big-name tour operator offering a small but reasonably priced range of Norwegian holidays from hiking in the fjords and city breaks in Bergen, through to fully escorted coach and boat tours.

Waymark Holidays ℗01753/516 477,
ⓦwww.waymarkholidays.co.uk. Cross-country skiing specialists concentrating on the mountains between Oslo and Bergen, in the south of Norway. Has a broad range of holidays to suit novice skiers and the experienced alike, as well as summer walking packages. Reckon on £600 per week for skiing, all-inclusive. Highly recommended.

Cruise companies in Britain

Fred Olsen Cruise Lines ℗01473/742 424,
ⓦwww.fredolsencruises.co.uk. Over a dozen Baltic and Norwegian cruises a year.

Norwegian Coastal Voyage ℗020/8846 2666,
ⓦwww.norwegiancoastalvoyage.com. UK agent for the Hurtigrute coastal boat. Extremely helpful and efficient.

Norwegian Cruise Line ℗ 0800/181 560,
ⓦwww.ncl.com. Among other sailings, this company operates a twelve-night Scandinavian capitals cruise and a fifteen-day, annual Path of the Vikings cruise. Also Nordkapp and fjord cruises.

P&O Cruises ℗0845/355 5333,
ⓦwww.pocruises.com). Two-week Norwegian coastal voyages, plus Arctic and Nordkapp cruises.

Flights from Ireland

The easiest route to Scandinavia from Ireland is on one of the twice daily SAS flights **from Dublin** to **Copenhagen** or **Stockholm**, from where you can fly onto Norway with ease. Through ticketing is commonplace, but SAS passengers can also take advantage of the Visit Scandinavia AirPass (see p.36). Official **fares** to Oslo start at around €228 plus tax for a midweek economy fare, although special offers are sometimes available, and a discount agent (see p.opposite) may have youth, student or discounted tickets for even less. Another good bet, which may work out even cheaper, is to fly from Ireland to Stansted and from Stansted to Oslo (Torp) with Ryanair. Ryanair has flights to Stansted from several Irish cities, Dublin, Knock, Shannon, Kerry, Cork and Londonderry. As a sample return fare, Dublin to Stansted with Ryanair should cost in the region of €65, then €149 from Stansted to Oslo (Torp).

From Belfast, there are no direct flights to Scandinavia, and your best bet is probably to fly via London or Dublin with British Midland or SAS. **Fares** to Oslo usually start at about £160 for an economy return, but special offers can take these as low as £120. Failing that, you should be able to get a reasonable deal through a discount agent, either in Northern Ireland or in mainland Britain.

Airlines in Ireland

Aer Lingus UK ☎0845/084 4444, Republic of Ireland ☎0818/365 000, ⓦwww.aerlingus.ie. Dublin to Copenhagen and Stockholm, via London Heathrow.
British Airways UK ☎0845/773 3377, Republic of Ireland ☎1800/626 747, ⓦwww.ba.com. Flights from Dublin and Cork to London for onward connections to Norway.
British Midland UK ☎0870/607 0555, Republic of Ireland ☎01/407 3036, ⓦwww.flybmi.com. Dublin to London or Manchester for onward connections to Norway.
Ryanair UK ☎0871/246 0000, Republic of Ireland ☎01/609 7800, ⓦwww.ryanair.com. Flights from Dublin, Shannon, Kerry, Cork, Knock and Londonderry to London Stansted, with onward flights to Oslo (Torp), 110km or so south of Oslo.
SAS Scandinavian Airlines UK ☎0845/607 2772, Republic of Ireland ☎01/844 5440, wwww.scandinavian.net. Direct flights from Dublin to Copenhagen and Stockholm. Onward flights to several cities in Norway, including Oslo and Trondheim.

Organized tours from Ireland

Not many operators run **package tours** to Scandinavia from Ireland, although where available these may be the cheapest way to travel, and sometimes the only way to reach remote parts of the region at inhospitable times of year. Likewise, city-break packages may well work out cheaper than arranging the same trip independently. British operators are listed on p.14, those based in Ireland are detailed below.

Travel agents and tour operators in Ireland

Co-op Travel Care Belfast ☎0870/902 0033, ⓦwww.travelcareonline.com. Flights and holidays to all parts of Scandinavia.
Crystal Holidays ☎01/433 1080. City breaks and skiing holidays.
Joe Walsh Tours Dublin ☎01/676 0991, ⓦwww.joewalshtours.ie. General budget fares agent.
McCarthy's Travel Cork ☎021/427 0127, ⓦwww.mccarthystravel.ie. General flight agent.
Premier Travel Derry ☎028/7126 3333, ⓦwww.premiertravel.uk.com. Discount flight specialists.
Rosetta Travel Belfast ☎028/9064 4996, ⓦwww.rosettatravel.com. General flight and holiday agent.
Student & Group Travel Dublin ☎01/677 7834. Student and group travel specialists.
Trailfinders Dublin ☎01/677 7888, ⓦwww.trailfinders.ie. One of the best-informed and most efficient agents for independent travellers; produces a very useful quarterly magazine worth scrutinizing for round-the-world routes.

Flights from the US and Canada

The only airline to fly non-stop **from North America** to Norway is SAS, which has daily flights from New York (Newark) to Oslo. There are, however, flights operated by both American and European carriers to the other Scandinavian countries, from where you can pick up swift onward connections to Norway. **Fares** to Copenhagen, Oslo and Stockholm are fairly similar, whichever carrier you choose, and if you can be fairly flexible with your departure dates you should be able to take advantage of the special promotional fares offered regularly by the airlines.

You may find it cheaper, however, to fly with one of the European carriers and **change planes** in a non-Scandinavian hub city. London is the obvious choice as it's one of the cheapest European cities to fly to and there are regular budget flights on to Norway from there (see p.12): alternatively, you could continue your journey by train (see p.20) or by ferry (see p.22). Other possible hub cities include Reykjavik, Brussels, Amsterdam, Paris, Frankfurt or Zurich. If you don't live in one of the gateway cities for flights in North America, however, this may involve changing planes more than once.

From New York you can fly non-stop to Oslo on SAS (7hr 30min), and to Stockholm, where you can pick up a connecting flight, on Delta; SAS also flies from **Washington DC** to Copenhagen. Round-trip fares from the East Coast are US$900–1000 in high season, and US$450–550 in low season. **From Chicago**, American Airlines flies direct to Stockholm (8hr 30min), while SAS flies to both Stockholm and Copenhagen. Round-trip fares are US$950–1100 in high season, US$450–500 in low. **From Seattle**, SAS flies direct to Copenhagen, but there are no direct flights **from Los Angeles** or **San Francisco** – your best bet is to change planes in New York, or one of the European hub cities. Round-trip fares from the West Coast are around US$1100–1300 (high season) and US$550–600 (low).

There are no non-stop flights **from Canada** to Norway; again, you'll need to change planes in New York, or one of the European hub cities. Flying time from Toronto is 9–13hr, and from Vancouver 13–18hr, depending on connections. Fares from Toronto or Montréal to Norway are CDN$1500–1650 (high season) and CDN$900–1200 (low). From Vancouver, fares are around CDN$1950 (high season) and CDN$1250 (low).

If you're thinking about travelling around Norway by plane, check out the **air passes** detailed on p.36.

Airlines in North America

Air Canada ☏ 1-888/247-2262, ⓦ www.aircanada.ca. Daily from Toronto (with connections from Vancouver) to Frankfurt and Zurich, and 5–7 weekly to Paris, with onward connections with SAS to Oslo and Trondheim.
Air France US ☏ 1-800/237-2747, ⓦ www.airfrance.com, Canada ☏ 1-800/667-2747, ⓦ www.airfrance.ca. Daily from many North American cities to Paris, with connecting flights to Oslo.
American Airlines ☏ 1-800/433-7300,

ⓦ www.aa.com. Daily from Chicago direct to Stockholm.
British Airways ☏ 1-800/247-9297, ⓦ www.british-airways.com. Daily flights from 22 North American cities to London, with onward connections to major Scandinavian cities.
British Midland ☏ 1-800/788-0555, ⓦ www.flybmi.com. Flights to London with onward connections to Oslo.
Continental Airlines domestic ☏ 1-800/523-3273, international ☏ 1-800/231-0856, ⓦ www.continental.com. Daily flights between various major North American cities and European cities with connections to Oslo.
Delta Air Lines domestic ☏ 1-800/221-1212, international ☏ 1-800/241-4141, ⓦ www.delta.com. Daily direct flights from New York (JFK) to Stockholm.
Icelandair ☏ 1-800/223-5500, ⓦ www.icelandair.com. Daily direct flights to Reykjavik from New York, Baltimore, Boston and Minneapolis plus two weekly from Orlando and Halifax, with onward connections to Oslo. Some flights allow a three-night stopover in Reykjavik.
Lufthansa US ☏ 1-800/645-3880, Canada ☏ 1-800/563-5954, ⓦ www.lufthansa-usa.com. Daily flights from major North American cities via Frankfurt to Scandinavia.
Northwest/KLM Airlines domestic ☏ 1-800/225-2525, international ☏ 1-800/447-4747, ⓦ www.nwa.com, ⓦ www.klm.com. Flights from major North American cities to Norway via Amsterdam.
SAS (Scandinavian Airlines) ☏ 1-800/221-2350, ⓦ www.scandinavian.net. Daily direct flights to Copenhagen, Stockholm and Oslo from New York (Newark); to Stockholm and Copenhagen from Chicago; to Copenhagen from Seattle and Washington DC.
Swiss ☏ 1-877/359-7947, ⓦ www.swiss.com. Daily to Zurich from Atlanta, Boston, Chicago, Cincinnati, Los Angeles, Miami, Newark, New York (JFK) and Montréal, with connections to Scandinavia.
Virgin Atlantic Airways ☏ 1-800/862-8621, ⓦ www.virgin-atlantic.com. Daily from various US cities to London, with onward connections to Scandinavia.

Discount travel companies in North America

Airtech ☏ 212/219-7000, ⓦ www.airtech.com. Standby seat broker; also deals in consolidator fares.
Airtreks.com ☏ 1-877-AIRTREKS or 415/912-5600, ⓦ www.airtreks.com. Specialists in round-the-world tickets. The website has an interactive database that lets you build and price your own round-the-world itinerary.

Council Travel ☏1-800/2COUNCIL, ⓦ www.counciltravel.com. Nationwide organization that mostly specializes in student/budget travel. Flights from the US only. Owned by STA Travel.

Educational Travel Center ☏1-800/747-5551 or 608/256-5551, ⓦ www.edtrav.com. Student/youth discount agent.

New Frontiers ☏1-800/677-0720 or 310/670-7318, ⓦ www.newfrontiers.com. French discount-travel firm based in New York City. Other branches in LA, San Francisco and Québec City.

Skylink US ☏1-800/247-6659 or 212/573-8980, Canada ☏1-800/759-5465, ⓦ www.skylinkus.com. Consolidator.

STA Travel ☏1-800/781-4040, ⓦ www.sta-travel.com. Worldwide specialists in independent travel; also student IDs, travel insurance, car rental, rail passes, etc.

Student Flights ☏1-800/255-8000 or 480/951-1177, ⓦ www.isecard.com. Student/youth fares, student IDs.

TFI Tours ☏1-800/745-8000 or 212/736-1140, ⓦ www.lowestairprice.com. Consolidator.

Travac ☏1-800/TRAV-800, ⓦ www.thetravelsite.com. Consolidator and charter broker with offices in New York and Orlando.

Travelers Advantage ☏1-877/259-2691, ⓦ www.travelersadvantage.com. Discount travel club; annual membership fee required (currently $1 for three months' trial).

Travel Cuts Canada ☏1-800/667-2887, US ☏1-866/246-9762, ⓦ www.travelcuts.com. Canadian student-travel organization.

Worldtek Travel ☏1-800/243-1723, ⓦ www.worldtek.com. Discount travel agency for worldwide travel.

Packages and organized tours from North America

There are a good number of companies operating **organized tours** of Norway, ranging from cruises to hiking holidays, and from dog-sledge rides to musk-ox safaris. Group tours can be expensive, and quoted prices occasionally do not include the air fare to Norway, so always check what you are getting. If your visit is centered on Oslo you could simply book a hotel-plus-flight package (which can work out cheaper than booking the two separately). Scanam and Passage Tours offer very reasonable weekend deals in the low season (see opposite and p.18). Tour reservations can usually be made either direct or through your local travel agent.

Tour operators and specialist agents in North America

Abercrombie and Kent ☏1-800/323-7308, ⓦ www.abercrombiekent.com. Upmarket company offering tailormade Scandinavian and Baltic coach tours and cruises.

Adventure Center ☏1-800/228-4747, ⓦ www.adventurecenter.com. Fifteen-day camping tour of Norway, Sweden and Finland from $800.

Adventures Abroad ☏1-800/665-3998, ⓦ www.adventures-abroad.com. Offers a variety of Scandinavian packages, specializing in small group tours.

Backroads ☏1-800/462-2848, ⓦ www.backroads.com. Has a six-day cycling holiday in the Vesterålen and Lofoten islands and a seven-day hiking tour of Norway's mountains, glaciers and fjords.

BCT Scenic Walking ☏1-800/473-1210, ⓦ www.bctwalk.com. Walking tours in Norway.

Borton Overseas ☏1-800/843-0602, ⓦ www.bortonoverseas.com. Company specializing in adventure vacations (hiking, rafting, birdwatching, dog-sledging, cross-country skiing, cycling) and farm and cabin stays throughout Norway. Agents for DNT (the Norwegian Mountain Touring Association; see p.51).

Brekke Tours ☏1-800/437-5302, ⓦ www.brekketours.com. A well-established company specializing in tours to Scandinavia with a host of sightseeing and cultural tours.

Contiki Tours ☏888 CONTIKI, ⓦ www.contiki.com. Tours of Scandinavia for 18- to 35-year-olds for around $1419 for 24 days. Campsite/cabin accommodation.

EuroCruises ☏1-800/688-3876, ⓦ www.eurocruises.com. Cruises of the Baltic Sea, the Norwegian fjords and the canals of Sweden.

Euroseven ☏1-800/890-3876, ⓦ www.euroseven.com. Hotel-plus-flight packages from New York, Baltimore or Boston to Scandinavia.

Loma Travel ☏1-888/665-9899. Canadian tour operator offering cheap flights, tours and cruises to Norway.

Nordic Saga Tours ☏1-800/848 6449, ⓦ www.nordicsaga.com. Packages, flights and information on air passes within Scandinavia.

Nordique Tours/Norvista ☏1-800/995-7997, ⓦ www.nordiquetours.com. A wide range of Scandinavian packages including "Scandinavian capitals", Lapland and the Norwegian fjords.

Norwegian Coastal Voyage ☏1-800/323-7436, ⓦ www.coastalvoyage.com. A mixture of escorted and independent cruises along the Norwegian coast on the Hurtigrute coastal boat (see p.35).

Passage Tours ☎1-800/548-5960, ⊛www.passagetours.com. Scandinavian specialist offering tours such as "The Northern Lights" and dog-sledging, ski packages and cheap weekend breaks.

Saga Holiday ☎1-800/343-0273, ⊛www.sagaholidays.com. Specialists in group travel for seniors, offering a cruise and coach tour of Sweden, Norway and Finland.

Scanam World Tours ☎1-800/545-2204, ⊛www.scanamtours.com. Scandinavian specialist with group and individual tours and cruises, plus cheap weekend breaks.

Scand-America Tours ☎1-800/886-8428 or 727/939-1505, ⊛www.scandamerica.com. Offers a wide variety of packages – everything from dog-sledging to garden tours – throughout Scandinavia.

Scanditours ☎1-800/432-4176, ⊛www.scanditours.com. Canadian Scandinavia specialist with wide range of travel options. Offices in Toronto and Vancouver.

Scantours ☎1-800/223-7226, ⊛www.scantours.com. Major Scandinavian holiday specialists offering vacation packages and customized itineraries, including cruises and city sightseeing tours.

Vantage Deluxe World Travel ☎1-800/322-6677, ⊛www.vantagetravel.com. Deluxe group tours and cruises in Scandinavia.

Flights from Australia and New Zealand

There are **no direct flights** from Australia or New Zealand to Norway, nor, indeed, to any other Scandinavian country. Instead you'll have to fly either via a European or an Asian gateway city, from where you can get a connecting flight, or continue your journey overland. Some of the airlines flying out of Australia and New Zealand can sell you a through-ticket, usually using SAS for the connecting services on to Norway. However, fares are pretty steep, so if you're on a tight budget it's worth flying to London (see "Flights from Britain", p.12), Amsterdam or Frankfurt first, and picking up a cheap flight from there. If you intend to take in a number of other European countries on your trip, it might be worth buying a Eurail pass before you go (see p.20).

Tickets purchased direct from the **airlines** tend to be expensive, with published fares ranging from A$2000/NZ$2500 (low season) to A$2500–3000/NZ$3000–3600 (high). Travel agents usually offer better rates on fares and have the latest information on spe-

cial deals, such as free stopovers en route and fly-drive-accommodation packages. Flight Centre and STA (see p.19 for details) generally offer the best discounts, especially for students and those under 26. For a discounted ticket to Norway from **Sydney**, **Melbourne** or **Auckland**, expect to pay A$1600/NZ$2000 (low season) and A$2500/NZ$2700 (high season). Fares from **Perth** and **Darwin** are slightly cheaper if you travel via Asia, rather more expensive if you go via Canada or the US. Fares from **Christchurch** and **Wellington** are around NZ$150–300 more than those from Auckland. Unless otherwise stated the fares we quote below are from East Coast cities in Australia and Auckland in New Zealand.

For a scheduled flight to Norway, count on paying fares of around A$1500/NZ$1900 (low season) up to A$2260/NZ$2800 (high season) on Alitalia or KLM; A$1900/NZ$2280 (low season) and A$2500/NZ$3000 (high) on SAS, Thai Airways and Lufthansa; and A$2400/NZ$2700 (low season) up to A$2850/NZ$3400 (high season) on British Airways, Qantas, Singapore Airlines, Air New Zealand and Canadian Airways. See the box on p.19 for a full rundown of airlines and routes.

Air passes which allow for discounted flights within Europe and Scandinavia, such as the SAS **Visit Scandinavia AirPass** (see p.36) and the British Airways/Qantas "One World Explorer", are available in conjunction with a flight to Scandinavia, and must be bought at the same time. Expect to pay around A$2400/NZ$2600 (low season) up to A$2850/NZ$3000 (high season). **Round-the-world** tickets that take in Scandinavia include the Star Alliance package (bookable through Ansett and Air New Zealand; around A$2800/NZ$3350), and the One World Alliance "Global Explorer" (bookable through Qantas; A$2400–2900/NZ$2900–3400).

There are very few agents specializing in **package trips** to Scandinavia. Your best bet is Bentours (see p.19 for details), who can put together a package for you, and is one of the few agents to offer skiing holidays in Norway. Alternatively, contact a European tour operator (see p.13).

If you're planning to travel a lot **by train**, or use trains to get to Norway from another European country, it's worth considering a train pass. **Eurail passes**, which come in numerous versions (see p.20 for a rundown) are available from most travel agents, or from branches of CIT (see below) or Bentours (see below). There is also a specific pass for Scandinavia, the **ScanRail** pass (further details on p.21), and another for Norway – the **Norway Rail Pass** (see p.33).

Airlines in Australia and New Zealand

Air New Zealand Australia ☎ 13 24 76, New Zealand ☎ 0800/737 000, ⓦ www.airnz.com. Daily flights from Auckland to London or Frankfurt via Los Angeles, then onward connections with SAS to Norway.

Alitalia Australia ☎ 02/9244 2445, New Zealand ☎ 09/308 3357, ⓦ www.alitalia.com. Six flights weekly from Sydney (with Ansett connections from other state capitals) to major Scandinavian cities, via Amsterdam or Milan.

British Airways Australia ☎ 02/8904 8800, New Zealand ☎ 0800/274 847 or 09/357 8950, ⓦ www.britishairways.com. Daily flights to London from Sydney, Perth or Brisbane with onward connections to Norway.

Cathay Pacific Australia ☎ 13 17 47 or 1300/653 077, New Zealand ☎ 09/379 0861 or 0508/800 454, ⓦ www.cathaypacific.com. Several flights weekly from Australia and New Zealand to Hong Kong, with onward connections to Scandinavia.

Lufthansa Australia ☎ 1300/655 727, ⓦ www.lufthansa-australia.com, New Zealand ☎ 09/303 1529, ⓦ www.lufthansa.com/ index_en.html. Daily flights to Norway from major cities via Bangkok or Singapore and Frankfurt.

Qantas Australia ☎ 13 13 13, ⓦ www.qantas .com.au, New Zealand ☎ 09/357 8900, ⓦ www.qantas.co.nz. Daily flights from state capitals via Asia or Europe to Norway.

Scandinavian Airlines (SAS) Australia ☎ 1300/727 707, New Zealand agent: Air New Zealand ☎ 09/357 3000, ⓦ www.scandinavian .net. No flights from Australia or New Zealand, but can organize connections to Norway via Bangkok, Beijing, Singapore or Tokyo.

Singapore Airlines Australia ☎ 13 10 11, New Zealand ☎ 09/303 2129, ⓦ www.singaporeair .com. Daily service from major Australian and New Zealand cities to Scandinavia via Singapore.

Flight and travel agents in Australia and New Zealand

Budget Travel New Zealand ☎ 0800/808 480, ⓦ www.budgettravel.co.nz. Discount flight specialist.

Flight Centre Australia ☎ 13 31 33 or 02/9235 3522, ⓦ www.flightcentre.com.au, New Zealand ☎ 0800/243 544 or 09/358 4310, ⓦ www. flightcentre.co.nz. One of the best discount flight specialists.

STA Travel Australia ☎ 1300/733 035, ⓦ www.statravel.com.au, New Zealand ☎ 0508/782 872, ⓦ www.statravel.co.nz. Worldwide specialists in low-cost flights and tours for students and under-26s, though other customers welcome. Also does rail passes.

Student Uni Travel Australia ☎ 02/9232 8444, New Zealand ☎ 09/300 8266, ⓦ www.sut.com.au. Specializes in low cost flights for students.

Thomas Cook Branches throughout Australia (call ☎ 13/1771 for nearest branch, ☎ 1800/801002 for telesales), New Zealand ☎ 09/379 3920, ⓦ www. thomascook.com.au. Flight deals and package holidays.

Trailfinders Australia ☎ 02/9247 7666, ⓦ www.trailfinders.com.au. One of the best-informed and most efficient agents for independent travellers, offering flight and accommodation advice.

Usit Beyond New Zealand ☎ 0800/788336, ⓦ www.usitbeyond.co.nz. Student and youth flight specialists.

Specialist agents and tour operators in Australia and New Zealand

Adventures Abroad New Zealand ☎ 0800/800 434, ⓦ www.adventures-abroad.com. Wide range of Scandinavian packages from one to three weeks.

Bentours Australia ☎ 02/9241 1353, ⓦ www. bentours.com.au. Ferry, rail, bus and hotel passes and a host of scenic tours throughout Scandinavia including fjord tours.

CIT Australia ☎ 02/9267 1255, ⓦ www.cittravel .com.au. Europe-wide rail passes.

Contiki Australia ☎ 02/9511 2200, New Zealand ☎ 09/309 8824, ⓦ www.contiki.com. Frenetic tours for 18–35-year-old party animals including a 22-day tour of Scandinavia.

Explore Holidays Australia ☎ 02/9857 6200 or 1300/731 000, ⓦ www.exploreholidays.com.au. Offers a 21-day adventure tour through central and northern Sweden and coastal Norway.

Travel Plan Australia ☎ 02/9958 1888 or 1300/130 754, ⓦ www.travelplan.com.au. Skiing specialist with some packages to Norway.

Viatour Australia ☎ 02/8219 5400, ⓦ www. viator.com. Booking agent for hundreds of travel suppliers worldwide, including those who offer tours to Norway.

By rail from the UK and Ireland

Taking a train can be a relaxed if long-winded way of getting to Norway, though it's likely to work out considerably more expensive than flying, especially if you're over 26. A number of deals involving rail passes (see p.20) make it possible to cut costs, however, and there's the added advantage of being able to break your journey – travelling to Oslo, for instance, you could stop off at Brussels, Hamburg and Copenhagen. If you are planning to travel from Ireland by train, the best option by far is to buy an InterRail pass.

The most straightforward and quickest way to get to Europe by train is through the Channel Tunnel on **Eurostar** from Waterloo International in London, or from Ashford in Kent, via Paris or Brussels. Almost all ticketing for train travel within Europe is now handled by **Rail Europe** (see p.21), who sell through-tickets to Norway. To get the best fares on Rail Europe you'll need to book a round-trip fourteen days in advance and spend at least one Saturday night away. With this type of ticket, the fare from London to Oslo is currently £330, and the journey takes around 28 hours, via Brussels, Hamburg and Copenhagen. As always, it's worth checking for special deals.

Alternatively, you could take the train and a **cross-channel ferry**, though this is much slower, and not always cheaper. Through-tickets are available from any major high street travel agent, or you could organize your own train and ferry tickets independently (for ferry operators, see p.23).

Rail passes

Rail passes can reduce the cost of train travel significantly, especially if you plan to travel extensively around Norway or visit as part of a wider tour of Europe. There's a huge array of passes available, covering regions as well as individual countries. Some have to be bought before leaving home, while others can only be purchased in the country itself. Rail Europe is the umbrella company for all national and international rail tickets, and its comprehensive website (ⓦwww.raileurope .com) is the most useful source of information on which rail passes are available, and their current prices. Described below are the two main pan-European rail passes, InterRail

and Eurail, as well as the ScanRail pass, which is valid for train travel in Scandinavia; details of the Norway Rail Pass, for Norway only, are given on p.33.

InterRail pass

The **InterRail pass** is available only to European residents, and you will be asked to provide proof of residency before being allowed to purchase one. They are divided into zones and you can buy up to three zones, or a global pass which covers all the zones. They are valid for 22 days (one zone only) or one month, and come in over-26 and (less expensive) under-26 versions. For current prices, consult ⓦwww.raileurope.com.

The pass covers 28 European countries (including Turkey and Morocco) grouped together in **zones**: **A** (Republic of Ireland/Britain); **B** (Norway, Sweden, Finland); **C** (Germany, Austria, Switzerland, Denmark); **D** (Czech & Slovak Republics, Poland, Hungary, Croatia); **E** (France, Belgium, Netherlands, Luxembourg); **F** (Spain, Portugal, Morocco); **G** (Italy, Greece, Turkey and Slovenia, plus some ferry services between Italy and Greece); and **H** (Bulgaria, Romania, Yugoslavia, Macedonia).

Inter-Rail passes do not include travel between Britain and the continent, although holders are eligible for discounts on rail travel in Britain and Northern Ireland and cross-Channel ferries. The pass also gives discounts on the London–Paris Eurostar service, on several international ferry routes, including Harwich to Esbjerg, and a whole raft of domestic Norwegian buses and ferries (see pp.33–35). The pass can be purchased from one of the agents listed on p.13 & p.15, or you can save £5 by booking it via the Inter-Rail website (ⓦwww.inter-rail.co.uk).

Eurail pass

The **Eurail Pass** is only available to non-Europeans, and must be purchased before arrival in Europe. It allows unlimited free first-class train travel in seventeen European countries, including Norway, and is available in increments of fifteen days, 21 days, one month, two months and three months. If you're under 26, you can save money with a **Eurail Youthpass**, which is valid for second-class travel or, if you're travelling with between one and four companions, a joint

Eurail Saverpass; both of these are available in the same increments as the Eurail Pass. You stand a better chance of getting your money's worth out of a **Eurail Flexipass**, which is good for ten or fifteen days' travel within a two-month period. This, too, comes in first-class, under-26/second-class (**Eurorail Youth Flexipass**) and group (**Eurail Saver Flexipass**) versions. For current prices of all the Eurail passes, consult Ⓦ www.raileurope.com. See the list below for details of where to buy the passes.

ScanRail pass

If you're planning to travel extensively by train within Scandinavia, your best bet is the **ScanRail pass**. It is available in both first and second class versions for five days' travel within two months, ten days' travel within two months, or 21 consecutive days. There are also **Youth** (12–25 year olds) and **Senior** (60+) versions of the pass: the Youth version gives a discount of about 25 percent on the full adult price, and the Senior version a discount of about fourteen percent. Note that on some intercity express trains a small supplement is charged. You can also buy a **ScanRail 'n' Drive Pass**, which allows five days of unlimited train travel and two days car rental with unlimited mileage in any two month period: extra car days can be purchased at a daily rate.

All the ScanRail passes can be purchased from the agents listed below, or from any major rail station within Scandinavia. For details of current prices check out Rail Europe's website (Ⓦ www.raileurope.com).

Rail contacts

In the UK and Ireland

Eurostar ☏ 0870/160 6600, Ⓦ www.eurostar.co.uk.
Rail Europe (SNCF French Railways) UK ☏ 0870/584 8848, Ⓦ www.raileurope.co.uk. Discounted rail fares for under-26s on a variety of European routes; also agents for Inter-Rail, and Eurostar, and sells ScanRail passes.

In North America

CIT Rail US ☏ 1-800/223-7987 or 212/730-2400, Canada ☏ 1-800/361-7799, Ⓦ www.cit-rail.com. Sells Eurail and ScanRail passes.

DER Travel US ☏ 1-888/337-7350, Ⓦ www.dertravel.com/rail. Sells Eurail and many individual country passes, including the ScanRail passes.
Europrail International Canada ☏ 1-888/667-9734, Ⓦ www.europrail.net. Sells Eurail and ScanRail passes.
Rail Europe US ☏ 1-800/438-7245, Canada ☏ 1-800/361-7245, Ⓦ www.raileurope.com/us. Official North American Eurail Pass agent; also sells ScanRail passes.
ScanTours US ☏ 1-800/223-7226 or 310/636-4656, Ⓦ www.scantours.com. Sells Eurail and ScanRail passes.

In Australia and New Zealand

Rail Plus Australia ☏ 1300/555 003 or 03/9642 8644, Ⓦ www.railplus.com.au. Sells Eurail and ScanRail passes.
Bentours Australia ☏ 02/9241 1353, Ⓦ www.bentours.com.au. Sells Scandinavian rail and bus passes.
CIT World Travel Australia ☏ 02/9267 1255 or 03/9650 5510, Ⓦ www.cittravel.com.au. Sells Eurail and ScanRail passes.
Trailfinders Australia ☏ 02/9247 7666, Ⓦ www.trailfinder.com.au. Sells all European coach and train passes.

By coach from the UK and Ireland

A **coach journey** from Britain to Norway is something of an endurance test, and with airfares falling it can actually prove more expensive than flying. It's only worth taking the bus if time is no object and you specifically do not want to fly.

The major UK operator of international coach routes is **Eurolines** (UK ☏ 0870/514 3219; Republic of Ireland ☏ 01/836 6111). Tickets are bookable on the internet at Ⓦ www.eurolines.co.uk, through most major travel agents (see p.13 & p.15), and at any Eurolines or National Express agent (☏ 0870/580 8080, Ⓦ www.nationalexpress.co.uk or Ⓦ www.gobycoach.com).

Eurolines runs eight services weekly to **Copenhagen** either via Brussels (20hr) or Amsterdam (26hr). In Copenhagen, you can pick up a connection on to **Oslo** (six weekly; 9hr 30min). **Euro-Apex** tickets are usually the least expensive fares, and must be booked seven days in advance, and you must return within one month. The current Euro-Apex fare from London to Oslo is £189 return, £5–20 less if you're **under 26**,

Useful timetable publications

The red book **Thomas Cook European Timetables** details schedules of over 50,000 trains in Europe, as well as times of more than 200 ferry routes and rail-connecting bus services. It's updated and re-issued every month, though the main changes are in the June edition (published at the end of May), which has details of the summer European schedules, and the October edition, (published at the end of September), which includes the winter schedules. The book can be purchased online (which gets you a ten percent discount) at ⓦwww.thomascookpublishing.com, or from branches of Thomas Cook (see ⓦwww.thomascook.co.uk for your nearest branch), and costs £9.50. Their useful *Rail Map of Europe* can also be purchased online for £6.95.

depending on the route. Note that in the peak summer months, all fares increase slightly.

There are no through services to Copenhagen and Norway from anywhere in Britain outside London, though **National Express** connects in London with Eurolines buses from all over the British Isles. Similarly, getting to Norway by coach from Ireland involves going to London and picking up a connection there.

By car and ferry from Britain

Regular **car ferries** link Britain with Norway, and whilst fares aren't cheap, discounts and special deals, such as DFDS Seaways' "All in one car" midweek return fare, can cut costs greatly. Prices vary enormously according to the season, number of passengers and type of cabin accommodation, but not surprisingly, are usually at their lowest during the winter months.

An alternative to sailing directly to Norway is to take a ferry **to Germany** or **Holland** (or even Belgium or France), and drive from there. DFDS Seaways' crossings from Harwich to Hamburg and Stena Line's from Harwich to the Hook of Holland are probably the most convenient options if you're heading straight for Norway.

By ferry from Newcastle and Aberdeen

The shortest sea route to Norway is on DFDS Seaways' (see p.23 for contact details) twice-weekly service from **Newcastle** to **Kristiansand** (18hr), which continues onto Gothenburg in Sweden (26hr). Prices to both destinations are the same and start at £64 one-way in low season, £104 return. The "All in

one car" fare is £374 return. Expect to pay more in the spring and summer months, and supplements at weekends. All fares include a cabin berth.

Alternatively, Fjord Line (see p.23 for contact details) runs two or three sailings a week from **Newcastle to Stavanger** (20hr), **Haugesund** (23hr) and **Bergen** (27hr) – not exactly a short trip, and in rough weather the crossing can seem interminable. Tickets cost the same to all three ports, with a minimum fare in winter of £62 each way (including a cabin berth), plus £60 each way for a car, rising in summer to £96 each way and £70 per car. During the summer months reclining seats are available instead of a cabin for £42. Motorbikes are carried for £30 each way, bicycles £10.

In addition, from May to September, Northlink Ferries (see p.23 for contact details) operate from **Aberdeen** to **Lerwick** in Shetland, from where Smyril Line (see p.23 for contact details) runs a service to **Bergen**, though there's currently no through-ticketing. The Aberdeen to Shetland one-way fares start at £26.50 (£60 extra for a cabin berth), plus £120 for a car. One-way Shetland to Bergen fares start at £52 (£70 extra for a cabin), plus £42 for a car. The journey from Aberdeen to Bergen takes about three days in all and involves a stopover in Lerwick – altogether a sea voyage of almost epic proportions.

Flights from the rest of Scandinavia

All seven of Norway's international airports – Oslo (Gardermoen), Oslo (Torp), Bergen, Stavanger, Kristiansand, Trondheim and Tromsø – have good links with the rest of Scandinavia. Most flights within Scandinavia are operated by SAS (see p.13, p.15, p16 and p.19), whose standard scheduled fares are expensive, but the airline does offer all sorts of special deals as well as the **Visit Scandinavia AirPass** (see p.36).

By rail from the rest of Scandinavia

By train, Norges Statsbaner (Norwegian State Railways; @www.nsb.no) and Sweden's SJ railways (@www.sj.se) combine to provide a regular service from **Stockholm to Oslo** (1–3 daily; 6hr). Fares vary enormously, but with advance booking a one-way ticket can cost as little as £41/US$62. SJ also operates a service **from Stockholm to Trondheim** (2 daily; 12hr; from £94/US$141 one-way), whilst another Swedish rail company, Tågkompaniet (@www.tagkompaniet.se), links **Stockholm with Narvik** (2 daily; 19hr; from £35/US$53 one-way).

Trains **from Copenhagen to Oslo** (2–4 daily; 6–8hr) use the Öresund bridge between the Danish coast and Malmö in Sweden, but you still have to change once en route, normally at Gothenburg (Göteborg). The standard one-way fare between the two capitals is £100/US$150, but this can be reduced to around £55/US$83 by booking in advance. InterRail, Eurail and ScanRail passes (see above) are valid on all these services.

By coach from the rest of Scandinavia

Norway's national bus company, **Nor-Way Bussekspress** (@0047/82 02 13 00 at 10kr per minute; @www.nor-way.no) runs six buses weekly from Copenhagen to Oslo via Gothenburg (Göteborg) in Sweden; the journey takes nine and a half hours. It also links Stockholm with Oslo (6 weekly; 8hr), and Hamburg with Kristiansand and Stavanger (2 weekly; 11hr/15hr) via the Hirsthals–Kristiansand ferry. Its only rival is Sweden's **Säfflebussen** (@www.safflebussen.se; @0047 22 19 49 00), whose buses also link Stockholm with Oslo (5 daily; 7hr 30min) and Copenhagen and Oslo (5 daily; 8hr). Säfflebussen charges 230 Norwegian kroner (330nkr at peak times) for Copenhagen to Oslo, and 250nkr (360nkr at peak times) for Oslo to Stockholm.

By ferry from the rest of Scandinavia

Several **car ferries** shuttle across the Skagerrak **from Denmark to Norway**. One of the most useful is DFDS Scandinavian Seaways' once-daily, year-round ferry from Copenhagen to Oslo (16hr). In addition, Stena Line links Frederikshavn with Oslo (1–2 daily; 8hr 30min), and Color Line ferries leave Hirsthals for Oslo (5 weekly to 1 daily; 8hr) and Kristiansand (1–4 daily; 5hr). There's also a Color Line ferry service **from Sweden to Norway**, linking Strömstad, north of Gothenburg, with Sandefjord (year-round; 2–5 daily; 2hr 30min).

Ferry **prices** vary enormously depending on the season and whether or not you have a cabin, but as a sample summertime fare DFDS charges passengers £50 one-way from Copenhagen to Oslo without a cabin, and cars £24. When booking, always look out for special deals, which can cut costs considerably. Note also that rail-pass holders get discounts on some routes.

Ferry contacts

Color Line Oslo @0047/22 94 44 00 @www.colorline.com. Hirsthals to Oslo and Kristiansand; Strömstad to Sandefjord; Kiel near Hamburg to Oslo.
DFDS Seaways UK @0870/533 3000, @www.dfdsseaways.co.uk. Newcastle to Gothenburg and Kristiansand; Copenhagen to Oslo.
Fjord Line UK @0191/296 1313, @www.fjordline.com. Newcastle to Stavanger, Haugesund and Bergen.
P&O Stena Line UK @0870/600 0600 or 01304/864 003, @www.posl.com. Dover to Calais.
P&O North Sea Ferries UK @0870/129 6002, @www.ponsf.com. Hull to Rotterdam and Zeebrugge.
Northlink Ferries UK @0845/600 0449. Aberdeen to Lerwick (Shetland) for onwards connection with Smyril line to Bergen.
Sea France @0870/571 1711, @www.seafrance.com. Dover to Calais.
Smyril Line @01595/690 845. Services from Lerwick (Shetlands) to Bergen.
Stena Line UK @0870/570 7070, Northern Ireland @028/9074 7747, Republic of Ireland @01/204 7777, @www.stenaline.com. Harwich to the Hook of Holland; Frederikshavn to Oslo.

Red tape and visas

The vast majority of people, including citizens of the USA, Canada, Australia, New Zealand and all members of the EU and EEA (European Economic Area), need only a valid passport to enter Norway for up to three months. All other nationals should consult the nearest Norwegian embassy or consulate about visa requirements.

A **residence permit** is necessary if you want to stay longer than the standard three-month limit. EU/EEA nationals can either apply for the permit within Norway itself, from the local police, or from a Norwegian embassy or consulate before arrival. If the application is successful, the residence permit will normally grant the holder the right to stay in Norway for five years (one year for students). In most cases, the permit is renewable, and also grants the holder the right to work (though EU/EEA nationals can start work before the residence permit has been obtained) and to reside anywhere in Norway. Particular conditions may be attached: for example, if you apply for a residence permit as a recipient of services (say, as a tourist), you would have to prove that you could both finance yourself and pay for the services you receive.

For non-EU/EEA nationals, the regulations are tighter. Applications must be submitted to a Norwegian embassy or consulate before arrival, and applicants must prove that they can finance themselves. If the application is successful, a residence permit issued to a non-EU/EEA national is rarely for longer than one year, takes time to renew, and does not include the right to work – for that a **work permit** is required. The applicant is also required to have a fixed address for the period concerned.

Finally, note that at the port of entry you may be asked to explain the reason for your visit to Norway and how long you intend to stay. You may also be asked to prove that you have enough money to support yourself during your stay. Be polite and never answer facetiously.

Norwegian embassies and consulates

Australia 17 Hunter St, Yarralumla, Canberra, ACT 2600 (00 61 2 6273 3444; ℮emb.canbera@mfa.no).
Canada Embassy: Royal Bank Centre, Suite 532, 90 Sparks St, Ottawa, Ontario, ONK1P 5B4 (℡613/238 6571, ℮emb.ottawa@mfa.no).
Ireland 34 Molesworth St, Dublin 2 (℡00 353 1 662 1800; ℮emb.dublin@mfa.no).
UK Embassy: 25 Belgrave Square, London SW1X 8QD (℡020/7591 5500, ℮konsulat.london @mfa.no); 86 George St, Edinburgh EH2 3BU (℡0131/226 5701, ℮konsulat.edinburgh @mfa.no).
USA 2720, 34th St NW, Washington, DC 20008 (℡202/333-6000, ℮emb.washington@mfa.no). Embassy in Washington DC, consulates in Seattle, San Francisco, Los Angeles, Houston, Minneapolis, Chicago, Miami and New York.

Duty-free restrictions

On arrival in Norway, EU nationals may bring in, duty-free, a maximum of 200 cigarettes (or 250g of tobacco), two litres of beer, one litre of wine, and one litre of strong spirits, per adult. Dispense with the hard liquor and you can take in an extra litre of wine or beer. Visitors from North America can import duty-free up to 400 cigarettes (or 500g of tobacco) and two litres of liquor or wine. Returning home, the limits are pretty much the same. There are also restrictions as to the value of other goods/purchases you can take home without paying tax – check with your airline or ferry company if you're unsure. Remember that the importing of food, plants or animals back into Britain, Ireland, the USA, Canada, Australia or New Zealand is severely restricted.

Information, websites and maps

B

BASICS | Information, websites and maps

Before you leave home, there's a wealth of information that you can pick up on the internet and from the offices of the Norwegian Tourist Board. Once inside the country, information is very easy to come by too, as every town and most of the larger villages have their own tourist offices. Maps are widely available in Norwegian bookshops and sometimes at the tourist offices as well, but buying one before you go helps in planning – and if you're driving you will, of course, need a good road map.

Tourist offices

With offices in half a dozen countries world-wide, the **Norwegian Tourist Board** offers an efficient service, stocking a wide range of glossy, free booklets. One of their most useful brochures is the official travel guide called *Norway: Facts and Information*. This has touring suggestions and all sorts of background information. There's also the free *NRI Guide to Transport and Accommodation*, an extensive listing that classifies all the country's hotels and most of its guest houses, and includes a digest of the main public transport routes. There are also brochures tailored to meet specific interests, for example *Camping*, which lists and grades several hundred major campsites. Furthermore, the Norwegian Tourist Board has a substantial collection of local material – mainly regional guides – and specific material on the more popular tourist destinations such as the fjords, Oslo and Bergen.

The tourist board works in conjunction with **NORTRA**, a commercial foundation jointly funded by the government and the private sector. Among its other functions, NORTRA publishes about ten titles on specific aspects of holidaying in Norway, including encyclopedic information on angling, motoring, mountain hiking, guest harbours and the Hurtigrute coastal ship. The tourist board has the complete list of NORTRA publications.

Inside Norway, **tourist offices** are ten-a-penny. In the smaller towns and larger villages, you can pretty much guarantee you'll get a free map and a list of local sights and hotels. The same applies in the larger towns and cities, but here the tourist offices often rent bikes, sell local discount cards, change money and have access to a small supply of

rooms in private houses. They will book these on your behalf (either free or for a minimal charge of around 30kr) as part of their accommodation service, which also includes the booking of hotel rooms, again for a minimal charge. Note, however, that you'll usually need to stump up a refundable deposit in addition to paying the booking fee. **Opening hours** vary considerably, but the larger urban offices are open all year, sometimes every day of the week, while the smaller concerns operate from April or May to September, from Monday to Friday and often during the weekend. Throughout the summer, many are open well into the evening. We've specified individual opening hours throughout the guide.

Norwegian Tourist Board offices abroad

Australia No tourist office, but the embassy handles tourist information: 17 Hunter St, Yarralumla, Canberra ACT 2600 (☏00 61 2 6273 3444, ℮emb.canbera@mfa.no).
Canada All travel enquiries dealt with by the US office (see below).
Ireland No tourist office, but the embassy handles tourist information: 34 Molesworth St, Dublin 2 (☏00 353 1 662 1800, ℮emb.dublin@mfa.no).
New Zealand No tourist office (see Australia).
UK 5th Floor, Charles House, 5 Lower Regent St, London SW1Y 4LR (☏0906/302 2003, calls cost 50p per minute; ℳwww.visitnorway.com).
USA 655 Third Ave, New York, NY 10022 (☏212/855 9700, ℳwww. visitnorway.com)

Maps

The Norwegian Tourist Board's *Norway: Facts and Information* brochure contains several general **maps** of the country and

Norway on the Net

Ⓦ**www.bike-norway.com** The best of the English-language cycling sites, this website suggests around a dozen routes and provides useful practical information about road conditions, traffic and cycle repair facilities and so forth.

Ⓦ**www.museumnett.no** Comprehensive information on the country's museums and current exhibitions.

Ⓦ**www.odin.dep.no** ODIN – Official Documentation and Information from Norway. A Norwegian government site, as its name suggests, and despite the plain presentation it has everything you ever wanted to know about Norway and maybe more. Especially good on politics.

Ⓦ**www.oslopro.no** Dedicated to Oslo with city listings and links.

Ⓦ**www.turistforeningen.no** DNT – the Norwegian Mountain Touring

Association – operates this excellent site, which outlines the country's most popular hiking routes, region by region. Also comprehensive information on local, affiliated hiking associations and DNT huts.

Ⓦ**www.unginfo.oslo.no/streetwise** An English guide to Oslo specifically designed for young people. Strong on practical information geared to the budget traveller.

Ⓦ**www.vandrerhjem.no** The official site of Norwegian Hostelling, providing clear and detailed information. You can make a reservation, order brochures and other publications, and there's a useful news section too.

Ⓦ**www.visitnorway.com** The official site of the Norwegian tourist board with links to all things Norwegian, and good sections on outdoor activities and events.

Norway's many tourist offices provide a wealth of free city, town and regional maps. Drivers, however, will need to invest in a good **road map**. Hallwag International's *Norge* map (1:1,000,000) is perhaps the best of the single-sheet, fold-up country maps: it's easy to follow, is widely available in Norway and elsewhere, includes an index and has a sliding distance guide on the back cover. Its main drawback, apart from the occasional error, is that the scale is too large, a criticism that applies – doubly so – to its more accurate rival, Michelin's map number 985 of Scandinavia (1:1,500,000).

The best book of Norwegian road maps is the *Veiatlas Norge*, produced by the state-run Statens Kartverk, an arm of the highways department. This consists of 57 two-page maps (1:300,000) and 80 city and town maps (1:20,000); it comes with an index and a distance chart and is widely available for about £20/US$32. Of the regional, single-sheet road maps, the best and most widely available is the series produced by Freytag & Berndt (1:400,000). These cover the country in four maps, have an index and are easy to follow except in the most congested parts of the country –

around Oslo and Bergen and so forth – where the scale is insufficient to pick out many of the roads.

Statens Kartverk also publishes authoritative **hiking maps** at a scale of 1:50,000. This series covers every part of the country and is extremely accurate. In addition, the same people publish maps to all the more popular hiking areas at a scale of 1:100,000, which gives the hiking trails greater prominence. Statens Kartverk maps are available abroad (see specialist map shops in the box below), though there's usually a twenty percent mark-up on the domestic price of 60–70kr. For more on hiking, see p.51-54. **Cycling maps**, with route suggestions, are usually on sale at tourist offices in the more popular cycling areas; for more on cycling see p.38. Finally, if you intend getting to know **Oslo** well, the fold-out *Falkplan* is the best on the market and is easy to get hold of both in Norway and abroad.

Map outlets

In the UK and Ireland

Easons Bookshop 40 O'Connell St, Dublin 1 ☏01/858 3881, Ⓦ www.eason.ie.

Heffers Map and Travel 20 Trinity St, Cambridge CB2 1TJ ☎ 01865/333 536, ⓦ www.heffers.co.uk.

Hodges Figgis Bookshop 56–58 Dawson St, Dublin 2 ☎ 01/677 4754, ⓦ www.hodgesfiggis.com.

The Map Shop 30a Belvoir St, Leicester LE1 6QH ☎ 0116/247 1400, ⓦ www.mapshopleicester.co.uk.

National Map Centre 22–24 Caxton St, London SW1H 0QU ☎ 020/7222 2466, ⓦ www.mapsnmc.co.uk.

Newcastle Map Centre 55 Grey St, Newcastle-upon-Tyne, NE1 6EF ☎ 0191/261 5622.

Ordnance Survey Ireland Phoenix Park, Dublin 8 ☎ 01/802 5300, ⓦ www.osi.ie.

Ordnance Survey of Northern Ireland Colby House, Stranmillis Ct, Belfast BT9 5BJ ☎ 028/9025 5755, ⓦ www.osni.gov.uk.

Stanfords 12–14 Long Acre, WC2E 9LP ☎ 020/7836 1321, ⓦ www.stanfords.co.uk.

The Travel Bookshop 13–15 Blenheim Crescent, W11 2EE ☎ 020/7229 5260, ⓦ www.thetravelbookshop.co.uk.

In the US and Canada

Adventurous Traveler.com US ☎ 1-800/282-3963, ⓦ www.adventuroustraveler.com.

Book Passage 51 Tamal Vista Blvd, Corte Madera, CA 94925 ☎ 1-800/999-7909, ⓦ www.bookpassage.com.

Distant Lands 56 S Raymond Ave, Pasadena, CA 91105 ☎ 1-800/310-3220, ⓦ www.distantlands.com.

Elliot Bay Book Company 101 S Main St, Seattle, WA 98104 ☎ 1-800/962-5311, ⓦ www.elliotbaybook.com.

Globe Corner Bookstore 28 Church St, Cambridge, MA 02138 ☎ 1-800/358-6013, ⓦ www.globecorner.com.

Map Link 30 S La Patera Lane, Unit 5, Santa Barbara, CA 93117 ☎ 1-800/962-1394, ⓦ www.maplink.com.

Rand McNally US ☎ 1-800/333-0136, ⓦ www.randmcnally.com. Around thirty stores across the US; dial ext 2111 or check the website for the nearest location.

The Travel Bug Bookstore 2667 W Broadway, Vancouver V6K 2G2 ☎ 604/737-1122, ⓦ www.swifty.com/tbug.

World of Maps 1235 Wellington St, Ottawa, Ontario K1Y 3A3 ☎ 1-800/214-8524, ⓦ www.worldofmaps.com.

In Australia and New Zealand

The Map Shop 6–10 Peel St, Adelaide, SA 5000 ☎ 08/8231 2033, ⓦ www.mapshop.net.au.

Specialty Maps 46 Albert St, Auckland 1001 ☎ 09/307 2217, ⓦ www.ubdonline.co.nz/maps.

MapWorld 173 Gloucester St, Christchurch ☎ 0800/627 967 or 03/374 5399, ⓦ www.mapworld.co.nz.

Mapland 372 Little Bourke St, Melbourne, Victoria 3000 ☎ 03/9670 4383, ⓦ www.mapland.com.au.

Perth Map Centre 1/884 Hay St, Perth, WA 6000 ☎ 08/9322 5733, ⓦ www.perthmap.com.au.

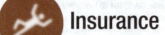

Insurance

Prior to travelling, you'd do well to take out an insurance policy to cover against theft, loss and illness or injury. Before paying for a new policy, however, it's worth checking whether you already have some degree of cover. As an EEA (European Economic Area) member, Norway has free reciprocal health agreements with other member states – and that includes all EU countries (see Health on p.29). In addition, some all-risks home insurance policies may cover your possessions when overseas, and many private medical schemes include cover when abroad. In Canada, provincial health plans usually provide partial cover for medical mishaps overseas, while holders of official student/teacher/youth cards in Canada and the US are usually entitled to meagre accident cover and hospital in-patient benefits. Students will often find that their student health cover extends during the vacations and for one term beyond the date of last enrolment.

After exhausting the possibilities above, you might want to contact a specialist travel insurance company. A typical travel insurance policy usually provides cover for the loss of baggage, tickets and – up to a certain limit – cash or cheques, as well as cancellation or curtailment of your journey. Most of them exclude so-called **dangerous sports** – climbing, rafting, skiing, and so forth – unless an extra premium is paid. Many policies can be chopped and changed to exclude cover that you don't need – for example, sickness and accident benefits can often be excluded or included at will. If you do take medical coverage, ascertain whether benefits will be paid as treatment proceeds or only after your return home, and whether there is a 24-hour medical emergency number. It is also worth noting that few private insurance policies cover prescription charges – the "excess" is usually greater than the cost of the medicines. When securing baggage cover, make sure that the per-article limit – typically under £500 – will cover your most valuable possession. If you need to make a claim, you should keep receipts for medicines and medical treatment, and in the event that you have anything stolen, you must obtain a crime report statement or number.

Rough Guides travel insurance

Rough Guides offers its own travel insurance, customized for our readers by a leading UK broker and backed by a Lloyd's underwriter. It's available for anyone, of any nationality and any age, travelling anywhere in the world.

There are two main Rough Guide insurance plans: **Essential**, for basic, no-frills cover; and **Premier** – with more generous and extensive benefits. Alternatively, you can take out **annual multi-trip insurance**, which covers you for any number of trips throughout the year (with a maximum of 60 days for any one trip). Unlike many policies, the Rough Guides schemes are calculated by the day, so if you're travelling for 27 days rather than a month, that's all you pay for. If you intend to be away for the whole year, the **Adventurer** policy will cover you for 365 days. Each plan can be supplemented with a "**Hazardous Activities Premium**" if you plan to indulge in sports considered dangerous, such as skiing, scuba-diving or trekking. For a policy quote, call the Rough Guide Insurance Line on UK freefone ☎0800/015 0906; US toll-free ☎1-866/220 5588, or, if you're calling from elsewhere ☎0044 1243/621 046. Alternatively, get an online quote or buy online at ⊛www.roughguidesinsurance.com.

Health

Under reciprocal health arrangements, all citizens of EU and EEA (European Economic Area) countries are entitled to free or discounted medical treatment within Norway's public health care system. Non-EU/EEA nationals should take out their own medical insurance to cover them while travelling in Norway. EU/EEA citizens may want to consider private health insurance too, in order to cover the cost of items not within the EU/EEA's scheme, such as dental treatment and repatriation on medical grounds. For more on insurance, see opposite.

All EU nationals should complete **form E111** before travelling as proof of entitlement to treatment under EU/EEA arrangements. The form is available from most post offices in the UK and from health boards in the Republic of Ireland. If you don't have an E111 form with you, you will have to pay upfront for any medical treatment you need. If you do have to stump up for treatment, make sure you get a receipt so that you can claim the money back either from your insurance company, or from the Department for Work & Pension Benefits Agency, Overseas Division Medical Benefits, Tyneview Park, Whitley Road, Newcastle-upon-Tyne NE98 1BA (☎0191/218 7547).

Pharmacies

Minor ailments can be dealt with at **pharmacies** (*apotek*), which supply prescription and non-prescription drugs as well as toiletries, tampons, condoms and the like. Most pharmacies are open Monday to Friday 9am to 5pm, and some on Saturday mornings too. In the cities a rota system keeps at least one pharmacy open 24 hours a day: the rota should be displayed in the window of every pharmacy, and tourist offices also have details, as do some of the better hotels. Outside the cities, you'll find a pharmacy in every town and in some of the larger villages, but the smaller the place, the less likelihood there is of late-night opening.

Seeking medical treatment

Health care in Norway is of a very high standard and widely available: even the remotest communities are within relatively easy – or well-organized – reach of medical attention. Rarely will **English speakers** encounter language problems – if the doctor or nurse can't speak English themselves (which is unlikely) there will almost certainly be someone at hand who can.

If you should fall ill, you can get the address of an **English-speaking doctor** from your local pharmacy, tourist office, hotel or even consulate. If you're seeking treatment under EU/EEA health agreements, double-check that the doctor is working within (and seeing you as) a patient of the public health care system. Even within the EEA/EU agreement, you still have to pay a significant portion of the doctor's consultation and prescription charges (senior citizens and children are exempt), as well as a proportion of the costs of any non-hospital treatment, although hospital treatment is free. If you do get landed with a bill, get a receipt at the time of payment, and take it and your passport to the local sickness office (Lokale Trygdekontor) of the district where treatment was obtained, or the National Office for Social Insurance Abroad (Folketrygdkontoret for utenlandersaker). EU citizens will subsequently be reimbursed.

In **medical emergencies**, call ☎113. If you're reliant on free treatment within the EEA/EU health scheme, try to remember to make this clear to the ambulance staff and, if you're whisked off to hospital, to the medic you subsequently encounter. To ensure your non-private status is clearly understood, it's a good idea to have your E111 or equivalent documentation with you always.

Costs, money and banks

Norway has a reputation as one of Europe's most expensive holiday destinations. In some ways (but only some) this is entirely justified, as most of what you're likely to buy – a cup of coffee, a roll of film, a book – is costly. On the other hand, certain major items are reasonably priced, including accommodation and public transport.

Costs

Accommodation can be remarkably inexpensive when compared with other north European countries. In particular, Norway's HI hostels, almost all of which have family and double rooms as well as dormitory bunks, are invariably first rate and exceptionally good value. Getting around is good news too. Most travellers use some kind of rail pass, there are a fistful of discounts and internal deals, and the state subsidizes the longer and more remote bus journeys. Furthermore, concessions are almost universally applied at attractions and on public transport, with infants (aged under 4) going everywhere free, children (under 16) and seniors (usually over 67) typically paying half the standard rate. Food is, however, a different matter. With few exceptions – for example tinned fish – it's expensive and the cost of alcohol is enough to make even a heavy drinker contemplate abstinence. Consequently, restaurants are also pricey, though costs remain manageable if you avoid the extras and concentrate on the main courses, for which around £12/$19 will normally suffice – twice that with a starter and dessert. You can, of course, pay a lot more – prices in top Oslo restaurants can be twice the average level, and then some. More economical are the café-bars, but these are largely confined to the bigger towns and cities.

On average, if you're prepared to buy your own picnic lunch, stay in youth hostels, and stick to the less expensive cafés and restaurants, you could get by on around **£30/$47 a day** excluding the cost of public transport. Staying in three-star hotels, eating in medium-range restaurants most nights (but avoiding drinking in a bar), you'll get through at least **£50/$80 a day** – with the main variable being the cost of your room. On **£120/$190** a day and upwards, you'll be limited only by your energy reserves – though if you're planning to stay in a five-star hotel and to have a big night out, this figure still won't be enough. As always, if you're travelling alone you'll spend much more on accommodation than in a group of two or more: most hotels and hostels do have single rooms, but at between sixty and eighty percent of the price of a double.

Currency and exchange rates

Norwegian currency consists of **kroner**, one of which, a krone (meaning crown and abbreviated **kr** or **NOK**), is divided into 100 **øre**. Coins in circulation are 50 øre, 1kr, 5kr and 10kr; notes are for 50kr, 100kr, 200kr, 500kr and 1000kr. You can bring in up to 25,000kr in notes and coins (there's no limit on travellers' cheques).

At the time of writing the **exchange rate** was 11.5kr to one pound sterling; 7.4kr to one US dollar; 4.7kr to one Canadian dollar; 4.1kr to one Australian dollar; 3.6kr to one New Zealand dollar; and 7.35kr to one euro.

ATMs: debit and credit cards

ATMs are commonplace in Norway, especially in the cities, and are undoubtedly the quickest and easiest way of getting money. Most ATMs give instructions in a variety of languages, and accept a host of **debit cards**, including all those carrying the Cirrus coding. If in doubt, check with your bank to find out whether the card you wish to use will be accepted – and if you need a new (international) PIN. You'll rarely be charged a transaction fee as the banks make their profits from applying different exchange rates. **Credit cards** can be used in ATMs too, but in this case transactions are treated as loans, with interest accruing daily from the date of withdrawal. All major credit cards, including American Express, Visa and Mastercard, are widely accepted in Norway.

Travellers' cheques

The main advantage of buying **travellers' cheques** is that they are a safe way of carrying funds. All well-known brands of travellers' cheque in all major currencies are widely accepted in Norway, with Euro and US dollar travellers' cheques being the most common. The usual fee for their purchase is one or two percent of face value, though this fee is often waived if you buy the cheques through a bank where you have an account. You'll find it useful to purchase a selection of denominations. When you **cash your cheques**, almost all banks make a percentage charge per transaction on top of a basic minimum charge.

In the event that your cheques are **lost or stolen**, the issuing company will expect you to report it immediately. Make sure you keep the purchase agreement, a record of cheque serial numbers, and the details of the company's emergency contact numbers or the addresses of their local offices, safe and separate from the cheques themselves. Most companies claim to replace lost or stolen cheques within 24 hours.

Banks and exchange

All but the tiniest of settlements in Norway has a **bank** or **savings bank**, the vast majority of which will change foreign currency and travellers' cheques. Many will also give cash advances on credit cards. **Banking hours** are usually Monday to Friday from 9am to 3.30pm, with many banks staying open until 5pm on Thursday. All major **post offices** change foreign currency and travellers' cheques at rates comparable to those at the bank, and they have longer opening hours, generally Monday to Friday 8am or 8.30am to 4pm or 5pm, and Saturday from 8am or 9am to 1pm.

For changing currency, a small transaction fee is the norm at both banks and post offices – they make their profits from the rate of exchange. Indeed, if the commission is

waived, double-check the exchange rate to ensure it's not unreasonable.

Outside banking and post office hours, most major hotels and some tourist offices, hostels and campsites will change money, but at less generous rates and with varying commissions.

Wiring money

Having **money wired** from home using one of the major money-wiring companies (see below) is never convenient or cheap, and should only be considered as a last resort. It can be slightly cheaper to have **your own bank** send the money through. For that, you need to nominate a receiving bank in Norway; any local branch will do, but those in the bigger cities will probably be more familiar with the process. Naturally you need to confirm the co-operation of the local bank before you set the wheels in motion back home. The sending bank's fees are geared to the amount being transferred and the urgency of the service you require – the fastest transfers, taking two or three days, start at around £25/$40 for the first £300–400/$450–600.

Money-wiring companies

Thomas Cook US ☏1-800/287-7362; Canada ☏1-888/823-4732; UK ☏01733/318 922; Republic of Ireland ☏01/677 1721; ⊛www.us.thomascook.com.
Travelers Express Moneygram US ☏1-800/926-3947; Canada ☏1-800/933-3278; ⊛www.moneygram.com.
Western Union US and Canada ☏1-800/325-6000; Australia ☏1800/501 500; New Zealand ☏09/270 0050; UK ☏0800/833 833; Republic of Ireland ☏1800/395 395; ⊛www.westernunion. com.

Tax-free shopping

Taking advantage of their decision not to join the EU, the Norwegians run a **tax-free shopping scheme** for tourists. If you spend more than 308kr at any of three thousand outlets in the tax-free shopping scheme you'll get a voucher for the amount of VAT you paid. On departure at an airport, ferry terminal or frontier crossing, present the goods, the voucher and your passport, and – provided you haven't used the item – you'll get an 11–18 percent refund, depending on the price of the item. Not all exit points from the country have a reclaim desk, however – pick up a leaflet at any participating shop to find out which do – and note that many of

the smaller reclaim points keep normal shop hours, closing for the weekend at 2pm on Saturday.

Getting around

Norway's public transport system – a huge mesh of trains, buses, car ferries and passenger express ferries – is comprehensive and reliable. In the winter services can be cut back severely (especially in the north), but no part of the country is inaccessible for long. Bear in mind, however, that Norwegian villages and towns usually spread over a large distance, so don't be surprised if you end up having to walk a kilometre or two from the station to where you want to go. It's this sprawling nature of the country's towns, and more especially the remoteness of many of the sights, that encourages many visitors to rent a car (see p.36).

With regard to public transport **timetables**, many of the principal air, train, bus and ferry services are detailed in the *NRI Guide to Transport and Accommodation*, a free and easy-to-use booklet available from Norwegian Tourist Board offices abroad (see p.25). Once you get to the country, you'll find that almost every tourist office carries a comprehensive range of free local and regional public transport timetables. In addition, all major train stations carry *NSB Togruter*, a free brochure detailing all Norway's train timetables, while long-distance bus routes operated by the national carrier, Nor-Way Bussekspress, are listed in the free *Rutehefte* (timetable), available at principal bus stations. However, for complex itineraries you might want to invest in the hefty *Rutebok for Norge*. Published five times a year, and costing around 200kr, this contains every schedule in the country as well as prices and lists of all government-approved accommodation. The book also gives the fixed-price taxi tariffs that apply to all town-to-town journeys – though expensive, these can be a real life-saver in remote regions – and a very useful route-planning section with maps. An English section helps you navigate round the guide. The *Rutebok* is available from larger bookshops, many travel agents and some tourist offices, as well as online at ⓦwww.reiseinfo.no (Norwegian only).

Trains

With the exception of the Narvik line into Sweden, operated by Tågkompaniet (☎0046/690 69 10 17; ⓦwww.tagkompaniet.se), all Norwegian **train** services are run by Norwegian State Railways (Norges Statsbaner or NSB; ☎81 50 08 88, then dial 4 for English, ⓦwww.nsb.no). Apart from a sprinkling of branch lines, NSB's services operate on three main domestic routes, linking Oslo to Kristiansand and Stavanger in the south, to Bergen in the west and to Trondheim and on to Bodø in the north. In places, the rail system is extended by a *TogBuss* (literally train-bus) service, with connecting buses continuing on from the train terminal. The nature of the country has made several of the routes engineering feats of some magnitude, worth the trip in their own right – the tiny **Flåm line** and the sweeping **Rauma line** from Dombås to Åndalsnes are exciting examples.

Prices are bearable, with the popular Oslo to Bergen run, for example, costing around 600kr one way, and Oslo to Trondheim 700kr. Both journeys take around six and a half hours. Costs can be reduced by purchasing a **rail pass** (see p.20 & p.33), or by taking advantage of one of NSB's various **discount fares**. The main ticket discount scheme is the **Minipris** (mini-price), which cuts up to fifty percent off the price of long-distance journeys. Under the scheme, tickets must be purchased at least one day in advance, are valid only on certain off-peak trains, and stopovers are not permitted; the trains you can take are indicated with a green dot on timetables. It's worth asking locally (and ahead of time) if any of NSB's discount deals apply on your specific route.

In terms of **concessionary fares**, there are group and family reductions; children under 4 travel free provided they don't take up a seat, while under-16s pay half fare, as do senior citizens (67+). It's worth noting that all long-distance, overnight and international services require an **advance seat reservation** (30kr) whether you have a rail pass or not. In high season it's wise to make a seat reservation on main routes anyway as trains can be packed. **Sleepers** are reasonably priced if you consider you'll save a night's hotel accommodation: a bed in a three-berth cabin costs 120kr, in a two-berth it's 260kr, and a single cabin costs 590kr, or 760kr ensuite.

NSB are in the middle of a long-term reorganization of their services. Ultimately, there will be just three types of train; *Puls* trains on short-haul commuter lines, mid-range *Agenda* trains, and long-distance, tilting *Signatur* trains. In the meantime, these new trains operate alongside older rolling stock, variously Local, Express and Night Trains. Even more confusingly, different trains have different **classes**: *Puls* trains have no separate classes; there are two classes on Signatur trains (*Signatur Pluss* and 2nd); and three on Express (Normal, Office and Saloon).

NSB **timetables** are available free at all train stations. The general timetable, the *NSB Togruter*, is supplemented by individual timetables on each of the lines and, in the case of the more scenic routes, by leaflets describing the sights as you go.

For further advance advice about passes, discounts and tickets, either contact the specialist agents listed in the "Getting There" section (pp.11–23) or NSB direct (see above).

Rail passes

InterRail, **Eurail** and **ScanRail** passes (see pp.20 & 21) are all valid on the Norwegian railway system. If you are only travelling within Norway, however, the **Norway Rail Pass** might be a better bet. It allows unlimited travel on almost all of Norway's rail lines on

a specified number of days within a specific period: three days in one month costs 1170kr; four days 1460kr; and five days 1620kr. The pass can be bought from major train stations inside Norway and from agents abroad (see p.21). Children under four travel free; under-sixteens get a fifty percent discount; and seniors twenty percent.

Holders of all rail passes have to pay a compulsory seat reservation fee (30kr) on all long-distance and international services and none of the passes are valid on the Gardermoen to Oslo express or the Flåm railway, though holders do get a thirty percent discount on the latter. All rail passes are also valid on connecting *TogBuss* services, while ScanRail and InterRail give a fifty-percent discount on scores of inter-city bus and boat routes.

Buses

Where the train network won't take you, **buses** will – and at no great cost, either: a substantial fjord journey, like the Sogndal–Florø trip, costs 259kr, while the ten-hour bus ride between Ålesund and Bergen is a reasonable 527kr. All tolls and almost all ferry costs are included in the price of a ticket, which can represent a significant saving. Long-distance express buses run between all Norway's major towns, but in the western fjords and the far north they are often the only means of public transport.

Most long-distance buses are operated by the national carrier, **Nor-Way Bussekspress** (☎82 02 13 00 calls charged at 10kr per minute; ⊛ www.nor-way.no), whose principal information office is at Oslo's main bus station. Their services are supplemented by a dense network of local buses, whose timetables are available at most tourist offices and bus stations. In general, most long-distance routes tend to operate once or twice daily, with one bus leaving early in the morning, while short hauls, although more frequent during the day, often tail off in the late afternoon. **Tickets** can usually be bought on board, but travel agents sell advance tickets on the more popular long-distance routes; be sure to keep your ticket till the journey is completed.

In terms of **concessionary fares**, there are student, group and family reductions; children under four years travel free, youngsters from four to fifteen pay half fare, and senior

Discount fares with rail passes on boats and buses

The following list is not comprehensive – it's always worth showing a rail pass to see if there are any special deals on buses and boats – but it does give details of some of the more useful **discount fares**. InterRail and ScanRail passes entitle holders to a reduction of fifty percent on the price of a ticket on the following **bus routes**: Fauske–Harstad; the Fauske–Lofoten Ekspressen; the Møreekspressen (Oslo–Otta–Ålesund); the Narvik–Lofoten Ekspressen; the Nordfjordekspressen (Oslo–Otta–Stryn); the Nord–Norgeekspressen (Bodø–Fauske–Narvik–Tromsø–Alta); the Sogn og Fjordane Ekspressen (Oslo– Sogndal–Førde); the Vestlandsbussen (Bergen–Stryn–Ålesund); and the Øst-Vestxpressen (Lillehammer–Flåm–Bergen).

In addition, InterRail and ScanRail passes give discounts of fifty percent on certain **Hurtigbåt** passenger express boats, principally on the Bergen–Haugesund–Stavanger, Narvik–Svolvaer and Bergen–Flåm routes.

citizens (over 67) get a 33 percent discount. Nor-Way Bussekspress also offers InterRail and ScanRail pass holders a fifty percent **discount** on certain bus services (see box above), and some local bus companies have comparable deals. Indeed, rail-pass and student-card holders should always ask about discounts when purchasing a ticket.

If you are going to travel much by bus, the Nor-Way Bussekspress **NOR-WAY BussPass** is excellent value, giving 21 days of unlimited travel for 2300kr. Valid on all Nor-Way Bussekspress services, the pass covers all toll and ferry costs, and guarantees a seat without advance booking (except for groups of more than eight) – the idea is that if one bus gets full, they will lay on another. It is not, however, valid on the majority of local bus services. Infants under three travel free; a pass for a child (aged 4–15) costs 75 percent of the adult rate. The pass can be purchased at any of the larger bus stations in Norway and a complimentary timetable detailing all Nor-Way Bussekspress services is included.

Ferries

Using a **ferry** is one of the highlights of any visit to Norway – and indeed among the western fjords and around the Lofoten they are all but impossible to avoid. The majority are roll-on, roll-off **car ferries** and they represent an economical means of transport, with prices fixed on a nationwide sliding scale: short journeys (10–15min) cost foot passengers 18–24kr, whereas a car and driver pay in the region of 45–65kr. **Ferry procedures** are straightforward: foot passengers walk on and pay the conductor,

drivers wait in line with their vehicles on the jetty till the conductor comes to the car window to collect the money. However, some busier routes have a drive-by ticket office. One or two of the longer car ferry journeys (in particular Bodø–Moskenes) take advance reservations, but the rest operate on a first-come first-served basis. Off-season, there's no real need to arrive more than twenty minutes before departure – with the possible exception of the Lofoten island ferries – but in the summer allow two to three hours to be safe.

Hurtigbåt passenger express boats

Norway's **Hurtigbåt** passenger express boats are catamarans that make up in speed what they lack in enjoyment: unlike the ordinary ferries, you're cooped up and view the passing landscape through a window, and in choppy seas the ride can be disconcertingly bumpy. Nonetheless, they're a convenient time-saving option: it takes just four hours on the Hurtigbåt from Bergen to Balestrand, for instance, and a mere two-and-a-half hours from Harstad to Tromsø, compared with six-and-a-half hours by Hurtigrute (see below). Hurtigbåt services are concentrated on the west coast around Bergen and the neighbouring fjords; the majority operate all year. Fares are significantly more expensive per kilometre than on the car ferry, and there's no fixed tariff table, so rates vary considerably. There are **concessionary fares** on all routes, with infants up to the age of three travelling free, and children (4–15) and senior citizens (over 67) getting a fifty percent discount. In addition, rail-pass holders and students are often eligible for a fifty percent reduction on the full adult rate – ask the operator.

The Hurtigrute

Norway's most celebrated ferry journey is the long and beautiful haul up the coast from Bergen to Kirkenes on the **Hurtigrute** coastal boat (literally "rapid route"; ⓦ www.hurtigruten.com; ☎81 03 00 00), or "coastal steamer", in honour of its past means of locomotion. Eleven ships combine to provide one daily service in each direction and the boat stops off at over thirty ports on the way. The service began in 1893, earning its nickname by completing the journey in a fraction of the time it took to travel overland. To many, the Hurtigrute remains the quintessential Norwegian experience and it certainly is the best way to observe the rigours of this extraordinary coastline. Until fairly recently, the ferry was a vital supply line to the remote towns of northern Norway, but the extension of the road system has taken away much of its earlier importance. Nonetheless, it continues to act as a delivery service, its survival assured by its popularity with tourists – and you may well find the lounges full of elderly British and American travellers. This combined role of supply and cruise ship is one of the Hurtigrute's real charms and it has a financial advantage too: unlike on a real cruise ship, sleeping in the lounges or on deck is allowed at, of course, a fraction of the cabin price. All the ships also have a first-rate restaurant and a 24-hour cafeteria; at busy times, reserve at the restaurant as early as possible. **Sailing schedules** are widely available; they are on the website, in the Norwegian Tourist Office's *NRI Transport and Accommodation* booklet and supplied by every Norwegian coastal tourist office.

The whole return trip from Bergen to Kirkenes and back again takes eleven days and **tickets**, which include all meals, cost anywhere between 10,000kr and 25,000kr, depending on the class of cabin and when you sail. April, May, September and October sailings, for example, can be up to thirty percent cheaper than those in June, July and August. There are also **concessionary fares** offering significant discounts for senior citizens (over 67), students, and families with children (aged 4 to 15). Infants under four years old travel free providing they do not occupy a separate berth. These discounts, however, are only valid for a limited number of cabins and on certain sailings, which makes pre-booking pretty much essential. Further details are available from, and bookings can be made at, most travel agencies back home. Making a Hurtigrute booking once you've got to Norway is easy too, and although some of the discount deals you can get back home can't be secured locally, other (often better) deals can. In Norway, contact either a travel agency or the general Hurtigrute telephone number or website.

A **short or medium-sized hop** along the coast on a section of the Hurtigrute route is also well worth considering. Fares are not particularly cheap, especially by comparison with the bus, but they are affordable. The standard, high-season, one-way passenger fare, excluding meals, for the sixteen-hour journey from Bodø to Harstad is 700kr (1180kr with a car); and for the six and a half hour trip from Harstad to Tromsø it's 470kr (790kr with a car). Bikes are transported at ten percent of the cost of a car. Last-minute bargains, however, can bring the rates right down to amazingly low levels. All the tourist offices in the Hurtigrute ports have the latest details and should be willing to telephone the captain of the nearest ship to make a reservation on your behalf.

Planes

Internal flights can prove a surprisingly inexpensive way of hopping about the country and are especially useful if you're short on time and want to reach, say, the far north: Tromsø to Kirkenes takes the best part of two days by bus, but it's just an hour by plane. Domestic air routes are served by several companies, but the major player is SAS (ⓦ www.scandinavian.net) along with its many subsidiaries, primarily Braathens (ⓦ www.braathens.no). Regular standard fares are around 1600kr one-way from Oslo to Bergen, 3000kr from Oslo to Tromsø, and 2400kr from Bergen to Trondheim. In addition, SAS/Braathens operates a variety of **discount** schemes, such as Braathens' special fare for under-25s, which knocks 50–75 percent off the full price. Both SAS and Braathens also have special **excursion fares** bookable at least seven days in advance and including a Saturday night away; these can discount the regular fare by fifty percent, sometimes more. Otherwise,

Hurtigrute sailing schedule

Northbound departure times from principal ports:

Bergen 20.00 (April–Sept); 22.30 (Oct–March)

Florø 02.15 (April–Sept); 04.45 (Oct–March)

Ålesund 09.30, via Geiranger, and 18.45 (April–Sept); 15.00 (Oct–March)

Geiranger 13.30 (April–Sept only)

Kristiansund 01.45 (April–Sept); 23.00 (Oct–March)

Trondheim noon (All year)

Bodø 15.00 (All year)

Stamsund 19.30 (All year)

Svolvær 22.00 (All year)

Harstad 08.00 (All year)

Tromsø 18.30 (All year)

Hammerfest 06.45 (All year)

Honningsvåg 15.30 (All year)

Arrive **Kirkenes** 10.30 (All year)

Southbound year-round departure times from principal ports:

Kirkenes 13.30

Honningsvåg 07.00

Hammerfest 13.00

Tromsø 01.30

Harstad 08.30

Svolvær 19.30

Stamsund 21.30

Bodø 04.00

Trondheim 10.00

Kristiansund 17.00

Ålesund 00.45

Doesn't stop at **Geiranger** southbound

Florø 08.15

Arrives **Bergen** 14.30

check out Braathens' and SAS's special offers, which often provide some great bargains.

In terms of **concessionary fares**, both SAS and Braathens permit infants under two to travel free on most flights and there are substantial – 30–40 percent – discounts for seniors (65+) and children under eighteen travelling in a family group including at least one full-fare-paying adult. The details of these various discounts vary year to year, so it's always worth shopping around.

Both Braathens and SAS have excellent-value **air passes**. Braathens' **Northern Lights Pass** (not available to Scandinavian residents) is valid on all the company's routes and comprises discount coupons with short one-way flights within either southern or northern Norway costing 620kr; long one-way flights between the south and the north cost 1170kr. The dividing line between north and south is drawn through Trondheim, which is counted as belonging to both zones. The coupons can be purchased both before you get to Norway, and in the country itself. Further details direct from Braathens in your home country (see "Getting There") or in Norway (⊕81 52 00 00).

The SAS **Visit Scandinavia AirPass** is also easily purchased before you arrive in Scandinavia, as well as in Norway itself, but is only available to those who fly to

Scandinavia on an SAS or Braathens flight. Like the Northern Lights Pass, it is not available to Scandinavian residents. It entitles holders to purchase up to eight AirPass vouchers for internal flights within Scandinavia, which are good for almost all SAS and Braathens flights within the region. The vouchers cost €70/505nkr to fly within any one country and €80/585nkr if you fly from one Scandinavian country to another; airport taxes are extra.

Driving and car rental

Norway's **main roads** are excellent, especially when you consider the vagaries of the climate, and now that most of the more hazardous sections have been ironed out or bypassed by tunnelling, driving is comparatively straightforward. That said, you still have to be careful on some of the higher sections and in the enormous tunnels, and once you leave the main roads for the narrow byroads that wind across the mountains, you'll be in for some nail-biting experiences – and that's in the summertime. In winter the Norwegians close many roads to concentrate their efforts on keeping the main highways open, but obviously blizzards and ice can make driving anywhere difficult, even dangerous–winter tyres, studs and chains notwithstanding. Always seek local advice especially if you're venturing onto minor roads; in the north you can't even assume that the

E6 Arctic Highway will be driveable. At any time of the year, the more adventurous the drive, the better equipped you need to be: on remote drives you should pack provisions, have proper hiking gear, check the car thoroughly before departure and carry a spare can of petrol.

Norway's main highways have an **E prefix** – E6, E18 etc; all the country's other significant roads are tagged "rv" (*riksvei*) followed by a number; as a general rule, the lower the rv number, the busier the road. In this guide, we've used the E prefix, but designated the other roads as Highways (followed by their numbers). Don't be too amazed if a road number given in the guide is wrong – the Norwegians are forever changing the numbers.

Tolls are imposed on certain roads to pay for construction projects such as bridges and tunnels. Once the costs are covered the toll is removed. The older building projects levy a fee of around 20–30kr, but the toll for some of the newer works (like the tunnel near Mundal) runs to well over 100kr per vehicle. There's also a modest toll (15–20kr) on entering the country's larger cities, but whether this is an environmental measure or a means of boosting city coffers is debatable. To avoid getting flustered at a toll booth, Norwegian drivers carry a supply of coins.

Fuel is readily available, even in the north, though here the settlements are so far apart that you'll need to keep your tank pretty full; if you're using the byroads extensively, remember to carry an extra can. Current fuel prices are around 8–10kr a litre and there are four main grades – unleaded (*blyfri*) 95 octane; unleaded 98 octane; super 98 octane; and diesel. It's worth remembering that many petrol stations don't accept credit cards, so make sure you have enough cash before filling up.

Major mountain passes' winter closing

Obviously enough, there's no preordained date for the **opening and closing of mountain roads** – it depends on the weather, and the threat of avalanches is often much more of a limitation than actual snowfall. The dates below should therefore be treated with caution; if in doubt seek advice locally. If you should head along a mountain road that's closed, sooner or later you'll come to a **barrier** and have to turn round.

E6: Dovrefjell (Oslo–Trondheim). Usually open all year.
E69: Skarsvåg–Nordkapp. Closed late Oct to early April.
E134: Haukelifjell (Oslo–Bergen/Stavanger). Usually open all year.
Hwy 7: Hardangervidda (Oslo–Bergen). Usually open all year.
Hwy 13: Vikafjellet (Voss–Vik). Closed Dec to April.
Hwy 51: Valdresflya (Otta to Gjendesheim and Fagernes). Closed Nov to early May.
Hwy 55: Sognefjellet (Skjolden to Lom). Closed Nov to early May.
Hwy 63: Trollstigen (Grotli–Geiranger–Åndalsnes). Closed late Sept to late May.

Documentation and rules of the road

EU, Canadian and USA **driving licences** are all honoured in Norway, but other nationals may need an **International Driver's Licence** (available at minimal cost from your home motoring organization). Any sort of provisional licence is, however, not acceptable. If you're bringing your own car, you must have vehicle registration papers, adequate insurance, a first-aid kit, a warning triangle and a green card (available from your insurer or motoring organization). Extra insurance coverage for unforeseen legal costs is also well worth having, as is an appropriate **breakdown policy** from a motoring organization. In Britain, for example, the AA (ⓦwww.theaa.co.uk) charges members and non-members about £95 for a month's Europe-wide breakdown cover, with all the appropriate documentation, including green card, provided.

Rules of the road are strict. You drive on the right, with dipped headlights required at all times, and seatbelts are compulsory for drivers and front-seat passengers (back-seat passengers too, if fitted). There's a speed limit of 30kph in residential areas, 50kph in built-up areas, 80kph on open roads and 90kph on motorways and some main roads. **Cameras** monitor hundreds of kilometres of main road – watch for the *Automatisk Trafikk Kontroll* warning signs – and speeding fines are so heavy that local drivers stick religiously within the speed limit. If you are filmed speeding in a rental car, expect your credit card to be stung by the rental company to the tune of at least 700kr. If you're stopped for **speeding**, you may face a large spot fine (700–3000kr), and leniency is rarely shown to unwitting foreigners. **Drunken driving** is also severely frowned upon. You can be asked to take a breath test during a routine traffic-check; if over the limit, you will have your licence confiscated and may face 28 days in prison.

If you **break down** in a rental car, you'll get roadside assistance from the particular repair company the car hire firm has contracted. The same principle applies to your own vehicle and its insurance/breakdown policy. Two major **breakdown companies** in Norway are Norges Automobil-Forbund (NAF; 24hr assistance on ☎81 00 05 05) and Viking Redningstjeneste (24hr assistance on ☎80 03 29 00). There are emergency telephones along some motorways, and NAF patrols many mountain passes between mid-June and mid-August.

Car rental

All the major international **car rental** companies are represented in Norway, and local contact details are given in the Guide's "Listings" sections for the larger cities. To rent a car, you have to be 21 or over (and have been driving for at least a year), and you'll need a credit card. Rental **charges** are fairly high, beginning around 3600kr per week for unlimited mileage in the smallest vehicle, but include collision damage waiver and vehicle (but not personal) insurance. To cut costs, watch for special deals offered by the bigger companies – a Friday to Monday weekend rental might, for example, cost you as little as 1000kr. If you go to a smaller, local company (of which there are many, listed in the telephone directory under *Bilutleie*), you should proceed with care. In particular, check the policy – it will usually be in Norwegian and in English – for the excess applied to claims, and ensure that it includes collision damage waiver (applicable if an accident is your fault) as well as adequate levels of financial cover. Bear in mind, too, that it's almost always less expensive to make your rental arrangements before you leave home and pick the car up at the airport on arrival.

In the UK

Avis ☎0870/606 0100, ⓦwww.avisworld.com.
Budget ☎0800/181 181, ⓦwww.budget.co.uk.
Europcar ☎0845/722 2525, ⓦwww.europcar.co.uk.
National ☎0870/536 5365, ⓦwww.nationalcar.com.
Hertz ☎0870/844 8844, ⓦwww.hertz.co.uk.

Holiday Autos ☎0870/400 00 99, ⓦwww.holidayautos.co.uk.
Thrifty ☎01494/751 600, ⓦwww.thrifty.co.uk.

In Ireland

Avis Northern Ireland ☎028/9024 0404, Republic of Ireland ☎01/605 7500, ⓦwww.avis.co.uk.
Budget Republic of Ireland ☎01/9032 7711, ⓦwww.budgetcarrental.ie.
Europcar Northern Ireland ☎028/9442 3444, Republic of Ireland ☎01/614 2800, ⓦwww.europcar.ie.
Hertz Republic of Ireland ☎01/660 2255, ⓦwww.hertz.ie.
Holiday Autos Republic of Ireland ☎01/872 9366, ⓦwww.holidayautos.ie.

In North America

Avis US ☎1-800/331-1084, Canada ☎1-800/272-5871, ⓦwww.avis.com.
Budget US ☎1-800/527-0700, ⓦwww.budgetrentacar.com.
Europe by Car US ☎1-800/223-1516, ⓦwww.europebycar.com.
Hertz US ☎1-800/654-3001, Canada ☎1-800/263-0600, ⓦwww.hertz.com.
National US and Canada ☎1-800/227-7368, ⓦwww.nationalcar.com.
Thrifty US and Canada ☎1-800/367-2277, ⓦwww.thrifty.com.

In Australia

Avis ☎13 63 33, ⓦwww.avis.com.
Budget ☎1300/362 848, ⓦwww.budget.com.
Hertz ☎13 30 39, ⓦwww.hertz.com.
National ☎13 10 45, ⓦwww.nationalcar.com.au.
Thrifty ☎1300/367 227, ⓦwww.thrifty.com.au.

In New Zealand

Avis ☎09/526 2847, ⓦwww.avis.co.nz.
Budget ☎09/976 2222, ⓦwww.budget.co.nz.
Hertz ☎0800/654 321, ⓦwww.hertz.co.nz.
National ☎0800/800 115 or 03/366 5574, ⓦwww.nationalcar.co.nz.
Thrifty ☎09/309 0111, ⓦwww.thrifty.co.nz.

Cycling

Cycling is a great way to take in Norway's scenery – just be sure to wrap up warm and dry, and don't be over-ambitious in the distances you expect to cover. Dedicated cycle tracks are few and far between, and mainly confined to the larger towns, but there's precious little traffic on most of the minor roads and cycling along them is a popular pastime. Furthermore, whenever a road is improved or re-routed, the old highway is often redesignated as a cycle route. At almost every town or village you're likely to stay in, you can anticipate that someone will **rent bikes** – either the tourist office, a sports shop, hostel or campsite. Costs are pretty uniform and you can reckon on paying between 120kr and 200kr a day for a seven-speed bike, plus a refundable deposit of up to 1000kr; mountain bikes are about thirty percent more.

A few tourist offices have maps of recommended cycling routes, but this is a rarity. It is, however, important to check your itinerary thoroughly, especially in the more mountainous areas. Cyclists aren't allowed through the longer **tunnels** for their own protection (the fumes can be life-threatening), so discuss your plans with whoever you rent the bike from. You'll also need good lights to ride through those tunnels that aren't prohibited. Bikes mostly go free on car ferries and attract a nominal charge on passenger express boats, but buses vary. The national carrier, Nor-Way Bussekspress accepts bikes only when there is space and charges the appropriate child fare, whilst local, rural buses sometimes take them free, sometimes charge and sometimes do not take them at all. As for trains, Norwegian Railways levies a modest charge of 90kr for carrying bicycles, though on international and express trains you have to book their carriage ahead of time.

If you're planning a **cycling holiday**, your first port of call should be the Norwegian Tourist Board (see p.25). They issue a free multilingual leaflet entitled *Sykkel-Norge*, which describes in detail twelve excellent cycling routes, mostly in the south (see chapter 2) or centre (see chapter 3) of the country, but also including the Rallarvegen in the fjords (see p.214) and a Lofoten route from Svolvær to Moskenes (see p.303–310). The shortest route is 75km, the longest 200km, and they come in varying degrees of difficulty.

In addition, a further twelve routes are detailed in a series of booklets published by **Sykkelturisme i Norge** (Cycle Tourism in Norway), Box 3132, Handelstorget, 3707 Skien (ⓦwww.bike-norway.com), an umbrella organization that promotes cycling in Norway. The routes are all between the south coast and Lofoten and from around 100km to 400km in length. Also included in the booklets is useful information about road conditions, tunnels, repair facilities and places of interest en route. The *Syklistenes Landsforening* (the Norwegian Cyclist Association), Storgata 23c, 0028 Oslo (ⓣ22 47 30 30; ⓦwww.slf.no), also publishes cycling books and maps, but they are nearly all in Norwegian.

The tourist office has a list of **tour operators** specializing in cycling holidays, such as *Freebike Norway Adventures*, Lillestrømvn 475, 1912 Enebakk (ⓣ64 92 65 41, ⓕ64 92 93 96; ⓦwww.freebike.no), who runs a variety of week-long cycling trips and weekend tours in the fjord region and around Lillehammer. Tour costs vary enormously, but an average price is about 5000kr a week all-inclusive.

Accommodation

Inevitably, hotel accommodation is one of the major expenses you will incur on a trip to Norway – indeed, if you're after a degree of comfort, it's going to be the costliest item by far. There are, however, budget alternatives, principally private rooms (arranged via the local tourist office), campsites and cabins, and last but certainly not least, an abundance of HI-registered hostels. Also bear in mind that most hotels offer 25–40 percent discounts in summer and often give substantial year-round weekend discounts too.

Hotels

Norwegian **hotels** are almost universally of a high standard: neat, clean and efficient. Summer prices and more impromptu weekend deals also make many of them, by European standards at least, comparatively economical. Another plus is that the price of a hotel room always includes a **buffet breakfast** – and especially in middle-ranking hotels and up, these can be sumptuous banquets. The main disadvantage is the rooms themselves, which tend to be small – especially the singles – and often lacking in character. Norway abounds in mundane concrete and glass high-rise hotels, though there is a fair smattering of original and often antique places too.

In summer you can take advantage of one of several **hotel discount and pass schemes** in operation throughout Norway (see below). There are four main ones to choose from and each serves to cut costs, but often at the expense of a flexible, or rather spontaneous, itinerary – advance booking is the norm – and diversity: you might prefer to mix hotel and hostel accommodation rather than staying in a hotel every night. Most Norwegian hotels are members of one discount/pass scheme or another. The majority of Norwegian hotels, their room rates, summer discounts and facilities, are listed in the free booklet *Transport and Accommodation*, available from Norwegian tourist offices.

Leading hotel discount and pass schemes

Best Western Summer Pass Costing 75kr, this pass ensures you get the lowest bed-and-breakfast rates at any of Best Western's twenty five Norwegian hotels during high summer (mid-June to late August). Prices vary enormously, depending on the hotel, but most Best Westerns are in price bands ❹–❻) and, with the pass, you can get a discount on the rack rate of around thirty percent. Advance reservations are required to guarantee a bed – either direct with any hotel in the chain, or through the website (ⓦwww.bestwestern.no).

Fjord Pass More than 200 hotels and guesthouses across most of Norway participate in this scheme, with prices for bed and breakfast ranging from 450kr to 1010kr per double room per night. Costing 95kr, the pass is valid for two adults and their children under the age of 15, and gives savings of around ten percent on rack rates. The pass is valid all year, but many of the hotels only participate for a limited period. The pass is widely available in Norway, at tourist offices, major NSB train stations, and at all accommodation in the scheme. Alternatively, you can get it direct from Fjord Tours, Strømgt 4, 5015 Bergen (☎55 55 76 60, Ⓕ55 31 20 60, ⓦwww.fjordpass.no).

Rica Holiday Pass (*Rica Feriepass*) All seventy Rica hotels in Norway participate in this scheme: most are in price category ❹–❻. The pass is valid from late June to mid-August and gives discounts of up to fifty percent on standard tariffs, with every fifth night free. The pass, which is free, can be obtained at any *Rica* hotel or via the website (ⓦwww.rica.no).

Scan + Hotel Pass This pass offers discounts of up to fifty percent at more than 200 hotels in Scandinavia, with around a third of them scattered throughout Norway. It also offers the fifth night's accommodation free. With the pass, double rooms start at 660kr including breakfast. The pass is valid

Accommodation price codes

All the accommodation detailed throughout this guide has been graded according to the following price categories. Prices given are for the **least expensive double room in high season**, although almost every hotel offers seasonal and/or weekend discounts, which can reduce the rate by nearly half. Wherever hotels have an **official summer or weekend rate** we've marked it (s/r), but bear in mind that many others will give impromptu summer and weekend discounts. Single rooms, where available, usually cost between 60 and 80 percent of a double.

The categories given are primarily intended as a guide to price, and the description of the level of facilities in each category provided below is no more than a rough outline of what you might reasonably expect, not a hard-and-fast rule. Throughout the Guide, we have also included cabin-style (*hytter*) accommodation, which is mostly found on campsites. These comfortable, if simple, wooden cabins usually sleep four and can be hired by the night. Almost every hostel has both dormitory beds and double rooms, so we have provided prices for both. The hostel rates given apply to HI members; non-members pay a surcharge of 25kr a night.

❶ **under 350kr** This category includes the majority of HI hostels, almost all of which have single- and double-bedded rooms, as well as dormitory accommodation. The price code refers to double rooms; single rooms range from 220kr to 360kr; while dorm beds usually cost between 125kr and 175kr per person per night, though the most expensive hostels charge around 200kr. Most dormitories have four bunks, some six, but few are larger. Showers and toilets are often shared between dormitories, though almost never to excess, while many singles and doubles are en suite.

❷ **350–600kr** In this category are the majority of rooms in private houses – private rooms – which are arranged through the local tourist office and normally cost in the region of 400–500kr per double room. This category also includes the least expensive guest houses and pensions, where the rooms are normally without private facilities except for washbasins or, sometimes, showers. Expect the rooms to be fairly simple, particularly in the cities. Also in this grade are the most expensive double rooms in HI hostels, many of which are en suite.

❸ **600–800kr** In this category are the more expensive pensions and the least expensive hotel rooms. Most of the hotel rooms in this category are plain but functional, though summer discounts can bring some of the smarter hotel rooms into this price band.

❹ **800–1000kr** In winter, this grade covers most of the country's less expensive chain hotels, where the en-suite rooms are comfortable, if hardly inspiring. In the summer, however, discounts can put some excellent hotels in this price band.

❺ **1000–1200kr** In winter, this grade covers most of the country's better hotels, from modern high-rises with all facilities to the older, more characterful, period places. Rooms are always en suite and mostly equipped with phone, TV, perhaps a mini-bar, and occasionally room service.

❻ **1200–1400kr** At this price, you can expect all mod cons – mini-bar, phone and TV and so forth – plus a good range of hotel facilities, usually a gym and sauna, sometimes a pool.

❼ **over 1400kr** The few hotels in this category are mostly the deluxe ones in Oslo and Bergen, which come with every facility – as you might expect.

at a number of different hotel chains, including the mid-price *Rainbow*, *Golden Tulip* and *Norlandia* hotels. It costs 90kr and is valid at weekends all year and all week from May to September. The pass can be purchased via the website (🌐www.scanplus.no) or from tour operators around the world – the website has a full list.

Pensions and guesthouses

For something a little more informal and less anonymous than the average hotel, **pensions** – *pensjonater* – are your best bet, small, intimate guesthouses usually available in the larger cities and more touristy towns. They cost in the region of 450–550kr for a single room, 600–700kr for a double, and breakfast is generally extra. A *gjestgiveri* is a **guesthouse** or **inn**, charging the same sort of price and sometimes occupying fine old premises. Facilities in all are usually adequate and homely without being overwhelmingly comfortable; more often than not bathrooms are communal. Some pensions and guesthouses have kitchens available for the use of guests, which means you're very likely to meet other residents – a real boon (perhaps) if you're travelling alone.

Hostels

For many budget travellers as well as hikers, climbers and skiers, the country's HI **hostels** (*Vandrerjhem*) provide the accommodation mainstay. There are almost one hundred in total, spread right across the country but with handy concentrations in the western fjords, the central hiking and skiing regions, and in and around Oslo. The Norwegian hostelling association, **Norske Vandrerhjem**, Torggata 1, Oslo (📞23 13 93 00, 🌐www.vandrerhjem.no), issues a free booklet, *Norske Vandrerhjem*, which details locations, opening dates, prices and telephone numbers; it's also possible to make bookings via its website. With the odd exception, the hostels themselves are nearly always very good, sometimes excellent, though those that occupy residential schools tend to be rather drab and institutional.

The average **price** at an HI hostel is around 150kr a night for a dormitory bed, 50kr for breakfast and 80–100kr for a hot meal. Almost all hostels also have a few

regular double and single rooms on offer: at 250–450kr a double, these are among the cheapest rooms you'll find in Norway. If you're not a member of Hostelling International (HI) you can still use the hostels, though it will cost an extra 25kr a night. If you don't have your own sheet sleeping bag, you'll have to rent one for around 40–50kr a time. It cannot be stressed too strongly that **pre-booking** a hostel bed will save you lots of unnecessary legwork.

Many hostels are only **open** from mid-June to mid-August and most close between 11am and 4pm. There's sometimes an 11pm or midnight curfew, though this is not much of a drawback in a country where carousing is so expensive. Breakfast is usually included – ask for a breakfast packet if you have to leave early – and often very good indeed, though other hostel **meals** can be of variable quality, ranging from the bland and filling to the delicious. Most, though not all, hostels have small **kitchens**, but often no pots, pans, cutlery or crockery, so self-caterers should take their own.

Hostelling International associations

In the UK

England and Wales: Youth Hostel Association (YHA) 📞0870/770 8868, 🌐www.yha.org.uk and www.iyhf.org. Annual membership £13; under-18s £6.50; lifetime £190 (or five annual payments of £40).

Ireland: Irish Youth Hostel Association 📞01/830 4555, 🌐www.irelandyha.org. Annual membership €15; under-18s €7.50; family €31.50; lifetime €75.

Northern Ireland: Hostelling International Northern Ireland 📞028/9032 4733, 🌐www.hini.org.uk. Annual membership £10; under-18s £6; family £20; lifetime £75.

Scotland: Scottish Youth Hostel Association 📞0870/155 3255, 🌐www.syha.org.uk. Annual membership £6; under-18s £2.50.

In the US

Hostelling International-American Youth Hostels 📞202/783-6161, 🌐www.hiayh.org. Annual membership $25; over-55s $15; under-18s free; groups of ten or more free; lifetime memberships $250.

In Canada

Hostelling International Canada ☎1-800/663 5777 or 613/237 7884, ⊛www.hostellingintl.ca. Up to 28 months' membership CDN$35; under-18s free; lifetime membership CDN$175.

In Australia

Australia Youth Hostels Association
☎02/9261 1111, ⊛www.yha.com.au. Annual membership AUS$52 for the first twelve months and then AUS$32 each year after; under-18s AUS$16.

In New Zealand

Youth Hostelling Association New Zealand
☎0800/278 299 or 03/379 9970, ⊛www.yha. co.nz. Adult membership NZ$40 for one year; NZ$60 for two years; NZ$80 for three years; lifetime membership NZ$300; under-18s free.

Private rooms

Tourist offices in the larger towns and the more touristy settlements can often fix you up with a **private room** in someone's house, which may include kitchen facilities. Prices are competitive – from 200–250kr single and 300–350kr double – though there's usually a booking fee (20–30kr) on top, and the rooms themselves are typically some way out of the centre. Nonetheless, they're often the best bargain available and, in some cases, an improvement on the local hostel. If you don't have a sleeping bag, check the room comes with bedding – not all of them do; and if you're cooking for yourself, a few basic utensils wouldn't go amiss either.

Cabins and mountain huts

The Norwegian countryside is dotted with hundreds of timber **cabins/chalets** (called *hytter*), ranging from simple wooden huts through to comfortable lodges. They are usually two- or four-bedded affairs with kitchen facilities and sometimes a bathroom, even TV, but not necessarily bed linen. Some hostels have them in their grounds and there are usually a handful of *hytter* at most campsites, where they are graded into five categories. One-star cabins are the most basic with just one room and few facilities; two-star must have electricity; three-star have a handy water supply; four- and five-star

always have hot and cold water and en-suite facilities. In the Lofoten islands cabins are the most popular form of accommodation, many occupying refurbished fishermen's huts called **rorbuer**, or their modern equivalents.

Costs vary enormously, depending on the location, size and amenities of the *hytter*, and there are significant seasonal variations too. However, a one-night stay in a four-bedded *hytter* will rarely cost more than 800kr – a more usual price would be about 400kr – and most of the larger versions fall within the 600kr to 800kr price band. If you're travelling in a group, they are easily the cheapest way to see the countryside. Many *hytter* are also hired out by the week as holiday cottages. All *hytter* can be booked in advance either direct or through travel agents (see p.13, p.15 p.16 and p.19; those that are attached to campgrounds can also be booked online at ⊛www.camping.no.

One further option for hikers is the chain of **mountain huts** (again called *hytter*) on hiking routes countrywide. Some are privately run, but the majority are operated by the Norwegian Mountain Hiking Association (DNT), and its affiliated regional hiking organizations. For further details see p.51.

Campsites

Camping is a popular pastime in Norway, and there are literally hundreds of campsites to choose from, anything from a field with a few spaces for tents through to extensive complexes with all mod cons. The Norwegian tourist authorities detail around four hundred campsites in their free *Camping* brochure (also online at ⊛www.camping.no), allocating them one to five stars based purely on the facilities offered (and not on the aesthetics of the location). Most sites are located with the motorist in mind and a good few occupy key locations beside the main roads. The majority are two- and three-star establishments, where prices are usually per tent pitch, plus a small charge per person; on average expect to pay 80–160kr per night for two people. At four- and five-star sites, overnight fees for two usually range from 120kr to 250kr. During peak season it can be a good idea to **reserve ahead** if you have a car and large tent or trailer; phone numbers are listed in the *Camping* booklet and throughout the

Guide. The Scandinavia **Camping Card** (Campingkort) brings faster registration at many campsites across Scandinavia and occasionally entitles the bearer to special camping rates. It is valid for one year, costs 90kr and can be purchased from participating campsites or online at ⓦ www.camping .no.

Camping rough in Norway is more than tolerated; indeed, as in Sweden, it is a tradition enshrined in law. You can camp anywhere in open areas as long as you are at least 150m away from any houses or cabins.

As a courtesy, ask farmers for permission to use their land – it is rarely refused. Between April 15 and September 15 fires are not permitted in woodland areas nor in fields, and throughout the year campervans are not allowed to stay overnight in lay-bys. For other countryside restrictions, see "Hiking" (p.51). A good sleeping bag is, not surprisingly, essential, since even in summer it can get very cold, and, in the north at least, mosquito repellent and sun-protection cream can be vital.

Food and drink

Norwegian food can, at its best, be excellent: fish is plentiful, and carnivores can have a field day trying meats like reindeer steak, elk, or even – conscience permitting – seal. Admittedly it's pricey, and those on a tight budget may have problems varying their diet, but by exercising a little prudence in the face of the average menu (which is almost always in Norwegian and English), you can keep costs down to reasonable levels. Vegetarians, however, will have slim pickings, except in big-city Oslo, and drinkers will have to dig very deep into their pockets to maintain much of an intake. Indeed, most drinkers end up visiting the supermarkets and state off-licences (Vinmonopolets) so that they can imbibe at home – in true Norwegian style – before setting out for the evening. For a full glossary of useful food and drink terms, see p.421.

Food

Many travellers exist almost entirely on a mixture of picnic food and home-made hot meals, with the odd café meal thrown in to boost morale. Frankly, this isn't really necessary (except on the tightest of budgets) as there are a number of ways to eat out inexpensively. To begin with, a satisfying buffet breakfast, served in almost every hostel and hotel, is an affordable way to vary your diet, whilst special lunch deals will get you a tasty, hot meal for around 60–80kr. Finally, alongside the regular restaurants – which are admittedly expensive – there's the usual array of budget pizzerias and cafeterias in most towns.

Breakfast, picnics and snacks

Breakfast (*frokost*) in Norway is a substantial self-service affair of bread, crackers, cheese, eggs, preserves, cold meat and fish, washed down by tea and coffee. It's usually first-rate at HI hostels, and often truly memorable in hotels, filling you up for the day for around 50–80kr where it's not included with the price of your room (a rare event).

If you're buying your own **picnic food**, bread, cheese, yoghurt and local fruit are all relatively good value, but other staple foodstuffs – rice, pasta, meat, cereals and vegetables – can cost up to around twice what they would at home. Anything tinned is particularly pricey, with the exception of tinned fish, coffee and tea. Beware of a sandwich spread called *Kaviar* – bright pink, sold in tubes and full of additives. Real caviar, on the other hand – from lump-fish rather than sturgeon – is widely available and relatively inexpensive (around 45–50kr for a small jar). **Supermarkets** are ten-a-penny – Rimi and Rema 1000 are the two biggest chains.

Fast food offers the best chance of a hot take-away snack. The indigenous Norwegian stuff, served up from **gatekjøkken** – street kiosks or stalls – in every town, consists mainly of rubbery hot dogs (*varm pølse*), while pizza slices and chicken pieces and chips are much in evidence too. Depressingly, American-style burger bars are also creeping in – both at motorway service stations and in the towns and cities, with McDonald's and Burger King particularly well represented.

A better choice, and usually not much more expensive, is simply to get a sandwich, normally a huge open affair called a **smørbrød** (pronounced "smurrbrur"), heaped with a variety of garnishes. You'll see *smørbrød* groaning under meat or shrimps, salad and mayonnaise, in the windows of bakeries and cafés, or in the newer, trendier sandwich bars in the cities. **Cakes** and **biscuits** are good, too: look out for doughnuts, Danish pastries (*wienerbrød*), butter biscuits (*kjeks*) and waffles (*vafler*).

Good **coffee** is available everywhere, served black or with cream, rich, strong, and, in a few places, free after the first cup, particularly at breakfast. **Tea**, too, is ubiquitous, but the local preference is for lemon tea or a variety of flavoured infusions. All the familiar **soft drinks** are also widely available.

Lunch and dinner

For the best deals, you should have your main meal of the day at lunchtime (*lunsj*), when **kafeterias** (often self-service restaurants) lay on **daily specials**, the *dagens rett*, for around 70–90kr. This is a fish or meat dish served with potatoes and a vegetable or salad, often including a drink, sometimes bread, and occasionally coffee too. Dipping into the menu is more expensive, but not cripplingly so if you stick to omelettes and suchlike. Many department stores – including the Domus chain – have *kafeterias*, as does every large train station. You'll also find them hidden above shops and offices, and next to hotels in larger towns, where they might be called *Kaffistova*. Most close at around 6pm and many don't open at all on Sunday. As a general rule, the food these places serve is plain, verging on the ordinary (though there are some excellent exceptions), but the same cannot be said of the continental-style **café-bars** which abound in Oslo and, increasingly, in all of Norway's larger towns and cities.

These eminently affordable establishments offer much tastier and more adventurous meals like pasta dishes, salads and vegetarian options.

In all of the cities, but especially in Oslo, there are first-class **restaurants**, serving dinner (*middag*) in quite formal surroundings. Apart from exotica such as reindeer and elk, the one real speciality is the seafood, characteristically simple in preparation and wonderfully fresh: whatever you do, don't go home without treating yourself at least once. In the smaller towns and villages, gourmets will be harder pressed – many of the restaurants are pretty mundane, though the general standard is improving rapidly. In all but the most exclusive places, main courses begin at around 150kr, starters and desserts around 60kr each. If in doubt, smoked salmon comes highly recommended, and so does the catfish and monkfish. Again, the best deals are at lunchtime, when a few restaurants put out a **koldtbord** (the Norwegian version of *smörgåsbord*), where for a fixed price of around 170–220kr you can get through as much as possible during the three or four hours it's served. Highlights include vast arrays of pickled herring, salmon (*laks*), cold cuts of meat, dried reindeer, a feast of breads and crackers, and usually a few hot dishes too – meatballs, soup and scrambled eggs. Similar prices apply to the help-yourself, all-you-can-eat **buffets** available in many of the larger hotels in the fjords from around 6pm; go early to get the best choice.

In the towns, and especially in Oslo, there is also a sprinkling of **ethnic restaurants**, mostly Italian with a good helping of Chinese and Indian places. Other cuisines pop up here and there too – Japanese and Moroccan to name but two – but the most affordable are usually the Chinese restaurants and the pizza joints.

Vegetarians

Vegetarians are in for a hard time. Apart from a couple of specialist restaurants in Oslo, you can do little except make do with salads, look out for egg dishes in *kafeterias* and supplement your diet from supermarkets. If you are a **vegan** the problem is greater: when the Norwegians are not eating meat and fish, they are attacking a fantastic selection of milks, cheeses and yoghurts. At least you'll know what's in every dish you eat, since everyone speaks English. If you're self-catering, look for **health food shops** (*helsekost*), found in some of the larger towns and cities.

Drink

One of the less savoury sights in Norway is the fall-over drunk. For reasons that remain obscure – or at least culturally complex – many Norwegians can't just have a drink or two, but have to get absolutely wasted. The majority of their compatriots deplore such behaviour and have consequently imposed what amounts to alcoholic rationing: thus, although booze is readily available in the bars and restaurants, it's taxed up to the eyeballs (half a litre of beer costs 35kr or more) and the distribution of wines and spirits is strictly controlled by a state-run monopoly, **Vinmonopolet**. Whether this type of paternalistic control makes matters better or worse is debatable, but the majority of Norwegians support it.

What to drink

If you decide to splash out on a few drinks, you'll find Norwegian **beer** is lager-like and comes in three strengths (class I, II or III), of which the strongest and most expensive is class III. Brands to look out for include Hansa and Ringsnes. There's hardly any domestically produced **wine** and most **spirits** are imported too, but one local brew worth experimenting with at least once is **aquavit**, served ice-cold in little glasses. At forty percent proof, it's real headache material, though more palatable with beer chasers: Linie aquavit is one of the more popular brands.

Retail outlets for drink

Beer is sold in supermarkets and shops all over Norway, though some local communi-

ties, particularly in the west, have their own rules and restrictions. It costs about half the price you'd pay in a bar. The strongest beer, along with wines and spirits, can only be purchased from the state-controlled **Vinmonopolet** shops. There's usually one in each medium-size town, though there are more branches in the cities (twenty or so in Oslo). Opening hours are generally Monday–Wednesday 10am to 4/5pm, Thursday 10am to 5/6pm, Friday 9am to 4/6pm, Saturday 9am to 1pm, though these times can vary depending on the area, and all shops close the day before a public holiday. At these stores wine is quite a bargain, from around 55kr a bottle, and there's generally a fairly idiosyncratic choice of vintages from various South American countries.

Where to drink

Wherever you **go for a drink**, a half-litre of beer will cost in the region of 45kr and a glass of wine about 35kr. You can get a drink at most outdoor cafés, in restaurants, and in bars, pubs and cocktail bars. That said, only in the towns and cities is there any kind of bar life and in many places you'll be limited to a drink in the local hotel bar or restaurant. However, in Oslo, Bergen, Stavanger, Trondheim and Tromsø you will be able to keep drinking in bars until at least 1am – until 4am in some places.

Norwegians are not as a general rule social drinkers, and **buying a round** is virtually unheard of: people normally pay for their own drink, something which, considering the prices, is worth remembering. Incidentally, a small number of people make their own brews in illegal **stills**. If you are invited over "for a drink", be very careful about what you are drinking. Swigging something akin to aviation fuel in any sort of quantity can leave you, quite literally, speechless.

Communications

Both postal and telephone systems are very efficient in Norway, and things are made even easier by the fact that the staff nearly all speak good English.

Mail

There's no shortage of **post offices** in Norway, and the usual opening hours are Monday to Friday 8/8.30am–4/5pm and Saturday 8/9am–1pm, though some urban post offices stay open longer. **Postage** costs 5.5kr for a postcard or a letter under 20g sent within Norway (7kr within Scandinavia, 9kr to the EU), and 10kr to countries outside. Mail to the USA takes a week to ten days, and two to three days within Europe. You can receive letters at any main city post office by having them addressed "Poste Restante" followed by the surname of the addressee (preferably underlined and in capitals), and then the name of the town and country. When collecting mail, take along your passport or identity card. If you're expecting post and your initial enquiry produces nothing, ask the clerk to check under all of your names and initials as letters sometimes get misfiled.

Telephones

Norway has a reliable **telephone** system, run by Telenor, and you can make domestic and international telephone calls with ease from public phones, which are plentiful and almost invariably work – if you can't find one, some bars have payphones. Most hotel rooms have phones too, but these always attract an exorbitant surcharge.

Public telephones are of the usual Western European kind, where you deposit the money before you make your call. They take 1kr, 5kr, 10kr and 20kr coins, though coin-operated public phones are gradually being phased out in favour of those that only take **telecards** (*TeleKort*). These phone cards can be purchased at newsstands, post offices, major train stations and some supermarkets, and come in 40kr, 90kr and 140kr denominations. An increasing number of public phones also accept the major credit cards.

Most phone booths have English instructions displayed inside. To make a direct call to the UK, dial the code listed below, wait for the tone and then dial the number, omitting the initial 0. To make a direct call to North America, dial the code below, wait for the tone and then dial 1 followed by the area code and number. All Norwegian telephone numbers have eight digits and there's no area code. Local telephone calls **cost** a minimum of 2kr, while 10kr is enough to start an international telephone call, but not much more. International calls are around fifteen percent cheaper from 10pm to 8am.

International dialling codes and useful numbers

To Norway ☎00 47
From Norway to:
  Australia ☎00 61
  Denmark ☎00 45
  Ireland ☎00 353
  New Zealand ☎00 64
  Sweden ☎00 46
  UK ☎00 44
  USA and Canada ☎00 1

Directory enquiries (Scandinavia) ☎180
Directory enquiries (International) ☎181
Emergencies (Fire) ☎110
Emergencies (Police) ☎112
Emergencies (Ambulance) ☎113
International operator assistance (inc. collect & reverse-charge calls) ☎115
Domestic operator assistance (inc. collect & reverse-charge calls) ☎117

Telephone charge cards

Various telephone companies, including British Telecom, issue **telephone charge cards** to their subscribers for use abroad. These cards can be used on any phone and the subsequent call is automatically billed to your home telephone number. To use them, you first dial a code for Norway, which accesses your own company's lines, and then you tap in your account number and PIN – and away you go. In most cases, there is no local charge, but some hotels apply a connection or access fee. For further details, ask your phone company.

Most of Norway is on the **mobile phone network**, which means hikers, skiers, climbers and other outdoors enthusiasts can contact someone by phone almost no matter where they are – invaluable if things go wrong. The Norwegian mobile network is on the **GSM** band common to the rest of Europe, Australia and New Zealand. This means that the vast majority of mobile phones from these countries will work here, though, if you haven't used your mobile abroad before, you should check with your phone company: some mobiles are, for example, barred from international use. It's also a good idea to check **call charges** as costs can be excruciating – particularly irritating is the supplementary charge that you pay on incoming calls.

Things are more complicated (and expensive) for Canadians and Americans. The **North American mobile network** is not compatible with the GSM system, so you'll need a Tri-Band phone which is able to switch from one band to the other.

Finally, international **texting** via the GSM band is – or can be – dead easy. Depending on the mobile, there's often no need to tap in international codes, you just send the message as you would back home. Again, your phone company will advise.

Email

One of the best ways to keep in touch while travelling is to sign up for a free **internet email address** that can be accessed from anywhere, with companies such as YahooMail (Ⓦwww.yahoo.com) or Hotmail (Ⓦwww.hotmail.com). Once you've set up an account, you can use these sites to pick up and send mail from any internet café, or hotel with internet access. In Norway, most of the smarter hotels have internet access of some description and there are a couple of internet cafés in all of the big cities – addresses are given in the Guide. Every public library has internet access too and, even better, it's free.

If you're **taking your own computer**, Ⓦwww.kropla.com is a useful website which gives details of how to plug your lap-top in when abroad. It also has a list of international access codes and information about electrical systems in different countries, including Norway.

Media

Most British and some American daily newspapers, plus the occasional periodical, are on sale in most towns at Narvesen kiosks, major train stations and airports. As for the Norwegian media, state advertising, loans and subsidized production costs sustain a wealth of smaller papers that would bite the dust elsewhere. Most are closely linked with political parties, although the bigger city-based papers tend to be independent. Highest circulations are claimed in Oslo by the independent Verdens Gang and the independent-conservative Aftenposten, and in Bergen by the liberal Bergens Tidende.

Norway's **television** network has expanded over the last few years, in line with the rest of Europe. Alongside the state channels, NRK1, NRK2 and TV2, there are satellite channels like TV Norge, while TV3 is a chan- nel common to Norway, Denmark and Sweden; you can also pick up Swedish TV broadcasts. Many of the programmes are English-language imports, and are always sub-titled, never dubbed, so there is invariably something on that you'll understand, though much of it is pretty unadventurous stuff. The big global cable and satellite channels like MTV and CNN are commonly accessible in hotel rooms.

Local tourist **radio**, giving details of events and festivals, is broadcast during the summer months; watch out for roadside signs advertising these stations. Otherwise, Radio Norway broadcasts English-language news updates on short wave several times daily. In Oslo, it's on FM (93 MHz). The **BBC World Service** is broadcast to all mainland Scandinavia. Frequencies vary according to area and often change every few months. For the latest details, visit ⓦwww.bbc.co.uk/worldservice or write for the free *Programme Guide* to BBC External Services Publicity, Bush House, PO Box 76, Strand, London WC2B 4PH. For reception information for **Radio Canada**, visit ⓦwww.rcinet.ca, and for **Voice of America** visit ⓦwww.voa.gov.

Opening hours, public holidays and festivals

Although there's recently been some movement towards greater flexibility, opening hours for shops and businesses remain fairly restrictive. On the other hand, tourist attractions and leisure amenities tend to have extended opening hours in the summer, but close down early (or completely) in winter especially outside the cities. On public holidays, most things close – though not, of course, restaurants, bars and hotels – and public transport is reduced to a limited (Sunday) timetable.

Opening hours

Normal **shopping hours** are Monday through Friday 10am to 4pm or 5pm, with late opening on Thursdays till 6pm or 8pm, plus Saturdays 10am to 1pm or 3pm. Most supermarkets stay open much longer – from 9am until 8pm in the week and from 9am to 6pm on Saturdays, but close on Sundays. In addition, the majority of kiosks-cum-newsstands stay open till 9pm or 10pm every night of the week (including Sundays), but much more so in the cities and towns than in the villages. Many petrol stations sell a basic range of groceries and stay open till 11pm daily. Vinmonopolet, the state-run liquor store chain, has limited opening hours that vary between stores. **Office hours** are normally Monday to Friday 8.30am or 9am to 5pm or 5.30pm.

Almost every Norwegian town and most of the larger villages have a **museum** of some description. Specific opening times are given in this guide, but in general they open from 10am to 6pm from May to September, and to around 4pm the rest of the year. Monday is a common closing day. However, travelling outside the May to September period, expect a lot of the less important and/or less popular museums to be closed. All the major museums and galleries in Norway are described in the guide, but the sheer number of municipal and minor museums, many of which are only of specialist or local interest, means we have had to be selective: the rest you can miss with a clear conscience.

Public holidays

National **public holidays** are a noticeable feature of the Norwegian calendar and act as a further unifying force in what remains an extremely homogeneous society. There are twelve national public holidays per year, most of which are keenly observed, though the tourist industry carries on pretty much regardless. Incidentally, some state-run museums adopt Sunday hours on public holidays, except on Christmas Day and New Year's Day (and often December 26) when they close. Otherwise most businesses and shops close, and the public transport system operates a skeleton or Sunday service. Most Norwegians take their holidays in the summer season, between mid-June and mid-August.

National public holidays

New Year's Day
Maundy Thursday (Thursday before Easter)
Good Friday
Easter Sunday
Easter Monday
Labour Day (May 1)
Ascension Day (early to mid-May)
National Day (May 17)
Whit Sunday (the seventh Sunday after Easter)
Whit Monday
Christmas Day
Boxing Day (day after Christmas Day)
Note, that when Labour Day or a comparable holiday falls on a Sunday, the next day usually becomes a holiday.

Festivals and events

Almost every town in Norway has some sort of summer shindig and there are winter celebrations too. For the most part, these are worth going to if you are already in the area rather than meriting a special journey. There are two main sorts of **festival**, one being celebrations of historical or folkloric events, the other more contemporary-based jazz and pop music binges and the like. As you might expect, most tourist-oriented events take place in summer and, as always, national and local tourist offices can supply details of exact dates, which tend to vary from year to year. Below we have listed the more important festivals, some of which are detailed in the guide.

A festivals calendar

January
The three- to four-day **Nordlysfestivalen** (Northern Lights Festival) of classical and contemporary music takes place in Tromsø, and features everything from jazz to chamber music. It coincides with the return of the sun, hence its name. For information and tickets contact ☎77 68 12 50 or ⊛www. nordlysfestivalen.no.

February
Ski events at Holmenkollen, in Oslo, run from early February to late March. All sorts of races take place in all sorts of disciplines, from ski marathons to the Nordic World Cup, ending with a massively popular ski jumping competition. Information on ☎75 12 41 20 and ⊛www. skiforeningen.no; tickets on ☎81 53 31 33 and ⊛www.billettservice.no.

March
In late March, Lillehammer stages the **Birkebeinerrennet**, a famous, 58km cross-country ski race from Rena to Lillehammer that celebrates the dramatic events of 1206 when the young prince Haakon Håkanson was rushed over the mountains to safety. The race follows what is thought to have been the original route. Information and tickets on ☎61 27 58 10 and ⊛ www.birkebeiner.no.

May
Constitution or **National Day** sees processions and flag-waving all over the country to celebrate the signing of the Norwegian constitution on May 17, 1814. The first-rate and diverse **Festspillene i Bergen** (Bergen International Festival) of contemporary music takes place from late May until early June. Information and tickets on ☎55 21 06 30 and ⊛www.fib.no.

June
Held in late June in Voss, the **Ekstremsportveko** (Extreme Sport Week) features adventure sports from paragliding and base jumping through to rafting. Information and tickets on ☎92 05 45 56 and ⊛www.ekstremsportveko.com.
The three-day **Norwegian Wood** open-air rock festival takes place in Oslo's Frogner Park amphitheatre, showcasing big-name international artists as well as up-and-coming local bands. Information on ⊛www.norwegianwood.no; tickets on ☎81 53 31 33 and ⊛www.billettservice.no.

July
Held over a five-day period in the middle of the month, the **Molde Jazz Festival** is one of the best of its type, attracting big international names as well as Scandinavian artists. Information and tickets on ☎71 20 31 50 and ⊛www.moldejazz.no.
The **Olavsfestdagene** takes place at the end of the month, with historical pageants and plays honouring Norway's first Christian king, Olav, being staged at Stiklestad, where Olav was killed in battle in 1030. The events are spread over several days leading up to the main attractions on St Olav's Day. Information on ☎73 84 14 50 and ⊛www.olavsfestdagene.no; tickets on ☎81 53 31 33 and ⊛www.billettservice.no.

August
The **Oslo Jazz Festival** is held around the middle of the month, a five-day event attracting some big international names. Information and tickets on ☎22 42 91 20 and ⊛www.oslojazz.no.

October The ten-day **Ultimafestivalen** (Ultima Contemporary Music Festival) features performances by international and Scandinavian talent at various venues across Oslo. Information and tickets on ☎ 22 42 99 99 and ⓦ www.ultima.no.

Outdoor pursuits

Norwegians have a love of the great outdoors. They enjoy many kinds of sports – from dog-sledging and downhill skiing in winter, through to mountaineering, angling and white-water rafting in the summer – but the two most popular activities are hiking and cross-country skiing.

Hiking

Norway boasts some of the most beautiful mountain landscapes in the world. A sequence of rugged mountain ranges, accentuated by icy glaciers, rocky spires and deep green fjords, traverses the country, creating some of the wildest terrain in Europe. Parts of these mountain ranges have been protected by the creation of a string of **national parks** (see p.53), and these are now the focus for the country's hikers. However, the parks incorporate only a fraction of the mountains and there are still little-known and little-visited areas, particularly in the north where the mountains give way to the vast upland plateau of the Finnmarksvidda.

The more popular hiking areas are usually easily reached by public transport, and are crisscrossed by **trails**. These are often dotted with strategically placed mountain huts and lodges (see below), which provide **meals** and **accommodation**. Each establishment is about a day's walk from its nearest neighbour. The **hiking season** is short and loosely defined by the opening and closing of the mountain lodges. It runs from early July (mid-June in some areas) through to late September. At this time of the year, the weather is mild and you can anticipate daytime mountain temperatures of between 20°C and 25°C: pleasant, comfortable, and ideal for hiking. And of course it's daylight for most of the time – beyond the Arctic Circle, all the time – so you're unlikely to be searching for a mountain lodge after dark.

Visitors attempting **long-distance hiking** tours in the mountains of Norway must have previous experience – the weather is too fickle and conditions too treacherous for novices – and no one, however experienced, should attempt a mountain walk alone. With this in mind, **DNT** (Den Norske Turistforening; the Norwegian Mountain Touring Association) runs **week-long guided tours** in the more popular hiking areas; contact DNT's main Oslo office (see below) for its English brochure, or check out its website. Most of the participants are Norwegian, but the tours are popular with visitors as well. Prices vary with the itinerary, but average 3000–4000kr for an all-inclusive package. Some specialist tour operators handle hiking tours too – see p.14, p.15, p.17 & p.19.

DNT (the Norwegian Mountain Touring Association)

Den Norske Turistforening (ⓦ www .turistforeningen.no) plays an active part in managing all aspects of hiking in Norway. Essentially an umbrella organization, it coordinates more than forty local hiking associations, which run mountain lodges, and take care of trails and waymarking. The association also sells maps, organizes tours and provides advice on equipment. DNT's **main office** is in Oslo at Storgata 3 (☎ 22 82 28 00, ℻ 22 82 28 01); its postal address is Postboks 7, Sentrum, 0101 Oslo.

DNT's **website** gives details of all its affiliated members (*Turomåder*), a full list of hiking areas (*Område*) with local details, as well as opening times, contact numbers and so forth, of every DNT and affiliate hut (*hytter*), but only in Norwegian. The larger affiliated hiking associations have their own offices and websites, of which two of the most useful are the **Bergen Turlag**, Tverrgata 4, Bergen (☎55 33 58 10, ⊛www.bergen-turlag.no) and Trondheim's **Trondhjems Turistforening**, Sandgt 30 (☎73 92 42 00, ⊛www.tt.no).

Mountain lodges and rough camping

DNT manages over 300 **mountain huts and lodges** throughout the country, and its regional affiliates maintain many more. Membership of DNT costs 400kr per annum, and although you don't have to be a member to use their huts, you'll soon recoup your outlay through reduced hut charges. For DNT members staying in staffed huts, a bunk in a dormitory costs 90kr, while a family or double room costs 140–175kr, with meals starting at 70kr for breakfast, 165kr for dinner. At unstaffed huts, where you leave the money for your stay in the box provided, an overnight stay costs 135kr. Non-members pay about fifty percent more. Membership can be purchased at any DNT office or staffed mountain lodge.

DNT-staffed mountain lodges, mostly located in the southern part of the country, are often large enough to accommodate over 100 guests, and provide a full service including meals, food and lodging. Some can be reached by road, others on foot only. They are clean, friendly, and well run. All three meals are available – your make your own lunch from the remains of the breakfast buffet. **Self-service huts**, with twenty to forty beds, are also concentrated in the mountains of southern Norway and offer lodging with bedding. Food can be purchased at the self-service lodges, and kitchen equipment is provided. **Unstaffed DNT huts**, often with less than twenty beds, are found mostly in the north. They provide bedding, stoves for heating and cooking, and all kitchen equipment, but you must bring and prepare your own food.

Reservations are accepted at DNT-staffed (and affiliated) lodges for stays of more than two nights, though the lodges are primarily designed to cater for guests in transit. Otherwise, beds are provided on a first-come, first-served basis. DNT members over 50 years of age are, however, guaranteed a bed. During high season, lodges may sometimes be full, although this is not common. If beds are not available, you are given a mattress and blankets for sleeping in a common area. Norwegians are proud that no one is ever turned away. In walks mentioned in this book, Gjendesheim, Glitterheim, Gjendebu and Rondvassbu are DNT-staffed lodges.

Private lodges, generally resembling the larger staffed DNT lodges, are also found in the mountains of Norway. Prices are somewhat higher than at DNT premises, although DNT members often qualify for a discount. In the walking routes described in this book, Østerbø and Memurubu are privately run and staffed. Private lodges accept reservations, and tourist offices have comprehensive details of those in their locality; many DNT brochures list this information too. Incidentally, lodges on the Finnmarksvidda are owned and operated by the government.

As an alternative to the mountain lodges, **rough camping** is allowed freely throughout Norway, although campfires are prohibited from April 15 to September 15. You may camp freely for one night only in any one spot, so long as you are not within 150 metres of a building. In some national parks and other walking areas, these rules have been modified: you must move a bit further away from a hut, or stay near to the hut in a designated camping area. Obviously enough, the main disadvantage of camping, as distinct from staying in a lodge, is the amount of equipment you have to carry; on the other hand, the remoter regions and national parks have few if any lodges.

Planning a hike

Safety should be a primary concern when walking in any mountain area. You should plan your route before starting out, study the maps, know how steep the elevation is, and estimate the time you will need to get to your next stopping point. You should not set out without emergency equipment, extra food, and clothing appropriate for cold and wet conditions. Notify someone of your route and dates of travel. In hunting areas (and seasons), it makes sense to wear brightly coloured clothes when walking in countryside and woodland.

The **equipment** you'll need is similar to what you'd use for hiking in other mountainous regions of Europe. If you plan on a day's hike here and there, you should carry warm clothing, including a hat, scarf and gloves, waterproofs, a sunhat, sunglasses, sun cream, food and water or a thermos, a first-aid kit, insect repellent, a map and compass. For long-distance hut-to-hut tours, you will need a sheet sleeping bag (blankets will be provided), extra clothes, thermals, a knife, toiletries and a torch. Up-to-date synthetic materials, such as polyester or fleece, do an excellent job of keeping you warm when wet, since they neither absorb nor retain moisture. Boots, not trainers, are necessary, and although the new lighter-weight boots may suffice for day walking, heavier boots are more comfortable on longer tours. For campers, a plastic survival bag will keep you and your pack dry; note also that Camping Gaz is only available from certain outlets (details at local tourist offices). Always thorough, DNT (see p.51) issues a comprehensive list of what to take, right down to types of underwear.

Hiking trails are typically marked at regular intervals by cairns. Most junctions are marked by signposts, some of which have stood for many years and are on the small side, making them hard to spot. Red T's are also painted on rocks – a welcome route marker when the weather is poor, as they are visible from farther away than the signposts. Although waymarking is quite good, you should purchase area hiking **maps**. These are available at DNT offices, many tourist offices, most larger book stores and train stations, and in village shops in some of the more popular hiking areas. The entire country has been mapped by the Norwegian highways department and their *M711 Norge* 1:50,000 series, with red and white covers and carrying the trademark *Statens Kartverk*, are the most detailed. They are extremely accurate and many have recently been updated. The department also publishes maps to all the more popular hiking areas at the scale of 1:100,000, which give the hiking trails greater prominence; the series carries the same *Statens Kartverk* trademark and has a maroon cover.

Guidebooks on mountain hiking in Norway are few and far between: probably the best is *Walking in Norway* by Constance Roos, published by Cicerone Press, 2 Police Square, Milnthorpe, Cumbria, LA7 7PY, England (℡01539/562 069, ℻01539/563 417, ℻www.cicerone.co.uk). This outlines an extensive range of mainly long-distance hiking routes.

Hiking areas and national parks

Thirty-six established mountain areas in Norway offer tremendous variety for the walker. From alpine peaks to flat upland plateaux, to green valleys and easy rolling hills, there is walking for everyone. Scramblers will enjoy summits on well-marked routes; older walkers or families with children can easily roam about on gentle slopes; and the athletic can hike out for days on end. The following is a brief description of the more important hiking areas and national parks, most of which are discussed at greater length in the guide.

Some 300km north of Oslo, Norway's most famous hiking area is the **Jotunheimen National Park** ("Home of the Giants" – see p.166), where pointed summits and undulating glaciers dominate the skyline. Covering only 3900 square kilometres, the park offers an amazing concentration of high peaks, more than two hundred of them rising above 1900 metres. There are no public roads; all visitors to the park's interior either walk or ski in. In Jotunheimen, you will find northern Europe's two highest peaks, Galdhøpiggen (2469m) and Glittertind (2464m). Norway's highest waterfall, Vettisfossen, with a 275-metre drop, is also located here.

About 100km east of Jotunheimen, the **Rondane National Park** (see p.163) is one of the country's most popular walking areas. The Rondane's 580 square kilometres, one-third of which is in the high alpine zone, appeal to walkers of all ages and abilities. Ten peaks exceed the 2000-metre mark; many are accessible to any reasonably fit and eager walker. In the eastern Rondane, the gentle Alvdal Vestfjell appeals to older walkers and families with small children.

Stretching east from the Hardangerfjord to Finse in the north and Rjukan in the east, the **Hardangervidda** (see p.210) is Europe's largest mountain plateau, one third of which – 3430 square kilometres – constitutes the protected Hardangervidda National Park. At one time it was home to 40,000 reindeer, the last wild reindeer in Europe, but overgrazing has reduced their numbers. Five tourist organizations work together here to maintain a network of trails, roads and tourist huts, and the entire plateau, with its distinctive lunar-like appearance, is a favourite haunt of hikers and cross-country skiers.

Southeast of Åndalsnes, the mountain ranges of **Tafjord** and **Sunnmøre** are less well-known, incorporating deep fjords, plunging valleys and jagged mountains. Not to be forgotten, either, are the stunning peaks of the **Trollheimen** ("Home of the Trolls"), a favourite with the country's mountaineers.

One of the most accessible of all Norwegian parks, the **Dovrefjell National Park** (see p.169) is bisected by the E6 and the Dombås–Trondheim railway. In Viking times, the Dovre mountain range was regarded as dividing the country in two – with "north of the mountains" and "south of the mountains" meaning north and south of the Dovre. In the eastern Dovre undulating mountains predominate, but as you hike west the steep and serrated alpine peaks of the Romsdal come into view. In the eastern Dovrefjell, there are marshes and open moors with rounded ridges. In the west you find the greatest concentration of high peaks outside the Jotunheimen.

East of Trondheim, the **Sylene Mountains** run along the Norwegian–Swedish border for 800km. In spite of hydroelectric development, this popular summer hiking area still feels very remote. With its rolling hills and gentle ascents, the Sylene presents a contrast to the wild and steep areas to the west. It's an ideal area for people who enjoy easy and fairly level walking. A second walking area located along the Norwegian–Swedish border, this time near Røros, is the **Femundsmarka** (see p.172), where open moorland is broken up by scores of lakes and a few bare peaks.

In the north, it's hard to beat the **Troms Border Trail**. This begins southeast of Tromsø near the Finnish border, and crosses fine mountain scenery in one of Norway's wildest spots. The trail also passes near Treriksrøysa, the point where Norway, Finland and Sweden meet. Cairned routes link up well-appointed unstaffed huts. Walkers seeking isolation will find this area to their liking. The rugged mountains near the northern city of Narvik are equally dramatic and easier to reach.

In the far north, the frozen wastes of Finnmark cover close to 48,000 square kilometres, or fifteen percent of Norway's total surface area. The interior of the region consists of a vast mountain plateau, the **Finnmarksvidda** (see p.331), which holds hundreds of lakes and several thousand kilo-

metres of streams and rivers. At an average height of 300–400m, the plateau's rolling terrain is covered by a carpet of heather turf interspersed with patches of brushwood and birch forest. A handful of lodges (*fjellstuer*) offer accommodation.

Skiing

Norway has as good a claim as anywhere to be regarded as the home of **skiing**: a 4000-year-old rock carving found in Northern Norway is the oldest-known illustration of a person on skis; the first recorded ski competition was held in Norway in 1767; and Norwegians were the first to introduce skis to North America. One of the oldest cross-country ski races in the world is the 55km Birkebeinerrennet from Rena to Lillehammer, held annually in late March; about five thousand skiers participate. The race follows the route taken by Norwegian mountain men in 1206 when they rescued the two-year-old Prince Håkon. The rescuers wore birch bark leggings known as Birkebeiners, hence the name of the race.

Downhill skiing and **snowboard** conditions in Norway are usually excellent from mid-November through to late April, though daylight hours are at a premium around the winter solstice. Temperatures tend to be a good bit colder than in the Alps, and Norway has a more consistent snow record. Broadly speaking Norwegian snow is deep, soft and forgiving. Resorts tend to be less crowded, have smaller class sizes and lift queues, and are at a lower altitude than their counterparts further south in Europe. The main centres for downhill skiing are at Voss (see p.212), Oppdal (see p.169), Geilo (see p.174), Hemsedal and Trysil.

Cross-country skiing is a major facet of winter life in Norway. Approximately half the population are active in the sport, and many Norwegians still use skis to get to work or school. Norwegian interest in the sport is such that in 1994, thousands waited overnight in temperatures of -25°C to see the final day of racing at the Lillehammer winter Olympics. In the classic style of cross-country skiing, the whole body is angled forwards and the skis remain parallel except when braking or turning. For forward propulsion the skier transfers all weight to one ski, then straightens that leg while kicking downwards and backwards. At the same time, the arm on the opposite side of the body pushes down and back on the ski pole close to the line of the unweighted ski, which glides forward. At the finish of the kick, weight is transferred to what was the gliding ski, ready for the next kick. An unweighted cross-country ski is arc shaped, with the central section not touching the ground until the skier's down-kick flattens it on to the snow; the ends of the skis glide while the middle grips. Near major ski resorts, sets of parallel ski tracks called *Loipe* are cut in the snow by machine. They provide good gliding conditions and help keep the skis parallel; some *Loipe* are floodlit.

Skis can be waxed or waxless. Waxless skis have a rough tread in the middle called "fishscales", which grips adequately at temperatures around zero. Waxed skis work better at low temperatures and on new snow. Grip wax is rubbed onto the middle third of the ski's length, but a sticky substance called *klister* is used instead in icy conditions. All skis benefit from hard glide wax applied to the front and back thirds of the base.

In the Telemark region of Southern Norway a technique has been developed to enable skiers to descend steep slopes on free-heel touring skis. This technique, known as "**Telemarking**", provides a stable and effective turning platform in powder snow. Essentially the skier traverses a slope in an upright position, but goes down on a right knee to execute a right turn and vice versa.

For companies specializing in downhill **ski packages** to Norway see p.14, p.15, p.17 and p.19; nearly all of them will also deal with cross-country skiing and other, more obscure winter activities such as frozen waterfall climbing and ice fishing. Several specialist operators organize **cross-country skiing tours** (see p.14, p.15, p.17 and p.19), and DNT (see p.51) organizes a limited range of guided excursions too. Touring skiers should adopt the precautions taken by winter hill walkers: if going out for more than a couple of hours the skier should have emergency clothing, food and a vacuum flask with a hot drink. Detailed advice about coping with winter conditions is available in the excellent *Welcome to the Norwegian Mountains in Wintertime* booklet available from DNT.

Although you may be tempted to go on a ski package, remember that in most places you should find it easy (and comparatively inexpensive) to go skiing independently. Even in Oslo, there are downhill ski runs within the city boundaries, and plenty of places from which to **rent equipment**. Per day, ski rental with boots and poles costs in the region of 150kr, snowboards 250kr, and passes for chair lifts 200kr. Cross-country skiers will also have few difficulties in renting skiing tackle by the day (or week), with costs similar to those for downhill gear. In terms of **preparation**, lessons on a dry slope are useful in so far as they develop confidence and balance, but cross-country skiing needs stamina and upper body as well as leg strength.

Finally, **summer skiing** on Norway's mountains and glaciers – both alpine and cross-country – is now very popular. Lots of places offer this, but one of the largest and most convenient spots is the **Folgefonn Sommar Skisenter** (late May to late Sept daily 10am–4pm; ☎94 56 78 40, ⓦwww.folgefonn.no), which has ski rental, a ski school, a café and a ski lift to the slopes; see p.208 for more details.

Fishing

Norway's rivers provide some wonderful opportunities for **anglers**. In particular, the fjord region's rivers offer fabulous freshwater fishing, as do the Arctic rivers further north, with common species including trout, char, pike and perch. Lakselv (see p.346) in Finnmark is one of several places renowned for its salmon fishing – *lakselv* actually means "salmon river" – and there is outstanding sea angling off the Lofoten Islands too. To go **freshwater fishing**, you need two licences – a national licence, which is free and available at any post office, and a local licence (*fiskeko-rt*), available from sports shops, a few tourist offices, some hotels and most campsites. The cost of the local licence varies enormously; in the Oslo area it is 165kr.

Seawater fishing has different rules: there's no local licence and you only need a national one if you go fishing for salmon, trout or sea char. This licence costs 180kr, can be purchased at any post office and also includes the freshwater national licence. If you take your own fishing tackle, you must have it disinfected before use.

For further information, NORTRA's Angling in Norway, available from the Norwegian Tourist Board, provides a comprehensive account of what you can catch and where, while the Norwegian Tourist Board's website (⊛ www.visitnorway.com) has details of organized fishing trips

River-rafting

Norway has literally dozens of top-notch **whitewater river-rafting** runs. Two of the

best places are Voss (see p.212) and Sjoa (see p.161). For a full list of **tour operators** offering rafting trips, contact Norges Padleforbund (the Norwegian Canoe Association), Service boks 1, Ullevål stadion, 0840 Oslo (☎21 02 98 35, ⊛ www.padling.no).

! Crime and personal safety

There's little reason why you should ever come into contact with the Norwegian police force. This is one of the least troublesome corners of Europe – in the whole of the country there's an average of only one murder per week. You will find that most public places are well lit and secure, most people genuinely friendly and helpful, and street crime and hassle relatively rare.

It would be foolish, however, to assume that problems don't exist. Oslo in particular has its share of **petty crime**, fuelled – as elsewhere – by drug addicts and alcoholics after easy money. But keep tabs on your possessions and you should have little reason to visit the police. If you do, you'll find them courteous, concerned, and usually able to speak English. If you have something stolen, make sure you get a police report – essential if you are to make a claim against your insurance.

As for offences *you* might commit, drinking alcohol in public places is not permitted, and being drunk on the streets can get you arrested. Drinking and driving is treated especially rigorously. Drugs offences, too, are met with the same attitudes that prevail throughout most of Europe. Women won't, however, be cautioned for topless sunbathing, which is universally accepted in the resorts (elsewhere there probably won't be anyone around to care), and camping rough is a tradition enshrined in law. Should you be **arrested** on any charge, you have the right to **contact your embassy or consulate** (see p.114 for details). Unfortunately, consular officials are notoriously reluctant to get involved, though most are required to assist you to some degree if you have your passport stolen or lose all your money. If you've been detained for a drugs offence, don't expect any sympathy or help.

Avoiding trouble

Almost all the problems tourists encounter in Norway are to do with **petty crime** – pickpocketing and bag-snatching – rather than more serious physical confrontations, so it's as well to be on your guard and know where your possessions are at all times. Sensible **precautions** include: carrying bags slung across your neck and not over your shoulder; not carrying anything in pockets that are easy to dip into; having photocopies of your passport, airline ticket and driving licence; leaving passports and tickets in the hotel safe; and noting down the numbers of your travellers' cheques and credit cards. When you're looking for a hotel room, never leave your bags unattended. Vehicle theft is still uncommon, but luggage and valuables left in cars do make a tempting target, so when parking ensure your possessions are not left in view. If you're on a **bicycle**, make sure it is well locked up. At **night**, you'd be well advised to avoid walking round the rougher parts of Oslo (to the east of the city centre and especially around the main train and bus station, Oslo S). Also, as general precautions, avoid unlit streets and don't go out loaded with valuables. Using public transport, even late at night, isn't usually a problem, but if in doubt, take a taxi.

Thieves often work in pairs and, although theft is far from rife, you should be aware of certain **ploys** to distract you, such as when a "helpful" person points out "birdshit" (shaving cream or similar) on your coat, while someone else relieves you of your money; being invited in the street to read a card or paper; someone in a café making a move for your drink with one hand and, as you try to prevent your drink being taken, exploring your bag with the other. If you're in a crowd, watch out for people moving in unusually close.

What to do if you're robbed

If you're robbed, you need to go to **the police** (℡112) to report it, not least because your insurance company will require a police report, so remember to make a note of the report number or, better still, ask for a copy of the statement itself. Don't expect a great deal of concern if your loss is relatively small, and don't be surprised if the formalities take

ages. In the unlikely event that you're **mugged** or otherwise threatened, *never* resist, and try to reduce your contact with the robber to a minimum. Either just hand over what's wanted, or throw money in one direction and take off in the other. Afterwards, go straight to the police, who will be much more sympathetic and helpful on these occasions.

Sexual harassment

In the normal course of events, **women travellers** in almost any part of Norway are unlikely to feel threatened or attract unwanted attention. The main exception is in the seedier areas of Oslo, where the atmosphere may feel frightening especially late at night, but with common sense and circumspection you shouldn't have anything to worry about. In terms of nightclubs and bars, the men who hang around in them pose no greater or lesser threat than similar operators at home, though the language barrier (where it exists) makes it harder to know who to trust.

Travellers with disabilities

As you might expect, the Norwegians have adopted a progressive and thoughtful approach to the issues surrounding disability and, as a result, there are decent facilities for travellers with disabilities across the whole country. An ever increasing number of hotels, hostels and campsites are equipped for disabled visitors, and are credited as such in the tourist literature by means of the standard wheelchair-in-a-box icon. Furthermore, on most main routes Norwegian State Railways has special carriages with wheelchair space, hydraulic lifts and a disabled toilet; domestic flights either cater for or provide assistance to disabled customers; new ships on the Hurtigrute coastal sea route have lifts and cabins designed for disabled people; and the newer fjord ferries also have lifts from the car deck to the lounge and toilets.

In the cities and larger towns, many **restaurants** and most **museums** and public places are wheelchair-accessible, and although facilities are not so advanced in the countryside, things are improving rapidly. Drivers will find that most motorway **service stations** are wheelchair-accessible and that, if you have a UK-registered vehicle, the disabled **car parking badge** is honoured. Note

also that several of the larger car rental companies have modified vehicles available. On a less positive note, city pavements can be uneven and difficult to negotiate and, inevitably, winter snow and ice can make things even worse.

Getting to Norway should be relatively straightforward too. Most airlines and shipping companies provide assistance to disabled travellers, while some also have specific facilities, such as DFDS Scandinavian Seaways ferries' specially adapted cabins.

Contacts for travellers with disabilities

In Norway

Euro Terra Nova, Rådhusgata 17, N-0164 Oslo (☎22 99 23 99, ℻22 99 23 90, ⓦwww.euroterranova.no). Recommended in the Official Travel Guide produced by the tourist office, this organization has information on hotel and car rental discounts as well as on coach tours round Norway especially designed for wheelchair users.
Norges Handikapforbund, Schweigaardsgt 12, 0185 Oslo (☎24 10 24 00, ℻24 10 24 99, ⓦwww.nhf.no). Postal address: Postboks 9217, Grønland, 0134 Oslo. This organization produces a wide range of useful information from general guidance on accessibility across the whole of the country through to comments about the major hotel chains and transport. The website is particularly good, and is in both English and Norwegian.

In the UK and Ireland

Access Travel 6 The Hillock, Astley, Lancashire M29 7GW ☎01942/888 844, ⓦwww.access-travel.co.uk. Tour operator that can arrange flights, transfers and accommodation that is suitable for people with disabilities.
Holiday Care 2nd floor, Imperial Building, Victoria Rd, Horley, Surrey RH6 7PZ ☎01293/774 535, Minicom ☎01293/776 943, ℻01293/784 647, ⓦwww.holidaycare.org.uk. Provides free lists of accessible accommodation.
Irish Wheelchair Association Blackheath Drive, Clontarf, Dublin 3 ☎01/818 6400, ℻01/833 3873, ⓦwww.iwa.ie. Useful information provided about travelling abroad with a wheelchair.
Tripscope Alexandra House, Albany Rd, Brentford, Middlesex TW8 0NE ☎0845/758 5641, ℻020/8580 7021,

ⓦwww.justmobility.co.uk/tripscope. A registered charity that provides a national telephone information service offering free advice on international transport for those with a mobility problem.

In the US and Canada

Access-Able ⓦwww.access-able.com. Online resource for travellers with disabilities.
Directions Unlimited 123 Green Lane, Bedford Hills, NY 10507 ☎1-800/533-5343 or ☎914/241-1700. Travel agency specializing in bookings for people with disabilities.
Mobility International USA 451 Broadway, Eugene, OR 97401 ☎541/343-1284, ℻541/343-6812, ⓦwww.miusa.org. Information and referral services, access guides, tours and exchange programmes. Annual membership $35 (includes quarterly newsletter).
Society for the Advancement of Travelers with Handicaps (SATH) 347 5th Ave, New York, NY 10016 ☎212/447-7284, ⓦwww.sath.org, ⓔsathtravel@aol.com. Non-profit-making educational organization that has actively represented travellers with disabilities since 1976.
Wheels Up! ☎1-888/389-4335, ⓦwww.wheelsup.com. Provides discounted airfare, tour and cruise prices for disabled travellers, also publishes a free monthly newsletter and has a comprehensive website.

In Australia and New Zealand

ACROD (Australian Council for Rehabilitation of the Disabled) PO Box 60, Curtin ACT 2605; Suite 103, 1st floor, 1–5 Commercial Rd, Kings Grove 2208; ☎02/6282 4333, TTY ☎02/6282 4333, ℻02/6281 3488, ⓦwww.acrod.org.au, ⓔacrodnat@acrod.org.au. Provides lists of travel agencies and tour operators for people with disabilities.
Disabled Persons Assembly 4/173–175 Victoria St, Wellington, New Zealand ☎04/801 9100 (also TTY), ℻04/801 9565, ⓦwww.dpa.org.nz. Resource centre with lists of travel agencies and tour operators for people with disabilities.

Gay Norway

Norway was one of the first countries in the world to pass a law (1981) making discrimination against homosexuals and lesbians illegal. In 1993, it became only the second country to pass legislation giving lesbian and gay couples the same rights as married couples, while retaining a bar on church weddings and the right to adopt children. This, however, had more to do with respect for the rights and freedoms of the individual than a positive attitude to homosexuality – Norway remains, in essence at least, very much a (heterosexual) family-oriented society. Nevertheless, the general attitude to gays is so tolerant that few feel the need to disguise their sexuality, and the age of consent is sixteen.

It's commonplace for bars and pubs to have a mixture of straights and gays in their clientele. There is something of a separate scene in Bergen, Trondheim and especially Oslo, but it's pretty low-key stuff and barely worth seeking out – and the same applies to the weekly gay and lesbian nights held in some small-town nightclubs. The best source of information on the Oslo scene is **ungdoms informasjonen**, at Møllergata 3 in the city centre (☏22 41 51 32; ⊛www.unginfo .oslo.no), whose website has a gay section in both English and Norwegian. The main gay event in the city's calendar takes place each June – the *Skeive Dager* (Queer Days) Festival, incorporating Gay and Lesbian Pride (see p.114 for full details).

There is also a strong and effective nationwide gay organization, **Landsforeningen for Lesbisk og Homofil frigjøing** (LLH; ☏22 11 05 09, ℱ22 20 24 05, ⊛www.llh.oslo.no), whose head office is in Oslo on the third floor at Nordahl Brunsgate 22. The postal address is LLH, Postboks 6838, St Olavs plass, 0130 Oslo. It also has branches throughout the country.

Contacts for gay and lesbian travellers

In the UK

⊛**www.gaytravel.co.uk** Online gay and lesbian travel agent, offering good deals on all types of holiday. Also lists gay- and lesbian-friendly hotels around the world. Also check out **adverts** in the weekly *Pink Paper*, handed out free in gay venues.

In the US and Canada

Damron ☏1-800/462-6654 or ☏415/255-0404, ⊛www.damron.com. Publishes *Men's Travel Guide*, a pocket-sized yearbook full of hotel, bar and club listings and resources for gay men; *Women's Traveler* provides similar listings for lesbians; and *Damron Accommodations* provides listings of over 1000 accommodations for gays and lesbians worldwide. All these titles can be bought at a discount on the website, where a search facility gives gay-friendly hotels and listings for major Scandinavian cities.

Gaytravel.com ☏1-800/429-8728, ⊛www.gaytravel.com. The premier site for trip planning, bookings and general information about international gay and lesbian travel – including city breaks to Bergen and Norwegian cruises.

International Gay & Lesbian Travel Association ☏1-800/448-8550 or ☏954/776-2626, ⊛www.iglta.org. Trade group that can provide a list of gay- and lesbian-owned or -friendly travel agents, accommodation and other travel businesses.

In Australia and New Zealand

Gay and Lesbian Tourism Australia ⊛www.galta.com.au. Directory and links for gay and lesbian travel worldwide.

Parkside Travel ☏08/8274 1222, ℰparkside@herveyworld.com.au. Gay travel agent dealing with all aspects of gay and lesbian travel worldwide.

Silke's Travel ☏1800/807 860 or ☏02/8347 2000, ⊛www.silkes.com.au. Long-established gay and lesbian specialist, with the emphasis on women's travel.

Tearaway Travel ☏03/9510 6644, ⊛www.tearaway.com. Gay-specific business dealing with international and domestic travel.

Directory

ADDRESSES In Norway, addresses are always written with the number after the street-name. In multi-storey buildings, the ground floor is referred to as the first floor, and so on (we have numbered floors accordingly in this guide).

ALPHABET The letters Æ, Ø and Å come at the end of the alphabet, after Z (and in that order).

BOOKS You'll find English-language books in almost every bookshop, though they are far more expensive than at home. Libraries, too, stock foreign-language books.

BORDERS There is little formality at either the Norway–Sweden or Norway–Finland borders, but the northern border with Russia is a different story. Despite the relaxation of tension in the area following the break-up of the Soviet Union, border patrols (on either side) won't be overjoyed at the prospect of you nosing around. If you have a genuine wish to visit Russia from Norway, it's best to sort out the paperwork – visas and so forth – before you leave home. Kirkenes (see p.348) is the main starting point for tours into Russia from Norway.

CHILDREN There are no real problems with taking children to Norway. They pay half-price (infants aged under 3 or 4 free) on all forms of public transport, and at almost every attraction, from museums through to theme parks. As for accommodation, family rooms are widely available in HI hostels, and in most hotels an extra (child's) bed will be placed in a room at no or little cost. Baby compartments (with their own toilet and changing room) are available for children aged 2

and under on most trains, and baby-changing rooms can be found at most larger train stations. Many restaurants have children's menus; if not, it's always worth asking for cheaper, smaller portions of a dish.

GLACIERS These slow-moving masses of ice are in constant, if generally imperceptible, motion, and are therefore potentially dangerous. People, often tourists, die on them nearly every year. Never climb a glacier without a guide, never walk beneath one and always heed the instructions at the site. Guided crossings can be terrific – see the relevant accounts in the guide.

LEFT LUGGAGE There are coin-operated lockers in most train and bus stations and at all major ferry terminals.

SMOKING Smoking is prohibited in all public buildings, including train stations, and forbidden on all domestic flights and bus services. Restaurants have to have non-smoking areas by law, and there are supposed to be dividing walls between smoking and non-smoking sections. Hoteliers have by law to designate fifty percent of their rooms as non-smoking.

TIME Norway is one hour ahead of the UK and six to nine hours ahead of continental USA.

TIPPING Some hotels, cafés, restaurants and bars add a service charge to their bills and this is – or at least should be – clearly indicated. Otherwise, few people tip at hotels or bars, but restaurant waiters will be disappointed not to get a tip of between 10 and 15 percent.

Guide

Guide

Oslo and the Oslofjord

CHAPTER 1 # Highlights

* **The National Gallery**
  Norway's largest collec-
  tion of fine art, with a bit
  of everything from
  Munch to Manet, Dahl to
  Degas. **See p.82**

* **The Viking Ships
  Museum** This excellent
  museum contains a trio
  of Viking longships
  retrieved from ritual burial grounds in the south
  of the country. **See p.92**

* **The Vigelandsparken**
  Take a stroll round the
  fantastical creations of
  Gustav Vigeland in this
  open-air sculpture park.
  See p.95

* **The Munch Museum**
  See *The Scream* and
  others in this huge collection of works by
  Norway's most eminent
  artist. **See p.98**

* **Hovedøya and
  Langøyene** You can
  swim, walk through
  woods or laze on the
  beach on these Oslofjord
  islands, just a short ferry
  ride from the city centre.
  See p.101

* **Engebret Café** Try the
  reindeer and other
  Norwegian specialities at
  one of Oslo's top-class
  restaurant. **See p.104**

Oslo and the Oslofjord

Oslo is a vibrant, self-confident city whose urbane, easy-going air bears comparison with any European capital. This was not always the case, however. Oslo was something of a poor relation until Norway's break with Sweden at the beginning of the twentieth century, remaining dourly provincial until the 1950s, and only since then has the city developed into a go-ahead and cosmopolitan commercial hub of half a million people. It is also the only major metropolis in a country brimming with small towns and villages, its nearest rival, Bergen, being less than half its size. This gives Oslo a powerful – some say overweening – voice in the political, cultural and economic life of the nation. Inevitably, Norway's big companies are mostly based here, as a rash of concrete and glass tower blocks testifies, but fortunately these monoliths rarely interrupt the stately Neoclassical lines of the late nineteenth-century **city centre**, Oslo's most beguiling region, boasting a lively street life and bar scene as well as a clutch of excellent museums. Indeed, Oslo's biggest single draw is its **museums**, which cover a hugely varied and stimulating range of topics: the fabulous Viking Ships museum, the Munch Museum showcasing a good chunk of the painter's work, the sculpture park devoted to the bronze and granite works of Gustav Vigeland, and the moving historical documents of the Resistance Museum, are enough to keep even the most weary museum-goer busy for a few days. There's also a decent **outdoor life** – Oslo is enlivened by a good range of parks, pavement cafés, street entertainers and festivals. In summer, when virtually the whole population seems to live outdoors, the city is a real delight. Winter's also a good time to visit, when Oslo's location amid hills and forests makes it a thriving and affordable ski centre.

Whilst its city centre may be compact, Oslo's outer districts spread over a vast 453 square kilometres, encompassing huge areas of forest, sand and water. Almost universally, its inhabitants have a deep and abiding affinity for the wide open spaces that surround their city: the waters of the Oslofjord to the south and the forested hills of the Nordmarka to the north, are immensely popular for everything from boating and hiking to skiing. For all but the shortest of stays, there's ample opportunity to join in – the open forest and **cross-country ski** routes of the Nordmarka and the **island beaches** just offshore in the Oslofjord are both easily reached by underground train or ferry.

Oslo curves round the innermost shore of the **Oslofjord**, whose tapered waters extend for some 100km from the Skagerrak, the choppy channel separating Norway and Sweden from Denmark. As Norwegian fjords go, Oslofjord is not spectacularly beautiful – the rocky shores are generally low and unprepossessing – but scores of islets diversify the seascape. These tiny forested bumps, which once housed the city's seaward defences, now accommodate

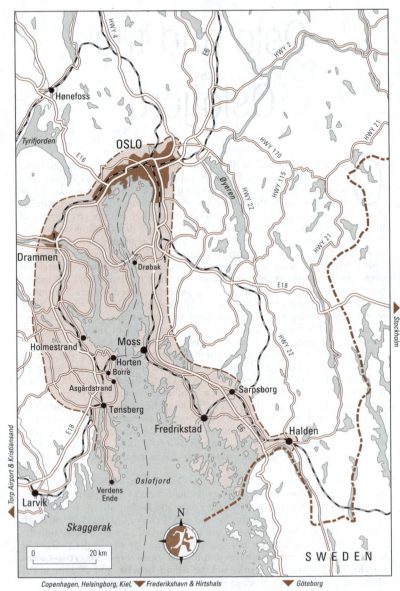

summer chalets. The towns that trail along the shoreline are of little immedi-ate appeal, being for the most part workaday industrial settlements. The few exceptions include, on the eastern shore, **Fredrikstad**, Norway's only surviv-ing fortified town, and the picturesque village of **Drøbak**, and on the western shore, the Viking burial mounds of **Borre** and the popular holiday resort of **Tønsberg**.

Oslo

If Oslo is your first taste of Norway, you'll be struck by the light – soft and brilliantly clear in the summer and broodingly gloomy in winter. The grand late nineteenth- and early twentieth-century buildings of central Oslo suit the climate well, doughty structures that once gave a sense of security to the emergent nation, and still look reassuringly sturdy today. Largely as a result, most of **downtown Oslo** remains easy and pleasant to walk around, a hum-ming, good-natured place whose airy streets and squares combine these appealing remnants of the city's early days with a clutch of good museums – in particular the Nasjonalgalleriet (National Gallery) and the Hjemmefrontmuseum (Resistence Museum) – and dozens of lively bars, cafés and restaurants.

The city's showpiece museums – most notably the remarkable Vikingskipshuset (Viking Ships Museum) – are located on the **Bygdøy penin-sula**, to which ferries shuttle from the jetty behind the **Rådhus** (City Hall); other ferries head south from the Vippetangen quay behind the Akershus to the string of rusticated **islands**, such as the pretty, wooded Hovedøya, that necklace the inner waters of the Oslofjord. Back on the mainland, **east Oslo** is the least prepossessing part of town, a gritty sprawl housing the poorest of the city's inhabitants, though the newly revived district of **Grünerløkka** is now home to a slew of fashionable bars and clubs. The main reason to head this way, howev-er, is for the **Munch Museum**, which boasts a superb collection of the artist's work; afterwards it's mildly tempting to pop along the eastern shore of Oslo's principal harbour for the views over the city and to look at the skimpy remains of the medieval town. **Northwest Oslo** is far more prosperous, with big old houses lining the avenues immediately to the west of the Slottsparken. Beyond is the **Frognerparken**, a chunk of parkland where the stunning open-air sculp-tures of Gustav Vigeland are displayed in the **Vigelandsparken**. Further west still, beyond the city limits in suburban Høvikodden, the **Henie–Onstad Kunstsenter** displays more prestigious modern art, enhanced by the museum's splendid setting on a headland overlooking the Oslofjord.

The city's enormous reach becomes apparent only to the north of the cen-tre in the **Nordmarka**. This massive forested wilderness, stretching far inland, is patterned by hiking trails and cross-country ski routes. Two T-bane lines pro-vide ready access, clanking their way up into the rocky hills that herald the region. The more westerly T-bane grinds on past **Holmenkollen**, a ski resort where the ski-jump makes a crooked finger on Oslo's skyline. The line termi-nates at **Frognerseteren** – although the station is still within the municipal boundaries, the forested hills and lakes nearby feel anything but urban. The more easterly T-bane is perhaps even more appealing, ending up near **Sognsvannet**, a pretty little lake set amidst the woods and an ideal place for an easy stroll and/or a picnic.

Compared to other European capitals, Oslo is extremely safe. However, the usual cautions apply to walking around on your own late at night, when you should be particularly careful in the vicinity of Oslo S, the main train station, where the junkies gather.

Some history

OSLO is the oldest of the Scandinavian capital cities. Its name is derived from *Às,* a Norse word for God, and *Lo,* meaning field. The city was founded around 1048 by Harald Hardrada, but it wasn't until Harald's son, Olav Kyrre, established a bishopric and built a cathedral here, that the city really began to take off. Despite this, the kings of Norway continued to live in Bergen – an oddly inefficient division of state and church, considering the difficulty of communication. At the start of the fourteenth century, **Håkon V** rectified matters by moving to Oslo, where he built himself the Akershus fortress, and the town boomed until 1349, when bubonic plague wiped out almost half the population. The slow decline that followed this catastrophe accelerated when Norway came under Danish control in 1397. No longer the seat of power, Oslo became a neglected backwater until its fortunes were revived by the Danish king **Christian IV**. He moved Oslo lock, stock and barrel, shifting it west to its present site and modestly renaming it **Christiania** in 1624. The new city prospered, and continued to do so after 1814, when Norway broke away from Denmark and united with Sweden. In the event, this political realignment was a short-lived affair and by the 1880s, Christiania – and the country as a whole – was clamouring for independence. This was eventually achieved in 1905, though the city didn't revert to its original name for another twenty years – and has hardly looked back since.

Arrival and information

Downtown Oslo is at the heart of a superb public transport system, which makes arriving and departing convenient and straightforward. The principal arrival hub is the area around **Oslo S** train station at the eastern end of the main thoroughfare, **Karl Johans gate**. The other hub is **Nationaltheateret** at the west end of Karl Johans gate, handier for most city centre sights and Oslo's main harbour. There's a **tourist information** office in Oslo S and another by the harbour, close to Nationaltheateret.

By air
Oslo's gleaming airport, **Gardermoen**, is a lavish affair very much in the Scandinavian style, with acres of cool stone floor, soft angles, slender concrete pillars and high ceilings. Departures is on the upper level, Arrivals on the lower, where there are also currency exchange facilities, car rental offices – see "Listings" on p.113 for details – and a **tourist information** office. The latter will make hotel reservations on your behalf for a small charge – see "Accommodation" on p.74.

Oslo Card

The **Oslo Card** is a useful pass that gives free admission to almost every museum and unlimited free travel on the whole municipal transport system, including local trains, plus free on-street parking at metered parking places. It also provides some discounts in shops, hotels and restaurants, though in winter, when opening hours for many sights and museums are reduced, you may have to work hard to make the card pay for itself. Valid for 24, 48 or 72 days, it costs 190kr, 280kr or 370kr respectively, with children aged four to fifteen charged 60kr, 80kr or 110kr. A 24-hour family card for two adults and two children costs 395kr. It's available at the city's tourist offices, most hotels and campsites in Oslo, the Trafikanten office (see p.73) and most downtown Narvesen newsagents. The card is valid for a set number of hours (rather than days) starting from the moment it is first used, at which time it should either be presented and stamped, or (for example, if your first journey is by tram) you should fill in the date and time yourself.

Gardermoen is located 45km north of the city, at the end of a 7km-long spur road off the E6 motorway. If you're heading into Oslo by **car**, there is a 15kr toll on all approach roads into the city – so have some kroner handy. **Express trains** to Oslo stop at Oslo S, with most continuing on to Nationaltheatret station (5.30am–12.30pm every 10–15 min; 25min; 140kr single). There are also less frequent **inter-city** trains into Oslo (70kr single) that take about twenty minutes longer, plus train services north to Lillehammer, Røros and Trondheim. Alternatively, **Flybussen** (Mon–Sat 5.30am–1am, Sun noon–midnight, every 10–15min; 45min; 95kr single and 150kr return) depart from outside the Arrivals concourse for the main downtown bus station, Oslo Bussterminal. They then continue on to Jernbanetorget, Grensen and the *Radisson SAS Scandinavia Hotel*. Incidentally, **for Gardermoen departures**, the Flybussen follows the same route in the opposite direction, but will stop at any city centre bus stop on the way. Finally, Nor-Way Bussekspress operates a variety of other bus services from the airport direct to the small towns surrounding Oslo.

Note that if you are flying from Stansted or Prestwick in the UK on the budget airline Ryanair, you'll land at **Oslo (Torp)** airport, just outside the town of Sandefjord, about 110km southwest of Oslo: there are connecting buses (150kr return, 98kr single) from Torp to the capital.

By train and bus

International and domestic **trains** use **Oslo Sentralstasjon**, known as Oslo S (train information and reservations ☎815 00 888, ⓦwww.nsb.no), sited on the Jernbanetorget, a square at the eastern end of the city centre. There are money exchange facilities here, as well as a post office, a tourist office, and two **train information** offices – one for enquiries, the other for tickets and seat reservations. (The latter are compulsory on many long-distance trains – see p.000). Many domestic trains also pass through the Nationaltheatret station, at the west end of Karl Johans gate, which is slightly more useful for the city centre.

The central **Bussterminalen** (bus terminal) is handily placed a short walk to the northeast of Oslo S, beneath the Galleriet centre. Long-distance buses arrive at and depart from here, though incoming services sometimes terminate on the south side of Oslo S, at the bus stands beside Havnegata. Oslo Bussterminal also handles most of the longer bus services within the city as well as those to and from the airport. For all bus enquiries, consult the Nor-Way Bussekspress Bussterminalen information desk (Mon–Fri 7am–10pm, Sat

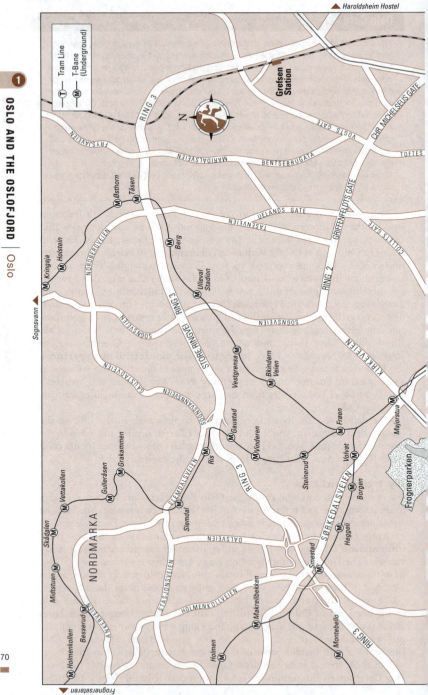

▲ Haroldsheim Hostel

Tram Line T
T-Bane (Underground) M

Grefsen Station

N

RING 3

FRYSJAVEIEN

CHR. MICHELSENS GATE

VOGTS GATE

TOFTES

MARIDALSVEIEN

BENTSEBRUGATA

UELANDS GATE

GRIFFENFELDTS GATE

COLLETS GATE

TÅSENVEIEN

RING 2

SOGNSVEIEN

KIRKEVEIEN

M Østhorn
M Tåsen

M Holstein

M Kringsjå

NORDBERGVEIEN

M Berg

M Ullevål Stadion

RING 3

STORE RINGVEI

SOGNSVEIEN

M Vestgrensa

M Blindern Veien

◄ Sognsvann

SOGNSVANNSVEIEN

GAUSTADVEIEN

M Gaustad

M Vinderen

M Steinerud

M Fraen

M Volvat

M Majorstua

STEINDALSVEIEN

M Gråkammen

M Gulleråsen

M Ris

RING 3

Frognerparken

M Vettakollen

M Skådalen

NORDMARKA

STASJONSVEIEN

M Slemdal

DALSVEIEN

Smestad

SØRKEDALSVEIEN

Borgen

Heggeli

M Midtstuen

ANKERVEIEN

M Besserud

HOLMENKOLLVEIEN

M Makrellbekken

M Montebello

RING 3

M Holmenkollen

M Holmen

▼ Frognerseteren

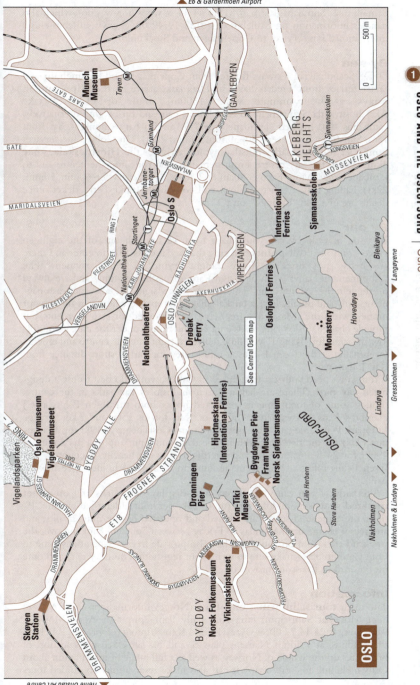

▲ E6 & Gardermoen Airport

1

500 m

0

Tøyen

Munch Museum Ⓜ

SARS GATE

GATE

Grønland Ⓜ

MARIDALSVEIEN

GAMLEBYEN

RING 1

Jernbane torget Ⓜ

Stortinget Ⓣ

NYLANDSVEIEN

EKEBERG HEIGHTS

Oslo S Ⓣ

KONGSVEIEN

GRØNLIGATA

Kongsveien Ⓣ

Sjømannsskolen

MOSSEVEIEN

PILESTREDET

Nationaltheatret Ⓜ

KARL JOHANS GATE

RÅDHUSGATA

International Ferries

Sjømannsskolen

PILESTREDET

VERGELANDVN

Nationaltheatret

OSLO TUNNELEN

AKERSHUSKAIA

VIPPETANGEN

Oslofjord Ferries

Bleikøya

DRAMMENSVEIEN

Drøbak Ferry

See Central Oslo map

Monastery

Hovedøya

Langøyene ▼

Vigelandsparken

Oslo Bymuseum
Vigelandmuseet

TH HEFTYES GATE

BYGDØY ALLE

DRAMMENSVEIEN

Hjortneskaia
(International Ferries)

OSLOFJORD

Lindøya

Gressholmen ▼

HALDAN SVARTES GT

FROGNER STRANDA

Dronningen Pier

Bygdøynes Pier
Fram Museum
Norsk Sjøfartsmuseum

Lille Herbern

▼

E18

Kon-Tiki Museet

LANGVIKSN

HUK AVENY

Store Herbern

Nakholmen & Lindøya ▼

DRAMMENSVEIEN

MUSEUMSVN

Nakholmen

Skøyen Station

DRONNING BLANCAS V

BYGDØYVEIEN

FREDRIKSBORGVEIEN

O. BJØRNSONS V.

STRØMSBORGVEIEN

Norsk Folkemuseum

Vikingskipshuset

BYGDØY

OSLO

◀ Henie Onstad Art Centre

8am–4pm & Sun 8am–10pm; ☎81 54 44 44, ⓦwww.nor-way.no), which also handles information on Säfflebussen (☎22 19 49 00, ⓦwww.safflebussen.se) international bus services to Copenhagen and Stockholm.

By sea

DFDS Scandinavian Seaways **ferries** from Copenhagen and Helsingborg, and Stena ferries from Fredrikshavn in Denmark, arrive at the **Vippetangen quays**, a twenty-minute walk (1300m) south of Oslo S: take Akershusstranda/Skippergata to Karl Johans gate and turn right. Alternatively, catch bus #60 marked "Jernbanetorget" (Mon–Fri 6am–midnight, Sat from 7am, Sun from 8am, every 20–30min; 10min; 22kr). On Color Line services from Kiel and Denmark's Hirsthals, you'll arrive at the **Hjortneskaia**, some 3km west of the city centre. From here, bus #56 runs into the centre and to Jernbanetorget (Mon–Fri 6–9.20am & 2.30–5.30pm, every 30–60min; 10min; 22kr). Failing that, a taxi to Oslo S will cost about 100kr. Ferry ticket office details are given in "Listings", on p.113.

By car

Arriving in Oslo by car, you'll have to drive through one of the eighteen video-controlled **toll-points** that ring the city; it costs 15kr to enter and there are hefty spot fines if you're caught trying to avoid payment. The "Abonnement" lanes (with blue signs) are for passholders only and are always on the left; the "Mynt/Coin" lanes (with yellow signs) are for exact cash payments only and usually have a bucket-shaped receptacle where you throw your money; while the "Manuell" (grey) lanes are also used for cash payments, but provide change. Oslo's ring roads encircle and tunnel under the city; if you follow the signs for "Ring 1" you'll be delivered right into the centre and emerge (eventually) at the Ibsen P-Hus, a multistorey car park a short distance from Karl Johans gate.

You won't need your car to sightsee in Oslo, so you'd do best to use a designated **car park**. There are half a dozen multistorey car parks in the centre, though some of them operate restricted hours: both the Ibsen P-hus at CJ Hambros Plass 1, two blocks north of Karl Johans gate, and Aker Brygge Europark P-hus, Sjøgata 4, are open 24 hours. Costs begin at 19kr for 30 minutes (23kr for the first hour) during the day (7am–5pm), up to a maximum of 190kr for 24 hours: evening and overnight rates are heavily discounted. The Ibsen P-hus offers a 20 percent discount to Oslo Card holders (see box on p.69).

Alternatively, you can park in **pay-and-display car parks** and **on-street metered spaces** around the city (up to 25kr per hour). Identified by blue "P" signs, these metered spaces are owned and operated by the municipality, and are free of charge from Monday to Friday between 5pm and 8am and over the weekend after 2pm on Saturday. They also provide free parking at any time to Oslo Card holders (make sure to write your registration number, date and time on the card in the space provided).

Information

The main **tourist information office** (Norges Informasjonssenter; May & Sept Mon–Sat 9am–5pm; June–Aug daily 9am–7pm; Oct–April Mon–Fri 9am–5pm; ☎24 14 77 00, ⓦwww.visitoslo.com, ⓔinfo@oslopro.no) is behind the Rådhus, at Fridtjof Nansens plass 5, and has an extensive selection of brochures on the whole of Norway, as well as a full range of information about Oslo, including free city maps: it can also make reservations on guided tours and book accommodation. In addition, there's a tourist office inside **Oslo S** (May–Sept daily 8am–11pm, Oct–April Mon–Sat 8am–5pm) with similar services. Both offices sell the Oslo Card and have free copies of various booklets and leaflets, including the excellent and very thorough *Oslo Official Guide* and *What's On in Oslo* – invaluable for listings of events and services.

The **Trafikanten** information office (see below) provides information on Oslo's public transport system.

City transport

Oslo's safe and efficient public transport system consists of buses, trams, a small underground rail system (the Tunnelbanen) and local ferries. It's run by AS Oslo Sporveier, whose information office, **Trafikanten**, is beneath the high-tech see-through clocktower, outside Oslo S on the Jernbanetorget (Mon–Fri 7am–8pm, Sat & Sun 8am–6pm; ☎ 177, ⓦ www.trafikanten.no). It sells all the tickets and passes detailed below and gives away a useful **transit route map**, the *Sporveiens hovedkart,* as well as the *Rutebok for Oslo* booklet, detailing every timetable for every route in the Oslo system.

Flat-fare **tickets** (bought on board the bus, tram or ferry, or at T-bane stations) cost 22kr and are valid for unlimited travel within the city boundaries for one hour; children four to sixteen years old travel half price, babies and toddlers free. There are several ways to cut costs. The best is to buy an **Oslo Card** (see p.69), which is valid on the whole network and on certain routes into the surrounding *kommunes* – but not on trains or buses to the airport. If you're not into museums, however, a straight **travel pass** might be a better buy. A Dagskort (24hr pass) is valid for unlimited travel within the city limits and costs 50kr, a seven day pass costs 160kr, while a monthly pass will set you back 620kr. Alternatively, there's the Flexikort which is valid for eight trips and costs 135kr. As well as the Trafikanten office, all these passes and tickets can be bought at most Narvesen kiosks and staffed T-bane stations, while the Dagskort and the Flexikort are also sold by bus and tram drivers.

On buses, the driver will check your ticket; on trams you're trusted to have one. Flexikort tickets need to be stamped at the beginning of a journey – by machine or manually – and thereafter you have one hour of travel on each ticket. Passes also need to be stamped and are valid from that time onwards. Though fare-dodging might seem widespread, if you're caught you'll get a hefty on-the-spot fine of 750kr.

Buses

Almost all city **bus** services originate at Jernbanetorget beside Oslo S, with buses to the outer suburbs usually departing from the Bussterminal. The vast majority of buses – city and suburban - pass through Jernbanetorget, with many also stopping at Nationaltheatret. Most buses stop running at around midnight, though on Friday and Saturday nights **night buses** (*nattbuss*) take over on certain routes (flat-rate fare 50kr; Oslo Card and other passes not valid); full details in the timetable, *Rutebok for Oslo*.

Trams

The city's **trams** run on eight routes through the city, crisscrossing the centre from east to west, and sometimes duplicating the bus routes. They are a bit slower than the buses, but are a handy and rather more enjoyable and relaxing way of getting about. Major stops include Jernbanetorget, Nationaltheatret and Storgata. Most operate regularly – every ten or twenty minutes, from 6am to midnight.

Tunnelbanen and trains

The Tunnelbanen – **T-bane** – has eight lines which converge to share a common slice of track crossing the city centre from Majorstuen in the west to Tøyen in the east, with Jernbanetorget, Stortinget and Nationaltheatret stations in between. From this central section, four lines run westbound (*Vest*) and four eastbound (*Øst*). The system mainly serves commuters from the suburbs, but you'll find it useful for trips out to Holmenkollen and Sognsvann – where the trains travel above ground. The system runs from around 6am until 12.30am. A series of **local commuter trains**, run by NSB, links Oslo with Moss, Eidsvoll, Drammen and other outlying towns; departures are from Oslo S, with many also stopping at Nationaltheatret. For details of services to and from the airport, see p.69.

Ferries

Numerous **ferries** shuttle across the northern reaches of the Oslofjord to connect the city centre with its outlying districts. To the Bygdøy peninsula and its museums, they leave from the piers behind the Rådhus (mid-April to Sept). The all-year services to Hovedøya, Lindøya and the other offshore islets (except Langøyene, June–Aug only) leave from the Vippetangen quay, 1300m south of Oslo S. To get to the Vippetangen quay, take bus #60 from Jernbanetorget. If you're venturing beyond the city limits, there are also boats to Nesodden (all year), and Drøbak (mid-May to early Sept 5 weekly), leaving from the Aker Brygge piers.

Taxis

The speed and efficiency of Oslo's public transport system means that you should rarely have to resort to a **taxi**, which is probably just as well as they are quite expensive. Taxi fares are regulated, with the tariff varying according to the time of day. At night you can expect to pay around 100kr for a ten-minute, five-kilometre ride; during the day about 25 percent less. Taxi ranks can be found round the city centre and outside all the big hotels; a convenient one is at the corner of Karl Johans gate and Lille Grensen. To call a cab ring Oslo Taxi ☎02 323 or Taxi2 ☎02 202.

Bicycles

Renting a **bicycle** is a pleasant option if you want to get around under your own steam: the city has a reasonable range of cycle tracks, and roads increasingly have cycle lanes. A **municipal bike** rental scheme is planned with bikes released like supermarket trolleys from points all over the city: Ask at the tourist office for the latest news.

Accommodation

Oslo has the range of hotels you would expect of a capital city, as well as B&Bs, a smattering of guesthouses (*pensjonater*) and a quartet of youth hostels. To appreciate the full flavour of the city, you're best off staying on or near the western reaches of Karl Johans gate – between the Stortinget and the Nationaltheatret – though the well-heeled area to the north and west of the

Royal Palace (Det Kongelige Slott) is enjoyable too. Many of the least expensive lodgings are, however, to be found in the vicinity of Oslo S, but this somewhat grimy district – along with the grey suburbs to the north and east of the station – hardly sets the pulse racing. That said, if money is tight and you're here in July and August, your choice of location may well be very limited as the scramble for **budget beds** becomes acute – or at least tight enough to make it well worth phoning ahead to check on space. For peace of mind, it is advisable to make an **advance reservation**, particularly for your first night.

One way to cut the hassle is to use the accommodation service provided by the tourist office in their three branches (at the airport, in Oslo S and near the Rådhus; see p.68 & p.72). Each office issues full accommodation lists and will make a booking on your behalf for 30kr per person, a real bargain when you consider that they often get discounted rates. Note also that the Oslo S office is especially good for B&Bs.

Hotels

In Oslo, 600–900kr will get you a fairly small and simple en-suite room. You hit the comfort zone at about 1000kr, and luxury from around 1200kr. However, special offers and **seasonal deals** often make the smarter hotels more affordable than this. Most offer up to forty percent discounts at weekends, while in July and August – when Norwegians leave town for their holidays – prices everywhere tend to drop radically. Also, most room rates are tempered by the inclusion of a good-to-excellent self-service buffet **breakfast**. The tourist offices keep lists of the day's best offers, or try the places on the following list – but always ring ahead first.

Central

Bondeheimen Rosenkrantz gate 8 ☎23 21 41 00, ℱ23 21 41 01, ⓦwww.bondeheimen.com. One of Oslo's most delightful hotels, handily located just two minutes' walk north of Karl Johans gate. Both the public areas and the extremely comfortable bedrooms are tastefully decorated in a modern, pan-Scandinavian style, with polished pine everywhere. The inclusive buffet breakfast, served in the *Kaffistova* (see p.107) is excellent, and there's free coffee, soup and bread in the foyer throughout the evening. The rack rate for a double is 1195r (single 995kr), but look out for weekend and summer discounts of up to forty percent. ❺, s/r ❸

Bristol Kristian IV's gate 7 ☎22 82 60 00, ℱ22 82 60 01, ⓦwww.bristol.no. Plush establishment distinguished by its sumptuous public areas with ornate nineteenth-century chandeliers, columns and fancifully carved arches. ❻, s/r ❹

City Skippergaten 19 ☎22 41 36 10, ℱ22 42 24 29, ⓦwww.cityhotel.no. This modest but pleasant hotel, a long-time favourite with budget travellers, is located above shops and offices in a typical Oslo apartment block near Oslo S. The surroundings are a little seedy, but the hotel is cheerful enough, with small but perfectly adequate rooms. ❹, s/r ❸

Continental Stortingsgata 24-26 ☎22 82 40 00, ℱ22 42 96 89, ⓦwww.hotel-continental.no. One of Oslo's most prestigious hotels. Sumptuous public areas and amazingly comfortable bedrooms furnished in immaculate modern style. The hotel is ideally located, a stone's throw from Karl Johans gate, and incorporates several high class bars and restaurants. ❼, s/r ❻

First Hotel Nobel House Kongens gate 5 ☎23 10 72 00, ℱ23 10 72 10, ⓦwww.firsthotels.com. Deluxe hotel with style – from the smart wooden floors to the cool, modernist decor. Great downtown location too, close to the restaurants and art museums of Bankplassen. ❼, s/r ❺

Grand Karl Johans gate 31 ☎23 21 20 00, ℱ23 21 21 00, ⓦ www.grand.no. Over 100 years of tradition, comfort and style in *the* prime position on Oslo's main street translates into stratospheric room rates. But breakfasts are sumptuous, the lobby opulent and the rooms eminently comfortable. Hefty weekend and summertime discounts make the *Grand* much more affordable. ❼, s/r ❹

Quality Savoy Universitets gate 11 ☎23 35 42 00, ℱ23 35 42 01, ⓦwww.choicehotels.no/quality/savoy. At the corner of Universitets gate and Kristian Augusts gate. Attractive choice with pleasant, comfortable rooms and wood-panelled public areas. Also has one of the city's most atmospheric bars, on the ground floor. In an interesting area too, with bookshops and cafés to suit every taste. ❻, s/r ❸

Rainbow Europa St Olavs gate 31 ☎23 25 63 00, ℻23 25 63 63, ⓦwww.rainbow-hotels.no. Large, modern chain establishment in dreary surroundings near the west end of St Olavs gate. Towards the lower end of its price range. ❹, s/r ❸

Rainbow Norrøna Grensen 19 ☎23 31 80 00, ℻23 31 80 01, ⓦwww.rainbow-hotels.no. Pleasantly modernized hotel with antique flourishes – stained glass windows and heavy brass doors. Occupies part of a nineteenth-century apartment block right in the middle of town, about 400m to the north of the Stortinget. The buffet breakfast is excellent and the breakfast room offers an attractive city view. ❹, s/r ❸

Rainbow Stefan, Rosenkrantz gate 1 ☎23 31 55 00, ℻23 31 55 55, ⓦwww.rainbow-hotels.no. Unremarkable but spick-and-span modern hotel above the ground floor shops in a five-storey building. Great location, just a couple of minutes' walk north of Karl Johans gate. Near the bottom of its price range, it's one of the city's better deals. ❹

Rica Holberg Holbergs plass 1 ☎23 15 72 00, ℻23 15 72 01, ⓦwww.rica.no. This grand, nineteenth-century building has recently been refurbished, both inside and out, but still retains some of its historic atmosphere. The public rooms are pleasant and appealing, while the bedrooms are spick, span and modern. Overlooks Holbergs plass, a pint-sized square about 500m to the north of the Slottsparken. ❼, s/r ❹

Rica Victoria Rosenkrantz gate 13 ☎24 14 70 00, ℻24 14 70 01, ⓦwww.rica.no. A large modern hotel, just south of Karl Johans gate. Its spacious rooms have every convenience, and it's justifiably popular with visiting business folk. ❼

Westside

Best Western Ambassadeur Camilla Colletts vei 15 ☎23 27 23 00, ℻22 44 47 91, ⓦwww.bestwestern.com/no/ambassadeur). One of a long sequence of attractive nineteenth-century town houses graced by wrought-iron balconies. The somewhat grimy pink exterior doesn't do justice to the elegantly furnished interior, where each of the bedrooms has a different theme such as "Shanghai" or "Amsterdam". A great location too, just three blocks west of the Slottsparken. ❻, s/r ❹

Frogner House Skovveien 8 ☎22 56 00 56, ℻22 56 05 00, ⓦwww.frognerhouse.com. Located in one of Oslo's ritziest neighbourhoods, this elegant hotel occupies a handsome Victorian townhouse. Each of the comfortable bedrooms is decorated in tasteful modern style, with stripped wood and thick carpets throughout. One kilometre west of the centre off Frognerveien – trams #12 or #15. ❼, s/r ❺

Gabelshus Gabels gate 16 ☎23 27 65 00, ℻23 27 65 60, ⓔgabelshus.hotel@os.telia.no. This delightful hotel, one of the most intimate in the city, boasts a beautifully maintained interior with ornate fireplaces and antique furnishings. Located in a smart residential area a couple of kilometres west of the city centre, off Drammensveien. Highly recommended. Tram #10 from the centre. ❻, s/r ❹

Rica Bygdøy Allé Bygdøy allé 53 ☎23 08 58 00 ℻23 08 58 08 ⓦwww.rica.no. With its forest of spiky, late nineteenth-century towers, this Rica possesses the most imposing hotel facade in the city. Inside, each of the rooms is individually decorated in tasteful modern style. On the first floor you'll also find the excellent *Restaurant Magma*, run by one of Norway's most high-profile chefs, Sonja Lee. The hotel is situated in a busy residential area about 2km west of the centre; to get there use buses #30–#32. ❺

Eastside

Anker Storgata 55 ☎22 99 75 00, ℻22 99 75 20, ⓦwww.anker.oslo.no. A large budget hotel in a glum high-rise block (also housing the *Albertine Hostel; see p.77*) beside the Akerselva river at the east end of Storgata. The clientele are mainly Norwegian, and the facilities are adequate, if somewhat frugal. Fifteen minutes' walk from Oslo S or five minutes by tram. ❹

Hostels, B&Bs and guesthouses

There are three very popular HI **hostels** in Oslo, all open to people of any age, though you'll need to be a member to get the lowest rate – non-members pay a surcharge of 30kr. Alternatively, the tourist office can book you into a **B&B**, which will cost a flat rate of 170kr for a single room, and 300kr for a double. This is something of a bargain especially as many also have cooking facilities, but they do tend to be out of the city centre, and there is often a minimum two-night stay. In addition, you could try a **guesthouse**, or *pensjonater*, which start at around 340kr for a single room, and 450kr for a double. They offer basic but generally adequate accommodation, either with or without en-suite facilities, but breakfast is not included, and at some places you may need to supply your own sleeping bag. Unfortunately, there are very few in Oslo, and only one is near the city centre.

Anker Hostel Storgata 55 ☎22 99 72 00, ℻22 99 72 20, ⓦwww.anker.oslo.no. This hostel has plain and simple rooms with dorm beds at 155kr in a 4-bedded room, or 135kr in a 6-bedded room. Serves an adequate breakfast and has self-catering facilities; utensils can be borrowed on payment of a refundable deposit. Bed linen and towels are for hire, or bring your own. The hostel occupies part of a glum high-rise block which also houses the *Anker* hotel (see above), in a cheerless neighbourhood at the east end of Storgata, fifteen minutes' walk from Oslo S or five minutes by tram #11, #12, #15 or #17. ❷

Cochs Pensjonat Parkveien 25 ☎23 33 24 00, ℻23 33 24 10, ⓦwww.cochs.no. No-frills guesthouse occupying the third floor of an old apartment block, in a handy location behind Slottsparken at the foot of Hegdehaugsveien. Some rooms have a kitchen unit; singles with shower and kitchenette cost 450–500kr (350kr without). Triples and quadruples are also available. ❷

Oslo Ekeberg Kongsveien 82 ☎22 74 18 90, ℻22 74 75 05, ⓔoslo.ekeberg.hostel @vandrerhjem.no. This small HI hostel, with just eleven rooms, occupies part of a school complex 4km southeast of Oslo S. Take tram #18 or #19 from outside Oslo S, and it's 100m from the Holtet tram stop. Dorm beds cost 175kr, doubles ❷

Oslo Haraldsheim Haraldsheimveien 4, Grefsen ☎22 22 29 65, ℻22 22 10 25,

ⓦwww.haraldsheim.oslo.no. Best of Oslo's three HI youth hostels, 4km northeast of the centre, and open all year except Christmas week. Has 270 beds in 71 rooms, most of which are four-bedded. The public areas are comfortable and attractively furnished and the bedrooms are frugal but clean: about 40 have their own showers and WC. There are self-catering facilities, a restaurant and washing machines. The basic dorm bed price (170kr) includes breakfast; doubles and single rooms (290kr, 360kr with shower) are also available. The only downside can be the presence of parties of noisy schoolchildren. It's a very popular spot, so advance booking is essential throughout the summer. To get there, take tram #15 or #17 from the bottom of Storgata, near the Domkirke, to the Sinsenkrysset stop, from where it's a ten-minute (signposted) walk. By road, the hostel is near – and signed from – Ring 3. ❷

Oslo Holtekilen Michelets vei 55 Stabekk ☎67 51 80 40, ℻67 59 12 30, ⓔoslo.holtekilen.hostel@vandrerhjem.no. Another HI hostel, but much smaller than Haraldsheim, this has kitchen facilities, a restaurant and a laundry. It's located 10km west of the city centre. From Oslo Bussterminalen, take bus #151 and the hostel is 100m from the Kveldsroveien bus stop. Dorm beds cost 180kr, including breakfast. Single and double rooms are also available. ❷

Camping and cabins

Camping is a fairly easy proposition in an uncrowded city, and of the sixteen sites dotted within a 50km radius, the nearest to the centre is just 3km away. If you're out of luck with rooms in town, most sites also offer **cabins**, but ring ahead to check availability.

Ekeberg Camping Ekebergveien 65 ☎22 19 85 68, ℻22 67 04 36. Large and fairly basic campsite in a rocky, forested piece of parkland just 3km east of the city centre; bus #34 from Jernbanetorget goes past. Open June-Aug.

Langøyene Camping Langøyene ☎22 11 53 21.

Extremely popular, no-frills campsite located on one of the nicest islets just offshore from downtown Oslo. Langøyene has the city's best beaches and an attractive wooded shoreline. To get there, take ferry #94 from the Vippetangen quay. Open June to mid-Aug.

Central Oslo

Despite the mammoth proportions of the Oslo conurbation, the city centre has remained surprisingly compact, and is easy to navigate by remembering a few simple landmarks. From the Oslo S train station, at the eastern end of the centre, the main thoroughfare, **Karl Johans gate**, heads directly up the hill,

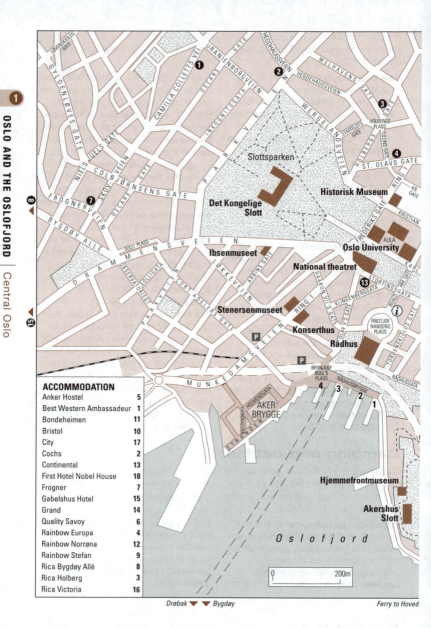

ACCOMMODATION

Anker Hostel	5
Best Western Ambassadeur	1
Bondeheimen	11
Bristol	10
City	17
Cochs	2
Continental	13
First Hotel Nobel House	18
Frogner	7
Gabelshus Hotel	15
Grand	14
Quality Savoy	6
Rainbow Europa	4
Rainbow Norrøna	12
Rainbow Stefan	9
Rica Bygdøy Allé	8
Rica Holberg	3
Rica Victoria	16

Drøbak ▼ ▼ Bygdøy   Ferry to Hoved

passing the **Domkirke** (Cathedral) and cutting a pedestrianized course until
it reaches the **Stortinget** (Parliament building). From here it sweeps down past
the **University** to the **Kongelige Slott**, or Royal Palace, situated in parkland
– the **Slottsparken** – at the western end of the centre. South of the palace, on
the waterfront, sits the brash harbourside **Aker Brygge** development, across

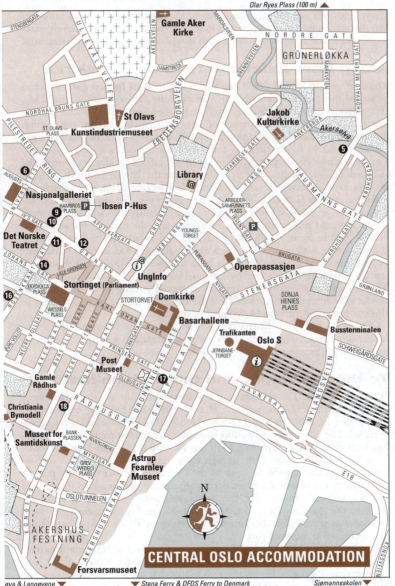

Olar Ryes Plass (100 m) ▲

Gamle Aker Kirke

NORDRE GATE

GRÜNERLØKKA

St Olavs

Kunstindustrimuseet

Jakob Kulturkirke

Akerselka

⑤

Library
@

Nasjonalgalleriet

⑥

Ibsen P-Hus

HAMBROS PLASS

⑨
⑩

ARBEIDER-
SAMFUNNETS
PLASS

Det Norske Teatret

⑪ ⑫

YOUNGS-
TORGET

Operapassasjen

BRUGATA

⑭

LILLE GRENSEN

UngInfo

SONJA
HENIES
PLASS

GRØNLAND

⑯

EIDSVOLLS
PLASS

Stortinget (Parliament)

STORTORVET

Domkirke

WESSELS
PLASS

Basarhallene

Trafikanten

Bussterminalen

SCHWEIGARDSGATE

Oslo S

JERNBANE-
TORGET

Post Museet

⑰

Gamle Rådhus

HAVNEGATA

E18

Christiania Bymodell

⑱

Museet for Samtidskunst

BANK-
PLASSEN

MYNTGATA

GREV
WEDELS
PLASS

Astrup Fearnley Museet

OSLOTUNNELEN

N

AKERSHUS FESTNING

CENTRAL OSLO ACCOMMODATION

Forsvarsmuseet

øya & Langøyene ▼   ▼ Stena Ferry & DFDS Ferry to Denmark   Sjømannsskolen ▼

from which lies the distinctive twin-towered **Rådhus** (City Hall). South of the Rådhus, on the lumpy peninsula overlooking the harbour, is the severe-looking castle, **Akershus Slott**. The castle, the Stortinget and Oslo S form a triangle enclosing a tight, rather gloomy grid of streets and high tenement buildings that was originally laid out by Christian IV in the seventeenth century. For many years this was the city's commercial hub and although Oslo's burgeoning suburbs undermined its position in the 1960s, the district is currently making a comeback, re-inventing itself with specialist shops and smart restaurants.

Along Karl Johans gate to the Domkirke

Heading west and uphill from Oslo S train station, **Karl Johans gate**, the city's principal street, is the most obvious starting point for exploring central Oslo. The street begins unpromisingly with tacky shops and hang-around junkies, but things pick up at the corner of Dronningens gate, where the curious **Basarhallene**, a circular, two-tiered building, is to be found. Its brick cloisters housed the city's food market in the last century, but it now serves as a tiny shopping complex complete with art shops and cafés. The adjacent **Domkirke** (Cathedral; daily 10am–4pm; free) dates from the late seventeenth century, though its heavyweight tower was remodelled in 1850. From the outside the cathedral appears plain and dour, but the elegantly restored interior is a delightful surprise, its homely, low-ceilinged nave and transepts awash with maroon, green and gold paintwork. At the central crossing, the flashy Baroque **pulpit**, where cherubs frolic among the foliage, faces a **royal box** that would look more at home at the opera. The **high altar** is Baroque too, its relief of the Last Supper featuring a very Nordic-looking sacrificial lamb. To either side are stained-glass **windows** created by Emanuel Vigeland in 1910 (for more on the Vigelands, see pp.95–96). The brightly coloured **ceiling paintings** are also modern, with representations of God the Father above the high altar, Jesus in the north transept and the Holy Spirit in the south.

Outside the Cathedral, **Stortorvet** was once the main city square, but it's no longer of much account, its nineteenth-century **statue** of a portly Christian IV merely the forlorn guardian of a second-rate flower market.

To the Stortinget and the Nationaltheatret

Returning to Karl Johans gate, it's a brief stroll up to the **Stortinget** (Parliament building), an imposing chunk of neo-Romanesque architecture. Completed in 1866, its stolid, sandy-coloured brickwork exudes bourgeois certainty. The Stortinget is open to the public by guided tour only (English-language tours July to mid-Aug Mon–Sat at 10am & 1pm; mid-Sept to mid-June Sat 10am & 1pm; free), though these reveal little more than can be gleaned from the outside. In front of the Parliament, a narrow **park-piazza** runs west to the Nationaltheatret, occupying the gap between Karl Johans gate and Stortingsgata. In summer, the park teems with promenading city folk, dodging the jewellery hawkers, ice-cream kiosks and street performers, while in winter its attraction is the compact, floodlit open-air ice rinks, where skates can be rented at minimal cost.

Lurking at the western end of the park is the Neoclassical **Nationaltheatret**, built in 1899 and flanked by two turgid statues of Henrik Ibsen and Bjørnstjerne Bjørnson. Inside, the red-and-gold main hall, which seats eight hundred, has been restored to its turn-of-the-century glory. Unless you understand Norwegian, the best way to see the interior is to take one of the occasional **guided tours** (ask for details at the box office or phone ☎22 00 14 00; theatre tickets on ☎815 00 811). It's also worth noting that Nationaltheatret is a useful transport interchange. Around the back of the building are two tunnels, the one on the right houses the westbound T-bane, the one on the left holds the eastbound. In addition, many city buses and the Flybussen stop beside the Nationaltheatret, on Stortingsgata.

The University and its museums

Opposite the Nationaltheatret, at the western end of Karl Johans gate, the nine-teenth-century buildings of the **University**, all classical columns and imperial pediments, sit well in this monument-rich part of the city centre. The **Aula** (late June to late Aug daily 10am–2.45pm; free), the main hall between the university's two symmetrical wings, has huge interior murals by Edvard Munch. The controversial result of a competition held by the university authorities in 1909, the murals weren't actually unveiled until 1916, after years of heated debate. Munch had just emerged (cured) from a winter in a Copenhagen psychiatric clinic when he started on the murals, and the major parts, *The History*, *Sun*, and *Alma Mater*, reflect a new mood in his work – con-fident and in tune with the natural world he loved.

Around the corner, the **Historisk Museum** (History Museum; mid-May to mid-Sept Tues–Sun 10am–4pm; mid-Sept to mid-May Tues–Sun 11am–4pm; free), at Frederiks gate 2, displays the university's hotch-potch of historical and ethnographical collections. The highlight is the **Viking and early medieval** section, on the ground floor: in the rooms to the left of the entrance are sev-eral magnificent twelfth- and thirteenth-century stave-church (see box on p.174) porches and gateposts, alive with dragons and beasts emerging from swirling, intricately carved backgrounds. There are weapons, coins, drinking horns, runic stones, religious bric-a-brac and bits of clothing here too, as well as a superb **vaulted room** dating from the late thirteenth century and retrieved from the stave church in Ål, near Geilo. The room's brightly coloured wood panels are painted in tempera – a technique where each pigment was mixed with glue, egg white and ground chalk – and feature a complicated Biblical iconography, beginning at the apex with the Creation, followed by depictions of Christ's childhood and ultimately his death and resurrection. An English-language leaflet, available in the room, gives the full low-down, but it's the dynamic forcefulness of these naive paintings, as well as the individuality of some of the detail that really impresses – look out, in particular, for the nasty-looking Judas at the Last Supper, and the pair of amenable donkeys peeping into the Christ's manger.

The rest of the ground floor is taken up by a pretty dire sequence of exhibi-tions on the Stone, Bronze, Iron and Viking ages. Geared towards school par-ties, the tiny dioramas are downright silly, and detract from the exhibits which (accompanied by long explicatory leaflets) illustrate various aspects of early Norwegian society, from religious beliefs and social structures through to mil-itary hardware, trade and craft. Nevertheless, the section entitled "The Love of Art" contains a modest but fascinating sample of early Viking decorative art, starting with the intensely flamboyant, ninth-century Oseberg and Borre styles and continuing into the Jellinge style, where greater emphasis was placed on line and composition. There's also a whole room of precious objects – finger rings, crucifixes, pendants, brooches, buckles and suchlike – illustrating the sus-tained virtuosity of Norse goldsmiths and silversmiths.

On the first floor, the first part of the **Etnografisk Museum** (Ethnographical Museum; same times) is devoted to the Arctic peoples and fea-tures an illuminating section on the Sami, who inhabit the northern reaches of Scandinavia. Incongruously, there's a coin collection here as well, while the upper floors contain a large and diverse collection of African and Asiatic art and culture, from Samurai suits to African masks and everything in between.

The Kongelige Slott and the Slottsparken

Standing on the hill at the west end of Karl Johans gate, **Det Kongelige Slott** (the Royal Palace) is a monument to Norwegian openness. Built between 1825 and 1848, when the monarchs of other European nations were nervously counting their friends, it still stands without railings and walls, its grounds – the **Slottsparken** – freely open to the public. A snappy changing of the guard takes place daily outside the palace at 1.30pm, and there are guided tours of certain sections of the interior in summer, though tickets are hard to come by – ask for details at the tourist office. Directly in front of the palace is an equestrian statue of **Karl XIV Johan** himself. Formerly the French General Bernadotte, he abandoned Napoleon and was subsequently elected King of Sweden. When Norway passed from Denmark to Sweden after the Treaty of Kiel in 1814, he became King of Norway as well. Not content, seemingly, with the terms of his motto (inscribed on the statue), "The people's love is my reward", Karl Johan had this whopping palace built, only to die before it was completed.

The Ibsen and Stenersen museums

The grand old mansions bordering the southern perimeter of the Slottsparken once housed Oslo's social elite. Here, in a fourth floor apartment at Arbins gate 1, **Ibsen** spent the last ten years of his life, strolling down to the *Grand Café* (see p.104) every day to hold court – a tourist attraction in his own life time. His old quarters are now maintained as the **Ibsen-museet** (Tues–Sun guided tours at noon, 1pm & 2pm; 40kr). Both Ibsen and his wife died here: Ibsen paralyzed in bed, but his wife, unwilling to expire in an undignified pose, dressed herself to die sitting upright in a chair. Only the study looks much as it did in Ibsen's day, but the reverential one-hour tour provides a fascinating background to his work, and helps to explain the importance of the playwright to his emergent nation. For more on Ibsen, see p.133.

East from the Ibsen Museum, it's a couple of minutes' walk to the **Stenersenmuseet**, Munkedamsveien 15 (Tues & Thurs 11am–7pm; Wed, Fri, Sat & Sun 11am–5pm; 40kr), home to an eclectic collection of modern art, the bulk of which was gifted to the city in 1936 by the author and art collector Rolf Stenersen (the same man who gave a second collection to Bergen, p.197). The first-floor entrance, across from the city's main concert hall, leads straight to the museum's pride and joy, its room of Munch paintings – Stenersen was a friend of Munch and bought many of his works. These include early paintings like *The Sick Room* and *Cabaret*, both dating from 1886, and disturbing later works, from the unnerving *Melancholy* to the forceful *Dance of Life*. Adjoining rooms hold an enjoyable sample of early- to mid-twentieth-century Scandinavian paintings, including the notable *Small Girl on a Sofa* by **Alex Revold** and **Per Krohg**'s aloof but finely observed *Two Children*, *Actress*, and *Dressmaker*. Other rooms are devoted to Munch sketches, the soft-hued Norwegian landscapes of **Amaldus Nielsen** (1838–1932), bright burlesques of Oslo life by **Ludvig Ravensberg** (1871–1958), and two portraits of Stenersen himself. There's also a lively programme of temporary exhibitions.

The Nasjonalgalleriet

Returning to Karl Johans gate, head up Universitets gata to see Norway's largest and best collection of fine art at the **Nasjonalgalleriet**, Universitets gata 13 (National Gallery; Mon, Wed & Fri 10am–6pm, Thurs 10am–8pm, Sat 10am–4pm, Sun 11am–4pm, Tues closed; free; ⓦwww.nasjonalgalleriet.no).

Housed in a grand nineteenth-century building, the collection may be short on internationally famous painters – apart from a fine body of work by Edvard Munch – but there's compensation in the oodles of Norwegian art, including work by all the leading figures up until the end of World War II. The only irritation is the way the museum is organized: the works of individual artists are often displayed in several different rooms and although the **free plan** available at reception sheds some light on matters, it's too skimpy by half. The text below mentions room numbers where it's helpful, but note that locations are sometimes rotated.

The **ground floor** is home to a somewhat garbled and quirky series of collections. The two rooms to the right of the entrance, beyond the gallery's shop, are crammed with **plaster casts** of Italian Renaissance sculptures (including a massive, militaristic equestrian statue by Donatello) and of a horde of Classical gods and Roman Caesars: these casts were very much in vogue during the second half of the nineteenth century, when plaster casters roamed the world to copy well-known works of art. To the left of the entrance, one room is devoted to Danish and Norwegian nineteenth-century sculpture, while another holds a workaday selection of Norwegian paintings from 1870 to 1910; the others are set aside for temporary exhibitions.

Heading up the wide and gracious **stairway**, you'll see a tortured bronze relief of *Helvete* (Hell) by Gustav Vigeland, before reaching the kernel of the gallery's collection on the **first floor**. Broadly speaking, this is divided between Norwegian painting on the right and non-Norwegian European art on the left. The latter section contains some enjoyable samples of work by the **Impressionists** and **Post-Impressionists**, with assorted bursts of colour from Manet, Monet, Degas and Cézanne, as well as a distant, piercing Van Gogh self-portrait, while the early twentieth century is represented by works from the likes of Picasso, Gris and Braque. There's also a set of religious paintings of the medieval Russian Novgorod school and a rather timid selection of **Old Masters**, among which Lucas Cranach's *The Golden Age*, some sketches by Goya, and two warm and melodramatic canvases by El Greco stand out. Nonetheless, for a national gallery there are few older works of significance, reflecting Norway's past poverty and its lack of an earlier royal or aristocratic collection to build upon.

Johan Christian Dahl and Thomas Fearnley

To the right of the staircase, the first room of **Norwegian paintings** (Room 17) features the work of the country's most important nineteenth-century landscape painters, **Johan Christian Dahl** (1788–1857) and his pupil **Thomas Fearnley** (1802–42). The Romantic Naturalism of their finely detailed canvases exposed Norway's growing sense of nationhood after the break-up of the Dano-Norwegian union in 1814. In a clear rejection of Danish lowland civil-servant culture, Dahl and Fearnley asserted the beauty (and moral virtue) of Norway's wild landscapes, which had previously been seen as uncouth and barbaric. This reassessment was clearly influenced by the ideas of the Swiss-born philosopher Jean Jacques Rousseau (1712–78), who believed that the peoples of mountain regions possessed an intrinsic nobility precisely because they were remote from the corrupting influences of (lowland) civilization. Dahl, who was a professor at the Academy of Art in Dresden for many years, wrote to a friend in 1841: "Like a true Poet, a Painter must not be led by the prevailing, often corrupt Taste, but attempt to create… a landscape [that]… exposes the characteristics of this Country and its Nature – often idyllic, often historical, melancholic – what they have been and are."

Dahl's giant 1842 canvas *Stalheim* is typical of his work, a mountain landscape rendered in soft and dappled hues, dotted with tiny figures and a sleepy village. His *Hjelle in Valdres* (1851) adopts the same approach, although here the artifice behind the apparent naturalism is easier to detect. Dahl had completed another painting of Hjelle the year before; returning to the subject, he widened the valley and heightened the mountains, sprinkling them with snow. Fearnley often lived and worked abroad, but he always returned to Norwegian themes, painting no fewer than five versions of the moody *Labrofossen ved Kongsberg* (The Labro Waterfall at Kongsberg); his 1837 version is displayed here.

Late nineteenth- and early twentieth-century Norwegian paintings

At the far end of Room 17, turn right into Room 29 for the work of **Hans Frederik Gude** (1825–1903) and **Adolph Tidemand** (1814–76), not so much for the quality of the painting as for their content. Tidemand's absurdly romantic, folkloric scenes reflect the bourgeois nationalism that swept Norway in the middle of the nineteenth century. The two men were the leading lights of a generation of Norwegian artists, though they actually lived in Düsseldorf, where they lectured at the art academy. They collaborated on the creation of *Spearing Fish by Night* and the *Bridal Voyage on the Hardanger Fjord*, with Gude painting the landscape and Tidemand the figures.

In the 1880s, Norwegian landscape painting took on a mystical and spiritual dimension. Influenced by French painters such as Théodore Rousseau, Norwegian artists abandoned the naturalism of earlier painters for more symbolic representations. **Gerhard Munthe** (1849–1929) dipped into lyrical renditions of the Norwegian countryside, and his cosy, folksy scenes were echoed in the paintings of **Erik Werenskiold** (1855–1938), who is well represented by *Peasant Burial*. There are examples of both artists' work in Room 23. During this period, **Theodor Kittelsen** (1857–1914) defined the Norwegian rendition of trolls, sprites and sirens in his illustrations for Asbjørnsen and Moe's *Norwegian Folk Tales*, published in 1883. Two modest examples of his other work – a self-portrait and a fairy-tale landscape – are in Room 18. **Harald Sohlberg** (1869–1935) clarified the rather hazy vision of many of his Norwegian contemporaries, painting a series of sharply observed Røros streetscapes and expanding into more elemental themes with such stunning works as *En blomstereng nordpå* (A Northern Flower Meadow) and *Vinternatt i Rondane* (Winter Night in the Rondane). These are exhibited in Room 31, alongside the comparable *Opptrekkende uvaer* (Approaching Storm) by **Halfdan Egedius** (1877–99).

Edvard Munch

The Nasjonalgalleriet's star turn, however, is its **Munch** collection. Representative works from the 1880s up to 1916 are gathered together in one central room (Room 24), with several lesser pieces displayed elsewhere. His early work is very much in the Naturalist tradition of his mentor Christian Krohg, though by 1885 Munch was already pushing back the boundaries in *The Sick Child*, a heart-wrenching evocation of his sister Sophie's death from tuberculosis. Other works displaying this same sense of pain include *Mother and Daughter, Moonlight, Madonna* and *The Scream*, a seminal canvas of 1893 whose swirling lines and rhythmic colours were to inspire the Expressionists. Munch painted several versions of *The Scream*, but this is the original, so it is hard to exaggerate the embarrassment felt by the museum when, in 1994, someone climbed in through the window and stole it. The painting was eventually recovered, but the thief was never caught. All in all, the gallery's sample of Munch's work serves as a good introduction to the artist, but those seeking a more comprehensive selection of his work should visit the Munch Museum (p.98).

Norwegian paintings from 1910

Aside from the work of Munch, who was always an exceptional figure, Norwegian art was reinvigorated in the 1910s by a new band of artists who had trained in Paris under Henri Matisse, whose emancipation of colour from Naturalist constraints inspired his Norwegian students. The most outstanding of them, **Henrik Sørensen** (1882–1962), summed up his influence thirty years later: "From Matisse, I learned more in fifteen minutes than from all the other teachers I have listened to." Such lessons inspired Sørensen's surging, earthy landscapes of the lowlands of eastern Norway, which he much preferred to the monumental scenery of the west coast. **Axel Revold** (1887–1962) was trained by Matisse too, but he also assimilated Cubist influences in paintings such as *The Fishing Fleet leaves the Harbour*. **Erling Enger** (1899–1990), in contrast, maintained a gently lyrical, slightly tongue-in-cheek approach to the landscape and its seasons. Examples of the work of these and other later artists can be found on the first and the second floors, where there is also a large collection of paintings from the rest of Scandinavia, mostly dating from the first half of the twentieth century.

The Kunstindustrimuseet

The **Kunstindustrimuseet** (Museum of Applied Art; Tues, Wed & Fri–Sun 11am–4pm, Thurs 11am–7pm; 25kr; ⓦ www.kunstindustrimuseet.no), St Olavs gate 1, occupies an imposing nineteenth-century building some five minutes' walk from the Nasjonalgalleriet – continue to the far end of Universitets gata, veer to the right and it's at the end of the street. Founded in 1876, it can lay claim to being one of the earliest applied art museums in Europe. Its multifaceted collection is particularly strong on **furniture**, with examples of all the major styles – both domestic and imported – that have been popular in Norway from the medieval period to the present day.

The museum spreads over four floors. The first floor accommodates temporary exhibitions (which sometimes raise the cost of admission), while one floor up, in the first room to the left of the stairs, there's an engaging hotchpotch of **Viking** paraphernalia, from drinking horns, brooches and belts, through to religious statuettes and church vestments. The museum's top exhibit is here too: dating from the early thirteenth century, the intricate and brightly coloured **Baldishol Tapestry** is one of the finest and oldest examples of woven tapestry in Europe. Next door, the elongated Norwegian Gallery boasts an enjoyable sample of carved wooden furniture, of which the cheerily painted **chests** from Gudbrandsdal, with their abundance of acanthus leaves, are especially fetching. Alongside is a charming selection of **bedspreads** decorated with religious and folkloric motifs. Using skills distantly inherited from Flemish weavers, the Norwegians took to pictorial bedspreads in a big way, their main modification being the elimination of perspective in the attempt to cover the joins. Of ceremonial significance, these bedspreads were brought out on all major occasions – weddings and festivals in particular. The bedspreads began as fairly crude affairs at the start of the seventeenth century, but achieved greater precision and detail throughout the eighteenth century, after which the art went into a slow decline. The two most popular subjects were the arrival of the Magi, and the Wise and Foolish Virgins, a suitably didactic subject for any newlyweds.

On the next floor is a sequence of period interiors illustrating foreign fashions from Renaissance and Baroque through to Chippendale, Louis XVI and Art Nouveau. Another floor up are ceramics and glassware from the early nineteenth century onwards, and displays on textiles and fashions. The highlight here is the collection of extravagant **costumes** worn by Norway's royal family at the turn of the twentieth century. Dresses is too prosaic a word for the fairy-tale affairs favoured by Queen Maud, daughter of England's Edward VII and wife of Haakon VII, not to mention Crown Princess Sonja's consecratory robe from the 1930s.

East from the Kunstindustrimuseet to Grünerløkka

Leaving the museum, walk round the dull, brown-brick pile of **St Olav Domkirke**, built for the city's Catholics in the middle of the nineteenth century, and follow Akersveien as far as the cemetery. There's a choice of routes here. If you keep straight on, it's a short stroll up the slope to the **Gamle Aker Kirke** (Mon–Sat noon–2pm; free), a sturdy stone building still in use as a Lutheran parish church. It dates from around 1100, which makes it the oldest stone church in Scandinavia, although most of what you see today is the result of a heavy-handed nineteenth-century refurbishment.

Alternatively, back at the cemetery, turn right down **Damstredet**, a steep cobbled lane lined with early nineteenth-century clapboard houses built at all kinds of odd angles. Lined with some of the few wooden buildings to have survived Oslo's developers, the street is a picturesque affair, a well-kept reminder of how the city once looked. At the bottom of Damstredet, there's another choice of routes. If you stroll south along **Fredensborgveien**, you'll thread your way past office blocks, regaining the city centre in around fifteen minutes. But if you head east for about five minutes along Hausmanns gate to the corner of Torggata, you'll reach the **Jakob Kulturkirke**, a disused church now housing a cultural centre where concerts, art exhibitions, and theatre are held (phone ☎22 99 34 50, ⓦ www.kkv.no for details).

Behind the church, head north along Torggata, and you'll soon reach **Ankerbrua** (Anker bridge) across the **River Akerselva.** Sporting sculptures by talented Norwegian sculptor Per Ung – look out, in particular, for Peer Gynt and his reindeer – the bridge marks the main approach to **Grünerløkka**. Formerly a run-down working-class district, Grünerløkka's recent regeneration has turned it into one of the most fashionable parts of the city, particularly amongst artists and students. Turn left just beyond the bridge, and you'll find yourself in **Markveien**, whose nineteenth-century buildings have been extensively gentrified and now accommodate a string of trendy cafés, bars, restaurants and designer shops. At Olav Ryes Plass, the first splash of greenery, cross over to **Thorvald Meyers gate** and press on north for the short stroll to **Birkelunden**, a grassy square that's especially popular for hanging out in the summer.

The quickest way to get back to the centre is on tram #11 or #12, which both run along Thorvald Meyers gate.

To the water: the Rådhus and Aker Brygge

Back in the city centre, just a couple of minutes' walk south of the Nationaltheatret, the **Rådhus** (City Hall: May–Aug daily 9am–5pm; Sept–April daily 9am–4pm; free: guided tours June & July daily at 10am, noon & 2pm; Aug–May Mon–Fri at 10am, noon & 2pm; 30kr) rears high above the waterfront. Oslo's controversial modern City Hall, nearly twenty years in the making, finally opened in 1950 to celebrate the city's nine-hundreth anniversary. Designed by Arnstein Arneberg and Manus Poulsson, the Modernist, twin-towered building of dark brown brick was a grandiose statement of civic pride. At first, few people had a good word for what they saw as an ugly and strikingly un-Norwegian addition to the city. But with the passing of time, the obloquy has fallen on more recent additions to the skyline, such as Oslo S, and the Rådhus has become one of the city's more popular buildings.

Initially, the interior was equally contentious. Many leading Norwegian painters and sculptors contributed to the decorations, which were intended to celebrate all things Norwegian. The **Rådhushallen** (main hall) is decorated with vast, stylized – and for some, completely over-the-top – murals. On the north wall, Per Krohg's *From the Fishing Nets in the West to the Forests of the East* invokes the figures of polar explorer Fridtjof Nansen (on the left) and dramatist Bjørnstjerne Bjørnson (on the right) to symbolize, respectively, the nation's spirit of adventure and its intellectual development. On the south wall is the equally vivid *Work, Administration and Celebration,* which took Henrik Sørensen a decade to complete. The self-congratulatory nationalism of these murals is hardly attractive, although the effect is partly offset by the forceful fresco in honour of the Norwegian Resistance of World War II, running along the east wall.

Outside, at the back of the Rådhus, a line of six muscular bronzes represents the trades – builders, bricklayers and so on – who worked on the building. Behind them, and beyond the tram lines, stand four massive granite female sculptures surrounding a fountain. Beyond, and shadowed by the bumpy Akershus peninsula, is the busy central **harbour**, with Bygdøy and the islands of the Oslofjord filling out the backdrop. This is one of downtown Oslo's prettiest spots, and a stone's throw away is the old Aker shipyard which has been turned into the swish **Aker Brygge** shopping-cum-office complex, a gleaming concoction of walkways, circular staircases and glass lifts, all decked out with neon and plastic; the bars and restaurants here are some of the most popular (and expensive) in town.

Around Rådhusgata

Running east from the Rådhus, Rådhusgata cuts off the spur of land on which Akershus Castle (see below) is built, and straddles a grid of streets laid out by Christian IV in the 1620s. The layout, however, is just about all that has survived; the old timber buildings were almost entirely replaced by grander stone structures in the nineteenth century, when the district flourished as the commercial heart of the city. An exception is the pint-sized **Gamle Rådhus**, Oslo's old town hall, at the corner of Nedre Slotts gate and Rådhusgata, though this was heavily restored after fire damage in 1996. In commemoration of the fact that Oslo's first theatrical performance took place here in 1667, its second floor contains the **Teatermuseet** (Theatrical Museum; Wed 11am–3pm, Thurs noon–6pm & Sun noon–4pm; 25kr), stuffed with relics including posters, puppets and costumes.

Museum enthusiasts might also be interested in the offbeat **Postmuseet** (Post Museum; Mon–Fri 10am–5pm, Sat 10am–2pm, Sun noon–4pm; free), a brief walk to the north at Kirkegata 20 and Prinsens gate. Outlining the history of the Norwegian postal service and displaying hundreds of stamps, the museum is really specialist viewing, except for a diorama revealing the exploits of a certain Gunnar Turtveit. A long-distance postman, Turtveit was buried by an avalanche near Odda in western Norway in 1903. Entombed for 56 hours, Turtveit survived thanks to his trusty bugle, which he used to dig a tunnel through the snow – a fine example of a man saved by his horn.

Museet for Samtidskunst

Arguably the city's most attractive square, **Bankplassen** lies one block south of Rådhusgata, along Kirkegata. Framed by Gothic Revival and Second Empire buildings, the square is a perfect illustration of the grand tastes of the Dano-Norwegian elite who ran the country at the start of the twentieth century. Bankplassen's proudest building, the 1907 Art Nouveau former Norges Bank headquarters at no. 4, has been superbly restored to house the enterprising **Museet for Samtidskunst** (Contemporary Art Museum; Tues, Wed & Fri 10am–5pm, Thurs 10am–8pm, Sat 11am–4pm, Sun 11am–5pm; Ⓦwww.museet.no; 40kr). Based on collections once jumbled together in the Nasjonalgalleriet, the museum owns work by every major post-war Norwegian artist and many leading foreign figures too.

For the most part, the **displays** take the form of a series of temporary, thematic exhibitions spread over three floors. The works, some of which are massive, are each allowed a generous amount of space, so – given that the museum also hosts prestigious international exhibitions – only a fraction of the permanent collection can be shown at any one time. Nonetheless, Norwegian names to look out for include Bjørn Carlsen, Frans Widerberg, Erik Killi Olsen, Knut Rose and Bjørn Ransve. There are also three permanent installations, including the weird *Inner Room V*, the fifth in a series of angst-rattling rooms made from recycled industrial junk by the Norwegian Per Inge Bjørlo. Tucked away in a room of its own on the top floor, there's also the peculiar – and peculiarly engaging – *The Man Who Never Threw Anything Away*. This is the work of the Russian Ilya Kabakov, who has spent over a decade collecting hundreds of discarded items from the recesses of his house – bits of toenail, string etc, etc – and assembled them here, each precisely labelled and neatly displayed. Kabakov continues turning up to add bits and pieces to his installation, which occupies a sort of parallel reality – originally a retreat from the bureaucratic illogicalities of the Soviet system, but now a tribute to the anally retentive.

The exhibits hang from every wall and offset every corner and stairwell, but it's still difficult not to be more impressed by the building itself, its polished, echoing halls resplendent with gilt and marble, ornamental columns and banisters. Visitors get to leave their bags inside one of the bank's old safes, and you can stop off in the first floor *Café Sesam* for cakes and coffee.

Astrup Fearnley Museet

Opened in 1993, the **Astrup Fearnley Museet for Moderne Kunst**, Dronningens gate 4 (Astrup Fearnley Modern Art Museum; Tues, Wed & Fri 11am–5pm, Thurs 11am–7pm, Sat & Sun noon–5pm; Ⓦwww.af-moma.no; 50kr, but free on Tues), about 200m to the east of the Samtidskunst, occupies a sharp modern building of brick and glass, with six-metre-high steel entrance doors. It's meant to impress – a suitably posh setting for the display of several private collections and for prestigious temporary exhibitions. The latter often leave little space for the permanent collection, which includes examples of the work of most major post-war Norwegian artists, as well as a smattering of foreign works by such celebrated artists as Francis Bacon, Damien Hirst and Anselm Kiefer.

Norway has a well-organized, high-profile body of professional artists whose long-established commitment to encouraging artistic activity throughout the country has brought them respect, not to mention state subsidies. In the 1960s, abstract and conceptual artists dominated the scene, but at the end of the 1970s there was a renewed interest in older art styles, particularly Expressionism, Surrealism and Cubism, plus a new emphasis on technique and materials. To a large degree these opposing impulses fused, or at least overlapped, but by the late 1980s several definable movements had emerged. One of the more popular trends was for artists to use beautifully attractive colours to portray disquieting visions, a dissonance favoured by the likes of **Knut Rose** and **Bjørn Carlsen**. The latter's ghoulish *Searching in a Dead Zebra* has been highly influential, and is now part of the museum's permanent collection. Other artists, the most distinguished of whom is **Tore Hansen**, have developed a naive style. Their paintings, apparently clumsily drawn without thought for composition, are frequently reminiscent of Norwegian folk art, and constitute a highly personal response drawn from the artist's emotions and subconscious experiences.

Both of these trends embody a sincerity of expression that defines the bulk of contemporary Norwegian art. Whereas the prevailing mood in international art circles encourages detached irony, Norway's artists characteristically adhere to the view that their role is to interpret, or at least express, the poignant and personal for their audience. An important exception is **Bjørn Ransve**, who creates sophisticated paintings in constantly changing styles, but always focused on the relationship between art and reality. Another exception is the small group of artists, such as **Bjørn Sigurd Tufta**, who have returned to non-figurative modernism to create works that explore the possibilities of the material, while the content plays no decisive role. An interest in materials has sparked a variety of experiments, particularly among the country's sculptors, whose installations incorporate everyday utensils, natural objects and pictorial art. These installations have developed their own momentum, pushing back the traditional limits of the visual arts in their use of many different media including photography, video, textiles and furniture. An opposing faction is led by the painter **Odd Nerdrum**, who spearheads the figurative rebellion against the modernists. The most prominent Norwegian sculptor today is **Bård Breivik**, who explores the dialogue between nature and human beings.

The Akershus complex

Though very much part of central Oslo by location, the thumb of land that holds the sprawling fortifications of the **Akershus complex** (outdoor areas daily 6am–9pm; free) is quite separate from the city centre in feel. Built on a rocky knoll overlooking the harbour in around 1300, the original **Slott** (castle) was already the battered veteran of several unsuccessful sieges when Christian IV (1596–1648) took matters in hand. The king had a passion for building cities and a keen interest in Norway – during his reign he visited the country about thirty times, more than all the other kings of the Dano-Norwegian union together. So, when Oslo was badly damaged by fire in 1624, he took his opportunity and simply ordered the town to be moved round the bay from its location at the mouth of the River Alna beneath the Ekeberg heights. He had the town rebuilt in its present position, renamed it Christiania – a name which stuck until 1925 – and transformed the medieval castle into a Renaissance residence. Around the castle he also constructed a new fortress – the **Akershus Festning** – whose thick earth-and-stone walls and protruding bastions were designed to resist artillery bombardment. Refashioned and enlarged on several later occasions, and now bisected by Kongens gate, parts of the fortress have remained in military use until the present day.

There are several **entrances** to the Akershus complex, but the most interesting is from the west end of Myntgata, where there's a choice of two marked footpaths. One leads to the **Christiania Bymodell** (June–Aug Tues–Sun 11am–6pm; free), which explains the city's history from 1624 to 1840 by means of an hourly audiovisual presentation and a large-scale model of Oslo as it appeared in 1838; drop by to get a better idea of the city's evolution and what the town looked like when it was protected by the fortress. The second footpath leads up to a side gate in the perimeter wall, just beyond which is a dull museum-cum-information centre that makes a strange attempt to tie in the history of the castle with modern environmental concerns. There's another choice of signposted routes here, with one path offering heady views over the harbour as it worms its way up to the castle.

The Hjemmefrontmuseum

In a separate building just outside the castle entrance is the **Hjemmefrontmuseum** (The Resistance Museum; mid-April to mid-June & Sept Mon–Sat 10am–4pm, Sun 11am–4pm; mid-June to Aug Mon, Wed, Fri & Sat 10am–5pm, Tues & Thurs 10am–6pm, Sun 11am–5pm; Oct to mid-April Mon–Fri 10am–3pm, Sat & Sun 11am–4pm; 25kr); its location is particularly apt as captured Resistance fighters were tortured and sometimes executed in the castle by the Gestapo. Labelled in English and Norwegian, the museum's mostly pictorial displays detail the history of the war in Norway, from defeat and occupation through resistance to final victory. There are tales of extraordinary heroism here – the determined resistance of hundreds of the country's teachers to Nazi instructions, and the story of a certain Petter Moen, who was arrested by the Germans and imprisoned in the Akershus, where he kept a diary by picking out letters on toilet paper with a nail: the diary survived, but he didn't. Another section deals with Norway's Jews, who numbered 1800 in 1939 – the Germans captured 760, of whom 24 survived. There's also an impressively honest account of Norwegian collaboration: fascism struck a chord with the country's petit bourgeois, and hundreds of volunteers joined the Germany army. The most notorious collaborator was **Vidkun Quisling** – pressing a button brings up his radio announcement declaring his assumption of power at the start of the German invasion in April 1940.

Akershus Slott

Next door, the severe stone walls and twin spires of the medieval **Akershus Slott** (Akershus Castle; May to mid-Sept Mon–Sat 10am–4pm, Sun 12.30–4pm; 30kr; free guided tour at 11am, 1pm & 3pm, Sun at 1pm & 3pm) perch on a rocky ridge high above the zigzag fortifications that Christian IV added in the seventeenth century. The castle is approached through a narrow tunnel-gateway, beyond which the stone-flagged courtyard is overlooked by the main gate. The interior is, however, a real disappointment, with a series of bare rooms only enlivened by the tapestries and bedspreads of the **Romerike Hall**. Also on view are the royal chapel and the royal mausoleum, the last resting place of Norway's current dynasty.

Back outside, a **path** leads off the courtyard, running down the side of the castle with the walls pressing in on one side and views out over the harbour on the other. At the foot of the castle, the path swings across a narrow promontory and soon reaches the **footbridge** over Kongensgate. Cross the footbridge for the Forsvarsmuseet (see below), or keep straight for the string of ochre-coloured barrack blocks that leads back to Myntgata.

Forsvarsmuseet

On the far side of the Kongensgate footbridge, among the buildings flanking the sprawling parade ground, is the **Forsvarsmuseet** (The Armed Forces Museum; June–Aug Mon–Fri 10am–6pm, Sat & Sun 11am–4pm; Sept–May Mon–Fri 10am–3pm, Sat & Sun 11am–4pm; free). However, compared to the quiet heroics of the Resistance museum, this is frankly a poor foil; it's a dreary account of the nation's military history illustrated by an assortment of uniforms, rifles and guns. The only real surprise is the number of wars the Scandinavian countries have waged against each other. From here, it's a short walk back to the main entrance of the Akershus complex at the foot of Kirkegata.

Southwest of the centre:
the Bygdøy peninsula

Other than the centre, the place where you're likely to spend most time in Oslo is the **Bygdøy peninsula**, across the bay to the southwest of the city, where **five museums** make for an absorbing cultural and historical trip. Indeed, it's well worth spending a full day or, less wearyingly, two half-days. The most enjoyable way to reach Bygdøy is by **ferry**. These leave from the Rådhusbrygge (pier 3) behind the Rådhus every forty minutes (May–Aug Mon–Fri 7.45am–9.05pm, Sat & Sun 9.05am–9.05pm; late April & Sept daily 9.05am–6.25pm), returning to a similar schedule. All the ferries to the peninsula call first at the Dronningen Pier (15min from Rådhusbrygge) and then the Bygdøynes Pier (20min). The two most popular attractions – the Viking Ships and Folk museums – are within easy walking distance of the Dronningen pier; the other three are a stone's throw from Bygdøynes. If you decide to walk between the two groups of museums, allow about fifteen minutes: the route is well signposted but dull. The alternative to the ferry is **bus** #30 (every 15min), which runs all year from Jernbanetorget and the Nationaltheatret to the Folk Museum and Viking Ships, and, when the ferry isn't running, to the other three museums as well.

Norsk Folkemuseum

About 700m uphill from Dronningen pier, the **Norsk Folkemuseum**, at Museumsveien 10 (Norwegian Folk Museum; mid-May to mid-Sept daily 10am–6pm; 70kr: mid-Sept to mid-May Mon–Fri 11am–3pm, Sat & Sun 11am–4pm; 50kr; Ⓦwww.norskfolke.museum.no), combines indoor collections on folk art, furniture, dress and customs with an extensive open-air display of reassembled buildings, mostly wooden barns, stables, storehouses and dwellings from the seventeenth to the nineteenth centuries. Look out also for the imaginative temporary exhibitions, for which the museum has a well-deserved reputation.

At the **entrance**, pick up a free map and English-language guide and begin by going upstairs to the Norwegian parliament chamber, a cosy nineteenth-century affair that has been reassembled here, complete with inkwells and quills at the members' seats. The adjoining complex of buildings holds a rather confusing sequence of exhibitions. Some are missable, but the **folk art** section has delightful samples of quilted bedspreads and painted furniture, as well as an intriguing sub-section devoted to **love gifts**, with fancily carved love spoons and mangle boards given by the boys, and mittens and gloves by the girls. In rural Norway, it was considered improper for courting couples to be seen together during the day, but acceptable (or at least tolerated) at night – and to assist the process parents usually moved girls of marrying age into one of the farm's outhouses, where tokens could be swapped without embarrassment. The **folk dress** section is excellent too. Rural customs specified the correct dress for every sort of social gathering, and it's the extravagant and brightly coloured bridal headdresses that grab the eye. The amount of effort that went into the creation of the folk costumes was quite extraordinary, although perhaps it should be remembered that the exhibits were mostly owned by wealthier Norwegians – many others could barely avoid starvation, never mind indulging in fancy dress.

The **open-air collection** consists of more than 150 reconstructed buildings. Arranged geographically, they provide a marvellous sample of Norwegian rural architecture, somewhat marred by inadequate explanations. That said, it's still worth tracking down the **stave church** (see box on p.174), particularly if you don't plan to travel elsewhere in Norway. Dating from the early thirteenth century but extensively restored in the 1880s, when it was moved here from Gol, near Geilo, the church is a good example of its type, with steep, shingle-covered roofs and dragon finials. You can't usually enter the building, but from the outside gallery you can make out the cramped, gloomy nave and the interior, decorated with robust woodcarvings, with a striking *Last Supper* behind the altar. Elsewhere, the cluster of buildings from **Setesdal** in southern Norway holds some especially well-preserved dwellings and storehouses from the seventeenth century, while the **Numedal** section contains one of the museum's oldest buildings, a late thirteenth-century house from Rauland whose door posts are embellished with Romanesque vine decoration. In summer, many of the buildings are open for viewing, and costumed guides roam the site to explain the vagaries of Norwegian rural life.

Vikingskipshuset

A five-minute walk south along the main road is the **Vikingskipshuset** (Viking Ships Museum; daily: May–Sept 9am–6pm; Oct–April 11am–4pm; 40kr; ⓦwww.ukm.uio.no/vikingskipsmuseet), a large hall specially constructed to house a trio of ninth-century Viking ships, with viewing platforms to enable you to see inside the hulls. The three oak vessels were retrieved from ritual burial mounds in southern Norway around the turn of the twentieth century, each embalmed in a subsoil of clay which accounts for their excellent state of preservation. The size of a Viking **burial mound** denoted the dead person's rank and wealth, while the possessions buried with the body were designed to make the afterlife as comfortable as possible. Implicit was the assumption that a chieftain in this world would be a chieftain in the next – slaves, for example, were frequently killed and buried with their master or mistress – a belief that would subsequently give Christianity, with its alternative, less fatalistic vision, an immediate appeal to those at the bottom of the Viking hierarchy. Quite how the Vikings saw the transfer to the after-life taking place is less certain. The evidence is contradictory: sometimes the Vikings stuck the anchor on board the burial ship in preparation for the spiritual journey, but at other times the vessels were moored to large stones before they were buried.

Neither was ship burial the only type of Viking funeral – far from it. The Vikings buried their dead in mounds and on level ground, with and without grave goods, in large and small coffins, both with and without boats – and they practised cremation too.

The museum's star exhibits are the Oseberg and Gokstad ships, named after the places on the west side of the Oslofjord where they were discovered in 1904 and 1880 respectively. The **Oseberg ship**'s ornately carved prow and stern rise high above the hull, where thirty oar-holes indicate the size of the crew. It is thought to be the burial ship of a Viking chieftain's wife and much of the treasure buried with it was retrieved and is displayed at the back of the museum. The grave goods reveal an attention to detail and a level of domestic sophistication not usually associated with the Vikings. There are marvellous decorative items like the fierce-looking animal-head posts and exuberantly carved ceremonial sleighs, plus a host of smaller, more mundane household items such as agricultural tools and a cooking pot. Here also are finds from another burial mound at Borre in Vestfold (see p.121), most notably a rare dark-blue glass beaker and a fancily decorated bridle.

The Oseberg ship is 22m long and 5m wide, and probably represents the type of vessel the Vikings would have used to navigate fjords and coastal waters. The **Gokstad ship** is slightly longer and wider, and quite a bit sturdier. Its seaworthiness was demonstrated in 1893 when a copy sailed across the Atlantic to the USA. Like the Oseberg mound, the Gokstad burial chamber was raided by grave robbers long ago – and to greater effect – but a handful of items were unearthed, and these are exhibited behind the third vessel, the **Tune ship**. Only fragments of this, the smallest of the three vessels, survive; these are displayed unrestored, much as they were discovered in 1867 on the eastern side of the Oslofjord.

The Kon-Tiki museet

A few metres from the Bygdøynes pier, the **Kon-Tiki museet** (Kon-Tiki Museum; daily: April–May & Sept 10.30am–5pm; Oct–March 10.30am–4pm; June–Aug 9.30am–5.45pm; 35kr; ⓦwww.kon-tiki.no) displays the eponymous balsawood raft on which, in 1947, the Norwegian **Thor Heyerdahl** made his famous journey across the Pacific from Peru to Polynesia. Heyerdahl wanted to prove the trip could be done: he was convinced that the first Polynesian settlers had sailed from pre-Inca Peru, and rejected prevailing opinions that South American balsa rafts were unseaworthy. Looking at the flimsy raft, you could be forgiven for agreeing with Heyerdahl's doubters – and for wondering how the crew didn't murder each other after a day, never mind several weeks in such a confined space. Heyerdahl's later investigations of Easter Island statues and cave graves lent further weight to his ethnological theory, which has now received a degree of acceptance. The whole saga is outlined here in the museum, and if you're especially interested, the story is also told in his book *The Kon-Tiki Expedition*. Preoccupied with transoceanic contact between prehistoric peoples, Heyerdahl went on to attempt several other voyages, sailing across the Atlantic in a papyrus boat, *Ra II*, in 1970, to prove that there could have been contact between Egypt and South America. *Ra II* is also displayed here and the exploit recorded in another of Heyerdahl's books, *The Ra Expeditions*.

The Frammuseet

Just across the road, in front of the mammoth triangular display hall that is the **Frammuseet** (Fram Museum; March–April daily 11am–3.45pm; early May & Sept daily 10am–4.45pm; mid-May to mid-June daily 9am–4.45pm; mid-June to Aug daily 9am–6.45pm; Oct daily 10am–3.45pm; Nov–Feb Mon–Fri 11am–2.45pm, Sat & Sun 11am–3.45pm; 30kr), stands the *Gjøa*, the one-time sealing ship in which **Roald Amundsen** made the first complete sailing of the Northwest Passage in 1906. By any measure, this was a remarkable achievement and the fulfilment of a nautical mission that had preoccupied sailors for several centuries. It took three years, with Amundsen and his crew surviving two ice-bound winters deep in the Arctic, but this epic journey was soon eclipsed when, in 1912, the Norwegian dashed to the South Pole famously just ahead of the ill-starred Captain Scott.

The ship that carried Amundsen to within striking distance of the South Pole, the *Fram*, is displayed inside the museum. Designed by Colin Archer, a Norwegian shipbuilder of Scots ancestry, and launched in 1892, the *Fram*'s design was unique, its sides made smooth to prevent ice from getting a firm grip on the hull, while inside a veritable maze of beams, braces and stanchions held it all together. Living quarters inside the ship were necessarily cramped, but – in true Edwardian style – the Norwegians found space for a piano. Look out also for the assorted knick-knacks the explorers took with them, exhibited in the display cases along the walls. There are playing cards, maps, notebooks, snowshoes and surgical instruments – but this was as nothing to the equipment carted around by Scott, one of the reasons for his failure. Scott's main mistake, however, was to rely on Siberian ponies to transport his tackle. The animals were useless in Antarctic conditions and Scott and his men ended up pulling the sledges themselves, whereas Amundsen wisely brought a team of huskies.

Norsk Sjøfartsmuseum

The adjacent **Norsk Sjøfartsmuseum** (Norwegian Maritime Museum; mid-May to Sept daily 10am–6pm; Oct to mid-May Mon–Wed & Fri–Sun 10.30am–4pm, Thurs 10.30am–6pm; 30kr) occupies two buildings, the larger of which is a well-designed, brick structure holding a varied collection of maritime artefacts. One of the more interesting exhibits is an electronic link with the Oslofjord traffic control system, which allows visitors to track (but not change!) local shipping movements. The museum's most popular attraction, however, is the "Supervideograph", a widescreen movie that tracks over Norway's coastline in dramatic style. There's also the so-called Gibraltar boat, a perilously fragile, canvas-and-board home-made craft on which a bunch of Norwegian sailors fled Morocco for British Gibraltar after their ship had been impounded by the Vichy French authorities.

The museum's second building, the **Båthallen** (boat hall), boasts an extensive collection of small and medium-sized wooden boats from all over Norway, mostly inshore sailing and fishing craft from the nineteenth century. Non-sailors may find it of limited interest – and head straight for the museum's fjordside café instead.

West of the centre: the Henie-Onstad Kunstsenter

Overlooking the Oslofjord just beyond the city boundary in Høvikodden, some 12km west of the centre, the **Henie-Onstad Kunstsenter** (Henie-Onstad Art Centre; Tues–Thurs 10am–9pm & Fri–Mon 11am–6pm; usually

70kr but varies with exhibitions; half-price with Oslo Card; ☎67 80 48 80; ⓦwww.hok.no) is one of Norway's more prestigious modern art centres. There's no false modesty here – it's all about art as an expression of wealth – and the low-slung, modernistic building is a glossy affair on a pretty, wooded headland landscaped to accommodate a smattering of sculptures. The centre was founded by the ice-skater-cum-movie-star **Sonja Henie** (1910–69) and her shipowner-cum-art-collector husband Niels Onstad in the 1960s. Henie won three Olympic gold medals (1928, 1932 and 1936) and went on to appear in a string of lightweight Hollywood musicals. Her accumulated cups and medals are displayed in a room of their own, and once prompted a critic to remark: "Sonja, you'll never go broke. All you have to do is hock your trophies." In the basement are the autographed photos of many of the leading celebrities of Sonja's day – though the good wishes of a youthful-looking Richard Milhous Nixon hardly inspire empathy.

The wealthy couple accumulated an extensive collection of twentieth-century painting and sculpture. Matisse, Miró and Picasso, postwar French abstract painters, Expressionists and modern Norwegians all feature, but these now fight for gallery space with temporary exhibitions by contemporary artists. It is, therefore, impossible to predict what will be on display at any one time, and telephoning ahead is a good idea, especially as the centre also hosts regular concert and theatre performances. After the museum, be sure to spend a little time wandering the surrounding **sculpture park**, where you'll see work by the likes of Henry Moore and Arnold Haukeland: you can pick up a plan of the park at reception.

Getting there is easy by public transport: buses #151, #161, #251, #252 and #261 leave Oslo S at regular intervals, and most services also stop at the Nationaltheatret. Ask the driver to let you off at the Høvikodden stop, and you'll be dropped on the main road about five minutes' walk from the Art Centre. By car, the Centre is close to – and signposted from – the E18 road to Drammen.

Northwest of the centre: the Frognerparken

The green expanse of **Frognerparken** (Frogner Park) lies to the northwest of the city centre and is accessible by tram #12 or #15 from the centre – get off at Vigelandsparken, the stop after Frogner plass. The park incorporates one of Oslo's most celebrated and popular cultural targets, the open-air **Vigelandsparken** which, along with the nearby museum, commemorates a modern Norwegian sculptor of world renown, **Gustav Vigeland**. Between them, park and museum display a good proportion of his work, presented to the city in return for favours received by way of a studio and apartment during the years 1921–30. The park is also home to Frogner Manor, now housing the **Oslo Bymuseum**.

The Vigelandsparken

A country boy, raised on a farm just outside Mandal, on the south coast, **Gustav Vigeland** (1869–1943) began his career as a woodcarver but later, when studying in Paris, he fell under the influence of Rodin, and switched to stone and bronze. He started work on the **Vigelandsparken** (always open;

free) in 1924, and was still working on it when he died almost twenty years later. It's a literally fantastic concoction, medieval in spirit and complexity. Here he had the chance to let his imagination run riot and, when the place was unveiled, many city folk were simply overwhelmed – and no wonder. From the monumental wrought-iron gates, the central path takes you into a world of frowning, fighting and posturing bronze figures, which flank the footbridge over the river. Beyond, the **central fountain**, part of a separate commission begun in 1907, is an enormous bowl representing the burden of life, supported by straining, sinewy bronze Goliaths, while underneath, water tumbles out around figures engaged in play or talk, or simply resting or standing.

But it's the twenty-metre-high **obelisk** up on the stepped embankment, and the granite sculptures grouped around it, which really take the breath away. It's a humanistic work, a writhing mass of sculpture which depicts the cycle of life as Vigeland saw it: a vision of humanity playing, fighting, teaching, loving, eating and sleeping – and clambering on and over each other to reach the top. The granite children scattered around the steps are perfect: little pot-bellied figures who tumble over muscled adults – the local favourite is *Sinnataggen* (the angry child) – and provide an ideal counterpoint to the real Oslo toddlers who splash around in the fountain, oblivious and undeterred.

The Vigeland-museet

A five-minute walk from the obelisk, on the other side of the river at the southern edge of the park, the **Vigeland-museet** (Vigeland museum; May–Sept Tues–Sat 10am–6pm, Sun noon–6pm; Oct–April Tues–Sun noon–4pm; 40kr; Ⓦ www.vigeland.museum.no), at the corner of Halvdan Svartes gate and Nobels gate, was the artist's studio and home during the 1920s. The city built it for him and let him live there rent free on condition that the building – and its contents – passed back to public ownership on his death. It's still stuffed with all sorts of items related to the sculpture park, including photographs of the workforce, discarded or unused sculptures, woodcuts, preparatory drawings, and scores of plaster casts: here and there are scraps of biographical information. Vigeland was obsessed with his creations during his last decades, and you get the feeling that given half a chance he would have had himself cast and exhibited. As it is, his ashes were placed in the museum's tower.

The Oslo Bymuseum

A couple of hundred metres north of the Vigeland-museet, the mildly diverting **Oslo Bymuseum** (City Museum; June–Aug Tues–Fri 10am–6pm, Sat & Sun 11am–6pm; Sept–Dec & mid-Jan to May Tues–Fri 10am–4pm, Sat & Sun 11am–4pm; 30kr) is housed in the expansive, eighteenth-century **Frogner Manor**. The buildings are actually rather more interesting than the museum: a central courtyard is bounded on one side by the half-timbered Manor House,

---

Emanuel Vigeland

Gustav Vigeland enthusiasts may be interested by the work of the great man's younger and lesser-known brother, Emanuel, a respected artist in his own right. His stained-glass windows can be seen in Oslo's **Domkirke** (see p.80), while the **Emanuel Vigeland Museum** (Sun only noon–4pm; 30kr), northwest of the city centre at Grimelundsveien 8 (T-bane #1 to Slemdal), has a collection of his frescoes, sculptures, paintings and drawings.

complete with its appealing clock tower, and by antique agricultural buildings on the other three. Each of the latter has a huge cellar with thick stone walls beneath a rough wooden superstructure, in typical Norwegian country style. The best part of the **museum** is in the renovated old barn, which holds a sequence of thematic displays exploring the history of the city. Amongst many, there are sections on prisons, kitchens, the fire brigade and the police, but it's the paintings and photos of old Oslo and its people that catch the eye. For once, the labelling is exclusively in Norwegian, so pick up the English brochure at reception, though frankly it's not nearly as detailed as it could be. The museum has its own café, though the park's two open-air cafés are more enticing – nurse a beer at either the *Herregårdskroen* or the *Frognerparkens Café*, both between the Bymuseum and the bridge.

North of the centre: the Nordmarka

Crisscrossed by **hiking trails** and **cross-country ski routes**, the forested hills and lakes that comprise the **Nordmarka** occupy a tract of land that extends deep inland from central Oslo, but is still within the city limits for some 30km. A network of byroads provides dozens of access points to this wilderness, which is extremely popular with the capital's outdoor-minded citizens. **Den Norske Turistforening** (DNT), the Norwegian hiking organization, maintains a handful of staffed and unstaffed huts here. Its Oslo branch, in the city centre at Storgata 3 (Mon–Fri 10am–4pm, Thurs 10am–6pm, Sat 10am–2pm; ☏22 82 28 00; ⊛www.turistforeningen.no), has detailed **maps** and can sell a year's DNT membership for 400kr, which confers a substantial discount at its huts; see p.51 for more on DNT and hiking in general.

Sognsvannet

For a day trip, one of the easiest and most obvious departure points is **Sognsvann station**, the terminus of T-bane #5, just twenty minutes from the city centre. Maps of the surrounding wilderness are posted at the station and show a network of hiking trails labelled according to season – blue for summer, red for winter and skiing. From the station, it's a signposted five-minute walk to **Sognsvannet**, an attractive loch flanked by forested hills and encircled by an easy 4km-long hiking trail. The lake is iced over until the end of March or early April, but thereafter it's a perfect spot for swimming, though Norwegian assurances about the warmth of the water should be treated with caution. With the proper equipment (see p.51), it's possible to **hike west** over the hills to Frognerseteren station (see below), an arduous and not especially rewarding trek of about 5km. Locals mostly shun this route in summer, but – approached from the other direction – it's really popular in winter with parents teaching their children to cross-country ski. There is also a longer and more interesting route to Frognerseteren via **Ullevålseter**, where a huddle of old wooden buildings houses a very good café serving excellent home-made applecake. The whole route is about 9km long, and takes about 3hours to walk.

Frognerseteren and Holmenkollen

T-bane #1 also delves into the Nordmarka, wriggling up into the hills to the **Frognerseteren terminus**, a thirty-minute ride north of the city centre. From the station, there's a choice of signposted trails across the surrounding countryside. The most popular is the easy but squelchy two-kilometre stroll to the **Tryvannstårnet TV Tower** (daily: May & Sept 10am–5pm; June 10am–6pm; July & Aug 10am–8pm; Oct–April 10am–4pm; 40kr), where a lift whisks you up to an observation platform. From here, there are panoramic views over to the Swedish border in the east, Oslo to the south and the forest-ed hills of the Gudbrandsdal valley to the north. Labels inside the platform point everything out for you, though it's not worth going up unless the weath-er is clear as even a light mist obscures the view. Alternatively, it's just a couple of hundred metres from the T-bane terminus to the *Frognerseteren Restaurant* (opens 11am; ☎22 92 40 40), a delightful wooden lodge whose terrace offers splendid views out over the Nordmarka. The self-service restaurant is excellent too, and much less expensive.

Forest footpaths link Frognerseteren with Sognsvannet (see above), or it's a twenty-minute tramp downhill to the flashy chalets and hotels of the **Holmenkollen ski resort**, whose main claim to fame is its international **ski-jump** – a gargantuan affair that dwarfs its surroundings. At its base, the diligent **Skimuseet** (Ski Museum; daily: Jan–April & Oct–Dec 10am–4pm; May & Sept 10am–5pm; June–Aug 9am–8pm; 80kr including access to ski-jump) exhibits skiing apparel and equipment through the ages, from the latest in com-petition wear to the seemingly makeshift garb of early Polar explorers like Nansen and Amundsen. The museum also gives access to the mountain of metal steps which leads up the **ski-jump** for a peek straight down at what is, for most people, a horrifyingly steep, almost vertical, descent. It seems impos-sible that the tiny bowl at the bottom could pull the skier up in time – or that anyone could possibly want to jump off in the first place. The bowl is also the finishing point for the 8000-strong cross-country skiing race that forms part of the Holmenkollrennene ski festival every March.

About 1km downhill from the ski jump is **Holmenkollen T-bane station** (line #1), from where it's a 25-minute ride back to central Oslo.

Northeast of the centre: the Munch Museum

Nearly everyone who visits Oslo makes time for the **Munch-museet** – and with good reason. In his will, Munch donated all the works in his possession to Oslo city council – a mighty bequest of several thousand paintings, prints, drawings, engravings and photographs, which took nearly twenty years to cat-alogue and organize before being displayed in this purpose-built gallery.

The museum itself (June to mid-Sept daily 10am–6pm; mid-Sept to May Tues–Fri 10am–4pm, Sat & Sun 11am–5pm; 60kr; ⓦwww.munch.museum .no) is located to the northeast of the city centre in the workaday suburb of Tøyen, at Tøyengata 53. Getting there by public transport couldn't be easier: take the T-bane to Tøyen station and it's a signposted, five-minute walk.

The Munch-museet

The collection is huge, and only a small – but always significant – part can be shown at any one time. In fact, this is something of an advantage as seeing the whole collection would take days, though naturally it does mean you can't be certain what will be displayed and when. One feature you can rely on is the

Edvard Munch

Born in 1863, **Edvard Munch** had a melancholy childhood in what was then Christiana, overshadowed by the early deaths of both his mother and a sister from tuberculosis. After some early works, including several self-portraits, he went on to study in Paris – a city he returned to again and again, and where he fell fleetingly under the sway of the Impressionists. In 1892 he went to Berlin, where his style evolved and he produced some of his best and most famous work, though his first exhibition here was considered so outrageous it closed after only a week: his paintings were, a critic opined, "an insult to art". Despite the initial criticism, Munch's work was subsequently exhibited in many of the leading galleries of the day. Generally considered the initiator of the Expressionist movement, Munch wandered Europe, creating and exhibiting prolifically. Meanwhile overwork, drink and problematic love affairs were fuelling an instability that culminated, in 1908, in a nervous breakdown. Munch spent six months in a Copenhagen clinic, after which his health was much improved – and his paintings lost the self-destructive edge characteristic of his most celebrated work. However, it wasn't until well into his career that he was fully accepted in his own country, where he was based from 1909 until his death in 1944.

permanent display on Munch's life and times in the basement, providing plenty of background information on the artist.

In the museum's **main gallery**, the landscapes and domestic scenes of Munch's **early paintings**, such as *Tête à Tête* and *At the Coffee Table*, reveal the perceptive if deeply pessimistic realism from which Munch's later work sprang. Even more riveting are the great works of the **1890s**, which form the core of the collection and are considered Munch's finest achievements. Among many, there's *Dagny Juel*, a portrait of the Berlin socialite Ducha Przybyszewska, with whom both Munch and Strindberg were infatuated; the searing representations of *Despair* and *Anxiety*; the chilling *Red Virginia Creeper*, a house being consumed by the plant; and, of course, *The Scream* – of which the museum holds several of a total of fifty versions. Consider Munch's words as you view it:

I was walking along a road with two friends. The sun set. I felt a tinge of melancholy. Suddenly the sky became blood red. I stopped and leaned against a railing feeling exhausted, and I looked at the flaming clouds that hung like blood and a sword over the blue-black fjord and the city. My friends walked on. I stood there trembling with fright. And I felt a loud unending scream piercing nature.

Munch's style was never static, however. **Later paintings** such as *Workers On Their Way Home* (1913), produced after he had recovered from his breakdown and had withdrawn to the tranquillity of the Oslofjord, reflect his renewed interest in nature and physical work. His technique also changed: in works like the *Death of Marat II* (1907) he began to use streaks of colour to represent points of light. Later still, paintings such as *Winter in Kragerø* and *Model by the Wicker Chair*, with skin tones of pink, green and blue, begin to reveal a happier, if rather idealized, attitude to his surroundings, though this is most evident in works like *Spring Ploughing*, painted in 1919.

The exhibition is punctuated by **self-portraits**, a graphic illustration of Munch's state of mind at various points in his career. There's a palpable sadness in his *Self-Portrait with Wine Bottle* (1906), along with obvious allusions to his heavy drinking, while the telling perturbation of *In Distress* (1919) and *The Night Wanderer* (1923) indicate that he remained a tormented, troubled man even in his later years. One of his last works, *Self-Portrait By the Window* (1940), shows a glum figure on the borderline between life and death, the strong red of his face and green of his clothing contrasted with the ice-white scene visible through the window.

Munch's **lithographs and woodcuts** are shown in a separate section of the gallery: a dark catalogue of swirls and fogs, technically brilliant pieces of work and often developments of his paintings rather than just simple copies. In these he pioneered a new medium of expression, experimenting with colour schemes and a huge variety of materials, which enhance the works' rawness: wood blocks show a heavy, distinct grain, while there are colours like rust and blue drawn from the Norwegian landscape. As well as the stark woodcuts on display, there are also sensuous, hand-coloured lithographs, many focusing on the theme of love (taking the form of a woman) bringing death.

East of the centre: medieval Oslo and rock carvings

Founded in the middle of the eleventh century by Harald Hardrada, **medieval Oslo** lay tucked beneath the Ekeberg heights at the mouth of the River Alna, some 3km round the bay to the east of today's city centre. The old town, which had a population of around 3000 by the early fourteenth century, had two palaces – one for the bishop and one for the king – reflecting the uneasy division of responsibility which dogged its history. The settlement was also plagued by fires, which ripped through the wooden buildings with depressing regularity. After one such conflagration in 1624, **Christian IV** moved the city to its modern location, widening the streets to combat the fire danger, and what remained of old Oslo became an insignificant outpost. In successive centuries the traces of the medieval town were almost entirely obliterated, and only recently has there been any attempt to identify the original layout of what is commonly called the **Gamlebyen** (Old Town). There are precious few fragments to see, but they're just about worth seeking out when combined with a peek at a group of nearby prehistoric **rock carvings**.

The rock carvings

From Jernbanetorget, it's a ten-minute tram ride (#18 or #19) up to the old **Sjømannsskolen** (Merchant Marine Academy) – now a business school – housed in a large and conspicuous building perched high on a hill. The tram stops opposite the academy, whose fjord-facing terrace offers some of the most extensive views in Oslo, stretching all the way across the inner reaches of the Oslofjord to the Holmenkollen ski-jump. To the rear of the academy, a narrow drive – Karlsborgveien – leads downhill into a little dell. Here, on the left-hand side, you'll spot a group of ochre **rock carvings** depicting elk, deer and matchstick people, around 6000 years old and the earliest evidence of settlement along the Oslofjord.

The Gamlebyen

Walking back down from the academy along Kongsveien and then Oslo gate, it takes about ten minutes to reach the junction of Bispegata and the heart of the **Gamlebyen**. On the corner, at Oslo gate 13, is the **Ladegård**, a comely eighteenth-century mansion built on the site of the thirteenth-century

Bishop's Palace, whose foundations are underneath. On the other side of Oslo gate are the battered, but clearly labelled, ruins of both St Hallvardskatedralen (St Halvard's Cathedral) and St Olavskloseret (St Olav's Monastery) behind.

South of the centre: the islands and beaches of the inner Oslofjord

The compact archipelago of low-lying, lightly forested **islands** to the south of the city centre in the **inner Oslofjord** is the city's summer playground, and makes going to the **beach** a viable option. The ferry trip out there is fun too, especially in the evening when the less populated islands become favourite party venues for the city's preening youth. **Ferries** to the islands (22kr each way, Oslo Card and all other transport passes valid) leave from the Vippetangen quay, at the foot of Akershusstranda – a twenty-minute walk or a five-minute ride on bus #60 from Jernbanetorget. Incidentally, extra ferries are usually laid on when things get busy, so don't let any queues put you off.

Hovedøya and Langøyene

Conveniently, **Hovedøya** (ferry #92; mid-March to Sept 7.30am–7pm, every hour or ninety minutes; Oct to mid-March 3 daily; 10min), the nearest island, is also the most interesting. Its rolling hills contain both farmland and deciduous woods as well as the overgrown ruins of a **Cistercian monastery** built by English monks in the twelfth century. There are also incidental remains from the days when the island was garrisoned and armed to protect Oslo's harbour. A map of the island at the jetty helps with orientation, but on an islet of this size – it's just ten minutes' walk from one end to the other – getting lost is pretty much impossible. There are plenty of footpaths to wander, you can swim at the shingle beaches on the south shore, and there's a seasonal café opposite the monastery ruins. Camping, however, is not permitted as Hovedøya is a protected area, which is also why there are no summer homes.

The pick of the other islands is wooded **Langøyene** (ferry #94; June–Aug hourly 9am–7pm; 30min), the most southerly of the archipelago and the one with the best beaches. The H-shaped island has a **campsite**, *Langøyene Camping* (June–Aug; ☎22 11 53 21), and at night the ferries are full of people with sleeping bags and bottles of drink, on their way to join swimming parties.

Eating and drinking

There was a time when eating out in Oslo hardly set the pulse racing, but things are very different today. At the top end of the market, the city possesses dozens of fine **restaurants**, the pick of which feature Norwegian ingredients, especially fresh North Atlantic fish, but also more exotic dishes of elk, caribou, and salted-and-dried cod – for centuries Norway's staple food. Many of these restaurants have also assimilated the tastes and styles of other cuisines – Mediterranean foods are very much in vogue – and there is a reasonable selection of foreign restaurants too, everything from Italian to Mongolian.

Many of Oslo's restaurants are fairly formal affairs with prices to burn your fingers. The city's ethnic restaurants, however, are usually much less expensive

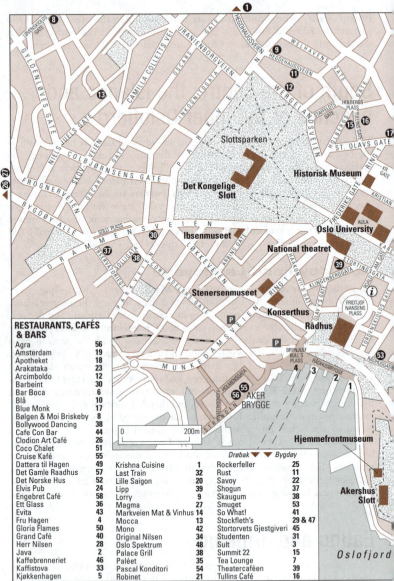

RESTAURANTS, CAFÉS & BARS

Agra	56
Amsterdam	19
Apotheket	18
Arakataka	23
Arcimboldo	12
Barbeint	30
Bar Boca	6
Blå	10
Blue Monk	17
Bølgen & Moi Briskeby	8
Bollywood Dancing	38
Cafe Con Bar	44
Clodion Art Café	26
Coco Chalet	51
Cruise Kafé	55
Dattera til Hagen	49
Det Gamle Raadhus	57
Det Norske Hus	52
Elvis Pub	24
Engebret Café	58
Ett Glass	36
Evita	43
Fru Hagen	4
Gloria Flames	50
Grand Café	40
Herr Nilsen	28
Java	2
Kaffebrenneriet	46
Kaffistova	33
Kjøkkenhagen	5

Krishna Cuisine	1
Last Train	32
Lille Saigon	20
Lipp	39
Lorry	9
Magma	27
Markveien Mat & Vinhus	14
Mocca	13
Mono	42
Original Nilsen	34
Oslo Spektrum	48
Palace Grill	38
Paléet	35
Pascal Konditori	54
Robinet	21

Drøbak ▼ ▼ Bygdøy

Rockerfeller	25
Rust	11
Savoy	22
Shogun	37
Skaugum	38
Smuget	53
So What!	41
Stockfleth's	29 & 47
Stortorvets Gjestgiveri	45
Studenten	31
Sult	3
Summit 22	15
Tea Lounge	7
Theatercaféen	39
Tullins Café	16

Ferry to Hove

–Vietnamese food, in particular, is currently in fashion – while **cafés** and **café-bars** are equally affordable. These run the gamut from homely family places, offering traditional Norwegian stand-bys, to student haunts and ultra-trendy hang-outs. Nearly all serve inexpensive lunches, and many offer excellent, competitively priced evening meals as well, though most self-service cafés close at 5 or 6pm. In addition, downtown Oslo boasts a vibrant **bar** scene, boister-

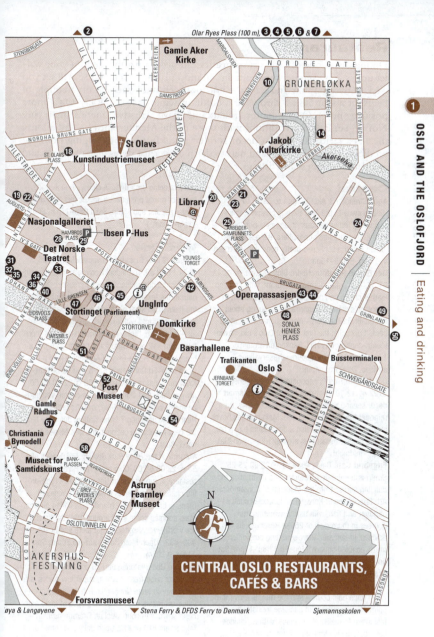

CENTRAL OSLO RESTAURANTS, CAFÉS & BARS

ous but generally good-natured, and at its most frenetic on summer weekends, when the city is crowded with visitors from all over Norway.

Finally, those carefully counting the kroner will find it easy to buy bread, fruit, **snacks** and sandwiches from stalls, supermarkets and kiosks across the city centre, while fast-food joints offering hamburgers and *pølser* (hot dogs) are legion.

Restaurants

Dining out at one of Oslo's **restaurants** can make a sizeable dent in your wallet unless you exercise some restraint. In most places, a main course will set you back between 150kr and 220kr – not too steep until you add on a couple of beers (at about 50kr a throw) or a bottle of wine (at least 240kr). On a more positive note, Oslo's better restaurants have creative menus marrying Norwegian culinary traditions with those of the Mediterranean – and a lousy meal is a rarity. Restaurant decor is often a real feature too, ranging from the predictable fishing photos and nets to sharp modernist styles, all pastel walls and angular furnishings and fittings.

Central

Agra Stranden 3, Aker Brygge ☎ 22 83 07 12. Hidden away in the Aker Brygge complex, this appealing, Indian restaurant serves super-tasty food in an authentic atmosphere. It's reasonably priced and the service is pretty good, too. Mon–Sat 4–11pm, Sun 3–10pm.

Det Gamle Raadhus Nedre Slotts gate 1 ☎ 22 42 01 07. This smart, formal restaurant, with its deep leather chairs and neo-baronial fittings, is not to everyone's taste, but there's no quibbling about the quality of the food – Norwegian cuisine at its best. It occupies the first floor of Oslo's old, seventeenth-century City Hall. Reckon on around 170–250kr for a main course. Reservations advised. Daily from 4pm.

Det Norske Hus Prinsengate 18 at Kongensgate ☎ 22 41 12 10. First-rate restaurant with smart decor serving traditional Norwegian cuisine, from reindeer through to salted cod. Main courses hover around 220kr. There's also a downstairs lunch bar, where similar meals cost around 100kr. Mon–Sat 11am–midnight.

Engebret Café Bankplassen 1 ☎ 22 82 25 25. Smart and intimate restaurant in an attractive old building across from the Museum of Contemporary Art. Specializes in Norwegian delicacies such as reindeer and fish, with mouth-watering main courses in the region of 250kr. Reservations advised. In summer, there's seating outside on the pretty cobbled square. Mon–Fri 11am–11pm, Sat noon–11pm.

Grand Café Karl Johans gate 31 ☎ 22 42 93 90. This is the *Grand Hotel*'s café-restaurant where Ibsen once held court – and the murals prove the point. Now popular with package tourists, the old-fashioned formality of the place, with its chandeliers, bow-tie waiters and glistening cutlery, is its main appeal, plus the reasonably priced set lunches. Also has a rooftop café with great views over Karl Johans gate, though service can be slow.

Theatercaféen *Hotel Continental* Stortingsgata 24–26 ☎ 22 82 40 50. Eat in splendid Art Nouveau surroundings and watch the city's movers and shakers doing their thing. A classy, though pricey, menu of mixed provenance makes this restaurant a very popular spot. Mon–Sat 11am–11pm, Sun 11am–10pm.

Westside

Bølgen & Moi Briskeby Løvenskioldsgate 26 ☎ 24 11 53 53. Traditional Norwegian cuisine with a hint of Mediterranean/nouvelle crossover served both in the (expensive) gourmet restaurant and at the (less expensive) bistro. Also serves fantastic breakfast buffets with everything you could wish for – and more. Highly recommended. To get there, take tram #12 or #15 from the centre. Also has a branch at the Henie-Onstad Art Centre (see p.94). Open Mon–Fri 8am–1am, Sat & Sun 9am–1am.

Krishna Cuisine Kirkeveien 59B ☎ 22 60 62 50. Always tasty and filling, the three-course vegetarian meals cost around 100kr, with free refills, too. Near the Majorstuen T-bane station, this is by far the best vegetarian option in the city. Mon–Fri noon–8pm.

Magma at the *Hotel Rica Bygdøy Allé* Bygdøy allé 53 ☎ 23 08 58 00. Chic and expensive first-floor restaurant, run by one of Norway's most high-profile chefs, Sonja Lee. Its inventive international menu is based on French and north Italian cuisine. Main courses come in at around 190–240kr, and are worth every kroner. To get there use buses #30–#32. Open Mon–Sat 11am–10.30pm, Sun 11am–9.30pm.

Shogun Observatoriegaten 2B ☎ 22 44 07 45. *Shogun*'s superfresh sushi at super low prices is a great way to taste Norwegian fish. It serves good value set meals of 8, 10 or 12 pieces of maki and nigiri sushi with soup. Just off Drammensveien – take trams #10 or #12. Open daily 2–11pm.

Grønland and Grünerløkka

Arakataka Mariboes gate 7 ☎ 23 32 83 00. This smart, modern restaurant serves outstanding food, mostly fish, at unbeatable prices, both à la carte

△Constitution Day, Royal Palace, Oslo

and with a set three-course menu for just 250kr. Highly recommended, though the service can be patchy. A 15-minute walk north of the Domkirke or bus #34 or #38 from Jernbanetorget. Sun–Thurs 4–10pm, Fri–Sat 4–11pm.

Lille Saigon Møllergata 32C ☎22 11 48 13. The best Vietnamese food in the city. Simple surroundings, but delicious, inexpensive meals – be sure to try the springrolls. Daily noon–11pm.

Markveien Mat & Vinhus Torvbakkgaten 26, entrance in Markveien ☎22 37 22 97. Mediterranean-influenced food and one of the best wine cellars in the city. High quality meals and excellent service. Mon–Sat 5–11pm, wine bar from 4pm.

Sult Thorvald Meyers gate 26 ☎22 87 04 67. One of the city's most popular restaurants, called "Hunger" after the novel by Knut Hamsun. Features an inventive, Norwegian-based menu, using only the freshest ingredients. Moderate prices. The adjacent bar *Tørst* (meaning Thirst) serves great frozen Strawberry Margarithas. Open Tues–Thurs 4–10pm, Fri 4–11pm, Sat 1–11pm, Sun 1–10pm.

Cafés, coffee houses and café-bars

For sit-down food, **cafés** represent the best value in town. Traditional *kafeterias* (often self-service) offer substantial portions of Norwegian food in pleasant surroundings, mostly decorated in crisp modern style. Oslo also has a slew of **café–bars** dishing up salads, pasta and the like in attractive, often modish premises. The best deals are generally at lunchtime, when there's usually a dish of the day. In addition, Oslo now contains dozens of specialist **coffee houses**. A couple of national chains are well represented – *Kaffe & Krem* and the rather more appealing *Kaffebrenneriet* – and there's a smattering of independent places too. Most of the cafés listed below close around 8 or 9pm, while the café-bars stay open much later. The coffee houses tend to close between 5 and 7pm on weekdays, and around 5pm at weekends.

Central

Amsterdam Universitetsgata 11. Entrance on Kristian Augusts gate. Decorated in the style of a traditional Dutch bar, this busy and agreeable café-bar has a moderately priced menu with an international flavour. Offerings include lasagne, satay, and ciabatta with shellfish, and prices are in the 70–90kr range. Kitchen closes around 9pm. Open Mon & Tues 11.30am–12.30am, Wed–Sat 11.30am–2.30am, Sun 1pm–midnight.

Apotheket St Olavs gate 2 at St Olavs Plass. Officially called Tekehtopa, but known to all and sundry as Apotheket, this grand old building used to be a pharmacy, and retains its high ceilings, old wooden panels and antique furniture. It's now a highly recommended café-bar serving excellent food, such as Greek meze and other Mediterranean treats at very affordable prices, all washed down by a good range of beers. Open Sun–Thurs 10am–2am, Fri & Sat noon–2.30am; kitchen closes at 10pm.

Coco Chalet Øvre Slottsgate 8. Leather booths, heavy drapes and Art Nouveau flourishes characterize this old-fashioned but fashionable café in the city centre. Inexpensive snacks from 35kr. Mon–Fri 8am–5pm, Sat 10am–5pm.

Ett Glass Karl Johans gate 33:entrance round the corner on Rosenkrantz gate. Trendy, candle-lit café-bar with an imaginative menu focusing on Mediterranean-influenced light meals and lunches. Moderate prices. Mon, Tues & Sun noon–midnight, Wed–Sat noon–2.30am; kitchen closes at 10pm.

Java Ullevålsveien 45B, St Hanshaugen district. Coffee connoisseur's paradise patronized by Norwegian royals, but lacking any corresponding pomp. Delicious sandwiches, too.

Kaffebrenneriet 45 Grensen at Akersgata. One of the most central branches of the popular Norwegian coffee house chain. Serves particularly good espressos, as well as tasty snacks and great cakes. Bright, modern decor. Mon–Fri 9am–6pm, Sat 9am–5pm.

Kaffistova Rosenkrantz gate 8. Part of the *Hotell Bondeheimen* (see p.75), this spick-and-span self-service café serves tasty, traditional Norwegian cooking at very fair prices. There's usually a vegetarian option, too. Mon–Fri 9.30am–7pm, Sat & Sun 10.30am–5pm.

Paléet Karl Johans gate 37–43. In the basement of this modern shopping mall is a "Food Street" comprising a dozen bargain places. What's on offer is, to all intents and purposes, fast food, but of a superior standard. Two stalls to look out for are *Italo's*, with its Italian pastas and pizzas, and *Hellas*, a Greek counter selling dishes from 80kr. You order at any of the counters before finding a seat. Mall open Mon–Fri 10am–8pm, Sat 10am–6pm.

Pascal Konditori Tollbugata 11. Wonderful pastries and tasty coffee in this little café, located in a former bakery. Delightfully decorated with ceramic tiles of cherubs and fruit. Mon–Fri 8am–5pm, Sat 10am–5pm, Sun noon–5pm.

Stockfleth's branches on Lille Grensen and CJ Hambros plass. Many locals swear by the coffee served at this small chain, which regularly wins awards for its brew.

Tullins Café Tullins gate 2. Ignore the glum exterior and venture inside this cosy little café, where they serve inexpensive meals and very filling snacks. The beer is (by Norwegian standards) a real snip at just 40kr per half-litre. Open Mon–Wed noon–2am, Thurs–Sat noon–3.30am & Sun noon–1am.

Westside

Arcimboldo Wergelandsveien 17. Fashionable but unpretentious self-service café-bar located inside the Kunstnernes Hus, a former art gallery facing onto the Slottsparken. Its imaginative menu features both Mediterranean-style and Norwegian dishes, with main courses in the region of 150kr. Mon–Wed 11am–midnight, Thurs 11am–1am, Fri & Sat 11am–3am, Sun noon–6pm.

Clodion Art Café Bygdøy Allé 63, entrance round the corner on Thomas Heftyes gate. Well to the west of the city centre, not far from Frognerparken, this café-bar, with its second-hand, brightly-painted furniture, hosts regular art displays and serves good food: soups at around 45kr, bowls of pasta for 70kr. Food served daily 10am–9pm, drinks until 1am.

Mocca Niels Juels gate 70. The only Oslo coffee-house to roast its own beans – the results speak

for themselves. Like its sister coffee house, *Java* (see above) it also serves great sandwiches.

Rust Hegdehaugsveien 22. Smart, loungy kind of place that's good for lunches and light meals during the day and early evening. Turns into a chic bar at night, with a fine selection of Calavados. Mon–Thurs 11am–1am, Fri–Sat 11am–2.30am & Sun noon–1am.

Eastside: Grønland and Grünerløkka

Dattera til Hagen Grønland 10 ☎ 22 17 18 61. Spin-off venture of *Fru Hagen* (see below), serving tapas, beer and coffee in the daytime, and turning into a happening bar at night with a good live DJ on the first floor. The outdoor area at the back is great on a hot summer's night. Mon–Wed 11am–12.30am, Thurs–Sat 11am–2.30am and Sun noon–12.30am.

Evita Brugata 17. The Grønland branch of this small coffee house chain, serving good coffee to an off-beat clientele.

Fru Hagen Thorvald Meyers gate 42. Long-standing colourful joint; still trendy, and serving tasty snacks and meals from an inventive menu with a Mediterranean slant. Filling sandwiches, salads and wok-cooked dishes too. Main courses from 80–130kr. The kitchen closes at 9.30pm, after which the drinking gets going in earnest. Very popular spot – so go early to be sure of a seat. Daily 11am–1.30am.

Kjøkkenhagen Thorvald Meyers gate 40. Next door to *Fru Hagen*, serving simple, straightforward snacks and light meals – tasty salads, quiche and so forth – at moderate prices. Open daily 11am–10pm.

Bars

Bar-hopping in Oslo is an enjoyable affair. The more mainstream bars are in the centre along and around Karl Johans gate, while the sharper, more fashionable spots are concentrated to the east in the Grønland and Grünerløkka districts. The westside of the city is home to the smart set, who gather in the chics bars of Hegdehaugsveien and Bogstadveien. Most of Oslo's bars stay open until around 1am on weekdays, and at the weekend, in some cases, until 3–4am: almost all are open daily. Drinks are uniformly expensive, so if you're after a big night out, it's a good idea to follow Norwegian custom and have a few warm-up drinks at home.

Central

Cruise Kafé Stranden 3, Aker Brygge. Standard-issue modern bar done out in pastel shades, with photographs of actors on the walls. It's all rather contrived, but the music – rock, and some rock and roll – is eclectic, and there are occasional live acts too. Mon, Tues & Sun noon–12.30am, Wed &

Thurs noon–2am, Fri & Sat 1pm–2.30am.

Last Train Karl Johans Gate 45, The best rock-pub in town. Good old-style rock played at volume to a leather and jeans clientele. Mon–Fri 3pm–3.30am, Sat 1pm–3.30am & Sun 6pm–3.30am.

Lipp Olavs gate 2. Part of the *Hotel Continental*,

this big and brash bar, all wide windows and wood, is popular with the young(ish) and well-heeled. Tues–Sat 3pm–2.30am, Sun & Mon 3pm–1.30am.

Savoy Universitetsgata 11. With its stained-glass windows and wood-panelled walls, this small, intimate bar is an agreeably low-key spot to nurse a beer. Part of the *Quality Savoy Hotel*, on the corner of Kristian Augusts gate. Daily 5pm–2am.

Studenten Karl Johans gate 45 at Universitetsgata. A huge copper vat gets centre stage in this bar that brews its own beer. There are views across to the Nationaltheatret from the window seats, and a youthful crowd. Mon, Tues & Sun 11am–1.30am, Wed & Thurs 11am–2.30am, Fri & Sat 11am–3.30am.

Summit 22 Holbergs gate 30. On top of the *Radisson SAS Scandinavia Hotel*, this bar-lounge looks like the interior of a cruiseship, but you can't fault the panoramic views over the city. Open daily until 3am.

Westside

Barbeint Drammensveien 20, close to Parkveien. If you're familiar with Scandinavian bands and films, you may recognize a few faces in this jam-packed, fashionable bar. Loud sounds – everything from rap to rock. Daily 8pm–3.30am.

Lorry Parkveien 12, at the corner of Hegdehaugsveien. Popular and enjoyable pub with old-fashioned fittings, attracting a mixed crowd. There's a wide choice of beers, and outdoor seating in the summer. Daily 11am–2.30am.

Palace Grill Solligata 2. A small American-style bar with Irish beers on draft. Roots, rock and jazz music, plus occasional live acts. Popular with everyone from yuppies to students. Mon–Thurs &

Sun 3pm–2am, Fri & Sat 3pm–3am.

Skaugum Solligata 2, same entrance as the *Palace Grill* (see above). The backyard behind the *Palace Grill* and *Bollywood Dancing* (see below) is home to a quirky summer-only outdoor bar, with rack upon rack of multi-coloured lightbulbs illuminating the thirty-odd sinks that have been attached to the walls. It's all very modish and successful – modern art with flair – and attracts an appreciative clientele. Open June–Sept daily 6pm–midnight.

Eastside: Grønland and Grünerløkka

Bar Boca Thorvald Meyers gate 30. Tiny 1950s-style bar serving the best cocktails in town. The bartenders take their work very seriously, and you need to get there early to avoid the crush.

Cafe con Bar Brugata 11. Hip-as-you-like with retro interior and a long bar that can make buying a drink hard work. Good atmosphere, loungy decor and unisex toilets for those surprise meetings.

Elvis Pub Christian Kroghs gate 43. A tiny place devoted entirely to Elvis images and paraphernalia. No guesses as to what's on the jukebox. At midnight the disco lights are turned on for yet more retro fun. Down by the River Akerselva near the north end of Storgata, it's not too easy to find, but hardcore Elvis fans will undoubtedly succeed. Open till 3am on the weekend.

Robinet Mariboes gate 7. Possibly the smallest bar in Oslo – 1950s retro kitsch combined with excellent drinks and an intellectual crowd.

Tea Lounge Thorvald Meyers gate 33B. Lounge-type bar with velvety red couches and huge windows. Fine place to have a quiet, or romantic, night out.

Entertainment and nightlife

Oslo has a vibrant **nightclub** scene, which is hardly surprising considering the number of Norwegians who flock to Ibiza every year. Tracking down live music is also straightforward. Though the domestic **rock** scene is far from inspiring, **jazz** fans are well served, with several first-rate venues dotted round the city centre, while **classical music** enthusiasts benefit from an ambitious concert programme. Most **theatre** productions are in Norwegian, but English-language theatre companies visit often, and at the **cinema** films are shown in the original language with Norwegian subtitles.

For **entertainment listings** it's worth checking the Norwegian-language weekly listings leaflet *Plakaten*, available free from downtown cafés, bars, shops and tourist offices. More detailed information and reviews are provided by *Natt & Dag* (ⓦ www.nattogdag.no), a free Norwegian-language monthly broadsheet, which is also widely distributed downtown. The main alternative is

What's On in Oslo, a monthly English-language freebie produced by the tourist office. Summer is the best time to be in Oslo for events of almost every description, but winter sees a fair range of happenings too.

For **tickets**, try Ticket Master (☎815 33 133), for whom larger Norwegian post offices also act as agents; otherwise, contact the venue direct.

Nightclubs and live music

Oslo's hippest **nightclubs** are located on the east side of the city in the Grønland and Grünerløkka districts, but there's also a selection of more mainstream places right in the centre of town around Karl Johans gate and on Rosenkrantz gate. Entry will set you back in the region of 100kr, and, surprisingly enough, drink prices are the same as anywhere else. Nothing gets going much before 11pm; closing times are generally around 3am. Almost all the clubs also host a variety of **live music**, ranging from local home-grown talent to the big-name bands – check the listings press (see above) for individual programmes.

Bollywood Dancing Solli gate 2 ☎22 55 11 66. Super-kitschy restaurant-bar-cum-disco that's one of the best – and trendiest – nightspots in town. Asian retro decor – fake red leather sofas and so forth – plus ingenious cocktails. Check out the excellent "Bollyburgers" and groove away on the dancefloor until the early hours. Lots of fun.

Blå Brenneriveien 9C ☎22 20 91 81, Ⓦwww.blx.no. Creative, cultural nightspot in Grünerløkka, featuring everything from live jazz and cabaret through to public debates and poetry readings. Also features some of the best DJs in town, keeping the crowd moving until 3.30am at the weekend. In summer, there's a pleasant riverside terrace and the food is pretty good too.

Blue Monk St Olavs gate 23, at the corner of Pilestredet ☎22 20 22 90. Crowded, earthy nightspot noted for its eclectic programme of live music, from blues through to Estonian funk. Below is the equally gritty *Sub Pub*, featuring punk, ska and rock.

Gloria Flames Grønland 18 ☎22 17 16 00. Not the easiest place to find – there's just a small sign on the door – but worth searching out if you're into hardcore rock and rockabilly.

Mono Pløens gate 4 ☎22 41 41 66, Ⓦwww.cafemono.no. Dark interior with plush old couches and retro 1970s fixtures and fittings. Attracts mostly students and music business types, and hosts live acts – mainly indie – several nights a week with diverse DJ sounds, too. Mon–Fri noon–2am, Fri & Sat noon–4am, Sun 2pm–2am.

Oslo Spektrum Sonja Henies plass 2 ☎22 05 29 00, Ⓦwww.oslospektrum.no. Major venue, close to Olso S, showcasing big international acts, as well as small-fry local bands.

Rockefeller Music Hall Torggata 16 ☎22 20 32 32, Ⓦwww.rockefeller.no. Accommodating up to 1500 people, one of Oslo's grandest nightspots occupies an imaginatively refurbished former bath house. It hosts well-known and up-and-coming rock groups, with a good sideline in reggae and salsa.

Smuget Rosenkrantz gate 22 ☎22 42 52 62, Ⓦwww.smuget.no. Large, long-established and still popular nightclub with bars, a disco and regular live acts, mostly by home-grown rock or blues bands.

So What! Grensen 8 ☎22 33 64 66, Ⓦwww.sowhat.no. Something of a national institution and long a mecca for indie bands, So What! offers an ambitious programme of live music in its darker-than-dark basement. When there isn't a gig, it hosts some high-octane dancing, whilst the ground floor bar features rock and indie music.

Festivals

Big-name rock bands often include Oslo in their tours, leavening what would otherwise be a pretty dull scene. The most prestigious annual event is **Norwegian Wood** (☎815 33 133, Ⓦwww.norwegianwood.no), a three-day open-air rock festival held in June in the outdoor amphitheatre at Frogner Park, a ten-minute ride from the city centre on tram #12 or #15. Previous years have attracted the likes of Iggy Pop, Lou Reed and Van Morrison, and the festival continues to pull in some of the best international artists, supported by a variety of Norwegian acts. The arena holds around six thousand people, but tickets, costing around 350kr per day, sell out long in advance.

Oslo also hosts the more contemporary **Øyafestivalen** (℡22 37 59 09, ⓦwww.oyafestivalen.com), a three-day event that showcases a wide range of artists, mostly Norwegian but with some imports too – 2002, for example, included Tortoise, Chicks On Speed and Saint Etienne. A club night kicks the whole thing off in style. The festival usually takes place in the middle of August, outside in the Middelalderparken – about 10min by tram #18 from Jernbanetorget. Less high-profile, but of equal appeal is the **Musikkens dag** (℡23 10 36 96, Ⓕ22 42 48 19, ⓦwww.musikkensdag.org), a one-day event in May with free, open-air concerts around the city. The main stage on Rådhusplassen hosts all the major acts, while a second stage Akersgata concentrates on blues and rockabilly.

Jazz venues

Oslo has a strong **jazz** tradition, and in early or mid-August its week-long **Jazz Festival** attracts internationally renowned artists as well as showcasing local talent. The Festival Office, at Tollbugata 28 (℡22 42 91 20, ⓦwww.oslojazz.no) has full programme details of all the gigs, including those where there's an admission charge as well as the many free outdoor performances. At other times of the year, try one of the following for regular jazz acts.

Herr Nilsen CJ Hambros plass 5 ℡22 33 54 05, ⓦwww.herrnilsen.no. Small and intimate bar whose brick walls are decorated with jazz memorabilia. Live jazz – often traditional and bebop – most nights. Air-conditioned; central location. Daily 1pm–2.30am.
Original Nilsen Rosenkrantz gate 11 ℡22 72 12 21 ⓦwww.originalnilsen.no. Popular bar featuring regular live jazz. Daily 1pm–3am.
Stortorvets Gjestgiveri Grensen 1 ℡23 35 63 70, ⓦwww.stortorvets-gjestgiveri.no. Near the Domkirke, at the junction of Grensen and Grubbegata this old rabbit-warren of a place incorporates a jazz café, where there's traditional and modern jazz every Thursday night and Saturday lunchtime.

Classical music and opera

Oslo's major orchestra, the **Oslo Filharmonien** (ⓦwww.oslofilharmonien .com), gives regular concerts in the city's Konserthus, Munkedamsveien 14, and has an information office at Haakon VII's gate 2 (℡23 11 60 60; Ⓔpublikumskontor@oslophil.com). As you would expect, programmes often include works by Norwegian and other Scandinavian composers. Tickets for most performances cost around 300kr. In August and September, the orchestra traditionally gives a couple of free evening concerts in the Vigeland sculpture park, as part of the city's summer entertainment programme, which also sees classical performances at a variety of other venues, including the Domkirke, the Munch Museum and the University Aula (for details of the summer programme, contact the tourist office; see p.72).

In October, the ten-day **Ultima Contemporary Music Festival** (ⓦwww.ultima.no, ℡22 42 99 99) gathers together more Scandinavian and international talent in an ambitious programme of concerts featuring everything from modern contemporary music to opera, ballet, classical and folk. The performances take place in a variety of venues throughout the city; for full details check Ultima's website or contact the tourist office.

Finally, **Den Norske Opera**, Norway's prolific opera company, offers a popular repertoire – Mozart, R. Strauss and the Italians – but also undertakes a number of contemporary works each year. Performances are usually held at the Opera House, Storgata 23 (information ℡23 31 50 00; booking office ℡815 444 88; ⓦwww.operaen.no).

Cinema

The facility with which the Norwegians tackle other languages is best demonstrated at the **cinema**, where films are shown in their original language with Norwegian subtitles. Given that American (and British) films are the most popular, this has obvious advantages for visiting English speakers. Oslo has its share of mainstream multi-screens, as well as a good art house cinema. Prices are surprisingly reasonable: tickets average around 65–75kr.

Cinema listings – including details of late-night screenings – appear daily in the local press and the tourist office has programme times too. The following is a selection of central screens.

Eldorado Torggata 9 ☎820 30 000. Mainstream cinema showing the usual bockbusters.

Filmens Hus Dronningens gate 16 ☎22 47 45 00. Art house cinema with a varied programme mixing mainstream and alternative films.

Filmteateret Stortingsgata; ☎820 30 000. Old theatre converted into a cinema with wonderful decor. Shows mainstream and classic films.

Gimle Bygdøy allé ☎820 30 000. A sympathetically revamped old cinema with the most comfortable seats in town. A winebar in the entrance adds a nice touch. Varied programme, mostly mainstream.

Saga Stortingsgata 28 at Olav V's gate ☎820 30 000. Mainstream cinema with six screens.

Theatre

Nearly all Oslo's theatre productions are in Norwegian, making them of limited interest to (most) tourists, though there are occasional English-language performances by touring theatre companies. The principal venue is the **Nationaltheatret**, Stortingsgata 15 (☎22 31 90 50; ⓦwww.nationaltheatret .no), which hosts the prestigious, annual Ibsen Festival. Touring companies may also appear at the more adventurous **Det Norske Teatret**, Kristian IV's gate 8 (☎22 42 43 44, ⓦwww. detnorsketeatret.no).

Sports

Surrounded by forest and fjord, Oslo is very much an outdoor city, offering a wide range of **sports** and active pastimes. In summer, locals take to the hills to hike the network of trails that lattice the forests and lakes of the Nordmarka (see p.97), where many also fish. Others use the city's open-air swimming pools and tennis courts, or head out to the offshore islets of the Oslofjord (see p.101) to sunbathe and swim. In winter, the cross-country ski routes of the Nordmarka are especially popular, as is downhill skiing at Holmenkollen. Indeed skiing is such an integral part of winter life here that the T-bane carriages all have ski racks. Sleigh-riding is possible too, and so is ice skating, with the handiest rinks right in the middle of town in front of the Stortinget (see p.80). An indoor option at any time of year is **ten-pin bowling** at – amongst several places – Oslo Bowlingsenter, Torggata 16 (☎22 20 44 42).

Summer sports

Oslo's main open-air **swimming pool**, Tøyenbadet (☎22 68 24 23; 50kr, children 30kr; free with the Oslo Card), is located at Helgesens gate 90, to the northeast of the city centre, close to the Munch Museum. To get there, take the T-bane to Tøyen station, from where it's a five-minute walk. Tøyenbadet comprises four unheated, seasonal swimming pools, a sauna, solarium, diving boards, water chute and keep-fit facilities. It also has a year-round indoor swimming pool. Similar outdoor swimming facilities are provided from May to August at the newly redecorated Frognerbadet baths (☎22 44 74 29; 60kr; children 30kr; free with the Oslo Card), in Frognerparken, northwest of the centre, reached on tram #12 and #15. Also in Frognerparken is Oslo's only set of municipal **tennis courts**, an inexpensive supplement to the city's many private tennis clubs. The public courts only cost 50kr per person (30kr for children) and as a result they're very popular, especially at weekends. Hiring a court is done locally at the kiosk.

With regard to **fishing**, the freshwater lakes of the Nordmarka are reasonably well stocked with such common species as trout, char, pike and perch. The Oslomarkas Fiskeadministrasjon, Kongeveien 5 (☎22 49 07 99), near the Holmenkollen ski-jump, provides information on fishing in the Oslo area. In particular, it can advise about fishing areas and has lists of where local licences can be bought; see p.55 for general information about fishing in Norway.

Winter sports

Skiing is extremely popular throughout Norway, and here in Oslo skis and equipment can be rented for 200–300kr a day from Skiservice Tomm Murstad, Tryvannsveien 2 (☎22 13 95 00; ⊛www.skiservice.no), at the Voksenkollen

---

Oslo with children

There's no shortage of things to do with children in Oslo, beginning with the open-air **Vigelandsparken** (see p.95). If the weather is good, the **beaches** of the Oslofjord islands (see p.101) are bound to appeal, or you can use the city's **swimming pools** (see "Sports" on p.111. In winter, ice-skating at one of the city's outdoor rinks (see p.113) is always popular, while pick of the activities is **sleigh riding** in the Oslo forest (see p.113).

Few children will want to be dragged round Oslo's main museums, except perhaps for the **Frammuseet** (see p.93), but there are several museums geared up for youngsters. The most popular is the **Norsk Teknisk Museum**, at Kjelsåsveien 143 (Technology Museum; late June to late Aug daily 10am–6pm; Sept to mid-June Tues–Fri 10am–4pm, Sat & Sun 10am–5pm; 60kr, children 30kr; ⊛www.tekniskmuseum.no). Out to the north of the city close to Lake Maridal (Maridalsvannet), this is an interactive museum, equipped with working models and a galaxy of things to push and touch, as well as a café and picnic area. To get there from the city centre, take bus #37 to Kjelsås station alongside the museum, or tram #11 or #12 to their Kjelsås terminus from where it's a couple of minutes' walk.

Alternatively, there's the rather more creative **Barnekunstmuseet** at Lille Frøens vei 4 (Children's Art Museum; Jan–June Tues–Thurs 9.30am–2pm, Sun 11am–4pm; July to early Aug Tues–Thurs & Sun 11am–4pm; mid-Sept to mid-Dec Tues–Thurs 9.30am–2pm, Sun 11am–4pm; closed mid-Aug to mid-Sept; 40kr, children 20kr; T-bane to Frøen). This has an international collection of children's art – drawings, paintings, sculpture and handicrafts – along with a children's workshop where painting, music and dancing are frequent activities; call ahead for details on ☎22 46 85 73.

The gallant (or foolhardy) can also head off to an **amusement park**, the Tusenfryd (June Mon–Fri 10.30am–5pm, Sat & Sun 10.30am–7pm; July to mid-Aug daily 10.30am–7pm; May, late Aug & Sept Sat & Sun only 10.30am–7pm; ☎64 97 66 99, ⊛www.tusenfryd.no), located about 20km southeast of Oslo along the E18. It has more than twenty varied rides, including a roller coaster and a "SpaceShot". In summer, special buses run to the park from the main city bus station.

Discounts for children are commonplace. Almost all sites let babies and toddlers in free, and charge half of the adult tariff for youngsters between 4 and 16 years of age. It's the same on public transport, and hotels are usually very obliging too, adding camp beds of some description to their rooms with the minimum of fuss and expense.

T-bane station – the penultimate stop on line #1. Both cross-country and downhill enthusiasts should call at the **Skiforeningen** (Ski Association) office, at Kongeveien 5 (☎22 92 32 00; ⊛www.skiforeningen.no), near the Holmenkollen ski-jump, on T-bane #1. It has lots of information on Oslo's floodlit trails, cross-country routes, downhill and slalom slopes, ski schools (including one for children) and excursions to the nearest mountain resorts. Guided ski tours are organized by Uten Grenser (☎22 22 77 40 or ☎908 71 621. For spectators, March sees the annual Holmenkollen Ski Festival: tickets and information from the Skiforeningen.

Three other winter sports are worth noting. **Horsedrawn sleigh rides** in the Nordmarka can be arranged through either Vangen Skistue, PO Box 29, Klemetsrud, N–1212 Oslo (☎64 86 54 81), or Helge Torp, Sørbråten Gård, Maridalen, Oslo (☎22 23 22 21). **Ice fishing** is another Nordmarka option, but follow what the locals do as it can be dangerous (see p.55 for information on fishing licences). Finally, there's a floodlit **skating rink**, Narvisen (Nov–March), in front of the Stortinget beside Karl Johans gate. Admission is free and you can hire skates on the spot at reasonable rates, with a modest discount if you have an Oslo Card.

Listings

Airlines Air France, Haakon VII's gate 9 (☎23 50 20 01); British Airways, at the airport (☎800 33 142); Finnair, Jernbanetorget 4a (☎810 01 100); KLM, booking and information only by phone (☎820 02 002); Lufthansa, Nygt. 3 (☎23 35 51 00); SAS, at the airport and at the airport train terminal at Oslo S (☎815 20 400); Widerøe's (☎810 01 200).

American Express Travel Service Offices at Fridtjof Nansens plass 6 (☎22 98 37 35; Mon–Fri 9am–4.30pm, Sat 10am–3pm).

Banks and exchange Among many, Den Norske Bank has downtown branches at Stranden 1, Aker Brygge, and Karl Johans gate 2; Sparebanken is at Oslo S, Storgata 1 and Kirkegata 18. Normal banking hours are mid-May to mid-Sept Mon–Fri 8.15am–3pm, Thurs till 5pm; mid-Sept to mid-May Mon–Fri 8.15am–3.30pm, Thurs till 5pm. ATMs are liberally distributed across the city centre and at Gardermoen airport. There are also late-opening bureaux de change at the airport in Arrivals (Mon–Fri 8am–10.30pm, Sat 8.30am–7pm & Sun 10am–10.30pm) and Departures (Mon–Fri 5.30am–8pm, Sat 5.30am–6pm & Sun 6.30am–8pm), plus another at the airport train terminal at Oslo S. (Mon–Fri 7am–7pm, Sat & Sun 8am–5pm). You can also change money and travellers' cheques at larger post offices, where the rates are especially competitive.

Bookshops Tanum, Karl Johans gate 37, has the city's widest selection of English fiction, while Nomaden, Uranienborgveien 4, just behind the Slottsparken, is Oslo's best shop for travel guides and maps. Tronsmo, Kristian Augusts gate 19, has long been the city's best-stocked leftist bookshop with many of its titles in English. Norlis Antikvariat, opposite the National Gallery at Universitetsgata 18, sells second-hand and some new English-language books, as does JW Cappelens Antikvariat, Universitetsgata 20, which is particularly good on Arctic explorers and their tales of derring-do. The shop of the Norwegian hiking organization, Den Norske Turistforening (DNT), Storgata 3, has a comprehensive collection of Norwegian hiking maps.

Buses For information on all long-distance domestic and most international bus services, contact Nor-Way Bussekspress, at the Bussterminalen information desk (Mon–Fri 7am–10pm, Sat 8am–5.30pm, Sun 8am–10pm; ☎23 00 24 00 for services to and from Oslo; ☎820 21 300 for all other services; ⊛www.nor-way.no). The information desk also has information on Säfflebussen (☎22 19 49 00, ⊛www.safflebussen.se) international bus services to Copenhagen and Stockholm. For city buses, see p.73.

Car breakdown There are three big, national breakdown companies and each has a 24hr help line. They are NAF Alarm (☎810 00 505); Falken Redningskorps (☎02 222); and Viking Redningstjeneste (☎800 32 900).

Car rental Avis, Munkedamsveien 27 (☎23 23 92 00), and at the airport (☎64 81 06 60); Bislet Bilutleie, Pilestredet 70 (☎22 60 00 00); Budget,

113

Biskop Gunerius gate 3, at *Royal Christiania Hotel* (☎23 16 32 40), and at the airport (☎800 30 210); Europcar, at the airport (☎22 60 70 22); see also under *Bilutleie* in the Yellow Pages.

Crafts For traditional and authentic Norwegian handicrafts, the best bet is Husfliden, Møllergata 4 (Mon–Fri 10am–5pm, Thurs 10am–6pm, Sat 9am–3pm, ☎24 14 12 80, ⓦ www.husfliden.no). For more modern, pan-Scandinavian gear, try Norway Designs, Stortingsgata 28 (Mon–Fri 9am–5pm, Thurs 9am–7pm, Sat 10am–3pm; ☎23 11 45 10), which features an amazing glass castle every Christmas.

Cycling The Syklistenes Landsforening, Storgata 23c (Norwegian Cyclist Association; ☎22 47 30 30, ⓦ www.slf.no), gives advice and information on route planning and sells cycling maps. For bike hire in Oslo, see p.74.

Dentist Municipal dental information on ☎22 67 30 00. Otherwise, see under *Tannleger* in the Yellow Pages.

Email and internet Internet access is available free at the main city library, Henrik Ibsen gate 1 (Mon–Fri 10am–8pm, Sat 9am–3pm), while many of the better hotels also provide facilities for guests. In addition, there are a number of internet cafés, including Networld, in the Galleriet shopping mall, above the main bus station (Mon–Fri 9am–11pm, Sat & Sun 10am–10pm; ☎22 17 19 00; ⓦ www.networld.no; 20kr for first 15min, 10kr for 15min thereafter), and the Studenten bar, Karl Johans gate 45 at Universitetsgata (daily noon–8pm; ☎22 42 56 80; ⓦ www.studenten-café.no; 40kr per hour).

Embassies and consulates Australia, Jernbanetorget 2 (☎22 47 91 70); Canada, Wergelandveien 7 (☎22 99 53 00); Germany, Oscars gate 45 (☎23 27 54 00); Ireland, c/o *Radisson SAS Scandinavia Hotel*, Holbergs gate 30 (☎22 20 43 70); Netherlands, Oscars gate 29 (☎23 33 36 00); Poland, Olav Kyrres plass 1 (☎22 55 55 36); UK, Thomas Heftyes gate 8 (☎23 13 27 00); USA, Drammensveien 18 (☎22 44 85 50). For others, look under *Ambassadeur og Legasjoner* in the Yellow Pages.

Emergencies Ambulance & medical assistance ☎113; Police ☎112; Fire brigade ☎110.

Ferries DFDS Seaways (to Helsingborg & Copenhagen), Vippetangen Utstikker (pier) #2, beside Akershusstranda (☎22 41 90 90, ⓦ www.dfds.no); Stena Line (to Frederikshavn in Denmark), Jernbanetorget 2 (☎02 010, ⓦ www.stenaline.no); and Color Line (to Kiel and Hirtshals, Denmark), Hjortneskaia (☎22 94 44 00, ⓦ www.dfds.no). Tickets from the companies direct or travel agents.

Gay Oslo There's not much of a scene as such, primarily because Oslo's gays and lesbians are mostly content to share pubs and clubs with heteros. However, the most popular lesbian club-cum-disco is *Potpurriet*, Øvre Vollgate 13 (☎22 41 14 40), where things warm up at about 11pm, while gay men congregate at the *London Pub*, CJ Hambros plass 5 (☎22 70 87 00), with a pub/bar on one floor and a disco downstairs. The main gay event is the *Skeive Dager* (Queer Days; ⓦ www.skeivedager.no) festival usually held over ten days in late June with parties, parades, political meetings, a film festival and incorporating Gay Pride. Gay activities and events in Oslo are organized by LLH (Landsforeningen for lesbisk og homofil frigjøring), 3rd Floor, Nordahl Brunsgate 22 (☎22 11 05 09, ⓦ www.llh.oslo.no), who can also provide advice.

Hiking Den Norske Turistforening (DNT), Storgata 3 (Mon–Fri 10am–4pm, Thurs 10am–6pm, Sat 10am–2pm; ☎22 82 28 00, ⓦ www.turistforeningen.no/codeland/), sells hiking maps and gives general advice and information on route planning – a useful first port-of-call before a walking trip in Norway. Join here to use its nationwide network of unstaffed mountain huts, and get substantial discounts on its staffed mountain huts; the subscription fee of 400kr gives a year's membership.

Jewellery Juhl's Silver Gallery, Roald Amundsens gate 6 (☎22 42 77 99, ⓦ www.juhls.no), is the Oslo outlet for the jewellers and silversmiths of national repute, who established its first workshop in remote Kautokeino (see p.332) forty years ago. Many of the designs are Sami-inspired.

Laundry Majorstua Myntvaskeri, Vibes gate 15 (Mon–Fri 8am–8pm, Sat 8am–5pm); Mr Clean, Parkveien 6, entrance on Welhavens gate (daily 7am–11pm); A-vask Selvbetjening, Thorvald Meyers gate 18, Grünerløkka (daily 10am–8pm).

Left luggage Coin-operated lockers (24hr) and luggage office at Oslo S.

Lost property (*hittegods*) Trams, buses and T-bane ☎22 08 53 61; NSB railways ☎23 15 00 00; police ☎22 66 98 65.

Markets and supermarkets Oslo's principal open-air market is on Youngstorget (Mon–Sat 7am–2pm), a brief stroll north of the Domkirke along Torggata. There's everything here from second-hand clothes to fresh fruit and veg. More central are the fresh produce stalls in the Basarhallene, beside Karl Johans gate. Supermarkets are thick on the ground in the suburbs, but rarer in the city centre. The biggest name is Rimi, which has a downtown outlet at Akersgata 45, near the corner with Grensen (Mon–Sat 8am–8pm, Sun 9am–5pm).

Newspapers Many English and American newspapers and magazines are available in downtown Oslo's Narvesen kiosks. There's an especially wide selection at the newsagents in Oslo S train station.

Pharmacy There is a 24hr pharmacy near Oslo S –Jernbanetorgets Apotek, Jernbanetorget 4b (☏22 41 24 82). Elsewhere, all city pharmacies display a rota of late-opening duty pharmacies.

Police In an emergency, ring ☏112.

Post offices The main post office, with poste restante, is at Dronningens gate 15 and Prinsens gate (Mon–Fri 8am–6pm, Sat 10am–3pm). There are lots of other post offices dotted around Oslo and usual opening hours are Mon–Fri 8am–5pm, Sat 9am–1pm. Downtown locations include Karl Johans gate 22, opposite the Parliament building; Universitetsgata 2; and inside Oslo S. All post offices exchange currency and cash travellers' cheques at very reasonable rates.

Taxis There are taxi ranks dotted all over the city centre. You can also telephone Oslo Taxi on ☏02 323 or Taxi 2 on ☏02 202.

Trains Enquiries and bookings on ☏815 00 888, ⓦwww.nsb.no.

Travel agents For discounted flights, train and bus tickets, try either Euro Terra Nova, Dronningens gate 26 (☏22 94 13 50); or KILROY travels, Nedre Slotts gate 23 (☏23 10 23 00). STA at Karl Johans gate 8 (☏815 59 905) is good for student deals, while Tourbroker Reisebyrå, Drammensveien 4 (☏22 83 27 15), specializes in Eurolines bus tickets. For the full list of Oslo travel agents, see under *Reisebyråer* in the Yellow Pages.

Vinmonopolet There are lots of branches of this state-run liquor and wine store in Oslo, including one at Møllergata 10 (Mon–Wed 10am–5pm, Thurs & Fri 10am–6pm, Sat 9am–3pm).

Women's movement The campaigning Norsk Kvinnesaksforening, Majorstuveien 39 (☏22 60 42 27, ⓦwww.kvinnesaksforening.no) can put you in touch with women's groups in Oslo and the rest of Norway; as well as providing information on events and activities.

Youth Hostel Association Norske Vandrerhjem has its main office in the centre of town, near Oslo S at Torggata 1 (☏23 13 93 00, ⓦwww. vandrerhjem.no). It issues a free and detailed booklet on all the country's hostels; its website carries the same information, too.

Youth information Oslo's youth information shop, UngInfo, Møllergata 3 (☏22 41 51 32, ⓦwww.unginfo.oslo.no), operates an advisory service on everything from sexual health to careers. It's also a good place to find out about live music and events. Open Mon–Fri 11am–5pm.

Around Oslo: the Oslofjord

Around 100km from top to bottom, the narrow straits and podgy basins of the **Oslofjord** link the capital with the open sea. This waterway has long been Norway's busiest, an islet-studded channel whose sheltered waters were once crowded with steamers shuttling passengers along the Norwegian coast. The young Roald Dahl, who spent his summer holidays here from 1920 to 1932, loved the area. In his autobiographical *Boy* he wrote: "Unless you have sailed down the Oslofjord… on a tranquil summer's day, you cannot imagine the sensation of absolute peace and beauty that surrounds you." Even now, though industry has blighted the shoreline and cars have replaced the steamers, the Oslofjord makes for delightful sailing, and on a summer's day you can spy dozens of tiny craft scuttling round its nooks and crannies. The **ferry** ride from Oslo to **Drøbak**, a pretty village on the fjord's east shore, does provide a pleasant introduction, though it's not quite the same as having your own boat.

Both sides of the fjord are dotted with humdrum industrial towns, and frankly there's not much to tempt you out of Oslo if your time is limited – especially as several of the major city sights are half-day or day excursions in themselves. But if you have more time, there are several places on the train and bus routes out of the city that do warrant a stop. The pick of the crop is **Fredrikstad**, down the fjord's eastern side on the train route to Sweden. The

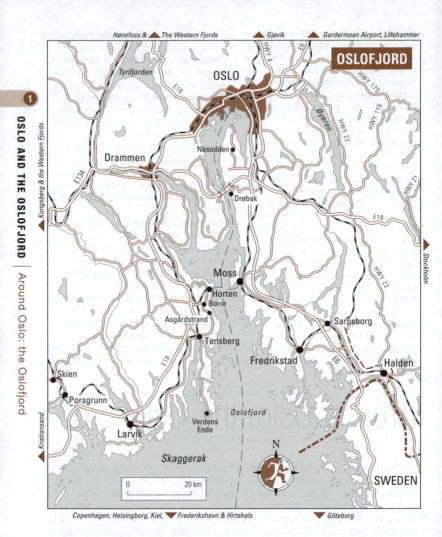

OSLOFJORD

Tyrifjorden

OSLO

HWY 4

E6

HWY 170

HWY 115

Øveren

Drammen

E16

Nesodden

HWY 22

E134

Drøbak

E18

HWY 22

◄ Kongsberg & the Western Fjords

Stockholm ►

Moss

Horten
Borre

Asgårdstrand

Sarpsborg

Tønsberg

E18

Fredrikstad

E6

Halden

Skien

Porsgrunn

Oslofjord

Verdens
Ende

Larvik

◄ Kristiansand

Skaggerak

N

0   20 km

SWEDEN

old part of the town consists of a riverside fortress whose gridiron streets and earthen bastions, dating from the late sixteenth century, have survived in remarkably good condition. The fortress was built to defend the country from the Swedes, as was the imposing hilltop stronghold that rears up above **Halden**, an otherwise innocuous town further southeast, hard by the Swedish border. Highlight of the fjord's western shore is the cluster of Viking burial mounds at **Borre**, just outside the ferry port of **Horten**, while the breezy town of **Tønsberg** gives easy access to the shredded archipelago that pokes a rural finger out into the Skagerrak.

   Motorways leave Oslo to strip along both sides of the Oslofjord – the E6 in the east, the E18 to the west – and there's a regular **train** service from Oslo S serving both sides too. On the east side, the train stops at Fredrikstad and Halden, but not Drøbak, which is best reached from Oslo by ferry. On the western side, trains run to Drammen and Tønsberg, but not Horten. To cross the Oslofjord, you can either use the 7km-long tunnel which runs west from Drøbak, or catch the **car ferry** (every 30min; 30min) between Horten and **Moss**, about 60km south of Oslo.

The east shore: Drøbak, Fredrikstad and Halden

The first place of any real interest on the Oslofjord's eastern shore is **DRØBAK**, a tiny port that slopes along the shoreline about 40km from the capital. It's at its prettiest round the old harbour, where a cluster of white clapboard houses covers the headland and straggles up towards a handsome timber church dating from the early eighteenth century.

Drøbak witnessed one of the few Norwegian successes during the German invasion of 1940, when the cruiser *Blucher* was sunk by artillery as it steamed towards Oslo. The gunners had no way of realizing just how important this was – the delay to the German flotilla gave the Norwegian king, Haakon VII, just enough time to escape the capital and avoid capture. The village's only other claim to fame comes from its specialist Christmas shop, the *Julehuset* (Mon–Fri 10am–5pm, Sat 10am–3pm & Sun noon–4pm, longer hours before Christmas), whose popularity is such that many Scandinavian children believe that Father Christmas really lives here. As for **cafés**, *Det Gamle Bakeri* (daily 11am–11pm) serves tasty snacks and light meals in an attractive wooden building with an open log fire, while the *Skipperstuen*, in the wooden house on the knoll next to the harbour (daily 11am–11pm), does excellent sandwiches.

The best way to get to Drøbak from Oslo is by **boat**, an enjoyable trip. From mid-May to early September, M/S Prinsessen (☎23 11 52 20; ⓦwww.nbds.no) departs Oslo's Aker Brygge pier for Drøbak five times weekly, clipping out across the islet-studded fjord and stopping off at a couple of small islands on the way. The journey takes about an hour and costs 60kr each way. The boat's timetable makes it possible to complete the return trip on the same day – though this isn't crucial as there's also a fast and frequent bus service between Drøbak and Oslo (#541 hourly to Jernbanetorget and several other downtown bus stops).

Fredrikstad

It's an hour-long, 90-kilometre train journey south from Oslo to **FREDRIK-STAD**, named after the Danish king Frederick II, who had the original fortified town built here at the mouth of the river Glomma in 1567. Norway was ruled by Danish kings from 1387 to 1814 and, with rare exceptions, the country's interests were systematically neglected in favour of Copenhagen. A major consequence was Norway's involvement in the bitter rivalry between the Swedish and Danish monarchies, which prompted a seemingly endless and particularly pointless sequence of wars lasting from the early sixteenth century until 1720. The eastern approaches to Oslo (then Christiania), along the Oslofjord, were especially vulnerable to attack from Sweden, and the area was ravaged by raiding parties on many occasions. Indeed, Frederick II's fortress only lasted three years before it was burnt to the ground, though it didn't take long for a replacement to be constructed – and for the whole process to be repeated again. Finally, in the middle of the seventeenth century, Fredrikstad's

fortifications were considerably strengthened. The central gridiron of cobbled streets was encircled on three sides by zigzag bastions which allowed the defenders to fire across and into any attacking force. In turn, these bastions were protected by a moat, concentric earthen banks, and outlying redoubts. Armed with 130 cannon, Fredrikstad was, by 1685, the strongest fortress in all of Norway – and it has remained in military use to this day, which partly accounts for its excellent state of preservation. The fort was also unaffected by the development of modern Fredrikstad, which grew up as a result of the timber industry: the new town was built on the west bank of the Glomma while the old fort – now known as the **Gamlebyen** (Old Town) – was on the east.

The town

From Fredrikstad's adjoining **train** and **bus** stations, located in the new part of town, it's a couple of minutes' walk to the river – head straight down Jernbanegata and take the first left along Ferjestedsveien. From the jetty, the **ferry** (Mon–Fri 5.30am–11pm, Sat 7am–11pm, Sun 9.30am–11pm; 5min; 8kr) shuttles over to the gated back wall of the Gamlebyen. Inside, the pastel-painted timber and stone houses of the old town, just three blocks deep and six blocks wide, make for a delightful stroll, especially as surprisingly few tourists venture this way except at the height of the season. Indeed, on a drizzly day the streets echo only to the sound of your own footsteps plus the occasional army boot hitting the cobbles as the garrison goes about its duties. A **museum** (mid-June to Aug Mon–Sat 11am–5pm, Sun noon–5pm; 30kr), housed in the Gamle Slaveri, where prisoners once did hard labour, dutifully outlines the history of the Old Town and displays a model of the fortress in its prime. Elsewhere, the main square holds an unfortunate statue of Frederick II, who appears to have a serious problem with his pantaloons, but it's the general appearance of the place that appeals rather than any specific sight.

Make sure also that you take in the most impressive of the town's outlying defences, the **Kongsten Fort**, about ten minutes' walk from the main fortress: go straight ahead from the main gate, take the first right along Heibergsgate and it's clearly visible on the left. Here, thick stone and earthen walls are moulded round a rocky knoll which offers wide views over the surrounding countryside – an agreeably quiet vantage point from where you can take in the lie of the land.

Back on the western side of the Glomma, a short walk along Ferjestedsveien, away from the river brings you to a small park and the adjacent **Domkirke** (late June to mid-Aug Tues–Sat noon–3pm), a brown, brick building with stained glass by Emanuel Vigeland (see p.96). Beyond the church is the centre of modern Fredrikstad, an uninteresting place on a bend in the river.

Practicalities

Although it's preferable to visit Fredrikstad as a day trip, there are a handful of **hotels**, of which the best is probably the *Victoria*, Turngaten 3 (☎69 31 11 65, ⓕ69 31 87 55; ⓦwww.victoria-fredrikstad.com; ❻, s/r ❹), a comfortable, newly refurbished establishment in an Art Nouveau building overlooking the park next to the Domkirke. Alternatively, the bargain basement *Fredrikstad Motel & Camping*, Torsnesveien 16 (☎69 32 05 32, ⓕ69 32 36 66; ❷), is located about 300m straight ahead outside the main gate of the Old Town; it provides tent space as well as inexpensive rooms. As for **food**, the Gamlebyen is dotted with cafés and patisseries, and is also home to the town's best restaurant, *Balaklava Gjestgiveri*, at Færgeportgata 78 (☎69 32 30 40), with an outdoor terrace and specializing in seafood.

Halden

Just 2km from the Swedish border and 35km from Fredrikstad, the workaday wood-processing town of **HALDEN** is bisected by the River Tista and hemmed in by steep forested hills, the closest of which is crowned by the commanding **Fredriksten Festning** (fortress). Work began on the stronghold in 1661 at the instigation of Frederick III, during a lull in the fighting between Sweden and Denmark. The stakes were high: the Swedes were determined to annihilate the Dano-Norwegian monarchy and had only just failed in their attempt to capture Oslo and Copenhagen. Consequently, Frederick was keen to build a fortress of immense strength to secure his northerly possessions. He called in Dutch engineers to design it and, after a decade, the result was a labyrinthine citadel whose thick perimeter walls, heavily protected gates, bastions and outlying forts were brilliantly designed to suit the contours of the two steep, parallel ridges on which they were built. The proof of the pudding was in the eating. The Swedes besieged Fredriksten on several occasions, but without success, though the town itself suffered badly. In 1716, the Norwegians razed it to the ground, a scorched earth policy that later prompted some nationalistic poppycock from the writer Bjørnstjerne Bjørnson: "We chose to burn our nation, ere we let it fall."

The town

Halden **train station** abuts the south bank of the Tista, while the **bus station** is a couple of minutes' walk away to the south on Tollbugata. The **fortress** (mid-May to Aug daily 10am–5pm & Sept Sun noon–3pm; 40kr) is on this side of the river too, its forested slopes climbed by several steep footpaths, the most enjoyable of which begins on **Peder Colbjørnsens gate** and leads up to the main gatehouse. Allow at least an hour for a thorough exploration of the fort, whose ingenuity and impregnability are its salient features. Although most of the buildings are labelled, only a handful are open to the public, most notably the **Historiske Samlinger** (History Museum) in the old prison in the eastern curtain wall. There are also hour-long guided tours (late June to mid-Aug 3 daily; 45kr), but you shouldn't require any help to absorb the obvious and powerful atmosphere. On the far side of the fortress, where the terrain is nowhere near as steep, you'll find a monument to the Swedish king Karl XII, who was killed by a bullet in the temple as he besieged the fort in 1718. An inveterate warmonger, Karl had exhausted the loyalty of his troops, and whether the bullet came from the fortress or one of his own men has been a matter of considerable Scandinavian speculation.

Practicalities

Despite its fortress, Halden is too routine a place to spend the night, but if you're marooned there's a reasonable range of accommodation. The **tourist office**, just to the south of the bus station at Langbrygga 3 (late-Aug to mid-June Mon–Fri 9am–3.30pm, late June to mid-Aug Mon–Fri 9am–4.30pm; ☏69 19 09 80, ⓦwww.haldentourist.no), has a full list, but the pick of the **hotels** is the *Park Hotel*, Marcus Thranes gate 30 (☏69 21 15 00, ⓕ69 21 15 01, ⓦwww.park-hotel.no; ❺, s/r ❹), a neat, trim, modern place on the northwest edge of the town centre. Alternatively, Halden has a plain and frugal 35-bed HI **hostel** (late June to early Aug; ☏69 21 66 00, ⓔhalden.hostel @vandrerhjem.no; dorm beds 100kr, doubles ❶), sited in a chalet-like school building on Flintveien, in the suburb of Gimle, 3km north of the train station and readily reached by several local buses.

The west shore: Drammen, Horten and Tønsberg

West of the city centre, Oslo's rangy suburbs curve round the final basin of the Oslofjord before bubbling up over the hills almost as far as **DRAMMEN**, a substantial industrial settlement some forty kilometres southwest of the capital. Built on an arm of the Oslofjord and astride the fast-flowing River Drammenselva, the town handles most of the vehicles imported into Norway. This is hardly a reason to visit, however, and nor do the modern office blocks and stuffy late nineteenth-century buildings of its centre conjure up much interest. From here, there's a choice of routes, with the E134 wriggling west through Kongsberg (see p.176) and on to the western fjords (see p.204), while the E18 presses on south down the Oslofjord. The latter road bypasses **HORTEN**, a small port and naval base from where a car ferry shuttles across the Oslofjord to Moss (every 30min; 30min). Appropriately enough, Horten is home to one of the region's better seafaring museums, the **Marinemuseet**, in part of the naval complex, a short drive to the north of the town centre on Karljohansvern (May–Sept daily noon–4pm, Oct–April Sun noon–4pm; free). The museum bounces smartly through the history of the Norwegian navy with the assistance of scale models and a hotchpotch of maritime artefacts – ships' bells, figureheads and suchlike.

Borre's Viking burial mounds and the Midgard Historical Centre

Heading south from Horten on Highway 19, it's about 4km along the fjord to **BORRE**, a scattered hamlet that boasts the largest collection of extant **Viking burial mounds** in all of Scandinavia. There are seven large and twenty-one small mounds in total, with the best preserved being clustered together in the woods by the water's edge – follow the "*Borrehaugene*" sign. These grassy bumps date from the seventh to the tenth century, when Borre was a royal burial ground and one of the wealthiest districts in southern Norway. The mounds are quite interesting and well worth a wander, but the setting is even better – in springtime wild flowers carpet the woods and the sea gently laps the shoreline, making this a perfect spot for a picnic. The area has been designated a national park, and the neighbouring **Midgard Historisk Senter** (Historical Centre; mid-April to mid-Sept Tues–Sun 11am–6pm; mid-Sept to mid-April Tues–Sun noon–5pm; 40kr; Ⓦwww.midgardsenteret.org), in a brand new, low-slung building by the village church, gives the historical lowdown. In a series of well-presented displays, the centre explores Borre's Viking history covering aspects such as Norse Religion and Mythology and Everyday Life in the Viking Era.

From Borre, it's just 17km south on Highway 19 to Tønsberg. On the way, you can detour east along Highway 311 to the seaside village of **ÅSGÅRDSTRAND**, where Munch's old summer home and studio have survived as a particularly dull attraction: the two timber buildings overlooking the fjord hold just a few Munch prints and bits and bobs of period furniture.

Tønsberg and around

The last town of any size on the Oslofjord's western shore, **TØNSBERG**, some 100km from Oslo, was allegedly founded by Harald Hårfagre in the ninth century, and rose to prominence in the Middle Ages as a major ecclesiastical and trading centre. The sheltered sound made a safe harbour – the plain was ideal for settlement, and once built, the town's palace and fortress assured it the patronage of successive monarchs. All of which sounds exciting, and you might expect Tønsberg to be one of the country's more important historical attractions. Sadly though, precious little survives from the town's medieval heyday, the best of a decidedly poor hand being the renovated, nineteenth-century warehouses of the **Tønsberg Brygge**, a pedestrianized area whose narrow lanes, dotted with bars and restaurants, hug the waterfront in the centre of town.

As for the castle, the **Slottsfjellet**, only the foundations have survived, fragmentary ruins perched on a wooded hill immediately to the north of the centre, though it takes little imagination to appreciate the castle's strategic and defensive position. The Swedes burned it down in 1503 and the place was never rebuilt – today's watchtower, the inelegant **Slottsfjelltårnet** (mid-May to late June Mon–Fri 10am–3pm, Sat & Sun noon–5pm; late June to mid-Aug daily 11am–6pm; late Aug to mid-Sept Sat & Sun noon–5pm; late Sept Sun noon–3pm; 10kr), was plonked on top in the nineteenth century.

Its medieval importance aside, Tønsberg was known for whaling, an industry common to the whole coast, and the **Vestfold Fylkesmuseum** (Vestfold County Museum; mid-May to mid-Sept Mon–Sat 10am–5pm, Sun noon–5pm; 30kr), on Farmannsveien, on the east side of the Slottsfjellet, has a rather sad array of whale skeletons on show. Rather more cheery are the displays devoted to the town's history and the evolution of Vestfold shipping, while outside, on the hillside, the grazing livestock is actually part of the "Farming" section.

Practicalities

From Tønsberg **train station**, it's a five- to ten-minute walk south to the main square, Torvet. From here, it's just a couple of hundred metres along Rådhusgaten to the waterfront Tønsberg Brygge, where you'll find the **tourist office** (late June & Aug Mon–Sat 8.30am–6.30pm; July daily 10am–8pm; Sept to mid-June Mon–Fri 8.30am–3.30pm; ☎33 35 02 00; ⓦwww.visittonsberg .com). Tønsberg has several central **hotels**, including the waterfront *Rica Klubben*, Nedre Lang gate 49 (☎33 35 97 00, ⓕ33 35 97 97, ⓦwww.rica.no ❺, s/r ❸), something of a brick-and-concrete monstrosity, but with comfortable rooms and fine views over the harbour. For frugal but well-kept rooms and a first-rate Norwegian breakfast, the HI **hostel**, Dronning Blancasgate 22 (☎33 31 21 75, ⓔtonsberg.hostel@vandrerhjem.no; dorm beds 170kr), is on a side street beneath (and to the east of) the Slottsfjellet: turn right out of the train station and follow the signs for the five-minute walk. The nearest **campsite**, *Furustrand Camping* (☎33 32 44 03, ⓕ33 32 74 03), overlooks the Oslofjord 5.5km east of town and has cabins. For **food**, there are several cafébars and restaurants in the Tønsberg Brygge: try the popular, harbourside *Esmeralda*, for its tasty seafood, or the nearby *Brygga Restaurant*, with its pleasant outside terrace.

Around Tønsberg

The low-lying islands and skerries that nudge out into the Skagerrak to the south of Tønsberg are a popular holiday destination. By and large, people come here for the peace and quiet, with a bit of fishing and swimming thrown in, and the whole coast is dotted with summer homes. To the outsider, this is not especially stimulating, but there is one wonderfully scenic spot, **Verdens Ende** – "World's End" – about thirty minutes' drive from Tønsberg, right at the southernmost tip of the southernmost island, Tjöme. In this blustery spot, rickety fishing jetties straggle across a cove whose blue-black waters are surrounded by bare, sea-smoothened rocks and islets. It would be nice to think a wandering Viking gave the place its name, but in fact this was a romantic gesture by visiting Victorians. To wet your whistle, pop along to the seashore restaurant.

Verdens Ende apart, the most enjoyable way to see the archipelago is by **boat**, and the Tønsberg tourist office has information about archipelago cruises. These include the *D/S Kysten I*, a 1909 tramp steamer that chugs round these waters in July (1 daily; 3hr 30min; 120kr; ☎33 31 25 89), departing from Honnørbryggen, the jetty just to the north of the tourist office.

Travel details

Trains

Oslo to: Bergen (3–4 daily; 6hr 30min); Dombås (4–5 daily; 4hr); Drammen (4–5 daily; 40min); Fredrikstad (hourly; 1hr); Geilo (3–4 daily; 3hr 20min); Halden (hourly; 1hr 45min); Hamar (7 daily; 1hr 30min); Hjerkinn (4–5 daily; 4hr 30min); Kongsberg (3–5 daily; 1hr 10min); Kristiansand (3–5 daily; 4hr 40min); Lillehammer (7 daily; 2hr); Myrdal (4–5 daily; 4hr 30min); Otta (4–5 daily; 3hr 30min); Røros (2–3 daily; 5hr); Stavanger (3–5 daily; 7hr 30min); Trondheim (4–5 daily; 6hr

50min); Tønsberg (2–7 daily; 1hr 40min); Voss
(3–4 daily; 5hr 20min); Åndalsnes (2–3 daily; 5hr
30min).

Buses

Oslo to: Alta via Sweden (3 weekly; 27hr; reserva-
tions obligatory); Arendal (1 daily; 4hr 15min);
Balestrand (3 daily; 8hr 15min); Bergen (1 daily;
11hr 40min); Drøbak (hourly; 40min); Mundal,
Fjaerland (3 daily; 7hr 50min); Grimstad (1 daily;
4hr 40min); Hamar (1 daily; 2hr); Hammerfest via
Sweden (3 weekly; 30hr; reservations obligatory);
Haugesund (1 daily; 10hr); Kongsberg (1 daily;
2hr); Kristiansand (1 daily; 5hr 40min);
Lillehammer (1 daily; 3hr); Lillesand (1 daily; 5hr);
Odda (1 daily; 8hr); Otta (2 daily; 5hr); Sogndal (3
daily; 7hr); Stavanger (1 daily; 10hr); Stryn (1 daily;
8hr); Voss (1 daily; 10hr 30min).

Ferries

Horten to: Moss (every 30min; 30min).
Oslo to: Bygdøynes (daily every 40min; 15min);
Drobak (mid-May to early Sept five weekly; 1hr);
Dronningen (daily every 40min; 10min); Hovedøya
(mid-March to Sept 9–12 daily; Oct to mid-March
3 daily; 10min); Langøyene (June–Aug hourly;
30min).

Domestic flights

Oslo to: Bergen (hourly; 1 hr); Bodø (6 daily; 1 hr);
Harstad/Narvik (5 daily; 1hr 40min); Tromsø (8
daily; 2 hr); Trondheim (10 daily; 1 hr).

International ferries

Oslo to: Copenhagen (1 daily; 16hr); Frederikshavn
(1–2 daily; 8hr 30min); Hirtshals (5 weekly to 1
daily; 8hr); Kiel (1 daily; 19hr).

The South

CHAPTER 2   # Highlights

* **The Clarion Hotel Tyholmen** Occupying a grand wooden building, Arendal's luxurious hotel is one of the finest places to stay on the south coast. **See p.131**

* **M/S Øya** Take a delightful three-hour cruise along the coast between Lillesand and Kristiansand on this pint-sized ferry boat. **See p.133**

* **Mandal** The prettiest resort on the south coast, with the country's finest sandy beach. **See p.137**

* **Norsk Hermetikkmuséet** Stavanger's Canning Museum displays a fascinating collection of sardine tin labels – commercial art at its best. **See p.143**

* **Preikestolen** A geological oddity near Stavanger, this great hunk of rock offers staggering views down to the Lysefjord on three of its sides. **See p.147**

The South

rcing out into the Skagerrak between the Oslofjord and Stavanger, Norway's **south coast** may have little of the imposing grandeur of other, wilder parts of the country, but its eastern half, in particular, is dotted with islands and undeniably lovely. Backed by forests, fells and lakes, it's this part of the coast that attracts Norwegians in droves, equipped not so much with bucket and spade as with boat and navigational aids – these waters, with their islands, rocky islets and narrow inlets, make for particularly enjoyable **sailing**. Camping on the offshore islands is easy too, with a few restrictions: you can't stay in one spot for more than 48 hours, nor light a fire either on bare rock or among vegetation, and must steer clear of anyone's home. Leaflets detailing further coastal rules and regulations are available at any local tourist office.

If boats and tents aren't your thing, the white-painted clapboard houses of tiny towns like **Lillesand**, **Arendal** and – to a lesser degree – **Grimstad** have an appropriately nautical, almost jaunty air. This portion of the coast is also important for Norway's international trade: it's just a short hop to Denmark from here, and several of the larger towns such as Sandefjord, Larvik and Porsgrunn have escaped their original roles as timber ports to become modern industrial centres in their own right. Most of these manufacturing towns are run-of-the-mill, except for the biggest of them, **Kristiansand**, a lively port and resort with enough sights, restaurants, bars and beaches to while away a night, maybe two. Beyond Kristiansand lies **Mandal**, an especially fetching holiday spot with a great beach, but thereafter the coast becomes harsher and less absorbing, heralding a sparsely inhabited region with precious little to detain you before **Stavanger**, a lively oil town and port within easy striking distance of some fine fjord and mountain scenery.

There are regular **trains** from Oslo to Kristiansand and Stavanger, but the rail line runs inland for most of its journey, only dipping down to the coast at the major resorts, which makes for a disappointing ride, the sea views mostly shielded behind the bony, forested hills. The same applies to the main **road and bus** route – the **E18/E39** – which, though convenient and fast, also sticks stubbornly inland for most of the 320km from Oslo to Kristiansand (E18) and again for the 250km on to Stavanger (E39). Thanks to the E18/E39, all but the tiniest of coastal villages are easy to get to, though exploring the surrounding area can be awkward without your own vehicle. Right along the south coast, **accommodation** of one sort or another is legion, and all the larger towns have at least a couple of hotels, but if you're after a bit of social bounce bear in mind the **season** is short, running from the middle of June to August; outside this period many attractions are closed and local boat trips curtailed.

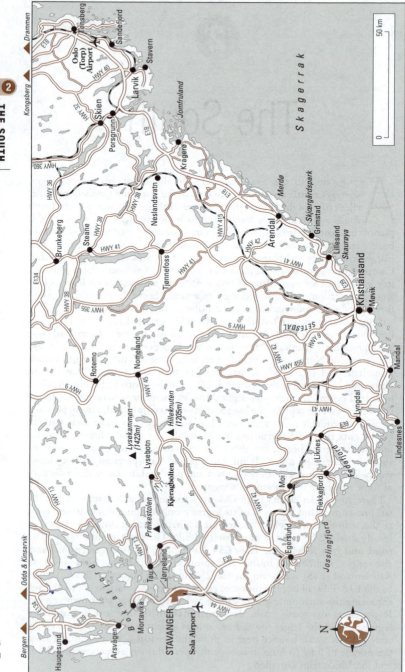

0   50 km

The E18 to Lillesand

The fretted shoreline that stretches the 200km south from Tønsberg (see p.121) to Lillesand is home to a series of small resorts that are particularly popular with weekenders from Oslo. The most interesting is **Grimstad**, with its Ibsen connections; the liveliest is **Arendal;** and the prettiest **Lillesand**. All three have decent places to stay, but only pint-sized **Kragerø** has an HI hostel. Many of the resorts, most notably Lillesand and Arendal, offer **boat trips** out to the myriad islets that dot this coast, for a spot of swimming and beach- (or at least rock-) combing. The islands were once owned by local farmers, but many are now in public ownership, and zealously protected from any development. In addition, most of the resorts offer summertime cruises along the coast, of which the delightful three-hour trip from Lillesand to Kristiansand is the most worthwhile.

Fast and frequent express **buses** scuttle along the **E18** from Sandefjord to Kristiansand, linking the key resorts, though you do have to change for Kragerø. A **train** line runs along the coast too, but it's not a particularly useful service – of the places described here only Arendal has its own train station.

Sandefjord

One hundred and twenty kilometres south of Oslo, the industrial town of **SANDEFJORD** is perhaps best known as the site of **Oslo (Torp) airport** (also known as Sandefjord Airport Torp), 8km north of the town. It has a wide range of domestic flights and a few international ones operated by SAS/Braathens, as well as being the Norwegian gateway for Ryanair services from Stansted, Glasgow and Frankfurt. Express **buses** from the airport (connecting with Ryanair flights) run to downtown Oslo (98kr each way; 2hr); there are also local buses to Sandefjord train station (Mon–Fri hourly; limited service at the weekend; 20min).

Whilst it's not the most obvious tourist destination, Sandefjord itself can be a convenient starting point if you've just arrived at the airport, or from Strømstad in Sweden by ferry (Color Line; ⓦwww.colorline.com), which docks right in the centre of town. Sandefjord is at its prettiest along the waterfront, where a breezy area of parks and gardens culminates in the old municipal baths, a grandiose complex built in 1899 in a Viking-inspired dragon style. The baths closed at the beginning of World War II and now house a civic centre. From the town's **train** and adjacent **bus station**, it's about 800m down Jernbanealleen to the waterfront and the **tourist office** at Thor Dahls gate 5 (ⓣ33 48 60 00; ⓦwww.vestfold.com). Of Sandefjord's several **hotels**, the most agreeable is the *Rica Park Hotel Sandefjord*, by the harbourfront at Strandpromenaden 9 (ⓣ33 44 74 00, ⓕ33 44 75 00, ⓦwww.rica.no; ❼, s/r ❹).

Kragerø

Pressing on down the E18, it's about 10km from Sandefjord to the turning for **Larvik**, where Color Line ferries depart for Frederikshavn in Denmark, and then another 20km to **Porsgrunn**, with a rare view of the sea as you cross the massive bridge spanning the fjord. After another 40km or so, Highway 38 branches off for the 13km jaunt to **KRAGERØ**, whose narrow harbour is protected by a pair of bumpy little islets. One of the busiest resorts on the coast, Kragerø's tiny centre, with its cramped lanes and alleys rising steeply from the harbourfront, makes a good living as a supply depot for the surrounding coves and rocky islets, where the Norwegians have built themselves scores of summer cottages.

Founded as a timber port in the seventeenth century, Kragerø later boomed as a shipbuilding centre, its past importance recalled by the antique gun battery on the harbour islet of **Gunnarsholmen**. To take a closer look at this relic of the Napoleonic Wars, walk across the causeway on the south side of town. The port was also a fashionable watering hole in the late nineteenth and early twentieth century. It was here that Edvard Munch produced some of his jollier paintings and where **Theodor Kittelsen** (1857–1914), a native of Kragerø, spent his summers. A middling painter but superb illustrator, Kittelsen defined the popular appearance of the country's folkloric creatures – from trolls through to sirens – in his illustrations for Asbjørnsen and Moe's *Norwegian Folk Tales*, published in 1883. Kittelsen's family home, the **Kittelsenhuset**, at Theodor Kittelsens vei 5, in the town centre (late June to Aug Mon–Sat 11am–3pm; 20kr), is now a lively little museum celebrating the artist's life and times with a smattering of his paintings and a few family knick-knacks. Kragerø's only other sight of note is its **church**, an imposing brown-brick structure perched on a hill on the north side of the centre.

The most popular excursion from Kragerø is the **ferry to Jomfruland** (mid-Aug to late Sept Mon–Fri 2 daily; 45min; 30kr each way; ℡35 98 58 58; ⓦwww.fjordbat.no), a long and slender island stuck out in the Skagerrak beyond the offshore skerries. Just 10km long and 600m wide, the island is popular for its easy walking trails which network the wooded interior, and its long rocky beaches. The ferry docks at **Tårnbrygga**, halfway along the north shore.

Practicalities

The main Oslo–Kristiansand **bus** stops in Tangen, where a connecting bus makes the twenty-minute journey to Kragerø. The nearest **train station** is at Neslandsvatn, where the *Togbuss* meets the Oslo–Kristiansand train for the forty-five minute journey to Kragerø. In Kragerø itself, the **bus station** is next door to the **tourist office** at the northern tip of the main harbour (mid-June to mid-Aug Mon–Fri 9am–8pm, Sat 9am–6pm & Sun 11am–6pm; mid-Aug to mid-June Mon–Fri 10am–2pm; ℡35 98 23 88).

Most holidaymakers shop and eat in Kragerø but few actually **stay** – if you are tempted, your best options are the modern *Victoria Hotel*, at PA Heuchs gate 31, on the harbourfront (℡35 98 75 25, ℻35 98 29 26; ⓦwww.aco.no; ❺), or the HI **hostel**, the *Kragerø Vandrerhjem*, at Lovisenbergveien 20, 2km out of town along Highway 38 (℡35 98 57 00, ℻35 98 57 01; ⓔkragero.hostel @vandrerhjem.no; dorm beds 220kr, doubles ❷; late June to mid-Aug). The hostel occupies an expansive wooden building beside a pretty bay, rents out rowing boats, and serves tasty if simple evening **meals** and breakfasts; buses travelling in to Kragerø on Highway 38 pass right by the hostel.

Arendal

Sixty-five kilometres beyond the Kragerø turning, small-town **ARENDAL** is one of the most appealing places on the coast. Its sheltered harbour curls right into the centre, which is further crimped by the forested hills pushing in from behind. The town's heyday was in the eighteenth century when its shipyards churned out dozens of the sleek wooden sailing ships that then dominated international trade. There's an attractive reminder of these boom times in the grand **Rådhus**, on Radhusgaten (Mon–Fri 9am–3pm; free), a four-storey, white timber building from 1812 that faces out over what was once the main city dock. The Rådhus was actually built as a private mansion for a wealthy family of merchants – as the formal rooms inside demonstrate – and there are more elegant old merchants' buildings immediately behind in the oldest part of town, known as **Tyholmen**. You can wander these few blocks and then stroll along the boardwalk flanking **Pollen**, the short rectangular inner harbour bordered by pavement cafés. For the architectural low-down on the Tyholmen, sign up for one of the tourist office's **walking tours** round the town (late June to early Aug 3 weekly; 1hr 30min; 50kr). Arendal's only other point of interest is the south coast's largest contemporary arts gallery, **Bomuldsfabriken**, Oddenveien 5 (Tues–Sun noon–4pm; 20kr; Ⓦwww.bomuldsfabriken.com), which hosts some excellent temporary exhibitions. It occupies an old lakeside factory a couple of kilometres north of the town centre and is signposted off Highway 410.

Also available at the tourist office are details of all sorts of **boat trips**, which leave from Pollen. The most enjoyable is to **Merdø** (hourly; 30kr), a low-lying, lightly wooded islet in the Skagerrak. Footpaths network the island, there's a beach, a café and the **Merdøgaard Museum** (late June to mid-Aug daily noon–4pm; 30kr), which occupies an eighteenth-century sea captain's house.

Practicalities

From Arendal **train station**, it's a five- to ten-minute walk west to the main square, Torvet – either through the smoky tunnel or up and over the steep hill along Iuellsklev and then Bendiksklev, the latter being a distinctly healthier route. Torvet is about 150m north of the inner harbour, Pollen. **Buses** stop in the larger square, west of Torvet and across from the huge red-brick church with the copper-green steeple. Arendal **tourist office** is on the east side of Pollen on Langbryggen (mid-June to mid-Aug Mon–Sat 9am–7pm, Sun noon–7pm; mid-Aug to mid-June Mon–Fri 9am–4pm; Ⓣ37 00 55 44; Ⓦwww.arendal.com).

Easily the nicest place **to stay** is the luxurious *Clarion Hotel Tyholmen*, Teaterplassen 2 (Ⓣ37 02 68 00, Ⓕ37 02 68 01; Ⓦwww.tyholmenhotel.no; ❼, s/r ❹), which occupies a handsome wooden building in the style of an old warehouse on the Tyholmen quayside. The more modest *Scandic Hotel Arendal*, Friergangen 1 (Ⓣ37 02 51 60, Ⓕ37 02 67 07; Ⓦwww.scandic-hotels.com; ❻, s/r ❹), is a straightforward modern hotel with well-appointed rooms, just off the west side of Pollen. For **food**, there are a couple of inexpensive cafés on Torvet and a string of more tempting places along and around Pollen, including *Madam Reiersen*, which offers delicious seafood and fresh pasta dishes from its harbourside premises at Nedre Tyholmsvei 3. Later on, the café-bars lining Pollen become lively **drinking** haunts till the early hours, especially on a warm summer's night.

Grimstad

From Arendal, it's a short 20km hop south on the E18 to **GRIMSTAD**, where a brisk huddle of white houses with orange-tiled roofs is stacked up behind the harbour. Nowadays scores of yachts are moored in the harbour, but at the beginning of the nineteenth century the town had no fewer than forty shipyards and carried on a lucrative import-export trade with France. It was not particularly surprising, therefore, that when **Henrik Ibsen** left his home in nearby Skien in 1844, aged sixteen, he should come to Grimstad, where he worked as an apprentice pharmacist for the next six years. The ill-judged financial dealings of Ibsen's father had impoverished the family, and Henrik's already jaundiced view of Norway's provincial bourgeoisie was confirmed here in the port, whose worthies Ibsen mocked in poems like *Resignation*, and *The Corpse's Ball*. It was here too that Ibsen picked up first-hand news of the Paris

Revolution of 1848, an event that radicalized him and inspired his paean to the insurrectionists of Budapest, *To Hungary*, written in 1849. Nonetheless, Ibsen's stay on the south coast is more usually recalled as providing the setting for some of his better-known plays (see box opposite), particularly *Pillars of Society*. The pint-sized pharmacy where Ibsen lived and worked is now home to the **Ibsenhuset og Grimstad bymuseum** (Ibsen House and Grimstad Town Museum; Jan–May & Aug–Dec Mon–Fri 10am–3pm; June–July Mon–Sat 11am–5pm & Sun 1–5pm; 40kr), just up from the harbour in the centre of town on Henrik Ibsens gate. With its creaking wooden floors and narrow-beamed ceilings, the building has maintained its nineteenth-century appearance and houses a selection of Ibsen memorabilia – look out for the glass case displaying the playwright's hat, coat, umbrella and boots as worn on his daily stroll down to Oslo's *Grand Hotel*. Also here, courtesy of Ibsen's son, is the dining-room furniture from his apartment in Oslo (see p.82).

From the museum, it's a couple of minutes' walk south to the pedestrianized part of Storgata, once the town's main street. Signposted off it as you near the harbourfront is the **Reimanngården**, an uninspiring collection of four replica eighteenth-century buildings, one of which is a reconstruction of another pharmacy where Ibsen worked – the original building was demolished in the 1950s – and now home to the town's art society. In the opposite direction from the Ibsen house, it's a short, steep hike north up to **Grimstad Kirke**, a large late nineteenth-century wooden church plonked on a hill above the harbour. Inside, many of the original fittings have survived, including some heavy-duty wrought-iron lamps and candelabras, and there's a tapestry of the Resurrection by the font.

Practicalities

With regular services from Oslo, Arendal and Kristiansand, Grimstad **bus station** is at the south end of the harbour, a couple of hundred metres along from the **tourist office** (Jan–May & Aug–Dec Mon–Fri 8.30am–4pm; June & July Mon–Fri 9am-6pm & Sat-Sun 10am–4pm; ☎37 04 40 41; ⓦwww.grimstad.net). Here, you can pick up all the usual information as well as detailed maps of the islands that dot the seaward approaches to Grimstad harbour. Many of the islands are protected within the **Skjærgårdspark**, and have public access moorings, as well as picnic and bathing facilities: the tourist office can also advise on local **boat hire** companies. In addition, there are a handful of **boat cruises** to choose from, though these don't stop at any of the islands: the most popular is a two-hour coastal cruise on the M/S Bibben (July Sun–Fri 1 daily; 150kr; ☎37 04 31 85).

Grimstad has an attractive and central **hotel**, the *Grimstad Hotell*, Kirkegaten 3 (☎37 25 25 25, ⓕ37 25 25 35; ⓦwww.grimstadhotell.no; ❻), in an old and cleverly converted clapboard complex amongst the narrow lanes near the Ibsen house; the hotel has the best **restaurant** in town, too. Wine buffs can check out the locally made fruit wines – Fuhr Rhubarb and Fuhr Vermouth are the two to try.

Lillesand

Bright, cheerful **LILLESAND**, just 20km south of Grimstad, is one of the most popular holiday spots on the coast, the white clapboard houses of its tiny centre draped prettily round the harbourfront. One or two of the buildings, notably the sturdy **Rådhus** (1734), are especially good-looking, but it's the general appearance of the place which appeals, best appreciated from the ter-

Ibsen

Henrik Johan Ibsen (1828–1906), Norway's most famous and influential playwright, is generally regarded as one of the greatest dramatists of all time, and certainly his central themes have powerful modern resonances. In essence, these concern the alienation of the individual from an ethically bankrupt society, loss of religious faith and the yearning of women to transcend the confines of their roles as wives and mothers. Ibsen's central characters often speak evasively, mirroring the repression of their society and their own sense of confusion and guilt. Venomous exchanges – a major characteristic of the playwright's dialogue – appear whenever the underlying tensions break through. Ibsen's protagonists do things which are less than heroic, often incompetent, even malicious. Nevertheless, they aspire to *dåd*, the act of the hero/heroine, arguably a throwback to the old Norse sagas.

These themes run right through Ibsen's plays, the first of which, *Catalina* (1850), was written while he was employed as an apothecary's assistant at Grimstad. The alienation the plays reveal was undoubtedly spawned by his troubled childhood: Ibsen's father had gone bankrupt in 1836, and the disgrace – and poverty – weighed heavily on the whole family. More humiliation followed at Grimstad, where the shy, young Ibsen worked for a pittance and was obliged to share a bed with his boss and two maids, which resulted in one of them bearing him a child in 1846.

Ibsen escaped provincial Norway in 1850, settling first in Oslo and then Bergen. But he remained deeply dissatisfied with Norwegian society, which he repeatedly decried as illiberal and small-minded. In 1864, he left the country and spent the next 27 years living in Germany and Italy. It was during his exile that Ibsen established his literary reputation – at first with the rhyming couplets of *Peer Gynt*, featuring the antics of the eponymous hero, a shambolic opportunist in the mould of Don Quixote, and then by a vicious attack on small-town values in *Pillars of Society*. It was, however, *A Doll's House* (1879) which really put him on the map, its controversial protagonist, Nora, making unwise financial decisions before walking out not only on her patronizing husband, Torvald, but also on her loving children – all in her desire to control her own destiny. *Ghosts* followed two years later, and its exploration of moral contamination through the metaphor of syphilis created an even greater furore, which Ibsen rebutted in his next work, *An Enemy of the People* (1882). Afterwards, Ibsen changed tack (if not theme), firstly with *The Wild Duck* (1884), a mournful tale of the effects of compulsive truth-telling, and then *Hedda Gabler* (1890), where the heroine is denied the ability to make or influence decisions, and so becomes perverse, manipulative and ultimately self-destructive.

Ibsen returned to Oslo in 1891. He was treated as a hero, and ironically – considering the length of his exile and his comments on his compatriots – as a symbol of Norwegian virtuosity. Indeed, the daily stroll he took from his apartment to the *Grand Hotel* in Karl Johans gate became something of a tourist attraction. He was incapacitated by a heart attack in 1901 and died from the effects of another five years later.

race of one of the town's waterfront café-restaurants: the *Sjøbua*, midway round the harbour, does very nicely.

To investigate Lillesand's architectural nooks and crannies, sign up at the tourist office (see below) for one of its hour-long **guided walks** (1 daily mid-June to Aug; 30kr). It also has details on a variety of local **boat trips**, including cruises along the coast, fishing trips and the *badeboot* (bathing boat; July only 4 daily; 15min; 40kr return), which shuttles across to Hestholm bay on the island of **Skaurøya**, where swimmers don't seem to notice just how cold the Skagerrak is. Better still is a three-hour cruise on the dinky **M/S Øya** passenger ferry (late June to early Aug Mon–Sat at 10am; 170kr each way; ☎94 58 33 97), which wiggles south to Kristiansand (see p.134) along a narrow channel separating the mainland from the offshore islets. Sheltered from the full force of the ocean, this channel – the **Blindleia** – was once a major trade route, but today it's trafficked by every sort of pleasure craft, from replica three-mast sailing ships to the sleekest of yachts. Other, faster, boats make the trip too, but the M/S Øya is the most charming.

Practicalities

Lillesand is not on the train line, but it is on the main Oslo-Kristiansand bus route. **Buses** pull in near the south end of the harbour, a brief stroll from the **tourist office**, located in the old waterfront customs house (mid-June to mid-Aug Mon–Fri 9am–6pm, Sat 10am–4pm & Sun noon–4pm; mid-Aug to mid-June Mon–Fri 9am–4pm; ☎37 26 16 80; Ⓦwww.lillesand.com). Lillesand has one central **hotel**, the first-rate *Hotel Norge*, Strandgaten 3 (☎37 27 01 44, Ⓕ37 27 30 70; Ⓦwww.hotelnorge.no; ❹, s/r ❼), which occupies a grand old wooden building near the bus stop. Refurbished in attractive period style, the interior holds some charming stained-glass windows and the rooms are named after some of the famous people who have stayed here – the novelist Knut Hamsun and the Spanish king Alfonso XIII for starters. Alternatively, try *Tingsaker Familiecamping*, on Øvre Tingsaker (☎37 27 04 21, Ⓕ37 27 01 47; Ⓦwww.tingsakercamping.no; May–Aug), a well-equipped waterfront campsite with cabins (❸). It's about 1km north of the centre – take Storgata and keep going – and has self-catering facilities, canoe hire, a pool and a playground. The *Hotel Norge* has an excellent **restaurant**, but it's more expensive and formal than the harbourfront *Sjøbua* (☎37 27 03 66), where you can sample excellent fish dishes for around 160kr, in surroundings kitted out like an old sailing ship.

Kristiansand

Norway's fifth largest town, with some 75,000 inhabitants, **KRIS-TIANSAND**, is something of a holiday resort; a genial, energetic place which thrives on its ferry connections with Denmark, its busy marinas and passable sandy beaches. In summer, the seafront and adjoining streets are a frenetic bustle of cocktail bars, fast-food joints and flirting holidaymakers, and even in winter Norwegians come here to live it up.

Like so many other Scandinavian towns, Kristiansand was founded by and named after **Christian IV**, who saw an opportunity to strengthen his coastal defences here. Building started in 1641, and the town has retained the spacious quadrant plan that characterized all Christian's projects. There are few specific sights, but it's worth a quick look around, especially when everyone else has gone to the beach and left the central pedestrianized streets relatively empty. Its main attraction, however, is a few kilometres out town at the **Kristiansand Kanonmuseum**, the forbidding remains of a large coastal gun battery built during the German occupation.

Arrival, information and accommodation

Trains, **buses** and Color Line **ferries** all arrive close to each other, by Vestre Strandgate, on the edge of the town grid. The main regional **tourist office** is here too, at Vestre Strandgate 32 (mid-June to mid-Aug Mon–Fri 8am–6pm, Sat 10am–6pm & Sun noon–6pm; mid-Aug to mid-June Mon–Fri 8.30am–3.30pm; ☎38 12 13 14; Ⓦwww.sorlandet.com). It provides free town maps, public transport timetables and information on boat times, island bathing

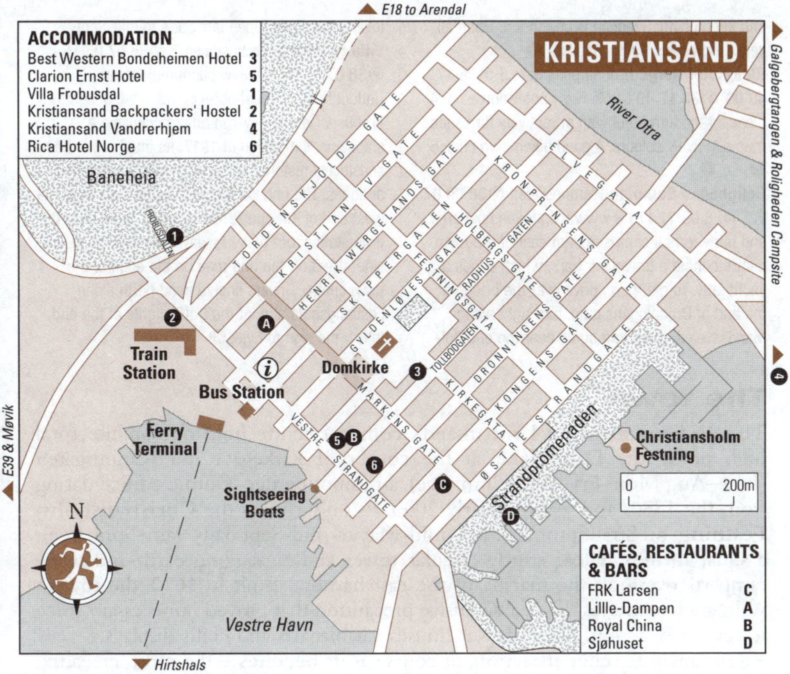
E18 to Arendal
KRISTIANSAND
ACCOMMODATION
Best Western Bondeheimen Hotel 3
Clarion Ernst Hotel 5
Villa Frobusdal 1
Kristiansand Backpackers' Hostel 2
Kristiansand Vandrerhjem 4
Rica Hotel Norge 6
Baneheia
River Otra
Galgebergtangen & Roligheden Campsite
Train Station
Bus Station
Ferry Terminal
Domkirke
Sightseeing Boats
Christiansholm Festning
Strandpromenaden
Vestre Havn
E39 & Møvik
Hirtshals
TORDENSKJOLDS GATE
KRISTIAN IV GATE
HENRIK WERGELANDS GATE
SKIPPERGATEN
GYLDENLØVES GATE
FESTNINGSGATA
TOLLBODGATEN
KIRKEGATA
MARKENS GATE
VESTRE STRANDGATE
ØSTRE STRANDGATE
KONGENS GATE
DRONNINGENS GATE
RADHUS-GATEN
HOLBERGS GATE
KRONPRINSENS GATE
ELVEGATA
0 200m
N
CAFÉS, RESTAURANTS & BARS
FRK Larsen C
Lille-Dampen A
Royal China B
Sjøhuset D

and beaches. **Parking** is easy throughout town, with car parks concentrated along Vestre Strandgate. The best way to explore the town centre is on **foot** – it only takes about ten minutes to walk from one side to the other – or, for journeys further afield, **bike rental** is available at Kristiansand Sykkelsenter, Grim Torv (Ⓣ38 03 68 35), where 21-gear bikes cost 150kr per day, 490kr for a week.

Accommodation

Kristiansand has a reasonably good choice of **accommodation** with a fair sprinkling of hotels, a guesthouse or two, a youth hostel and a nearby campsite.

Centrum Park Hotel Bondeheimen Kirkegata 15 Ⓣ38 02 44 40, Ⓕ38 02 73 21, Ⓦwww.centrumpark.no. A converted nineteenth-century town house right in the middle of town, near the Domkirke, with modern and comfortable if uninspiring rooms. ⑤, s/r ④

Clarion Ernst Hotel Rådhusgaten 2 Ⓣ38 12 86 00, Ⓕ38 02 03 07, Ⓦwww.ernst.no. Housed in a flashily modernized building, this hotel has large doubles with standard-issue modern furnishings and fittings. The air conditioning can be stuffy, so try to get a room where you can open a window and which doesn't face the interior courtyard. ⑥, s/r ⑤

Kristiansand Backpackers' Hostel Jernbanetomta, Vestre Strandgate 49 Ⓣ38 02 79 69, Ⓕ38 09 48 96, Ⓦwww.backpackers.no. Hard by the train station, this hostel provides frugal lodgings at budget prices, though all the rooms – from singles and doubles through to six-bunk rooms – are en suite. Self-catering facilities and a laundry. ②–③

Kristiansand Vandrerhjem Skansen 8 Ⓣ38 02 83 10, Ⓕ38 02 75 05, ⒺKristiansand.hostel@vandrerhjem.no. This youth hostel is pricey for what you get – cramped rooms in an ugly, prefabricated 1960s building in the middle of an industrial estate. The facilities are, however, quite good with self-catering, a laundry and a café. The hostel is about fifteen minutes' walk east of the ferry terminal on the tiny peninsula – Tangen – edging the marina. Take any street up to Elvegata, turn right

and keep going: Skansen is on the left. Open all year. Dorm beds 190kr, doubles ❷
Rica Hotel Norge Dronningens gate 5 ☎38 17 40 00, ℱ38 17 40 01, ⊕www.hotel-norge.no. A pleasant modern hotel with attractively furnished rooms in lively colours. A good downtown choice. ❺, s/r ❹
Roligheden Camping Framnesveien ☎38 09 67 22, ℱ38 09 11 17, ⊕www.roligheden.no. Large and fairly formal campsite 3km east of the town centre behind a gravel car park, which edges a yacht jetty. To get there, drive over the bridge at the end of Dronningens gate, turn right along Marviksveien, then right again near the end, fol-

lowing the signs. Open late June to mid-Sept.
Villa Frobusdal Frobusdalen 2 ☎38 07 05 15, ℱ38 07 01 15, ⊕www.bednbreakfast.no. Undoubtedly the best hotel in town, the delightful *Frobusdal* is a family-run affair occupying a shipowner's mansion of 1917. Its interior has been sensitively restored and is crammed with period antiques. The only problem is location: it's near the west end of Kirkegata, five minutes' walk from the train station, but tucked away down a hard-to-find side-street off the ring road on the edge of the town centre. Drivers should head north along Festningsgata and, at the traffic lights at the end, follow the sign to Evje. ❹

The town

The gridiron streets of Kristiansand's compact centre hold one architectural high point, the **Domkirke** at the corner of Kirkegata and Rådhusgaten (June–Aug Mon–Fri 10am–2pm; free), an imposing neo-Gothic edifice dating from the 1880s and seating nearly 2000. Its only rival is the **Christiansholm Festning**, on Strandpromenaden (mid-May to mid-Sept daily 9am–9pm; free), a squat fortress whose sturdy circular tower and zigzagging earth-and-stone ramparts overlook the marina in the east harbour. Built in 1672, the tower's walls are five metres thick, a defensive precaution that proved unnecessary since it never saw action. These days it houses various arts and crafts displays.

Kristiansand's other attraction, of course, is its **beaches** – the most appealing being is **Galgebergtangen** (Gallows' Point), an attractive rocky cove with a small sandy beach, 2km east of the town centre. To get there, go over the bridge at the end of Dronningens gate, take the first major right (at the lights) and follow the signs.

The Kristiansand Kanonmuseum

An easy 10km drive south along the coast at **Møvik** – take Highway 456 out of Kristiansand, then Highway 457 for the last 3km – is the **Kristiansand Kanonmuseum** (May to mid-June Mon–Wed 11am–3pm; mid-June to mid-Aug daily 11am–6pm; mid-Aug to Sept Wed–Sun 11am–6pm; 50kr), a former World War II coastal battery built using the forced labour of POWs. Around 1400 men worked on the project, which involved the construction of protective housings for four big guns at the narrowest part of the Skagerrak. Guns on the Danish shore complemented those here, so that any enemy warship trying to slip through the straits could be shelled. Only a small zone in the middle was out of range, and this the Germans mined. The complex once covered 220 acres, but today the principal remains hog a narrow ridge, with a massive, empty artillery casement at one end, and a whopping 38cm-calibre **gun** in a concrete well at the other. The gun, which could fire a 500kg shell almost 55km, is in pristine condition, and visitors can explore the loading area, complete with the original ramrods, wedges, trolleys and pulleys. Below is the underground command post and soldiers' living quarters, again almost exactly as they were in the 1940s – including the odd bit of German graffiti.

Work started on the fortress in 1941, largely because Hitler overestimated both Norway's strategic importance, and the likelihood of an Allied counter-invasion in the north. These two judgements of error prompted him to garrison the country with nigh on half a million men, and build several hundred artillery batteries round the coast – a huge waste of resources that were desperately needed elsewhere.

Eating and drinking

There are lots of **restaurants** and **cafés** in the centre of Kristiansand, but the standard is very variable – we've given a few of the choicer places below. There's also a fairly active nightlife based around a handful of **bars** which stay open until 2am.

FRK Larsen Markensgate 5. Near the corner of Kongensgate, this laid-back café-bar is an appealing, fashionable place. Also serves meals, such as salted cod (*bacalao*), for a very reasonable 175kr.

Lille-Dampen Henrik Wergelandsgate 15. First-rate and inexpensive bakery, with delicious takeaway baguettes. Mon–Fri 8am–4.30pm.

Royal China Tollbodgaten 7 ☏ 38 07 02 77.

Surprisingly plush Chinese restaurant offering tasty main courses from as little as 90kr.

Sjøhuset, Østre Strandgate 12a ☏ 38 02 62 60. In an old converted warehouse by the harbour at the east end of Markensgate, this excellent restaurant serves superb fish courses for 190–2100kr. Nautical fittings and wooden beams set the scene. Open daily in summer; closed Sun rest of the year.

West from Kristiansand to Stavanger

From Kristiansand, the **E39** weaves its way west for 240km to **Stavanger**, staying inland for the most part and offering only the odd glimpse of the coast. The **train line** follows pretty much the same route until **Egersund**, when it returns to the coast for the final eighty kilometres, slicing across long flat plains with the sea on one side and distant hills away to the east.

Both road and train line pass through a sparsely inhabited region, where the rough uplands and long valleys of the interior lead down to a shoreline that is pierced by a string of inlets and fjords. The highlight of this coast is undoubtedly **Mandal**, a fetching seaside resort with probably the best sandy beach in the whole of Norway, but thereafter the region has little to inspire. Aside from a brief stroll round the old port of **Flekkefjord**, there's nothing to detain you until Stavanger.

Mandal

MANDAL, just 40km from Kristiansand along the E39, is Norway's southernmost town. This old timber port reached its heyday in the eighteenth century, when pines and oaks from the surrounding countryside were much sought after by the Dutch to support their canal houses and build their trading fleet. Although it's now bordered by a modern mess, Mandal has preserved its quaint **old centre**, a narrow strip of white clapboard buildings spread along the north bank of the Mandalselva river just before it rolls into the sea. It's an attractive spot, well worth a stroll and you can also drop by the municipal **museum** (late June to mid-Aug Mon–Fri 11am–5pm, Sat 11am–2pm & Sun 2–5pm; March to late June & mid-Aug to Oct Sun only 2–5pm; 20kr), whose rambling collection – from agricultural implements to seafaring tackle – occupies an old merchant's house overlooking the river. Its exhibits also include a small but enjoyable collection of nautical paintings, and outside by the front door is a statue of the town's most famous son, Gustav Vigeland (see p.95). It's not its antiquities that make Mandal a popular tourist spot, however, but its fine beach, **Sjøsanden**. An 800-metre stretch of golden sand backed by pine trees and framed by rocky headlands, it's touted as Norway's best beach – and although this isn't saying a lot, it's a perfectly enjoyable place to unwind for a few hours. The beach is about 1.5km from the town centre: walk along the harbour, past the tourist office to the end of the road and turn left; keep going until you reach the car park at the beach's eastern end.

If you have your own transport, you should also consider an excursion to the windy headland of **Lindesnes** (literally "where the land curves round"), 40km away to the southwest – take the E39 and turn down Highway 460. This is Norway's most southerly point, a bare, lichen-stained promontory surmounted by a sturdy red-and-white lighthouse that is exposed to extraordinarily ferocious storms, especially when the warm westerly currents of the Skagerrak meet cold easterly winds.

Practicalities

There are no trains to Mandal, but buses from Kristiansand (Mon–Sat hourly, 6 on Sun; 50min; 70kr) and Stavanger (1–3 daily; 3hr 30min), pull in at an ugly modern **bus station** by the bridge on the north bank of the Mandalselva river; from here it's a brief walk west to the old town centre, just beyond which is the **tourist office**, facing the river at Bryggegata 10 (mid-June to Aug Mon–Fri 9am–7pm; Sept to mid-June Mon–Fri 9am–4pm; ☎38 27 83 00; ⓦwww.visitregionmandal.com). There are a couple of good places to **stay**, beginning with the handy and economical *Kjøbmandsgaarden Hotel*, which occupies an old timber house in a street of such buildings, across from the bus station at Store Elvegaten 57 (☎38 26 12 76, ⓕ38 26 33 02; ⓦwww.kjg-hotel.no; ❹). All the dozen or so rooms are spick and span and the decor is bright and cheerful. More upmarket is the appealing *First Hotel Solborg*, Neseveien 1 (☎38 26 66 66, ⓕ38 26 48 22; ❼, s/r ❺), an odd-looking but somehow rather fetching modern structure with every mod con; it's on the west side of the town centre, a good ten-minute walk from the bus station, tight against a wooded escarpment. Alternatively, you can camp or rent a cabin (❷) very close to the western end of the beach at the *Sjøsanden Feriesenter*, Sjøsandvei 1 (☎38 26 14 19), signposted 2km from the town centre.

The *First Hotel Solborg* has the best **restaurant** in town, but for something less pricey and more informal, head into the centre where you'll find several places, including the lively pizzeria-restaurant, *Jonas B Gundersen*. The café-restaurant of the *Kjøbmandsgaarden* comes highly recommended too, offering a tasty range of Norwegian dishes at inexpensive prices.

Flekkefjord

From Mandal, the **E39** runs past the turning for the Lindesnes lighthouse (see above) and heads west for 80km before reaching **FLEKKEFJORD**, the first town of any interest. With a population of just 6000, Flekkefjord has an old and picturesque centre whose timber houses line the banks of a short (500m) channel that connects the Lafjord and the Grisefjord. The town's heyday was in the sixteenth century, when Dutch traders came to purchase timber for their houses and granite for their dykes and harbours. Later, in the 1750s, the herring industry came to prominence, along with shipbuilding and tanning, but the Flekkefjord economy had pretty much collapsed by the end of the nineteenth century when sailing ships gave way to steam. The oldest and prettiest part of Flekkefjord – known as **Hollenderbyen** after the town's Dutch connections – is on the west side of the channel, and only takes a few minutes to explore, though you can extend this pleasantly enough by visiting the nearby nineteenth-century period rooms of the **Flekkefjord Museum** (June–Aug Mon–Fri 11am–5pm, Sat & Sun noon–5pm; 15kr).

Buses pull in on Løvikgata, about 200m east of the central waterway, while the **tourist office** is on the west side of the same waterway at Elvegaten 15 (mid-June to mid-Aug Mon–Fri 9am–6pm, Sat & Sun 10am–2pm; mid-Aug to mid-June Mon–Fri 9am–4pm; ⊤38 32 21 31). There's no pressing reason to overnight here, but if you do want **to stay**, the unassuming *First Hotel Maritim* (⊤38 32 33 33, Ⓕ38 32 43 12; Ⓦwww.firsthotels.com; ❻, s/r ❸), overlooking the east side of the central waterway at Sundgaten 15, is the best bet.

Egersund and the Jossingfjord

At Flekkefjord, the E39 turns inland for the last 120km to Stavanger. Alternatively, you can take the more southerly, but slightly longer (130km), **Highway 44** which offers occasional glimpses of the sea, especially where it wiggles across the narrow **JOSSINGFJORD**. It was here, in 1940, that 300 Allied POWs were liberated from the German supply ship *Altmar* by the Royal Navy destroyer *Cossack*. This rare British success prompted those Norwegians who were opposed to the Germans – the vast majority of the population – to call themselves "Jossings" for the rest of the war.

From the Jossingfjord, it's a further 35km or so to **EGERSUND**, a port and minor manufacturing centre that spreads over a jigsaw of bays and lakes at the end of a deep and sheltered ocean inlet. Apart from an assortment of old timber houses in the centre, along Strandgaten, Egersund's tranport links are the main reason to visit: it's on the Kristiansand–Stavanger **train line** and has Fjord Line **ferry** connections with Bergen and Hantsholm in Denmark.

From Egersund, it's 10km north to the E39 and a further 65km to Stavanger.

Stavanger and around

STAVANGER is something of a survivor. While other Norwegian coastal towns have fallen foul of the precarious fortunes of fishing, Stavanger has grown and flourished, and is now the proud possessor of a dynamic economy which has swelled the population to over 100,000. It was the herring fishery that first put money into the town, crowding its nineteenth-century wharves with coopers and smiths, net makers and menders. When the fishing industry failed, the town moved into shipbuilding and ultimately oil: the port builds the rigs for the offshore oilfields and refines the oil as well.

None of which sounds terribly enticing, and certainly no one could describe Stavanger as picturesque. However, it's an easy city to adjust to, has a couple of enjoyable museums, and a raft of excellent restaurants and lively bars. You'll also hear lots of English spoken, as well-paid foreign oil-workers gather here for their leave. If you stay a few days, you might want to sally out into the surrounding fjords, where the hike to the **Preikestolen** rock is one of the most popular jaunts in southern Norway.

Arrival, information and city transport

Stavanger's international **airport** is 14km southwest of the city centre at **Sola**. There's a Flybussen into Stavanger (Mon–Fri 6am–9pm, Sat 6am–8pm & Sun 7am–9pm every 20–30min; 45kr), which stops at major downtown hotels, the ferry terminals and the bus and train stations. The **bus terminal** and the **train station** (⊤51 56 96 10) are adjacent to each other on the southern side of the Breiavatnet, a tiny lake that's the most obvious downtown landmark. Also at the bus station is Rogaland Kollektivtrafikk, an agency run collectively by several transport companies (Mon–Fri 7am–9pm, Sat 8am–3.30pm & Sun noon–7pm; ☎51 53 96 00; ⓦwww.ruteservice.no), which provides comprehensive details of buses, boats and trains in the city and surrounding area.

Fjord Line **ferries** (☎815 33 500; ⓦwww.fjordline.com) from Newcastle,

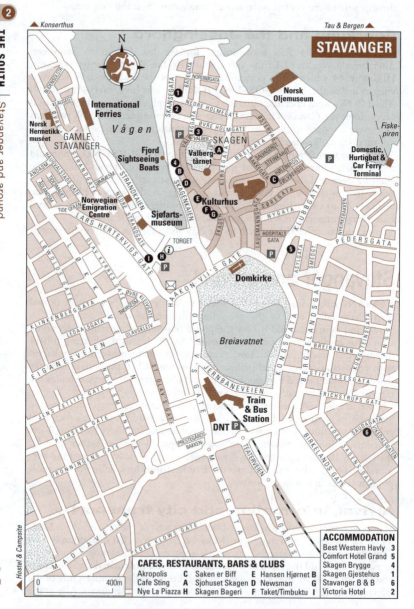

▲ Konserthus

Tau & Bergen ▲

STAVANGER

International Ferries

Vågen

Norsk Hermetikk-muséet

GAMLE STAVANGER

Norsk Oljemuseum

Fiske-piren

SKAGEN

Fjord Sightseeing Boats

Valberg-tårnet

Domestic, Hurtigbåt & Car Ferry Terminal

Norwegian Emigration Centre

Sjøfarts-museum

Kulturhus

TORGET

Domkirke

Breiavatnet

JERNBANEVEIEN

Train & Bus Station

DNT

140

▲ Hostel & Campsite

0   400m

CAFES, RESTAURANTS, BARS & CLUBS

Akropolis	C	Saken er Biff E	Hansen Hjørnet B
Cafe Sting	A	Sjøhuset Skagen D	Newsman G
Nye La Piazza	H	Skagen Bageri F	Taket/Timbuktu I

ACCOMMODATION

Best Western Havly	3
Comfort Hotel Grand	5
Skagen Brygge	4
Skagen Gjestehus	1
Stavanger B & B	6
Victoria Hotel	2

Haugesund and Bergen berth on the west side of the harbour, beside Strandkaien, a five-minute walk from the main square, Torget, which is itself immediately to the north of the central lake. All **Hurtigbåt** passenger express boats and **car ferries** bound for the islands and fjords around Stavanger use the Fiskepiren terminal, about 800m northeast of the train and bus stations. Finally, most pleasure cruises depart from Skagenkaien, on the east side of the main harbour.

On-street **parking** is difficult, but not impossible: central car parks include those beside the bus station, the main post office and Skagenkaien. See "Listings", p.146, for addresses of car rental agencies.

Information

The **tourist office** overlooks the Torget from its bright and breezy premises at Rosenkildetorget 1 (Jan–May Mon–Fri 9am–4pm & Sat 9am–2pm; June–Aug daily 9am–8pm; Sept–March Mon–Fri 9am–4pm & Sat 9am–2pm; ☎51 85 92 00; ⓦwww.visitstavanger.com). It publishes the useful, free *Stavanger Guide* and supplies free copies of *På Gang*, a monthly listings brochure. It also provides local bus and ferry timetables, as well as free cycling maps of both the city and its surroundings, along with route suggestions, and can book visitors on guided tours (see below).

City transport and tours

All Stavanger's key attractions are clustered in or near the centre within easy walking distance of each other, while the town's environs can be reached by a variety of local boats and buses departing from the terminals detailed above. A number of operators also provide regular summertime **fjord sightseeing tours**, with the **Lysefjord** (see p.146) being the most popular trip. Most of the tours depart from Skagenkaien and prices start at around 250kr for a three- to four-hour excursion; tickets are available at the quayside. For a more formal introduction to the city and its immediate environs, consider taking the tourist office's two-hour **guided coach tour** (June–Aug 1 daily; 195kr) that starts at the tourist office and takes in the historic quarter of Gamle Stavanger (see p.142).

Accommodation

There's no shortage of accommodation to choose from in Stavanger. Half a dozen **hotels** are dotted around the town's compact centre, each offering substantial weekend and summer discounts. Alternatively, there are a couple of convenient, no-frills **guesthouses** and, further afield, an HI **hostel** and **campsite**.

Hotels and guesthouses

Best Western Havly Hotel Valberggata 1 ☎51 89 67 00, ⓕ51 89 50 25, ⓦwww.havly-hotell.no. Unassuming, recently refurbished modern hotel in the narrow side streets off Skagenkaien. Comfortable, quiet rooms. ➍, s/r ➌

Comfort Hotel Grand Klubbgata 3 ☎51 20 14 00, ⓕ51 20 14 01, ⓦwww.choicehotels.no. A good central choice, close to all the bars and restaurants. The rooms are smart, modern and spacious and the price includes a very good buffet breakfast. ➍, s/r ➌

Skagen Hotell & Gjestehus Skansegata 7 ☎51 93 85 00, ⓕ51 93 85 01, ⓦwww.shg.no. This hotel-cum-guesthouse in an old wooden building on the east side of the harbour has recently been revamped. Has 28 en-suite rooms, the best of which are kitted out in a brisk and pleasant modern style. ➌

Skagen Brygge Hotell Skagenkaien 30 ☎51 85 00 00, ⓕ51 85 00 01, ⓦwww. skagenbryggehotell.no. A delightful quayside hotel, built in the style of an old warehouse but with lots of glass, and great views over the harbour. The rooms are modern and tastefully decorated, the buffet breakfast outstanding and delicious mid-afternoon nibbles are on offer, free – cheese, pickled herring etc. The only quibble concerns the noise from outside on summer weekends, when your best bet is probably to get a room at the back or on the top floor. **7**, s/r **4**

Stavanger Bed and Breakfast Vikedalsgaten 1a ⊤51 56 25 00, ⊕51 56 25 01, ⓦwww. stavangerbedandbreakfast.no. Straightforward modern place in an unexciting residential area five minutes' walk southeast of the central lake. An inexpensive option. **3**

Victoria Hotel Skansegata 1 ⊤51 86 70 00, ⊕51 86 70 10, ⓦ www.victoria-hotel.no. Part of the *Rica* chain, this large hotel occupies a big old building, with a fancy portico, overlooking the east side of the harbour. The foyer has kept much of its Victorian appearance, complete with wood panelling, leather sofas and ships' models, while the

comfortable bedrooms beyond are also in a broadly period style. The summer rate applies to weekends, too. **7**, s/r **3**

Hostels and campsites

Mosvangen Camping Tjensvollveien 1 ⊤51 53 29 71. By the lake, next door to the youth hostel, with cabins (**2**) as well as spaces for tents and caravans. Open mid-May to mid-September.

Stavanger Vandrerhjem Mosvangen Henrik Ibsens gate 21, ⊤51 87 29 00, ⊕51 87 06 30, ⓔstavanger.mosvangen.hostel@vandrerhjem.no. This plain HI youth hostel occupies a lakeside setting, a 3km walk from the centre: take Madlaveien west from near the station and turn left just beyond the lake, Mosvatnet, on to Tjensvollveien – Henrik Ibsens gate is its continuation. The hostel has self-catering and laundry facilities; advance reservations are advised. Open June–Aug. Dorm beds 145kr, doubles **1**

The City

Much of central Stavanger was built with oil money – a modern, flashy but surprisingly likeable ensemble of mini tower-blocks. The only relic of the medieval city is the twelfth-century **Domkirke** (mid-May to mid-Sept Mon & Tues 11am–6pm, Wed–Sat 10am–6pm & Sun 1–6pm; mid-Sept to mid-May Wed–Sat 10am–3pm; free), above the Torget, whose pointed-hat towers signal a Romanesque church that has suffered from several poorly conceived renovations. The simple interior, originally the work of English craftsmen, has fared badly too, spoilt by ornate seventeenth-century additions including an intricate pulpit and five huge memorial tablets adorning the walls of the aisles – a jumble of richly carved angels, crucifixes, death's-heads, animals and apostles. Organ recitals are held here every Thursday at 11.15am.

A brief stroll away, beyond the fresh fish and flower stalls of **Torget**, is the **Skagen** area, built on the bumpy promontory that forms the eastern side of the harbour. It's an oddly discordant district, a clumsy mixture of old and new incorporating the town's main shopping zone, whose mazy street plan is the only legacy of the original Viking settlement. The spiky nineteenth-century firewatch **Valbergtårnet** (Valberg tower), sits atop Skagen's highest point, guarded by three rusty cannons and offering sweeping views of the city and its industry.

Beside the waterfront on the far side of Skagen, the oil industry celebrates its achievements by way of the gleaming **Norsk Oljemuseum** (Norwegian Petroleum Museum; June–Aug daily 10am–7pm, Sept–May Mon–Sat 10am–4pm & Sun 10am–6pm; 75kr; ⓦwww.norskolje.museum.no). Housed in a hangar-like building, the museum has displays on North Sea geology, oil extraction and the like, complete with drill bits and other oil-rig paraphernalia. There are several hands-on exhibits too – including a diving bell – plus an honest account of the accidents and occasional disasters that have befallen the industry.

Gamle Stavanger

The town's star turn is **Gamle Stavanger** (Old Stavanger), on the western side of the harbour. Though very different in appearance from the modern structures back in the centre, the buildings here were also the product of a boom. From 1810 until around 1870, herring turned up just offshore in their millions, and Stavanger took advantage of this slice of luck. The town flourished and expanded, with the number of merchants and ship owners increasing dramatically. Huge profits were made from the exported fish, which were salted and later, as the technology improved, canned. Today, some of the wooden stores and warehouses flanking the western quayside hint at their nineteenth-century pedigree, but it's the succession of narrow, cobbled lanes behind them that shows Gamle Stavanger to best advantage. Formerly home to local seafarers, craftsmen and cannery workers, the area has been maintained as a residential quarter, mercifully free of tourist tat; the long rows of white-painted, clapboard houses are immaculately maintained, complete with gas lamps, picket fences and tiny terraced gardens. There's little architectural pretension, but here and there flashes of fancy wooden scrollwork must once have raised eyebrows among the Lutheran population.

The Norsk Hermetikkmuséet

Right in the heart of Gamle Stavanger at Øvre Strandgate 88, the **Norsk Hermetikkmuséet** (Canning Museum; early June & late Aug Mon–Thurs 11am–3pm; mid-June to mid-Aug daily 11am–4pm; Sept–May Sun 11am–4pm; 40kr) occupies an old **sardine-canning factory** and gives a glimpse of the industry that saved Stavanger from collapse at the end of the nineteenth century. The herring largely disappeared from local waters in the 1870s, but the canning factories switched to imported fish, thereby keeping the local economy afloat. They remained Stavanger's main source of employment until as late as 1960: in the 1920s there were seventy canneries in the town, and the last one only closed down in 1983. A visit to an old canning factory may not seem too enticing, but actually the museum is very good, not least because of its collection of **sardine tin labels**, called *iddis* in these parts from the local pronunciation of *etikett*, the Norwegian for label. Hundreds of labels have survived, in part because they were avidly collected by the town's children. The hobby prompted bouts of adult anxiety – "Label thefts – an unfortunate collection craze", ran a 1915 headline in the *Stavanger Aftenblad*. The variety of design is extraordinary – anything and everything from representations of the Norwegian royal family to surrealistic fish with human qualities. Spare a thought here for a Scottish seaman by the name of **William Anderson**: it was his face, copied from a photograph, that beamed out from millions of *Skippers'* sardine tins, a celebrity status so frowned upon by shipowners that Anderson couldn't find work. But the story ended happily when Anderson wrote to the cannery concerned and they put him on the payroll for the remainder of his working life. You can watch the museum **smoking its own sardines** on the first Sunday of every month and every Tuesday and Thursday from mid-June to mid-August – and very tasty they are too.

The Sjøfartsmuseum and the Norwegian Emigration Centre

Walk back through the old town towards the centre and you'll pass the **Sjøfartsmuseum** (Maritime Museum; same times as Canning Museum; 40kr), at Nedre Strandgate 17. Sited in a restored warehouse, this museum gives another insight into the history of Stavanger, with the exhibits mostly exploring the various trades that served the shipping industry. There are some nice touches like the old sailmakers' room, and some reconstructed shop and office interiors.

Just around the corner from the Sjøfartsmuseum, on the west side of the harbour at Strandkaien 31, the **Norwegian Emigration Centre** (☎51 53 88 60, ⓦwww.emigrationcenter.com) might be of interest if you have Norwegian ancestors. Among a wide portfolio of historical data, it holds parish registers, ship passenger lists and census records covering all of Norway. This database enables them to trace an enquirer's Norwegian forebears, but to stand a good chance of success, they really need to have the exact name, date of birth and year of emigration. The research is charged for by the hour, which can become very expensive, but if you want to do it yourself, you'll need to be able to read Danish and Norwegian, often in Gothic script.

Eating, drinking and nightlife

Although prices are marginally inflated by oil-industry expense accounts, Stavanger is a great place to **eat**, with several fine seafood restaurants clustered on the east side of the harbour along Skagenkaien. For something less expensive, the best option is to stick to the more mundane cafés and restaurants near the Kulturhus in the heart of the Skagen shopping area.

Stavanger is lively at night, particularly at weekends when a rum assortment of oil workers, sailors, fishermen, executives, tourists and office workers gathers in the **bars and clubs** on and around Skagenkaien to live (or rather drink) it up. Most places stay open until 2am or later, with rowdy – but usually amiable – revellers lurching from one bar to the next.

For more subdued evenings, check out the programme at the **Stavanger Konserthus** (Concert Hall; ☎51 53 70 00; ⓦwww.stavanger-konserthus.no) in Bjergsted park, north of the centre beyond Gamle Stavanger, where there are regular concerts by the Stavanger Symphony Orchestra and visiting artists. There's an eight-screen **cinema**, Stavanger Kinematografer, inside the Kulturhus, on Sølvberggaten (☎51 51 07 00).

Cafés and restaurants

Akropolis Sølvberggata 14. Near the Kulturhus, this is a medium-priced Greek restaurant housed in a white wooden building on a cobbled street. Closed Mon.

Café Sting Valbergjet 3 ☎51 89 38 78, ⓦwww.café-sting.no. Right next to the Valbergtårnet, this laid-back café-bar is probably the coolest place in town. The food is tasty and inexpensive, with mostly Mediterranean and Norwegian dishes. Also doubles as an art gallery and live music venue, hosting anything from indie through to rock.

Nye La Piazza Rosenkildetorget 1. Above the tourist office, this smart Italian restaurant serves delicious pizzas, pasta and more.

Saken er Biff Skagen 28 ☎51 89 60 80. No self-respecting oil town could do without a steakhouse – and this is it. A couple of stuffed cattle heads remind you what you're eating, and fish dishes, reindeer and ostrich are available too. Around 200kr for a main course.

Sjøhuset Skagen Skagenkaien 16 ☎51 89 51 80. Fine fish and seafood restaurant on the harbour, with monkfish a speciality. Main dishes are around 200kr.

Skagen Bageri Skagen 18. This pleasant coffee house, with its finely carved antique door and lintel, occupies the prettiest of the old wooden buildings on Skagen, one block up from the quayside. Great pastries, cakes and snacks at reasonable prices.

Bars and clubs

Hansen Hjørnet Skagenkaien 18. Down on the harbour, this is one of Stavanger's most popular spots, particularly on a sunny day, when the outside terrace fills up fast.

Newsman Skagen 14. One block back from the east side of the harbour, this attractive, busy bar has papers to read and a well-heeled clientele. Open until 2am.

Taket Nedre Strandgate 15 ☎51 84 37 20, ⓦwww.herlige-stavanger.com. The best club in town, across the harbour from most of the bars, just metres from the tourist office; don't be surprised if you have to queue. Open Mon–Wed & Sun midnight to 4am, Thurs–Sat 10pm–4am.

Timbuktu Nedre Strandgate 15. Flashy café-bar beneath *Taket*. Noted for its imaginative modern decor and trendy atmosphere.

△ Old town, Gamle Stavanger

Listings

Airlines Braathens, at the airport (☎815 20 000); SAS, at the airport (☎81 00 33 00); Widerøes, at the airport (☎81 00 12 00).

Car rental Avis, Skansegaten 15 (☎51 93 93 60); Hertz, Olav V's gate 13 (☎51 52 00 00) and at the airport (☎51 65 10 96).

Emergencies Fire ☎110; Police ☎112; Ambulance ☎113.

Exchange Competitive rates at the main post office (see below).

Ferries: International: Fjord Line, Strandkaien (☎81 53 35 00). **Domestic**: Rogaland Kollektivtrafikk for regional bus, boat and train enquiries (☎51 53 96 00; locally also ☎177); Flaggruten (☎51 86 87 80) for Hurtigbåt passenger express boat services to Haugesund and Bergen.

Hiking The DNT-affiliated Stavanger Turistforening, Olav V's gate 18 (Mon–Wed & Fri 10am–4pm, Thurs 10am–6pm; ☎51 84 02 00; www.stavanger-turistforening.no), will advise on local hiking routes and sells a comprehensive

range of hiking maps. It maintains around 900km of hiking trails and runs more than thirty cabins in the mountains east of Stavanger, as well as organizing ski schools on winter weekends. It also offers general advice about local conditions, weather, etc, and you can obtain DNT membership here.

Laundry Renseriet, Kongsgata 40, by Breiavatnet. Coin-operated machines.

Left luggage At the Fiskepiren Hurtigbåt terminal (Mon–Fri 6.30am–11.30pm, Sat 6.30am–8pm, Sun 8am–10pm); and at the bus/train station (Mon–Fri 8am–5pm, Sat 8am–2.30pm, closed Sun).

Pharmacist Løveapoteket, Olav V's gate 11 (daily 9am–11pm; ☎51 52 06 07).

Post office The main post office is at Haakon VII's gate 9 (Mon–Fri 8am–5pm & Sat 9am–1pm).

Taxis Norgestaxi (☎08000).

Vinmonopolet State-run liquor and wine outlet at Olav V's gate 13; across the street from Stavanger Turistforening.

Around Stavanger: Lysefjord

Stavanger sits on a long promontory that pokes north towards the wide waters of the Boknafjord, a deep indentation in the coast speckled with islets. To the east of the town, longer, narrower fjords drill far inland, the most diverting being the blue-black **Lysefjord**, famous for its precipitous cliffs and an especially striking rock formation, the **Preikestolen**. This distinctive 25-metre-square table of rock boasts a sheer 600m drop down to the fjord below on three of its sides.

Along the Lysefjord

There are several ways to visit Lysefjord by boat from Stavanger. One option is a three-and-a-half-hour round trip half-way up the fjord, with **Rødne Clipper Fjord Sightseeing** (☎51 89 52 70; ⓦwww.rodne.no), departing from the Skagenkaien (Jan–April & Oct–Dec 4–7 monthly, May & Sept 3 weekly; June–Aug 1–2 daily; 280kr). Despite the gushing multilingual commentary, however, the fjord seems disappointingly gloomy when seen from the bottom of its cliffs, and from this angle the Preikestolen hardly makes any impression at all. A rather more dramatic trip (run by the same company) takes you the full length of the fjord to **Lysebotn** (June–Aug 1–2 weekly; 7hr; 450kr), where a connecting bus heads up the mountainside, tackling no less than 27 switchbacks, on its way to the minor road that leads back to Stavanger. You can do the trip independently, using Ruteservice Rogaland ferries from Stavanger's Fiskepiren to Lysebotn (June–Sept 1–2 daily; 4hr; 135kr per person, 305kr for car and driver; advance booking is required for vehicles). If you're returning from Lysebotn to Stavanger by bus, check with the tourist office first to find out which ferry is met by a bus.

The road from Lysebotn offers spectacular views as it wiggles its way up the mountainside, but even better views are to be had from the very demanding **hiking trail** which leads west from the car park of the **Øygardstøl** café and information centre, just above the last hairpin on the Lysebotn road. The trail leads to a much-photographed boulder, the **Kjeragbolten**, wedged between two rock faces high above the ground. Allow between five and six hours for the round trip – and steel your nerves for the 1000m drop down to the fjord below.

Preikestolen

Lysefjord's most celebrated vantage point, **Preikestolen** ("Pulpit Rock"), offers breathtaking views, though on sunny summer weekends you'll share them with a fair crowd. To get to the rock, take the **ferry** east from Stavanger to **Tau** (every 30min to 1hr; 40min; passengers 30kr, car & driver 90kr) and then drive south along Highway 13 until, after about 14km, you reach the signed side road leading to Preikestolen. A local **bus** runs between Tau and Preikestolen too (4 daily; 25min); check first with the tourist office which of the ferries it connects with. From the car park at the end of the road, it's a two-hour hike to Preikestolen (and two hours back) along a clearly marked trail. The first half is steep in parts and paved with uneven stones, while the second half – over bedrock – is easier. The change in elevation is 350m; take food and water.

Back at the car park, a short sharp hike leads down to **Refsvatn**, a small lake encircled by a footpath which takes three hours to negotiate, taking in birch and pine woods, marshes, narrow ridges and bare stretches of rock. It also threads through **Torsnes**, an isolated farm that was inhabited until 1962. The lake footpath connects with a rough path that careers down to the Refsa quay on the Lysefjord.

Also by the car park, a first-rate HI **hostel**, *Preikestolen Vandrerhjem* (℡97 16 55 51, Ⓕ51 74 91 11, Ⓦwww.preikestolhytta.no; dorm beds 140kr, doubles ❷; June–Aug) is perched high on the hillside, with great views over the surrounding mountains. Built on the site of an old mountain farm, the hostel comprises a small complex of turf-roofed lodges, each of which has a spick-and-span pine interior. There are self-catering facilities and boat rental, but no laundry; reservations are advised as the place is popular with school groups.

North to Haugesund

With great ingenuity, Norway's road builders cobbled together the E39 coastal road, the **Kystvegen**, which traverses the country's west coast from Stavanger to Haugesund and ultimately Bergen – a distance of about 190km – with two ferry trips breaking up the journey. The highway slips across a string of islands, which provide a pleasant introduction to the scenic charms of western Norway – and hint at the sterner beauty of the fjords beyond. Perhaps surprisingly, the region is primarily agricultural. The intricacies of the shoreline, together with the prevailing westerlies, made the seas so treacherous that locals mostly stuck to the land, eking out a precarious existence from the thin soils that had accumulated on the leeward sides of some of the islands.

By **car**, it takes between five and six hours to get from Stavanger to Bergen. The first of the two E39 **ferries** shuttles across the Boknafjord from Mortavika to Arsvågen, about 30km out of Stavanger (every 20–40min; 25min; car & driver 110kr); the second, another 120km beyond, links Sandvikvåg with Halhjem (every 30min to 1hr; 50min; car & driver 120kr), 40km short of Bergen. A fast and frequent **bus** service – the Kystbussen – plies the E39, taking a little under six hours to get to Bergen (8–11 daily; 390kr); it's slower, but offers much better views, than the **Hurtigbåt** passenger express boat which plies the same route (2–4 daily; 4hr; 590kr).

Haugesund

The routine industrial town of **HAUGESUND**, 90km north of Stavanger and 12km off the E39, is a small and lively port that thrived on the herring fisheries in the nineteenth century and now booms as a major player in the North Sea oil industry. It was here that the first ruler of a united Norway, **Harald Hårfagri** (Harald the Fair-Haired), was buried, and a granite obelisk, the **Haraldshaugen**, now marks his supposed resting place, by the seashore about 2km north of the centre. He gained sovereignty over these coastal districts during a decisive sea battle in 872, an achievement that, according to legend, released him from a ten-year vow not to cut his hair until he became king of all Norway. Haugesund's other claim to fame is as the town from where a local baker emigrated to the USA in an attempt to improve his fortunes; his daughter, Marilyn Monroe, was born in 1926.

Buses to Haugesund pull in on the east side of the centre, about 500m from the waterfront and the **Hurtigbåt** terminal. The **tourist office** is on the waterfront as well, at Kaigaten 1 (June–Aug Mon–Fri 10am–6pm & Sat 10am–4pm; Sept to May Mon–Fri 8am–3.30pm; ☎52 73 45 23; ⓦwww.visithaugalandet.no). Although there's no particular reason **to stay**, if you do need to, the *Rica Travel Hotel*, Skippergata 11 (☎52 86 30 00, ⒡52 86 28 25; ⓦwww.rica.no; ❺), has pleasant, comfortable doubles, and is one of several straightforward modern hotels right in the centre of town.

From Haugesund, you can either continue north on the E39 to Bergen (see p.187), or branch off east along the **E134** to Lofthus (see p.209) and Kinsarvik (see p.208), on the Hardangerfjord.

Travel details

Trains

Kristiansand to: Oslo (3–5 daily; 4hr 40min); Stavanger (3–5 daily; 3hr).
Oslo to: Arendal – change at Nelaug (3–5 daily; 4hr 40min); Egersund (3–5 daily; 6hr 40min); Kristiansand (3–5 daily; 4hr 40min); Neslandsvatn – for Kragerø (3–5 daily; 2hr 40min); Sandefjord (6–8 daily; 1hr 50min); Stavanger (3–5 daily; 7hr 30min).
Sandefjord to: Oslo (6–8 daily; 1hr 50min); Tønsberg (6–8 daily; 20min).
Stavanger to: Kristiansand (3–5 daily; 3hr); Oslo (3–5 daily; 7hr 30min).

Buses

Arendal to: Lillesand (4–5 daily; 45min); Oslo (4–5 daily; 4hr).
Grimstad to: Lillesand (4–5 daily; 15min); Oslo (4–5 daily; 4hr 30min).
Kristiansand to: Flekkefjord (1–3 daily; 2hr); Mandal (Mon–Sat hourly, 6 on Sun; 50min); Oslo (4–5 daily; 5hr 30min); Stavanger (1–3 daily; 4hr).
Oslo to: Arendal (4–5 daily; 4hr); Grimstad (4–5 daily; 4hr 30min); Kristiansand (4–5 daily; 5hr 30min); Lillesand (4–5 daily; 4hr 45min).
Lillesand to: Arendal (4–5 daily; 45min); Kristiansand (4–5 daily; 45min); Grimstad (4–5 daily, 15min); Oslo (4–5 daily; 4hr 45min).
Mandal to: Kristiansand (Mon–Sat hourly, 6 on Sun; 50min); Stavanger (1–3 daily; 3hr 30min).
Stavanger to: Bergen (8–11 daily; 5hr 40min); Haugesund (8–11 daily; 2hr); Kristiansand (1–3 daily; 4hr); Mandal (1–3 daily; 3hr 30min).

Car ferries

Egersund to: Bergen (2–4 weekly; 8hr). With Fjord line; originates in Hantsholm, Denmark.
Stavanger to: Bergen (2–6 weekly; 7hr); Haugesund (2–6 weekly; 2hr 30min). With Fjord Line; originates in Newcastle, UK.

Hurtigbåt passenger express boats

Stavanger to: Bergen (2–4 daily; 4hr); Haugesund (2–4 daily; 1hr 15min).

Central Norway

CHAPTER 3

Highlights

✳ **Sygard Grytting** Stay in
a beautifully preserved
eighteenth-century farm-
stead, near Hundorp.
See p.160

✳ **Whitewater rafting**
Brave some of Norway's
most exiting whitewater
rafting runs on the River
Sjoa. See p.161

✳ **Lake Gjende** A boat trip
along one of Norway's
most beautiful icy lakes
provides a scenic intro-
duction to the mighty
Jotunheimen mountains.
See p.166

✳ **Kongsvold Fjeldstue**
This lovely hotel occu-
pies a tastefully restored
complex of old timber
buildings, and is conven-
ient for exploring the
Dovrefjell National Park.
See p.169

✳ **Borgund stave church**
One of the best pre-
served and most harmo-
nious of Norway's 28
remaining stave
churches. See p.173

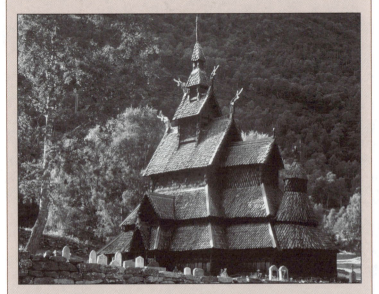

Central Norway

P reoccupied by the fjords and the long road to Nordkapp, few tourists are
tempted to explore central Norway. The Norwegians know better.
Trapped between Sweden and the fjords, this great chunk of land boasts
some of the country's finest scenery, with the forested dales that trail north and
west from Oslo heralding the region's rearing peaks. It's here, within shouting
distance of the country's principal train line and the E6 – long the main line
of communication between Oslo, Trondheim and the north – that you'll find
three of Norway's prime hiking areas. These comprise a trio of mountain
ranges, each partly lying within the Jotunheimen, Rondane and the Dovrefjell
national parks respectively. Of the three, Jotunheimen is the harshest and most
stunning, with its string of icy, jagged peaks; the Dovrefjell is more varied with
severe mountains in the west and open moors and rounded ridges in the east;
whilst Rondane, a high alpine zone, has more accessible mountains and low
vegetation. Each of the parks is equipped with well-maintained walking trails
and DNT huts, and Otta and Kongsvoll, on both the E6 and the train line,
make particularly good starting points for hiking expeditions.

Despite these attractions, it's easy to think of the whole region as little more
than a **transport corridor** whose main highways rush from Oslo across the
interior heading north and west. Of these, the **E6** is the most interesting, as it
runs up the **Gudbrandsdal** valley past several historic sights, on its way to the
Jotunheimen and Dovrefjell parks. The E6 also passes within comfortable striking distance of the intriguing old iron town of **Røros** and even better, it's the
starting point for **Highway 15** and the **E136**, two wonderful roads which
thread through the mountains to the fjords: the first goes to Lom (see p.228)
and Geiranger (see p.238), the second to Åndalsnes (see p.241). To the west of
Oslo, the **E16** is the fastest of the three main roads to the fjords, as it thumps
across to Lærdal and through the series of tunnels that enable it to fast track to
Bergen. It has much to recommend it west of Flåm (see p.216), but its dull eastern reaches are enlivened only by the handsome **Borgund stave church**.
Further south, the easterly sections of **Highway 7** and the **E134** are also pretty routine, with the attractive former silver town of **Kongsberg** being the
principal bright spot.

As you might expect, **bus** services along these main highways are excellent,
although, once you get onto the smaller roads, the bus system thins out and
travelling becomes difficult without your own vehicle. **Trains** are fast and frequent too, along the two main railway lines that cross Central Norway. The
Oslo to Bergen line shadows Highway 7 until just before Geilo, while the more
run-of-the-mill Oslo to Trondheim line passes through Hamar, where you
change for the branch line to Røros, before reaching Dombås, the junction for

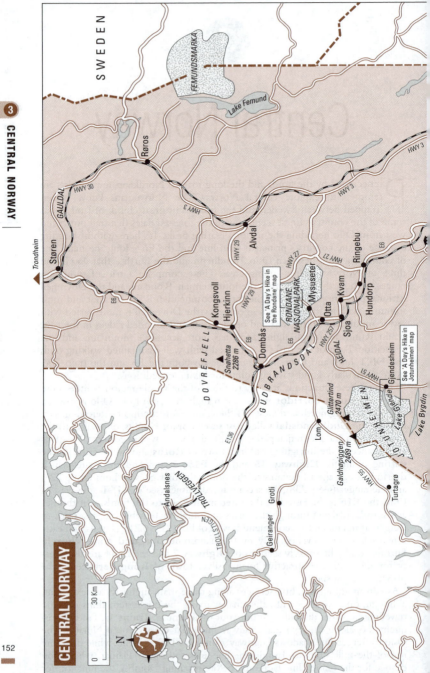

SWEDEN

FEMUNDSMARKA

Lake Femund

Central Norway

Røros

GAULDAL
HWY 30

HWY 3

HWY 3

HWY 3

Støren

HWY 29

Alvdal

HWY 27

HWY 27

Ringebu

E6

E6

Kongsvoll
Hjerkinn

HWY 29

Mysuseter

Kvam

Hundorp

See 'A Day's Hike in
the Rondane' map

RONDANE
NASJONALPARK

Otta

Sjoa

E6

E6

Dombås

HWY 257

HEIDAL

HWY 51

Gjendesheim

See 'A Day's Hike in
Jotunheimen' map

▲ Snøhetta
2286 m

DOVREFJELL

GUDBRANDSDAL

Lake Gjende

Lake Bygdin

Glittertind
2470 m

JOTUNHEIMEN

E136

Lom

Galdhøpiggen
2469 m

HWY 55

Turtagrø

Åndalsnes

TROLLVEGGEN

Grotli

Geiranger

TROLLSTIGEN

N

CENTRAL NORWAY

0   30 Km

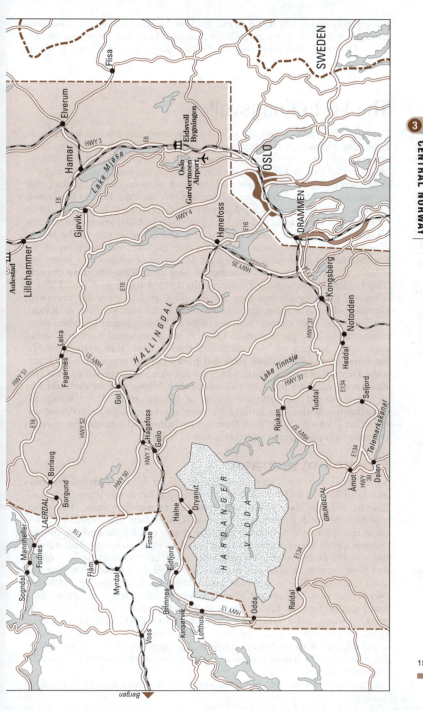

SWEDEN

Flisa

Elverum

Hamar

HWY 3

E6

Eidsvoll
Bygningen

Lake Mjøsa

Oslo
Gardermoen
Airport

OSLO

Gjøvik

HWY 4

Hønefoss

DRAMMEN

Aulestad

Lillehammer

E6

E16

E16

HWY 35

E18

Kongsberg

Leira

HALLINGDAL

7

HWY 37

Notodden

HWY 51

Fagernes

Heddal

E134

Seljord

Lake Tinnsjø

HWY 37

Telemarkskanal

Gol

HWY 52

Hagafoss

Geilo

Tuddal

Rjukan

HWY 31

Borlaug

HWY 7

HWY 50

Borgund

Dryanut

Halne

HARDANGER
VIDDA

GRUNGEDAL

E134

Åmot

HWY
38

Dalen

LÆRDAL

E16

Mannheller

Fodnes

Flåm

Finse

7

Eidfjord

Bruimnes

HWY 13

Odda

Raldal

E134

Sogndal

Myrdal

Kinsarvik

Lofthus

Voss

Bergen ▼

153

the superbly scenic run down to the fjords at Åndalsnes. In terms of **accommodation**, roadside campgrounds are commonplace, there's a reasonable supply of HI hostels, and every town and village has at least one hotel or guesthouse.

The E6 to Kongsvoll

Rushing from Oslo to Trondheim and points north, the **E6** remains the most important highway in Norway, and the only one with more than two lanes, although only in certain sections: consequently, it's kept in excellent condition, and often has the roadworks to prove it. Inevitably, the road is used by many of the region's long-distance **buses**, and for much of its length it's also shadowed by Norway's principal **train** line. Leaving Oslo, both the E6 and the railway connect with the international airport at Gardermoen (see p.68) before following the north bank of Lake Mjøsa en route to **Lillehammer**, where the 1994 Winter Olympic Games were staged, and home to one of the best of Norway's open-air folk museums. Thereafter, road and rail sweep on up the **Gudbrandsdal** river valley, within sight of a string of modest little towns and villages, with the first significant attraction here being **Ringebu stave church**. The Gudbrandsdal witnessed some of the fiercest fighting of World War II when the Norwegians and their British allies tried to stem the northward German advance, a campaign remembered at the war museum in **Kvam**. Pushing on, it's just a few kilometres more to **Sjoa**, a centre for white-water rafting, and a little further north, **Otta**, an undistinguished town but within easy reach by bus of the magnificent mountains and uplands of the **Jotunheimen** and **Rondane national parks**. Further north still is the handsome **Dovrefjell** national park, which is most pleasingly approached from tiny **Kongsvoll**. All three parks are famous for their hiking, and are networked by an extensive and well-planned system of **hiking trails**. From Kongsvoll, Trondheim is within easy striking distance; alternatively, you can detour east via either Highway 29 or 30 to **Røros**, a fascinating old iron-mining town on the mountain plateau that stretches across to Sweden.

Eidsvoll-bygningen

Some 70km from Oslo and clearly signposted off the E6, **Eidsvoll-bygningen** (mid-May to mid-June Mon–Fri 10am–3pm, Sat & Sun 10am–5pm; mid-June to mid-Aug daily 10am–5pm; mid-Aug to mid-Sept daily 10am–3pm; mid-Sept to Oct & April to mid-May Sat & Sun 11am–2pm; 40kr) is a handsome and spacious old manor house that gives a real insight into the tastes of Norway's early nineteenth-century upper class. This two-storey timber house has just over thirty rooms, with what were once the owners' living areas on the first floor, beneath the servants' quarters and above the basement kitchens. The main entrance hall is in the Neoclassical style much favoured by the Dano-Norwegian elite, its columns a suitably formal introduction to the spacious suites that lie beyond. The library is well stocked, there's a billiard room and smoking room, and a string of elegant dining rooms and bedrooms. Oriental knick-knacks and English furniture appear throughout, and the occasional mural depicts Greek mythological figures. The house was owned by the Ankers family, who made their money from the local iron works – hence the splendid cast-iron stoves.

It's a delightful ensemble, but the house owes its preservation to its historical significance rather than its aesthetics. One of the Ankers, Carsten, was a close friend and ally of the Danish crown prince **Christian Frederik**, and this connection has given the house national importance. Towards the end of the Napoleonic Wars, the Russians and British insisted the Danes be punished for their alliance with the French, and proposed taking Norway from Denmark and handing it over to Sweden. In an attempt to forestall these territorial shenanigans, the Danes dispatched Christian Frederik to Norway, where he set up home in Carsten Ankers' house in 1813, and proceeded to lobby for Norwegian support. In April of the following year more than a hundred of the country's leading citizens gathered here at Eidsvoll manor house to decide whether to accept union with Sweden or go for independence with Christian Frederik on the throne. The majority of this **National Assembly** chose independence, and set about drafting a liberal constitution based on that of the United States. Predictably, the Swedes would have none of this. Four years earlier, the Swedes had picked one of Napoleon's marshals, **Jean-Baptiste Bernadotte**, to succeed their previous king who had died without an heir. As King Karl Johan, Bernadotte was keen to flex his military muscles and, irritated by these developments, he invaded Norway in July 1814. Frederik was soon forced to abdicate and the Norwegians were pressed into union, though Karl Johan did head off much of the opposition by guaranteeing the Norwegians' new constitution and parliament, the Storting.

Carsten Ankers converted the upper storey of his home into premises for the National Assembly, comprising a handful of administrative offices plus the **Room for the Constitutional Committee**, where the original wooden benches have survived along with various landscape paintings. There's a rusticated modesty to it all which is really rather charming, and a statue of Venus has been put back in the room after years of being shunted up and down the adjoining corridors: it had originally been removed, after prolonged discussion, because the representatives considered it an erotic distraction.

The house is in the country just to the south of the industrial town of **Eidsvoll Verk**: it's signed off the E6, 2km down a byroad.

Hamar

Just beyond Eidsvoll Verk, the E6 curves round the eastern shore of Norway's largest lake, **Lake Mjøsa**, a favourite retreat for Norwegian families, whose second homes dot the surrounding farmland, woods and pastures. Before the railroad arrived in the 1880s, the lake was an important transport route, crossed by boats in summer and by horse and sleigh across its frozen surface in winter. It's also halfway country: the quiet settlements around the lake give a taste of small-town southern Norway before the E6 plunges into the wilder regions further north.

Midway round the lake, some 130km from Oslo, lies **HAMAR**, an easygoing little place of 25,000 souls, whose marinas and waterside cafés make a gallant attempt to sustain a nautical flavour. Unlikely though it may seem today, Hamar was once the seat of an important medieval bishopric, and the battered remains of its **Domkirke** (cathedral), now protected by an ambitious glass roof, are stuck out on the Domkirkeodden (cathedral point), a low, grassy headland about 2km west of the centre. The cathedral is thought to have been built by the "English pope" Nicholas Breakspear, who spent a couple of years in Norway as the papal legate before becoming Adrian IV in 1154. During the Reformation, the building was ransacked, along with the surrounding episcopal complex, and local road-builders subsequently helped themselves to the stone. Today, the ruins – whose most distinct remains are a set of four sturdy Gothic arches – form part of the **Hedmarksmuseet** (daily: mid-May to mid-June & mid-Aug to early Sept 10am–4pm; mid-June to mid-Aug 10am–6pm; 65kr), which also comprises an archeological museum and an open-air folk museum. The latter contains fifty buildings brought here from all over the region and, although it's not as comprehensive as the one in Lillehammer (see p.157), it does contain one or two particularly fine buildings, including the parsonage of Bolstad with its beautifully decorated log walls.

DS Skibladner

Hamar is as good a place as any to pick up the 130-year-old **paddle steamer**, the *DS Skibladner*, which shuttles up and down Lake Mjøsa between late June and late August: on Tuesdays, Thursdays and Saturdays the boat makes the return trip across the lake from Hamar to Gjøvik and on up to Lillehammer; on Wednesdays, Fridays and Sundays it chugs south down to Eidsvoll and back; there's no Monday service. Sailing times are available at any local tourist office or direct from the company (☎61 14 40 80; ⓦ www.skiblander.no). Tickets are bought on board: return trips from Hamar to Eidsvoll cost 250kr and last two and a half hours, those to Lillehammer cost 300kr and last eight hours. Travellers heading north may find the trip to Lillehammer tempting at first sight, but the lake is not particularly scenic, and after four tedious hours on the boat you may well feel like jumping overboard. The best bet is to take the shorter ride to Eidsvoll instead.

Practicalities

Hamar's **train station** is in the town centre beside the lake; **buses** stop outside. It's here that some trains from Oslo pause before heading up the branch line to Røros (see p.170), a fine three-and-a-half-hour ride over hills and through huge forests. Some 100m from the train station – turn left out of the terminal building along Stangevegen – is the **tourist office**, at Parkgata 2 (daily: mid-May to mid-June 10am–4pm & mid-June to mid-Aug 10am–6pm; ☎62 51 02 26). The jetty for the *DS Skibladner* ferry is 500m further along the lakeshore.

There's no pressing reason to overnight in Hamar, but the town does have a fair choice of central hotel **accommodation**. The most attractive option is the *First Hotel Victoria*, a brisk modern place down by the lakeshore not far from the train station, at Strandgata 21 (☎62 02 55 00, ⓕ62 53 32 23; ⓦ www .first-hotel-victoria.no; ❹). Alternatively, there's an HI **hostel**, *Hamar Vandrerhjem Vikingskipet*, about 2km east of the station at Åkersvikavegen 24 (☎62 52 60 60, ⓕ62 53 24 60; ⓦ www.vikingskipet-motell.no; dorm beds 135kr, doubles ❷). The hostel occupies a plain and modern, two-storey chalet complex which it shares with a motel; it's in the middle of nowhere, just across from the massive skating arena built for the 1994 Winter Olympics in the shape of an upturned Viking ship.

Lillehammer and around

LILLEHAMMER (literally "Little Hammer"), 50km north of Hamar and 180km from Oslo, is Lake Mjøsa's most worthwhile destination. In **winter**, it's one of the top Norwegian ski centres, a young and vibrant place whose rural lakeside setting and extensive cross-country ski trails contributed to its selection as host of the 1994 Olympic Winter Games. In preparation for the games, the Norwegian government spent a massive two billion kroner on the town's **sporting facilities**, which are now among the best in the country. Spread along the hillsides above the town, they include a ski-jumping tower and chair lifts, an ice hockey arena, a bobsleigh track and a cross-country skiing stadium giving access to about 30km of ski trails. Several local companies, including Saga Arrangement, Gudbrandsdalsveien 203 (☎61 26 92 44, ⓕ61 26 24 22, ⓦwww.sagaarrangement.no), offer all-inclusive winter sports and activity holiday packages. As you would expect, most Norwegians arriving here in winter come fully equipped, but it's possible to rent or buy equipment locally – the tourist office (see below) will advise.

Lillehammer remains a popular holiday spot in **summer** too. Hundreds of Norwegians hunker down in their second homes in the hills, popping into the town centre for drinks or meals. Cycling, walking, fishing and canoeing are popular pastimes at this time of year, with all sorts of possibilities for guided tours. Yet, however appealing the area may be to Norwegians, the countryside hereabouts has little of the wonderful wildness of other parts of Norway, and unless you're someone's guest or bring your own family, you'll probably feel rather out on a limb. That said, Lillehammer is not a bad place to break your journey, and there are a couple of attractions to keep you busy for a day or two – principally the **Maihaugen** open-air museum, and the country home of Norwegian author Bjørnstjerne Bjørnson, a short drive out of town at **Aulestad**. Incidentally, if you're intent on visiting several of Lillehammer's museums, a **museum pass** (200kr) makes sense; it's sold at the tourist office and participating museums.

The town

Lillehammer's briskly efficient centre, just 700m across, is tucked into the hillside above the lake, the E6 and the railway. It has just one really notable attraction, the **Kunstmuseum** at Stortorget 2 (Art Museum; late June to late Aug daily 11am–5pm; late Aug to late June Tues–Sun 11am–4pm; 60kr). Housed in a flashy modern edifice, the gallery is renowned for its temporary exhibitions of contemporary art (which often attract an extra admission charge), but the small permanent collection is also very worthwhile, comprising a representative sample of the works of most major Norwegian painters, from Johan Dahl and Christian Krohg to Munch and Erik Werenskiold. In particular, look out for the striking landscapes by one of the less familiar Norwegian artists, **Axel Revold** (1887–1962). A student of Matisse and an admirer of Cézanne, Revold spent years working abroad before returning home and applying the techniques he had learnt to his favourite subject, northern Norway: his beautifully composed and brightly coloured *Nordland* is typical.

A twenty-minute walk southeast of the town centre, on Anders Sandvigsgate, the much-vaunted **Maihaugen** (late May & late Aug to Sept daily 10am–5pm; June to mid-Aug daily 9am–6pm; Oct to mid-May Tues–Sun 11am–4pm; 70kr, late June to late Aug 90kr; ⓦwww.maihaugen.no) is the largest open-air folk museum in northern Europe. Incredibly, the whole collection represents the lifetime's work of one man, a dentist by the name of Anders Sandvig. Maihaugen holds 185 relocated buildings, brought here from all over the region, including a charming seventeenth-century presbytery (*prestegårdshagen*), a thirteenth-century stave church from Garmo, sturdy log storehouses and smokehouses, summer grazing huts and various workshops.

The key exhibits, however, are the two **farms** from Bjørnstad and Øygarden, dating from the late seventeenth century. Complete with their various outhouses and living areas, the two farms comprise 36 buildings, each with a specific function, such as food-store, sheep-shed, hay barn, stable and bathhouse. This set-up may have worked, and it certainly looks quaint, but it was, in fact, forced upon farmers by their tried-and-tested method of construction, **laft**. Based on the use of pine logs notched together at right angles, the technique strictly limited the dimensions of every building, as the usable part of the pine tree was rarely more than eight metres long. Indeed, it seems likely that many farmers would have preferred to keep their winter supplies in the main farmhouse rather than in a separate store, as implied by a draconian medieval law that stated, "When a man discovers another in his storehouse… then he may kill the man if he so wishes." Outside there are farmyard animals, and costumed guides give the lowdown on traditional rural life; in the summertime there's often the chance to have a go at domestic activities such as spinning, baking, weaving and pottery – good, wholesome fun. You can spend time too in the main museum building, which features temporary exhibitions on folkloric themes. Allow a good half-day for a visit and take advantage of the free forty-minute English-language **guided tour** (June to mid-Aug only; every other hour, on the hour, until 2hr before closing), although these are not as informative as perhaps they might be. To get to the museum, walk up Jernbanegata from the train station, turn right onto Anders Sandvigsgate, and keep going.

You might also be tempted by the **Norges Olympiske Museum** (Norwegian Olympic Museum; mid-May to Aug daily 10am–6pm; Sept to mid-May Tues–Sun 11am–4pm; 60kr), which offers a jaunty run-through of the history of the games. It's housed in Håkon Hall, one of the arenas built for the 1994 Olympics, which is itself located in Olympiaparken, about 1.5km northeast of the train station. To get there, head east from the centre along Bankgata, turn left onto Sigrid Undsets way and Olympiaparken is on the right beyond the river.

To get a glimpse the countryside surrounding Lillehammer, you might want to take a ride on the antique **DS Skibladner** paddle steamer as it shuttles up and down Lake Mjøsa: catch it from the jetty about 800m south of the centre (see p.156 for further details).

Practicalities

The E6 runs along the lakeshore about 700m below the centre of Lillehammer, where the ultra-modern **Skysstasjon**, on Jernbanetorget, incorporates both the **train station** and the **bus terminal**. The main **tourist office** is a five-minute walk uphill, off the main street, Storgata, at Elvegata 19 (early June to mid-Aug Mon–Sat 10am–8pm, Sun 11am–6pm; mid-Aug to early June Mon–Fri 10am–4pm, Sat 10am–2pm; ☎61 25 02 99; ⓦwww.lillehammerturist.no), with the usual free brochures, public transport timetables and information on local activities. **Orientation** couldn't be easier, with all activity focused on the pedestrianized part of Storgata, which runs north from Bankgata, across Jernbanegata to the tumbling River Mesnaelva; Anders Sandvigsgate and Kirkegata run parallel to Storgata – to the east and west respectively.

The tourist office can help with finding **accommodation**, or you could head straight for the popular, year-round HI **hostel**, *Lillehammer Vandrerhjem Skysstasjonen* (☎61 24 87 00, ⓕ61 26 25 66; ⓔlillehammer.hostel @vandrerhjem.no; dorm beds 175kr, doubles ❷), which occupies part of the Skysstasjon. It has thirty or so four-bunk rooms, as well as a few doubles, kitted out with smoked-glass windows and smart modern furnishings. A further budget option is the *Gjestebu Overnatting*, housed in a Swiss-style chalet just north of the centre beyond the river, at Gamleveien 110 and Løkkgata (☎ & ⓕ61 25 43 21 ⓔss-bu@online.no; ❶). It has a variety of accommodation here, from eight-bunk dorms at 100kr per person, through to apartments with kitchenettes from just 500kr per night; there are self-catering facilities too. If you're around for longer, you may want something rather more cosy, such as the *Gjestehuset Ersgaard*, Nordseterveien 201 (T61 25 06 84, F61 25 31 09; Wwww.ersgaard.no; ➍), a couple of kilometres above the centre towards Nordseter. The rooms here are neat and trim, the breakfasts are excellent, and there are fine views over the town and lake. For downtown **hotel** accommodation, a good bet is the *First Hotell Breiseth*, a large chain hotel with comfortable rooms, across from the Skysstasjon at Jernbanegata 1 (T61 24 77 77, F61 26 95 05; Wwww.firsthotels.com; ➏).

Lillehammer has a good supply of downtown **cafés** and **restaurants**. The busy *Bøndernes Hus Kafeteria*, at Kirkegata 68 (Mon–Fri 8.30am–7pm, Sat 8.30am–4pm, Sun noon–6pm), is a big, old-fashioned place with cheap and filling self-service meals. Moving up a rung, the *Vertshuset Solveig*, down an alley off the pedestrianized part of Storgata, is cafeteria-style too, but the meals are first-rate with main courses averaging around 120kr. To ring the changes, the *Teppanyaki*, Storgata 73 (T61 25 74 44), is a very good and affordably priced Japanese restaurant. In sunny weather, head for the *Rica Hotel's Terrassen*, a large and moderately priced outdoor restaurant serving all the Norwegian favourites; it's by the river on Storgata. Lillehammer also has an animated nightlife, with **bars** clustered around the river end of Storgata. Places come and go pretty fast, but the liveliest spot at the time of writing is *Nikkers Spiseri*, at Elvegata 18, a stone's throw from the main tourist office.

Around Lillehammer: Aulestad

Eighteen kilometres north of Lillehammer in the village of Follebu, is **AULESTAD** (daily: late May & Sept 11am–2.30pm, June & Aug 10am–3.30pm, July 10am–5.30pm; 50kr), a good-looking villa perched on a leafy knoll, and packed with mementoes of its former owner **Bjørnstjerne Bjørnson** (1832–1910). Little known outside Norway today, Bjørnson was a major figure in the literary and cultural revival that swept the country at the end of the nineteenth century, and made his name with the peasant tales of *Synnøve Solbakken* in 1857. Thereafter, he churned out a veritable flood of novels, stories, poems and plays, many of which romanticized Norwegian country folk and, unusually for the time, were written in Norwegian, rather than the traditional Danish. He also championed all sorts of progressive causes, from Norwegian independence through to equality of the sexes and crofters' rights, albeit from a liberal viewpoint. Nowadays, however, his main claim to fame is as author of the poem that became the national anthem. Bjørnson moved to Aulestad in 1875, and an audio-visual display inside the house gives further details on the man and his times.

To get to Aulestad, head north from Lillehammer on the E6 and turn onto Highway 255 for about 6km. To get back onto the E6 heading north, follow Highway 255 from the Bjørnson house, then turn onto Highway 254: this brings you out on the E6 halfway between Lillehammer and the Ringebu church (see below).

The Gudbrandsdal

Heading north from Lillehammer, the E6 and the railway leave the shores of Lake Mjøsa to run along the **Gudbrandsdal**, a 160km-long river valley, which was for centuries the main route between Oslo and Trondheim. Enclosed by mountain ranges, the valley has a comparatively dry and mild climate, and its fertile soils have nourished a string of farming villages since Viking times, though there was some light industrialization at the beginning of the twentieth century.

Ringebu stave church

The Gudbrandsdal begins pleasantly enough, the easy sweep of its forested hills interrupted by rocky outcrops and patches of farmland dotted with brightly coloured farmhouses. After 60km, the E6, swings past the distinctive maroon spire of **Ringebu stave church** (daily: late May & early Sept 10am–4pm; early June & late Aug 9am–4pm; mid-June to mid-Aug 8am–8pm; 40kr), which stands on a hill 1km off the E6, and a couple of kilometres south of Ringebu village. Dating from the thirteenth century, the original church was modified and enlarged in the 1630s, reflecting both an increase in the local population and the new religious practices introduced after the Reformation. At this time, the nave was broadened, the chancel replaced and an over-large tower and spire plonked on top. The exterior is rather glum, but the western **entrance portal** sports some superb if badly weathered zoomorphic carvings from the original church. **Inside**, the highlights are mainly eighteenth-century Baroque – from the florid pulpit and altar panel through to a memorial to the Irgens family, complete with trumpeting cherubs and intricate ruffs.

Hundorp and Sygard Grytting

From the church, it's 15km to the straggling village of **HUNDORP**, where a neat little quadrangle of old farm buildings has been tastefully turned into a roadside tourist stop, with a café, art gallery, shop and **hotel**. The *Hundorp Dale-Gudbrands gard* (℡61 29 71 1, ℻61 29 71 03; ⓦwww.hundorp.no; ④) is an attractive two-storey building of traditional design – timber planking on top of a stone cellar. There has been a farm here since prehistoric times, its most famous owner being a Viking warrior by the name of Dalegudbrand, who became a bitter enemy of St Olav after his enforced baptism in 1021. With a little time to spare, you can nose around the complex's immediate surroundings, where there are six small but distinct **Viking burial mounds**, as well as a rough circle of standing stones – a map in the courtyard shows how to get to them all. The stones, which date from around 700AD, mark the spot where freemen gathered in the *allthing* to discuss issues of local importance. Presided over by the most powerful local chieftain, *allthings* were held in the open-air and the assembled freemen showed their approval for any decisions taken by brandishing their weapons. The hotel is 500m from Hundorp **train station**: to get there, follow the railway lines to the north and then turn right up the access road. **Buses** stop in front of the hotel on the E6.

A further 5km north, overlooking the E6, the ancient farmstead of *Sygard Grytting* (mid-June to mid-Aug; ℡ & ℻61 29 85 88; ⓔpost@grytting.com; ④) nestles amongst the orchards, providing some of the best lodgings in Norway. The eighteenth-century farm buildings are in an almost perfect state of preservation, a beautiful ensemble with the assorted barns, outhouses and main house facing onto a tiny courtyard. One of the barns – now housing bunk beds for dormitory accommodation (300kr per person) – dates from the fourteenth century, when its upper storey was used to shelter pilgrims on the long haul north to Trondheim cathedral (p.262). Most of the double rooms are in the main house, which has been superbly renovated to provide extremely comfortable lodgings amidst antique furnishings, faded oil paintings and open fires. Breakfast is splendid too – the bread is baked on the premises – and dinner is available by prior arrangement.

The nearest **train station** is at Hundorp, 5.8km away, where long–distance **buses** will drop you too.

Kvam

Pressing on, the E6 weaves north following the course of the river to reach, after 25km, **KVAM**, a modest chipboard-producing town that witnessed some of the worst fighting of World War II. Once the Germans had occupied Norway's main towns, they set about extending their control of the main roads and railways, marching up the Gudbrandsdal in quick fashion. At Kvam, they were opposed by a scratch force of Norwegian and British soldiers, who delayed their progress despite being poorly equipped – the captain in charge of the British anti-tank guns had to borrow a bicycle to patrol his defences. The battle for the Gudbrandsdal lasted for two weeks (April 14–30, 1940) and is commemorated at the **Gudbrandsdal Krigsminnesamling** (War Museum; early May to late June & mid-Aug to mid-Sept Wed–Sun 10am–4pm; late June to mid-Aug daily 9am–5pm; 40kr), in the centre of Kvam beside the E6. In the museum, a series of first-rate multilingual displays runs through the campaign, supported by a substantial collection of military mementoes and lots of fascinating photographs. There are also informative sections on the rise of Fascism and the Norwegian resistance, plus a modest display on the role played by the villagers of Otta in the Kalmar War of 1611–13 (see p.162). Across the main street from the museum, in the **church graveyard**, is a Cross of Sacrifice, honouring the 54 British soldiers who died here while trying to halt the German advance in 1940.

Buses travel through Kvam on the E6 and there's a request stop metres from museum; Kvam **train station** is about 200m south of the museum.

Sjoa

From Kvam, it's 9km further up the valley to **SJOA** train station (a request stop), sitting below the E6 at its junction with Highway 257. The latter cuts west along the **Heidal** valley, which boasts some of the country's most exciting **white-water rafting** on the River Sjoa. The rafting season lasts from May to September, and an all-inclusive one-day rafting excursion costs around 700kr; a more strenuous two-day expedition inclusive of meals and lodgings will set you back almost three times that amount. For further details, contact local specialists, Heidal Rafting (T61 23 60 37, F61 23 60 14, Wwww. heidalrafting.no), who are based at Sjoa HI **hostel**, *Sjoa Vandrerhjem*, (T61 23 62 00, F61 23 60 14; Esjoa.hostel@vandrerhjem.no; dorm beds start at 135kr, doubles ❶; mid-May to Sept), 1300m west of Sjoa train station, near Highway 257. The hostel is perched on a wooded hillside high above the river, its main building an old log farmhouse dating from 1747, where meals are now served. Breakfasts are banquet-like, and dinners (by prior arrangement only) are reasonably priced if rather less spectacular. The hostel offers two types of accommodation: there's a no-frills dormitory block at the bottom of the slope and a handful of spacious and comfortable chalets up above. Reservations are advisable for the chalets at weekends. It's a fifteen-minute walk to the hostel from the station: head south, then turn tight into a minor road, and continue beneath the railway bridge and over the river on a suspension bridge. Once over the river, turn left at the T-junction and then follow the signs. If you're driving, just turn off the E6 along Highway 257 and watch for the sign.

Beyond the Heidal valley, Highway 257 continues west to meet Highway 51, the main access road to the east side of the Jotunheimen National Park at Gjendesheim (see p.167).

Otta

Just 10km beyond Sjoa lies **OTTA**, an unassuming little town at the confluence of the rivers Otta and Lågen. It may be dull, but if you're reliant on public transport, Otta makes an ideal base for hiking in the nearby Rondane and Jotunheimen national parks (see below), though staying in one of the parks' mountain lodges is infinitely preferable. In Otta, everything you need is within easy reach: the E6 passes within 300m of the town centre, sweeping along the east bank of the Lågen, while Highway 15 bisects the town from east to west with the few gridiron streets that pass for the centre lying a few metres to the south.

There are no sights as such, but the **statue** outside the Skysstasjon, north of Highway 15, commemorates a certain **Pillarguri**, whose alertness made her an overnight sensation. During the Kalmar War of 1611–13, one of many wars between Sweden and Denmark, a band of Scottish mercenaries hired by the king of Sweden landed in the Romsdalsfjord, intent on crossing Norway to join the Swedish army. The Norwegians – Danish subjects at that time – were fearful of the Scots, and when Pillarguri spotted them nearing Otta she dashed to the top of the nearest hill and blew her birch-bark horn to sound the alarm. The locals hastily arranged an ambush at one of the narrowest points of the trail and all but wiped the Scots out – a rare victory for peasants over professionals. One of Pillarguri's rewards was to have a hill named after her and today the stiff hike along the footpath up the forested slopes to the summit, **Pillarguritoppen** (853m), across the Otta river south of the centre, is a popular outing.

Clumped together in the Skysstasjon on the north side of Highway 15, are the **train station**, **bus terminal** and exceptionally helpful **tourist office** (July–Aug Mon–Fri 8.30am–7pm, Sat & Sun 11am–6pm; Sept–June Mon–Fri 8.30am–4pm; ☎61 23 66 50, ⓦwww.vistrondane.com), which can provide local bus timetables, book accommodation, reserve Lake Gjende boat tickets, and sell DNT membership, fishing licences and a good range of hiking maps. One of the best **accommodation** options is *Grand Gjestegård*, a large pension-cum-hotel with simple rooms furnished in modern style (☎61 23 12 00, Ⓕ61 23 04 62; ❸): it's across from the train station at the corner of Ola Dahls gate. A few metres further to the west along Ola Dahls gate, the recently revamped chain hotel *Norlandia Otta Hotell*, (☎61 23 00 33, Ⓕ61 23 15 24; ⓦwww. norlandia.no; ❹) makes a reasonable alternative. The nearest **campsite**, the year-round *Otta Camping* (☎61 23 03 09) lies about 1500m from the town centre on the wooded banks of the River Otta, with cabins (❷) and space for tents: to get there, cross the bridge on the south side of the centre, turn right and keep going. Otta's choice of **places to eat** is rather poor, too, though there is one good spot, the *Pillarguri* on Storgata (☎61 23 01 04), a cosy café–restaurant, offering a good range of traditional Norwegian dishes; it's normally open daily from noon to 10pm.

Otta is within easy striking distance of the main access points to two **national parks** – **Rondane**, just 20km or so to the east, and the **Jotunheimen**, about 90km to the southwest along highways 15 and 51. There are **buses** from Otta bus station to the parks too, but only in summer. These are Otta to Spranget for the Rondane (late June to mid-Aug 2 daily; 50min) and Otta to Gjendesheim for Jotunheimen (late June to Aug 1–2 daily; 2hr). Return buses leave about five hours after the arrival of the first bus of the day.

From Otta to the western fjords

Running west from Otta, **Highway 15** sweeps along a couple of wide river valleys to **Lom** (see p.228), where there's a choice of wonderful routes into the western fjords: You can either carry on along Highway 15 towards Stryn (see p.233), or branch off north onto the nerve-jangling **Ørnevegen** (Eagle's

Highway; Highway 63) to Geiranger (see p.238). Alternatively, you can turn off Highway 15 at Lom, onto the **Sognefjellsveg** (Highway 55) which climbs steeply to the south, travelling along the western flank of the Jotunheimen National Park and offering breathtaking views of its jagged peaks before careering down to Sogndal (see p.235).

Three times a day, the Nor-Way Bussekspress Oslo–Måløy **bus** runs along Highway 15 from Otta to Stryn. From mid-June to August, there is a connecting bus service from Grotli or Langvetn on Highway 15, which runs along Highway 63 to Geiranger and ultimately Åndalsnes (1–2 daily). The journey time from Otta to Lom is one hour, three hours to Stryn. There are no bus services along the Sognefjellsveg.

Rondane Nasjonalpark

Spreading north and east from Otta towards the Swedish border, the **Rondane Nasjonalpark**, established in 1962 as Norway's first national park, is now one

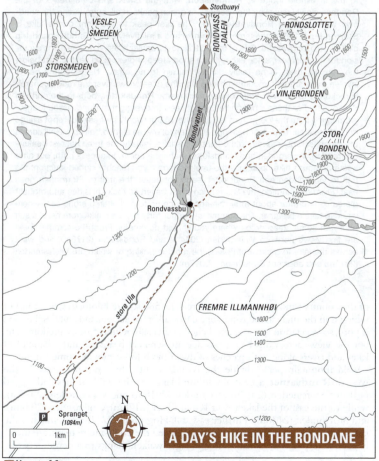

A DAY'S HIKE IN THE RONDANE

A day's hike in the Rondane

Start and finish: Spranget car park (altitude 1084m).
Distance: 17km return.
Time: 8hr.
Highest point: Storronden (2138m).
Maps: 1718 I Rondane (M711); Rondane 1:100,000.
Transport: Bus from Otta to Spranget car park (late June to mid-Aug 2 daily; 50min); or taxi.
Accommodation: *Rondvassbu* staffed DNT lodge (see p.166); or in Otta (see p.161).

Branching off the E6 near Otta, a signposted, 20km-long mountain road wriggles its way up to **Mysuseter**, a sprawling chalet settlement on the edge of the Rondane national park. Beyond the village, a narrow toll road nudges 5km further east to the **Spranghet car park**, the starting point of this one-day hike, and no more than a wind-buffeted field with uninterrupted views into the park.

From the car park, it's a ninety-minute level walk along the service road northeast to the lakeshore lodge at **Rondvassbu**, with the bleak and bare peaks of the Rondane slowly revealing themselves – a dozen peaks in all, surrounding the shadowy waters of the **Rondvatnet lake**. The first peak to the right of the lake is **Storronden** (2138m), the target of this hike and a relatively easy five-hour round-trip climb from Rondvassbu. One of the park's most popular hikes, it makes a fine excursion for the beginner, since except for a short steep and exposed section just below the summit, there is no really difficult terrain to negotiate. Neighbouring peaks involve more arduous mountain hiking with the finest views over the range generally reckoned to be from **Vinjeronden** and nearby **Rondslottet**, both to the north of Storronden. For these longer hikes, you'll need to overnight at *Rondvassbu* lodge.

Emerging from the lodge, turn left and after about twenty metres you'll spot a large map of the area. Take your bearings and then follow the signed trail up the hill across the rough, scrabbly terrain to the right of the lake. Initially, the three nearest peaks – Storronden, Vinjeronden and Rondslottet – share a common access path, but after about an hour's hike up across the treeless terrain you reach a signed junction: the trail to Vinjeronden and Rondslottet leads northeast, the trail to Storronden goes east. From the junction, the Storronden track traverses rocky hillsides and modest plateaux, and after about forty minutes you come to a sheltered stone seat where you can take a breather. The summit is another forty minutes' hike from here, a stiff haul with some steep drops where you should be careful. From the summit, there are fine views north to Vinjeronden (2044m) and Rondslottet (2178m), and west across the lake to a circle of peaks, the most imposing of which are Veslesmeden (2015m) and adjacent Storsmeden (2017m).

of the country's most popular hiking areas. Its 580 square kilometres, one third of which is in the high alpine zone, appeal to walkers of all ages and abilities. The soil is poor, so vegetation is sparse and lichens, especially reindeer moss, predominate, but the views across this bare landscape are serenely beautiful, and a handful of lakes and rivers along with patches of dwarf birch forest provide some variety.

Wild mountain peaks divide the Rondane into three distinct areas. To the west of **Rondvatnet**, a centrally located lake, are the wild cirques and jagged peaks of Storsmeden (2017m), Sagtinden (2018m) and Veslesmeden (2015m), while to the east of the lake tower Rondslottet (2178m), Vinjeronden (2044m), and Storronden (2138m). Further east still, Høgronden (2115m) dominates the landscape. The mountains, ten of which exceed the 2000-metre mark, are mostly accessible to any reasonably fit and eager walker, thanks to a dense network

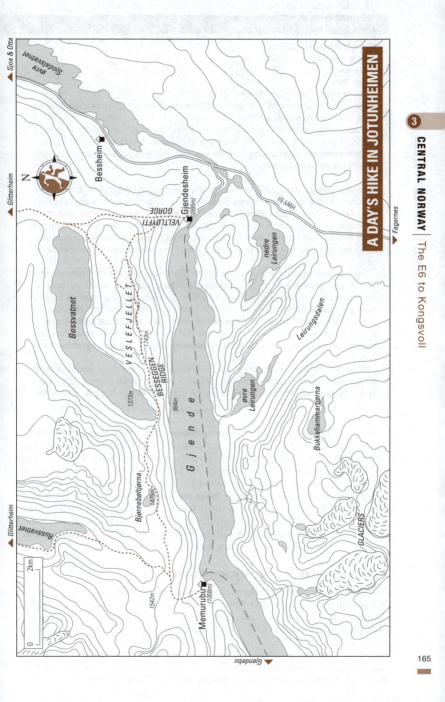

N

▲ *Sjoa & Otta*

øvre Sjodalsvatnet

Bessheim

▲ *Glitterheim*

GJENDESHEIM

VETLÅFELL GORGE

Gjendesheim
(995m)

HWY 51

▲ *Fagernes*

Bessvatnet

VESLEFJELLET

nedre
Leirungen

Leirungsdalen

1743m

BESSEGGEN RIDGE

1373m

984m

G j e n d e

øvre
Leirungen

Bukkehammartjørna

Bjørnebøltjørna

1475m

▲ *Glitterheim*

Russvatnet

1542m

Memurubu
(1008m)

GLACIERS

2km

0

▼ *Gjendebu*

A day's hike in Jotunheimen

Start: Memurubu (1008m).
Finish: Gjendesheim (995m).
Distance: 15km.
Time: 6hr.
Highest point: Besseggen Ridge (1743m).
Maps: 1617 IV Gjende (M711); 1618 III Glittertinden (M711). Jotunheimen (No. 45) 1:100,000. All produced by Statens Kartverk.
Transport: Bus from Otta to Gjendesheim (late June to Aug 1–2 daily; 2hr); boat from Gjendesheim to Memurubu (late June to mid-Sept 1–3 daily; ☏61 23 85 09).
Accommodation: *Gjendesheim*, full-service DNT hut (see p.167); *Memurubu*, full-service private hut (see p.167).

Norway's best-known day hike, across the **Besseggen ridge** high above Lake Gjende, links the **mountain lodges** of Memurubu and Gjendesheim. Stretching west from Gjendesheim, **Lake Gjende** is one of Norway's most beautiful and most famous lakes – not least because Ibsen had his character Peer Gynt tumble from the ridge into the lake on the back of a reindeer. Some 18km long and 146m deep, the lake's glacially-fed waters are tinted green due to the presence of myriad clay particles.

The hike east from the *Memurubu* lodge to Gjendesheim is easy to complete in a day. If you do the hike in the opposite direction, you can return by boat to Gjendesheim in the evening, but you'll have to calculate your speed accurately to meet the boat at *Memurubu* – and that isn't easy. Whichever direction you take, be sure to confirm boat departure times before you set out, and check weather conditions too, as snow and ice can linger into July. If you have more time, consider spending another day hiking back from **Gjendebu** lodge, at the western end of Lake Gjende.

Starting at the **Memurubu** jetty, begin by walking behind the lodge along the vehicle access road until – after about two minutes – you encounter a sign to Gjendebu. Ignore this and keep to the road as far as the gate. Go through the gate and on the

of trails and hiking huts. For **accommodation**, the *Rondvassbu lodge* (late June to mid-Sept; ☏61 23 18 66; ❶) is a typical staffed DNT lodge, with more than one hundred beds, filling meals and pleasant service. For all but the briefest of hikes, it's best to arrive at the lodge the day before to have a chance of starting first thing the next morning. If, however, visibility is poor or you don't fancy a climb, there is a charming summer **boat service** (July–Aug 2–3 daily; 30min each way; 35kr each way, 50kr return) to the far end of Rondvatnet, from where it takes about two and a half hours to walk back to *Rondvassbu* along the lake's steep western shore. In the eastern Rondane, the gentle **Alvdal Vestfjell** appeals to older walkers and families with small children.

Jotunheimen Nasjonalpark

Norway's most celebrated hiking area, **Jotunheimen** ("Home of the Giants") **Nasjonalpark** lives up to its name. Pointed summits and undulating glaciers dominate the skyline, soaring high above river valleys and lake-studded plateaux. Covering only 3900 square kilometres, the park offers an amazing concentration of high peaks, more than two hundred of which rise above 1900 metres. In Jotunheimen, you will find Norway's (and Northern Europe's) two highest peaks, Galdhøpiggen (2469m) and Glittertind (2464m), while Norway's highest waterfall, **Vettisfossen**, with a 275-metre drop, is here too, a far side you'll see the clearly signposted trail to Besseggen ridge, Gjendesheim and Glitterheim. Follow the trail up towards the first ridge with the *Memurubu* lodge behind. The path, up to 4m wide, is marked by DNT "T"s and worn to a different colour from its surroundings. After about twenty minutes you pass the Glitterheim turn-off, and about thirty minutes after that you reach the first ridge, from where the path offers extravagant views of the lake. Here the path is clearly marked by cairns and DNT "T"s. Some 1hr 30min into the walk, you cross a plateau beside the southern shore of tiny lake **Bjørnbøltjørna** (altitude 1475m). Afterwards, continue to climb up the path across the boulder-strewn terrain until – some two hours from *Memurubu* – you catch sight of **Bessvatnet**, a lake that's frozen for most of the year but otherwise blue, in contrast with Lake Gjende. After 2hr 30min you arrive at the base of the **Besseggen ridge**. This is a good spot to take a break and enjoy the views over the two lakes before tackling the ridge itself.

The thirty-minute scramble up to the peak of the ridge is very steep, with ledges that are, on occasion, chest high; you need to be moderately fit to negotiate them. In places, the ridge narrows to fifty metres with a sheer drop to either side, but you can avoid straying close to the edge by following the DNT "T"s. The views are superlative, the drops disconcerting – and a head for heights is essential. Beyond the peak of the ridge, the trail crosses a small plateau before meeting rising ground at the start of another, much less demanding thirty-minute scramble up to a wide plateau, where a huge cairn is clearly visible. Hike along the path to the cairn, from where you can readily discern the wide trail that leads across the mountainsides to the lodge at Gjendesheim, a two-hour hike from this point. Beyond the cairn, ignore a second turning to Glitterheim and push on across the wide plateau that leads to the **Veltløyfti gorge**, where a slippery scramble with steep drops requires care. The trail is, however, well-marked and the final destination clearly visible. **Gjendesheim**, with its lodge and ferry dock, has long been a popular base for explorations of Jotunheimen; the first huts at Gjendesheim and Memurubu were built in the 1870s. Indeed, the original hut at Gjendesheim is still visible, located on the south side of the River Sjoa and accessible by row-boat.

short walk from the Vetti lodge on the west side of the park. A network of footpaths and mountain lodges lattices the park, but be warned that the weather is very unpredictable and the winds can be bitingly cold – take care and always come well equipped.

There are no public roads into the park; visitors usually walk or ski into the interior from the Sognefjellsveg (Hwy 55) in the west (see p.227) or make the slightly easier approach from the east via **Gjendesheim**, 2km off Highway 51, some 90km from Otta. Gjendesheim is no more than a couple of buildings, but one of them is the excellent *Gjendesheim* DNT lodge (mid-June to mid-Sept & mid-Feb to mid-April; ☎61 23 89 10; ❶), at the eastern tip of long and slender Lake Gjende. **Boats** (late June to mid-Sept 1–3 daily; ☎61 23 85 09) travel the length of the lake, connecting with mountain trails and dropping by two more **lodges**. These are the privately-owned lodge at *Memurubu* (mid-June to mid-Sept; ☎61 23 89 99; ⓦwww.memurubu.no; ❷), halfway along the lake's north shore, and *Gjendebu's* staffed DNT lodge (late June to mid-Sept & early March to early April; ☎61 23 89 44; ❶), right at the lake's western end. A single fare from Gjendesheim to Memurubu costs 60kr, Gjendebu 80kr; returns are twice that unless you make the round trip on the same day, in which case fares are 80kr and 120kr respectively. It takes the boat twenty minutes to reach Memurubu, forty five for Gjendebu. Obviously enough, you get to see a slice

…d avoid a hike by riding the boat and sleeping at the lodges
…e in bad weather.

…s and the route to Åndalsnes

…the E6 and the railway lead 45km north to **DOMBÅS**, a mundane …settlement that boasts little more than a couple of good **places to** …se to the junction of the E6 and the E136 is the best option, the *Dombås Ho…* (☎61 24 10 01, ℱ61 24 14 61; ❺, s/r ❹), whose main building, with its distinctive high gables and handsome public rooms, overlooks the Gudbrandsdal. Most of the bedrooms are tucked away in the modern annexe round the back, and those in the main building, dating from the 1910s, are a little worse for wear, though the views down the valley more than compensate. A cheaper option, but also with good valley views is Dombås' HI **hostel** (☎61 24 09 60, ℱ61 24 13 30; ⓦwww.dombas-hotel.no; ❷, dorm beds 180kr), a comfortable complex of mountain huts way up on the hillside above the E6. To get there, head north out of town along the E6 for around 1km and follow the signs up the hill.

Beyond Dombås, the E6 and the main train line head north through the mountains towards Kongsvoll (see below) and ultimately Trondheim (p.258), whilst the E136 and the dramatic Rauma branch line lead west to the port of Åndalsnes (see p.241).

The E136 and the Rauma branch line

Dombås is where the **E136** and the **Rauma train line** (2–3 daily; 1hr 20min) branch west for the thrilling 110-kilometre rattle down to Åndalsnes (see p.241). The journey begins innocuously enough with road and rail slipping along a ridge high above a wide, grassy valley, but soon the landscape gets wilder as both nip into the hills. After 65km, they reach **Kylling bru**, an ambitious stone railway bridge, 56m high and 76m long, which spans the Rauma river. Pressing on, it's a further 20km to the shadowy hamlet of **Marstein** with the grey, cold mass of the **Trollveggen** ("Troll's Wall") rising straight ahead. At around 1100m, the Trollveggen incorporates the highest vertical overhanging mountain wall in Europe and as such is a favourite with experienced mountaineers, though it wasn't actually scaled until 1967. Somehow, the E136 and the railway manage to defile through the mountains and soon afterwards they slide down to Åndalsnes, the fjord glistening beyond.

Hjerkinn

Staying on the E6 north of Dombås, it's just 30km to the outpost of **HJERKINN**, stuck out on bare and desolate moorland, its pint-sized military base battered down against the wind and snow of winter. The base overlooks the junction of the E6 and Highway 29, as does the adjacent wooden **train station**, with its brightly painted window frames. Since medieval times there's been a mountain inn at Hjerkinn, a former staging post on the long trail to Trondheim, 170km away. The present structure, the *Hjerkinn Fjellstue* (☎61 24 29 27, ℱ61 24 29 49; ⓦwww.hjerkinn.no; ❹) is a fitting successor, its two expansive wooden buildings featuring big open fires and breezy pine furniture. The restaurant is good, too – try the reindeer culled from local herds – and there's horse-riding from the stables next door. Set on a hill overlooking the moors, the inn sits beside Highway 29, just over 2km from the train station.

Branching off the E6 onto Highway 29 at Hjerkinn is the shortest route to Røros (see p.170) if you're travelling from the south though, taking Highway 30, further north (see below), is a much more scenic approach.

Kongsvoll and the Dovrefjell Nasjonalpark

Beyond Hjerkinn, the E6 slices across the barren uplands before descending into a narrow ravine, the **Drivdal**. Hidden away here, just 12km from Hjerkinn, is **KONGSVOLL**, home to a tiny train station and the delightful *Kongsvold Fjeldstue* (☎72 40 43 40, ℻72 40 43 41; ⓦwwwkongsvold.no; ➍), which provides some of Norway's most charming accommodation. As at Hjerkinn, an inn has stood here since medieval times and the present complex, a huddle of tastefully restored timber buildings with sun-bleached reindeer antlers tacked onto the outside walls, dates back to the eighteenth century. Once a farm as well as an inn, its agricultural days are recalled by several outbuildings such as the little turf-roofed storehouses (*stabbur*), the lodgings for farmhands (*karstuggu*) and the barn (*låve*), atop which is a bell that was rung to summon the hands from the fields. The main building retains many of its original features and also holds an eclectic sample of antiques. The bedrooms, dotted round the compound, are of the same high standard – and the old vagabonds' hut (*fantstuggu*), built outside the white picket fence that once defined the physical limits of social respectability, contains the cosiest family rooms imaginable. Dinner is served in the excellent **restaurant**, where prices are reasonable, and the complex also includes a **café** and a Dovrefjell Nasjonalpark **information centre**. The inn makes a lovely spot to break your journey and an ideal base for hiking into the park, which extends to the east and west. If you're arriving by **train**, note that only some services stop at Kongsvoll station, 500m down the valley from the inn – and then only by prior arrangement with the conductor.

From Kongsvoll, it's about 40km to **Oppdal**, an uninspiring crossroads town where the Kristiansund road (Highway 70) meets the E6. Moving on, it's another 70km north to **Støren**, just 50km short of Trondheim, where you can turn off onto Highway 30 for the 100km drive along the picturesque **Gauldal** valley to Røros (see p.170).

Dovrefjell Nasjonalpark

Bisected by the railway and the E6, **Dovrefjell Nasjonalpark** is one of the more accessible of Norway's national parks. A comparative minnow at just 265 square kilometres, it comprises two distinct zones: spreading east from the E6 are the marshes, open moors and rounded peaks that characterize much of eastern Norway, while to the west the mountains become increasingly steep and serrated as they approach the jagged spires backing onto Åndalsnes (see p.241).

Hiking trails and **huts** are scattered across the western part of the Dovrefjell. **Kongsvoll** (see above) makes an ideal starting point: it's possible to hike all the way from here to the coast, but this takes all of nine or ten days. A more feasible expedition for most visitors is the two-hour circular walk up to the mountain plateau, or a two-day, round-trip hike to one of the four ice-tipped peaks of mighty **Snøhetta**, at around 2200m. There's accommodation five hours' walk west from Kongsvoll at the unstaffed **Reinheim hut** (mid-Feb to mid-Oct). On the first part of any of these three hikes, you're likely to spot **musk ox**, the descendants of animals imported from Greenland in the 1950s. Conventional wisdom is that these chunky beasts will ignore you if you ignore them and keep at a distance of at least 100m. They are, however, not afraid of humans and will charge if irritated – retreat as quickly and quietly as possible if one starts snorting and scraping. Further hiking details and maps are available at the park **information centre** in the *Kongsvold Fjeldstue* (see above).

Røros and around

Located on a treeless mountain plateau, **RØROS** is a blustery place even on a summer's afternoon, when it's full of day-tripping tourists surveying the old part of town. Little changed since its days as a copper-mining centre, Røros is a unique and remarkable survivor – until the mining company went bust in 1977, mining had been the basis of life here since the seventeenth century. This dirty and dangerous work was supplemented by a little farming and hunting, and life for the average villager can't have been anything but hard. Unusually, Røros' wooden houses, some of them 300 years old, have escaped the fires that have devastated so many of Norway's timber-built towns and as a consequence the town is on UNESCO's World Heritage list. Firm regulations now protect this rare townscape and changes to its grass-roofed cottages are strictly regulated. Film companies regularly use the town as a backdrop for their productions – it featured as a labour camp in the 1971 Anglo-Norwegian film of *One Day in the Life of Ivan Denisovich*, a choice of location that gives something of the flavour of the place.

The town centre

In the town centre, **Røros kirke** (early to mid-June & mid-Aug to mid-Sept Mon–Sat 11am–1pm; late June to mid-Aug Mon–Sat 10am–5pm, Sun 2–4pm; mid-Sept to May Sat 11am–1pm; 25kr) is the most obvious target for a stroll, its heavy tower reflecting the wealth of the early mine owners. Built in 1784, and once the only stone building in Røros, the church is more like a theatre

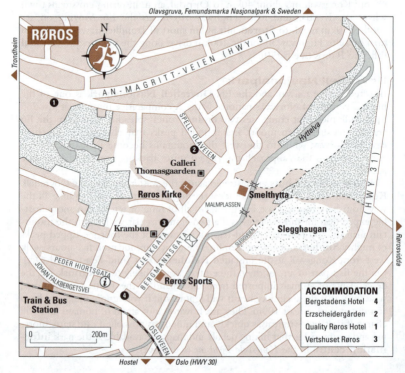

Olavsgruva, Femundsmarka Nasjonalpark & Sweden ▲

RØROS N

AN-MAGRITT-VEIEN (HWY 31)

Trondheim

SPELL-OLAVEIEN

Hyttelva

Galleri
Thomasgaarden ▣

Røros Kirke ✝
MALMPLASSEN

■ Smelthytta

Krambua ▣

Slegghaugan

KJERKGATA

BERGMANNSGATA

SLEGGVEIEN

HWY 31

Rørosvidda

PEDER HIORTSGATA

ℹ

JOHAN FALKBERGETSVEI

Røros Sports

Train & Bus
Station

ACCOMMODATION	
Bergstadens Hotel	4
Erzscheidergården	2
Quality Røros Hotel	1
Vertshuset Røros	3

0   200m

Hostel ▼   ▼ Oslo (HWY 30)

OSLOVEIEN

than a religious edifice. A huge structure capable of seating 1600 people, it was designed, like the church at Kongsberg (see p.176), to overawe rather than inspire. Its pulpit is built directly over the altar to emphasize the importance of the priest's word, and a two-tiered gallery runs around the nave. Occasional mine labourers were accommodated in the gallery's lower level, while "undesirables" were compelled to sit above, and even had to enter via a separate, external staircase. Down below, the nave exhibited even finer distinctions: every pew nearer the front was a step up the social ladder, while mine managers vied for the curtained boxes, each of which had a well-publicized annual rent; the monarch (or royal representative) had a private box commanding views from the back. These byzantine social arrangements are explained in depth during the **guided tour** (late June to mid-Aug, 1 daily in English), the cost of which is included in the admission fee.

Immediately below the church, on either side of the river, lies the oldest part of Røros. A huddle of sturdy cross-timbered smelters' cottages, storehouses and workshops squat in the shadow of the **slegghaugan** (slagheaps) – more tourist attraction than eyesore, and providing fine views over the town and beyond. Here, next to the river, the rambling main works, the *Smelthytta*, has been tidily restored and faces on to **Malmplassen** ("ore-place"), the wide earthen square where the ore drivers arrived from across the mountains to have their cartloads of ore weighed on the outdoor scales. In the square too, hung in a rickety little tower, is the smelters' bell, which used to be rung at the start of each shift. Malmplassen is at the top of Bergmannsgata which, together with parallel Kjerkgata, forms the heart of today's Røros. Conspicuously, the smaller artisans' dwellings, some of which have become **art and craft shops**, are set near the works, away from the rather more spacious dwellings once occupied by the owners and overseers, which cluster round the church.

The main works, the **Smelthytta** (literally "melting hut"; late June to mid-Aug daily 10am–7pm; early June & mid-Aug to Sept daily 10am–4pm; Oct-May daily 11am–2pm; 60kr) has been converted into a museum, a large three-storey affair whose most interesting section explains the intricacies of copper production in the cavernous hall which once housed the smelter. Dioramas illuminate every part of the process, and there are production charts, samples of ore and a potted history of the company – supported by a comprehensive English-language leaflet available free at reception. There's actually not that much to look at – the building was gutted by fire in 1975 – and so the museum is perhaps for genuine mining enthusiasts only.

Practicalities

The **train** and **bus stations** are at the foot of the town centre, a couple of minutes' walk from the **tourist office** on Peder Hiortsgata (late June to late Aug Mon–Sat 9am–6pm, Sun 10am–4pm; late Aug to mid-June Mon–Fri 9am–3.30pm, Sat 10.30am–12.30pm; ☎72 41 11 65; ⓦwww.rorosinfo.com), where you can pick up a comprehensive booklet on Røros and the surrounding region. It also has details of local **hikes** across the uplands that encircle the town, one of the more popular being the five-hour trek east to the self-service DNT hut at Marenvollen. The uplands are also popular with **cross-country skiers** in the winter, and the tourist office has a leaflet mapping out several possible skiing routes.

Røros makes for a pleasant overnight stay, which is just as well given its solitary location and the infrequency of trains onto Trondheim. There's a reasonable range of central **accommodation** too. Easily the best deal in town is the *Erzscheidergården* guesthouse, Spell-Olaveien 6 (☎72 41 11 94, ⓕ72 41 19 60;

❹), with a handful of charming, unassuming rooms in its main wooden building. Some of the rooms have fine views over the town, and there's an attractive subterranean breakfast area and a cosy lounge. With less charm, but also worth considering are the *Quality Røros Hotel*, An-Magritt-veien (☎72 40 80 00, ⓕ72 40 80 01; ⓦwww.choicehotels.no; ❻, s/r ❹), a big modern place on the northern edge of the centre, and *Vertshuset Røros*, Kjerkgata 34 (☎72 41 24 11, ⓕ72 41 03 64; ⓦwww.roroshotel.no; ❹), a guesthouse with cramped doubles that's bang in the centre of town. Last choice would be *Bergstadens Hotel*, Osloveien 2 (☎72 40 60 80, ⓕ72 40 60 81; ⓦwww.bergstaden.no; ❺, s/r ❹), conveniently located at the foot of Bergmannsgata, but otherwise a routine, modern hotel with workaday double rooms. The year-round HI **hostel** *Røros Vandrerhjem*, Øra 25 (☎72 41 10 89, ⓕ72 41 23 77, ⓔroros.hostel @vandrerhjem.no; dorm beds 190kr, doubles ❷) is situated in an unappealing concrete block, next to a sports ground, about 800m south of the train station.

When it comes to **food**, Røros is no gourmet's paradise, but there are enough choices to get by. The cosiest café is at *Galleri Thomasgaarden,* Kjerkgata 48, which doubles as a ceramics gallery and serves up tasty snacks and sandwiches as well as waffles (Mon–Fri 10am–4.30pm, Sat 10am–3pm & Sun noon–4pm). Further along Kjerkgata, at no. 28, is another good option, the *Krambua* restaurant and bar (Mon–Sat 11am to midnight or later, Sun noon–midnight), which offers filling daily specials, and traditional Norwegian dishes such as *Kjøttkaker i Brun saus* (meatballs in brown sauce) for around 100kr. Finally, the *Hotel Røros* has a good, if slightly formal, restaurant that's generally reckoned to serve the best seafood in town (daily until 10pm).

Around Røros: Olavsgruva copper mine and Femundsmarka Nasjonalpark

Some 13km east of Røros off Highway 31, the **Olavsgruva**, one of the old copper mines, has been kept open as a museum, and there are daily guided tours of its workings throughout the summer (early to mid-June & late Aug to early Sept Mon–Sat 2 daily, Sun 1 daily; late June to mid-Aug 5 daily; by prior arrangement early Sept to May Sat 1 daily; 60kr; book at Røros tourist office). The temperature down the mine is a constant 5°C, so remember to take something warm to wear – you'll need sturdy shoes too.

Still further east, some 40km from Røros, tucked in tight between the Swedish border and the elongated Lake Femund, the 385 square kilometres that make up the remote **Femundsmarka Nasjonalpark** encompass a wide variety of terrains. In the north are pine forests, marshes, lakes and rivers, which give way in the south to bare mountains and plateaux. There is no road access into the Femundsmarka, but a minor road leads from Røros to **Synnervika**, on the west side of **Lake Femund**, from where a **passenger boat**, the *M/S Fæmund* (early June to late Sept 2–4 weekly), shuttles around the lake, stopping at several remote outposts and jetties. Among the latter, several give access to the limited network of unstaffed DNT huts and hiking trails which cross the park; the jetties at **Røa** (30 min from Synnervika) and **Haugen** (1hr 15min) are perhaps the handiest. Sailing schedules are available from Røros tourist office. Several Røros-based operators run canoeing and fishing expeditions into the park – *Røros Sports*, at Bergmannsgata 13 (☎72 41 12 18), is as good as any.

From Oslo to the western fjords

The forested dales and uplands that fill out much of central Norway between Oslo and the western fjords rarely inspire: in almost any other European country, these elongated valleys would be attractions in their own right, but here in Norway they simply can't compare with the mountains and fjords of the north and west. Almost everywhere, the architecture is routinely modern and most of the old timber buildings, which once lined the valleys, are long gone – except in the open-air museums that are a feature of nearly every town hereabouts. Neither does it help that the towns and villages of the region almost invariably string along the roads in long, seemingly aimless ribbons.

Of the three major trunk roads crossing the region, the **E16** is the fastest, a quick 320-kilometre trip from Oslo to both the fjord ferry near Sogndal (see p.225) and the 24km-long tunnel leading to Flåm (see p.216). Its closest rival, the slower **Highway 7**, branches off the E16 at Hønefoss and, after a scenic wiggle along the edge of the Hardangervidda plateau, finally reaches the coast at Eidfjord near Hardangerfjord, a distance of 334km; Highway 7 also intersects with **Highway 50**, offering another possible route to Flåm. For most of its length, Hwy 7 is shadowed by the **Oslo–Bergen railway**, though they part company when the train swings north for its spectacular traverse of the mountains. The third road, the **E134**, covers the 418km from Drammen near Oslo to Haugesund, passing near Odda on the Sørfjord after 323km. Again, it's a slower route, but has the advantage of passing through the attractive town of **Kongsberg**, and near to **Rjukan**, with its fascinating World War II history.

Regular long-distance **buses** serve all three of the major roads.

The E16 to Leira and Borgund

It's 180km along the **E16** from Oslo through a series of river valleys to ribbon-like **LEIRA**, where you can break your journey at the HI **hostel** (☎61 35 95 00, ⓔleira.hostel@vandrerhjem.no; late May to early Aug; dorm beds 115kr, doubles ❶), which occupies part of a roadside high-school complex. At the next village of **Fagernes,** Highway 51 branches north, to run along the eastern edge of the Jotunheimen Nasjonalpark, passing near Gjendesheim and its lodge (see p.166) before finally joining Hwy 15 west of Otta (see p.161).

Back on the E16, about 30km west of Fagernes, the scenery begins to improve as you approach the coast. The road dips and weaves from dale to dale, slipping between the hills until it reaches the **Lærdal valley,** whose wooded slopes shelter the stepped roofs and angular gables of the **Borgund stave church** (daily: mid-June to mid-Aug 8am–8pm; May to mid-June & mid-Aug to Sept 10am–5pm; 50kr). One of the best preserved stave churches in Norway, Borgund was built beside what was one of the major pack roads between east and west, until bubonic plague wiped out most of the local population in the fourteenth century. Much of the church's medieval appearance has been preserved; its tiered exterior is protected by shingles and decorated with finials in the shape of dragons and Christian crosses, that culminate in a slender ridge turret. A rickety wooden gallery runs round the outside of the church, and the doors sport an intense swirl of carved animals and foliage. Inside, the dark, pine-scented nave is framed by the upright wooden posts that define this style of church architecture.

Beyond the church, the valley grows wilder as the E16 travels the 45km down to **Fodnes**, where a 24hr car ferry zips over to **Manheller** (every 30min;

Stave churches

Of Norway's 29 surviving **stave churches**, the majority are in the central region. They represent the country's most distinctive architectural attribute. The key feature of their design is that the timbers are placed vertically into the ground – in contrast to the log-bonding technique used by the Norwegians for everything else. Thus, a stave wall consisted of vertical planks slotted into sills above and below, with the sills connected to upright posts – or **staves**, hence the name – at each corner. Within this general concept, which originated in the twelfth century, there are several variations: in some churches, nave and chancel form a single rectangle; in others the chancel is narrower than, and tacked on to, the nave. External wooden galleries are a common feature, as are shingles and finials. The most distinctive and fetching of these churches are those where the central section of the nave has been raised above the aisles to create – from the outside – an almost pagoda-like effect. In virtually all the stave churches, the **door frames** (where they survive) are decorated from top to bottom with surging, intricate carvings which clearly hark back to Viking design. The dragons in particular are long-limbed creatures, often entwined in vine tendrils.

The **origins** of stave churches have attracted an inordinate amount of academic debate. Some scholars argue that they were originally pagan temples, converted to Christian use by the addition of a chancel, while others are convinced that they were inspired by Russian churches. In the nineteenth century, the stave churches acquired symbolic importance as reminders of the time when Norway was independent. Many had fallen into a dreadful state of repair, and were clumsily renovated – or even remodelled – by enthusiastic medievalists with a nationalist agenda. Undoing this renovation has been a major operation, and one that continues today. For most visitors, seeing one or two stave churches suffices – and two of the finest are those at Heddal (see p.178) and Borgund (see p.173).

15min; car & driver 80kr, passengers 27kr), some 18km from Sogndal (see p.225). On the way, you'll pass the entrance to the 24km-long tunnel that extends the E16 to Flåm (see p.216) and on to Bergen.

Highway 7 to Geilo and the fjords

Highway 7 branches off the E16 about 60km from Oslo at **Hønefoss**, and then cuts an unexciting course along the **Hallingdal valley**, shadowed by the main Oslo–Bergen railway. Some 180km from Hønefoss, the road forks at **Hagafoss**, with Highway 50 descending the dales to reach, after 100km, the Aurlandsfjord just round the coast from Flåm (see p.216). Meanwhile, Highway 7 presses on west to the winter ski resort of **GEILO**, 240km from Oslo. It's a boring town out of the skiing season, but it does have several inexpensive places to stay, including an HI **hostel** (℡32 08 70 60, ℻32 08 70 66; mid-June–Aug & Dec–April; dorm beds 120–150kr, doubles ❷), housed in large barrack-like buildings in the town centre just off the main drag. Details of other accommodation are available from the nearby **tourist office** (June & late Aug Mon–Fri 8.30am–6pm, Sat 9am–3pm; July to mid-Aug daily 8.30am–8pm; Sept–May Mon–Fri 8.30am–4pm; ℡32 09 59 00).

Just beyond Geilo, the rail line ceases to follow the road, and breaks off to barrel its way over the mountains to Finse, Myrdal (where you change for the scenic branch line down to Flåm; see p.216) and Bergen. Highway 7 continues west for a further 100km, slicing across the Hardangervidda mountain plateau (see p.210). It's a lonely, handsome road that passes several places, such as Halne and Dyranut, where you can pick up the Hardangervidda's network of hiking

△Fish market

trails (for more on hiking in the Hardangervidda, see p.210). On the far side of the plateau, Highway 7 rushes down a steep valley to reach the fjords at Eidfjord (see p.209).

The E134 to Kongsberg

Up in the hills some 80km from Oslo, **KONGSBERG** is one of the most interesting towns in the region and the main attraction along the **E134**, the third main road linking Oslo with the western fjords. A local story claims that the **silver** responsible for Kongsberg's existence was discovered by two goatherds, who stumbled across a vein of the metal laid bare by the scratchings of an ox. True or not, Christian IV was quick to exploit the find, creating a mining industry here that boosted his coffers no end: appropriately the town's name means "King's Mountain". In the event, it turned out that Kongsberg was the only place in the world where silver could be found in its pure form, and there was enough of it to sustain the town for a couple of centuries. By the 1750s, it was the largest town in Norway, with half its 8000 inhabitants employed in and around the 300-odd mine shafts that littered the area. The silver works closed in 1805, but by this time Kongsberg was also the site of a royal mint and then an armaments factory, which still employs people to this day.

To appreciate the full economic and political clout of the mine owners, it's necessary to visit the church they funded – **Kongsberg kirke** (mid-May to mid-Aug Mon–Fri 10am–4pm, Sat 10am–1pm & Sun 2–4pm; mid- to late Aug Mon–Fri 10am–noon; Sept to mid-May Tues–Thurs 10am–noon; 30kr), the largest and arguably most beautiful Baroque church in Norway. It dates from 1761, when the mines were at the peak of their prosperity, and sits impressively in a square surrounded on three sides by period wooden buildings. Inside, too, it's a grand affair, with an enormous, showy mock-marble western wall incorporating the altar, pulpit and organ. This arrangement was dictated by political considerations: the pulpit is actually *above* the altar, to ram home the point that the priest's stern injunctions to work harder on behalf of the mine owners were an expression of God's will. The **seating arrangements** were rigidly and hierarchically defined, and determined the church's principal fixtures. Facing the pulpit are the King's Box and boxes for the silverworks' managers, while other officials sat in the glass enclosures. The pews on the ground floor were reserved for their womenfolk, while the sweeping balcony was divided into three tiers to accommodate the Kongsberg petit bourgeoisie, the workers and, squeezing in at the top and the back, the lumpen proletariat.

As for the rest of Kongsberg, it's an agreeable if quiet place in summer, with plenty of green spaces. The **River Lågen** tumbles through the centre, and statues on the town bridge at the foot of Storgata commemorate various local activities, including foolhardy attempts to locate new finds of silver – one of which involved the use of divining rods. Mining enthusiasts will enjoy the **Norsk Bergverksmuseum**, Hyttegata 3 (Mining Museum; daily: mid-May to June & late Aug 10am–4pm; July to mid-Aug 10am–5pm; Sept to mid-May noon–4pm; 50kr), housed in the old smelting works at the river's edge along with a tiny ski museum and coin collection, but merely wandering around the town is as enjoyable a way as any of spending time here.

One set of **silver mines**, the Sølvgruvene, is open for tours and makes a fine excursion, especially if you have children to amuse. It's hidden in green surroundings 8km west of town in the hamlet of **SAGGRENDA**. To get there, drive (or take the local bus from outside the train station) along the E134 in

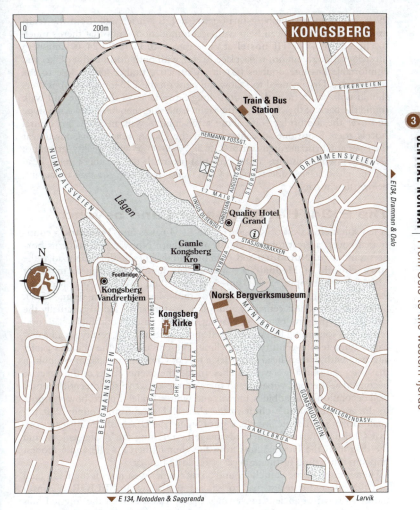

the direction of Notodden and look for the sign leading off to the right. The informative eighty-minute **tour** (early July to mid-Aug 4 daily; 60kr) includes a ride on a miniature train into the shafts through dark tunnels. Ask at the Kongsberg tourist office (see below) for times; also, take a sweater as it's cold underground. Back outside, just 350m down the hill, the old ochre-painted timber workers' compound – the **Sakkerhusene** – has been restored and contains a **café** as well as some rather half-hearted displays on the history of the mines.

Kongsberg practicalities

Kongsberg **tourist office**, at Karsches gata 3 (May to late June & mid-Aug to mid-Sept Mon–Fri 9am–4pm, Sat 10am–2pm; late June to mid-Aug Mon–Fri 9am–7pm, Sat & Sun 10am–4pm; mid-Sept to April Mon–Fri 9am–4pm; ☎32

29 90 50, Ⓦ www.kongsberg-turistservice.no), is a brief walk from the **train and bus station**, and can help with accommodation – not that there's much to choose from. The HI **hostel** at Vinjesgata 1 (Ⓣ 32 73 20 24, Ⓔ kongsberg .hostel@vandrerhjem.no) is *the* place to stay, with both dorm beds (195kr) and comfortable en-suite doubles (❷) in an attractive timber lodge close to the town centre. Drivers need to follow the signs on the E134; train and bus users should walk south from the station along Storgata, cross the bridge and walk round the back of the church on the right-hand side, then head down the slope and over the footbridge – it's about a ten-minute walk in all. As for central **hotels**, there is just one appealing option, the *Quality Hotel Grand*, down near the river at Christian Augusts gate 2 (Ⓣ 32 77 28 00, Ⓦ www.quality-grand.no; ❻, s/r ❹), which also has a first-class **restaurant**. If the weather's good, head for the pleasant riverside terrace of the *Gamle Kongsberg Kro* café-restaurant, below the church.

The E134: Heddal, Seljord and beyond

A few kilometres west of Kongsberg, the E134 passes into **Telemark**, a county that covers a great forested chunk of southern Norway. Just inside its borders is industrial **Notodden** and, 6km beyond that, beside the main road, is the **stave church of Heddal** (late May to late June & late Aug to mid-Sept Mon–Sat 10am–5pm, Sun 1pm–5pm; late June to late Aug Mon–Sat 9am–7pm, Sun 1pm–7pm; Sept to mid-May Sun 1pm–5pm; 25kr). Surrounded by a neat cemetery and rolling pastureland, Heddal is actually the largest surviving stave church in Norway, its pretty cascade of shingle-clad roofs restored to something like its medieval appearance in 1955, rectifying a heavy-handed nineteenth-century remodelling. The crosses atop the church's gables alternate with dragon-head gargoyles, a mix of Christian and pagan symbolism that is typical of many stave churches. Inside, the twenty masts of the nave are decorated at the top by masks, and there's some attractive seventeenth-century wall decoration in light blues, browns and whites. Pride of place, however, goes to the ancient **bishop's chair** in the chancel. Dating from around 1250, the chair carries a relief retelling the saga of Sigurd the Dragonslayer, a pagan story that Christians turned to their advantage by recasting the Viking as Jesus and the dragon as the Devil. Across from the church, there's a café and a modest museum illustrating further aspects of Heddal's history.

There's another fine church around 55km further west just off the E134 (and past the first and quickest road to Rjukan; see below) in **SELJORD**, a small industrial town of ancient provenance that spreads between the forested hills and Lake Seljordsvatnet. Dating from the twelfth century, this church (open for guided tours by appointment only; call Ⓣ 35 06 59 88) is built of stone and as such is something of a medieval rarity. The town also seems to have attracted more than its fair share of "Believe It or Not" stories: a monster is supposed to lurk in the depths of the lake; elves are alleged to gather here for some of their soirées; and the 570kg stone outside the church was, so the story goes, lifted only once, by an eighteenth-century strongman by the name of Nils Langedal. Elves and sea serpents apart, there's nothing much to delay you.

Grungedal and Røldal

Beyond Seljord, it's a further 50km west along the E134 to the **Åmot crossroads** (from where roads lead to Rjukan and Dalen; see below), and a further 30km to the handsome **Grungedal** valley, whose string of antique farmsteads lie between lake and mountain. Pushing on, the scenery bordering E134 becomes wilder and more dramatic as the road slips across the Hardangervidda mountain plateau (see p.210) before snaking its way to the hamlet of **RØL-DAL,** home to a further **stave church** (daily: late May 11am–3pm, June 10am–5pm, July 9am–7pm, Aug 10am–5pm; 30kr). It's a trim, rusticated affair dating from the twelfth century but much amended. In medieval times, the church was a major point of pilgrimage on account of the crucifix with healing powers that still hangs above the altar.

Just beyond Røldal, the E134 turns sharply to the north, where it meets the coastal Highway 13 running up from Stavanger. For 18km, the two highways share a common stretch of road before the E134 veers west bound for Haugesund (see p.148), 140km away, while Highway 13 continues north to the waterfalls at **Latefossen**, where two huge torrents empty into the river with a deafening roar. From here, it's a further 14km north on Highway 13 to **Odda**, an ugly industrial centre and an unfortunate introduction to the fjords: try to allow enough time to avoid the place altogether and carry on to the much more appealing hamlet of Lofthus (see p.209).

Dalen and Rjukan

The Åmot crossroads is a starting point for two excursions off the E134, south to Dalen and north to Rjukan, though an earlier turning off the E134 – before Seljord – is a faster route to Rjukan.

From Åmot, it's just 20km south on Highway 38 to tiny **DALEN**, the starting point for the passenger ferry that wends its way southeast along the **Telemarkskanal** to **Skien**, a journey of ten hours. No less than 105km long, the canal links the lakes and rivers of the district by means of eight locks that negotiate a difference in water levels of 72m. Completed in 1892, the canal was once an important trade route into the interior, but today it's mainly used by pleasure craft and two **passenger ferries** which make the trip most days of the week from mid-May to early September. Ferries leave Dalen around 8am in the morning and the one-way fare is 310kr; contact Telemarkreiser (Ⓣ35 90 00 30, ⓦwww.visittelemark.com) for further details and bookings. Dalen also possesses one of the region's more noteworthy country **hotels** in the comfortable *Hotel Dalen*, signposted 1km from Dalen bridge (Ⓣ35 07 70 00, ⓕ35 07 70 11; ⓦwww.dalenhotel.no; ❻; May–Dec). Built two years after the canal in a style influenced by stave churches, its gables are festooned with dragon heads and gargoyles.

Back at Åmot, but this time heading north, Highway 37 threads its way into forested hills en route to the **Vemork** industrial works, 53km from Åmot, and 7km short of **RJUKAN**, a hydroelectricity-generating town in a fine river valley set against a backdrop of harsh, rough mountains. Despite its dramatic position, Rjukan manages to be pretty humdrum, its 4000 inhabitants sharing a modest gridiron town centre originally assembled by the Norsk Hydro power company. The town is, however, a useful base for exploring the Hardangervidda (see p.210), the mountain plateau whose southeast corner is above the town.

Rjukan's prime attraction is the **Norsk Industriarbeidermuseum** (Norwegian Industrial Workers' Museum; May to mid-June daily 10am–4pm; mid-June to mid-Aug daily 10am–6pm; mid-Aug to Sept daily 10am–4pm; early Oct Mon–Fri noon–3pm, Sat & Sun 11am–4pm; 55kr), housed in the old hydroelectric station at Vemork. When it was opened in 1911, the power station had the greatest generating capacity in the world – its ten turbines provided a combined output of 108 megawatts. It is a fine example of industrial architecture pretending to be something else: with its high gables and symmetrical windows it looks more like a country mansion. Inside, the museum explores the effects of industrialization on what was then a profoundly rural country, has displays on hydroelectric power and the development of the trade unions, and features a gallery of propagandist paintings about workers and the class struggle by Arne Ekeland.

Yet, most foreigners come here because of the plant's role in World War II, when it was the site chosen by the Germans for the manufacture of **heavy water** – necessary for regulating nuclear reactions and hence for a nuclear bomb. Aware of the plant's importance, the Americans bombed it on several occasions and the Norwegian resistance mounted a string of guerrilla attacks; as a result, the Nazis decided to move the heavy water they had made to Germany. The only way they could do this was by train, and part of the journey was across Lake Tinnsjø – ingeniously the ferry was fitted with a set of railway tracks. This was the scene of one of the most spectacular escapades of the war, when the Norwegian resistance sunk ferry and train on January 20, 1944. All the heavy water was lost, but so were the fourteen Norwegian passengers – a story recounted in the film *The Heroes of Telemark*, in which Kirk Douglas played the cinematic stereotype of the Norwegian: an earnest man with an honest face, wearing a big pullover. The museum has an excellent exhibition on these wartime escapades, including a film entitled *If Hitler had the Bomb*, and does **guided tours** which follow the saboteurs' route. The tours leave from the car park outside the museum (late June to July 3 weekly; 100kr; 2hr): contact the museum (☎35 09 90 00) for reservations and the schedule.

Rjukan practicalities

Long-distance **buses** to Rjukan from Kongsberg pull in at the **bus station** on the south side of the river. The town centre is a couple of minutes' walk away, across the bridge on the other side of the river and it's here you'll find the **tourist office**, at Torget 2 (mid-June to Aug Mon–Fri 9am–7pm, Sat & Sun 10am–6pm; Sept–May Mon–Fri 9am–3.30pm; ☎35 09 12 90; ⓦwww .rjukan-turistkontor.no). Apart from the usual services, it can also supply useful bus timetables. Rjukan is a starting point for long-range hikes across the Hardangervidda: a **cable car**, the Krossobanen, carries passengers up to the plateau from a station about 2km from the tourist office, at the west end of town.

For **accommodation**, the best bet is the modern *Park Hotell Rjukan*, Sam Eydes gate 67 (☎35 08 21 88, fax 35 08 21 89; ❹), an efficient, medium-sized place with comfortable rooms right in the centre of town. As for **food**, there's a very good café-restaurant at the Norsk Industriarbeidermuseum: otherwise eat at the *Park Hotell*, where they serve traditional Norwegian dishes at moderate prices.

Travel details

Trains

Dombås to: Oslo (4–5 daily; 4hr); Åndalsnes (2–3 daily; 1hr 20min).
Geilo to: Oslo (3–4 daily; 3hr 20min).
Hamar to: Oslo (7 daily; 1hr 30min).
Hjerkinn to: Oslo (4–5 daily; 4hr 30min).
Kongsberg to: Kristiansand (3–5 daily; 3hr

30min); Oslo (3–5 daily; 1hr 10min).
Lillehammer to: Dombås (4–5 daily; 2hr); Oslo (7 daily; 2hr); Trondheim (4–5 daily; 4hr 30min).
Oslo to: Bergen (3–4 daily; 6hr 30min); Dombås (4–5 daily; 4hr); Drammen (3–5 daily; 40min); Geilo (3–4 daily; 3hr 20min); Hamar (7 daily; 1hr 30min); Hjerkinn (4–5 daily; 4hr 30min); Kongsberg (3–5 daily; 1hr 10min); Kongsvoll

(request stop; 1–2 daily; 4hr 50min); Kristiansand (3–5 daily; 4hr 40min); Lillehammer (7 daily; 2hr); Myrdal (3–4 daily; 4hr 30min); Otta (4–5 daily; 3hr 30min); Røros (2–3 daily; 5hr); Sjoa (request stop; 1–2 daily; 4hr 30min); Trondheim (4–5 daily; 6hr 50min); Åndalsnes (2–3 daily; 5hr 30min).
Otta to: Oslo (4–5 daily; 3hr 30min).
Røros to: Hamar (2–3 daily; 3hr 30min); Oslo (2–3 daily; 5hr); Trondheim (1–2 daily; 2hr 30min).
Åndalsnes to: Dombås (2–3 daily; 1hr 30min); Oslo (2–3 daily; 5hr 30min).

Buses

Kongsberg to: Drammen (4 daily; 50min); Haugesund (3 daily; 8hr 30min); Oslo (4 daily; 1hr 30min); Rjukan (2–3 daily; 2hr).
Lillehammer to: Bergen (1 daily; 9hr); Dombås (1 daily; 3hr); Fagernes (1 daily; 2hr); Lom (3 daily; 3hr 40min); Oslo (every 2–3 hours; 3 hr); Otta (3–4 daily; 2hr); Stryn (3 daily; 5hr 50min).
Oppdal to: Kristiansand (1–3 daily; 3hr 30min).
Otta to: Gjendesheim for Jotunheimen (late June to Aug 1–2 daily; 2hr); Lom (3 daily; 1hr 20min); Oslo (3–4 daily; 5hr 45min); Spranget for Rondane (late June to mid-Aug 2 daily; 50min); Stryn (3 daily; 3hr); Trondheim (2 daily; 5hr).
Rjukan to: Kongsberg (2–3 daily; 2hr); Oslo (2–3 daily; 3hr 30min).
Røros to: Oslo (6 weekly; 6hr); Trondheim (2–4 daily; 3hr 10min).

Bergen and the
Western Fjords

CHAPTER 4

Highlights

* **The Flåmsbana** Take a trip on the exhilarating Flåm railway as it careers down the mountainside providing spectacular views of the fjord below. **See p.216**

* **Troldhaugen** Visit the lakeside home of Edvard Grieg, Norway's most famous composer. **See p.199**

* **Urnes stave church** The oldest stave church in Norway is renowned for its Viking woodcarvings. **See p.227**

* **Jotunheim mountains** View the sharp, ice-tipped peaks of Norway's most imposing mountain range from the Sognefjellsveg mountain road. **See p.227**

* **Josteldalsbreen glacier** Take a walk out onto this mighty 500-square-kilometre ice plateau from the Kjenndalsbreen. **See p.231**

* **Geirangerfjord** Rugged and severe, the Geirangerfjord is one of the region's smallest but most beautiful fjords. **See p.235**

* **Union Hotel, Øye** Follow in the footsteps of Karen Blixen and Kaiser Wilhelm II, stay at the fjordland's most original hotel. **See p.237**

* **Ålesund** A beguiling ferry and fishing port, whose streets are flanked by appealing Art Nouveau buildings. **See p.243**

4

Bergen and the Western Fjords

f there's one familiar and enticing image of Norway it's the **fjords**: giant clefts in the landscape that run from the coast deep into the interior. Wild, rugged and serene, these huge wedge-shaped inlets are visually stunning; indeed, the entire fjord region elicits inordinate amounts of purple prose from tourist office handouts, and for once it's rarely overstated. The fjords are undeniably beautiful, especially around early May, after the brief Norwegian spring has brought colour to the landscape. In winter, the fjords are unerringly quiet, their blue-black waters contrasting with the blinding white of the snow that blankets the landscape, whereas in summer the mountains are filled with hikers and the waters patrolled by a steady flotilla of bright-white ferries. But don't be put off: the tourists are rarely in such numbers as to be intrusive, and even in the most popular regions, a brief walk off the beaten track will bring solitude.

The fjords run all the way up the coast to the Russian border, but are most easily – and impressively – seen near **Bergen**, the self-proclaimed "Capital of the Fjords". Norway's second largest city, Bergen is a welcoming place with an atmospheric old warehouse quarter, a relic of the days when it was the northernmost port of the Hanseatic trade alliance. It's also – as its tag suggests - a handy springboard for the nearby fjords, beginning with the gentle charms of the **Hardangerfjord** and the Flåmsdal valley, where the inspiring **Flåmsbåna** mountain railway trundles down to the Aurlandsfjord, a small arm of the mighty **Sognefjord**. Lined with pretty village resorts, the Sognefjord is the longest and deepest of the country's fjords and is perhaps the most beguiling, rather more so than the **Nordfjord**, lying parallel to the north. Between the Sognefjord and Nordfjord lies the **Jostedalsbreen glacier**, mainland Europe's largest ice sheet, while north of the Nordfjord is the narrow, S-shaped **Geirangerfjord**, a rugged gash in the landscape that is both the most celebrated and the most-visited of the fjords. Further north still, the scenery becomes even more extreme, reaching pinnacles of isolation in the splendid **Trollstigen** mountain highway, a stunning prelude to both the amenable town of **Åndalsnes** and the ferry port of **Ålesund**, with its attractive Art Nouveau buildings.

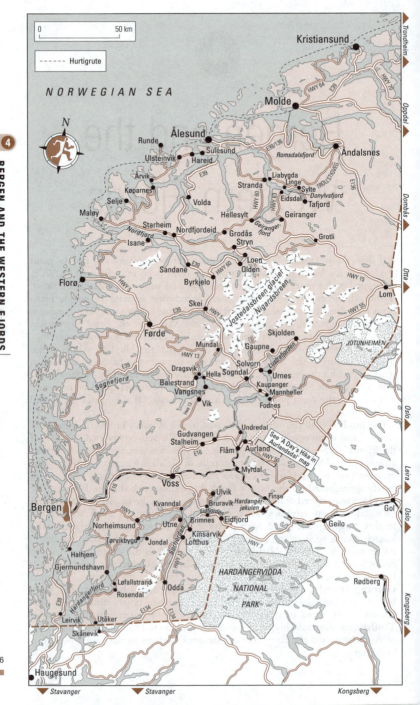

NORWEGIAN SEA

N

0   50 km

----- Hurtigrute

Kristiansund

Molde

Ålesund

Andalsnes

Runde

Ulsteinvik   Sulesund

Hareid

Arvik

Køparnes

Selje

Maløy

Starheim

Nordfjordeid

Isane

Sandane

Byrkjelo

Florø

Skei

Førde

Mundal

Dragsvik   Hella

Balestrand

Vangsnes

Vik

Gudvangen

Stalheim

Voss

Bergen

Norheimsund

Tørvikbygd

Halhjem

Gjermundshavn

Leirvik

Utåker

Skånevik

Volda

Hellesylt

Grodås

Stryn

Loen

Olden

Gaupne

Solvorn

Sogndal

Flåm

Aurland

Myrdal

Ulvik

Kvanndal   Bruravik

Brimnes

Utne   Kinsarvik

Jondal   Lofthus

Løfallstrand

Rosendal

Odda

Sulesund

Liabygda

Stranda   Linge   Sylte

Eidsdal   Tafjord

Geiranger

Grotli

Skjolden

Urnes

Kaupanger

Mannheller

Fodnes

Undredal

Finse

Eidfjord

Eidfjord

Geilo

Rødberg

Haugesund

Romsdalsfjord

Geiranger-
fjord

Donvlvsfjord

Jostedalsbreen glacier

Nigardsbreen

JOTUNHEIMEN

Lustrafjorden

Sognefjord

See "A Day's Hike in
Aurlandsdal" map

Hardanger-
jøkulen

HARDANGERVIDDA

NATIONAL

PARK

Lom

Nordfjord

HWY 5

HWY 60

HWY 55

HWY 15

HWY 13

HWY 7

HWY 13

HWY 134

E39

E39

E16

E136

E39/136

TROLLSTIGVEG

Trondheim

Oppdal

Dombås

Otta

Oslo

Leira

Oslo

Kongsberg

Stavanger   Stavanger   Kongsberg

186

Bergen

As it has been raining ever since she arrived in the city, a tourist stops a young boy and asks if it always rains here. "I don't know," he replies, "I'm only thirteen." The joke isn't brilliant, but it does contain a grain of truth. Of all the things to contend with in the western city of **BERGEN**, the weather is the most predictable: it rains on average 260 days a year, often relentlessly even in summer. But despite its dampness, Bergen is one of Norway's most enjoyable cities. Its setting – surrounded by seven hills, sheltered to the north, south and west by a series of straggling islands – is spectacular. There's plenty to see in town too, from sturdy old stone buildings and terraces of tiny wooden houses to a whole series of good **museums**, and just outside the city limits are Edvard Grieg's home, **Troldhaugen** as well as the charming open-air **Gamle Bergen** (Old Bergen) museum.

More than anything else, though, it's the general flavour of the place that appeals. Although Bergen has become a major port and something of an industrial centre in recent years, it remains a laid-back, easy-going town with a nautical air. Fish and fishing may no longer be the economic lynchpins of the city, but the bustling main harbour, **Vågen**, is still very much the focus of attention. If you stay more than a day or two – perhaps using Bergen as a base for viewing the local fjords – you'll soon discover that the city also has the region's best choice of **restaurants**, some impressive **art galleries**, and a decent **nightlife**.

Arrival and information

Bergen's stone-built **train station** (local ☎55 96 69 00, national ☎815 00 888) is located on Strømgaten, just along the street from the entrance to the Bergen Storsenter shopping mall, within which is the **bus station** (☎177). From Strømgaten, it's a five- to ten-minute walk west to the most interesting part of the city, the waterfront at Bergen's main harbour, **Vågen**, via the pedestrianized shopping street Marken; a taxi to the harbour will set you back about 60kr. The **airport** is 20km south of the city at Flesland, and is connected to the centre by the **Flybussen** (Mon–Fri & Sun 5am–9pm, Sat 5am–4pm, every 15–20min; 45min; 60kr). This pulls in beside the *SAS Hotel Norge* on Ole Bulls plass and then at the bus station, before proceeding to the harbourfront *SAS Royal Hotel*. Taxis from the rank outside the airport arrivals hall charge around 300kr into the centre of the city.

By boat

As well as being a hub for ferry and catamaran links with the fjords, **Bergen** is a busy international port. Ferries from Denmark, Iceland, Shetland and the Faroe Islands all arrive at Skoltegrunnskaien, the quay just beyond Bergenhus fortress, as do those from Newcastle, which call at Stavanger and Haugesund on the way here. **Hurtigbåt** passenger express boats from Haugesund, Stavanger and the Hardangerfjord, as well as those from Sognefjord and Nordfjord, line up on the opposite side of the harbour at the Strandkaiterminalen; local ferries from islands and fjords immediately north of Bergen mostly arrive here too, though short excursions round the Byforden, adjoining Bergen harbour, leave from beside the Torget.

Bergen is also a port of call for the **Hurtigrute** coastal boat, which arrives at the Frieleneskaien harbour on the southern edge of the city centre, beyond the university and close to the Puddefjordsbroen bridge (Highway 555). City bus #5 links the Frieleneskaien with the central Torget (Mon–Sat 6am–11pm every 30min to 1hr; Sun 8am–10pm hourly; 20kr); by taxi the journey costs about 70kr. Alternatively, it's a steep 25-minute walk to the centre up through the university and down the other side.

For ferry and boat **ticket and timetable information**, see "Ferries" under "Listings" (p.204).

By car

If you're driving into Bergen, note that a **toll** (10kr) is charged on all vehicles over 50cc entering the city centre from Monday to Friday between 6am and 10pm; pay at the tollbooths. There's no charge for driving out of the city. In an attempt to keep the city centre relatively free of traffic, there's a confusing and none-too-successful one-way system in operation, supplemented by rigorously enforced on-street parking restrictions. Outside peak periods, **on-street parking** is relatively easy and free, but during peak periods (Mon–Fri 8am–5pm, Sat 8am–6pm), metered parking is available only for a maximum of two hours and costs 18kr an hour. Your best bet, therefore, is to make straight for one of the four central **car parks**: the largest is the 24hr Bygarasjen, a short walk from the centre on Vestre Strømkaien, behind the Storsenter shopping mall and bus station, while the Parkeringshuset, on Rosenkrantzgaten (Mon–Fri 7am–11pm, Sat 8am–6pm & Sun 9am–6pm), has shorter opening hours but is handier for the harbourfront. To get there, follow the international ferry signs until you pick up the car park signs. **Tariffs** vary, but reckon on 13kr per hour up to a maximum of 130kr for 24hrs.

Information

The **tourist office** is in a large, mural-clad hall at Vågsallmenningen 1 (May & Sept daily 9am–8pm; June–Aug daily 8.30am–10pm; Oct–April Mon–Sat 9am–4pm; ☎55 55 20 00; ⓦwww.visitbergen.com), across the road from Torget, at the east end of the main harbour, the Vågen. It gives away copies of the exhaustive *Bergen Guide* and numerous other free brochures, as well as booking hotels and rooms in private houses, reserving places on guided tours, selling tickets for fjord sightseeing boats, and changing foreign currency. In high season, expect long queues. Widely available across the city centre is Bergen's excellent, free bi-monthly **newssheet**, containing local news, entertainment listings and reviews – the Bergen edition of the Oslo-based *Natt & Dag*. Naturally enough, it's in Norwegian, but the listings section is still easy to use.

City transport

Most of Bergen's key attractions are located in the compact city centre, which is best explored **on foot**. For outlying sights and accommodation, however, you'll need to take a city **bus**. Bergen and its environs are served by a dense network of local buses, whose hub is the bus station, in the Storsenter shopping mall on Strømgaten (☎177). Flat-fare tickets, available from the driver, cost 20kr and are valid for an hour; if your journey involves more than one bus, ask the driver for a free transfer. Another useful link is the **Attractions bus**, which links the city centre with most of the outlying sights, including Grieg's Troldhaugen and Gamle Bergen (hourly June–Aug daily 10am–5pm). It stops at several central points, including the tourist office and near the *Radisson SAS Royal Hotel*, on the Bryggen: a hop-on, hop-off day ticket costs 40kr. Finally, a tiny **orange ferry** (Mon–Fri 7am–4.15pm; 12kr) bobs across

The Bergen Card

The **Bergen Card** is a 24-hour (165kr) or 48-hour (245kr) pass which provides free use of all the city's buses and free or substantially discounted admission to most of the city's sights, and on many sightseeing trips. It also gives free on-street parking within the two-hour limit – if you can find a space. The pass comes with a booklet listing all the various concessions. Obviously, the more diligent a sightseer you are, the better value the card becomes, doubly so if you're staying a bus ride from the centre. The card is sold at a wide range of outlets, including the tourist office, major hotels and the train station.

Vågen to provide a shortcut between Munkebryggen, along Carl Sundts gate, and a point near the Bryggens Museum on the Bryggen.

Guided tours and sightseeing

The tourist office offers a plethora of **local tours**, including bus tours of the city, a mini-train ride around the city environs and fjord sightseeing trips: prices and departure times of all tours are detailed in the *Bergen Guide*. However, it's much cheaper to arrange your own visits than go on an organized tour; details as to how to get around on your own are given throughout this chapter. A couple of tours to be recommended, though, are the guided tours of **Bryggen** (see p.193) and the much-vaunted **Norway in a Nutshell** tour to Flåm, which involves a quick zip through the fjords by train, boat and bus (see p.206).

Accommodation

Budget **accommodation** is no great problem in Bergen. There are three hostels, a choice of private rooms and guesthouses, and some of the central hotels are surprisingly good value. Among the better deals are the **rooms** in private houses, that can be booked through the tourist office. The vast majority provide self-catering facilities and some are fairly central, though most are stuck out in the suburbs. Prices are at a fixed nightly rate – currently 340kr for a double room without en-suite facilities (230kr single), 400kr for en suite (260kr single), and 500kr for an apartment. They are all very popular, so in summer you'll need to arrive at the tourist office early to secure one for the night.

In addition, there are several **campsites** on the outskirts of the city, most of which also have four-bunk timber **cabins,** but you'll be far from the action at any of them.

Hotels

Hotel Dreggen Sandbrugaten 3 ☎ 55 31 61 55, ⓕ 55 31 54 23, ⓦ www.hotel-dreggen.no. Modest, three-star hotel in a plain modern block, but in a great location – just off the Bryggen. Thirty plain and fairly small rooms kitted out in modern style, both en suite and with shared facilities. ❸
Golden Tulip Rainbow Rosenkrantz Rosenkrantzgaten 7 ☎ 55 30 14 00, ⓕ 55 31 14 76, ⓦ www.rainbow-hotels.no. Efficient mid-range hotel in an old building just behind the Bryggen. Has everything you'll need and the rooms are tidy

and trim. On the upper floors, the best rooms have pleasing views over the harbour. Shame about the aluminium windows stuck in the attractive facade. ❼, s/r ❹
Grand Hotel Terminus, Zander Kaaes gate ☎ 55 21 25 00, ⓕ 55 21 25 01, ⓦ www .grand-hotel-terminus.no. There was a time when the tweed-jacketed visitors of prewar England headed straight for the *Grand* as soon as they arrived in Bergen – and not just because the hotel is next door to the train station. Those ritzy days are long gone, but the hotel has reinvented itself,

making the most of its quasi-baronial flourishes, notably its extensive wood panelling, chandeliers and stained glass. Breakfasts are superb and the bedrooms attractive and quiet, though some are rather pokey – if you can, have a look before you commit. ⑤, s/r ④

Hotel Park Pension, Harald Hårfagres gate 35 ℡55 54 44 00, ⑤55 54 44 44, ⓦwww.parkhotel .no. This excellent, family-run hotel occupies two handsome late nineteenth-century townhouses on the edge of the town centre near the university. The charming interior is painted in soft pastel colours and the public areas are dotted with antiques. The bedrooms are smart, neat and appealing. It's a very popular place, so advance reservations are advised. ④

Radisson SAS Hotel Norge Ole Bulls plass 4 ℡55 57 30 30, ⑤55 57 30 01 ⓦwww .radissonsas.com. Swish and swanky top-class hotel, right in the thick of things and with a full range of facilities from bar to heated swimming pool. ⑦

Radisson SAS Royal Hotel Bryggen ℡55 54 30 00, ⑤55 32 48 08, ⓦwww.radissonsas.com. Full marks here to the architects, who have built an extremely smart, first-rate hotel behind a brick facade that mirrors the style of the old timber buildings that surround it. All facilities – pool, health club and so forth, plus attractively appointed rooms. Popular with visiting business people. ⑦

Steens Parkveien 22 ℡55 31 40 50, ⑤55 32 61 22. One of an attractive terrace of high-gabled townhouses, overlooking a mini-lake on the edge of the town centre near the university, this well-established hotel offers inexpensive lodgings. The interior has lots of late Victorian flourishes, but the overall effect is rather gloomy. ④, s/r ③

Tulip Inn Rainbow Bryggen Orion Bradbenken 3 ℡55 30 87 00, ⑤55 32 94 14, ⓦwww .rainbow-hotels.no. Deservedly popular mid-range hotel with unassuming but comfortable modern rooms, in a handy location, a stone's throw from the Bergenhus fort. The breakfasts are magnificent banquets, involving every type of pickled herring you can think of. Hard to beat. ⑤, s/r ④

Guesthouses

Crowded House Travel Lodge Håkonsgaten 27 ℡55 90 72 00, ⑤55 90 72 01, ⓦwww .crowded-house.com. Traditionally, Bergen's guesthouses have been a little dowdy, but this lively, appealing place is the opposite – from the pastel-painted foyer to the bright and airy, if spartan, bedrooms. There are thirty-three rooms in total – 15 single, 14 double and 4 triples, all with shared bathrooms. There are self-catering facilities and a laundry too. Located halfway along traffic-clogged

Håkonsgaten, about five minutes' walk from the city centre. Singles 390kr, doubles ②.

Crowded House Travel Lodge Sandviken Sandviksveien 94 ℡55 90 72 00, ⑤55 90 72 01, ⓦwww.crowded-house.com. Similar in style and substance to its sister, the Håkonsgaten *Crowded House*, but located about 2km north from the city centre, and with parking facilities. Also singles 390kr, doubles ②

Skansen Pensjonat Vetrlidsallmenningen 29 ℡55 31 90 80, ⑤55 31 15 27, ⓔmail@ skansen-pensjonat.no. This simple little guesthouse occupies a nineteenth-century stone house of elegant proportions just above – and up the steps from – the terminus of the Fløibanen funicular railway, near Torget. It's a great location, in one of the most beguiling parts of town. The guesthouse has eight perfectly adequate if simple rooms, one of which is en suite. A real snip – at ②

Hostels and campsites

Bergen Vandrerhjem Montana Johan Blyttsveien 30 Landås ℡55 20 80 70, ⑤55 20 80 75, ⓦwww.montana.no. This large and comfortable HI hostel occupies lodge-like premises in the hills overlooking the city. Great views and great breakfasts, plus self-catering facilities, a laundry and internet/email access. Dorm accommodation, family rooms and doubles, the pick of which are en suite in a newly added wing. The hostel is 6km east of the centre – 15min on bus #31 (stop Montana) from Nygaten. Popular with school parties, who are (usually) housed in a separate wing. Dorm beds 185kr, doubles ②

Bergen Vandrerhjem YMCA Nedre Korskirkealmenning 4 ℡55 60 60 55, ⑤55 60 60 51, ⓔbergen.ymca.hostel@vandrerhjem.no. No-frills, HI hostel in the centre, a short walk from Torget. Has room for 175 guests, but fills up fast in summer. Facilities include a café, self-catering and a laundry. Open May to mid-Sept. Dorm beds cost just 100kr, plus 40kr for breakfast; single and doubles, with shared showers ②

Intermission Kalfarveien 8 ℡55 30 04 00. Christian-run, private hostel in a two-storey, oldish wooden building, a five-minute walk from the train station – just beyond one of the old city gates. Open mid-June to mid-Aug. Breakfast 30kr, dorm beds 100kr.

Lone Camping Hardangerveien 697 ℡55 39 29 60, ⑤55 39 29 79, ⓦwww.lonecamping.no. Bergen's main campsite, 20km east from the centre on Highway 580, is really only practical for those with their own transport. It has a lakeside location, tent and caravan pitches as well as simple cabins for rent. Open all year.

The City

Founded in 1070 by King Olav Kyrre ("the Peaceful"), **Bergen** was the largest and most important town in medieval Norway and a regular residence of the country's kings and queens. In the fourteenth century Bergen also became a Hanseatic League port, a prosperous enclave linked to other European cities by a vigorous trading life. It was a religious centre too – and at the height of its influence the city supported thirty churches and monasteries. The League was, however, controlled by German merchants and, after Hansa and local interests started to diverge, the Germans came to dominate the region's economy, reducing the locals to a state of dependency. Neither could the people of Bergen expect help from their kings and queens. Indeed it was the reverse: in return for easily collected taxes from the Hansa merchants, Norway's medieval monarchs compelled west-coast fishermen to sell their catch to the merchants – and at prices the merchants themselves set. As a result, the German trading station that flourished on the Bryggen, Bergen's main wharf, became wealthy and hated in equal measure, a self-regulating trading station with its own laws and an administration that was profoundly indifferent to local sentiment. In the 1550s, with Hansa power finally evaporating, a local lord – one Kristoffer Valkendorf – reasserted Norwegian control, but not out of the goodness of his heart. Valkendorf and his cronies simply took over the monopolies that had enriched their German predecessors, and continued to operate this iniquitous system, which so pauperized the region's fishermen, right up to the late nineteenth century. Indeed, it is only after World War II that local fishermen started to receive their financial dues, a prerequisite of the economic boom that has, since the 1960s, transformed Bergen from a fish-dependent backwater to a prosperous city.

Very little of medieval Bergen has survived, although parts of the fortress, the **Bergenhus** – which commands the entrance to the harbour – date from the thirteenth century. The rest of the city centre divides into several distinct parts, the most interesting being the harbourside **Bryggen**, which accommodates an attractive ensemble of stone and timber eighteenth- and nineteenth-century merchants' trading houses. The Bryggen ends at the head of the harbour and Bergen's main square, the **Torget**, which features an open-air fish market. East of here, stretching up towards the train station, is one of the older districts, a mainly nineteenth-century quarter that's at its prettiest along **Lille Øvregaten** and around the narrow lanes which clamber up the adjacent hillside. The main thoroughfare of this quarter, **Kong Oscars gate**, has been roughly treated by the developers, but it does lead to the city's most endearing museum, the **Lepramuseet** (Leprosy Museum). A stone's throw from here, the modern concrete blocks surrounding the central **lake**, Lille Lungegårdsvann, form the cultural focus of the city, containing Bergen's art galleries and main concert hall, while the chief commercial area is a few metres to the west along pedestrianized **Torgalmenningen**. The steep hill to the south of the central lake is crowned by the **university**.

Most of the main sights and museums are concentrated in these areas, but no tour of the city is complete without a stroll out along the **Nordnes peninsula**, where fine timber houses pepper the bumpy terrain and the old USF sardine factory now contains a first-rate arts complex and café.

Torget

In 1890, Lilian Leland, author of *Traveling Alone: A Woman's Journey Around the World*, complained of Bergen that "Everything is fishy. You eat fish and drink fish and smell fish and breathe fish." Those days are long gone, but now that Bergen is every inch a go-ahead, modern city, tourists in search of all things piscine, flock to **Torget's** open-air **fish market** (June–Aug daily 7am–5pm, Sept–May Mon–Sat 7am–4pm). It's not a patch on the days when scores of fishing vessels crowded the quayside to empty their bulging holds, but the stalls still display mounds of prawns and crab-claws, dried cod, buckets of herring and a hundred other varieties of marine life on slabs, in tanks, under the knife, and in packets. Fruit, vegetables and flowers – as well as souvenirs – have a place in today's market too, and there's easily enough variety of produce to assemble an excellent picnic lunch. At the end of the jetty beside Torget, take a peek at the **statue** of Leif Andreas Larsen, one of Norway's most renowned World War II heroes; for more on the man, see p.272.

The Bryggen

The site of the original settlement at Bergen, **BRYGGEN** is the city's best-preserved quarter, whose medieval provenance is recalled by a string of wooden warehouses with distinctive gables fronting the wharf. The area was once known as Tyskebryggen, or "German Quay", after the **Hanseatic** merchants who operated their **trading station** here, but the name was unceremoniously dropped after World War II. Hansa influence dated back to the thirteenth century, and derived from trading grain and beer for fish shipped here from northern Norway. Only later did the Germans come to dominate local affairs, much to the consternation of local landowners. By the middle of the sixteenth century, however, the Hanseatic League was in decline; the last German merchant hung on till 1764 but by then economic power had long since passed to the Norwegian bourgeoisie.

The **medieval buildings** of the Bryggen were destroyed by fire in 1702, to be replaced by another set of wooden warehouses. In turn, many of these were later replaced by stone warehouses in a style modelled on that of the Hansa period, but a significant number of timber buildings have survived. The first you'll come to, across from Torget, is the **Hanseatisk Museum** (Hanseatic Museum; June–Aug daily 9am–5pm; Sept–May daily 11am–2pm; 40kr, includes Schøtstuene), a well-preserved, early eighteenth-century merchants' dwelling, kitted out in late Hansa style. Among the assorted bric-a-brac are the possessions and documents of contemporary families, including several fine pieces of furniture, but more than anything else it's the gloomy, warren-like layout of the place that impresses, as well as the narrow bunk-beds and the all-pervading smell of fish.

A few metres further on is the main block of the remaining **timber buildings**, now housing souvenir shops, restaurants and bars. Despite the crowds of tourists, it's well worth nosing around here, wandering down the passageways in between wherever you can. Interestingly, these eighteenth-century buildings carefully follow the original building line: the governing body of the Hansa trading station stipulated the exact depth and width of each merchant's build-

Guided tours of Bryggen

The informative and amusing English-language **guided tours** of the Bryggen start from the Bryggens Museum (see overleaf) daily between June and August at 11am and 1pm, and take roughly an hour and a half. Tickets (70kr) are on sale at the museum, and after the tour you can reuse them to get back into the Bryggens and Hanseatic museums as well as the Schøtstuene – but only on the same day.

ing, and the width of the passage separating them – a regularity that's actually best observed from Øvregaten (see below). The planning regulations didn't end there: trade had to be carried out in the front section of the building, with storage rooms at the back; above were the merchant's office, bedroom and dining room. Up above those, on the top floor, were the living quarters of the employees, grouped into rooms by rank – junior merchants, journeymen/clerks and foremen, wharf hands and last (and least) errand-boys. Every activity in this rigidly hierarchical, all-male society was tightly controlled – employees were forbidden to fraternize with the locals and stiff fines were imposed for hundreds of "offences" including swearing, waking up the master and singing at work.

The Bryggens Museum and the Mariakirken

Just round the corner, the basement of the **Bryggens Museum** (May–Aug daily 10am–5pm; Sept–April Mon–Fri 11am–3pm, Sat noon–3pm, Sun noon–4pm; 30kr) features all manner of things dug up in archeological excavations that started on the Bryggen in 1955. A wide range of artefacts – domestic implements, handicrafts, maritime objects and trade goods – illustrates the city's early history, and provides some colourful background to a set of twelfth-century foundations, left *in situ* where they were unearthed. The museum's upper floors are given over to temporary exhibitions exploring other aspects of Bergen's past.

Beside the museum, the perky twin towers of the **Mariakirken** (St Mary's Church; late May to Aug Mon–Fri 11am–4pm; Sept to late May Tues–Fri noon–1.30pm; 10kr, free in winter) are the most distinctive features of what is Bergen's oldest extant building, a Romanesque-Gothic church dating from the twelfth century. It's still used as a place of worship and was, from 1408 to 1706, the church of the Hanseatic League merchants, who bought it and subsequently installed an ostentatious Baroque pulpit and altar. Several ecclesiastical bits and pieces in the nave and choir date from medieval times, most notably the choir's fifteenth-century altar reredos, a gaudy north German triptych with crude depictions of saints and apostles and exquisite framing. Over the southern portal hangs the best of the church's paintings – a finely detailed portrait of *Pastor Lammers* in his Sunday best, by the seventeenth-century Dutch artist, Lambert von Haven.

Øvregaten: the Schøtstuene and the Fløibanen funicular railway

Directly opposite the Mariakirken, the **Schøtstuene,** Øvregaten 50 (May & Sept daily 11am–2pm; June–Aug daily 10am–5pm; Oct–April Sun 11am–2pm; 40kr, includes Hanseatisk Museum), comprises the old Hanseatic assembly rooms, where the merchants would meet to lay down the law or just relax – it was the only building in the trading post whose occupants were allowed to have heating, as the wooden structures were a very real fire hazard. As you explore the comfortable rooms, it's hard not to conclude that the merchants cared not a jot for their employees shivering away nearby.

From the Schøtstuene, **Øvregaten** heads east, an attractive cobbled street which has marked the boundary of the Bryggen for the last 800 years. The Hanseatic warehouses once stretched back from the quayside to this street, and the old layout of the trading station is still easy to discern as you walk along the street – a warren of tiny passages separating warped and crooked buildings. On the upper levels, the eighteenth-century loading bays, staircases and higgledy-piggledy living quarters are still much in evidence, while the overhanging eaves of the passageways were designed to shelter trade goods.

At the far end of Øvregaten, back near the Torget, stands the terminus of the quaint **Fløibanen** funicular railway (May–Aug Mon–Fri 7.30am–midnight, Sat 8am–midnight, Sun 9am–midnight; Sept–April Mon–Fri 7.30am–11pm, Sat 8am–11pm, Sun 9am–11pm; departures every 30 min; return fare 50kr), which shuttles up **Mount Fløyen** ("The Vane"). When the weather is fine you get a bird's-eye view of Bergen and its surroundings from the top (320m above sea level), where there is a popular if rather staid café-restaurant. Several well-marked, colour-coded footpaths lead off through the woods or you can walk back down to the city in about 45 minutes. Simple walking maps are available free from the tourist office.

From the funicular teminus, you can either continue east along Lille Øvregaten (see p.196) or double back along Øvregaten to the Bergenhus.

The Bergenhus

Just to the west of the Bryggens Museum lies the **Bergenhus**, a large and roughly star-shaped fortification now used mostly as a park (daily 7am–11pm). Very little of the original medieval structure remains: the thick stone-and-earth walls enclosing the fortress date from the nineteenth century, while all the buildings within are reconstructions, the originals having been destroyed in 1944 by a German ammunition ship exploding just below the Bergenhus. Of the two main medieval replicas, the more diverting is the **Rosenkrantztårnet** (mid-May to Aug daily 10am–4pm; Sept to mid-May Sun noon–3pm; 20kr), a sturdy stone tower with thirteenth-century spiral staircases, low rough corridors, and rooftop battlements giving views over the harbour: its top floor contains an exhibition on medieval life. The tower is named after Erik Rosenkrantz, governor of Bergen from 1560 to 1568, who turned it into a grand fortified residence, equipping his own room, the Rosenkrantz chamber, with fine large windows and a handsome Renaissance chimneypiece, which have survived in pristine condition. Rosenkrantz was known principally as the architect of a new law under which anyone found guilty of an illegitimate sexual affair had to confess before a priest, before being fined. The law applied initially to men and women in equal measure, but by the 1590s women bore the brunt of any punishment. In Bergen, for example, women who could not pay the fine had to stand naked at the entrance to a church before being thrown out of town – the men just got exiled.

Across the cobbled courtyard, flanked by nineteenth-century officers' quarters, is the **Håkonshallen** (mid-May to Aug daily 10am–4pm; Sept to mid-May daily except Thurs noon–3pm, Thurs 3–6pm; 20kr), a careful reconstruction of the Gothic ceremonial hall built for King Håkon Håkonsson in the middle of the thirteenth century. Surplus to requirements once Norway lost its independence, no-one knew quite what to do with the capacious hall for several centuries, but it was revamped in 1910 and rebuilt after the 1944 explosion and is now in use once again for public ceremonies.

Beyond the Bergenhus, at the foot of the international ferry dock, is the disappointing **Norges Fiskerimuseum** (Norwegian Museum of Fisheries; June–Aug Mon–Fri 10am–6pm, Sat & Sun noon–4pm; Sept–May Mon–Fri 10am–4pm, Sat & Sun noon–4pm; 20kr). Charting the importance of the fishing industry to Bergen, the museum trawls through models of various types of boat with illustrations of different fishing techniques – line fishing, trawling, and so forth – plus sections on whaling and sealing, but it's all pretty predictable.

From here, it's a ten-minute walk back down Bryggen to the Torget.

Lille Øvregaten to the Lepramuseet

Running east from the Fløibanen terminal (see p.194), **Lille Øvregaten** is home to an appealing mix of expansive nineteenth-century villas and old timber houses, with bright-white clapboard planking and tiny windows. Yet more pretty wooden houses line the hill in the angle between the Fløibanen terminal and Lille Øvregaten – if anything these are even quainter, pressing in against steep cobbled lanes, which steer around occasional hunks of stone too large to move. Meanwhile, Lille Øvregaten curves round to the **Domkirke** (Cathedral; mid-May to Aug Mon–Sat 11am–5pm, Sun 10am–1pm; Sept to mid-May Tues–Fri 11am–2pm, Sat 11am–3pm, Sun 10am–1pm; free), a doughty edifice whose stern exterior has been restored and rebuilt several times since its original construction in the thirteenth century. Neither does the interior set the pulse racing, though some fancy wooden staircases – two leading to the organ and one to the pulpit – add a little fillip to the dour surroundings.

More promising by far is the fascinating **Lepramuseet**, just up from the Domkirke at Kong Oscars gate 59 (Leprosy Museum; late May to Aug daily 11am–3pm; 30kr). This endearingly antiquated collection is housed in the eighteenth-century buildings of **St Jørgens Hospital** (St George's Hospital), ranged around a charming cobbled courtyard, and tells the tale of the Norwegian fight against leprosy. The disease first appeared in Scandinavia in Viking times and became especially prevalent in the coastal districts of western Norway, with around three percent of the population classified as lepers in the early nineteenth century. The hospital specialized in the care of lepers, assuming a more proactive role from 1830, when a series of Norwegian medics tried to find a cure for the disease. The most successful of them was Armauer Hansen, who in 1873 was the first person to identify the leprosy bacillus. The last lepers left St Jørgens in 1946 and the hospital has been left untouched, the small rooms off the central gallery revealing the patients' cramped living quarters. Also on display are medical implements (including cupping glasses for drawing blood) and a few gruesome sketches and paintings of sufferers. Dating from 1702, the adjoining hospital **chapel** is delightful, its rickety, creaking timbers holding a lovely folksy pulpit and altarpiece decorated with cherubs and dainty scrollwork. The two altar paintings are crude but appropriate – *The Ten Lepers* and *Canaanite's Daughter Healed*.

Lille Lungegårdsvann: Bergen's art galleries

Bergen's central lake, **Lille Lungegårdsvann**, is a focus for summertime festivals and events, and its southern side is flanked by the city's four principal art galleries. Also on its southern side, on Lars Hilles gate, lurks the **Grieghallen** concert hall, an ugly concrete structure that serves as the main venue for the annual Bergen International Festival (see p.203).

Bergen Kunstmuseum – Rasmus Meyers Samlinger

The easternmost – and most diverting – of the four art museums is the **Bergen Kunstmuseum – Rasmus Meyers Samlinger**, Rasmus Meyers Allé 7 (Bergen Art Museum – the Rasmus Meyers Collection; mid-May to mid-Sept daily 11am–5pm; mid-Sept to mid-May Tues–Sun 11am–5pm; 50kr, combined ticket with the Bergen Billedgalleri and the Stenersen Collection), housed in a large building with a pagoda-like roof. Gifted to the city by one of its old merchant families, the collection contains an extensive range of Norwegian painting from early landscape painters like Dahl and Fearnley (see p.83) through Christian Krohg to later figures such as Alex Revold and Henrik Sørensen. There's also a particularly good sample of the work of Erik Werenskiold (1855–1938) and Theodor Kittelsen (1857–1914), who are best known for their illustrations of the folk stories collected by Asbjørnsen and Moe in rural Norway. Although the stories had already been published several times when the duo got working on them, it was Werenskiold and Kittelsen who effectively defined the appearance of the various folkloric figures in the popular imagination. It is, however, for its large sample of work by **Edvard Munch** that the museum is usually visited – if you missed out in Oslo (see p.98), this is the place to make amends. There are examples from all Munch's major periods, with the disturbing – and disturbed – works of the 1890s stealing the spotlight from the calmer paintings that followed his recovery from the nervous breakdown of 1908. Apart from the paintings, there's also a substantial collection of his woodcuts and lithographs.

Bergen Billedgalleri and Stenersens Samling

Just along the street, the **Bergen Billedgalleri** (Bergen Art Gallery; same times and price as the Rasmus Meyers Collection) is noted for its temporary exhibitions of contemporary art, whilst the adjacent **Bergen Kunstmuseum – Stenersens Samling** (Bergen Art Museum – the Stenersen Collection; same times and price as the Rasmus Meyers Collection) features both changing exhibitions and the modern art collection of Rolf Stenersen. Something of a Renaissance man, Stenersen (1899–1978) – one-time athlete, financier and chum of Munch – seems to have had a successful stab at almost everything; he even wrote some highly acclaimed short stories in the 1930s. In 1936 he donated his first art collection to his hometown of Oslo (see p.82), and 35 years later he was in a similar giving mood, the beneficiary being his adopted town of Bergen. The collection is especially strong on one of Stenersen's favourites, the Bauhaus painter Paul Klee, and there's a smattering of work by more familiar artists too, featuring the likes of Toulouse-Lautrec, Picasso, Miró, Ernst and Léger. Among the Norwegians, there are several Munch paintings and a selection of watercolours and oils by the versatile Jakob Weidemann (b. 1923), whose work was much influenced by French cubists during the 1940s, though he is now associated with the shimmering, pastel-painted abstracts he churned out in the 1960s.

Vestlandske Kunstindustrimuseum

The westernmost gallery of the four, the **Vestlandske Kunstindustrimuseum** (West Norway Applied Art Museum; mid-May to mid-Sept Tues–Sun 11am–4pm; mid-Sept to mid-May Tues–Sun noon–4pm; 40kr), occupies the Permanenten building, a whopping neo-Gothic structure at the corner of Christies gate and Nordahl Bruns gate. A lively exhibition programme with the focus on contemporary craft and design brings in the crowds, and some of the displays are very good indeed – which is more than can be said for the permanent collection and its Chinese marble statues. Fans of Ole Bull (see p.200) will, however, be keen to gawp at one of the great man's violins, made in 1562 by the Italian Salò.

Torgalmenningen and the Nordnes peninsula

The broad sweep of pedestrianized **Torgalmenningen** is a suitable setting for the commercial heart of modern Bergen, lined with shops and department

stores and decorated at its harbour end by a vigorous large-scale sculpture celebrating figures from the city's history. Around the corner, **Ole Bulls plass**,
also pedestrianized, sports a rock pool and fountain, above which stands a
rather jaunty statue of local boy Ole Bull, the nineteenth-century virtuoso violinist and heart-throb – his island villa just outside Bergen is a popular day trip
(see p.200). Ole Bulls plass stretches up to the municipal **theatre**, Den
Nationale Scene, at the top of the hill, worth the short walk for a look at the
fearsome, saucer-eyed statue of Henrik Ibsen that stands in front. Near here
too, just down the hill, at the east end of Strandgaten, is the imposing bulk of
an old **town gate**, built in 1628 to control access to the city but soon used by
the authorities to increase their revenues by the imposition of a toll.

Beyond the theatre, the hilly **Nordnes peninsula** juts out into the fjord, its
western tip accommodating the large **Akvariet** (Aquarium; May–Sept daily
9am–8pm; Oct–April daily 10am–6pm, 80kr; bus #11) and a pleasant park. It
takes about fifteen minutes to walk there from Ole Bulls plass – via
Klostergaten/Haugeveien – but the effort is much better spent in choosing a
different, more southerly route along the peninsula. This takes you past the
charming timber villas of Skottegaten and Nedre Strangehagen before it cuts
through the bluff leading to the old, waterside United Sardines Factory, imaginatively converted into an arts complex, the **Kulturhuset USF**, often called
Verftet; this incorporates a groovy café-bar, *Kafe Kippers* (see p.202).

Out from the centre

The lochs, fjords and rocky wooded hills surrounding central Bergen have
channelled the city's **suburbs** into long ribbons which trail off in every direction. These urban outskirts are not in themselves appealing, though they are
extraordinarily handsome when viewed from the highest of the seven hills
around town, the 642-metre **Mount Ulriken**. It's reached by the
Ulriksbanen cable car (June–Aug daily 9am–10pm; Sept–May daily
10am–sunset; 70kr return), whose terminal is behind the Haukeland Sykehus
(hospital) and near the *Montana* youth hostel, about 6km east of the Bryggen;
there are walks and a café at the hill-top. From May to September, a double-
decker shuttle bus "Bergen in a Nutshell" departs for the Ulriksbanen from the
Torget (daily 9.15am–8.45pm; every 30 min; bus and cable car 120kr return).
The rest of the year, take city bus #2 from the main post office.

Tucked away among the city surroundings is a trio of first-rate attractions,
each of which could happily occupy you for half a day. Two of them,
Troldhaugen, Edvard Grieg's home, and **Lysøen**, Ole Bull's island villa, are
south of the city, whereas the open-air **Gamle Bergen** (Old Bergen) is just to
the north. A trip to the Troldhaugen is often combined with a quick visit to
Fantoft stave church, which you pass en route. All four attractions are accessible by **public transport** with varying degrees of ease, though in summer the
Attractions bus (see p.189 for details) makes visiting Troldhaugen and Gamle
Bergen, two of its stops, quick and straightforward. There are also organized
excursions to Troldhaugen and Gamle Bergen – tickets and details from the
tourist office – though these are more pricey.

Fantoft stave church and Troldhaugen

Some 5km south of downtown Bergen, just off the E39 and clearly signposted, **Fantoft stave church** (mid-May to mid-Sept daily 10.30am–2pm &

2.30–6pm; 30kr) was moved here from a tiny village on the Sognefjord in the 1880s. The first owner, a government official, had the structure revamped along the lines of the Borgund stave church (see p.173), complete with dragon finials, high-pitched roofs and an outside gallery. In fact, it's unlikely that the original version looked much like Borgund, though this is somewhat irrelevant considering that the Fantoft church got burnt to the ground in 1992. Extraordinarily, the present owner has had built a replica of the destroyed church, a finely carved affair with disconcertingly fresh timbers, set amongst beech and pine trees just 600m from the main road.

Back on the E39, it's a further 2km south to the prominently-signposted turning that leads to **Troldhaugen** (Hill of the Trolls; May–Sept daily 9am–6pm; Oct & Nov Mon–Fri 10am–2pm, Sat & Sun noon–4pm; mid-Jan to April Mon–Fri 10am–2pm; 50kr), the lakeside home of **Edvard Grieg** (see box) for the last 22 years of his life – though "home" is something of an exaggeration, as he spent several months every year touring the concert halls of

Edvard Grieg

Composer of some of the most popular works in the standard orchestral repertoire, **Edvard Grieg** (1843–1907) was born in Bergen, the son of a salt-fish merchant – which, considering the region's historical dependence on the product, was an appropriate background for a man whose romantic compositions have come to epitomize western Norway, or at least an idealized version of it. Certainly, Grieg was quite happy to accept the connection, and as late as 1903 he commented that "I am sure my music has the taste of codfish in it." In part this was sincere, but he had an overt political agenda too. Norway had not been independent since 1380, and after centuries of Danish and Swedish rule its population lacked political and cultural self-confidence – a situation which the Norwegian nationalists of the time, including Ibsen and Grieg, were determined to change. Such was their success that they played a key preparatory role in the build-up to the dissolution of the union with Sweden, and the creation of an independent Norway in 1905.

Musically, it was Grieg's mother, a one-time professional pianist, who egged him on, and at the tender age of 15 he was packed off to the Leipzig Conservatoire to study music, much to the delight of his mentor, **Ole Bull** (see p.200). In 1863, Grieg was on the move again, transferring to Copenhagen for another three-year study stint and ultimately returning to Norway an accomplished performer and composer in 1866. The following year he married the Norwegian soprano Nina Hagerup, helped to found a musical academy in Oslo and produced the first of ten collections of folk-based *Lyric Pieces* for piano. In 1868, Grieg completed his best known work, the *Piano Concerto in A minor* and, in 1869, his *25 Norwegian Folk Songs and Dances*. Thereafter, the composer's output remained mainly songs and solo piano pieces with a strong folk influence, incorporating snatches of traditional songs.

During the 1870s he collaborated with a number of Norwegian writers, including **Bjørnstjerne Bjørnson** and **Henrik Ibsen**, setting their poetry to music. Grieg also providing incidental music (1876) for Ibsen's *Peer Gynt*, music which he later reworked to create the two popular *Peer Gynt Suites*. In 1884, he composed the *Holberg Suite*, written to commemorate the Dano-Norwegian philosopher and playwright, Ludvig Holberg. It is these orchestral suites, along with the piano concerto, for which he is best remembered today. In 1885, now well-to-do and well-known, Grieg and his family moved into **Troldhaugen** (see above), the house they had built for them near Bergen. By that time, Grieg had also established a pattern of composing during the spring and summer, and undertaking extended performance tours around Europe with his wife during the autumn and winter. This gruelling schedule continued until – and contributed to – his death in Bergen in 1907.

Europe. Norway's only composer of world renown, Grieg has a good share of commemorative monuments in Bergen – the statue in the city park and the Grieghallen concert hall to name but two – but it's here that you get a sense of the man, an immensely likeable and much-loved figure of leftish opinions and disarming modesty: "I make no pretensions of being in the class with Bach, Mozart and Beethoven," he once wrote. "Their works are eternal, while I wrote for my day and generation."

A visit begins at the **museum**, where Grieg's life and times are exhaustively chronicled, and a short film provides yet further insights. From here, it's a brief walk to the **house**, a pleasant and unassuming villa built in 1885, and still pretty much as Grieg left it, with a jumble of photos, manuscripts and period furniture. If you can bear the hagiographical atmosphere, the obligatory conducted tour is quite entertaining – especially the revelation that Grieg was only 1.52m tall and that he and Einstein bore an uncanny resemblance to each other. Grieg, in fact, didn't compose much in the house, but preferred to walk round to a tiny **hut** he had built just along the shore. The hut has survived, and today it stands beside a modern concert hall, the **Troldsalen**, where there are **recitals** of Grieg's works from mid-June through to November. Recital tickets (200kr), covering admission and transport, can be bought from Bergen tourist office. The bodies of Grieg and his wife – the singer Nina Hagerup – are inside a curious **tomb** blasted into a rock face overlooking the lake, and sealed with twin memorial stones; it's only a couple of minutes' walk off from the main footpath but few people venture out to this beautiful, melancholic spot.

As well as the Attractions bus (see p.189), several public **buses** go to Troldhaugen: take any bus from platforms 19, 20 or 21 at the city bus station, get off at the Hopsbroen stop, walk back along the road for about 200m and then turn left up Troldhaugsveien for a stiff and uninteresting twenty-minute walk. The Attractions bus doesn't stop at Fantoft, so, again, take any bus from platforms 19, 20 or 21 and ask to be put off at the Fantoft stop. From here, cross the road, turn right and walk up the hill behind the car park, a ten-minute stroll.

Ole Bull's villa on Lysøen

Around 25km south of Bergen, the leafy, hilly islet of **Lysøen** boasts the eccentrically ornate summer **villa** of the violinist **Ole Bull** (1810–1880), which, like Grieg's home, has now been turned into a museum packed with personal artefacts. With its onion dome and frilly trelliswork, Bull's villa was supposed to break with what Bull felt to be the dour architectural traditions of Norway, but whether it works or not is hard to say: inside, the arabesque columns and scrollwork of the capacious music hall-cum-main room look muddled rather than inventive. Bull may have chosen to build in a foreign style, but he was a prominent member of that group of nineteenth-century artists and writers, the Norwegian Romanticists, who were determined to revive the country's traditions – his special contribution having been the promulgation of its folk music. He toured America and Europe for several decades, his popularity as a sort of Victorian Mantovani dented neither by his fervent utopian socialism, nor by some of his eccentric remarks: asked who taught him to play the violin, he once replied, "The mountains of Norway". Then again, people were inclined to overlook his faults because of his engaging manner and stunning good looks – smelling salts were kept on hand during his concerts to revive swooning women. The **guided tour** of the house (mid-May to Aug Mon–Sat noon–4pm; Sun 11am–5pm; Sept Sun noon–4pm; 25kr) is a little too reverential for its own good and could do with a bit more pace, but the island's wooded footpaths, laid out by the man himself, make for some energetic walks afterwards. Maps of the island are given away free at the house, from where it's a stiff, steep but short walk over the hill to **Lysevågen**, a sheltered cove where you can go for a dip – but take Norwegian assurances about the warmth of the water with a pinch of salt.

To reach the villa from Bergen, take the Lysefjordruta **bus** from the bus station (platform 19 or 20; Mon–Fri 7 daily), and after about fifty minutes you'll reach Buena Kai, from where a **passenger ferry** makes the ten-minute crossing to Lysøen (hourly, on the hour, when the villa is open; last ferry back from the island at 4.30pm, 5.30pm on Sun; 40kr return). By **car**, drive south along E39, then take the Fana road (Highway 553) and follow the signs to Lysøen.

Gamle Bergen

Four kilometres north of the city centre along the coast, **Gamle Bergen** (Old Bergen) is an open-air complex comprising forty wooden houses that are representative of eighteenth- and nineteenth-century Norwegian architecture. Entry to the site as well as the adjacent park, which stretches down to the water's edge, is free and there's open access, but the **buildings** can only be visited on a guided tour (every hour on the hour; mid-May to Aug daily 10am–4pm; 50kr). Immaculately maintained, the interiors give a real idea of small-town life and although the site, with its careful cobbled paths and trim gardens, is a little too cute, the anecdote-heavy tour is bound to make you grin. The enduring impression is one of social claustrophobia: everyone knew everyone else's business – grim or scandalous, mundane or bizarre. It was this enforced uniformity that Ibsen loathed and William Heinesen explored in *The Black Cauldron* – see "Books", p.396.

Gamle Bergen is served by the Attractions **bus** (see p.189), or catch bus #9 (Mon–Sat hourly) from Torget.

Eating, drinking and nightlife

Bergen has a good supply of **restaurants**, the best of which tend to focus on seafood – the city's main gastronomic asset. The pricier tourist haunts are concentrated on the Bryggen, but these should not be dismissed out of hand – as several are first-rate. Other, marginally less expensive restaurants dot the side streets behind the Bryggen and the narrow lanes east of Torget, though locals tend to eat more economically and informally at the city's many **café-bars**. The best of these are gathered in the vicinity of Ole Bulls plass, where you'll also find some of the most fashionable **cafés** and **late-night bars**, as well as the heart of Bergen's fairly limited **club** scene.

The **fish market** on the Torget (June–Aug daily 7am–5pm, Sept–May Mon–Sat 7am–4pm) is outstanding for picnic lunches, offering everything from dressed crab, prawn rolls and smoked-salmon sandwiches to pickled herring and canned caviar. The covered market, **Kjøttbasaren**, a long and narrow gabled building at the Torget end of the Bryggen, also has stalls selling all sorts of fine picnic food.

Cafés, coffee houses and café-bars

Aroma Kaffebar Rosenkrantzgaten 1. Specialist coffee house with a good line in lattes and cappuccinos. Convivial atmosphere, frugal decor; also serves snacks. Mon–Fri 8am–11pm, Sat & Sun 11am–11pm.

Baker Brun Kjøttbasaren. There are several *Baker Brun* café-bakery franchises in Bergen, but this is probably the best, inside the covered market – the Kjøttbasaren – at the Torget end of the Bryggen. Mon–Sat 9am–6pm.

Dromedar Kaffebar Fosswinkels gate 16. Good coffee, and excellent cheesecake and carrot cake. A student favourite. Mon–Fri 7.30am–6pm, Sat 10am–6pm, Sun noon–7pm.

Fusion Kaffe and Bar Håkonsgaten 27. Snacks and salads, juices and coffees during the day, a busy bar at night. Attached to the *Soho Restaurant* (see below). Open Mon–Fri 1pm–1am, Sat & Sun 1pm–2am.

Godt Brød Vestre Torggate 2 and Nedre Korskirkealmenning 12. Eco-bakery and café (in that order), with great bread and good pastries, plus coffee and made-to-order sandwiches too. Mon–Fri 7.15am–6pm, Sat 7.15am–3pm.

Kafe Kippers Kulturhuset USF Georgernes Verft, on the Nordnes peninsula. ☎55 31 55 70. Part of the city's adventurous contemporary arts complex, this laid-back café-bar serves tasty, inexpensive food – the reindeer is highly recommended – occasionally rustles up great barbecues and, with its sea views and terrace, is *the* place to come on a sunny evening. Puts on live music too, notably during its own jazz festival in late May. Mon–Fri 11am–midnight, Sat & Sun noon–midnight.

Det Lille Kaffekompaniet Nedre Fjellsmug 2. Many locals swear by the coffee here, reckoning it to be the best in town. Great selection of teas too, and charming premises – just one medium-sized room in an old wooden building one flight of steps above the funicular terminal. Mon–Fri 5–11pm, Sat 11am–6pm, Sun noon–11pm.

Café Opera, Engen 24, near Ole Bulls plass. Inside a white wooden building with plant-filled windows, a fashionable crowd gathers to drink beer and good coffee. Tasty, filling snacks from as little as 50kr. DJ sounds – mostly house – at the weekend. Daily 11am–midnight.

Restaurants

Bryggeloftet and Stuene Bryggen ☎55 31 06 30. This restaurant may be a little old-fashioned, but it serves the widest range of seafood in town – delicious, plainly served meals featuring every North Atlantic fish you've ever heard of, and some you might not have heard of at all. Main courses around 190kr. Mon–Sat from 11am, Sun from 1pm.

Enhjørningen Bryggen ☎55 32 79 19. On the second floor of a superbly restored eighteenth-century merchant's house – all low beams and creaking floors – this smart restaurant serves a mouth-watering range of fish and shellfish, with main courses from around 220kr. Worth every krone for an indulgent evening out. Normal hours are Mon–Sat 4–11pm, but from June to August there's also a daily buffet lunch (Mon–Sat noon–4pm, Sun 1–4pm), a slightly more affordable alternative, with heaps of salmon, prawns and herring, along with salads, hot dishes, bread, cheese and desserts.

Naboen Restaurant Neumannsgate 20 ☎55 90 02 90. Easy-going restaurant featuring a lively, inventive menu – and Swedish specialities. Offers a wide range of fish dishes, including unusual offerings such as sea bass with blood-orange sauce; the pollack is especially good. Reckon on 170–200kr for a main course. Open Mon–Sat 4–11pm, Sun 4–10pm.

Nama Lodin Lepps gate 2b. Behind the Bryggen, this popular sushi and noodle restaurant is a modern affair, crisply decorated with pastel-painted walls and angular furniture. It may be popular, but it's not cheap – each piece of sushi will set you back around 25kr.

På Høyden Fosswinckelsgate 18 ☎55 32 34 32. Café-restaurant near the Grieghallen with modern decor and a student clientèle. Straightforward food – burgers, chicken and so forth – at inexpensive prices. The Greek salad (75kr) is particularly good. Mon–Fri 11am–6pm, Sat noon–6pm.

Pars Sigurdsgate 5 ☎55 56 37 22. First-rate Persian food in pleasantly kitsch surroundings. A good range of vegetarian dishes – eggplant casserole with rice, for instance, at 90kr; meat dishes in the region of 130kr. Open Tues–Thurs 4–11pm, Fri & Sat 4pm–midnight, Sun 3–10pm.

Smauet Mat og Vinhus Vaskerelvsmuget, off Ole Bulls plass ☎55 21 07 10. Excellent, smart and fairly formal restaurant offering traditional Norwegian cuisine – including oodles of seafood – plus more exotic dishes like ostrich and antelope. Reckon on 220kr for a main course. Open Sun–Thurs 4–10pm, Fri 4pm–midnight, Saturday 5pm–midnight.

Soho Håkonsgaten 27 ☎55 90 19 60. Chic and ultra modern restaurant with a creative and flexible menu – from full set meals to a one-course snack. Has a great line in traditional Norwegian dishes – try the *klippfisk* (dried and salted fish). Main courses average around 190kr. Open daily 4–10.30pm.

To Kokker Bryggen ☎55 32 28 16. Similar to – and metres from – the *Enhjørningen*, but without the buffet. First-class seafood, plus regional dishes – the oven-baked reindeer is a house speciality. Main courses around 230kr. Open Mon–Sat 5–11pm.

Clubs

Agora Chr Michelsensgate 4 ☎ 55 96 08 40. Popular student hang-out with house and DJ music from Wednesday through Saturday, 10pm till 3am. Regular live bands too – currently offers the city's best programme.

Garage, at the corner of Nygårdsgaten and Christies gate ☎ 55 32 19 80, ⓦ www.garage.no. Very busy place with a mixed crowd. Two bars on the ground floor, and a live music area in the basement – mostly rock and pop. Packed at the weekend.

Landmark Rasmus Meyers Allé. Club/pub with a boisterous atmosphere; occasional live music and DJ sounds. Next door to the Rasmus Meyers collection. Open daily noon–1am.

Festivals and the performing arts

With some justification, Bergen takes pride in its performing arts, especially during the annual **Festspillene i Bergen** (Bergen International Festival; ☎ 55 21 06 30, ⓦ www.festspillene.no), which presents an extensive programme of music, ballet, folklore and drama. The festival lasts for twelve days at the end of May, and its principal venue is the **Grieghallen**, on Lars Hille gate (☎ 55 21 61 50), where you can pick up programmes, tickets and information (also available at the tourist office). In addition, the city's contemporary arts centre, the **Kulturhuset USF**, down on Georgernes Verft on the Nordnes peninsula (☎ 55 31 55 70, ⓦ www.kulturhuset-usf.no) hosts **Nattjazz** (☎ 55 30 72 50, ⓦ www.nattjazz.no), a prestigious international jazz festival held at the same time as the main festival.

Throughout the summer, Bergen contrives to have an event of some kind almost every day of the week: the tourist office tabulates these activities in its *Sommer Bergen* leaflet and website (ⓦ www.sommerbergen.no). Part of the summer programme is devoted to **folk music and dancing**, which can be seen at the Bryggens Museum (mid-June to late Aug, weekly at 9pm; 95kr), or at Fana Folklore's Country Festivals" (☎ 55 91 52 40), a mix of Norwegian music, food and dancing held on a private estate outside the city. It takes place from June to August several times a week at 7pm and costs 260kr per person, including meal and transport: tickets can be bought from most of the major hotels and from FløIo, at Torgalmenning 9. There are also **chamber music and organ recitals** at the Mariakirken in June, July and August, and **Grieg recitals** at Grieg's home, Troldhaugen, from mid-June to October (see p.200 for details).

Outside of the peak summer season, the Kulturhuset (see above) puts on an ambitious programme of concerts, art-house films and contemporary plays, while the **Bergen Philharmonic** performs regularly in the Grieghallen from September to May (☎ 55 21 61 00; ⓦ www.harmonien.no). Bergen's main **theatre**, Den Nationale Scene, Engen (☎ 55 54 97 10; Sept–June), has three stages that host performances in Norwegian as well as occasional appearances by English-speaking troupes. Finally, Bergen has one large city-centre **cinema**, Bergen Kino, Konsertpaleet, Neumannsgate 3 (☎ 82 05 00 05), a five-minute walk south of Ole Bulls plass. Here, as is usual in Norway, films are shown in their original language with Norwegian subtitles if necessary. Predictably, American films rule the roost, so English speakers are at an advantage. **Entertainment listings** (in Norwegian) are provided in *Natt & Dag* (ⓦ www.nattogdag.no), a free monthly newssheet widely available across the city.

Listings

Airlines Braathens, Bergen airport (☎815 20 000); SAS, Bergen airport (☎810 03 300).

Bookshop Norli, Torgalmenningen 7, right in the city centre, is easily the best bookshop in town, with a wide range of English books and French, German and Spanish titles too. The travel section is especially good and the staff extremely helpful. Very competitive prices also. Mon–Fri 9am–8pm, Sat 9am–4pm.

Bus enquiries Timetable information on ☎177.

Car rental All the major international car rental companies have offices in town, including Hertz, Nygårdsgaten 89 (☎55 96 40 70); and Avis at Lars Hilles gate 20b (☎55 55 39 55). Statoil Bilutleie has an outlet at the airport (☎55 99 14 90) and so does Budget (☎55 14 39 00).

Consulates Netherlands, Carl Sundts gate 29 (☎55 54 42 80); UK, Carl Konows gate 34 (☎55 94 47 05).

Emergencies Ambulance ☎113; Fire ☎110; Police ☎112.

Dentists Emergency dental care is available at Vestre Strømkai 19 (Mon–Fri 4–9pm, Sat & Sun 3–9pm; ☎55 56 87 17).

Exchange The main post office offers competitive exchange rates for foreign currency and travellers' cheques, with longer opening hours (Mon–Fri 8am–6pm & Sat 9am–3pm) than the banks. The tourist office will also change foreign currency and travellers' cheques but their rates are poor, as are rates at the city's big hotels. There are ATMs dotted all over the city centre.

Ferries: Domestic: Hurtigbåt passenger express boats depart from the Strandkaiterminalen. The principal operators are HSD (south to Haugesund and Stavanger; north to Hardangerfjord; ☎55 23 87 80), and FSF (to Sognefjord and Nordfjord; ☎55 90 70 70). The Hurtigrute coastal boat sails daily at 8pm from the Frielenskaien on the southern edge of the city centre, about 1500m from the

train station. Tickets from local travel agents or the operator.

Ferries: International: Fjord Line, Skoltegrunnskaien (☎81 53 35 00), operates a car ferry service to Haugesund, Stavanger and Newcastle, and another to Egersund and Hantsholm in Denmark; Smyril Line, Slottsgaten 1 (☎55 32 09 70), has car-ferry sailings from the Skoltegrunnskaien to Shetland, the Faroes and Iceland.

Gay scene Information on Bergen's low-key scene at the city's main gay café-bar, *Café Finken*, Nygårdsgaten 2a (☎55 32 13 16).

Hiking The DNT-affiliated Bergen Turlag, Tverrgaten 4–6 (Mon–Wed & Fri 10am–4pm, Thurs 10am–6pm; ☎55 32 22 30), will advise on hiking trails in the region, sells hiking maps and arranges guided weekend walks.

Internet and email The *Cyberhouse Internet Café*, just below the funicular at Vetrlidsalmenning 30 (☎55 36 66 16, Ⓦwww.cyberhouse.no), has lots of PCs and is open daily until late at night. Thirty minutes cost 20kr, an hour costs 35kr.

Laundry Coin operated and service wash at *Jarlens Vaskoteque*, Lille Øvregate 17, near the funicular (☎55 32 55 04).

Pharmacy *Apoteket Nordstjernen*, at the bus station (Mon–Sat 8am–midnight, Sun 9.30am–midnight; ☎55 21 83 84).

Post office Main post office on Olav Kyrres gate, at the corner of Rådhusgaten (Mon–Fri 8am–6pm, Sat 9am–3pm). Travellers' cheques and foreign currency can be exchanged here at competitive rates.

Taxi Bergen Taxi ☎07000.

Trains National timetable information on ☎81 50 08 88.

Vinmonopolet There is a branch of this state-owned liquor store in the Bergen Storsenter, Strømgarten.

The Western Fjords

From Bergen, it's a mere skip and a jump over the mountains to the nearest of the major western fjords, the much-visited **Hardangerfjord**, whose narrow subsidiaries wiggle their way deep inland, towards **Voss**, an adventure sports centre of some renown. From here, it's a short train ride to Myrdal, start of a spectacularly dramatic train journey down the Flåmsdal valley to **Flåm**, draped beside the **Aurlandsfjord**. Scenic as all this is, it pales beside the nearby **Sognefjord**, whose stirring beauty is amplified by its sheer size, stretching inland from the coast for some 180km. Smaller at 120km long, the **Nordfjord** runs parallel to the north, and has a more varied landscape, with patches of the **Jostedalsbreen glacier** visible. Further north again, the **Geirangerfjord** is a marked contrast – narrow, sheer and rugged – while, a short distance to the west, is the forbidding **Norangsdal** valley, with the wild and beautiful **Hjørundfjord** beyond. Hop over a mountain range or two, via the dramatic **Trollstigen**, and you'll reach the town of **Åndalsnes**, in a handsome setting between rearing peaks and the Romsdalsfjord, at whose western end perches **Ålesund**, the region's prettiest town.

This is not a landscape to be hurried – there's little point in dashing from fjord to fjord. Stay put for a while, go for at least one hike or cycle ride, and it's then that you'll really appreciate the western fjords in all their grandeur. The sheer size is breathtaking – but then the geological movements that shaped them were on a grand scale. During the Ice Age, around three million years ago, the whole of Scandinavia was covered in ice, mountainously thick inland but thinner towards the coast. The weight of the ice pushed the existing river valleys deeper and deeper to depths well below that of the ocean floor – the Sognefjord, for example, descends to 1250m, ten times deeper than most of the Norwegian Sea. As the ice retreated, it left huge coastal basins that filled with seawater to become the fjords, which the warm Gulf Stream keeps ice-free.

Visiting the fjords: practicalities

Bergen is the obvious springboard from which to explore the fjords and, indeed, its tourist board organizes a barrage of fjordland excursions, such as the much-touted "Norway in a nutshell" (see below). However, there's no shortage of smaller towns around the region in which to base yourself: in the Hardangerfjord, **Ulvik** and **Lofthus** are the most appealing bases, Sognefjord has **Mundal** and **Balestrand**, while further north **Loen**, **Åndalsnes** and **Åle-sund** are all worth considering. An added bonus to staying outside the city, is that you won't have to use the **E16,** the main road east from Bergen, which is prone to congestion and passes through more than twenty tunnels, many of which are horribly noxious. Avoid it if you can, or at least branch off onto the relatively tunnel-free and much more scenic **Highway 7** the first chance you get.

The convoluted topography of the western fjords has produced a dense and complex **public transport** system that is designed to reach all the larger villages and towns at least once every weekday, whether by train, bus, ferry, Hurtigrute coastal boat or Hurtigbåt passenger express boat. By **train**, you can reach Bergen and Flåm in the south and Åndalsnes in the north. For everything in between – the Nordfjord, Jostedalsbreen glacier and Sognefjord – you're confined to **buses** and **ferries**, although virtually all services connect up with each other. Bear in mind also that although there may be a transport connection to the town or village you want to go to, many Norwegian settlements are scattered and you may be in for a long walk after you've arrived – a particularly dispiriting experience if it's raining.

We've covered the region **south to north** – from the Hardangerfjord to Sognefjord, Nordfjord, Geirangerfjord, Åndalsnes and Ålesund. There are certain obvious connections – from Bergen to Flåm, and from Geiranger over the Trollstigen to Åndalsnes, for example – but otherwise routes are really a matter

Norway in a nutshell

Of all the myriad excursions organized by fjordland tour operators, the most trumpeted is the whistle-stop **Norway in a nutshell**, which can be booked at any tourist office in the region. The full trip takes seven hours, and is an exhausting but exhilarating romp that gives you a taste of the fjords in one day. The tour starts in Bergen with a train ride to Voss and Myrdal, where you change for the dramatic Flåmsbåna branch line down to Flåm. Here, a two-hour cruise heads along the Aurlandsfjord and the Nærøyfjord to Gudvangen, where you get a bus back to Voss, and the train again to Bergen. You can pick up the tour in Voss for an affordable 420kr: the full excursion from Bergen costs 630kr.

of personal choice. Bear in mind also that the **E39**, which cuts across the western edge of the fjord region, is potentially useful as a quick way of getting between Bergen and Ålesund, as is the Hurtigrute coastal boat; see p.246 for details.

Throughout the text there are numerous mentions of fjord **car ferries** and **Hurtigbåt** passenger express boats. Hurtigbåt services are usually fairly infrequent – three a day at most – whereas many car ferries shuttle back and forth every hour or two from around 7am in the morning until 10pm at night every day of the week; we've given times of operation where they are either different from the norm or particularly useful. **Hurtigbåt fares** are fixed individually with prices starting at around 100kr for every hour travelled: the four-hour trip from Bergen to Balestrand, for example, will cost around 400kr. Rail pass holders (see pp.20 & 33) are often entitled to discounts of up to fifty percent and on some routes there are special excursion deals – always ask. **Car ferry fares**, on the other hand, are priced according to a nationally agreed sliding scale, with ten-minute crossings running at around 17kr per person and 41kr per car and driver, 19kr and 49kr respectively for a twenty-five minute trip.

The Hardangerfjord

To the east of Bergen, the obvious initial target is the 100-kilometre **Hardangerfjord**, whose wide waters are overlooked by a rough, craggy shoreline and a scattering of tiny settlements. At its eastern end the fjord divides into several lesser fjords, and it's here you'll find the district's most appealing villages, **Utne** and **Lofthus** and **Ulvik**, each of which has an attractive fjordside setting and at least one good place to stay. To the east of these tributary fjords rises the **Hardangervidda**, a mountain plateau of remarkable, lunar-like beauty and a favourite with Norwegian hikers. The plateau can be reached from almost any direction, but one favourite starting point is **Kinsarvik**, though this approach does involve a stiff day-long climb up from the fjord.

Of the two principal **car ferries** negotiating the Hardangerfjord, one shuttles between Kvanndal, Utne and Kinsarvik, the other links Brimnes with Bruravik. There are no trains in the Hardangerfjord area but **buses** are fairly frequent, allowing you to savour the scenery and get to the three recommended villages without too much difficulty, except possibly on Sundays when services are reduced.

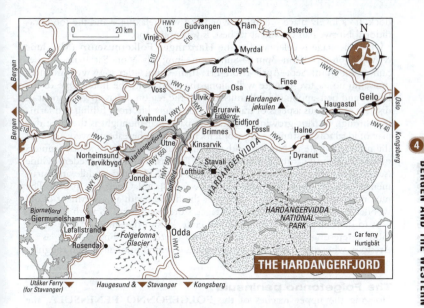

East from Bergen to the Kvanndal ferry

Heading east from Bergen by bus or car bound for the **Hardangerfjord**, you first have to put behind you the polluted tunnels of the E16, an unpleasant 30km journey, before you can head off down Highway 7. By contrast, this is a rattling trip, with the road twisting over the mountains and down the valleys, past thundering waterfalls and around tight bends before racing down to the tiny port and furniture-making town of **Norheimsund**. Sheltered in a bay along the Hardangerfjord, it's a modest place and there's little reason to hang around, other than to take the **Hurtigbåt** passenger express boat service to Utne, Kinsarvik, Lofthus, Ulvik or Eidfjord.

Leaving Norheimsund by road, Highway 7 sticks to the rugged shoreline as it travels east to the ferry dock at **Kvanndal**, another pleasant journey with every turning bringing fresh mountain and fjord views as the Hardangerfjord begins to split into its various subsidiaries. There's a choice of routes from Kvanndal: you can either press on down the northern shore of the Hardangerfjord towards Ulvik and Voss (see pp.211 and 212), or take the Kvanndal **ferry** over to Utne and/or Kinsarvik (1 or 2 hourly; 20min/50min).

Utne and the Folgefonno peninsula

The tiny hamlet of **UTNE**, the Kvanndal ferry's midway point, occupies a splendid location, its huddle of houses overlooking the fjord from the tip of the peninsula that divides the Hardangerfjord from the slender Sørfjord. For years, Utne's economy was dependent on the orchards that still trail along the Sørfjord's sheltered slopes, supplemented by fishing and furniture-making. Classic examples of the village's distinctive brightly painted furniture are on display in the delightful *Utne Hotel* (☎53 66 10 88, ℱ53 66 69 50; ℮kildehot@online.no; ❹), whose twenty-four rooms, mostly en-suite, occupy an immaculately maintained old clapboard complex metres from the ferry dock. It's a lovely place – family-owned and very relaxing – and the food, traditional Norwegian cuisine at its best, is top-notch too.

Utne's heritage is celebrated at the **Hardanger Folkemuseum** (May, June & Aug Mon–Fri 10am–3pm & Sun noon–4pm; July Mon–Sat 10am–6pm & Sun noon–4pm; Sept–April Mon–Fri 10am–3pm; 40kr; ⓦwww.hardanger .museum.no), a five-minute walk along the fjord from the hotel. One of the largest and best-appointed folk museums in the region, it has an assortment of displays on various aspects of traditional Hardanger life, from fishing and farming through to fruit-growing and trade. A particular highlight is the large display of local folk costume – the women's headdresses hereabouts were amongst the most elaborate in Norway and a popular subject for the romantic painters of the nineteenth century, notably Adolph Tidemand and Hans Frederik Gude (see p.84). There are also some fine examples of the Hardanger fiddle, an instrument much loved by both Ole Bull (see p.200) and Grieg (see p.199). The museum's open-air section rambles over the hillside with an assortment of old wooden buildings – farmhouses, cottages, store houses and so forth – playing host to demonstrations of farming and craft skills in the summer. One of the more interesting buildings is a thirteenth-century dwelling, known as an Årestova, whose dark and dingy interior has a central smokehole and roughly-hewn log walls.

The Folgefonno peninsula

Hogging the upper reaches of the **FOLGEFONNO PENINSULA**, the sprawling **Folgefonna glacier** boasts some excellent summer skiing. The conditions here are good for both Alpine and Telemark skiing, as well as snowboarding and there's even a purpose-built sledge run. On the edge of the glacier at 1200m above sea level, the Folgefonn Sommar Skisenter (late May to late Sept daily 10am–4pm; ⓣ94 56 78 40, ⓦwww.folgefonn.no) has ski rental, a ski school, a café and a ski lift to the slopes, while Folgefonni Breførarlag (ⓣ55 29 89 21, ⓦwww.welkome.to/folgefonni) runs guided hikes and climbs on the glacier, such as a six-hour blue ice tour (390kr, including equipment). To get there head southwest from Utne on Highway 550 for 36km to **Jondal**, then turn east along the signposted mountain toll-road (50kr) for the bumpy nineteen-kilometre ride up to the glacier. Home of the Hardanger's largest church, Jondal also has a useful **tourist office** (mid-June to mid-Aug Sun–Fri 11am–6pm & Sat 11am–3pm; ⓣ53 66 85 31) and car ferry connections over the Hardangerfjord to Tørvikbygd (hourly; 20min) just a few kilometres along Highway 49 from Norheimsund (see p.207).

Heading east from Utne, Highway 550 strips along the shore of the Sørfjord to the ugly industrial town of **Odda**, 45km away. Just before Odda, the road passes the entrance to the new 11km-long **Folgefonntunnelen** (55kr toll), which bores beneath the glacier to cross the Folgefonno peninsula. When you emerge from the tunnel, it's only 30km or so south to **Rosendal**, home of one of Norway's few country houses, the **Baroniet Rosendal** (daily: May–June 11am–4pm, July to early Aug 10am–6pm; mid-Aug to end of Aug 11am–5pm; 75kr). Dating from the seventeenth century, the house was in private hands until 1927, when the last owner bequeathed it to the University of Oslo. It boasts a string of period rooms, of which the Baroque library is the most handsome.

Kinsarvik

From Utne, the car ferry (every 1–2hr; 30min) bobs over the mouth of the Sørfjord to **KINSARVIK**, a humdrum little town which was once an important Viking marketplace. The Vikings stored their boats in the loft of the town's sturdy stone **church** (May to Aug daily 10am–7pm; free), though the building was clumsily restored in the 1880s, leaving only hints of its previous appearance, most notably a series of faint chalk wall paintings dating from the thirteenth century. Kinsarvik also lies at the mouth of the forested **Husedalen valley**, with its four crashing waterfalls. The valley makes an enjoyable hike in itself, though it's mostly used as an access route up to the Hardangervidda plateau. From Kinsarvik, it takes seven hours to reach the nearest DNT hut, the self-service **Stavali**, but the route is very steep and in rainy conditions very slippery. Hiking maps can be purchased at Kinsarvik **tourist office** (early & mid-May Mon–Fri 9am–3pm; late May to late June & late Aug to late Sept Mon–Fri 9am–5pm; late June to late Aug daily 9am–7pm; ⓣ53 66 31 12). Kinsarvik has a couple of places to stay – try the *Best Western Kinsarvik Fjord Hotel* (ⓣ53 66 31 00, ⓕ53 66 33 74; ⓦwww.kinsarvikfjordhotel.no; ❺, s/r ❻), a large, modern, ivy-clad block by the ferry dock – though nearby Lofthus is far more enticing.

Lofthus

Draped beside the Sørfjord 11km to the south of Kinsarvik, with the Folgefonna glacier glinting in the distance, **LOFTHUS** is an idyllic hamlet of narrow lanes and mellow stone walls, with a scattering of old grass-roofed houses sitting among the orchards, pinky-white with blossom in the springtime. Its **church** (May to Aug daily 10am–7pm; free) dates from 1250, a good-looking stone structure with immensely thick walls and several bright but crude wall and wood paintings. As at Kinsarvik, a steep **hiking trail** leads up from Lofthus to the Hardangervidda plateau; part of the trail includes the *Munketreppene*, stone steps laid by the monks who farmed this remote spot in medieval times. It takes about four hours to reach the plateau at Nosi (950m), and about seven or eight hours up to the Stavali self-service DNT hut.

The best place **to stay** in Lofthus is the delightful *Ullensvang Gjesteheim* (ⓣ53 66 12 36, ⓕ53 66 15 19; ⓔullensvang.gjesteheim@c2i.net; ❸), a huddle of antique timber buildings close to a bubbling stream, with thirteen cosy and unassuming rooms – and great food. Less distinctive is the modern, plush *Hotel Ullensvang* (ⓣ53 67 00 00, ⓕ53 67 00 01; ⓦwww.hotel-ullensvang.no; ❼, s/r ❺), a massive, solitary affair plonked on the water's edge, 1km to the north of the village.

Eidfjord and around

Heading north from Kinsarvik, Highway 13 runs the 19km to Brimnes, where a **car ferry** (1-2 hourly; 10min) shuttles over the fjord to Bruravik, for Ulvik (see p.211) and Voss (see p.212). Beyond Brimnes, Highway 13 becomes Highway 7, whose first significant port of call, after another 11km, is the village of **EIDFJORD**, which straggles over a narrow and hilly neck of land between the fjord and a large and deep lake, the Eidfjordvatnet. There's been a settlement here since prehistoric times and for centuries the village prospered as a trading centre at the end of one of the main routes over the Hardangervidda. Nowadays, however, it's a quiet spot, whose main attraction is the **Hardangervidda Natursenter** (daily: April–May & Sept–Oct 10am–6pm, June–Aug 9am–8pm; 70kr), with some mildly diverting displays on the Hardangervidda's natural history and geology. The *Eidfjord Hotell*, perched on a knoll high above the Eidfjord (ⓣ53 66 52 64, ⓕ53 66 52 12; ⓦwww.eidfjordhotel.no; ❹), makes an excellent base for exploring the area – it's a crisply designed, modern place with tastefully furnished rooms, and a very good restaurant. Alternatively, the village **tourist office** (late June & late Aug Mon–Sat 9am–6pm; July to mid-Aug Mon–Fri 9am–8pm, Sat 9am–6pm & Sun 11am–8pm; Sept to mid-June Mon–Fri 8.30am–4pm; ☎53 67 34 00; Ⓦwww.eidfjordinfo.com) has details of a handful of private rooms, as well as providing plenty of information on the surrounding attractions.

If you have your own transport, there are a handful of places in the vicinity of Eidfjord that are worth a visit. Head northeast out of Eidfjord up the Simdal valley and, after about 6km, a tortuous lane wiggles up to the remote **Kjeåsen mountain farm**, where you'll be rewarded with spectacular views over the Simadalsfjord below. The narrow road is single-track and restrictions apply – from o'clock to half-past the hour, you can drive up to the farm, and from half-past the hour to o'clock, you can return.

Heading east from Eidfjord along Highway 7, after some 18km, a signed footpath leads for a couple of hundred metres to the foot of the mighty, 145m-high **Vøringfossen** waterfalls. Further views of the falls, but this time from the top, can be had from the nearby hamlet of **Fossli**, perched on a cliff-top, about 1km off Highway 7. Fossli is also home to the unassuming, family-owned *Fossli Hotel* (☎53 66 57 77, Ⓕ53 66 50 34; Ⓦwww.fossli-hotel.com; May–Sept; ❹), where Grieg wrote his Opus 66. Founded in 1891, the hotel has been updated and now has sixty modern and fairly modest rooms in an impressive setting.

The Hardangervidda plateau

The **Hardangervidda** is Europe's largest mountain plateau, occupying a one-hundred-square-kilometre slab of land east of the Hardangerfjord and south of the Oslo–Bergen railway. The plateau is characterized by rolling fells and wide stretches of level ground, its rocky surfaces strewn with pools, ponds and rivers. The whole plateau is above the treeline, and at times has an almost lunar appearance, though the landscape does have some variation: there are mountains and a glacier, the **Hardangerjøkulen**, to the north, near Finse, while the west is wetter – and the flora somewhat richer – than the barer moorland to the east. The lichen that covers the rocks is savoured by herds of reindeer, who leave their winter grazing lands on the east side of the plateau in the spring, chewing their way west to their breeding grounds before returning east again after the autumn rutting season.

Stone Age hunters once followed the reindeer on their migrations and traces of their presence – arrowheads, pit-traps, etc – have been discovered over much of the plateau. Later, the Hardangervidda became one of the main crossing points between east and west Norway, with horse traders, cattle drivers and Danish dignitaries all cutting across the plateau along cairned trails. These are often still in use as part of a dense network of trails and tourist huts that has been developed by several DNT affiliates in recent decades. Roughly one third of the plateau has been incorporated within the **Hardangervidda Nasjonalpark**, but much of the rest is protected too, so hikers won't notice a deal of difference between the park and its immediate surroundings. The entire plateau is also popular for winter cross-country hut-to-hut skiing. Many hikers and skiers are content with a day on the Hardangervidda, but some find the wide-skyed, lichen-dappled scenery, particularly enchanting and travel from one end of the plateau to the other, a seven- or eight-day expedition.

Access to the plateau can be gained from the **Oslo–Bergen train** line which calls at Finse (see p.214), from where hikers and skiers head off across the plateau in all directions, or via **Highway 7**, which runs across the plateau between Eidfjord (see p.209) and Geilo (see p.174). There's precious little in the way of human habitation on this lonely 100km-long stretch of road, but you can pick up the plateau's hiking trails easily enough at several points, including **Dyranut** and **Halne**, 39km and 47km respectively from Eidfjord. Some hikers prefer to walk eastwards onto the Hardangervidda from Kinsarvik and Lofthus (see p.209), an arduous day-long trek up from the fjord, or from Rjukan (see p.179), to the southeast of the plateau, where a cable-car eases the uphill part of the trek.

Ulvik

Tucked away in a snug corner of the Hardangerfjord, the tiny village of **ULVIK** sits prettily along the shoreline with orchards covering the green hills behind. There's nothing specific to see – the town's main claim to fame as the place where potatoes were first grown in Norway in 1765 just about sums things up – but it's an excellent place to unwind, a popular little resort with a cluster of good hotels. **Hiking trails** lattice the rough uplands to the north of Ulvik and explore the surrounding shoreline. One of the most enjoyable is the easy half-day walk up to the **Ljonakleiv crofter's farm**, an old farmstead in the hills above the village: maps and details of the walk are available from the tourist office (see below). Another option is to walk or drive the 9km-long country road that leads east from Ulvik, across the adjacent promontory and up along the Osafjord, to the smattering of farmsteads that constitute **OSA**. Here, in the forested hills about 1km above the fjord, is one of the region's more unusual sights, the timber and brick **Stream Nest sculpture** (mid-May to mid-Aug daily 10am–4pm; 40kr), resembling a gigantic bird's nest and perched above a green river valley framed by stern hills. The sculpture was built by Takamasa Kuniyasu for the 1994 Lillehammer Winter Olympics, and moved here afterwards. As you near the site of the sculpture, the road passes the **Hjadlane Gallery for Samtidskunst** (Gallery of Contemporary Art; May–Sept daily 11am–6pm; 25kr), which has a programme of temporary exhibitions.

Practicalities

Ulvik is off the main **bus** routes, but there are regular local buses here from Voss (Mon–Sat 2–5 daily, Sun 1 daily; 1hr), which are routed via Bruravik to pick up passengers who've come from Odda, Lofthus, Kinsarvik and Eidfjord (1–4 daily) on the Brimnes–Bruravik ferry. There are also **Hurtigbåt** passenger express boat services to Ulvik from Norheimsund via Kinsarvik, Lofthus (1 daily; 2hr 10min). Buses pull into the centre of the village, metres from the jetty, from where it's a couple of minutes' walk along the waterfront to the **tourist office** (late May to late Sept Mon–Sat 8.30am–5pm, Sun 1–5pm; late Sept to late May Mon–Fri 8.30am–1.30pm; ☎56 52 63 60; Ⓦwww.ulvik.org/ulvikinfo). It issues all the usual information, including bus and ferry timetables, sells detailed hiking maps and rents out bikes (150kr per day).

The most prominent of the local **hotels** is the *Rica Brakenes Hotel* (☎56 52 61 05, Ⓕ56 52 64 10; Ⓦwww.brakanes-hotel.no; ❻, s/r ❹), a large and luxurious modern place occupying a lovely fjordside location in the centre of the village. Less obtrusive, the *Rica Ulvik* (☎56 52 62 00, Ⓕ56 52 66 41; ❺, s/r ❹), is a five-minute walk east along the waterfront, with fifty-odd balconied modern rooms overlooking the fjord. More low-key still, the *Ulvik Fjord Pensjonat* (☎56 52 61 70, Ⓕ56 52 61 60; ❹; May to late Sept) is a well-maintained and appealing **guesthouse**, a ten-minute walk west of the centre along the waterfront. The rooms in the main building are plain but comfortable, and there's a modern annexe too. Breakfasts are first-rate, but for evening **meals**, head to either of the *Rica* hotels – the *Ulvik* has the edge in terms of price and informality.

Voss and around

Whether by train or along the E16, the 100km jaunt east from Bergen to **Voss** is thoroughly enjoyable, with road and rail weaving past mountains and fjords before pressing on beside the rushing River Vosso. Beyond Voss, the next section of the rail line scuttles up the Raun Valley, an especially scenic journey and easily done on a day trip from Voss. The most popular target on this stretch of the line is the **Myrdal** junction, but only because the railway to Flåm meets the main line here. You can also disembark at two isolated hiking bases – **Ørneberget** (served by slow trains only) and **Finse**, both of which make excellent starting points for hiking and skiing the Hardangervidda plateau (see p.210). Drivers, however, should note that the mountain road heading east from Voss stops at Ørneberget – leaving Myrdal and Finse accessible only by train.

Voss

First impressions of **VOSS** are generally favourable: it has an attractive lakeside setting, boasts a splendid thirteenth-century church and is ringed by snow-capped hills. However, the town is primarily an **adventure sports** centre and winter **ski resort**, benefiting from the hills that encircle it to offer everything from skiing and snowboarding in winter through to summertime rafting, kayaking and horse riding.

With the lake on one side and the River Vosso on the other, the town has long been a trading centre on one of the main routes between west and east Norway – though you'd barely guess this from its modern appearance. In 1023, King Olav visited to check that the population had all converted to Christianity, and stuck a big stone cross here to make his point. Two centuries later another king, Magnus Lagabøte, built a church in Voss to act as the religious focal point for the region. The church, the **Vangskyrkja** (mid-May to mid-Sept Mon–Sat 10am–4pm & Sun 2–5pm; 15kr), still stands, its eccentric octagonal spire rising above stone walls which are up to two metres thick. The interior is splendid, a surprisingly flamboyant and colourful affair with a Baroque reredos and a folksy rood screen showing a crucified Jesus attended by two cherubs. The ceiling is even more unusual, its timbers painted in 1696 with a cotton-wool cloudy sky inhabited by flying angels – and the nearer you approach the high altar, the more of them there are. From opposite the church, the leafy Prestegardsalléen footpath heads south along the shore of **Lake Vangsvatnet** making for a pleasant stroll, while the central shops and cafés are worth a browse, particularly if you've come from the hamlets and villages further north.

Voss sports

In summer, Voss is a magnet for Norwegian **watersports** enthusiasts, who flock to the town to raft, kayak and canoe on the region's three rivers – the relatively placid Vosso, and the much wilder Stranda and Raundalen. The leading operator is Voss Rafting Senter (☎56 51 05 25, ℻56 51 06 30; ⓦwww .vossrafting.no), whose 4hr-whitewater rafting trips cost 650kr (690kr on Saturdays), including a swimming test and a snack. It also offers river-boarding

4

(a 5hr-trip) and sports rafting, which is akin to canoeing (4hr), for a similar price. Other operators include Nordic Ventures (☎56 51 00 17, ℱ56 51 00 18; Ⓦwww.nordicventures.com), who offers tandem paragliding as well as all sorts of kayaking excursions; **Voss Fallskjermklubb** (☎56 51 10 00; Ⓦwww .skydivevoss.no) for parachuting; and Stølsheimen Fjellridning, based at the Engjaland Fjellstove (mountain lodge), about thirty minutes drive from Voss (☎56 51 91 66; Ⓦwww.engjaland.no), for mountain horse-riding.

The **skiing** season in Voss starts in late November and continues until mid-April. From behind the train station, a **cable car** – the Hangursbanen – climbs 700m to give access to several short runs as well as the first of three chair lifts which take you up another 300m. A one-day lift pass costs 240kr (200kr for half a day), and in January and February some trails are floodlit. There's a choice of red, green and blue downhill ski routes. Full **equipment** for both downhill and cross-country skiing can be rented for around 200–300kr a day from Voss Skiskule & Skiutlege, at the upper Hangursbanen station (☎56 51 00 32), who also offers skiing and snowboarding lessons.

Practicalities

Buses stop outside the **train station** at the western end of the town centre, from where it's a five-minute walk to the **tourist office** (June–Aug Mon–Sat 9am–7pm, Sun 2–7pm; Sept–May Mon–Fri 9am–4pm; ☎56 52 08 00; Ⓦwww.visitvoss.no) on the main street, Uttrågata – veer right round the Vangskyrkja church and it's on the right. Here, you can get the free *Voss Guide*, detailing hiking, rafting, skiing and touring in the vicinity, as well as public transport timetables, help with accommodation, and bookings for the "Norway in a Nutshell" guided tour (see box on p.206), which costs 420kr from here.

Voss has a good selection of budget accommodation, of which the best is the excellent HI **hostel**, *Voss Vandrerhjem* (☎56 51 20 17, ℱ56 51 08 37; Ⓔvoss.hostel@vandrerhjem.no; Feb to mid-Nov; dorm beds 220kr, doubles ❷), sited in a modern chalet complex overlooking the water about 700m from the train station. To get there, turn right outside the station building and head along the lake away from the town centre. The hostel serves large, inexpensive evening meals and good breakfasts, has its own sauna, laundry, internet access and self-catering facilities and also rents out bikes and canoes; advance booking is recommended. The pick of the town's **guest houses** is the *Kringsjå Pensjonat*, Strengjarhaugen 6 (☎56 51 16 27, ℱ56 51 63 30; Ⓦwww.kringsjaa .no; ❷), just to the north of – and up above – the town centre and the railway line. Run by the Ole Bull music academy, it's bright, cheerful and modern, with seventeen plain rooms and a dining room dishing up tasty Norwegian food and pleasing views over Voss; again, advance booking is recommended. The rudimentary **campsite**, *Voss Camping* (☎56 51 15 97) is just a short walk south of the Vangskyrkja church – turn left from the train station, take the right fork at the church and then turn right again, along the Prestegardsalléen footpath. It's open all year and has a few cabins, bicycle- and boat-rental, and washing machines. Easily the best **hotel** is *Fleischer's Hotel* (☎56 52 05 00, fax 56 52 05 01; Ⓦwww.fleischers.no; ❻), next to the train station. Dating from the 1880s, the hotel's high-gabled and towered facade overlooks the lake and fronts the original building and a modern wing built in the same style. Many of the bedrooms are luxurious, but others seem a little down-market and jaded – further renovations are planned. The hotel **restaurant** serves the best food in town, and there's a terrace bar as well.

Around Voss: Ørneberget, Myrdal and Finse

All the trains pulling east out of Voss head up the Raun Valley, but only local trains stop – after forty minutes – at **ØRNEBERGET**, the remote mountain home of the *HI Mjølfjell Vandrerhjem* (T56 52 31 50, F56 52 31 51; W www.mjolfjell.no; dorm beds 195kr, doubles ❷). With its attractive setting, this well-equipped hostel in a comfortable mountain lodge is popular as a base for a range of sporting activities, from fishing and hiking on the Hardangervidda, to skiing in winter. It has self-catering facilities, a café, laundry, heated outdoor pool, and cycle- and canoe-rental, as well as single, double and family rooms, some of which are en suite: advance reservations are obligatory from September to February and May to mid-June. Despite the hostel's name, it is actually 6km from Mjølfjell train station, and only 300m from Ørneberget station. You can drive here, too, just about – the hostel is at the end of a narrow minor road that begins in Voss – but you can't drive any further east to Myrdal and Finse.

Finse

Beyond Ørneberget, the higher reaches of the railway line are desolate even in good weather. All trains stop at **Myrdal**, a remote railway junction where you change for the extraordinary train ride down to Flåm (see box on p.216), and then proceed onto **FINSE**, the railway's highest point, a solitary lakeside outpost on the northern periphery of the Hardangervidda. Heading east from Finse, the train takes forty minutes to reach Geilo (see p.174), three and a half hours more to Oslo.

Finse consists of nothing more than its station and a few isolated buildings, bunkered down against the howling winds that rip across the plateau in wintertime. One of buildings, just east of the station, houses the **Rallarmuseet** (Feb to early July Mon–Fri 10am–3pm; early July to Sept daily 10am–10pm; 30kr), containing a pictorial record of the planning and construction of the Oslo–Bergen railway, which was completed in 1909. The old black-and-white photos are the most interesting exhibits and a tribute to the navvies, who survived such grim conditions.

There's snow here from the beginning of November until well into June, and the **cross-country skiing** is particularly enthusiastic, with locals actually skiing off from the station. You can rent cross-country ski equipment at the *Finse 1222 Hotel* (see below), but you'll need to book it in advance. Outside of the ski season, **hiking** is popular, in particular the four-hour trail to the Blåisen snout, on the northeast edge of the **Hardangerjøkulen glacier**. Other, longer trails skirt the glacier to traverse the main body of the Hardangervidda plateau (see p.210). From Finse, it's an eleven-hour hike to reach Highway 7 at Dyranut (see p.211), so most hikers overnight after around eight hours at the self-service **Kjeldebu** DNT hut (March to mid-Oct).

Mountain bikes can be rented from the bike shop on the station platform for the ride along the old construction road, the **Rallarvegen**, which was originally laid to provide access for men and materials during the building of the mountain section of the railway. Surfaced with gravel and sometimes asphalt, the Rallarvegen runs west from Haugastøl to Finse and then continues to Flåm, a total distance of 80km; there's also an extension from the Myrdal junction to Ørneberget and the Raun Valley. The most popular stretch of the road passes through fine upland scenery as it leads the 35km west from Finse to Myrdal, though the first 21km (to Hallingskeid) is the highest part of the route and can be blocked by snow as late as July; check conditions locally. Most cyclists travel east to west as Finse is a good deal higher than Myrdal, and do the return trip by train: NSB railways will transport bikes for a small fee.

Finse has two **places to stay**: both are lodge-cum-chalet complexes, geared up for hikers, cyclists and skiers, and offering advice and guided excursions of various types – glacier-walking, in particular. Of the two, the *Finse 1222 Hotel* (☎56 52 71 00, ℉56 52 67 17; ⓦwww.finse1222.no; closed mid-Oct to Jan; ❼) is far more comfortable, with pleasant rooms, a good restaurant, plus a sauna, ice baths and a Turkish bath. The more frugal option is DNT's fully staffed *Finsehytta* (☎56 52 67 32, ℉56 52 67 60; mid-March to late May & July to mid-Sept; dorm beds 130kr; doubles ❶), which sleeps up to 150.

North from Voss to Flåm

Heading north from Voss, the **E16** covers the 65km to Flam, providing fine mountain and valley views and even boring beneath the mountains themselves in two stretches of tunnel – one of 11km and one of 5km – both constructed at colossal expense. This road now forms part of the fast route between Oslo and Bergen, but you can avoid most of the traffic by branching off at the Vinje crossroads, 20km out of Voss, onto **Highway 13**, which winds a scenic, 57km route north over the mountains to Vangsnes and the Sognefjord.

The E16 is served by regular **express buses** (2–6 daily) from Voss bound for Gudvangen, Flåm and ultimately Sogndal, while eastbound **trains** from Voss stop at Myrdal, where you change for the branch line to Flåm (see box on p.216). There are no buses serving Highway 13 to Vangsnes.

Highway 13 to Vangsnes

If you have your own transport, a tempting proposition, when driving north from Voss, is to turn off the E16 along **Highway 13**, a much quieter road but just as handsome. A quintessential fjordland journey, the highway begins by clambering up the Myrkdal valley passing waterfalls and wild ravines, before cutting an improbable route across the bleak and icy wastes of Vikafjell mountain, then weaving down to the stave church at Vik (see p.225). The highway is closed in winter – usually from late November to April – and snow is piled high on either side of the road until at least the end of May. Just beyond Vik, at **Vangsnes**, the ferry (see p.223) crosses the Sognefjord to give ready access to Balestrand (see p.221) and the fjord's beautiful northern shore.

The E16 to Stalheim, Gudvangen and Undredal

Back on E16, it's about 35km from Voss to **STALHEIM** and the 1.5km-long road that threads its way up to the *Stalheim Hotel* (☎56 52 01 22, ℉56 52 00 56, ⓦwww.stalheim.com; ❻), one of the region's finest. There has been a hotel here since the late nineteenth century, but today's building, a large and solid-looking lodge, dates from the 1960s. Parts of the interior have been kitted out in antique Norwegian style and the modern bedrooms are very well-appointed, but the highlight is the view – a simply breathtaking vista down along the Nærøyfjord.

From Stalheim, it's a further 10km or so along the E16 to the dreary miniport of **GUDVANGEN**, a forlorn little place at the southern tip of the

The Flåm railway (Flåmsbana)

Lonely **Myrdal**, just forty minutes by train from Voss, is the start of one of Europe's most celebrated branch rail lines, the **Flåmsbana** (mid-June to mid-September 10 daily; mid-September to mid-June 4 daily; 125kr single, 205kr return; ⓦwww. flaamsbana.no). Plummeting 900 metres down the Flåmsdal valley to **Flåm**, this fifty-minute, 20-kilometre train ride is not to be missed under any circumstances. The track, which took four years to lay in the 1920s, spirals down the mountainside, passing through hand-dug tunnels and, at one point, doubling back on itself to drop nearly 300m. The gradient of the line is one of the steepest in the world and as the tiny train squeals down the mountain, past cascading waterfalls, it's reassuring to know that it has five separate sets of brakes, each capable of bringing it to a stop. The service runs all year round, a local lifeline during the deep winter months.

It is possible to do the five-hour **walk** from the railway junction at Myrdal down the old road into the valley, instead of taking the train, but much the better option is to disembark about halfway down and walk in from there. **Berekvam** station, halfway along at an altitude of 343m, will do very nicely, leaving an enthralling two-to three-hour hike through changing mountain scenery down to Flåm. **Cycling** down the valley road is also perfectly feasible, though it's too steep to be relaxing.

Nærøyfjord. In the summertime, hundreds of tourists pour through here partly because of the car ferry connections to Kaupanger, but mainly because it's on the "Norway in a Nutshell" itinerary (see box on p.206). A modern complex down by the jetty incorporates souvenir shops, a café and a **hotel** of unusual design, the *Gudvangen Fjordtell* (ⓣ57 63 39 29, ⓕ57 63 39 80; late March to mid-Dec; ❸), consisting of a series of hut-like structures with turf roofs.

Just beyond Gudvangen, the E16 disappears into an 11km-long tunnel to emerge a few kilometres short of Flåm and a few hundred metres before the 6km-long byroad that romps down a boulder-strewn valley to **UNDREDAL**. Perched on the edge of the Aurlandsfjord, it's a peculiar little place, with narrow lanes overshadowed by the severity of the surrounding mountains. There's been a settlement here since Viking times as evidenced by the village **church** (mid-May to late June & late Aug to mid-Sept Sat & Sun 10am–5pm; late June to late Aug daily 10am–5pm; 25kr), parts of which date back to the twelfth century. A tiny affair, it's decorated in fine folkloric style – from the floral patterns on the walls and the stars and naïve figures on the ceiling, through to Christ crucified above the high altar.

Flåm

Fringed by meadows and orchards, the village of **FLÅM** sits beside the Aurlandsfjord, a slender branch of the Sognefjord, with mountains glowering behind. Despite its splendid setting, first impressions are poor: the fjordside complex adjoining the train station is crass and commercial – souvenir trolls and the like – and on summer days the tiny village heaves with tourists, who pour off the train, have lunch, and then promptly head out by bus and ferry. But a brief stroll is enough to leave the crowds behind at the harbourside, while out of season, or in the evening when the day-trippers have all moved on, Flåm is a pleasant spot – and an eminently agreeable place to spend the night. If you are prepared to risk the weather, mid-September is perhaps the best time to visit; the peaks already have a covering of snow and the vegetation is just turning its autumnal golden brown.

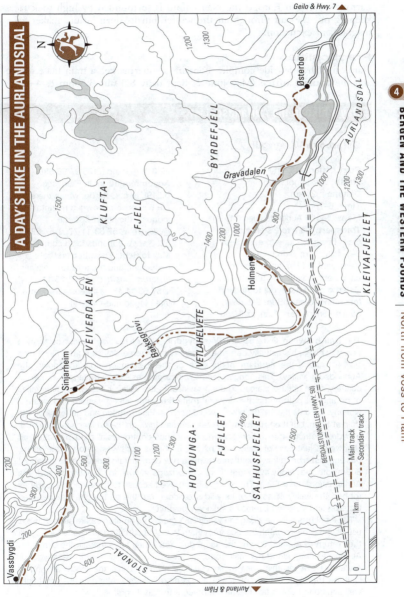

A DAY'S HIKE IN THE AURLANDSDAL

Geilo & Hwy. 7 ▲

Østerbø

BYRDEFJELL

Gravadalen

AURLANDSDAL

KLUFTA-

FJELL

KLEIVAFJELLET

Holmen

VEIVERDALEN

Bakkegrovi

VETLAHELVETE

Sinjarheim

HOVDUNGA-

FJELLET

SALHUSFJELLET

BERDALSTUNNELLEN (HWY. 50)

— Main track
····· Secondary track

0   1km

Vassbygdi

STONDAL

Aurland & Flåm ▼

Flåm is also the starting point for one of the most stupendous **ferry trips** in the fjords, the two-hour cruise up the Aurlandsfjord and down its offshoot, the **Nærøyfjord**, to Gudvangen (1-4 daily; 170kr single, 210kr return). The narrowest fjord in Europe, the Nærøyfjord is surrounded by high rock faces keeping out the sun throughout the winter, but its stern beauty makes for a magnificent excursion.

Practicalities

Flåm's ugly harbourside complex contains a supermarket, a train ticket office and the **tourist office** (May, June & Sept daily 8.30am–3.30pm & 4–8pm;

Day's hike in the Aurlandsdal

Østerbo to Vassbygdi

Start: Østerbø (820m).
Finish: Vassbygdi (94m).
Distance: 21 km.
Time: 6–7hr.
Maps: 1416 I Aurlandsdalen (M711).
Transport: Flåm to Østerbø on the Geilo bus (mid-June to early Sept 2–3 daily; 1hr); Østerbø and Vassbygdi to Flåm (mid-June to early Sept 1 daily; 1hr 10min/30min). Østerbø and Vassbygdi to Aurland (mid-June to early Sept 2–5 daily; 55min/15min). Taxi: Flåm (T 94 50

49 31); Aurland (T 95 97 98 68).
Accommodation: In Flåm (see p.219), or in Østerbø, where there are two privately-owned mountain lodges – the smart *Østerbø Fjellstove* (T 57 63 11 77, F 57 63 11 52; W www.aurlandsdalen.com; late May to Sept; ❸), with a first-rate restaurant, and the adjacent, plainer *Østerbø Turisthytte* (T 57 63 11 41, F 57 63 11 18; E ingeos@online.no; late May to mid-Oct; ❷).

The **trail between Østerbø and Vassbygdi** is one of Norway's most celebrated one-day hikes. It's actually part of a classic two- or three-day hike from Finse (see p.214), across the northern peripheries of the Hardangervidda and down the Aurlandsdal valley. This longer journey incorporates an extravagant range of scenery, from upland plateau to deep ravines; in the valley, it traces the final miles of an ancient path and cattle drovers' route that once linked eastern and western Norway. Up until the 1970s, hikers would begin at Finse station and get back on the train at Flåm, but then **Highway 50** was rammed through the Aurlandsdal as part of a hydroelectricity generation scheme. This once-controversial road branches off Highway 7 just east of Geilo (see p.174), and runs northwest through the valley, passing **Østerbø**, a lonely settlement with a pair of mountain lodges, situated about 800m off the highway. From here, it zigzags down to Vassbygdi and the Aurlandsfjord, near Flåm. Though it has improved access to the area, the road has robbed the valley of some of its wild splendour, but the part of the trail between Østerbø and Vassbygdi remains strikingly beautiful.

The local **bus** service along the valley isn't great, but timetables are such that it is usually possible to catch the bus from Flåm to Østerbø, make the hike to Vassbygdi then return to Aurland by bus the same day. You'll then have to walk the 6km from Aurland to Flåm along the main road, as there's nowhere to stay in Vassbygdi or Aurland. However, this does mean you'll be hiking against the clock; arriving at Østerbø the night before can make things more leisurely. Alternatively, you might well decide to book a taxi for the return leg from Vassbygdi.

Start your walk in Østerbø by locating the vehicle access track behind the large, red mountain lodge and, with the lake to your rear, hike uphill and through a gate. A

July–Aug daily 8.30am–8pm; ☎57 63 21 06), which sells hiking maps and ferry tickets, and gives out a useful free booklet containing public transport timetables and all sorts of local information. Flåm's only **hotel** is the *Fretheim* (☎57 63 63 00; ⓕ57 63 64 00; ⓦwww.fretheim-hotel.no; ➎), a rambling building whose attractive older part, with high-pitched roofs and white-painted clapboard, is flanked by a modern extension containing well-appointed rooms. The hotel is set back from the water a couple of hundred metres from the station. Alternatively, the *Heimly Pensjonat* (☎57 63 23 00, ⓕ57 63 23 40; ➌, s/r ➍) provides simple but adequate lodgings in a mundane, modern block that overlooks the fjord, about 450m east of the train station along the shore. For budget

few hundred metres on, cross the bridge you see to your left; it's here you pick up the first DNT sign to Vassbygdi. The path continues downhill towards the lake and eventually passes a small farmhouse. With the Østerbø huts now behind you, the track starts to head steadily uphill. It is etched into the hillside and clearly delineated by worn stones and the occasional red "T".

After 45minutes, you cross over some large slabs of rock to reach a gate. Go through the gate, and almost immediately the track drops down a steep hillside and under a rock overhang, with a marvellous view of the river valley and the **Gravadalen** waterfall. About one hour into the hike you cross the bridge over the Gravadalen river and arrive at a farmhouse with solar panels. Walking alongside the farmhouse, you cross a small meadow to go through another gate, which brings you to a wide stretch of the river. With the river on your left, keep going past the bridge and, half an hour on from the farmhouse, you reach a cairn marked **Grimerodl**. The next bit of the track can get quite boggy as it cuts across numerous streams, but soon you start to climb away from the valley floor, the hillsides dusted with pine and birch trees.

Two hours into the hike, the track reaches a sign marked **Sondrelli**. At this point there is a steep 150-metre descent to the river and the track is cut into the rock. A rope handrail is provided for reassurance, and the track itself is never less than 0.75m wide. About forty-five minutes later, the river disappears from sight to your left and you push on through the trees to a fork in the track – keep to the right. A few minutes later, you're heading down towards the river again and, three hours into the hike, you reach a bridge. Don't cross it, but instead follow the "T"s across the scree and boulder-studded mountainside.

Three-and-a-half hours from the start of your hike, you will come to the sign for **Vetlahelvete** (Little Hell Cave), a sombre and partly water-filled cave with a domed ceiling, a short walk off the trail. The walls are smooth, and there is a narrow open space at the top that lets in a bit of light. Back on the main track, it's another half-hour to the **Bakkegrovi** stream, which you cross, and then there's a further half-hour scramble downwards with the vegetation becoming thicker: wild raspberries, geraniums and ferns all grow freely here.

About five hours into the hike, you cross the spray-splattered bridge over the **Veiverdalselvi** and then head up towards the **Sinjarheim** summer farmhouse. Fifteen minutes' walk after and below the farmhouse, the route – blasted through rock walls – follows the riverside and there are rope handholds to assist hikers. Having traversed this tricky section, scramble down the rocky hillside, crossing several streams by a mixture of stepping stones and bridges, until, nearly six hours' walk from your starting point, you reach the start of a stretch of tree-lined river. An hour on from here and you leave the footpath for a country lane, which brings you down to the car park and bus stop in dreary **Vassbygdi**.

accommodation, the neat and trim *Flåm Camping*, a couple of minutes' sign-posted walk from the train station, has tent spaces and cabins (**❶**), and incorporates a small and well-kept HI **hostel** (May–Sept; ☎57 63 21 21, ☏57 63 23 80; ✉flaam.hostel@vandrerhjem.no; dorm beds 115kr, doubles **❶**). The only good place to **eat** in Flåm is the *Fretheim Hotell*, where they serve a banquet-like buffet every night; go early to get the pick of the dishes.

Moving on from Flåm

From Flåm, there are daily **Hurtigbåt** passenger express boat services up the Aurlandsfjord and then along the Sognefjord to Bergen; ports of call include Vik, Balestrand and Vangsnes. The one-way trip to Bergen takes five-and-a-half hours and costs 490kr; Balestrand is an hour-and-a-half away and costs 140kr. By **train**, Myrdal, at the top of the Flåmsbana, is on the main Oslo-Bergen line, while Sognebussen **express buses** (2-6 daily) pass through Flåm bound for a variety of destinations, including Bergen, Voss, Gudvangen and Sogndal. From mid-June to early September, **local buses** run south past the Aurlandsdal hamlets of Vassbygdi and Østerbø en route to Geilo (see box on p.218 for details). Heading east **by car**, it's tempting to use the brand new, free 24-kilometre-long tunnel from Aurlandsdal to Lærdal, that completes the fast road – the E16 – from Bergen to Oslo, though the 45km-long mountain road that the tunnel replaced has survived to provide splendid views and some hair-raising moments. Known as the **Snøvegen,** or snow road, it's open from the beginning of June to around the middle of October.

The Sognefjord

Profoundly beautiful, the **Sognefjord** drills in from the coast for some 200km, its inner recesses splintering into half a dozen subsidiary fjords. None of the villages and small towns that dot the fjord quite lives up to the splendid setting, but **Balestrand** and **Mundal**, on the Fjærlandsfjord, come close and are easily the best bases. Both are on the north side of the fjord which, given the lack of roads on the south side, is where you want (or pretty much have) to be, unless you're arriving from Flåm (p.216).

For almost its whole length, the Sognefjord's north bank is hugged by Highway 55, which slices northeast at **Sogndal** to clip past the **Lustrafjord**. Side roads lead off this part of the highway to a pair of top-notch attractions, **Urnes stave church** and, further north, to the east side of the Jostedalsbreen glacier at Nigardsbreen (see p.227). Thereafter – as the **Sognefjellsveg** - the road climbs steeply to run along the western side of the **Jotunheimen mountains**, an extraordinarily beautiful journey even by Norwegian standards and one which culminates with the road heading down to Lom on Highway 15.

Public transport to and around the Sognefjord is generally excellent. Operating about halfway along the fjord, perhaps the most useful of the **car ferries** links Vangsnes, Hella and Dragsvik (for Balestrand), but in the east of the fjord the 24-hour shuttle between Fodnes and Manheller is useful too, especially if you're arriving from Oslo on the E16 (see p.173). **Hurtigbåt** passenger express boat services connect Bergen, Balestrand, Vangsnes and Flåm, and long-distance **buses** come up from Bergen via Voss and the Fodnes-Mannheller ferry, bound for Sogndal. Here, further bus services shadow the Sognefjord's northern shore, running west to Hella and Balestrand and east to

Oslo, while other buses run up Highway 5 to Mundal and the Nordfjord (see p.229). There are no buses, however, along the Sognefjellsveg (Highway 55).

Balestrand and around

An appealing first stop, **BALESTRAND** has been a tourist destination since the middle of the nineteenth century, when it was discovered by European travellers in search of cool, clear air and picturesque mountain scenery. Kaiser Wilhelm II was a frequent visitor, too, sharing his holiday spot with the British bourgeoisie. These days, the village is used as a touring base for the immediate area, as the battery of small hotels and restaurants above the quay testifies, but it's all very small scale and among the 1000-strong population, farming still remains the principal livelihood. An hour or so will suffice to take a peek at Balestrand's two attractions. The **English church of St Olav** (free) is a spiky brown-and-beige wooden structure built in 1897 in the general style of a stave church at the behest of a British émigré, Margaret Kvikne, who moved here after she married a local curate. One of those curious relics from Britain's imperial past, the church remains part of the Diocese of Gibraltar, which arranges English-language services during the summer. The Germans have left their mark too. About 300m south of the church along the fjord are two humpy **Viking burial mounds**, supposedly the tombs of King Bele and his wife. On the larger of them is a statue of the king in heroic pose, put there by the kaiser in 1913, to match the statue of Bele's son-in-law that stands tall across the fjord in Vangsnes (see p.225).

Several **hiking trails** ascend the rocky slopes immediately to the west of the village clambering up to the peaks and lakes of the plateau beyond. None of them are easy – all begin with a short, stiff climb and pass through boggy ground, while several have steep drops – but the scenery is splendid. Balestrand

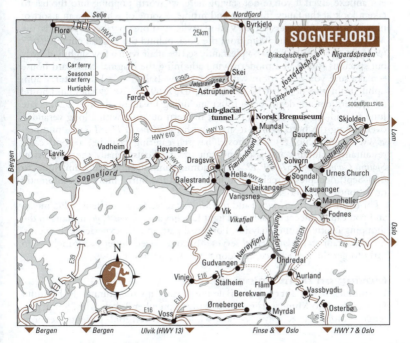

tourist office (see below) sells a detailed hiking map with multilingual trail descriptions, though if the weather is poor you'd be advised to leave the mountains alone, and stick to a much easier 4hr-hike along the bottom of the **Norddal valley** to the prettily situated Norddalsvatnet lake. To get to the trail head, drive west from Balestrand along Highway 55, for 24km, to **Nessane**, where a short and narrow byroad leads up the valley, past the Nessadalsvatnet lake to the car park; the trail head is just beyond. Note that after heavy rain, the trail gets far too squelchy to be much fun.

Practicalities

The only **car ferry** to Balestrand is the summertime service from Mundal, on the Fjærlandsfjord (see below); otherwise, the nearest you'll get is Dragsvik, 9km to the north of Balestrand, with ferries from Hella and Vangsnes (see below). Balestrand is served, however, by the **Hurtigbåt** which – like the Mundal ferry – docks at the quayside, plumb in the centre of the village. **Buses** stop beside the quayside too, in front of the Spar supermarket, behind which is the **tourist office** (early June & late Aug to Sept Mon–Fri 7.30am–1pm & 3.30–6pm, Sat 7.30am–1pm & 3.30–6.30pm & Sun 8am–12.30pm & 3.30–5.30pm; late June to late Aug Mon–Fri 7.30am–1pm & 3.30–9pm, Sat 7.30am–1pm & 3.30–6.30pm & Sun 8am–12.30pm & 3.30–6.30pm; Oct–May Mon–Fri 9am–3pm; ℡57 69 12 55; Ⓦwww.sognefjorden.no), which sells local hiking maps (70kr), issues bus and ferry timetables and rents bikes (30kr per hour; 75 kr per half-day; 150kr per day).

Balestrand's priciest **accommodation** is at *Kvikne's Hotel* (℡57 69 42 00, Ⓕ57 69 42 01; Ⓦwww.kviknes.no; ❹; May–Sept), whose various buildings dominate much of the waterfront. The best and most expensive rooms are old and overlook the fjord, while the cheaper rooms are round the back in a modern annexe. Even if you're not staying here, it's worth popping into the bar to take a look at the fancy furniture and fittings – some of which are in a sort of nineteenth-century version of Viking style. A more low-key option is the *Midtnes Pensjonat*, about 300m from the dock behind the English church (℡57 69 11 33, Ⓕ57 69 15 84; ❸), a pleasantly sedate affair with a few slightly dowdy but spacious rooms in a modern wing adjoining the original clapboard house – make sure you get a room with a fjord view. Balestrand's HI **hostel,** 150m uphill from the dock (℡57 69 13 03, Ⓕ57 69 16 70; Ⓔbalestrand.hostel @vandrerhjem.no; dorm beds 180kr including breakfast, doubles 520kr; late June to mid-Aug), occupies a pleasant modern building with a long verandah overlooking the fjord, which it shares with the *Kringsjå Hotell* (same number; Ⓦwww.kringsja.no; ❷). The hostel has self-catering facilities, a good café-restaurant, a laundry, and also rents out rowing boats. Finally, the **campsite**, *Sjøtun Camping* (℡57 69 12 23; Ⓔsjotun_camping@hotmail.com; June to mid-Sept) occupies a treeless field just beyond the burial mounds, a kilometre or so south of the dock.

For **food**, both the *Kringsjå* and the *Midtnes* serve tasty, excellent-value meals, and you can get decent snacks and light lunches at *Gekkens Café*, upstairs in the shopping centre on the quayside. For a real gastronomic experience, however, the restaurant at *Kvikne's Hotel* serves a banquet-sized buffet every night – go early to get the best choice, and don't miss the lemon mousse.

Moving on from Balestrand

In summer, a **car ferry** from Balestrand runs up the stunningly beautiful Fjærlandfjord to Mundal (late May to early September 2 daily; 1hr 25min; passengers 140kr; car & driver 245kr), while the **Hurtigbåt** passenger express boat links Balestrand with Vik and Bergen in one direction, Vangsnes, Sogndal and Flåm in the other (year-round 2-3 daily). From Balestrand, the *Sogn og Fjordane* **express bus** heads west to Førde (Mon–Fri 1 daily; 2hr), where you can change for the coastal town of Florø (see p.246) or Stryn and the Nordfjord (see p.229), and east to Sogndal (3 daily; 1hr 50min) and ultimately Oslo. At Sogndal, you can change for Mundal (see p.223), though services rarely connect and you're likely to have to wait for at least an hour or two.

Driving north from Balestrand, Highway 13 cuts a scenic route over the mountains on its way to the junction with the E39, which itself proceeds north to the Nordfjord, while Highway 55 runs east to Sogndal via the Dragsvik to Hella **car ferry** (15min; passengers 19kr, car & driver 50kr). The same ferry also runs to Vangsnes on the fjord's southern coast (25min; passengers 21kr, car & driver 57kr): sailings to both destinations are every forty minutes or so from mid-June to mid-August, hourly the rest of the year, and run from around 6am to 10pm or 11pm daily.

Mundal and around

To the north of Balestrand, the **Fjærlandsfjord** is a wild place, its flanks blanketed with a thick covering of trees extending down to the water's edge, while a succession of thundering waterfalls tumble down vast clefts in the rock up above. The village of **MUNDAL** – sometimes referred to as Fjærland – matches its surroundings perfectly, a gentle ribbon of old wooden houses edging the fjord, with the mountains as a backcloth. It's one of the region's most picturesque places, saved from the developers by its isolation: it was one of the last settlements on the Sognefjord to be connected to the road system, with Highway 5 from Sogndal only being completed in 1986. Moreover, it's eschewed the crasser forms of commercialism and become the self-styled "Norwegian Book Town" (Den norske bokbyen), with a dozen old buildings accommodating antiquarian and second-hand **bookshops** (mostly open mid-May to early September daily 10am–6pm). Naturally enough, most of the books are in Norwegian, but there's a liberal sprinkling of English editions too.

Bookshops aside, the village has two good-looking buildings, the first of which is the **Hotel Mundal** (see p.224), whose nineteenth-century turrets, verandahs and high-pitched roofs overlook the fjord from amongst the handful of buildings that amount to the village centre. Next door, the 1861 **church** (June–Aug daily 10am–6pm; free) is a serious affair, lacking in ornamentation but immaculately maintained; its graveyard hints at the hard but healthy life of the district's farmers – most of them seem to have lived to a ripe old age. Many locals are still farmers, but in summer hardly any of them herd their cattle up to the mountain pastures as was the custom until the 1960s. The disused tracks to these summer farms (*støls*) now serve as **hiking trails** of varying length and difficulty. The tourist office (see p.224) will advise, but one of the easier routes is the two-hour (each way) jaunt west along a country lane up **Mundalsdal** to **Heimastølen**, from where a track continues up to the marshy pastures of **Mundalsfjellstølen**.

Around Mundal

The marshes at the head of the Fjærlandsfjord, about 2km north of Mundal are frequented by a wide range of migratory birds in spring and autumn, enough to have prompted the establishment of the **Bøyaøyri nature reserve**. Along a quiet byroad that links Mundal with Highway 5, the reserve isn't huge and there are no hides, but with a pair of binoculars it's easy enough to watch the birds from the roadside. About 500m beyond the reserve, just off the main road, the **Norsk Bremuseum** (Norwegian Glacier Museum; April, May, Sept & Oct daily 10am–4pm; June–Aug daily 9am–7pm; information and enquiries free but displays 75kr; ☎57 69 32 88, ⓦwww.bre.museum.no) tells you more than you ever wanted to know about glaciers and then some. It features several lavish hands-on displays – like a simulated walk below a glacier – and screens films about glaciers; package tourists turn up in droves.

The museum is one of the Jostedalsbreen Nasjonalpark's three information centres (see p.227 and p.232) for details of the others), and has details of all the various guided glacier walks on offer across the park, as outlined in its "Breturar" (glacier walks) leaflet. The usual target from Mundal is the **Supphellebreen**, the Jostedalsbreen's nearest hikeable arm, or, to be precise, that part of it called **Flatbreen**. This challenging section of the glacier is not that easy to get to, however, and the whole excursion takes between six and eight hours: advance reservations, at least a day beforehand, are also essential (July only; ☎57 69 32 33; 400kr per person). If all that doesn't deter you, the Flatbreen does pay dividends with its fabulous scenery. The excursion begins at the Øygarden car park, about 3km off Highway 5 – watch for the sign just 2km north of the Bremuseum. From the car park, it's a stiff two-hour hike up the trail to the meeting point, the **Flatbrehytta**, an unstaffed DNT mountain hut. Thereafter, you spend two to three hours on the glacier. The hike up from Øygarden to the hut is a fine excursion in itself, so you might decide to dispense with the glacier walk. In this case, don't go back the way you came, but instead walk east from the Flatbrehytta along the less clearly defined trail that traverses the glacier's lateral moraine, providing superb views over the ice, and return to the car park via the next valley along.

At the other extreme, you can get close to the glacier without breaking sweat just 10km north of Mundal on Highway 5. Here, just before you enter the tunnel, look out for the signposted side road on the right, leading the 200m to the *Brævasshytta* restaurant (May–Sept daily 9am–5/8pm). This smart, modern place, a package-tour favourite, overlooks the slender glacial lake fed by the **Bøyabreen** arm of the glacier up above. It takes a couple of minutes to stroll down from the restaurant to the lake, close to the sooty shank of the glacier.

Mundal practicalities

The nearest you'll get to Mundal by regular **bus** is the Norsk Bremuseum on Highway 5, from where it's an easy 2.5-kilometre stroll south along the fjord to the village. **Ferries** arriving from Balestrand dock in the centre of Mundal where they connect with excursion buses (bookable here or in Balestrand), which take passengers to the Bremuseum for an hour or so, and then on to the Bøyabreen. Arriving **by car** from the south, you'll have a whopping 150kr toll to pay on Highway 5, just before you reach the turning for the village. Mundal **tourist office**, metres from the boat dock (late May to early Sept daily 9.30am–5.30pm; ☎57 69 32 33), advises on local hiking routes, sells hiking maps and has bus and ferry timetables; it also rents out **bikes** at 25kr per hour, 125kr per day.

There are two fjordside **hotels** in Mundal. The obvious choice is the splendid *Hotel Mundal* (☎57 69 31 01, ⓕ57 69 31 79; ⓦwww.fjordinfo.no/mundal; May to late Sept; ❺), a quirky place, whose public rooms display many original features, from the parquet floors and fancy wooden scrollwork through to the old-fashioned sliding doors of the cavernous dining room. The bedrooms are frugal and some show their age, but somehow it doesn't matter much. If you do stay, look out for the old photos on the walls of men in plus-fours and hob-nail boots clambering round the glaciers – only softies bothered with gloves. Nearby, the *Fjærland Fjordstue Hotell* (☎57 69 32 00, ℉57 69 31 61; ⓦwww.home.sol.no; ③) is very different – a well-tended family hotel with smart modern furnishings and a conservatory overlooking the fjord. Alternatively, *Bøyum Camping* (☎57 69 32 52) near the Bremuseum, has huts (❶) as well as spaces for tents. Both hotels offer good, wholesome **food**.

Moving on from Mundal, you can pick up long-distance **buses** along Highway 5 from the bus stop close to the Bremuseum. Services head south to Sogndal and Oslo along the E16 (3–4 daily), and north to Skei and Førde (3 daily): change at Skei for onward services north to Stryn and the Nordfjord (see p.229).

Vangsnes and Vik

From Balestrand, Highway 55 loops for 9km around the Esefjord, an inlet of the Sognefjord, to the quayside at **Dragsvik**, from where car ferries cross the mouth of the Fjærlandsfjord to Hella for the road to Sogndal (see below). They also shuttle across the Sognefjord to **VANGSNES**, where local farmers must have had a real shock when, in 1913, Kaiser Wilhelm erected a twelve-metre high **statue** of the legendary Viking chief Fridtjof the Bold on the hilltop above their jetty. The Fridtjovstatuen still stands, an eccentric monument to the Kaiser's fascination with Nordic mythology – Fridtjof the Bold was in love with Ingebjorg, daughter of King Bele, whose statue, also commissioned by the Kaiser, is back across the fjord at Balestrand. You can walk the 500m up from the jetty to take a closer look at Fridtjof, also gaining fine views of the fjord from the top.

From Vangsnes, it's a straight 11km south along the water's edge to **VIK**, a rather half-hearted village that sprawls up a wide valley. The only reason to stop here is to see the **Hopperstad stave church** (mid-May to mid-June & mid-Aug to mid-Sept daily 10am–5pm; mid-June to mid-Aug daily 9am–7pm; 40kr), sat on a hillock just off Highway 13, about 1500m from the fjord. In the 1880s the locals were about to knock it down, but a visiting architect and his antiquarian chum persuaded them to change their minds. The pair promptly set about repairing the place and did a good job. Today the church is one of the best examples of its type, its angular roofing surmounted by a long and slender tower. The interior has its moments too, with a Gothic side-altar canopy, parts of which may have been swiped from France by the Vikings, and a so-called lepers' window through which the afflicted listened to church services.

Beyond Vik, Highway 13 begins its long scramble up and over the windswept wastes of the **Vikafjell** mountain to Voss, 70km to the south (see p.212).

Sogndal and Kaupanger

From **Hella**, across the fjord from Dragsvik, it's 40km along the water's edge to **SOGNDAL** – bigger and livelier than Balestrand, but still hardly a major metropolis, with a population of just 6000. Neither is Sogndal as appealing: it has a pleasant fjord setting in a broad valley, surrounded by low, green hills dotted with apple and pear trees, but its centre is a rash of modern concrete and glass. Frankly, there are other much more agreeable spots within a few kilometres' radius and your best option is to keep going.

Buses drop passengers at the **station** – a major interchange – on the west side of the town centre at the end of Gravensteinsgata, the long main drag. From here, it's about 500m east along Gravensteinsgata to the **tourist office** (late June to late Aug Mon–Fri 9am–8pm, Sat 10am–5pm, Sun 3–8pm; late Aug to late June Mon–Fri 9am–4pm; ☎57 67 30 83; ⓦwww.sognefjorden.no), housed in one of the street's flashy modern buildings. It issues bus and ferry timetables, and has a list of local **accommodation**, though choices are fairly limited. The best of a poor bunch is the *Hofslund Fjord Hotel*, a stone's throw from the tourist office (T57 67 10 22, F57 67 16 30; W www.hofslund-hotel.no; ❸), in an old wooden building with a modern annexe; ask for a room with a fjord view. A cheaper option is the HI **hostel** (T57 67 20 33, F57 67 31 45; E sogndal.hostel@vandrerhjem.no; dorm beds 100kr, doubles ❶; mid-June to mid-Aug), which manages to feel quite homely despite being housed in a boarding school: it's signposted near the bridge at the east end of town, about 400m beyond the roundabout that marks the eastern extent of Gravensteinsgata. This same roundabout – about 50m from the tourist office – also marks the start of Fjøravegen, Sogndal's other main drag, which cuts through the town's commercial heart. For **food**, the choice is uninspiring, but the restaurant at the *Quality Hotel Sogndal*, Gravensteinsgata 5 (T57 62 77 00), is reliable, offering tasty Norwegian dishes at affordable prices.

Moving on from Sogndal, the **Hurtigbåt** passenger express boat goes to Flåm in one direction, Balestrand, Vik and Bergen in the other. **Express buses** head northwest to Fjærland and Skei (for Stryn) and southeast to Oslo via the 24hr Manheller-Fodnes **car ferry** (every 30min; 15min; car & driver 80kr, passengers 27kr), and the E16. **Local buses** run from Sogndal up Highway 55 to the beginning of the Sognefjellsvegen, serving Solvorn (Mon-Sat 1–2 daily; 25min), Elvekrok, for access to the Nigardsbreen glacier (2–5 daily; 1hr 30min), and Skjolden (1–2 daily; 1hr 30min). Note that there are currently no through services to Lom.

Kaupanger

About 10km southeast of Sogndal on Highway 5, the village of **KAUPANGER** is worth a quick detour. Here, the red and white timber houses of the old part of the village slope up from the harbour towards the **stave church** (early June to mid-Aug daily 10am–5.30pm; 30kr), a much modified thirteenth-century structure whose dourness is offset by its situation: the church stands on a hillside amid buttercup meadows with views of the fjord on one side and forested hills on the other. The interior has a couple of unusual features, too, including a musical score painted on one of the walls and a sad portrait of a Danish bailiff and his family with three stillborn babies. Afterwards, head down to the dock to visit the **Sognefjord Båtmuseum** (Boat Museum; June–Aug daily 10am–6pm; 50kr), with its assortment of mostly nineteenth-century wooden boats. Exhibits range from sturdy inshore fishing boats and ice boats (fitted with runners for use on frozen fjord inlets) to daintier, faster craft used by Danish dignitaries.

Solvorn and Urnes stave church

Some 15km northeast of Sogndal, a steep 3km-long road branches off Highway 55 to snake its way down to **SOLVORN**, an attractive little hamlet beneath the mountains on the sheltered foreshore of the **Lustrafjord**. Solvorn is home to the *Walaker Hotell* (T57 68 20 80, F57 68 20 81; W www.walaker .com; ❹), whose conspicuous, ugly, motel-style modern block contrasts dramatically with the old house, a comely pastel-painted building with a lovely garden, and first-rate period bedrooms.

Urnes stave church

From Solvorn, a local **car ferry** (early June to Aug hourly Mon-Fri 10am–4pm, Sat & Sun 11am–4pm; Sept to early June Mon-Fri 2–4 daily, Sun

1 daily; 20min; passenger 22kr, car & driver 60kr) shuttles across the Lustrafjord to **Ornes**, from where it's a stiff, ten-minute hike up the hill to **Urnes stave church** (early June–Aug guided tours only; daily 10.30am–5.30pm; 40kr). Magnificently sited with the fjord and the snow-dusted mountains as its backdrop, this is the oldest stave church in Norway, dating from the twelfth century, and famous for its wonderful **carvings**. On the outside, incorporated into the north wall, are two exquisite door panels, the remains of an earlier church dating from around 1070 and alive with a swirling filigree of strange beasts and delicate vegetation. These forceful, superbly crafted panels bear witness to the sophistication of Viking woodcarving, and indeed this distinctively Nordic art form, found in many countries where Viking influence was felt, is generally known as the Urnes style. Much of the church's interior is seventeenth-century, including some splendidly bulbous pomegranates, but there is Viking woodcarving here too, notably the strange-looking figures and beasts carved on the capitals of the staves and the sacred-heart bench-ends. The guided tour fills in all the details and a small display in the house-cum-ticket office has enlarged photos of carvings that are hard to decipher inside the poorly-lit church. If you don't wish to return to Solvorn after seeing the stave church, you can head north along the minor road that follows the east shore of the Lustrafjord, rejoining Highway 55 at Skjolden.

The Nigardsbreen

From the Solvorn turning, it's about 15km north along Highway 55 to **Gaupne**, where Highway 604 forks off for the delightful 34km trip up a wild, forested river valley to the **Breheimsenteret Jostedal information centre** (May to late June & late Aug to Sept daily 10am–5pm; late June to late Aug daily 9am–7pm; ☎57 68 32 50; ⓦwww.jostedal.com; displays 50kr). This bleak, ultra-modern structure fits in well with the bare peaks that surround it and, as you sip a coffee on the terrace, you can admire the glistening glacier known as the **Nigardsbreen**, an eastern arm of the Jostedalsbreen (see p.224). From here, it's an easy 3km walk or drive along a toll road (20kr) to the shores of an icy green lake, where a tiny **boat** (early June to Aug daily 10am–6pm; 20kr) shuttles across to the bare rock slope beside the glacier, a great rumpled and seamed wall of ice that sweeps between high peaks. It's a magnificent spectacle that can be easily viewed on a forty-minute hike up from the jetty to the glacier's shaggy flanks.

However, if you want something more taxing, there's a plethora of **guided glacier walks** available, ranging from an easy one- to two-hour jaunt suitable for children over six (daily July to mid-Aug; 140kr, children 60kr), through steeper four- (daily late May to mid-Sept; 285kr including boat) and seven-hour hikes (daily late May to early Sept; 600kr including boat), up to full-scale three-day expeditions over the glacier to Fjærland (early August; 1850kr): all prices include equipment. Tickets for the family walks can be bought from the guides at the starting point, beside the glacier, while all other tickets must be pre-purchased at the information centre at least an hour before departure; these walks start at the car park at the end of the toll road. Advance reservations for the overnight trips are essential and must be made at least four weeks beforehand: for further information on glacier walks, see p.231.

Highway 55: the Sognefjellsveg

Back at Gaupne, Highway 55 continues 26km northeast to **Skjolden**, a dull little town at the head of the Lustrafjord, that marks the start of the 85km-long

SOGNEFJELLSVEG over the mountains to Lom. The road, whose highest parts are closed by snow from late October to May, follows the course of one of the oldest trading routes in Norway, with locals transporting goods by mule or even on their shoulders. Salt and fish went east, while hides, butter, tar and iron went west. The section of the road that climbs over the highest part of the mountains – 1434 metres above sea level – was only completed in 1938 under a work creation scheme, which kept a couple of hundred men busy for two years in the harshest of conditions and with the crudest equipment – pickaxes, spades and wheelbarrows.

Beyond Skjolden, the Sognefjellsveg wiggles its way up the valley to a mountain plateau which it traverses, providing stunning views of the jagged, ice-crusted Jotunheimen peaks to the east. En route are several roadside lodges, the best of which is the *Turtagrø Hotel* (☎57 68 08 00, ℗57 68 08 01; Ⓦwww.turtagro.no; ❻; Easter–Oct), 15km from Skjolden. There's been a lodge here since 1888, but the present structure, a large and attractive red-timber building, was only built in 2001, after fire destroyed its predecessor. Its smart interior consists of Scandinavian pine, and the food is first-rate, with a three-course dinner costing around 400kr. The hotel is a favourite haunt for mountaineers, but it also provides ready access to the **hiking trails** that lattice the Jotunheimen Nasjonalpark. However, the terrain is unforgiving and the weather unpredictable, so novice hikers beware. One tough hike from the hotel is the six-hour haul southeast along the well-worn (but not especially well-signed) path up **Skagastøldalen** to DNT's self-service **Skagastølsbu** hut, though you can of course make the hike shorter by only going some of the way. The valley is divided into a number of steps, each preceded by a short, steep ascent; the hotel is 888m above sea level, the hut, a small stone affair surrounded by a staggering confusion of ice caps, mini-glaciers and craggy ridges, is at 1758m. If you'd rather have a guide, Turtagrø Føring, based at the *Turtagrø Hotel* (☎57 68 08 08), organizes a variety of guided mountain and glacier walks, as well as summer cross-country skiing trips (Easter to October).

Elveseter

On the far side of the plateau, the Sognefjellsveg clips down through forested **Leirdal** and **Bøverdal**, to the old farmstead of **ELVESETER**, some 45km from Turtagrø. Here a complex of old timber buildings comprises a mini historical theme park, dominated by a bizarre 33-metre-high plaster and cyanite column, the **Sagasøyla**. It's topped by a figure of the redoubtable Viking Harald Hardrada, who sits on his horse while, down the column below him, a romantic interpretation of Norwegian history unfolds. Dating from the 1830s, the column was brought to this remote place because no one else would have it – not surprising really.

Lom

Marking the end of the Sognefjellsveg, 23km beyond Elveseter, the crossroads settlement of **LOM** has been a trading and transport centre for centuries, benefiting – in a modest sort of way – from the farms which dot the surrounding valleys. Today, with a population of just 700, it's hardly a boom town, but it does make a comfortable living from the passing tourist trade, with motorists pausing here before the last thump down Highway 15 to the Geirangerfjord (see p.235). Lom's eighteenth-century heyday is recalled by its **stave church** (late May to mid-June & mid-Aug to mid-Sept daily 10am–4pm; mid-June to mid-Aug daily 9am–9pm; 40kr), an enormous structure perched on a grassy knoll above the river. The original church was built here about 1200, but it was remodelled and enlarged after the Reformation, when the spire and transepts were added and the flashy altar and pulpit installed. Its most attractive features are the dinky, shingle-clad roofs, adorned by dragon finials, and the Baroque acanthus vine decoration inside.

Nearby is the town's open-air museum, the **Lom Bygdamuseum Presthaugen** (July daily 1–4pm; 20kr), a surprisingly enjoyable collection of old log buildings in a forest setting. Norway teems with this type of museum, but Lom's is better than most. It is distinguished by the Olavsstugu, a modest hut where St Olav is said to have spent a night, and also by what must be the biggest and ugliest Storstabburet (storehouse) in the country. Museum enthusiasts will also want to visit the **Norsk Fjellmuseum** (Norwegian Mountain Museum; May & Sept Mon–Fri 9am–4pm, Sat & Sun 10am–5pm; early June & late Aug Mon–Fri 9am–6pm, Sat & Sun 10am–5pm; mid-June to mid-Aug Mon–Fri 9am–9pm, Sat & Sun 10am–8pm; Oct–April Mon–Fri 9am–4pm; 60kr), which shares its premises with the tourist office (see below). This modern museum covers all apects of the Jotunheimen mountains in admirable detail – from the fauna and the flora, to the landscapes, farmers and past mountaineers.

Practicalities

Buses to Lom pull in a few metres west of the main crossroads, and most of what you're likely to need is within easy walking distance of here. The church and the open-air museum are across the bridge on the other side of the river, as is the mountain museum and **tourist office** (Oct–April Mon–Fri 9am–4pm; May & Sept Mon–Fri 9am-4pm, Sat & Sun 10am–5pm; early June & late Aug Mon–Fri 9am–6pm, Sat & Sun 10am–5pm; mid-June to mid-Aug Mon–Fri 9am–9pm, Sat & Sun 10am–8pm; ⓣ61 21 29 90; ⓦwww. visitlom.com). The best **accommodation** is at the *Fossheim Turisthotell* (ⓣ61 21 10 05, ⓕ61 21 15 10; ❹), about 300m east of the crossroads along Highway 15. The main lodge here is neat and smart, with an abundance of pine, and behind, trailing up the wooded hillside, are some delightful little wooden cabins (also ❹), some of which are very old and all of which are en suite. The excellent hotel **restaurant** specializes in traditional Norwegian cuisine, and is reasonably priced. A reasonable second choice is the modern *Fossberg* hotel (ⓣ61 21 22 50, ⓕ61 21 22 51; ❹), a large, mostly wooden place by the crossroads. The nearest HI **hostel**, *Bøverdalen Vandrerhjem* (ⓣ & ⓕ61 21 20 64, ⓔboeverdalen.hostel@vandrerhjem.no; dorm beds 95kr, doubles ❶; June–Sept) is actually 20km back down the Sognefjellsveg, occupying a series of glum modern buildings right by the roadside.

Moving on from Lom, there are daily express **bus** services west along Highway 15 to Grotli, Stryn and ultimately Måløy, and east to Otta, on the main E6 highway, then onto Lillehammer and Oslo. From mid-June to the end of August, a local bus runs from Grotli to the Geirangerfjord, but check connections with Lom tourist office before you depart. There are no buses along the Sognefjellsveg from Lom to Sogndal.

The Nordfjord and the Jostedalsbreen glacier

The most direct way to get from the Sognefjord to the **Nordfjord**, the next great fjord system to the north, is via Highway 5's Fjærland tunnel, which bores

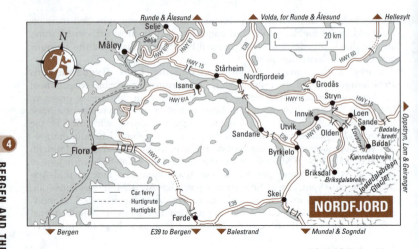

Selje
Måløy
Selja
HWY 61
HWY 15
Stårheim
Nordfjordeid
Grodås
Isane
Stryn
HWY 15
HWY 614
Innvik
Loen
Sande
Utvik
Olden
Bødals-
breen
Sandane
HWY 60
Lovatnet
Bødal
Florø
HWY 5
Byrkjelo
Kjenndalsbreen
Briksdal
Briksdalsbreen
Jostedalsbreen Glacier
Skei
NORDFJORD
Førde

Car ferry
Hurtigrute
Hurtigbåt

0 — 20 km

N

Oppstryn, Lom & Geiranger

4

BERGEN AND THE WESTERN FJORDS | The Nordfjord and the Jostedalsbreen glacier

beneath an arm of the vast **Jostedalsbreen glacier**. A short detour off Highway 5 leads to the charming **Astruptunet**, home of the artist Nikolai Astrup, while the main road heads north towards the Nordfjord itself. The inner recesses of the Nordfjord are best explored along **Highway 60**, which weaves a tortuous course through a string of unexciting little towns between the fjord and the Jostedalsbreen. Two mountain roads lead off Highway 60 to different glacial arms, one road branching off at Olden for **Briksdalsbreen**, the other at the pretty village of **Loen** for **Kjenndalsbreen**.

The dreary town of **Stryn** is an important crossroads, where Highway 60 crosses Highway 15 and runs on north to **Grodås**, home of the Anders Svor Museum, and Hellesylt (see p.236). Meanwhile Highway 15 runs west along the northern shore of the Nordfjord, dipping and diving between deep-green reflective waters and severe peaks. It's a handsome enough journey, but the Nordfjord does not have the allure of its more famous neighbours, at least in part because its roadside hamlets lack real appeal. Indeed, the main reason to head this way is to make the 100km haul to visit the solitary monastic remains of **Selja** island.

The Astruptunet

Heading north from Mundal (see p.223), it's about 30km to the **Kjøsnes junction**, where a byroad runs for 11km along the southern shore of Lake Jølstravatnet to the **ASTRUPTUNET** (June to late Aug daily 11am–5pm; Sept Sun only 11am–5pm; 50kr; ⓦ www.astruptunet.com; ⓣ 57 72 67 82), farmstead home and studio of **Nikolai Astrup** (1880–1928). On the steep slope above the lake, this huddle of old turf-roofed timber buildings looks pretty much the same as it did during the artist's lifetime, though the old barn has been replaced by a modern gallery, used for temporary exhibitions of, usually Norwegian, modern art. A versatile artist, Astrup's work included sketches, prints, and woodcuts, of which a good selection are on display here. However, the bulk of the collection is his landscape paintings, romanticized rural scenes in bright colours, with soft, flowing forms. Unlike many of his contemporaries, Astrup eschewed realism in favour of Neo-impressionism and, as such, he bridged the gap between his generation of Norwegian painters and the Matisse-inspired artists who followed.

Back on Highway 5, the Kjøsnes junction is just a couple of kilometres short of **Skei**, where you can either head west for the 100km journey to the coast at Florø (see p.246), or turn north for 20km up the valley to the Byrkjelo crossroads. From here, it's 40km along Highway 60 to Olden, where you turn off for the Briksdalsbreen (see p.232), and 7km more to Loen, at the start of the road to the Kjenndalsbreen (see p.233).

The Jostedalsbreen glacier

Lurking in the mountains and dominating the whole of the inner Nordfjord region, the **Jostedalsbreen glacier** is a five-hundred-square-kilometre ice plateau that reaches out towards Sognefjord and the Jotunheim mountains. The glacier stretches northeast from Highway 5 to Highway 15, its myriad arms nudging down into nearby valleys, the clay particles of its meltwater giving the local rivers and lakes their distinctive light-green colouring. Catching sight of the ice nestling between peaks and ridges can be unnerving: the overwhelming feeling is that it shouldn't really be there. As the poet Norman Nicholson wrote:

A malevolent, rock-crystal
Precipitate of lava,
Corroded with acid,
Inch by inch erupting
From volcanoes of cold

Nicholson's lines are an evocative and accurate description of a phenomenon that, for centuries, presented an impenetrable east–west barrier in Norway, crossed only at certain points by determined farmers and adventurers.

It's no less daunting today, but access is much freer since the creation of the **Jostedalsbreen Nasjonalpark** in 1991: roads have been driven deep into the glacier's flanks, the movement of the ice has been closely monitored and there has been a proliferation of guided glacier walks (*breturar*) on its various arms (see box). Independent access to the glacier is possible at several points, including the **Bøyabreen** on its south side near Mundal (see p.233) and the **Nigardsbreen** on its east side (see p.227), though the most popular access point is the **Briksdalsbreen** on the west side, off Highway 60, a forty-five

---

Guided glacier walks on the Jostedalsbreen

Most **guided glacier walks** on the Jostedalsbreen are scheduled between early July and mid-August, though on some arms of the glacier the season extends from May until late September, and even longer on the Briksdalsbreen. The walks range from two-hour excursions to five-day expeditions, with day-trip prices starting at 140kr per person for a two-hour stroll, rising to 400kr for a six- to eight-hour hike.

Booking arrangements for the shorter glacier walks vary. At the Nigardsbreen, for example, it's sufficient to turn up at the information centre an hour or two beforehand, but in general it's a good idea to make a reservation at least a day ahead. Sometimes this is best done through the information centre, sometimes direct with the tour operator. In the case of the overnight trips, however, advance booking is essential, often a minimum of four weeks beforehand. In all cases, basic **equipment** is provided, though you'll need to take good boots, waterproofs, warm clothes, gloves, hat, sunglasses, and your own **food** and **drink**. Finally, glaciers are in constant motion and are potentially very dangerous: never, under any circumstances, climb a glacier without a guide, and never walk beneath a glacier.

minute walk from the end of the road (see p.232). Far prettier and much less crowded, however, is the easy fifteen-minute walk to the **Kjenndalsbreen**, near Loen (see p.233).

Information on all the walks is widely available across the region and at the national park's three **information centres**: the **Norsk Bremuseum**, on the south side of the glacier near Mundal (see p.223); the **Breheimsenteret Jostedal** on the east side at the Nigardsbreen (see p.227); and the **Jostedalsbreen Nasjonalparksenter** in Oppstryn, 20km east of Stryn on Highway 15 (daily: May & late Aug to late Sept 10am–4pm; June to late-Aug 10am–6pm; ☎57 87 72 00; ⓦwww.museumsnett.no/jostedalsbreen; exhibitions 60kr). All three have displays on all things glacial and sell books, souvenirs and hiking maps.

The Briksdalsbreen

The uninspiring hamlet of **Olden** is notable only as the point where you turn off Highway 60, along the 24 kilometre-long byroad south to **Briksdal**. Here, a scattering of mountain chalets marks the starting point for the easy 45-minute walk to the **BRIKSDALSBREEN**, the most visited arm of the Jostedalsbreen. The path skirts waterfalls and weaves up the river until you finally reach the glacier, surprisingly blue except for streaks of dust and dirt. It's a simple matter to get close to the ice as the only precaution is a flimsy rope barrier with a small warning sign – be careful. The less energetic can hire a **pony and trap** by the café at the start of the trail (250kr per trap), though you'll still have to hike the last bit of the path. Guided glacier walks begin by the café area: contact Briksdal Breføring (☎57 87 68 00; ⓦwww.briksdalsbre .no) for details.

Local **buses** run once daily from Styrn, Loen and Olden to Briksdal, giving passengers about three hours at Briksdal before returning.

Loen and the Kjenndalsbreen

LOEN spreads ribbon-like along the Nordfjord's low-lying, grassy foreshore with ice-capped mountains breathing down its neck. Its main attraction is the outstanding *Hotel Alexandra* (☎57 87 50 00, ⓕ57 87 50 51, ⓦwww.alexandra .no; ❼, s/r ❺), renowned for its banquet-like breakfasts and wonderful evening buffets (from 7pm; 375kr). First impressions are of a large and fairly undistinguished modern block overlooking the fjord: inside, however, the public rooms are splendid – wide, open and extremely well-appointed – while the spacious bedrooms are infinitely comfortable and furnished in bright modern style. The hotel has all the facilities you'd expect, including a sauna and solarium. Over the road, at the water's edge, the *Hotel Loenfjord* (☎57 87 57 00, ⓕ57 87 57 51; ⓦwww.loenfjord.no; ❺, s/r ❹) is a cheaper, but still excellent, alternative. A cross between a motel and a lodge, it has expansive public rooms and also serves a very decent evening buffet (250kr).

Both hotels are located on land reclaimed from the fjord and the handful of dwellings that make up the old village are located about 500m inland. Here, perched on top of a gentle ridge, is Loen **church**, a tidy structure dating from 1837. Its interior is unremarkable, though the folksy furnishings and fittings are pretty enough, but the views from outside over the fjord are delightful. Its churchyard also holds a couple of items of interest, namely a stone Celtic Cross that is at least a thousand years old, and a pair of **memorial plinths** to the villagers who were drowned in the disasters of 1905 and 1936. On both occasions, a great hunk of the Ramnefjellet mountain on the south side of the valley fell into Lake Lovatnet and the ensuing tidal wave swept dozens of local farmsteads away. The second disaster was particularly tragic as the government had only just persuaded the villagers to return after the first time.

Loen is also the starting point of a popular five-hour hike east up to the plateau-top of **Mount Skåla** (1848m), from where the fjord and mountain views are fantastic. The path is clearly marked, but you'll have to be in good physical condition and have proper walking gear to undertake the trek: also, check locally for snow and ice conditions at the summit before setting out. The hike back down again takes about three hours, or you can overnight in the circular stone tower at the summit, the **Skålatårnet**, which serves as a self-service DNT hut with twenty beds and a kitchen. Curiously, the tower was built in 1891 at the behest of a local doctor – one Dr Kloumann – as a recuperation centre for TB sufferers.

The Kjenndalsbreen

Beginning beside the *Hotel Alexandra*, the 21km byroad leading to the **KJEN-NDALSBREEN** slips up the river valley past lush meadows before pressing on along the northerly shore of Lake Lovatnet. After 13km, the road reaches **Bødal**, whose grassy foreshore was the sight of the village that bore the brunt of the two tidal waves (see above); today's handful of houses perch cautiously on the ridge well above the water. Five kilometres from here up a bumpy, signposted road is a car park near the Bødalseter DNT hut, which marks the starting point for a guided glacier walk on the **Bødalsbreen** (June to mid-Sept; ☎57 87 68 00). Back on the Kjenndalsbreen road, it's another 3km or so beyond Bødal to a toll post (30kr), then another 5km to the end of the road and a car park. From here it's an easy and very pleasant twenty-minute ramble through rocky terrain to the **ice**, whose fissured, blancmange-like blue and white folds tumble down the rock face, with a furious white-green river, fed by plummeting meltwater, flowing beneath.

There are no local **buses** to the Kjenndalsbreen; the nearest you'll get is the once daily service – in each direction – from Stryn and Loen to Bødal and the Bødalseter car park. Far easier, and more scenic, is to take an organized **boat trip** along the glacial blue **Lake Lovatnet**, which docks beside the *Kjendalsstova Café*, 5km short of the glacier – it's a delightful cruise through a beguiling landscape. From the café, a bus takes you to the car park at the end of the Kjenndalsbreen road for the twenty-minute walk to the glacier, before heading back to the jetty and the return boat-trip; in total, the round trip takes four hours and costs 120kr per person. Boats leave daily (early June to August) from the tiny Sande jetty, 4.5km from *Hotel Alexandra,* down the Kjenndalsbreen road. The hotel issues tickets and takes bookings and will, at a pinch, give you a lift down to Sande, though the Stryn-Loen-Bødal bus connects with boat departures.

Stryn

STRYN, just 12km around the fjord from Loen, is the biggest town hereabouts, though with a population of 1200 that's hardly a major boast. For the most part, it's a humdrum modern sprawl straggling beside its long main street, but there is a pleasant pocket of antique **timber houses** huddled round the old bridge, down by the river, just to the south of the main drag.

The **bus station** is beside the river to the west of the town centre, from where it's a six-hundred-metre walk to the **tourist office** (June & Aug daily 8.30am–6pm, July daily 8.30am–8pm, Sept–May Mon–Fri 8.30am–3.30pm;

☎57 87 40 40; ⓦwww.nordfjord.no), bang in the centre, just off the main street – Tonningsgata – and behind *Johan's Kafeteria*. It issues free town maps and sells hiking maps, as well as renting out mountain bikes. There's no real reason to overnight here, but Stryn does have a good HI **hostel**, *Stryn Vandrerhjem* (☎57 87 13 36, ℉57 87 11 06, ⓔstryn.hostel@vandrerhjem.no; dorm beds 170kr, doubles ❷; June–Aug), perched high above the centre at Geilevegen 14. The chalet-like hostel has self-catering facilities, a laundry and internet access, plus splendid views over Stryn and its surroundings. It's a stiff 1km-long trek up Bøavegen, signposted from the main drag, on the east side of the centre. Alternatively, the well-equipped, four-star *Stryn Camping* (☎57 87 11 36, ℉57 87 20 25) is just a couple of hundred metres up Bøavegen, and has cabins (❷) as well as tent pitches. As for **food**, the best of a poor selection is the *Restaurant Bacchus*, Tonningsgata 33, on the east side of the centre, serving routine Italian dishes.

West of Stryn to the islet of Selja

Heading west out of Stryn, highways 15 and 60 share the same stretch of road until, after 10km, Highway 60 veers north to the town of Grodås and the Geirangerfjord (see p.235), while Highway 15 continues west to follow the northern coast of the Nordfjord. After 70km, Highway 15 comes to the junction of Highway 61, which leads the final thirty-five kilometres up to **Selje village**, a light scattering of houses straggling along a wide bay. Selje has a long sandy beach, but more importantly is the starting point for two-hour guided tours of the nearby **ISLET OF SELJA** (late May to mid-June Sat & Sun 1 daily; mid-June to late Aug 1–3 daily; 110kr including the boat). The islet is the site of several medieval remains, easily the most significant of which are the ruins of **Selja Kloster**, a monastery built in the tenth century by Benedictine monks. It was originally named after the legendary St Sunniva, an Irish princess who refused to marry the pagan selected by her father. Royal blood and loyalty to the Catholic faith were prime considerations for beatification – and Sunniva got her saintly reward, but only after spending the rest of her life hidden away in a cave on this lonely island. The best preserved part of the kloister is the church tower, but otherwise the dilapidated masonry is rather less impressive than the setting.

For details of the boat times and to make a reservation, contact the **tourist office** in Selje village (April to late May & late Aug to Sept Mon–Fri 8am–3pm; late May to mid-June & mid-Aug daily 10am–4pm; late June & early Aug daily 10am–6pm; July daily 10am–8pm; ☎57 85 66 06). The village has one **hotel**, the *Selje* (☎57 85 88 80, ℉57 85 88 81; ⓦwww.seljehotel.no; ❸), a large, modern lodge right behind the beach, which specializes in health treatments, and comes complete with indoor and outdoor pools, massage facilities and jacuzzi.

From Selje, you can continue to Ålesund (see p.243), 120km north, along highways 618, 620 and 61, via the **Koparneset to Årvik** ferry (every 30min to 1hr; 15min; passengers 18kr, car & driver 43kr) and the **Hareid to Sulesund** ferry (every 30min; 25min; passengers 25kr, car & driver 71kr).

Grodås: the Anders Svor Museum

Back on Highway 60, 6km north of the junction with Highway 15, the town of **GRODÅS** is strung along the eastern tip of Hor.indalsvatn, at 514m Europe's deepest and Norway's clearest lake. A straggly little place, it's distinguished only by the **Anders Svor Museum** (June to late Aug Mon–Sat

11am–5pm, Sun 1–5pm; 30kr), which occupies a comely Neoclassical structure built in 1953. Hardly a household name today, Svor (1864–1929) was a native of Grodås who established something of an international reputation as a sculptor of romantic figures that were much admired by the bourgeoisie. Some of the more clichéd pieces on display at the museum, such as *Bøn* (Prayer), *Sorg* (Grief) and *Lita jente* (A Small Girl), are typical of his work, though busts of his family and friends, in particular those of his wife, Brit, and his mother, reveal much more originality and talent. Svor's career is typical of his generation, too: like other Norwegian artists, he was keen to escape the backwoods, moving to Kristiania (Oslo) in 1881 and four years later to Copenhagen, the start of an extended exile that only ended after Norway's independence in 1905.

Whilst there's no pressing reason to overnight here, Grodås does have a pleasant **hotel**, the *Best Western Raftevolds* (☎57 87 96 05, ⓕ57 87 96 06; ⓔpost@raftevold.no; ❺), a mostly modern complex that spreads out along the lakeshore. Beyond Grodås, Highway 60 zips up the valley and over the hills to reach, after 25km, the turning for the Norangsdal valley (see p.237) and shortly afterwards Hellesylt, on the Geirangerfjord (see p.236).

The Geirangerfjord and Norangsdal

The **Geirangerfjord** is one of the region's smallest fjords, but also one of its most breathtaking. A convoluted branch of the Storfjord, the Geirangerfjord cuts well inland and is marked by impressive waterfalls, with a village at either end of its snake-like profile – **Hellesylt** in the west and **Geiranger** in the east. Of the two, Geiranger has the smarter hotels as well as the tourist crowds, while Hellesylt is smaller and quieter with the added bonus of its proximity to the magnificent **Norangsdal** valley, where the hamlet of **Øye** boasts one of Norway's most enjoyable hotels.

You can reach Geiranger in dramatic style from both north and south along the nerve-jangling Highway 63 – the **Ørnevegen**, or Eagle's Highway – which makes the approach to Hellesylt along Highway 60 seem comparatively demure. In addition, **car ferries** (May–Sept 4–8 daily; 1hr; passengers 90kr each way; car & driver 180kr each way) run between Hellesylt and Geiranger. This is one of the most celebrated trips in the entire region, the S-shaped waters about 300m deep and fed by a series of plunging waterfalls up to 250m in height. The falls are all named, and the multilingual commentary aboard the ferry does its best to ensure that you become familiar with every stream and rivulet. More interesting are the scattered ruins of abandoned farms, built along the fjord's 16km length by fanatically optimistic settlers during the eighteenth and nineteenth centuries. The cliffs backing the fjord are almost uniformly sheer, making farming of any description a short-lived and back-breaking occupation – and not much fun for the children either: when they went out to play, they were roped to the nearest boulder to stop them dropping into the fjord.

Long-distance **buses** travelling west along Highway 15 link Otta (see p.161) and Lom (see p.228) with either Grotli or Langvatn (depending on the service), at either of which you can change for the local bus north to Geiranger, though this connecting service only operates from mid-June to August. The same local bus pushes on from Geiranger to Åndalsnes via the northerly section of the Ørnevegen, the Eidsdal–Linge ferry and the dramatic Trollstigen mountain road (see p.241). Hellesylt is on the main Bergen–Ålesund bus route,

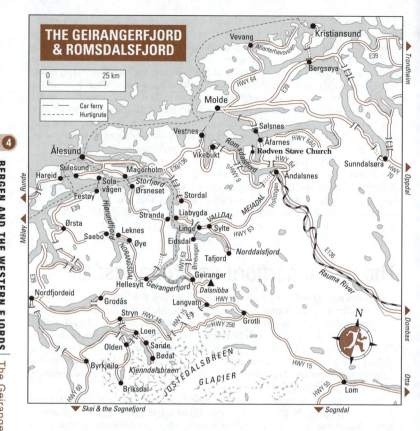

THE GEIRANGERFJORD & ROMSDALSFJORD

0   25 km

— — — Car ferry
- - - - Hurtigrute

Kristiansund

Vevang   *Atlanterhavsveien*

Bergsøya   E39

HWY 64   E39

Molde

Trondheim

Sølsnes

Vestnes   Åfarnes   HWY 660

Vikebukt   **Rødven Stave Church**

Ålesund   *Romsdalsfjord*   HWY 64

Sunndalsøra   HWY 70

Sulesund

Hareid   Sola-   Magerholm   *Storfjord*   HWY 9   Åndalsnes

vågen   Ørsneset   Stordal   *MEIADAL*   Trollstigen

Festøy   E39   *Hjørundfjord*   Stranda   Liabygda   *VALLDAL*

Ørsta   Leknes   Linge   Sylte

Saebo   Øye   Eidsdal   HWY 63

  NORANGSDAL   Tafjord   *Norddalsfjord*

Måløy   Runde

Nordfjordeid   Hellesylt   *Geirangerfjord*   Geiranger   *Dalsnibba*   HWY 15

Grodås   Langvatn

Stryn   HWY 15   Grotli

Loen   HWY 258

Olden   Sande   Bødal

Byrkjeilo   *Kjenndalsbreen*

Briksdal   *JOSTEDALSBREEN GLACIER*

HWY 60   HWY 15   HWY 55   Lom

Rauma River   E136

N

Oppdal

Dombås

Otta

▼ *Skei & the Sognefjord*   ▼ *Sogndal*

which passes along the appealing Highway 60 through Loen and Stryn; there are at least a couple of services daily. Finally, a limited local bus service runs from Hellesylt along the Norangsdal valley to Øye and Leknes (late June to mid–Aug Mon–Fri 1 daily): in the opposite direction, the bus runs all year, but it departs well before the other bus arrives.

Hellesylt

In Viking times, **HELLESYLT** was an important and well-protected port. Traders and warriors sallied forth from the village to England, France and Russia, and many old Viking names survive in the area. Nowadays it's primarily a stop-off on tourist itineraries, most visitors staying just long enough to catch the ferry down the fjord to Geiranger. For daytime entertainment, there is a tiny **beach** near the ferry quay, the prelude to some very cold swimming. Or you could splash about (as many do) in the waterfall in the village centre. By nightfall, once the day-trippers have departed, Hellesylt is quiet and peaceful.

The **tourist office** (June & late Aug to Sept Mon–Fri 9am–6pm, Sat & Sun noon–6pm; July to late Aug daily 9am–8pm; ☎70 26 38 80) is a five-minute walk from the jetty in a modern building that doubles as an **art gallery** (same times; 50kr). Its exhibits consist of a bizarre set of rather kitsch, Baroque wood-carvings illustrating Ibsen's *Peer Gynt*, by a certain Oddvin Parr. Hellesylt has one **hotel**, the *Grand* (ⓣ70 26 51 00, ⓕ70 26 52 22; ❸), whose fancy wooden scrollwork and high-pitched gables have been a local landmark since 1871, though guests stay in the modern annexe next door. The hotel's main competitor is the HI **hostel** (ⓣ70 26 51 28; ⓕ 70 26 36 57; dorm beds 120kr, doubles ❶; June–Aug), pleasantly set on the hillside above the village beside Highway 60 – a steep 350-metre walk up the signed footpath from the jetty. They have cabins (❶), which suit a family of four nicely, and self-catering facilities. Rowing boats can be rented here and from the *Grand*, which also sells fishing licences and rents out fishing equipment. *Hellesylt Camping* (ⓣ70 26 51 88) is in a shadeless field beside the fjord, about 400m from the quay.

The Norangsdal valley: Øye and Leknes

A century ago, ponies and traps took cruise-ship tourists from Hellesylt down through the majestic **Norangsdal** valley to what was then the remote hamlet of **ØYE**. Today, it's a simple 24km car journey – go 5km south on Highway 60 and watch for the turning on the right – but the scene appears not to have changed at all: steep, snow-tipped peaks rise up on either side of a wide, boulder-strewn and scree-slashed valley, dented by a thousand rock falls. Near the top of the valley, the road (8km of which is gravel) slips past mountain pastures, dotted with spartan timber cabins where local women once spent the summers tending their cattle. The best preserved of the cabins bear plaques illustrating and explaining the harshness of life on these mountain pastures. Further along, the road runs alongside lake **Lyngstøylvatnet**, which was created when a large rock slide dammed the valley's stream in 1908. The lake covers the remains of a group of shacks and the water is so clear that you can still make out their outlines. Pushing on, the road dips down to a string of farmsteads, which straggle along the valley, before arriving at Øye, at the eastern tip of the Norangsfjord.

The village's pride and joy is the splendid *Hotel Union* (ⓣ70 06 21 00, ⓕ70 06 21 16; ⓦwww.unionoye.no; closed mid-Oct to April; ❺), a delightfully restored High Victorian establishment that was built in 1891 to accommodate touring aristocrats. Its interior is crammed with period antiques and bygones seemingly hunted down from every corner of the globe by the present owner. Each of the bedrooms is individually decorated in elaborate style and most celebrate the famous people who stayed here, like King Haakon VII and Kaiser Wilhelm II, not to mention the Danish author Karen "*Out Of Africa*" Blixen: enthusiasts might be pleased to see a pair of her lover's boots. It's a great place to spend the night – though you have to turn a blind eye to the occasional period excesses, like the four-posters – and the food is first-rate too. Telephones are banned, which is inducement enough to sit on the terrace and watch the weather fronts sweeping in off the glassy green **Norangsfjord**, or have a day's fishing – the hotel sells licences and dispenses advice.

No ferries dock at Øye: the nearest leaves from **LEKNES**, 8km to the west. This minuscule port occupies a magnificent location at the point where the Norangsfjord meets the **Hjørundfjord**: to the south the mountains bear down on the fjord, to the north the blue-black waters widen out with pyramid-shaped peaks leading off into the distance on either side. Only 40km long, the Hjørundfjord is one of the most visually impressive fjords in the country; it takes its name from the days when the Black Death swept Norway, leaving just one person, a woman called Hjørund, alive in the area. The best way to see it is to leave your car at Leknes and take a round trip by **ferry**, which stops at various destinations along the shore. The shortest and most convenient journey, however, is across the Hjørundfjord to **Saebo** (every 1-2 hours; 15min each way).

Geiranger

Any approach to **GEIRANGER** is spectacular. Arriving by ferry slowly reveals the little village tucked in a hollow at the eastern end of the fjord, while approaching from the north by road involves thundering along a fearsome set of switchbacks on the Ørnevegen – the Eagle's Highway – for a first view of the village and the fjord glinting in the distance. Similarly, the road in from Highway 15 to the south begins innocuously enough, but soon you're squirming down the zigzags to arrive in Geiranger from behind. It's a beautiful setting, one of the most magnificent in western Norway, diminished only by the excessive number of tourists in peak season. That said, the congestion is limited to the centre of the village and it's easy enough to slip away and discover the true character of the fjord, hemmed in by sheer rock walls interspersed with hairline waterfalls, tiny-looking ferries and cruise ships bobbing about on its blue-green waters.

The first ever cruise boat arrived in Geiranger in 1869, packed with Quakers bearing tracts. These missionaries may not have had much luck converting the locals, who already considered themselves Christians, but they were certainly taken with the beauty of the Geirangerfjord and spread the word on their return home: within twenty years the village was receiving a regular supply of visitors. Seizing their chance, local farmers mortgaged, sold and borrowed anything they could to buy ponies and traps, and by the end of the century tourists were being carted up from the jetty to the mountains by the score. In 1919, the horse was usurped when a group of farmer-cum-trap owners clubbed together to import cars, which they kitted out with a municipal livery. The present owner of the *Union Hotel* (see below) has restored a dozen or so of these **classic cars**, including a 1922 Hudson, a 1932 Studebaker, and a 1931 Nash, and garaged them at the hotel: they can be admired free most afternoons – ask at the hotel reception.

Geiranger's other man-made attraction is the brand new **Norsk Fjordsenter** (mid-June to mid-Aug daily 10am–10pm, May to mid-June & mid-Aug to Sept daily 10am–5pm Ⓦwww.fjordsenter.info; 75kr), just across from the *Union Hotel*. Devoted to different aspects of the region's history, the museum covers topics ranging from communications and transport through to fjord farms and the evolution of tourism. Perhaps the most interesting display examines the problem of fjordland avalanches. Whenever there's a major rock fall into a fjord, the resulting tidal wave can have disastrous consequences – Tafjord in 1934 (see p.240) being an especially tragic example.

Geiranger's main attraction, however, is the scenery. A network of **hiking trails** lattices the mountains around Geiranger, giving access to thundering waterfalls, abandoned mountain farmsteads, and vantage points where the views over the fjord are exhilarating if not downright scary. One popular excursion to the mountain farm of **Skageflå** involves a boat ride (Geiranger Fjordservice; June–Aug 4–5 daily; 75kr) from the quay beside the tourist office to the farm's old jetty, followed by a stiff hour-long hoof up from the fjord to the farm, then a three-hour hike back to Geiranger. Note that the boat only docks at the Skageflå jetty on request; tickets can be bought on board or beforehand at the tourist office. A much shorter, but just as precarious, hike is the ten-minute trail to the **Flydalsjuvet**, an overhanging rock high above the Geirangerfjord. To get there, drive south from the Geiranger jetty and watch for the sign after about 5km; from the car park, which offers extravagant views itself, a slippery and rather indistinct track leads the 200m up to Flydalsjuvet.

Practicalities

Buses to Geiranger stop a stone's throw from the waterfront and a couple of hundred metres from the **ferry terminal**. The **tourist office** (May–Sept daily 9am–7pm, Oct–April Mon–Fri 9am–5pm; ☎70 26 30 99; ⓦwww .geirang.no) is close by, on the waterfront, beside the sightseeing boat dock, and issues bus and ferry timetables, sells boat trip tickets, and supplies free village maps, which outline local hiking routes.

Geiranger has several **hotels** to choose from, but advance reservations are strongly advised in July and August. The most upmarket is the large and lavish *Union* (☎70 26 83 00, ⓕ70 26 83 51, ⓦwww.union-hotel.no; ❼, s/r ❺; March to late Dec), high up the hillside, but just 300m from the jetty. There's been a hotel here since 1891, and while the present building, with its retro flourishes, is nothing special, its public rooms are large and lodge-like, and there's a sauna and both indoor and outdoor pools. The bedrooms are pleasantly furnished in modern style, many with balconies overlooking the fjord; those on floor four and above have the best views. Alternatively, there's the ultramodern timber-built *Grande Fjordhotell* (☎70 26 30 90, ⓕ70 26 31 77; ❹; May–Sept), which has a pleasant fjordside location about 2km north of the centre, on the road to Eidsdal. It also has **cabins** (❸) and a **campsite**, which is adjacent to the similar *Grande Turisthytter og Camping* (☎70 26 30 68, ⓕ70 26 31 17). The main campsite, *Geiranger Camping* (☎&ⓕ70 26 31 20), sprawls along the fjordside a couple of hundred metres to the east of the tourist office, but gets jam-packed with caravans, cars and motor bikes in summer. Finally, there's the family-run *Vinjebakken* **hostel**, (☎70 26 32 05; July to mid-Aug; dorm beds 180kr), near the octagonal church up the road from the jetty and off to the left. For **food,** easily the best option in town is the *Union's* first-rate help-yourself buffet dinner at 325kr per person.

From mid-June to August, local **buses** run north into Geiranger from either Grotli or Langvatn on Highway 15. There are two buses daily, one going straight into Geiranger (1hr), the other (2hr) making a dramatic detour up a rough mountain toll-road to the **Dalsnibba viewpoint** (1476m), overlooking the Geirangerfjord. This same local bus pushes north out of Geiranger heading for Åndalsnes (see p.241) via the Trollstigen, a journey of just over three hours. Geiranger is also served by the **Hurtigrute** coastal boat – but northbound only: to head south, you have to change boats at Ålesund. The boat takes all day to sail from Ålesund to Geiranger and back, leaving Geiranger at 1.30pm.

Highway 63 to Åndalsnes

The Golden Route, an 80km journey **from Geiranger to Åndalsnes** along Highway 63, is famous for its mountain scenery – and no wonder. Even by Norwegian standards, it's of outstanding beauty, the road bobbling past an army of dauntingly cold and severe peaks. The journey incorporates a short ferry ride across the picturesque Norddalsfjord, but it's the **Trollstigen** that is the most memorable section – a spectacular mountain road cutting an improbable course between the Valldal valley and Åndalsnes. A couple of places along the Norddalsfjord make for good detours en route – one west to the hamlet of

Stordal, home of an especially fine church, the other east to the intriguing village of Tafjord. At the end of the trip, small-town Åndalsnes makes a good base for further fjordland explorations and has a couple of excellent places to stay. It's also the northern terminus of the dramatic Rauma train line from Dombås (see p.168) in the east.

Twice-daily from mid-June to August, a special bus travels the length of the Golden Route, negotiating its hairpin bends and scary corners. If you're brave enough to drive yourself, note that the higher parts of the road are generally closed from early October to mid-May – longer if the snows have been particularly heavy.

Linge and Stordal

Heading north from Geiranger, the first 22km of the Golden Route is the knuckle-whitening jaunt up the Ørnevegen, or Eagle's Highway, to Eidsdal on the Norddalsfjord. From here, a car ferry (every 30–45min; 10min; passengers 18kr, car & driver 43kr) shuttles over to the LINGE jetty, where there's a choice of routes: travel east for the Trollstigen and Tafjord (see below), or head west for 21km along Highway 650 to STORDAL. A dull furniture-making town, that straggles along a wide valley shelving gently into the Storfjord, Stordal's only point of interest is the remarkable Rosekyrkja (Rose Church; mid-June to mid-Aug daily 11am–4pm; 20kr), standing right beside the road. Dating from the 1780s, the church has a modest exterior, with whitewashed planking and a dinky tower, contrasting with its extravagent interior which is awash with floral decoration, swirling round the pillars, across the ceiling and down the walls. There's an intensity of religious feeling here that well illustrates the importance of Christianity to Norway's country folk, an effect amplified by its naïve, almost abstract Biblical paintings.

If you're not going via the Trollstigen, you can continue along Highway 650 for the pleasant 60km drive to Ålesund (see p.243).

Sylte and Tafjord

From Linge, it's just 3km east to SYLTE, a shadowy, half-hearted village that strings along the Norddalsfjord. The handful of pretty, old wooden houses that once formed its main street are attractive enough, but more importantly Sylte marks the beginning of the Valldal valley leading up towards the Trollstigen. It's also where a byroad leads off Highway 63 to follow the Norddalsfjord 14km east to the remote, back-of-beyond village of TAFJORD. Ignore the ugly defunct power station at the entrance to the village then cross the river, and you'll find a pint-sized harbour, noteable only for its complete lack of old buildings. For it was here that, in 1934, a great hunk of mountain dropped into the fjord, creating a 16m tidal wave that simply washed this part of the village away, killing 23 locals in the process. Some 400m up the hillside, however, the greater part of Tafjord did survive and, unlike most of its neighbours, has been preserved in its original condition. As a result, its string of old buildings, with their thatched roofs, cairn-like chimneys and clapboard walls, show what these fjord villages looked like as late as the 1950s – and make for a fascinating hour or so's wander. If you want to stay longer, there's a couple of options in the old village: the plain and straightforward *Tafjord Gjestgård* (☎70 25 80 48; ⓕ70 25 81 33; ❷), or *Tafjord Camping* (☎70 25 80 79, ⓕ70 25 70 44; May–Sept), with a few modern cabins (❷). A local bus makes the twenty-minute journey between Sylte and Tafjord once or twice daily on weekdays.

Over the Trollstigen

The alarming heights of the **Trollstigen** ("Troll's Ladder"), a trans-mountain route between Valldal and Åndalsnes, are equally compelling in either direction. The road negotiates the mountains by means of eleven hairpin bends with a maximum gradient of 1:12, but it's still a pretty straightforward drive – unless you meet a tour bus coming the other way. Drivers (and cyclists) should also be particularly careful in wet weather.

The southern end of the Trollstigen starts gently enough with the road rambling up the **Valldal** valley, passing dozens of stalls selling fresh strawberries in June and July. Thereafter, the road swings north, as it bowls up **Meiadal** bound for the barren mountains beyond. It's here that the road starts to climb in earnest, before reaching the bleak and icy plateau-pass that marks the road's high point.

At the top, there are the inevitable cafés and souvenir shops, but it's all pretty low-key and a fast-flowing river muffles every sound as it barrels down the mountain below. A five-minute walk leads to the **Utsikten** (viewing point), with its magnificent panorama over the surrounding mountains and valleys. It is from here that the sheer audacity of the road becomes apparent, zigzagging across the face of the mountain and somehow managing to wriggle round the tumultuous, 180m **Stigfossen Falls**. Clearly visible to the west are some of the region's most famous mountains peaks: Bispen and Kongen (the "Bishop" and the "King") are the two nearest, at 1462m and 1614m respectively.

The north side of the Trollstigen brings stomach-churning hairpins, before the road resumes its easy ramblings, scuttling along the Isterdal to meet the E136 just 6km from Åndalsnes.

Åndalsnes

At the end of the splendid Rauma train line from Dombås, **ÅNDALSNES** is, for many travellers, their first – and sometimes only – contact with the fjord country, a distinction it doesn't really warrant. Despite a wonderful setting between lofty peaks and chill waters, the town itself is unexciting: small (with a population of just 3500), modern and industrial, and sleepy at the best of times. That said, Åndalsnes is an excellent place to orientate yourself and everything you're likely to need is near at hand, not least some first-rate accommodation. Åndalsnes also makes an ideal base for further fjord explorations. Within easy reach by ferry, bus and/or car is some wonderful scenery, from the stern peaks inland to the fretted fjords stretching towards the open sea. There's also **Rødven stave church** (late June to late Aug daily 11am–4pm; 30kr), just half an hour's drive away – from Åndalsnes, head east round the Isfjord and after 22km take the signed byroad for the final 10km. In an idyllic setting – amid meadows, by a stream and overlooking a slender arm of the Romsdalsfjord – the church dates from around 1300, though its distinctive wooden supports may have been added in 1712 during the first of several subsequent remodellings. Every inch a country church, the place's creaky interior holds boxed pews, a painted pulpit and a large medieval crucifix, but it's the bucolic setting which most catches the eye.

Practicalities

Buses all stop outside the **train station**, where you'll also find the **tourist office** (late June to Aug Mon–Sat 10am–7pm, Sun 1–7pm; Sept to late June Mon–Fri 9am–5pm; ☎71 22 16 22; ⓦ www.andalsnes.net). It provides bus timetables, regional guides, and the free *Dagsturer* (day trips) booklet with details of local motoring excursions and short hikes. The tourist office also has details of fishing trips to the fjord (3 daily; 4hr; 250kr), local day-long hikes and guided climbs (from 1500kr), as well as fixed-rate sightseeing expeditions with Åndalsnes Taxi (℡71 22 15 55), who charge – for example – 500kr for a brief scoot down the Trollstigen. This is, however, hardly a bargain when you consider that local car hire firms, such as Åndal Bil (℡71 22 22 55), charge around 650kr for a 24-hour car rental: check the current special deals with the tourist office. Local **hiking maps** are sold at *Romsdal Libris*, a couple of minutes' walk from the tourist office in the centre of town.

The tourist office also has a small supply of en-suite **private rooms** (❷), with self-catering facilities and bed linen provided – though most are a good walk from the town centre. Alternatively, Åndalsnes has a delightful HI **hostel** (mid-May to mid-Sept; ℡71 22 13 82, ℻71 22 68 35; Ⓔaandalsnes.hostel @vandrerhjem.no; dorm beds 180kr, doubles ❷), 2km west of town. To get there, head up the hill out of the centre onto the E136, go past the turning to Dombås staying on the E136 in the direction of Ålesund; cross the river and it's signed on the left-hand side. The hostel has a pleasant rural setting and its simple rooms, in a group of modest wooden buildings, are extremely popular, making reservations pretty much essential. The buffet-style **breakfast**, with its fresh fish, is one of the best hostellers are likely to get in the whole country. Unfortunately, the hostel doesn't do evening meals (though there are cooking facilities) and reception is closed from 10am to 4pm. Bikes can also be rented here. The other excellent choice, the *Grand Hotel Bellevue*, Åndalsgata 5 (℡71 22 75 00, ℻71 22 60 38; Ⓦwww.grandhotel.no; ❺), occupies a large white-washed block with attractive Art Deco touches on a hillock just up from the train station. The rooms on the top floors – four and five - have great views, and are well worth the extra 100kr or so. Otherwise, the modern *Rauma Hotell*, centrally located near the station at Vollan 16 (℡71 22 32 70, ℻71 22 32 71; ❹), is a bit cheaper, but despite its recent refurbishment lacks character. Among several local **campsites**, *Åndalsnes Camping og Motell* (℡71 22 16 29, ℻71 22 62 16; Ⓦwww.andalsnescamp.no) has a fine riverside setting about 3km from the town centre – follow the route to the youth hostel but turn first left immediately after the river. It's a well-equipped site with cabins (❶) as well as bikes, boats, canoes and cars available for rent.

For **food**, the *Buona Sera* pizzeria, a brief walk from the station up the hill out of town, serves filling Italian food at reasonable prices, but much better is the evening (6–9.45pm) buffet served at the *Grand Hotel Bellevue* for 175kr per person; go early to catch the best spread.

Moving on from Åndalsnes

Travelling west from Åndalsnes, there are regular **express buses** to Ålesund (3–4 daily; 2hr 25min), where you can pick up the Hurtigrute southbound at 12.45am, and northbound via Geiranger at 9.30am, then again at 6.45pm. Alternatively, **local buses** (Mon–Sat 5–8 daily, Sun 3 daily; 1hr 20min) run northwest from Åndalsnes to Molde (see p.248), a pretty fjord journey involving a short **ferry** trip from Åfarnes to Sølsnes (passengers 18kr, car & driver 45kr; 15min). At Molde you can either pick up a bus north on the coastal E39 to Kristiansund (4–9 daily; 1hr 35min), or carry straight on to Trondheim (1–2 daily; 5hr). Molde, Kristiansund and Trondheim are all **Hurtigrute** ports, providing yet more possibilities. Note that InterRail and ScanRail pass holders get a fifty-percent discount on E39 buses; also be careful to distinguish between Kristiansund and the southern coastal town of Kristiansand: to save confusion, in listings and brochures they are often written as Kristiansund N and Kristiansand S.

Heading southwest from Åndalsnes, a summertime **bus and ferry** service (mid-June to late Aug 2 daily; 140kr) travels over the Trollstigen (see p.241) to Geiranger (see p.238), where one of the daily services connects with the ferry to Hellesylt (see p.236).

Ålesund and around

At the end of the E136, some 120km west of Åndalsnes, the fishing and ferry port of **ÅLESUND** is immediately – and distinctively – different from any other Norwegian town. Neither old clapboard houses nor functional concrete and glass is much in evidence, but instead its centre boasts a conglomeration of pastel-painted frontages, lavishly decorated and topped with a forest of towers and turrets. There are dragons and human faces, Neoclassical and mock-Gothic facades, decorative flowers and even a pharaoh or two, the whole ensemble set amid the town's several harbours. These architectural eccentricities sprang from disaster: in 1904, a dreadful fire left 10,000 people homeless and the town centre destroyed, but within three years a hectic reconstruction programme saw almost the entire area rebuilt in a bizarre Art Nouveau style, which borrowed heavily from the German *Jugendstil* movement. The Norwegian architects added local folksy and often whimsical flourishes to the more austere foreign influences of the time, and Kaiser Wilhelm II, who used to holiday around Ålesund, footed the bill.

Ålesund has a couple of attractions nearby – the **Atlanterhavsparken** and the **Sunnmøre Museum** – both of which merit visits of an hour or two. The

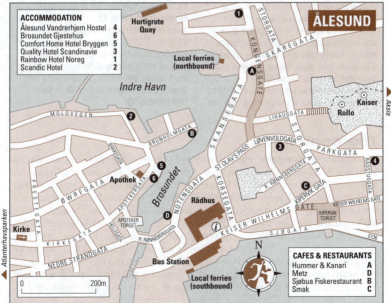

ACCOMMODATION
Ålesund Vandrerhjem Hostel	4
Brosundet Gjestehus	6
Comfort Home Hotel Bryggen	5
Quality Hotel Scandinavie	3
Rainbow Hotel Noreg	1
Scandic Hotel	2

CAFES & RESTAURANTS
Hummer & Kanari	A
Metz	D
Sjøbua Fiskerestaurant	B
Smak	C

town also makes a good base from which to venture further afield to the island of **Runde**, a bird watchers' paradise.

Arrival, information and accommodation

From north to south, Ålesund's town centre is about 700m wide. The **bus station** is situated on the southern waterfront, across from the **tourist office** in the Rådhus (June–Aug Mon–Fri 8.30am–7pm, Sat 9am–5pm, Sun 11am–5pm; Sept–May Mon–Fri 8.30am–4pm; ☎70 15 76 00; ⊛www .visitalesund.com). Here, you can pick up a free, but verbose, guide to Ålesund's architectural attractions, *On Foot in Ålesund* or, better still, sign up for a guided walking tour (mid-June to mid-Aug 1 daily; early May to early June & late Aug to late Sept Sat only; 1hr 30min; 60kr). Southbound local ferries depart from beside the bus station, northbound from the other side of the harbour, just metres from the **Hurtigrute** quay (see box p.246); southbound 12.45am, northbound 9.30am for Geiranger, 6.45pm for Trondheim). **Internet** and email access is available for free at the library inside the Rådhus (Mon–Fri 10am–5pm & Sat 10am–2pm).

Accommodation

Brosundet Gjestehus Apotekergata 5 ☎70 12 10 00, ⊕70 12 12 95, ⊛www.brosundet.no. An excellent guesthouse occupying an attractively converted waterside warehouse. It has a sauna, washing machines and self-catering facilities, and offers an excellent breakfast. ❹

Comfort Home Hotel Bryggen Apotekergata 1 ☎70 12 64 00, ⊕70 12 11 80, ⊛www .bryggen-hotel.no. A smart hotel in a carefully modernized old waterside warehouse. It has good facilities and well-appointed rooms. ❼, s/r ❹

Quality Hotel Scandinavie Løvenvoldgata 8 ☎70 15 78 00 ⊕70 15 78 01. Efficient chain hotel inhabiting a grand old Art Nouveau edifice that has, unfortunately, been spoiled by an ugly set of automatic front doors. Modern standard-issue chain-hotel bedrooms. ❹, s/r ❸

Rainbow Hotel Noreg Kongens gate 27 ☎70 12 29 38, ⊕70 12 66 60, ⊛www.rainbow-hotels.no.

A recently revamped modern block, with adequate rooms – those on the upper floors have sea views. ❺, s/r ❸

Scandic Hotel Ålesund Molovegen 6 ☎21 61 45 00, ⊕21 61 45 11, ⊛www.scandic-hotels.com. It may be part of a chain and occupy a harsh, modern block, but there's something very appealing about this relaxed and friendly hotel. The rooms are bright and cheerful, each comfortably furnished in contemporary style. Ask for a room on the top floor – they have the best sea views. Recommended. ❼, s/r ❹

Ålesund Vandrerhjem Parkgata 14 ☎70 11 58 30, ⊕70 11 58 59, ⓔaalesund.hostel@ vandrerhjem.no. Small and central HI hostel in a pleasant 1920s building at the top of Rådstuggata. Has a laundry, self-catering facilities and a café. Clean and cosy. Open May–Sept. Dorm beds 180kr, doubles ❷

The centre

Pedestrianized **Kongens gate** is Ålesund's main drag, and features several attractive Art Deco buildings, as does **Apotekergata**, just over the bridge on the other side of the harbour. Here, the old **Apothek** building, on the corner of Bakkegata, is of particular merit, its chunky bay windows, columns and tower lending it a decidedly neo-baronial appearance. Neighbouring **Kirkegata** is perhaps the most harmonious street of all, its long line of Art Nouveau houses decorated with playful turrets and towers reminiscent of a Ruritanian film set. It's also home to Ålesund's finest building, its **kirke** (church; June–Aug Tues–Sun 10am–2pm; free), completed in 1909. The church is Romanesque in style, from its roughly dressed stone blocks and heavy-duty tower through to its hooped windows, though the interior is far from sombre, thanks principally to the brilliant **frescoes** flanking the high altar. The work of

Enevold Thømt in the 1920s, the frescoes are startlingly original – with both Art Nouveau and Arts and Crafts influences – and keenly religious. The left-hand wall carries an image of the birth of Christ, the right the Ascension, while the vaulting of the arch above displays a variety of religious symbols – for baptism, communion, and so forth.

Aside from strolling through Ålesund's lively centre, draped around the **Brosundet** harbour, the town's only other attraction is the **park** at the top of Lihauggata. Here, you'll find monkey puzzle and copper beech trees, as well as a large statue of **Rollo**, a Viking chieftain born and raised in Ålesund, who seized Normandy and became its first duke in 911: he was also an ancestor of William the Conqueror. Close by, there's a much smaller bust of the town's benefactor, the kaiser, in which he looks disarmingly youthful. From the park, several hundred steps lead to the top of **Aksla hill**, from where the view out along the coast and its islands is fabulous.

Atlanterhavsparken and the Sunnmøre Museum

Three kilometres west of Ålesund on a low-lying headland, is the **Atlanterhavsparken** (Atlantic Sea-Park; mid-June to mid-Aug Mon–Fri & Sun 10am–7pm, Sat 10am–4pm; mid-Aug to Sept & May to mid June Mon–Sat 11am–4pm, Sun noon–5pm; Oct–April Tues–Sat 11am–4pm, Sun noon–5pm; 85kr), a giant marine complex. Inside are several enormous fish tanks, which are home to a variety of North Atlantic marine species. It also has an outside area with several easy footpaths and some decent bathing beaches.

Far more appealing, however, is the **Sunnmøre Museum** (late May to late June Mon–Fri 11am–4pm & Sun noon–4pm; late June to Aug Mon–Sat 11am–5pm & Sun noon–5pm; Sept to late May Mon, Tues & Fri 11am–3pm & Sun noon–4pm; ⓦwww.sunnmore.museum.no; 55kr), about 4km east of the centre just off the E136. One of Norway's more ambitious heritage museums, it occupies an attractive location, spread over wooded hills by the water's edge. Inside the large, modern complex, a series of displays explores various aspects of local life from medieval times onwards, whilst, outside, a collection of thirty-odd **boats**, some antique and others (such as the Viking longship) replicas, marks the start of a hiking trail that heads over the hills past sixty old **timber buildings**. Moved here from other parts of the Sunnmøre district, the buildings include assorted cowsheds, storehouses, stables and dwellings, as well as a row of eighteenth-century *kyrkjebuer* (shacks), where local country folk once kept their Sunday best clothes. By law, Norwegians had to go to church, and as this involved many of them in long and arduous journeys, *kyrkjebuer* were built next to parish churches, so the peasantry could rest and change into their clothes before the service. The *kyrkjebuer* also played a romantic role: it was here that many a Norwegian caught the eye of their future wife or husband.

Cafés, restaurants and bars

Ålesund has several first-rate **restaurants**. One of the best is the *Sjøbua Fiskerestaurant*, Brunholmgata 1 (☎70 12 71 00; closed Sun), which serves wonderful seafood in chic surroundings, and even has its own lobster tank – something of a rarity in Norway. It's expensive, with main courses from around 190kr, but very popular, so reservations are advised. An excellent second choice is *Hummer & Kanari*, Kongens gate 19 (Mon–Thurs 11.30am–1am, Fri & Sat 11.30am–2am; ☎70 12 80 08), which also specializes in seafood, as well as more unusual offerings from lamb to ostrich. In addition, it serves that old

4

The Hurtigrute from Ålesund to Bergen, via Florø

If time is short and you need to fast-track back south to Bergen, the best way is to take the **Hurtigrute** coastal boat, a thirteen-hour journey. The Hurtigrute goes via the west coast town of Florø, where, if you have some spare time, you might want to break your journey. Alternatively, you could **drive** south along the **E39** coastal highway, a 380km journey from Ålesund to Bergen involving four ferry rides. It takes a full day's motoring to complete the trip, and you'll need to pick up ferry timetables from the tourist office at Ålesund before you set out. The route covers some fine coastal scenery, but misses almost everything of any real interest, unless you detour west from Førde, for the 70km run along Highway 5 to Florø.

Norway's westernmost town, **FLORØ** has much in common with its west coast neighbours: it has a blustery island setting, its economy has been boosted by the oil industry, it offers tourists sea-fishing trips and excursions to a whole string of off-shore islands, and its mostly modern centre is wrapped around the traditional focus of coastal town life, the harbour. Once an important Viking centre, Florø's early days are recalled on the offshore islet of **Kinn**, where the stone **Kinnakyrkja** (church), with its intriguing carvings and Baroque altar piece, is a much modified Romanesque structure dating from the twelfth century. Passenger **boats** to Kinn leave from Florø harbour once or twice daily (mid-June to mid-August Mon–Fri; 30min). Ferry schedules are available at the **tourist office**, by the harbour at Strandgata 30 (mid-June to mid-Aug Mon–Fri 8am–7pm, Sat 10am–5pm, Sun noon–7pm; mid-Aug to mid-June Mon–Fri 8am–3.30pm; ☎57 74 75 05; ⊛www.vestkysten.no). It also has a list of local **accommodation**, with the best option being the waterfront *Quality Maritim Hotel*, Hamnegata 7 (☎57 75 75 75, ℱ57 75 75 10; ⊛www.florahotel.no; ❺, s/r ❹), a smart chain hotel built in the style of an old warehouse; ask for a room with a sea view. An alternative route back to Bergen from Florø is on the regular **Hurtigbåt** passenger express boat, which leaves from the main town dock (1–2 daily; 3hr 30min; 430kr).

Norwegian standby, *klippfisk* (salted and dried cod), cooked every which way and costing about 220kr. This restaurant is smart, but not as formal as the *Sjøbua*, and after the kitchen closes down – at about 9.30pm – it turns into one of the most agreeable **bars** in town. Less expensive if rather more mundane food is on offer at the hip *Smak Art Café and Gallery*, Kipervikgata 5 (11am–3.30pm & 4–8pm); here lunches cost around 70kr, main courses in the evening about 100kr. In sunny weather, the terrace of the *Metz*, beside the Brosundet harbour at Notenesgata 1, is the place for drinks.

Around Ålesund: bird-watching on Runde

The small island of **Runde**'s steep and craggy cliffs are the summer haunt of several hundred thousand **sea birds**. Common species include gannets, kitti-wakes, fulmars, razorbills and guillemots, but the most numerous of all is the **puffin**, whose breeding holes honeycomb the island's higher ground. Most species congregate here between late March and August, though some – like the Grey Heron and the Velvet Scoter – winter here. A network of footpaths provides access to a number of bird-watching vantage points, though these invariably involve a fair climb up from the foreshore.

The easiest way to visit Runde is to **drive** the 70km from Ålesund – Runde is connected to the mainland by a road bridge – though the journey does involve using the Sulesund to Hareid ferry (every 30min; 25min; passengers 25kr, car & driver 71kr). The trip is pretty straightforward by public transport, too: take the **Hurtigbåt** boat from Ålesund to Hareid (11 daily; 30min; 60kr

△ Performance at the Stiklestad National Cultural Centre

each way), several of which connect with an onward bus to Runde – check first with the Ålesund tourist office as to which buses connect. Once in Runde, if you don't fancy clambering around the island, you can get a two-and-a-half-hour **bird-watching boat trip** from the harbour (May to Aug 3 daily; 120kr; reservations on ☎70 08 59 16). Alternatively, a longer boat trip to Runde leaves from Ulsteinvik, about 40km from Ålesund: the "Charming Ruth" runs three times a week from late June to mid-August, takes around four hours and costs 200kr (bookings on ☎70 01 30 00). Neither of the boat trips sail in inclement weather.

Although you're most likely to visit Runde on a day-trip from Ålesund, there is **accommodation** on the island: the HI hostel and campsite *Runde Camping & Vandrerhjem* (☎70 08 59 16, ⑤ 70 08 58 70; ⓦwww.runde.no; dorm beds 110kr, doubles ❶) is on the southeast shore of the island, 300m from the harbour, with frugal, modern rooms.

North to Kristiansund

Ålesund is within easy striking distance of the next major towns up along the coast – **Molde** and **Kristiansund**, at 80km and 150km respectively. Neither is especially riveting: Molde's highlight is its annual jazz festival, while Kristiansund boasts a fine coastal location and a handful of mildly interesting sights recalling its heyday as a centre of the *klippfisk* (salted, dried cod) industry. The main road from Ålesund to Molde – the **E39** – is a pleasant coastal run culminating with a ferry crossing of the Romsdalsfjord. From Molde, there's a choice of routes to Kristiansund: the scenic **Highway 64**, incorporating the **Atlanterhavsveien**, a short but dramatic stretch of highway that hops from islet to islet on the very edge of the ocean; and the faster, but more mundane, continuation of the E39.

Ålesund, Molde and Kristiansund are also linked by the **Hurtigrute** coastal boat. Northbound, it leaves Ålesund for both destinations – as well as Trondheim – at 6.45pm, taking three hours to Molde, seven to Kristiansund, and thirteen and a half hours to Trondheim. Alternatively, there are one or two daily express **buses** from Ålesund to Molde, Bergsøya toll station – where you change for Kristiansund – and Trondheim; Ålesund to Molde takes two and a quarter hours; Ålesund to Kristiansund takes a little over fours hours, but check the Bergsøya connection before you set out. Local buses also provide a limited weekday service from Molde to Bremsnes, a twenty-minute ferry journey from the centre of Kristiansund; journey time is two hours.

Molde

From Ålesund, it's about 80km along the E39 to the **Vestnes ferry** (every 30min; 35min; passengers 27kr, car & driver 80kr), which scuttles over the Romsdalsfjord to the industrial town of **MOLDE**, sprawling along the seashore with a ridge of steep, green hills behind. Despite its modern appearance, Molde is one of the region's older towns, but it was blown to smithereens by the Luftwaffe in 1940, an act of destruction watched by King Håkon from these same hills just weeks before he was forced into exile in England. The new town that grew up in its stead is unremarkable, but it does host the week-long **Molde Jazz Festival**, held annually in the middle of July. Tickets are relatively cheap (100–250kr) and there's a smattering of big names among the home-grown talent. Programme details are widely available across the region and tickets can be purchased from the ticket office in Molde Rådhus (℡71 20 31 50, ℻71 20 31 51, ⓦwww.moldejazz.no). Naturally, the big-name concerts are sold out months in advance and accommodation is impossible to find during the festival, but the authorities operate a large official campsite, *Jazzcampen*, 3km west of the centre, for the duration. Outside of festival time, you're unlikely to want to stay in Molde, but if you do get stuck a good central option is the *Rica Hotel*, a well-appointed chain hotel on the waterfront at Storgata 8 (℡71 20 35 00, ℻71 20 35 01; ⓦwww.rica.no; ❺, s/r ❹).

All Molde's amenities are within easy each of each other: the **ferry terminal** is on the east side of the centre, about 400m from the **bus station**, which is itself close to the **tourist office** at Storgata 31 (mid-June to Aug Mon–Fri 9am–6pm, Sat 9am–3pm & Sun noon–5pm; Sept to mid-June Mon–Fri 8.30am–3.30pm; ℡71 25 71 33; ⓦwww.visitmolde.com).

From Molde to Kristiansund

There are two routes from Molde to Kristiansund. The quicker, but less interesting, option is to take the **E39**, which begins with a 50km canter northeast to a massive suspension **bridge** (55kr toll) between the mainland and the tiny islet of **Bergsøya**. Here, **Highway 70** spears north for the 25km trip to Kristiansund via the 5km Freifjord tunnel (60kr toll), while the E39 continues for 170km to Trondheim (see p.258).

A far more picturesque route, however, is to take **Highway 64**, which forks north off the E39 just to the east of Molde. It starts off by tunnelling through the mountains, before rounding the head of the slender Malmefjord. Afterwards, it rattles over the hills, down the valley and along the edge of the **Kornstadfjord** to reach the coast at the start of the **Atlanterhavsveien** (Atlantic Highway), some 50km from Molde. A spirited piece of engineering, the Atlanterhavsveien is a scenic 8km stretch of road that negotiates the mouth of the Kornstadfjord, manoeuvring from islet to islet by a sequence of bridges and causeways. In calm conditions, it's an attractive run, but in blustery weather it's exhilarating with the wind whistling round the car, the surf roaring and pounding away at the road.

Beyond, Highway 64 ploughs on across the island of **Averøy**, a 20km run that ends at the **Bremsnes car ferry** to Kristiansund (hourly Mon–Sat 5.30am–11pm, Sun 8am–11pm; 20min; passengers 20kr, car & driver 51kr). On Averøy, the **Kvernes stavkirke** (mid-June to mid-Aug daily 10am–5pm; 30kr) merits a brief detour – it's 10km south of Highway 64, along the island's eastern shore. Dating from the thirteenth century, the church was built on what had previously been a pagan ceremonial site as proved by the discovery here of a Viking phallus stone. Much modified over the centuries, the church is a simple barn-like affair distinguished by its Biblical wall paintings, added in the 1630s.

Kristiansund

Despite **KRISTIANSUND's** attractive coastal setting, straddling three rocky islets and the enormous channel-cum-harbour that they create, it somehow still contrives to look quite dull. The town was founded in the eighteenth century as a fishing port, and there are a handful of antique clapboard houses along **Fosnagata**, immediately to the north of the main quay – but once again the Luftwaffe polished off most of the old town in 1940. Up the slope to the west of the quay are the few modern streets that now serve as the town centre and nearby too, at the quay's south end, is the modern **klippfiskkjerringa statue** of a woman carrying a fish. The statue recalls the days when salted cod was laid out along the seashore to dry, producing the *klippfisk* that was the main source of income in these parts well into the 1950s. Appropriately, the town is home to the **Norsk klippfiskmuseum** (mid-June to mid-Aug Mon–Sat noon–5pm, Sun 1–4pm; 30kr), housed in an old and well-worn warehouse, the Milnbrygga, across the harbour to the east of the main quay. The most pleasant way to reach the museum is by a small passenger boat, the *Sundbåt* (Mon–Fri 6.30am–4pm, Sat 8.30am–1.30pm; 2 hourly; 15kr), which leaves from beside the statue to call at each of the town's three islets. The service was once crucial for getting around Kristiansund, but the islands are now connected by bridge and the boats are, essentially, an exercise in nostalgia. If you're visiting the *klippfiskmuseum*, you may want to drop by its waterfront warehouse neighbours, the **Hjelkrembrygga** (mid-June to mid-Aug Sun 1–4pm; 20kr), which displays old sepia photographs of the locality, and the **Woldbrygga** (same details), whose old boats and rope-making equipment are displayed in a nineteenth-century barrel factory. Of more general interest are the handful of venerable timber houses that make up the **Gamle Byen** (Old Town), situated on the smallest of the three islets, Innlandet – south across the harbour from the main quay. Look out here, too, for the distinctive **Lossiusgården**, a large and handsome house that belonged to an eighteenth-century merchant; unfortunately, you can't go inside.

Grip

Kristiansund's most popular attraction, however, is the boat trip to minuscule **GRIP**. A low-lying islet that's part of a slender archipelago 14km offshore, Grip is dotted with brightly painted timber houses and has a much-modified stave church dating from the fifteenth century. The islanders took refuge in the church whenever they were threatened by a storm, as they often were – indeed, when you look at the place, it's amazing anyone ever lived here at all. There are no permanent residents now, but in the summertime fishermen dock in the sliver of a harbour and there are even some basic guesthouse-style **lodgings** (❷); these are bookable via the Kristiansund tourist office (see below) and advance reservations are advised. There's a claustrophobia-inducing air about the islet and if you're here when the weather's up the effects can be quite overpowering. In summer, there's a daily **boat** from Kristiansund to Grip (June to mid-Aug 1–4 daily; May & late Aug Sat & Sun 1 or 2 daily; 150kr return); reservations should be made at the tourist office (see below).

Practicalities

Buses to Kristiansund pull in beside the Nordmørskaia quay at the north end of the main town quay, five minutes' walk from the *klippfiskkjerringa*. **Hurtigbåt** services also dock and leave from here, bound for Trondheim, as does the boat for Grip (see above). The **Hurtigrute** coastal boat (daily departures northbound at 1.45am, southbound at 5pm) docks at Holmakaia, a few metres to the east. From here, it's a short stroll up Kaibakken to the **tourist office** at Kongens plass 1 (mid-June to mid-Aug Mon–Fri 9am–7pm, Sat 10am–3pm & Sun 11am–4pm; mid-Aug to mid-June Mon–Fri 8.30am–4pm; ☎71 58 54 54; ⓦwww.visitkristiansund.no).

Kristiansund's first choice for **accommodation** is the modern *First Hotel Grand*, Bernstorrfstredet 1 (☎71 57 13 00, ⓕ71 57 13 10; ⓦwww .choicehotels.no; ❻, s/r ❹), just south of Kaibakken, the short street linking the south end of the main quay with the main square, Kongens plass. Alternatively, there's the *Rica Hotel Kristiansund*, a short walk to the west at Storgata 41 (☎71

67 64 11, ⓕ71 67 79 12; ⓦwww.rica.no; ➏, s/r ➍). For **food**, the *Smia* restaurant, at Fosnagata 30 (ⓣ71 67 11 70), stands head and shoulders above its competitors. Housed in a converted boat shed metres from the north end of the main quay, it serves superb fish dishes from around 150kr. Otherwise, try the *Sjøstjerna*, at Skolegata 8 (closed Sun), an inexpensive café-restaurant in the pedestrianized area, a short walk behind the tourist office; it specializes in seafood, with the marinated salmon being particularly tasty.

Travel details

Trains

Bergen to: Finse (3–4 daily; 2hr 15min); Geilo (3–4 daily; 3hr); Myrdal (3–4 daily; 1hr 50min); Oslo (3–4 daily; 6hr 30min); Voss (3–4 daily; 1hr 10min).
Dombås to: Trondheim (2–3 daily; 3hr); Åndalsnes (2–3 daily; 1hr 20min).
Myrdal to: Flåm (mid-June to mid-Sept 10 daily; mid-Sept to mid-June 4 daily; 50min).
Åndalsnes to: Dombås (2–3 daily; 1hr 20min); Oslo (2–3 daily; 5hr 30min).

Buses

Balestrand to: Oslo (3 daily; 8hr 15min); Sogndal (3 daily; 1hr 15min).
Bergen to: Dombås (2 daily; 11hr); Grotli (1–2 daily; 8hr); Flåm (2–6 daily; 3hr 10min); Hellesylt (1–2 daily; 8hr 15min); Loen (3–4 daily; 6hr 30min); Norheimsund (1–3 daily; 1hr 30min); Odda (1–3 daily; 3hr 30min); Oslo (1–3 daily; 11hr); Skei (3 daily; 5hr); Sogndal (2–6 daily; 4hr 30min); Stavanger (3–6 daily; 5hr); Stryn (2 daily; 7hr); Trondheim (1–2 daily; 14hr); Utne (1–3 daily; 2hr 45min); Voss (4 daily; 1hr 45min); Ålesund (1–2 daily; 10hr).
Geiranger to: Åndalsnes (mid-June to Aug 2 daily; 3hr).
Kristiansund to: Molde (1–3 daily; 1hr 15min); Trondheim (1–3 daily; 5hr); Ålesund (1–3 daily; 2hr 40min).
Molde to: Kristiansund (1–3 daily; 1hr 15min); Trondheim (1–3 daily; 5hr); Ålesund (1–3 daily; 2hr 15min); Åndalsnes (2–5 daily; 1hr 30min).
Mundal to: Oslo (3 daily; 7hr 50min); Sogndal (3 daily; 30min).
Sogndal to: Balestrand (3 daily; 1hr 15min); Bergen (2–5 daily; 4hr 30min); Mundal (3 daily; 30min); Oslo (3 daily; 7hr); Voss (2–6 daily; 3hr).
Stryn to: Bergen (2 daily; 7hr); Hellesylt (1–2 daily; 1hr); Oslo (3 daily; 8hr 30min); Trondheim (2 daily; 5hr 30min).

Voss to: Bergen (4 daily; 1hr 45min); Flåm (2–6 daily 1hr); Gudvangen (2–6 daily; 50min); Sogndal (2–6 daily; 3hr).
Ålesund to: Bergen (1–2 daily; 10hr); Hellesylt (2–3 daily; 2hr 40min); Molde (1–3 daily; 2hr 15min); Stryn (1–2 daily; 3hr); Trondheim (1–3 daily; 8hr); Åndalsnes (3–4 daily; 2hr 25min).
Åndalsnes to: Geiranger (mid-June to Aug 2 daily; 3hr); Molde (2–5 daily; 1hr 30min); Ålesund (3–4 daily; 2hr 25min).

Car ferries

Balestrand to: Mundal (late May to early September 2 daily; 1hr 25min).
Bruravik to: Brimnes (1–2 hourly; 10min).
Dragsvik to: Hella (every 40min to hourly; 15min); Vangsnes (every 40min to hourly; 25min).
Flåm to: Gudvangen (1–4 daily; 2hr).
Fodnes to: Manheller (every 30min; 15min).
Geiranger to: Hellesylt (May–Sept 4–8 daily; 1hr).
Gudvangen to: Flåm (1–4 daily; 2hr); Kaupanger (mid-May to Sept 4 daily; 2hr).
Hella to: Dragsvik (every 40min to hourly; 15min); Vangsnes (every 40min to hourly; 15min).
Kvanndal to: Kinsarvik (1 or 2 hourly; 50min); Utne (1 or 2 hourly; 20min).
Kaupanger to: Gudvangen (mid-May to Sept 4 daily; 2hr).
Utne to: Kinsarvik (1 or 2 hourly; 30min).

Hurtigbåt passenger express boats

Bergen to: Balestrand (2–3 daily; 4hr); Flåm (1 daily; 5hr 30min); Florø (1–2 daily; 3hr 30min); Selje (1–2 daily; 5hr); Sogndal (Mon–Sat 1–2 daily; 5hr).
Flåm to: Balestrand (1–3 daily; 1hr 30min); Bergen (1–2 daily; 5hr); Sogndal (Mon–Fri 1 daily; 50min).
Kristiansund to: Trondheim (2–3 daily; 3hr 40min).
Norheimsund to: Eidfjord (1 daily 2hr 40min);

Kinsarvik (1–3 daily; 1hr 15min); Lofthus (Mon–Sat 1–3 daily; 1hr 15min); Odda (1–3 daily; 1hr 40min); Utne (3–4 daily; 50min).

Hurtigrute coastal boat

Northbound departures: daily from Bergen at 8pm; Florø at 2.15am; Ålesund at 9.30am for Geiranger, 6.45pm for Molde; Geiranger at 1.30pm; Molde at 10pm; Kristiansund at 1.45am; arrives Trondheim at 8.15am.

Southbound departures: daily from Trondheim at 10am; Kristiansund at 5pm; Molde at 9.30pm; Ålesund at 12.45am; Florø at 8.15am; arrives Bergen, where the service terminates, at 2.30pm. Southbound, the Hurtigrute does not stop at Geiranger.

Trondheim to the
Lofoten islands

CHAPTER 5

Highlights

* **Bakklandet** The trendy bars and restaurants of this attractive, old district in Trondheim are *the* place to go for a lively night out. **See p.268**

* **Trondheim Cathedral** Scandinavia's largest medieval building makes a stirring focal point for the city. **See p.262**

* **Ofotbanen railway** A dramatic train ride from Narvik over the Swedish border through stunningly beautiful mountain scenery. **See p.289**

* **Whale-watching at Andenes** From late May to mid-September, whale-watching safaris from this remote port almost guarantee a sighting. **See p.296**

* **Henningsvær** One of the Lofoten islands, most picturesque fishing villages, with brightly painted wooden houses framing its attractive harbour. **See p.306**

* **The Norsk Fiskevaers-museum** History combines with a stunning setting at Å's Norwegian Fishing Village Museum. **See p.310**

* **Bird colonies on Værøy and Røst** The two remote Lofoten islands are renowned for their birdlife, including puffins, eiders, gulls, terns, cormorants, kittiwakes, guillemots, and rare sea eagles. **See p.311**

Trondheim to the Lofoten islands

The 900-kilometre-long stretch of Norway from Trondheim to the island-studded coast near Narvik marks the transition from the rural south to the blustery north. Readily accessible from Oslo by train, **Trondheim** is easily the biggest town hereabouts and capital of the fertile – by Norwegian standards – **Trøndelag** province: its easy-going air and imposing cathedral, the finest medieval building in the country, make it an enjoyable place to spend a few days. But travel on one of the express trains that thunder further north, and you begin to feel far removed from the capital and the more intimate, forested south. Distances between places grow ever greater, and travelling becomes more of a slog. As Trøndelag gives way to **Nordland** province things get increasingly wild – "Arthurian", thought Evelyn Waugh – and, the scenery apart, there is little of interest between Trondheim and the engaging industrial towns of **Mosjøen** and **Mo-i-Rana**.

Just north of Mo-i-Rana, on the E6, you cross the **Arctic Circle** – one of the principal targets for many travellers – at a point where the cruel and barren scenery seems strikingly appropriate. On the Arctic Circle, the midnight sun and 24-hour polar night occur once a year, at the summer and winter solstices respectively; the further north from here you go, the longer the period during which you can experience these two phenomena (see box, p.320).

Beyond the Arctic Circle, the mountains of the interior lead down to a fretted, craggy coastline and even the towns, the largest of which is the port of **Bodø**, have a feral quality about them. The iron-ore port of **Narvik**, in the far north of Nordland, has perhaps the wildest setting of them all, and was the scene of some of the fiercest fighting between the Allied and Axis forces in World War II. To the west lies the offshore archipelago that makes up the **Vesterålen and Lofoten islands**. In the north of the Vesterålen islands, between **Harstad** and **Andenes**, the coastline is mauled by massive fjords, whereas to the south, the Lofoten islands are backboned by a mighty and ravishingly beautiful mountain wall – a highlight of any itinerary. Among a handful of idyllic fishing villages the pick is **Å**, though **Henningsvær** and **Stamsund** come a very close second.

As for **accommodation**, the region has a smattering of strategically located hostels, and there are at least a couple of hotels in all the major towns, though

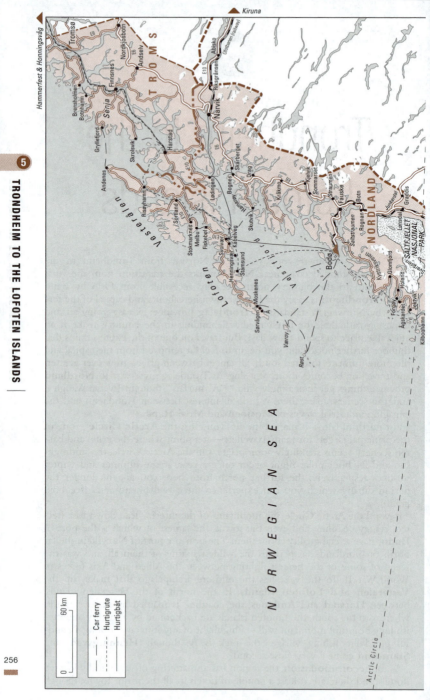

▲ *Kiruna*

◄ *Hammerfest & Honningsvåg*

T R O M S

N O R D L A N D

Vesterålen

Lofoten

Vestfjorden

N O R W E G I A N   S E A

Arctic Circle

SALTFJELLET
NASJONAL
PARK

Tromsø
Breivikeidet
Botnhamn
Gryllefjord
Andenes
Risøyhamn
Sortland
Stokmarknes
Melbu
Fiskebøl
Svolvær
Henningsvær
Stamsund
Sørvågen
Moskenes
Å
Finnsnes
Skrolsvik
Harstad
Lødingen
Bognes
Skutvik
Kjøpsvik
Kåringen
Kabelvåg
Nordkjosbotn
Andselv
Abisko
Oftoten (railway)
Riksgrensen
Narvik
Skarberget
Drag
Kjelvik
Sommarset
Straumen
Bodø
Saltstraumen
Rognan
Fauske
Botn
Kåkern
Værøy
Røst
Junkerdal
Graddis
Lønsdal
Storjord
Kystveien
Glomfjord
Holandsfjord
Holand
Jektvik
Førøy
Åskårdet
Kilboghamn

Senja

60 km
0

Car ferry
Hurtigrute
Hurtigbåt

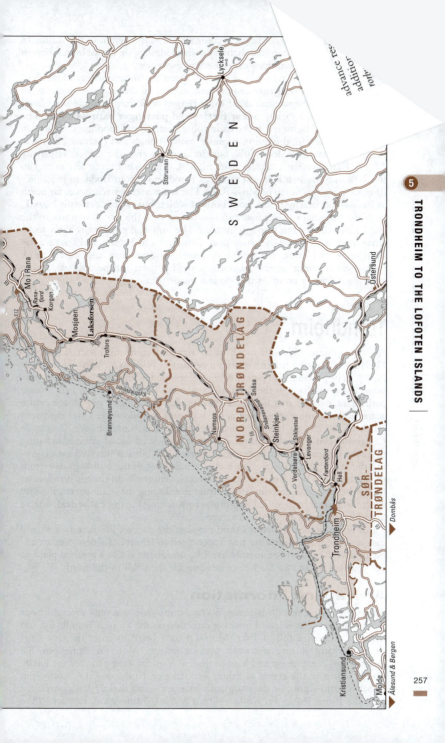

SWEDEN

Lycksele

Storuman

Östersund

Mo i Rana
Rana-fjord
Korgen
Mosjøen
Laksforsen
Trofors

Brønnøysund
Kystriksveien

Namsos
Snåsavatn Snåsa
Steinkjer
Verdalsøra Sliklestad
Levanger
Fættenfjord
Hell
Trondheim

NORD-TRØNDELAG

SØR-TRØNDELAG

Kristiansund
Molde

▼ Ålesund & Bergen

▼ Dombås

vations are strongly recommended in the height of the season. In ⌐on the Lofoten islands, inexpensive lodgings are available in scores of ⌐r (see p.301), small huts once used by fishermen.

Transport is good, which is just as well given the isolated nature of much of the region. The **Hurtigrute** coastal boat stops at all the major settlements on its route up the Norwegian coast from Bergen to Kirkenes, while the islands are accessible via a variety of **car ferries** and **passenger express boats**. The **E6**, or "Arctic Highway", is the main route north from Trondheim: it's kept in excellent condition, though in summer motor-homes and caravans can make the going very slow. Slower still, but stunningly scenic, the coastal **Highway 17**, or "Kystriksveien", utilizes road, tunnels, bridges and seven ferries to run the 700km from Steinkjer, just north of Trondheim, up to Bodø: its most picturesque stretch is north of Mo-i-Rana. The **train** network reaches as far north as Fauske and nearby Bodø, from both of which **buses** connect with Narvik, itself the terminal of a separate rail line which runs the few kilometres to the border and then south through Sweden. The only real problem is likely to be **time**: it's a day or two's journey from Trondheim to Fauske, and another day from there to Narvik. Unless you've several days to spare, you should think twice before venturing further north: travelling there can be arduous, and in any case it's pretty pointless if done at a hectic pace.

Trondheim

An atmospheric city with much of its antique centre still intact, **TROND-HEIM** was known until the sixteenth century as Nidaros ("mouth of the river Nid"), its importance as a power base underpinned by the excellence of its harbour and its position at the head of a wide and fertile valley. The early Norse parliament, or *Ting*, met here, and the cathedral was a major pilgrimage centre at the end of a route stretching all the way back to Oslo. After a **fire** destroyed much of the city in 1681, a military engineer from Luxembourg, Caspar de Cicignon, rebuilt Trondheim on a gridiron plan, with broad avenues radiating from the centre to act as firebreaks. Cicignon's layout has survived intact, giving the city centre an airy, elegant air, though most of the buildings date from the commercial boom of the late nineteenth century. With timber warehouses lining the river and doughty stone structures dotting the main streets, the city centre is a suitably dignified and prosperous setting for the **cathedral**, one of Scandinavia's finest medieval structures.

Trondheim is now Norway's third city, but the pace of life here is slow and easy, and the main **sights** are best appreciated in leisurely fashion over a couple of days. Genial and eminently likeable, Trondheim is also a pleasant place to get your last hit of city life before heading for the wilds of the north.

Arrival and information

Trondheim is on the E6 highway, 500km from Oslo, a seven- or eight-hour drive. A toll of 35kr is levied in either direction on the E6 near Trondheim, and there's a municipal toll of 15kr (Mon–Fri 6am–6pm) to enter the city. On-street **parking** during restricted periods (mostly Mon–Fri 8am–6pm, Sat 10am–1pm) is expensive and hard to find, so head for a car park: try the handy Torget P-hus, in the centre at Erling Skakkes gate 16 (Mon–Fri 6.30am–9pm & Sat 6.30am–7pm), or the marginally cheaper – and slightly less convenient – Bakke P-hus (Mon–Fri 6.30am–11pm & Sat 6.30am–9pm), east across the

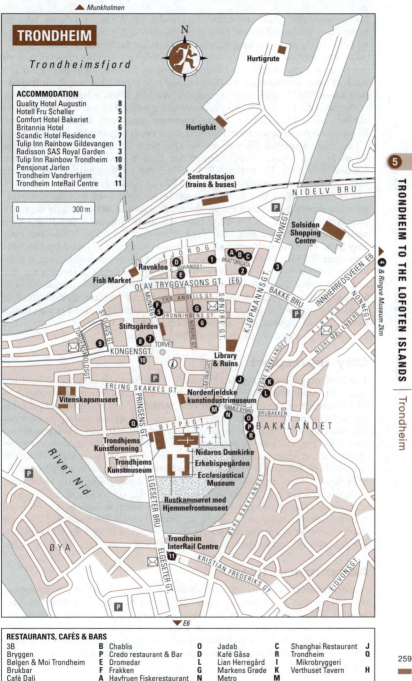

TRONDHEIM

Trondheimsfjord

5

TRONDHEIM TO THE LOFOTEN ISLANDS | Trondheim

Munkholmen

Hurtigrute

Hurtigbåt

Sentralstasjon (trains & buses)

NIDELV BRU

Solsiden Shopping Centre

ACCOMMODATION

Quality Hotel Augustin	8
Hotell Fru Schøller	5
Comfort Hotel Bakeriet	2
Britannia Hotel	6
Scandic Hotel Residence	7
Tulip Inn Rainbow Gildevangen	1
Radisson SAS Royal Garden	3
Tulip Inn Rainbow Trondheim	10
Pensjonat Jarlen	9
Trondheim Vandrerhjem	4
Trondheim InteRail Centre	11

0   300 m

Ravnkloa

Fish Market

FJORDGT.

JOHANSGT.

BRATTØRGATA

OLAV TRYGGVASONS GT. (E6)

THS. ANGELLS GT.

DRONNINGENS GT.

Stiftsgården

SØNDRE GT.

NORDRE GT.

TORVET

KONGENSGT.

ERLING SKAKKES GT.

Vitenskapsmuseet

PRINSENS GT.

Library & Ruins

VÅR FRUEGATE

Nordenfjeldske kunstindustrimuseum

GAMLE BYBRO

BAKKLANDET

BRUBAKKEN

NEDRE BAKKLANDET

NEDRE MØLLENBERG

KJØPMANNSGT.

BAKKE BRU

HAVNEGT.

INNHERREDSVEIEN E6

NONNEGT.

KIRKEGT.

Trondhjems Kunstforening

BISPEGT.

Trondhjems Kunstmuseum

ELGESETER BRU

Nidaros Domkirke
Erkebispegården
Ecclesiastical Museum

Rustkammeret med Hjemmefrontmuseet

ØYRE BAKKLANDET

ØYA

River Nid

ST. OLAVS GT.

TORDENSKJOLDSGT.

MUNKEGT.

Trondheim InteRail Centre

ELGESETER GT.

KRISTIAN FREDERIKS GT.

EIDVONSGT.

E6

Sverresborg Folkemuseum

Tram to ① & ◀

4 & Ringve Museum 2km

RESTAURANTS, CAFÉS & BARS

3B	**B**	Chablis	**O**	Jadab	**C**	Shanghai Restaurant	**J**
Bryggen	**P**	Credo restaurant & Bar	**D**	Kafé Gåsa	**R**	Trondheim	**Q**
Bølgen & Moi Trondheim	**E**	Dromedar	**L**	Lian Herregård	**I**	Mikrobryggeri	
Brukbar	**F**	Frakken	**G**	Markens Grøde	**K**	Verthuset Tavern	**H**
Café Dali	**A**	Havfruen Fiskerestaurant	**N**	Metro	**M**		

259

bridge from the centre at Nedre Bakklandet 60. Rates are around 10kr an hour. There is also a 24hr car park at Sentralstasjon, but outside of the restricted periods, on-street parking is free and spaces are fairly easy to find.

The **Hurtigrute** coastal boat docks at the harbour (northbound services from pier 1, quay 1, and southbound from pier 1, quay 2). These twin piers are 600m north of **Sentralstasjon**, the modern bus and train terminal, where the **information kiosk** (☎177) deals with all transport enquiries. If you're heading for the city centre from the Hurtigrute quay, consider taking a taxi (60kr) as it's a dull twenty-minute walk. The all-year **Kystekspressen** passenger express boat from Kristiansund docks at the Pirterminalen, 300m north of Sentralstasjon.

Trondheim **airport** is 35km northeast of the city at Værnes. From here, Flybussen (Mon–Fri 5am–9pm every 15min; Sat 5am–5.45pm every 30min; Sun 6.45am–9pm every 15–30min; 45 min; 55kr) run to Sentralstasjon and various points in the city centre, including the *SAS Royal Garden Hotel*.

From Sentralstasjon, you simply cross the bridge southwards to reach the triangular island on which central Trondheim sits. The **tourist office**, at Munkegata 19 (mid-May to early June & late Aug Mon–Fri 8.30am–6pm, Sat & Sun 10am–4pm; mid- to late June & mid-Aug Mon–Fri 8.30am–8pm, Sat & Sun 10am–6pm; early Aug Mon–Fri 8.30am–10pm, Sat & Sun 10am–8pm; Sept to mid-May Mon–Fri 9am–4pm; ☎73 80 76 60, ✉turistinfo@taas.no, ⊛www.trondheim.com), is right in the centre of town on a corner of the main square, Torvet. It provides the free and very useful *Trondheim Guide* (also available from the information racks at Sentralstasjon) as well as a wide range of other tourist literature including a cycle map of the city and its surroundings; it also has a limited supply of private rooms (see below). In addition, you can buy hiking maps and change money here – the latter service is especially handy outside banking hours.

City transport

The best way of exploring the city centre is **on foot** – it only takes about ten minutes to walk from one end to the other – but a convenient alternative is to take advantage of the city's **free bicycle rental**. Bright green municipal bikes are available from racks all over the city centre and are released upon payment of a small deposit (20kr); the money is returned automatically when you return your bike. The bikes are popular, so don't be surprised if you come across an empty rack. A map marking the locations of the racks is available from the tourist office. For longer excursions, **mountain bikes** can be rented from Ila Sykkelsenter, Steinberget 1 (☎73 51 09 40), at about 160kr a day. Otherwise, transport in town is by **buses** and **trams** with flat-fare tickets, from the driver, costing 22kr. If you need to travel outside town, to one of the outlying museums or the campsite, it might be worth buying the unlimited 24-hour public transport ticket, the *dagskort*, from the driver: it costs 55kr (70kr including the suburbs) and is valid on all local buses and trams.

Accommodation

Accommodation is plentiful in Trondheim, with a choice of private rooms, two hostels, and a selection of reasonably priced hotels and guesthouses (*pensjonater*). What's more, most of the more appealing places are dotted round the city centre, though the private rooms booked via the tourist office are usually out in the suburbs. These **private rooms** are good value, however, at a fixed rate of 400–440kr per double per night (250–320kr single), plus a 20kr booking fee and a 30kr deposit.

Hotels

Britannia Hotel Dronningens gate 5 ☎73 80 08 00, ℻73 80 08 01, ⓦwww.britannia.no. Right in the middle of town, this long-established hotel has a magnificent Art Nouveau breakfast room, complete with a Moorish fountain, Egyptian-style murals and Corinthian columns. The comfortable rooms are heavily discounted in summer. ❼, s/r ❹

Comfort Hotel Bakeriet Brattørgata 2 ☎73 99 10 00, ℻73 99 10 01, ⓦwww.choicehotels.no. Competent chain hotel in a pleasantly modernized former bakery. Central location. ❺, s/r ❸

Hotell Fru Schøller Dronningens gate 26 ☎73 87 08 00, ℻ 73 87 08 01, ⓦwww.scholler.no. Spick-and-span hotel whose 25 rooms have modern furnishings and fittings. It's in a central location, above the *Café Livingstone*. ❺, s/r ❹

Quality Hotel Augustin Kongens gate 26 ☎73 54 70 00, ℻73 54 70 01, ⓦwww. hotel-augustin.no. Routine chain hotel in a big, old brick building not far from the Torvet. Functional and perfectly adequate rooms. ❺, s/r ❹

Radisson SAS Royal Garden Kjøpmannsgata 73 ☎73 80 30 00, ℻73 80 30 50, ⓦwww. radissonsas.com. Stylish modern hotel with sweeping architectural lines and wonderfully comfortable beds. Good summer deals make this more affordable than you might expect. Banquet-like breakfasts too. Highly recommended. ❼, s/r ❹

Scandic Hotel Residence Torvet ☎73 52 83 80, ℻73 52 64 60, ⓦwww.scandic-hotels.com. Package-tour favourite, with standard double rooms. More expensive than most of its competitors except in summer, when there's a thirty-percent discount. ❼, s/r ❹

Tulip Inn Rainbow Gildevangen Hotell Søndre gate 22b ☎73 87 01 30, ℻73 52 38 98, ⓦwww.rainbow-hotels.no. In a sturdy Romanesque Revival stone building, a couple of minutes' walk northeast of Torvet, this chain hotel offers eighty or so comfortable, modern rooms

with a touch of style. ❻, s/r ❹

Tulip Inn Rainbow Trondheim Kongens gate 15 ☎73 50 50 50, ℻73 51 60 58, ⓦwww. rainbow-hotels.no. Big and popular chain hotel in a plain and chunky modern block, right in the centre. The bar here is one of the few places where you can get home-made mead (*mjød*), once – as in medieval England – Norway's most popular brew. ❺, s/r ❹

Guesthouses, hostels and camping

Trondheim InterRail Centre Elgeseter gate 1 ☎73 89 95 38. In an unusual, big, red, round building – the *Studentersamfundet* (university student centre) – just over the bridge at the south end of Prinsens gate, a five-minute walk from the cathedral. Offers basic bed-and-breakfast accommodation in a couple of hundred double rooms at 120kr per person per night; inexpensive café too. ❶

Pensjonat Jarlen Kongens gate 40 ☎73 51 32 18, ℻73 52 80 80. Basic rooms at bargain prices, and handy for the sights – but otherwise not much fun. ❷

Trondheim Vandrerhjem Rosenborg Weidemannsvei 41 ☎73 87 44 50, ℻73 87 44 55, ⓦwww.trondheim-vandrerhjem.no. This large and well-equipped HI hostel is mostly parcelled up into four-bed dorm rooms. Looks more like a hospital than somewhere you'd want to stay from the outside, but the interior is pleasant enough – especially the comfortable, newer rooms. It has self-catering facilities, a laundry and a canteen. A twenty-minute, 2km hike east from the centre: cross the Bakke bru onto busy Innherredsveien (the E6) and walk uphill; turn right onto Wessels gate and it's on the left at the fourth crossroads. To save your legs, take any bus up Innherredsveien and ask the driver to let you off as close as possible. Open all year. Dorm beds 195kr, doubles ❷

The city centre

The historic **centre of Trondheim** sits on a small triangle of land bordered by a loop of the River Nid, with the curve of the long and slender Trondheimsfjord beyond. **Torvet** is the main city square, a spacious, open area anchored by a statue-cum-sundial of Olav Tryggvason, Trondheim's founder (see p.360), perched on a tall stone pillar like a medieval Nelson. The broad avenues that radiate out from here were once flanked by long rows of wooden buildings, which served all the needs of a small town and administrative centre. Most of these older structures are long gone, replaced largely by uninspiring modern buildings, but one notable survivor is the **Stiftsgården**, a fine timber mansion erected in 1774. This is, however, small beer compared with the

Nidaros Domkirke (cathedral), an imposing, largely medieval structure that is the city's architectural high point. The cathedral dominates the southern part of the centre and close by is the much-restored **Erkebispegården** (Archbishop's Palace) and the pick of Trondheim's several museums, the **Nordenfjeldske Kunstindustrimuseum** (Museum of Decorative Arts) and the **Trondheim Kunstmuseum** (City Art Gallery). Near here too, on the far side of the **Gamle Bybro** – the old town bridge – is a clutter of old warehouses and timber dwellings that comprises the prettiest and most fashionable part of town, **Bakklandet**, home to the best restaurants and bars.

The cathedral

The goal of Trondheim's pilgrims in times past was the colossal cathedral, **Nidaros Domkirke**, Scandinavia's largest medieval building (May to mid-June & late Aug to mid-Sept Mon–Fri 9am–3pm, Sat 9am–2pm, Sun 1–4pm; mid-June to late Aug Mon–Fri 9am–6pm, Sat 9am–2pm, Sun 1–4pm; mid-Sept to April Mon–Fri noon–2.30pm, Sat 11.30am–2pm, Sun 1–3pm; 35kr, also includes the Erkebispegården). Dedicated to Saint Olav, the cathedral is the traditional burial place of Norwegian royalty, and has been the scene of every coronation since 1814. Gloriously restored following several fires and the upheavals of the Reformation, it remains the focal point of any visit to the city and is best explored in the early morning, when it's reasonably free of tour groups.

A magnificent blue and green–grey soapstone edifice, the cathedral has a copper-green spire and roof, and a fancy set of gargoyles on the choir. At first sight, it looks homogeneous, but closer examination reveals a true amalgam of architectural styles. The Romanesque transepts, with their heavy hooped windows and dog-tooth decoration, were built by English stonemasons in the twelfth century, whilst the choir, with its pointed arches, flying buttresses and intricate tracery, is early Gothic – and clearly influenced by contemporaneous churches in England. The nave was built in the early thirteenth century, also in the early Gothic style, but was destroyed by fire in 1719; the present structure is a painstakingly accurate late nineteenth-century replica.

Inside the cathedral, the half-light hides much of the lofty decorative work, but it is possible to examine the striking early twentieth-century **choir screen**, whose wooden figures are the work of Gustav Vigeland (see p.95). Vigeland was also responsible for the adjacent soapstone **font**, a superb piece of medievalism sporting four bas-reliefs respectively depicting Adam and Eve, John the Baptist baptizing the Christ, the Resurrection and a beguiling Noah and the Ark; Noah peers apprehensively out of his boat, not realizing that the dove, with the tell-tale branch, is up above. The other item of particular interest is a famous fourteenth-century **altar frontal** (front panel of an altar painting) displayed in a chapel off the ambulatory, directly behind the high altar. At a time when few Norwegians could read or write, the cult of St Olav (see box) had to be promoted visually, and the frontal is the earliest surviving representation of Olav's life and times. In its centre, Olav looks suitably beatific holding his axe and orb; the top left-hand corner shows the dream Olav had before the battle of Stiklestad, of Jesus dropping a ladder down to him from heaven. In the next panel down, Olav and his men are shown at prayer before the battle and, in the bottom right hand corner, Olav meets a sticky end, speared and stabbed by three cruel-looking soldiers. The final panel shows church officials exhuming Olav's uncorrupted body and declaring his sainthood.

At no extra charge, there are English-language **guided tours** of the church during the summer (mid-June to mid-Aug at 11am, 2pm & 4pm; 30min), and you can also take a peek at the assorted Norwegian **crown jewels** (April &

Saint Olav

Born in 995, **Olav Haraldsson** followed the traditional life of the Viking chieftain from the tender age of 12, "rousing the steel-storm" (as the saga writers described his bloody antics) from Finland to Ireland. He also served as a mercenary to both the duke of Normandy and King Ethelred of England, and it was during this time that he converted to Christianity. In 1015, he invaded Norway, defeated his enemies and became king, his military success built upon the support of the more prosperous farmers of the Trøndelag, an emergent class of yeomen who were less capricious than the coastal chieftains of Viking fame. However, Olav's zealous **imposition of Christianity** – he ordered the desecration of pagan sites and the execution of those who refused baptism – alienated many of his followers. The bribes of Olav's rival Knut (Canute), King of England and Denmark, did the rest: Olav's retainers deserted him, and he was forced into exile in 1028. Two years later, he was back in the Trøndelag, but the army he had raised was far too weak to defeat his enemies, and Olav was killed near Trondheim at the battle of **Stiklestad** (see p.271).

Olav might have lost his kingdom, but the nationwide Church he founded had no intention of losing ground. Needing a local **saint** to consolidate its position, the Church carefully nurtured the myth of Olav, a sanctification assisted by the oppressive rule of the "foreigner" Knut. After the battle of Stiklestad, Olav's body had been spirited away and buried on the banks of the River Nid at what is today Trondheim. There were rumours of miracles in the vicinity of the grave and when the bishop – who had come to investigate these strange goings-on – exhumed the body, he found it undecayed. Olav was declared a saint and his body placed in a silver casket. In 1066, Olav Kyrre, son of Olav's half-brother Harald the Fair-Haired, became King of Norway, and ordered work to begin on a grand church to house the remains in appropriate style. Over the years the church was altered and enlarged to accommodate the growing bands of medieval pilgrims, achieving cathedral status in 1152, when Trondheim became the seat of an archbishopric whose authority extended as far as Orkney and the Isle of Man.

May & late Aug to Oct Fri noon–2pm; June to late Aug Mon–Thurs & Sat 9am–12.30pm, Sun 1–4pm; free), kept at the west end of the church. What you won't see is St Olav's silver casket-coffin: this was taken to Denmark and melted down for coinage in 1537. Before you move on, you should certainly climb the cathedral **tower** (late June to late Aug Mon–Fri 10am–5pm, Sat 10am–12.30pm, Sun 1–3.30pm, every 30min; 5kr). From the top, there's a fine view of the city and the forested hills that surround it, with the fjord trailing away in one direction, the river valley in the other.

The Archbishop's Palace

Behind the Domkirke, to the south, lies the heavily restored **Archbishop's Palace** (Erkebispegården). This courtyard complex was originally built in the twelfth century for the third archbishop, Øystein, but two stone-and-brick wings are all that survive of the original quadrangle – the other two were added later.

After the archbishops were kicked out during the Reformation, the palace became the residence of the Danish governors. It was subsequently used as the city armoury, and many of the old weapons are now displayed in the **west wing** in the **Rustkammeret med Hjemmefrontmuseet** (Army and Resistance Museum; June–Aug Mon–Fri 9am–3pm, Sat & Sun 11am–4pm; Sept–Oct & March–May Sat & Sun only 11am–4pm; free). The museum's **first floor** gives the broad details of Norway's involvement in the interminable **Dano–Swedish wars** that racked Scandinavia from the fifteenth to the nineteenth century. As part of the Danish state, Norway was frequently attacked from the east along the Halden–Oslo corridor, the most memorable incursions being by the bellicose Swedish king, Karl XII. Much to the Danish king's surprise, Karl came a cropper in Norway: defeated for the first time and, when he came back for more, shot (possibly by one of his own men) while besieging Fredriksten fortress (see p.119) in 1718.

Of more general interest, the **second floor** describes the German invasion and occupation of **World War II**, dealing honestly with the sensitive issue of collaboration. In particular, you can hear **Vidkun Quisling**'s broadcast announcing – in a disarmingly squeaky voice – his coup d'état of April 9, 1940. There are also some intriguing displays on the daring antics of the Norwegian Resistance, notably an extraordinary – perhaps hare-brained – attempt to sink the battleship *Tirpitz* as it lay moored in an inlet of the Trondheimsfjord in 1942 (see box, p.272). This escapade, like so many others, involved Resistance hero **Leif Larsen**. Larsen worked closely with the Royal Navy organizing covert operations in occupied Norway from their base in the Shetlands. Supplies and personnel were transported across the North Sea by Norwegian fishing boats – a lifeline known, in that classically understated British (and Norwegian) way, as the "Shetland bus"; the book of the same name by David Howarth (see p.393) tells the tale of this remarkable enterprise.

Moving on, the **south wing** of the palace holds a smart **ecclesiastical museum** (May & early Sept Tues–Fri 11am–3.30pm, Sat 11am–3pm & Sun noon–4.30pm; early & mid-June & late Aug Mon–Fri 11am–3.30pm, Sat 11am–3pm & Sun noon–4.30pm; late Jun to late Aug Mon–Fri 10am–5pm, Sat 10am–3pm & Sun noon–5pm; mid-Sept to April Tues–Sat 11am–3pm Sun noon–4pm; 35kr or free with cathedral ticket), largely devoted to a few dozen medieval statues retrieved from the nave and west facade of the cathedral during its nineteenth-century reconstruction. Frankly, many of the statues are too battered to be particularly engaging, but they are well displayed and several are finely carved. In particular, look out for a life-size sculpture of **St Denis**, his head in his hands, in accord with the legend that he was beheaded, and subsequently spotted carrying his own head to his grave. Downstairs, an assortment of artefacts unearthed during a lengthy 1990s archeological investigation of the palace demonstrates the economic power of the archbishops: they employed all manner of skilled artisans – from glaziers and shoemakers to rope-makers, armourers and silversmiths – and even minted their own coins. There are English-language **guided tours** (late June to late Aug Mon–Fri at 10.30am & 3pm, Sat 10.30am & 2pm, Sun 3pm; no extra charge) of both the museum and the **north wing** – which is otherwise off-limits – but the latter's chambers and halls are fairly uninspiring.

From the back of the Erkebispegården, you can stroll out onto the grassy **lawns** beside the River Nid. A trio of rusting bastions are reminders of the military defences that once protected this side of town, but it's the setting that appeals. Footpaths snake round to the sturdy old tombs and wildflowers of the **graveyard**, just to the east of the cathedral's main entrance.

The Trondhjems Kunstmuseum and the Trondhjems Kunstforening

Near the cathedral, at Bispegata 7b, the **Trondhjems Kunstmuseum** (City Art Museum; June–Aug daily 10am–5pm, Sept–May Tues–Sun 11am–5pm; 40kr) is quite small, but features an enjoyable selection of works by Johan Dahl and Thomas Fearnley, the leading figures of nineteenth-century Norwegian landscape painting, as well as the romantic canvases of Hans Gude and his chum Adolph Tidemand. Also displayed is the first overtly political work by a Norwegian artist: *The Strike* (*Streik*) was painted in 1877 by the radical Theodor

Kittelsen, better known for his illustrations of the folk tales collected by Jorgen Moe and Peder Asbjørnsen. There's also a diverting selection of Munch's woodcuts, sketches and lithographs here, including several of those disturbing, erotically charged personifications of emotions – *Lust, Fear* and *Jealousy* – that are so characteristic of his oeuvre. Munch's works are not clearly labelled, but an inventory is available free at reception. Be aware that most of the permanent collection is removed from view during major temporary exhibitions, and even Munch can get the shove.

Next door, at Bispegata 9a, the **Trondhjems Kunstforening** (City Art Society; Tues–Fri 10am–4pm, Sat & Sun noon–4pm; 25kr) hosts temporary exhibitions of contemporary art, mostly Norwegian – or at least Scandinavian – but with a smattering of international works.

The Nordenfjeldske Kunstindustrimuseum

The delightful **Nordenfjeldske Kunstindustrimuseum** is at Munkegata 5, a couple of minutes' walk north from the cathedral (Museum of Decorative Arts; June to late Aug Mon–Sat 10am–5pm, Sun noon–5pm; late Aug to May Tues–Wed & Fri–Sat 10am–3pm, Thur 10am–5pm, Sun noon–4pm; 40kr; Ⓦwww.nkim.museum.no). The museum's collection is too extensive to be shown in its entirety at any one time and there's an ambitious programme of special exhibitions, so the exhibits are regularly rotated: nevertheless, you can expect to see most of the pieces mentioned below. Start in the **basement**, where the historical collection illustrates bourgeois life in Trøndelag from 1500 to 1900 by means of an eclectic assemblage of furniture, faïence, glassware and silver. There are twentieth-century pieces on display here too, notably a fine selection of Art Nouveau ceramics and furniture. This modern, domestic theme is developed on the **first floor**, where an entire room has been kitted out by the Belgian designer and architect **Henri van de Velde**. Also exhibited on the first floor is an unusual display of early twentieth-century **tapestries**. Produced in Trondheim, these were based on depictions of medieval folk tales painted by the Norwegian Gerhard Munthe. More modern works can be found on the **second floor**, but the highlight here is the room largely devoted to fourteen tapestries by **Hannah Ryggen**. Born in Malmø in 1894, Ryggen moved to the Trondheim area in the early 1920s and stayed until her death in 1970. Her tapestries are classically naive, the forceful colours and absence of perspective emphasizing the feeling behind them. This is committed art, railing in the 1930s and 1940s against Hitler and Fascism, later moving on to more disparate targets such as the atom bomb and social conformism. But she still made time to celebrate the things she cherished: *Yes, we love this country* (tapestry no. 9) is as evocative a portrayal of her adopted land as you're likely to find.

Bakklandet and the medieval church ruins

It's a couple of minutes' walk east of the cathedral to the **Gamle Bybro** (Old Town Bridge), an elegant wooden construction with splendid views over Kjøpmannsgata's early eighteenth-century gabled and timbered warehouses, now mostly restaurants and offices. There are more restaurants and several trendy bars at the far end of the bridge in tiny **Bakklandet**, Trondheim's own "Left Bank", a one-time working class district of brightly painted timber houses.

Doubling back over the Gamle Bybro from Bakklandet, and following the river north along **Kjøpmannsgata**, you soon come to the **medieval church ruins** discovered under the **library** at the east end of Kongens gate. A twelfth-century relic of the days when Trondheim had fifteen or more religious buildings, it is thought to have been a chapel dedicated to St Olav, although the evidence for this is a bit shaky. Excavations revealed nearly 500 bodies in the immediate area, which was once the church graveyard, and some skeletons are neatly displayed under glass. Entry is free and the site is accessible during library opening hours (July to mid-Aug Mon, Tues, Thurs & Fri 9am–4pm, Wed 9am–7pm & Sat 10am–3pm; mid-Aug to June Mon–Thurs 9am–7pm, Fri 9am–4pm, Sat 10am–3pm; plus Sept–April Sun noon–4pm). From the library, it's just a few minutes' walk west to Torvet and the Stiftsgården.

The Stiftsgården and north to the Ravnkloa

One conspicuous remnant of old timber-town Trondheim survives in the city centre – the **Stiftsgården**, which stretches out along Munkegata just north of Torvet (guided tours every hour on the hour till 1hr before closing: early to mid-June Mon–Sat 10am–3pm, Sun noon–5pm; late June to late Aug Mon–Sat 10am–5pm, Sun noon–5pm; 50kr). Built in 1774–78, this good-looking yellow structure is claimed to be the largest wooden building in northern Europe. These days it serves as an official royal residence, a marked improvement in its fortunes as it was originally built to house the provincial governor. Inside, a long series of period rooms are decorated with fanciful Italianate wall-paintings and furniture in a range of late eighteenth- to early nineteenth-century styles, from Rococo to Biedermeierstil, that reflect the genteel tastes of the early occupants. The anecdotal guided tour brings a smile or two – but not perhaps 50kr worth.

If the sight of Bakklandet's old wooden buildings has whetted your appetite, you'll enjoy the tangle of narrow alleys and pastel-painted clapboard frontages that fills out the sidestreets **north of Kongens gate** and west of Prinsens gate. There's nothing special to look at, but it's a pleasant area for a stroll, after which you can wander over to **Ravnkloa**, the jetty at the north end of Munkegata where the fish market is held – and where ferries leave for Munkholmen (see p.267).

The Vitenskapsmuseet

Back at Torvet, it's a five- to ten-minute walk southwest to the university's **Vitenskapsmuseet** at Erling Skakkes gate 47 (Museum of Natural History and Archeology; May to mid-Sept Mon–Fri 9am–4pm, Sat & Sun 11am–4pm; mid-Sept to Dec Tues–Fri 9am–2pm, Sat & Sun noon–4pm; 25kr), comprising several collections. At the front, the main building contains an assortment of forgettable stuffed animals and a largely incomprehensible ragbag of archeological finds. Don't bother with these, but instead pop into the smaller building on the left, where there's a small but enjoyable **church history** section (*kirkehistorie*; May to mid-Sept Mon–Fri 9am–4pm, Sat & Sun 11am–4pm; mid-Sept to Dec weekends), with ecclesiastical knick-knacks from pulpits and fonts through to processional crosses and statues of the saints. Even better, in the old *suhmhuset* (hay storehouse), a low, long building at the rear, is a first-rate **medieval exhibition** (*middelalder*), which tracks the development of Trondheim from its foundation in the tenth century to the fire of 1681. Its thoroughly researched, multilingual text is supported by an excellent range of archeological finds, and departs from the predictable "Kings and Queens" approach, investigating everything from sanitary towels and reliquary jars to popular games and attitudes to life and death.

Out from the centre

While most of Trondheim's attractions are neatly packed within walking distance of each other, on or around the city's central island, there are a few sights to lure you out of the centre. The historic **Munkholmen Island** is an easy ten-minute ferry ride away, while a couple of museums – the **Ringve**, to the northeast of the centre and the **Sverresborg Trøndelag Folkemuseum** in the southwest – both merit a visit.

Munkholmen island

Poking up out of the Trondheimsfjord just 2km offshore, the tiny islet of **Munkholmen** is easily reached by boat from the Ravnkloa jetty (late May to early Sept every hour on the hour 10am–6pm; 45kr return). The island has an eventful history. In Viking times it was used as the city's execution ground, and St Olav went to the added trouble of displaying the head of one of his enemies on a pike here, which must have made approaching mariners a tad nervous. In the eleventh century, the Benedictines founded a monastery on the island – hence its name – but it was not one of their more successful ventures: the archbishop received dozens of complaints about, of all things, the amount of noise the monks made, not to mention alleged heavy drinking and womanizing. After the Reformation, the island was converted into a prison, which doubled as a fortress designed to protect the seaward approaches to the city; later still it became a customs house. The longest-serving prisoner was the Danish count **Peder Griffenfeld** (1635–99), who spent eighteen years cooped up here until his eventual release in 1698. One of the most powerful men in Denmark, Griffenfeld played a leading role in the assumption of absolute power by King Frederick III (see p.366), but was outmanoeuvred and imprisoned by his rivals after the king's death.

Sturdy stone walls encircle almost the entire island, and behind them, sunk in a circular dip, is a set of quaint, almost cottage-like, **prison buildings** surrounding a cobbled courtyard. There are thirty-minute guided tours of the central part of the **fortress** (late May to early Sept daily 10.30am–5.30pm; 25kr), a cheerful romp through its galleries and corridors. The tour includes a visit to the spacious cell occupied by Griffenfeld, and a glimpse of the gun emplacement the Germans installed during World War II. After the tour you can wander over to the **café** or scramble along outside the walls and round the rocks beneath to either of a couple of rough, pebbly beaches.

The Ringve museum

The **Ringve Museum** (mid-May to June & Aug to mid-Sept daily 11am–3pm; July daily 11am–5pm; mid-Sept to mid-May Sundays 11am–4pm; ⓦwww.ringve.com; 70kr) occupies a delightful eighteenth-century country house and courtyard complex on the hilly Lade peninsula, some 4km northeast of the city centre. Devoted to musical history and to musical instruments from all over the world, the museum is divided into two sections. In the main building, the collection focuses on **antique European instruments** in period settings, with several demonstrations included in a lengthy – and obligatory – guided tour. The second section, in the old barn, contains an **international selection of musical instruments** and offers a self-guided zip through some of the key moments and movements of **musical history**. There are themes like "the invention of the piano" and "pop and rock", not to mention the real humdinger, "the marching band movement in Norway". Immaculately maintained, the surrounding **botanical gardens** (daily; free) make the most of the scenic setting. To get there, take bus #3 or #4 to Lade from Munkegata.

The Sverresborg Trøndelag Folkemuseum

Three kilometres southwest of the city centre lies one of the Norway's best folk museums, the **Sverresborg Trøndelag Folkemuseum** (June–Aug daily 11am–6pm, Sept–May Mon–Fri 11am–3pm, Sat & Sun noon–4pm; 75kr; ⓦ www.trondelag-folkemuseum.no). In a pleasant rural setting, with views over the city, the museum's indoor section kicks off with some well-presented displays tracing everyday life in the Trøndelag from the eighteenth century onwards. Outside, you'll see sixty relocated Trøndelag timber buildings, including a post office, grocery store, stave church and all sorts of farm houses and outhouses, built for a variety of purposes from curing meat to drying hay. Finally, it's worth staying for lunch here at the museum's *Vertshuset Tavern*, which serves up traditional Norwegian dishes (see p.269 for details). To get here, take bus #8 or #9 from Dronningens gate.

Eating and drinking

As befits Norway's third city, Trondheim has a healthy selection of first-rate **restaurants**, serving a variety of cuisines, though the Norwegian places almost always have the gastronomic edge. The **Bakklandet** district, in particular, by the eastern end of Gamle Bybro, has a cluster of excellent restaurants, as well as a string of laid-back, fashionable **café-bars** serving good food at very reasonable prices, while the **Brattørgata** district near the west end of Bakke bru, is renowned for its lively weekend **bar** scene. Finally – if needs must – the city's mobile **fast-food** stalls are concentrated around Sentralstasjon and along Kongens gate, on either side of Torvet.

As for **opening hours**, some restaurants open for a couple of hours at lunchtime and then in the evening, but many just stick to the evenings; some also close one day a week. Café-bars and bars almost invariably open from around 11am until the early hours of the morning – or at least until there's no-one left.

Café-bars

Café Dali Brattørgata 7. Ground-floor café serving small portions of international food from Tom Yam soup to tapas. Good place for a coffee or a light meal. At the upstairs bar, the cocktails are good and the decor industrial.

Dromedar Nedre Bakklandet 3a. A modern café-bar with a laid-back atmosphere, located a few metres north of the Gamle Bybro. The best coffee in the city plus snacks and light meals – filled bagels, sandwiches, etc.

Kafé Gåsa Øvre Bakklandet 58. With its traditional Norwegian decor and clutter of folksy bygones, this intimate café-bar is a charming place. Good Norwegian food and a great terrace in sunny weather.

Restaurants

Bryggen Øvre Bakklandet 66 ☎73 87 42 42. This is a superb, smart and classy seafood restaurant at the east end of the Gamle Bybro. The daily specials, mostly featuring the catch of the day, are a delight. Main courses average about 200kr. Mon–Sat 6pm–midnight; closed Sun.

Bølgen & Moi Trondheim Carl Johans gate 5 ☎73 56 89 00. Part of a small chain, this new, upmarket restaurant is where the Norwegian princess Mærtha Louise had her pre-wedding party when she married the writer Ari Behn in 2002. Top-notch seasonal ingredients are used to create a stylish and innovative menu featuring both Norwegian and international dishes. Open daily till 2am, but the kitchen closes at 10pm.

Chablis Øvre Bakklandet 62 ☎73 87 42 50. Just metres from the Gamle Bybro, this polished brasserie-restaurant, with its modish furnishings and fittings, serves up excellent food – Norwegian but with a Mediterranean slant. Has the same kitchen as the neighbouring *Bryggen* (see above), but the prices are a good deal lower. Open daily from 5pm.

Credo Restaurant & Bar Ørjaveita 4 ☎73 53 03 88. Smart and very popular Mediterranean/Spanish-influenced restaurant with delicious daily specials at very competitive prices. The restaurant is on the ground floor, with the stylish, modern *Credo Bar* upstairs.

Havfruen Fiskerestaurant Kjøpmannsgata 7 ☎73 87 40 70. An excellent fish restaurant near the cathedral – one of the best in town, with prices to match. Try to book in advance. Main courses from 200kr. Mon–Fri 4–11pm, Sat 6pm–midnight.

Jadab Brattørgata 3a ☎73 52 46 00. Indian food without the kitsch decor; all the standard dishes, friendly service and inexpensive prices.

Lian Herregård Lianveien 36 ☎72 55 90 77. Up in the forested hills about 8km west of the city centre, this traditional Norwegian restaurant has a terrace bar affording panoramic views over the Trondheimsfjord. Getting there is enjoyable too – catch the Lian tram, the Gråkallbanen, from St Olavs gate and stay on till you reach the terminus, from where it's a couple of minutes' walk up the hill to the restaurant; note that at weekends it can get very busy. Open April–Sept Tues–Sun noon–6pm; the rest of year, phone for times.

Markens Grøde Nedre Bakklandet 58 ☎73 53 16 11. The city's main vegetarian restaurant, featuring tasty food, a creative menu and a friendly atmosphere. Main courses at around 70kr. Open Tues–Sat 1–11pm, Sun 1–8pm.

Shanghai Restaurant Kjøpmannsgata 21 ☎73 51 47 77. Excellent Chinese restaurant specializing in Szechuan dishes at affordable prices.

Vertshuset Tavern Sverresborg allé 7 ☎73 87 80 70. In business since 1739, this restaurant-tavern has moved lock, stock and barrel from the town centre to the Folk Museum. Its low-ceilinged tim-

ber rooms are furnished in appropriate period style and the food is traditional Norwegian "Husmannskost": the *Kjøttkaker i brun saus med erterstuing* (meatballs in brown gravy served with pea stew) is hard to beat, closely followed by the *spekemat* (cured meat) at 220kr, the *rømmegrøt* (sour-cream porridge; 65kr) and the *fiskekaker* (fish cakes; 95kr). Open Mon–Fri 4pm–midnight, Sat 2pm–midnight, Sun noon–midnight.

Bars and nightclubs

Brukbar Munkegata 26. Interesting, colourful bar catering for everyone from business folk dropping in after work, to hardcore student boozers. Note the peculiar bee-shaped wall-lamps.

Frakken Dronningens gate 12, at the corner with Nordre gate. High-octane bar and nightclub – all tight trousers and highlit hairdos. Popular generally, and raucous at the weekends.

Metro Kjøpmannsgata 12 ☎73 52 05 52. Trondheim's only gay and lesbian bar. DJ sounds at the weekend. Open Wed 8pm–2am, Fri & Sat 10pm–2am.

3B Brattørgata 3B ☎73 51 15 50. Rock 'n' roll and indie club-cum-bar, where you can drink well into the wee hours.

Trondheim Mikrobryggeri Prinsens gate 39. Mainstream bar serving up its own microbrewery brews. Serves filling pub food too, in a friendly atmosphere.

Listings

Airlines Braathens ☎74 84 32 00; SAS ☎74 80 41 00; Widerøe ☎81 00 12 00.

Banks & exchange ATMs are dotted across the city centre; there's also a currency exchange at Kredittkassen, Olav Tryggvasons gate 39.

Car breakdown NAF ☎810 00 505; Viking Redningstjeneste ☎73 82 28 00.

Car rental Avis, Kjøpmannsgata 34 (☎73 84 17 90); Budget, Elgeseter gate 21 (☎73 94 10 25) and at the *Radisson SAS Royal Garden Hotel*, Kjøpmannsgata 73 (☎73 52 69 20); Europcar, at the airport (☎74 82 67 00).

Consulates UK, Beddingen 8 (☎73 60 02 00); Poland, TMV-Kaia 23 (☎73 87 69 00).

Crafts The best place to buy traditional Norwegian clothes and crafts is Husfliden, Olav Tryggvasons gate 18 (☎73 83 32 30).

Dentists Dental emergencies ☎73 50 55 00.

DNT *Trondhjems Turistforening*, just west of the centre at Sandgata 30 (☎73 92 42 00; Ⓦwww.tt.no), is the DNT's local branch, offering advice on the region's hiking trails and huts. It also organizes a variety of guided walks and cross-

country skiing trips, with activities concentrated in the mountains to the south and east of the city. There are one-day excursions and longer expeditions to suit different levels of skill and fitness.

Emergencies Ambulance ☎113; Fire ☎110; Police ☎112.

Internet access There's free internet access at the library, Peter Egges plass 1 (☎72 54 75 00; July to mid-Aug Mon, Tue, Thurs & Fri 9am–4pm, Wed 9am–7pm & Sat 10am–3pm; mid-Aug to June Mon–Thur 9am–7pm, Fri 9am–4pm, Sat 10am–3pm; Sept–April also Sun noon–4pm).

Pharmacy St Olav Vaktapotek, Kjøpmannsgata 65 (☎73 88 37 37), and Løveapoteket Byhaven, Olav Tryggvasons gate 28 (☎73 83 32 83), open late and at weekends.

Police station Kongens gate 87 (☎73 89 90 90); emergencies (☎112).

Post office Main office, with poste restante, at Dronningens gate 10 (Mon–Fri 8am–5pm, Sat 9am–2pm).

Swimming Pirbadet, Havnegata 12 (☎73 83 18 00), is Norway's biggest indoor swimming facility with pools, jacuzzis, waterslides etc. Open Mon, Wed & Fri 6.30am–9pm, Tues & Thurs 3–9pm, Sat & Sun 10am–7pm, though times vary, so call ahead to confirm: admission is 95kr.

Taxis Eight ranks in and around the city centre including those at Torvet, Sentralstasjon, Søndre

gate and the *Radisson SAS Royal Garden Hotel*, or call Trønder Taxi (℡73 90 90 73; 24hr).

Vinmonopolet There's a city-centre branch of this government-run liquor and wine store at Kjøpmannsgata 32.

North from Trondheim to Bodø

North of Trondheim, it's a long haul up the coast to the next major places of interest: **Bodø**, the main ferry port for Lofoten, and the gritty but likeable port of Narvik – respectively 720km and 910km distant. The easiest way to make the bulk of the trip is by **train**, a rattling good journey with the scenery becoming wilder and bleaker the further north you go – and you usually get a blast from the whistle as you cross the Arctic Circle. The train takes nine hours to reach **Fauske**, where the line reaches its northern limit and turns west for the final 65-kilometre dash across to Bodø. At Fauske, there are **bus** connections north to Narvik, a five-hour drive away, but many travellers take an overnight break here – though in fact nearby Bodø makes a far more pleasant stopover.

If you're **driving**, you'll find the main highway, the **E6**, which runs all the way from Trondheim to Narvik and points north, too slow to cover more than three or four hundred kilometres comfortably in a day. Fortunately, there are several pleasant places to stop, beginning with **Steinkjer** and **Snåsa** in Trøndelag. Steinkjer is a modest little town with a couple of good hotels, Snåsa, a relaxed – and relaxing – village, again with somewhere good to stay. Further north, in Nordland, the next province up, **Mosjøen** and **Mo-i-Rana**, two renovated former industrial towns, make pleasant pit stops, with Mo-i-Rana serving as a handy starting point for a visit to the **Svartisen glacier**, crowning the coastal peaks close by. The glacier is on the western rim of the **Saltfjellet Nasjonalpark**, a wild and windswept mountain plateau that extends east towards the Swedish border. The E6 and the railway cut through the park, giving ready access, but although this is a popular destination for experienced hikers, it's too fierce an environment for the novice or the lightly equipped.

A slower, but more scenic, option to the E6 north, is to take the "Kystriksveien", coastal **Highway 17**, from Steinkjer to Bodø, using seven ferry crossings en route. If you can't spare the time to do the whole route, you could join Highway 17 to the west of Mo-i-Rana, cutting out five ferries and the first 420km, but still taking in the most dramatic part of the journey, including fabulous views of the **Melfjord** and the Svartisen glacier.

The E6 to Stiklestad

Leaving Trondheim, the **E6** tunnels and twists its way round the Trondheimsfjord to **Hell**, a busy rail junction, where one line forks north to slice through the dales and hills of Trøndelag en route to Fauske, while the other shadows the E14 east for the 70km haul to the Swedish frontier, with Östersund beyond. Hell itself has nothing to recommend it except its name, though paradoxically *hell* in Norwegian means good fortune. Continuing along the E6, it's about 30km to the **Fjættenfjord**, a narrow inlet of the Trondheimsfjord and one-time hideout of the battleship *Tirpitz* (see box on p.272). Beyond the Fjættenfjord, the E6 clips past the tedious little towns of

Levanger and **Verdalsøra**, a centre for the fabrication of offshore oil platforms.

Stiklestad

From Verdalsøra, it's just 6km inland along Highway 757 to **STIKLESTAD**, probably Norway's most famous village. It was here in 1030 that Olav Haraldsson, later St Olav, was killed in battle, his death now commemorated by the **Stiklestad Nasjonale Kultursenter** (Stiklestad National Culture Centre; early June to mid-Aug daily 9am–8pm; mid-Aug to early June Mon–Fri 9am–4pm, Sat & Sun 11am–5pm; ☎74 04 42 00, 🌐www.stiklestad.no), whose assorted museums and open-air amphitheatre are spread out over the pastoral landscape. A descendant of Harald Hårfagre (the Fair-Haired), **Olav Haraldsson** (see p.263) was one of Norway's most important medieval kings, a Viking warrior turned resolute Christian monarch whose misfortune it was to be the enemy of the powerful and shrewd King Knut of England and Denmark. It was Knut's bribes that did for Olav, persuading all but his most loyal supporters to change allegiances – as a Norse poet commented in the cautionary *Håvamål* (the Sayings of Odin), "I have never found a man so generous and hospitable that he would not take a present." Dislodged from the throne, Olav returned from exile in Sweden in 1030, but was defeated and killed here at the Battle of Stiklestad. His role as founder of the Norwegian Church prompted his subsequent canonization, and his cult flourished at Trondheim until the Reformation.

The government has spent millions developing the Stiklestad Nasjonale Kultursenter, one of the results being the broad-beamed **Kulturhus**, whose prime attraction is a pleasingly melodramatic **museum** (80kr) that uses shadowy dioramas and a ghoulish soundtrack to chronicle the events leading up to Olav's death. Nonetheless, the dioramas contain few artefacts of note, other than one or two bits of armour and jewellery dating from the period, and neither is the text particularly revealing, which is a pity, since something more could have been made of Olav's position in medieval Christian folklore. One such tale, passed down through the generations, relates how Olav spent the night on a remote Norwegian farm, only to discover the family praying over a pickled horse's penis. Expressing some irritation – but no surprise – at this pagan ceremony, Olav threw the phallus to the family dog and took the opportunity to explain some of the finer tenets of Christianity to his hosts. There's a second display on St Olav upstairs in the museum, this one focuses on his cult and how it spread across western Europe.

Across from the Kulturhus, the much modified, twelfth-century stone **kirke** (church) reputedly marks the spot where Olav was stabbed to death. Claims that the stone on which the body was first laid out had been incorporated into the church's high altar were abandoned during the Reformation, in case of damage by Protestants. Just up the hill from the Kulturhus, a five-minute walk away, is the open-air **amfiteater** (amphitheatre), where the colourful Olsokspelet (St Olav's Play), a costume drama, is performed each year as part of the **St Olav Festival**. This is held over several days either side of the anniversary of the battle, July 29, and thousands of Norwegians make the trek here; tickets need to be booked months in advance with the Kultursenter. The amphitheatre also adjoins an open-air **folkemuseum** (folk museum), containing a few indoor exhibits, and some thirty seventeenth- to nineteenth-century buildings, moved here from all over rural Trøndelag.

Stiklestad is difficult to reach without your own transport, and there's nowhere to stay when you get there. A once or twice-daily **train** from

Leif Larsen and the attack on the Tirpitz

The German battleship *Tirpitz,* commissioned in 1941, spent most of its three-year existence hidden away in the **Fjættenfjord** (see p.270), where it was protected from air attack by the mountains and from naval attack by a string of coastal gun emplacements. With the fjord as its base, the *Tirpitz* was able to sally forth to attack Allied convoys bound for Russia and as such was a major irritant to the Royal Navy, who dreamt up a remarkable scheme to sink it. The navy had just perfected a submersible craft called the **Chariot**, which was six metres long, powered by electric motors, and armed with a torpedo. A crew of two volunteer divers manned the craft, sitting astride it at the rear – which must amount to some kind of definition of bravery. The plan was to transport two of these Chariots across from Shetland to Norway in a Norwegian fishing boat and then, just before the first German checkpoint, to attach them to the outside of the boat's hull. Equipped with false papers and a diversionary load of peat, the fishing boat would, it was thought, stand a good chance of slipping through the German defences. Thereafter, as soon as the boat got within reasonable striking distance, the Chariots could be launched towards the *Tirpitz* and, once they got very close to the ship, their torpedoes would be fired.

The boat selected was the *Arthur,* skippered by the redoubtable **Leif Larsen,** a modest man of extraordinary courage, who, over the course of the war, ran over fifty trips to Norway from the Shetlands. The *Arthur* had a crew of four Norwegian and six British seamen – four to pilot the Chariots and two to help them get into their diving suits. At first the trip went well. As soon as they reached Norway's coastal waters, the crew moved the Chariots from their hiding place in the hold and attached them to the hull. They then fooled the Germans and were allowed into the Trondheimsfjord, but here the weather deteriorated and the Chariots broke loose from the boat, falling to the bottom of the ocean before they could be used. There was, therefore, no choice but to abort the mission, scuttle the *Arthur* and row ashore in the hope that the crew could escape over the mountains to neutral Sweden. They divided into two parties of five, one of which made it without mishap – except for a few lost toes from frostbite – but the other group, led by Larsen, ran into a patrol. In the skirmish that ensued, one of the Englishmen, a certain AB Evans, was wounded and had to be left behind; the Germans polished him off.

On September 11, 1944, the *Tirpitz* was caught napping in the Kåfjord (see p.328) by Allied bombers, which flew in from a Russian airfield to the east, screened by the mountains edging the fjord. The *Tirpitz* was badly damaged in the attack, especially its engines. It managed to limp off to Tromsø, just outside of which it was finally sunk on November 12 by a combined bombing-and-torpedo attack.

Trondheim runs to Verdalsøra, 6km away, from where you have to walk, or use one of the taxis that usually wait outside the station. During the St Olav Festival, however, special trains and buses take visitors to the site; details from the Trondheim tourist office.

Steinkjer and Snåsa

Back on the **E6**, it's a further 30km to **STEINKJER**, a pleasant, unassuming town that sits in the shadow of wooded hills, at the point where the river that gave the place its name empties into the fjord. The Germans bombed the town to bits in 1940 when it was the site of an infantry training camp, and the modern replacement is a tidy, appealing ensemble that fans out from the long main street, **Kongens gate.** The E6 bypasses Steinkjer town centre, running parallel to – and about 400m to the west of – Kongens gate, with the **train station** in between. The E6 also passes the **tourist office** (mid-June to mid-Aug Mon–Sat 9am–8pm & Sun noon–8pm; mid-Aug to mid-June Mon–Fri

8am–4pm; ⓣ74 16 36 17, ⓦwww.steinkjer-turist.com). Right in the centre of town across from the train station is the *Quality Hotel Grand Steinkjer*, Kongens gate 37 (ⓣ74 16 47 00, ⓕ74 16 62 87, ⓔfirmapost@grandhotell.no; ❺, s/r ❸), which manages to seem quite old-fashioned even though it occupies a modern tower block. The rooms on its upper floors have splendid views along the coast, and the hotel restaurant serves tasty Norwegian dishes at reasonable prices. There are several other places to eat nearby, the pick of these being *Café Madam Brix*, Kirkegata 7 (ⓣ74 16 74 60), a cosy café-restaurant, which takes its name from the redoubtable widow who founded an inn here in 1722. A good second choice is the *Istanbul*, an inexpensive Turkish & Persian restaurant at Ølvegata 22 (ⓣ74 16 40 66). There's a year-round municipal **campsite**, *Guldbergaunet Camping* (ⓣ74 16 20 45, ⓕ74 16 47 35, ⓔguldsch@online.no) in the park on the south bank of the river, about 2km inland from the train station.

A few kilometres north of Steinkjer is the point where the **Krystiksveien** (Highway 17; see p.277) branches off the E6 to begin its scenic 700km journey north to Bodø. Alternatively, there's a choice of routes west to Snåsa: you can either take the E6 along the northern shore of the long and slender lake **Snåsavatnet**, or opt for the more agreeable (and slower) Highway 763, which meanders along the southern side of the lake through farmland and wooded hills.

Taking the faster E6, it's 60km to the far end of the lake and the sleepy, scattered hamlet of **SNÅSA**, a fine example of a Trøndelag rural community. It looks as if nothing much has happened here for decades, yet there is one sight of note, a pretty little hilltop **church** of softly-hued grey stone, dating from the Middle Ages and very much in the English style. On the west side of the village – and 6km from the E6 – is the *Snåsa Hotell* (ⓣ74 15 10 57, ⓕ74 15 16 15, ⓦwww.snasahotell.no; ❹, s/r ❸), a modern place with somewhat spartan decor, but comfortable bedrooms and a lovely setting overlooking the lake; it's a peaceful spot, ideal if you want to rest after a long drive. The hotel also operates a small **campsite** (same numbers; all year) with huts (❷) as well as spaces for tents and caravans. There's a restaurant here too, serving mundane but filling Norwegian staples, but if you're likely to arrive after 7pm, you should telephone ahead to check it will still be open.

Into Nordland: Mosjøen

Beyond Snåsa, the E6 leaves the wooded valleys of the Trøndelag for the wider, harsher landscapes of the province of **Nordland**. The road bobs across bleak plateaux and scuttles along rangy river valleys before reaching, after about 190km, the short, signposted side-road that leads to the **Laksforsen waterfalls**, a well-known beauty spot where the River Vefsna takes a 17-metre tumble. The café here offers a grand view of the falls, which were once much favoured by British aristocrats for their salmon-fishing.

Back on the E6, it's another 30km to the town of **MOSJØEN**, first impressions of which are not especially favourable. The setting is handsome enough, with the town wedged amid fjord, river and mountain, but a huge aluminium plant dominates, hogging the north side of the waterfront. Persevere, for Mosjøen was a small-time trading centre long before the factory arrived, and **Sjøgata**, down by the river just to the south of the plant, is lined by attractive old timber dwellings, warehouses and shops dating from the early nineteenth century. It's an appealing streetscape, especially since the buildings are still in everyday use. It only takes a few minutes to walk from one end of Sjøgata to the other, and on the way you'll encounter the mildly diverting **Vefsn Museum**, Sjøgata 31b (mid-Aug to May Mon–Fri 10am–3.30pm, Sat 10am–2pm; June to mid-Aug Mon–Fri 8am–3.30pm & Sun 11am–4pm; 25kr), which has displays on life in old Mosjøen and exhibits some interesting work by contemporary Nordland artists.

Mosjøen practicalities

Mosjøen **train station** is beside the E6 on the north side of town, in front of the aluminium plant. From here, it's about 1200m to the east end of Sjøgata – just follow the signs. The **bus station** is about 100m from the west end of Sjøgata and it's here, at CM Havigsgate 39, that you'll also find the **tourist office** (late June & July Mon–Fri 9am–7pm, Sat 11am–4pm & Sun 1–6pm; Aug to late June Mon–Fri 8am–3.30pm; ☎75 11 12 40, Ⓦwww.visithelgeland .com).

The pick of the town's several **hotels** is *Fru Haugans*, metres from the tourist office at Strandgata 39 (☎75 11 41 00, Ⓕ75 11 41 01, Ⓦwww.fruhaugans.no; ❺, s/r ❸). There's been an inn here since the eighteenth century and the present building is a well-judged amalgamation of the old and the new. Rather more unusual is the accommodation offered by the *Kulturverkstedet*, Sjøgata 22–24 (☎75 17 27 60), a local heritage organization that has refurbished a couple of old wooden houses on Sjøgata for rent – they are simple lodgings, with or without bed linen (❷–❸). *Kulturverkstedet* also has a charming, old-fashioned **café**, serving coffee and traditional Nordland pastries, but the best **restaurant** in town is *Ellenstuen*, at *Fru Haugans Hotel*, which provides tasty, mainly Norwegian dishes at competitive prices. Otherwise, for a daytime coffee or an evening **drink**, *Lilletorget*, at Strandgata 42, is the liveliest spot in town.

Mo-i-Rana and around

Beyond Mosjøen, the E6 cuts inland to weave across the mountains of the interior, whilst the railway stays glued to the seashore down below. Either way, it's an enjoyable journey, though the E6 has the scenic edge, especially when it starts its long climb up the slopes of **Korgfjellet**. The road falls well short of the summit, but its highest point still offers panoramic views and is the site of a motel and a monument honouring the 550 Yugoslav prisoners of war who built this section of the road during World War II. Thereafter, the E6 hairpins down to **Korgen**, sitting pretty beneath the mountains in the bend of a river, before it slips along the fjord to Mo-i-Rana, 90km from Mosjøen.

Hugging the head of the Ranafjord, **MO-I-RANA**, or more usually "Mo", was a minor port and market town until World War II, after which its fortunes, and appearance, were transformed by the construction of a steel plant. The plant dominated proceedings until the 1980s, when there was some economic diversification and the town began to clean itself up: the fjord shore was cleared of its industrial clutter and the E6 re-routed to create the pleasantly spacious, surprisingly leafy town centre of today. Most of Mo is resolutely modern, but the prettiest building is the good-looking **Mo kirke**, built in 1832, with a high-pitched roof and an onion dome, perched on a hill on the eastern edge of the centre. Enclosed by a mossy stone wall, the well-tended graveyard contains a communal tomb for unidentified Russian prisoners of war and the graves of six Scots Guards killed hereabouts in May 1940. In front of the church is a bust commemorating Thomas van Westen, an eighteenth-century evangelist-missionary who spearheaded early attempts to convert the Sami. Mo's only unusual sight is its Anthony Gormley sculpture, **Havmannen**, a disconsolate-looking figure who stands in the shallows of the harbourfront gazing down the fjord.

Arrival, information and transport

Mo's **bus** and **train stations** are close together, down by the fjord on Ole Tobias Olsens gate. The compact town centre lies east of this street, with the foot of the main pedestrianized street, Jernbanegata, opposite the bus station. The **tourist office** is about 300m to the south of the bus and train stations, also on Ole Tobias Olsens gate (mid-June to mid-Aug Mon–Fri 9am–8pm, Sat 9am–4pm & Sun 1–7pm; mid-Aug to mid-June Mon–Fri 9am–4pm; ☎75 13 92 00, ⓔinfomo@arctic-circle.no, ⓦwww.arctic-circle.no). It has the usual

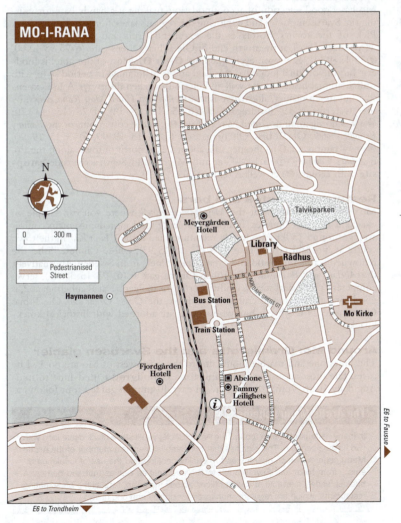

MO-I-RANA

N

0   300 m

Pedestrianised Street

Haymannen ⊙

Talvikparken

Meyergården Hotell

Library

Rådhus

Bus Station

Mo Kirke

Train Station

Fjordgården Hotell

Abelone

Fammy Leilighets Hotell

ⓘ

E6 to Fausue ▶

E6 to Trondheim ▼

local leaflets, provides free town maps and issues a free booklet detailing the Highway 17 Coastal Route (see box on p.277). It also has bus timetables, but local services are much too patchy for any serious exploration of the town's environs without your own transport. **Car rental** is available from Avis, at the Hydro Texaco Røssvoll gas station (℡75 14 81 57), for around 700kr a day, or the tourist office can arrange a **shared taxi** ride to the Svartisen glacier (see below), and will check whether the **boats** that give access to the glacier are running. Finally, the tourist office can make reservations for a wide range of **guided excursions**, from rafting, kayaking and fishing through to caving, climbing and trekking. The leading local **operator** is Rana Spesialsport, Øvre Idrettsvei 35 (℡75 12 70 88 or 909 51 108, Ⓦwww.spesialsport.no).

Accommodation

Mo has a good selection of accommodation, making it a handy base for visiting the Svartisen glacier and exploring the region's lakes, fjords and mountains. Pick of the town's **hotels** is the excellently run and very comfortable *Meyergården Hotell*, at the north end of Ole Tobias Olsens gate (℡75 13 40 00, Ⓕ75 13 40 01, Ⓦwww.meyergarden.no; ❺, s/r ❸). Most of the hotel is modern, but the original lodge has survived and is maintained in period style, with stuffed animal heads on the wall and elegant panelled doorways. A less expensive, but much plainer, alternative is the *Fjordgården Hotell Mo i Rana*, down by the waterfront at Søndregate 9 (℡75 15 28 00, Ⓕ75 15 43 70; Ⓦwww.fjordgarden.no; open May to Aug; ❸), or the cosy rooms of the *Fammy Leilighetshotell*, Ole Tobias Olsens gate 4 (℡75 15 19 99, Ⓕ75 15 19 90, Ⓦwww.fammy.no; ❸). Cheaper still, about 12km north of town along the E6, is *Anna's Camping* (℡75 14 80 74; mid-May to mid-Sept), a riverside **campsite** with cabins (❷) as well as tent pitches.

Restaurants, cafés and bars

Mo's best **restaurant** is at the *Meyergården Hotell*, where you can sample an excellent range of Norwegian dishes featuring local ingredients; main courses average around 150kr. Also highly recommended is the *China Kro*, in the town centre at Nordahl Griegs gate 9 (℡ 75 15 15 93), whose Chinese dishes are renowned across Nordland and even attract diners from Sweden. Alternatively, the *Abelone mat & vinstue*, Ole Tobias Olsens gate 6 (℡ 75 15 38 88), serves competent pizzas and steaks, whilst *Babettes*, in the centre at Ranheimgata 2, is good for light meals and coffee. For a drink, the *Onkel Oskar Bar*, Ole Tobias Olsens gate 28 is a lively **bar** whose walls are adorned with historical knick-knacks.

Around Mo: Grønligrotta and the Svartisen glacier

The limestone and marble mountains to the northwest of Mo are pocked by caves. The most accessible is the limestone **Grønligrotta** (mid-June to mid-Aug daily 10am–7pm; 70kr), where an easy 40-minute guided tour follows a

The Arctic Menu scheme

In many restaurants north around the Arctic Circle, you'll see a black circle icon with two flashes beneath. This signifies that the establishment is a member of the **Arctic Menu** scheme, which guarantees top quality cooking and the use of local ingredients – from meat and fowl through to fish and seal as well as fruit and berries. A booklet, widely available at tourist offices across the north, lists all the participating restaurants, which are regularly monitored for quality and originality.

subterranean river. Grønligrotta is lit by electric lights – it's the only illuminated cave in Scandinavia – and it's reached via the signposted road between the E6 and the Svartisen glacier.

Norway's second largest glacier, **Svartisen** – literally "Black Ice" – covers roughly 370 square kilometres of mountain and valley between the E6 and the coast. It's actually divided into two sections – east and west – by the Vesterdal valley, though this cleft is a recent phenomenon: when it was surveyed in 1905, the glacier was one giant block, about 25 percent bigger than it is today; the reasons for this change are still obscure. The highest parts of the glacier lie at around 1500m, but its tentacles reach down to about 170m – the lowest-lying glacial arms in mainland Europe. Mo is within easy reach of one of the glacier's eastern nodules: to get there, drive north from Mo on the E6 for about 12km and then take the signed turning to the glacier, a straightforward 23-kilometre trip ending beside the ice-green, glacial lake **Svartisvatnet**. Here, **boats** (late June to Aug 10am–4pm, every 1–2hrs; 20min each way; 75kr return) shuttle across the lake, though services can't begin until the ice has melted – usually by late June – so check with the tourist office in Mo before you set out. Viewed from the boat, the great convoluted folds of the glacier look rather like bluish-white custard, but close up, after a stiff three-hour hike past the rocky detritus left by the retreating ice, the sheer size of the glacier becomes apparent – a mighty grinding and groaning wall of ice edged by a jumble of ice chunks, columns and boulders.

The west side of the Svartisen glacier can be seen – and accessed – from the "Kystriksveien" Coastal Route, or Highway 17 (see box below). It can also be visited on **organized bus and ferry trips** from Bodø (see p.283).

The Kystriksveien Coastal Route – Highway 17

Branching off the E6 just beyond Steinkjer (see p.272) is the tortuous **Kystriksveien** Coastal Route (ⓦwww.rv17.no), or Highway 17, which threads its way up the west coast, linking many villages that could formerly only be reached by sea. This is an obscure and remote corner of the country, but apart from the lovely scenery there's little of special appeal, and the seven ferry trips that interrupt the 688-kilometre drive north to Bodø (there are no buses) make it expensive and time consuming. A free booklet describing the route can be obtained at tourist offices throughout the region – including Mo – and it contains all Highway 17's car-ferry timetables.

If you're short of time, the section of Highway 17 between **Mo-i-Rana** and **Bodø** takes in most of the scenic highlights, can be negotiated in a day, and cuts out five of the ferry trips. To sample this part of the route, drive 37km west from Mo along the E12 for the Highway 17 crossroads, from where it's some 60km north to the **Kilboghamn–Jektvik** ferry (3–6 daily; 1hr; driver and car 112kr) and a further 30km to the ferry linking **Ågskardet** with **Forøy** (5–14 daily; 10min; driver and car 41kr). On the first ferry you cross the Arctic Circle with great views of the beautiful **Melfjord**, and on the second, you get a chance to see a westerly arm of the **Svartisen** glacier (see above), viewed across the slender Holandsfjorden. For an even closer look at the glacier, stop at the information centre in **HOLAND**, 12km beyond Forøy, and catch the **passenger boat** (June to early Sept Mon–Fri 8am–9pm, Sat & Sun 10am–5.30pm, every 45min to 1hr 30min; 15min; 40kr return; ☏94 86 55 16), which zips across the fjord to meet a connecting bus; this travels the couple of kilometres up to the *Svartisen Turistsenter* (☏75 75 00 11), a mere 250m from the ice. The *Turistsenter* has a café, rents cabins (❷) and is the base for four-hour guided **glacier walks** (mid-June to mid-Aug only; prior booking is essential). For more on glacier walks see p.231. From Holand, it's 140km to the Saltstraumen (see p.284) and another 30km more to Bodø (see p.280).

The Arctic Circle Centre

Given its appeal as a travellers' totem, and considering the amount of effort it takes to actually get here, crossing the **Arctic Circle**, about 80km north of Mo, is a bit of a disappointment. The landscape, uninhabited for the most part, is undeniably bleak, but the gleaming **Polarsirkelsenteret** (Arctic Circle Centre; daily: May to early June & Aug 9am–8pm, late June to July 8am–10pm & early Sept 10am–6pm; ⓦwww.polarsirkelsenteret.no) disfigures the scene, like a giant lampshade plonked by the roadside and stuffed with every sort of tourist bauble imaginable. Both the bus and train whizz by, the latter tooting its whistle as it does so, and drivers can, of course, shoot past too, though the temptation to brave the crowds is strong. Even if you resist the Arctic exhibition (60kr), you'll probably get snared by either the "Polarsirkelen" certificate, or the specially stamped postcards. Outside the centre are poignant reminders of crueller times: a couple of simple stone **memorials** pay tribute to the Yugoslav and Soviet POWs who laboured under terrible conditions in World War II to build the Arctic railroad to Narvik – the Nordlandsbanen – for the Germans.

Saltfjellet Nasjonalpark: Lønsdal and Graddis

The louring mountains in the vicinity of the Arctic Circle Centre are part of the vast **Saltfjellet Nasjonalpark**, a mountain plateau whose spindly pines, stern snow-tipped peaks and rippling moors extend west from near the Swedish border to the Svartisen glacier. The E6 and the railway cut inland across this range between Mo-i-Rana and Rognan, providing access to the cairned hiking trails that lattice the mountains. You can also reach the trails from Highway 77, which forks east off the E6 to Sweden down the **Junkerdal**. The region, however, is the preserve of experienced hikers: the trails are not sufficiently clear to dispense with a compass, weather conditions can be treacherous and, although there's a good network of DNT-affiliated huts, none is staffed, nor do any of them supply provisions. Keys to these huts (most of which are owned by BOT, Bodø's hiking association; see p.280) are available locally, but clearly you have to sort this out with BOT before you set off.

Among several possible bases for venturing into the Saltfjellet, **LØNSDAL**, around 110km north of Mo and 20km beyond the Arctic Circle, is the most easily reached either on the E6 or by train from Trondheim, Mo or Bodø (1–3 daily, but some trains only stop at Lønsdal by request; check with the conductor). Not that there's actually much to reach: a one-kilometre-long turning off the E6 leads first to the *Polarsirkelen Høyfjellshotell* (ⓣ75 69 41 22 ⓕ75 69 41 27; ❸), a long wooden building in a sheltered location and with a cosy modern interior, and then to the lonely train station. The hotel has the only restaurant for miles around, and the food is good.

From Lønsdal, **hiking trails** lead off into the Saltfjellet. One of the more manageable options is the four-hour hike to **GRADDIS**, 18km east of the E6, where there's a **guesthouse** and **camping**: the *Graddis Fjellstue og Camping* (ⓣ75 69 43 41, ⓕ75 69 43 88, ⓔgraddis@c2i.net; late June to late Aug) has single rooms, doubles (❸), and rudimentary cabins (❷) in a farmstead on the wooded slopes of the **Junkerdal**, a remote and rather unwelcoming river valley cut into the Saltfjellet. Despite its gloominess, the Junkerdalen is a favourite spot from which to explore the Saltfjellet, not least because it's easy to reach by road from Sweden.

Botn

Some 45km north of Lønsdal, the E6 regains the coast at **Rognan**, from where it pushes along the east side of the Saltdalsfjord. About 5km after Rognan, at **BOTN**, keep your eyes peeled for the signposted, one-kilometre-long road up to the **Krigskirkegårder**, truly one of Nordland's most mournful and moving places. Buried here, in a wooded glade high above the fjord, are the Yugoslav prisoners of war and their German captors who died in the district during World War II. The men are interred in two separate **graveyards** – both immaculately maintained, though, unlike the plainer Yugoslav cemetery, the German section is entered by a sturdy granite gateway. Mostly captured Tito partisans, the Yugoslavs died in their hundreds from disease, cold and malnutrition, not to mention torture and random murder, during the construction of the Arctic railroad to Narvik. In order to avoid the dangerous voyage along the coast, the Germans tried to extend the railway line, which in 1940 terminated at Mosjøen, through here to Bodø and then onto Narvik. This line, the Nordlandsbanen, involved the labour of 13,000 POWs, but the Germans failed to complete it, and it was not until 1962 that the railway finally reached Bodø.

Fauske

From Botn, it's another 30km up the E6 to **FAUSKE**, which, but for a brief stretch of line from Narvik into Sweden, marks the northernmost point of the Norwegian rail network. For journeys further north, the twice-daily Nord-Norgeekspressen, express **bus** service, to Narvik and Tromsø leaves from beside Fauske **train station**: tickets can be purchased from the driver or in advance at any bus station. Note that there is a fifty percent discount for InterRail and Scanrail pass holders on the route to Narvik (see p.286), a gorgeous five-hour run past fjords, peaks and snow.

From Fauske's train and long-distance bus station, it's a five- to ten-minute walk down the hill and left at the T-junction to the local bus station and a few metres more to the main drag, **Storgata**. Also the E6, Storgata runs parallel to the fjord and holds the handful of shops that passes for the town centre: the **tourist office** (late Aug to mid-June Mon–Fri 8.30am–3.30pm, mid-to late June & mid-Aug daily 9am–4pm, July to early Aug Mon–Fri 9am–7.30pm & Sat–Sun 10am–7pm; ☎75 64 33 03, ⓦwww.saltenreiseliv.no) is at its eastern end at no. 86.

There's no real reason to linger in Fauske – you're better off changing onto the connecting bus to Narvik, or carrying on to Bodø, just forty minutes to the west and a much more palatable place to stay. However, if you are stranded here, Storgata holds the better of the town's two **hotels**, the *Fauske Hotell*, Storgata 82 (☎75 60 20 00, ⓕ75 64 57 37, ⓔfirmapost@fauskehotell.no; ❻, s/r ❹), a chunky square block whose rather sickly interior is dominated by a surfeit of salmon-coloured streaky marble. Quarried locally, the marble is exported all over the world, but is something of an acquired taste. Nonetheless, the hotel rooms are comfortable enough, and the big, tasty breakfast is a real snip. The most popular budget choice is the hostel-like *Seljestua*, 500m from the train station at Seljeveien 2 (☎90 73 46 96; late June to mid-Aug; ❷), but a much better bet is the *Lundhøgda* **campsite** (☎75 64 39 66, ⓕ75 64 92 49, ⓔlundhogda@c2i.net; May–Sept; cabins ❷), in a splendid location about 3km west of the town centre, overlooking the mountains and the fjord: head out of town along the E80 Bodø road, and look out for the campsite sign which will take you down a country lane, flanked by old timber buildings.

Bodø and around

Sixty-three kilometres west of Fauske along the E80, **BODØ** was founded in 1816. The town struggled to survive in its early years, but was saved from insignificance when the herring fishery boomed in the 1860s, a time when the town's harbourfront was crowded with the net-menders, coopers, oilskin-makers and canneries that kept the fleet going. In the early twentieth century, it accrued several industrial plants and became an important regional commercial and administrative centre, but was then heavily bombed during World War II, and nowadays there's precious little left of the proud, nineteenth-century buildings that once flanked the waterfront. Nonetheless, Bodø achieves a cheerful modernity, a bright and breezy place within comfortable striking distance of the old trading post of **Kjerringøy**, one of Nordland's most delightful spots. Bodø is also a regular stop on the Hurtigrute coastal service and much the best place from which to hop over to the choicest parts of the **Lofoten islands** (see p.300).

Arrival and information

Readily reached by train or bus from Fauske, Bodø is the terminus of the Trondheim train and the starting point of the Nord-Norgeekspressen express bus to points north. Bodø's **train station** is at the eastern end of the town centre, just off the long main street, Sjøgata. The **bus station** is a further 700m west along Sjøgata, adjoining the dock for the **Hurtigbåt** passenger express boat to Lofoten (most usefully to and from Svolvær; see p.303). The southern **Lofoten ferry** (to and from Moskenes, Værøy and Røst) and the **Hurtigrute** coastal boat use the docks 500m and 700m respectively northeast along the waterfront from the train station. Bodø **airport** is 2km south of the centre; regular local buses, marked *Sentrumsrunden,* link the airport with the bus station, or you can catch a cab to the centre for around 70kr. SAS has a ticket office at the airport (☎815 20 400) as well as several authorized agents in the centre – Bennett, Moloveien 20 (☎75 50 60 70), is as good as any.

The **tourist office** shares the Hurtigbåt and bus station terminal building at Sjøgata 3 (June–Aug Mon–Fri 9am–8pm, Sat 10am–8pm, Sun noon–8pm; Sept–May Mon–Wed & Fri 9am–4pm, Thurs 9am–6pm & Sat 10am–3pm; ☎75 54 80 00, ℱ75 54 80 01, ℮destinasjon@bodoe.com, ℗www.bodoe.com). It gives out information on connections to the Lofoten islands, rents out bikes and also issues an excellent town and district guide. You can join the **DNT** at Bodø og Omegn Turistforening (BOT), 2nd Floor, Storgata 17 (Tues, Wed & Fri noon–3pm, Thurs noon–5pm; ☎75 52 14 13; ℗www.bot.no), which also dispenses advice about the region's hiking trails and cabins.

Accommodation

Bodø has a reasonable supply of **accommodation**, including half a dozen hotels, an HI hostel and a couple of guesthouses. In addition, the tourist office has a small supply of **private rooms** in the town and its environs, at a fixed tariff of 300–350kr per double, plus a modest booking fee.

Hotels

Bodø Hotell, Professor Schyttesgate 5 ☎75 54 77 00, ℱ75 52 57 78, ℮booking@bodohotell.no. Mid-sized, mid-range hotel in a five-storey block right in the centre of town. Well-kept rooms with the usual mod cons decorated in the Scandinavian style with oodles of pine. Reasonably priced at ❹, s/r ❸

Comfort Home Hotel Grand Storgata 3 ☎75 54 61 00, ℱ75 54 61 50, ℗www.grand-bodo.no.

Upmarket chain hotel in a smart block with appealing Art Deco flourishes. **6**, s/r **4**

Norrøna Hotell Storgata 4b ⓣ 75 52 55 50, ⓕ 75 52 33 88, ⓦ www.norrona-hotell.bedre.no. Standard issue chain hotel in a large modern block metres from the bus station. At the lower end of the market, but still reliable and comfortable. **3**, s/r **2**

Radisson SAS Hotel Bodø Storgata 2 ⓣ 75 52 41 00, ⓕ 75 52 74 93, ⓦ www.sales.radissonsas.com. Occupying a huge, modern concrete-and-glass tower block, this is the best hotel in town, with well-appointed, well-appointed rooms. The upper floor rooms have great views out to sea. **7**, s/r **4**

Hostel, guesthouse and camping

Bodø Gjestegård Storgata 90 ⓣ 75 52 04 02, ⓕ 75 52 04 03, ⓔ johansst@online.no. Bargain accommodation in this twenty-room guesthouse not far from the railway station. Breakfast included. **2**

Bodø Vandrerhjem Sjøgata 55 ⓣ 75 52 11 22, ⓕ 75 52 16 35, ⓔ bodo.hostel@vandrerhjem.no. This spartan HI hostel is next door to the train station, but – apart from the location – it has precious little to commend it. Open May to September. Dorm beds 150kr.

Bodøsjøen Camping Bodøsjøen ⓣ 75 56 36 80, ⓕ 75 56 36 89. Year-round lakeside campsite located about 3.5km to the southeast of the centre, not far from the Bodin kirke. Tent pitches, caravan hook-ups and cabins (**2**).

The town

Although Bodø rambles over a low-lying peninsula poking out into the Saltfjorden, its **centre** is concentrated along two parallel streets, Sjøgata and Storgata. The town is short of specific sights, but 2km southeast of the centre on Olav V's gate, is its most popular attraction, the imaginative **Norsk Luftfartsmuseum** (Norwegian Aviation Museum; mid-June to mid-Aug Sun–Fri 10am–7pm, Sat 10am–5pm; mid-Aug to mid-June Mon–Fri 10am–4pm, Sat & Sun 11am–5pm; ⓦ www.aviation-museum.com; 70kr), which runs through the general history of Norwegian aviation. It adopts an imaginative approach to the subject, with its own building having been constructed in the shape of a two-bladed propeller: one "blade" houses air force and defence exhibits, the other civilian displays. The spot where the two blades meet straddles the ring road and is topped by part of the old Bodø airport control tower. Among the planes to look out for are a Spitfire – a reminder that two RAF squadrons were manned by Norwegians during World War II – and a rare Norwegian-made Hønningstad C-5 Polar seaplane. Bodø was frequently used by the US air force throughout the Cold War, and you can also see one of their U2 spy planes.

If you have your own transport, consider driving a further 1km south along Gamle Riksvei to the onion-domed **Bodin kirke** (late June to mid-Aug Mon–Fri 10am–3pm; free), a pretty little stone church sitting snugly among meadows. Dating from the thirteenth century, the church was modified after the Reformation by the addition of a tower and the widening of its windows – dark, gloomy churches were then associated with Catholicism. It is, however, the colourful seventeenth-century fixtures that catch the eye, plus the lovingly carved Baroque altarboard and pulpit, both painted in the eighteenth century by an itinerant German artist, Gottfried Ezechiel.

Cafés, bars and restaurants

Bodø is hardly a gourmet's paradise, but there are one or two competent **cafés** and **restaurants**, kicking off with the traditional and inexpensive *Løvolds Kafé* (closed Sun), down by the quay at Tollbugata 9: its Norwegian menu features local ingredients, with main courses averaging around 100kr, and daily specials

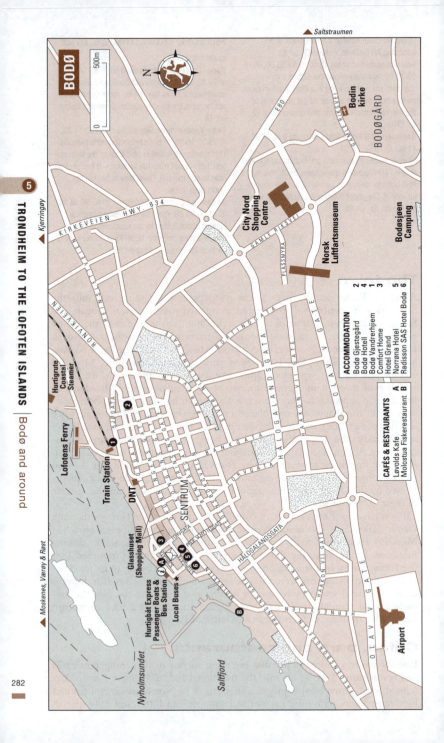

▲ Saltstraumen

BODØ

0   500m

N

▲ Kjerringøy

KIRKEVEIEN HWY 834

RØNVIKVEIEN

Hurtigrute
Coastal
Steamer

▲ Moskenes, Værøy & Røst

Nyholmsundet

Lofotens Ferry

Train Station

DNT

Glasshuset
(Shopping Mall)

Hurtigbåt Express
Passenger Boats &
Bus Station

Local Buses

SENTRUM

TORVGATA

PROF. SCHYTTES GT.

SIGDGATA

SJØGATA

BANKGATA

DRONNINGENSGATE

STORGATA

NEDRE

KONGENSGT.

HENRIKHENRIKSENSGT.

SENTRUM

Saltfjord

HÅLOGALANDSGATA

Airport

PRINSENSGT.

OLAV V GATE

HÅKON VII GATE

HÅLOGALANDSGATA

PARKVEIEN

NORDSTRANDVEIEN

OLAV V GATE

HERNESVEIEN

HÅKON VII GATE

City Nord
Shopping
Centre

Norsk
Luftfartsmuseum

Bodsjøen
Camping

PLASSMYRA

GAMLE RIKSVEI

OLAV V GATE

BODØGÅRD

Bodin
kirke

GAMLE RIKSVEI

E80

ACCOMMODATION
Bodø Gjestegård   2
Bodø Hotell   4
Bodø Vandrerhjem   1
Comfort Home   3
Hotel Grand   5
Norrøna Hotel   5
Radisson SAS Hotel Bodø 6

CAFÉS & RESTAURANTS
Løvolds Kafe   A
Molostua Fiskerestaurant B

70kr. More upmarket, the first-rate, waterfront *Molostua Fiskerestaurant og Kafé*, Moloveien 9 (☎75 52 05 30), is a café in the daytime and restaurant at night, serving tasty seafood and classic Norwegian dishes jazzed up with French-style sauces. In addition, the *En Kopp* coffee bar at the *SAS Radisson Hotel* serves the best coffee in town, while the hotel's top-floor **bar**, *Top 13,* has the best view.

Out from Bodø: the Svartisen glacier, Kjerringøy and Saltstraumen

The obvious excursions from Bodø are to head northeast to the old trading station at **Kjerringøy**, and southeast to the tidal phenomenon known as the **Saltstraumen**. In addition, every day except Saturday from June to August, Bodø tourist office runs organized tours to the **Svartisen glacier** (see p.277). The excursions take twelve hours, leaving Bodø bus station at 7.45am and arriving at the glacier at 11.30am; the cost is 390kr, but this doesn't include food. Be sure to have warm clothing. Finally, the glacier and the Saltstraumen can also be reached by car or bike from Highway 17, the "Kystriksveien" (see p.277).

Kjerringøy

Forty kilometres north along the coast from Bodø, the **KJERRINGØY** trading post (late May to mid-Aug daily 11am–5pm; 40kr; ☎75 51 12 57), boasts a superbly preserved collection of nineteenth-century timber buildings set beside a slender, islet-sheltered channel. This was once the domain of the **Zahl** family, merchant suppliers who bought fish from Lofoten's fishermen and sup-plied them with everything from manufactured goods and clothes to farmyard foodstuffs. It was not, however, an equal relationship: the Zahls, who operated a local monopoly until the 1910s, could dictate the price they paid for the fish, and many of the islanders were permanently indebted to them. This social divi-sion is still very much in evidence at the trading post, where there's a marked distinction between the guest rooms of the main house and the fishermen's bunk beds in the boat- and cookhouses. Indeed, the **family house** is remark-ably fastidious, with its Italianate busts and embroidered curtains – even the medicine cabinet is well-stocked with formidable Victorian remedies like the bottle of "Sicilian Hair Renewer".

There are enjoyable, hour-long **guided tours** around the main house (late May to mid-Aug, daily, every hour on the hour; 25kr) and, when you've fin-ished with the tour, you can nose around the reconstructed general store, drop in at the café and stroll the fine sandy beach in front of the complex. It's a peaceful and picturesque spot, that film-goers may recognize from the movie *I am Dina*, based on *Dina's Book*, by the Norwegian author Herbjørg Wassmo, which was filmed here.

Getting here **by car** is easy enough – a straightforward coastal drive from Bodø along Highway 834, using the Festvåg-Misten ferry (daily every 30min or hour; 10min; passengers 18kr, car & driver 43kr return; ☎948 94 288). **By bus** (1–2 daily except Sat; 73kr return inc. ferry) a day-return from Bodø bus station is possible Monday through Friday, but if you want **to stay** the night, the old parsonage, *Kjerringøy prestegård*, about 1km north of the trading post along the main road (☎75 51 07 80, ℱ75 50 77 10, ℰronvik.menighet @kirken.bodo.no), has simple double rooms in the main building (❶) and slightly pleasanter ones in the renovated cow-shed next door (❷).

Saltstraumen

Less interesting than Kjerringøy, but more widely publicized, is the maelstrom known as the **Saltstraumen**, 33km east of Bodø on Highway 17. Here, billions of gallons of water are forced four times a day through a narrow, 150m-wide channel, which links the inner and outer parts of the fjord. The whirling creamy water is at its most turbulent at high tide, and its most violent when the moon is new or full – a timetable is available from Bodø tourist office.

Although scores of tourists troop here for every high tide, you can't help but feel they wish they were somewhere else – the scenery is, in Norwegian terms at least, rather dull, and the view from the bridge which spans the channel unexciting. **Fishing** enthusiasts, however, will be impressed by the force of the water which pulls in all sorts of fish: cod, catfish and coley are common catches – one coley caught here weighed a remarkable 22.7 kilos (or so they say). Rods can be hired at several places, including the **Saltstraumen Opplevelsessenter** (Saltstraumen Adventure Centre; May–Aug daily 11am–6pm, Sept Sat & Sun only 11am–6pm; 60kr), housed in two adjoining buildings near the eastern end of the bridge. The centre tells you all you'd ever wanted to know about tidal currents, and then some, and also has several pools where you can take a close look at local marine life.

It takes about fifty minutes to **drive** from Bodø to the Saltstraumen, or you could take local **bus** #819 (Mon–Sat 5-7 daily, Sun 1 daily; 1hr; 46kr one way), though its times rarely coincide with the high tide. In this case, you can kill a couple of hours very pleasantly at *Kafé Kjelen*, a little red house on the west side of the bridge, whose balcony offers views over the maelstrom – don't miss its *Møsprumlefse*, a traditional, burrito-like pancake stuffed with a mix of sweet brown-cheese sauce, sour cream and melted butter.

North to Narvik

The 240-kilometre journey north from Fauske to Narvik is spectacular, with the **E6** rounding the fjords, twisting and tunnelling through the mountains and rushing over high, pine-dusted plateaux. The scenery is the main event, and there's little en route to merit a stop, with a couple of notable exceptions: the fascinating old farmstead at **Kjelvik**, where the hardship of rural life in Norway is revealed in idyllic surroundings, and the remote former trading-post of **Tranøy**. At the end of the journey, **Narvik** is an eminently likeable industrial town that witnessed some of the fiercest fighting in Norway during the German invasion of 1940. It's a good place for an overnight stop and a useful launching pad for the long haul to the far north, or a visit to the Vesterålen and Lofoten islands.

This stretch of the E6 between Fauske and Narvik presents two opportunities to catch a **car ferry** to Lofoten – one at Skutvik, the other at Bognes. The more southerly of the two is **Skutvik**, 37km to the west of the E6, with ferries to Svolvær in Lofoten. At **Bognes**, on the E6, there's a choice of ferries: one sails to Lødingen and the E10 on Lofoten, while a second hops across the Tysfjorden to **Skarberget** to rejoin the E6 80km south of Narvik. Long-distance **buses** link Bodø, Fauske and Narvik twice daily; the journey from Fauske to Narvik takes six hours.

The E6 north to Bognes

Beyond Fauske, the E6 scuttles over the hills to the small industrial town of **Straumen** and then threads along the coast to **Sommarset**, an old ferry point where boats crossed the **Leirfjord** until a new stretch of road was built around the fjord in 1986. This new section is an ambitious affair that drills through the mountains with the fjord glistening below. It also passes within 250m of the old farmstead of **KJELVIK**, 58km from Fauske, where a scattering of old wooden buildings, including a cottage, woodshed, forge and mill, nestle in a green, wooded valley. It's a beautiful spot, but the tenant farmers who worked the land finally gave up the battle against their harsh isolation in 1967. There was no electricity, no water, the soil was thin, and the only contact with the outside world was by boat; supply vessels would come up the Leirfjord to the Kjelvik jetty, from where it was a steep two-kilometre hike to the farm, 200m above the fjord. Today, there's open access to the farm, which is kept in good condition, and wandering around is a delight: you can also follow the old footpath down to the Kjelvik jetty. **Guided tours** of Kjelvik are available (late June to late August daily 11am–6pm; 30kr) and, on the last Saturday of the season, the **Kjelvik festival** sees the old buildings put to their original uses. Griddle-cakes are cooked on the wood stove, and dollops of sour cream and porridge are doled out to visitors.

After Kjelvik, the E6 bores through the mountains to reach, after about 40km, the couple of houses that make up **KRÅKMO**, with the lake on one side and the domineering mass of a mighty mountain, Kråkmotind, on the other. This was once a favourite haunt of that crusty reactionary Knut Hamsun (1859-1952), a one-time leading light among Norway's writers, but disgraced by his admiration for Hitler.

From Kråkmo, it's another 50km or so to the point where Highway 81 branches off to Skutvik and the car ferry to Svolvær, on the Lofoten islands (see below). Continuing up the E6 for a further scenic 20km, you'll reach **Bognes**, where one ferry heads west to Lødingen on Lofoten (mid-June to mid-Aug 12 daily, mid-Aug to mid-June 5 daily; 1hr; car and driver 122kr; ☎177), while a second travels to **Skarberget** for the E6 and the remaining 80km to Narvik (15–21 daily, every 1hr or 90min; 25min; car and driver 67kr; ☎177). In summer, it's worth arriving two hours before departure to be sure of a space.

West to Skutvik, Hamsund and Tranøy

Spearing off the E6 20km before Bognes, **Highway 81** heads to **SKUTVIK**, the departure point for car ferries to Svolvær, on the Lofoten islands (June to mid-Aug 8 daily; Sept–May 2–3 daily; 2hr; car & driver 200kr; ☎177). The road is only 35km long, but it takes a good hour to drive and passes some dramatic scenery as it weaves across the island of **Hamarøy**, all craggy shorelines and imposing peaks. About halfway along, the highway passes through the hamlet of **HAMSUND**, site of Knut Hamsun's boyhood home, now the tiny **Hamsun Museum** (summer only; irregular hours, call ☎75 77 02 94).

A more rewarding detour, however, is to the old trading post of **TRANØY**, in superb, remote scenery on Hamarøy's northern coast, some 15km north of Highway 81. Here, in these unlikely surroundings, you'll find a couple of art galleries: the **Hamsungalleriet på Tranøy** (Hamsun Gallery; mid-June to mid-Aug 11am–7pm, 30kr), in the old general store where Hamsun worked as a youth, exhibits the work of Norway's Karl Erik Harr, focusing on his illustrations of Hamsun's novels, while the **Tranøy Galleri** (late June to mid-Aug daily 11am–7pm; 30kr), also features illustrations of Hamsun's books, this time by Tor Arne Moen.

Tranøy has a couple of excellent **places to stay**: the *Edvardas hus* (☎75 77 21 82, ℉75 77 22 21, ⊛www.edvardashus.no, ℮visit@edvardashus.no; ➍), has nine extremely comfortable bedrooms in a substantial villa, and outstanding food, while *Tranøy Fyr* (☏ 75 77 23 00, ⓕ 75 77 23 01, ⓦ www.tranoyfyr.no, ⓔ tranoyfyr@online.no; mid-June to mid-Aug; ❹), has ten straightforward rooms in the old lighthousemen's quarters, on the edge of the ocean beneath the lighthouse. *Tranøy Fyr* also has its own café-restaurant with outdoor seating in the summertime. Cheaper, slightly plainer rooms (❷) can be had at *Edvardas Søster*, run by the same people as *Edvardas hus* (see above for contact details).

Narvik and around

A relatively modern town, **NARVIK** was established just a century ago as an ice-free port to handle the iron ore brought by train from northern Sweden. It makes no bones about its main function: the **iron-ore docks** are immediately conspicuous, right in the centre of town, the rust-coloured machinery dominating the whole waterfront. Yet, for all the mess, the industrial complex is strangely impressive, its cat's cradle of walkways, conveyor belts, cranes and funnels oddly beguiling. In recent years, Narvik has developed a second string to its bow, as an **extreme sports** centre with skiing, paragliding and scuba-diving becoming increasingly popular.

Arrival and information

Fifteen minutes' walk from one end to the other, Narvik's sloping centre straggles along the main street, **Kongens gate**, which doubles as the E6. The **train station** is at the north end of the town and from here it's a five- to ten-minute walk along Kongens gate to the **bus station**, in the basement of the Amfi

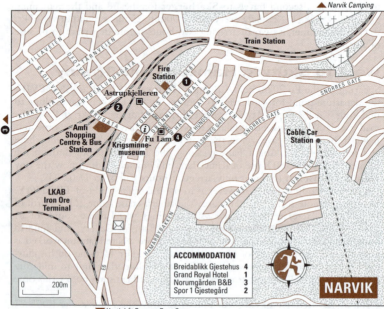

▲ *Narvik Camping*

Train Station

Fire Station ❶

Astrupkjelleren

VILLAVEIEN

SKOLE GATE

TÅRNVEIEN

LØFTENLUNDSGATA

FRYDENLUNDSGATA

KONGENS GATE (E6)

DRONNINGENS GATE

BRUGATA

KIRKEGATA

Amfi Shopping Centre & Bus Station

Krigsminne-museum

ⓘ Fu Lam ❹

HARENS GATE

TORE HUNDS GATE

SELSBANES GATE

SNORRES GATE

SNORRES GATE

TÅVEIEN

Cable Car Station

FJELLVEIEN

SKISTUAVEIEN

LKAB Iron Ore Terminal

HAMNØYBAKKEN

N

ACCOMMODATION

Breidablikk Gjestehus	4
Grand Royal Hotel	1
Norumgården B&B	3
Spor 1 Gjestegård	2

NARVIK

0   200m

▼ *Hurtigbåt Express Boat Quay*

shopping centre on the west side of the street. The **tourist office,** a few metres further along Kongens gate on the main square (early June Mon–Fri 9am–5pm, Sat & Sun 11am–5pm; mid-June to mid-Aug Mon–Fri 9am–5pm, Sat 10am–5pm & Sun 11am–5pm; late Aug Mon–Fri 9am–5pm, Sat 10am–3pm; Sept–May Mon–Fri 8.30am–3.30pm; ☏76 94 33 09; ✆post @narvikinfo.no; ✇www.narvikinfo.no), has the full range of bus and ferry timetables and provides lots of information on outdoor pursuits; it can also assist with ferry and activity reservations. For **mountain climbing** and guided **glacier walking**, contact Nord-Norsk Klatreskole (☏76 95 13 53), and for **scuba diving** amidst the wreck-studded waters around Narvik, try Narvik Dykk & Eventyr (☏995 12 205), which also rents out equipment and provides diving tuition.

From the tourist office, it's another five-minute walk south along Kongens gate to the dock for the **Hurtigbåt** passenger express boat service to Svolvær on Lofoten.

Accommodation

Breidablikk Gjestehus Tore Hunds gate 41 ☏76 94 14 18, ☏76 94 57 86, ✇www.narviknett.no/breida. This pleasant, unassuming guest house is neat and trim, with homely en-suite rooms. Those on the upper floors have attractive views over town and a good, hearty breakfast is included in the room rate. It's located at the top of the steps at the end of Kinobakken, a side road leading east off Kongens gate, just up from the main town square. ❷

Grand Royal Hotel Kongens gate 64 ☏76 97 77 00, ☏76 97 77 07, ✇www.grandroyalhotelnarvik .no. Although some of Narvik's hotels have seen better days, the *Grand*, just up from the tourist office, is well kept; its public rooms are wood-panelled and elegant, while the bedrooms are perfectly comfortable. ❻, s/r ❹

Narvik Camping Rombaksveien 75 ☏76 94 58 10, ☏76 94 14 20, ✆opofoten@opofoten.no. Year-round campsite, about 2.5km north of the centre on the E6; nothing special, but with tent pitches, hook-ups and cabins (❶).

Norumgården Bed & Breakfast Framnesveien 127 ☏76 94 48 57, ☏76 94 48 57, ✇norumgaarden.narviknett.no. Lavish but good value B&B in a 1920s timber villa. The Germans used the place as an officers' mess during the war and today, tastefully restored, it holds three large guest rooms, two of which have kitchenettes. Antiques are liberally distributed across the house and breakfast is included in the room rate. ❸

SPOR 1 Gjestegård Brugata 2A ☏76 94 60 20, ☏76 94 38 44, ✆post@spor1.no, ✇www.spor1.no. This trim guest house is the pick of the budget/backpacker options with clean and comfortable rooms in a brisk, modern style. Doubles, quads and a larger dorm room plus kitchen facilities, a sauna and a bar. Occupies a creatively recycled railway building, just below the main town bridge. Dorm beds 160kr, doubles ❷

The town

Narvik's first modern settlers were the navvies who built the nineteenth-century railway line, the **Ofotbanen** (see box, p.289), to the mines in Kiruna, over the border in Sweden – a herculean task commemorated every March by a week of singing, dancing and drinking, when the locals dress up in period costume. The town grew steadily up until World War II, when it was demolished by fierce fighting for control of the harbour and iron-ore supplies. Perhaps inevitably, the rebuilt town centre is rather lacking in appeal, with modern concrete buildings replacing the wooden houses that went before, but it still musters a breezy northern charm. It also possesses the fascinating **Nordland Røde Kors Krigsminnemuseum** (Red Cross War Memorial Museum; March to early June & late Aug to Sept daily 10am–4pm; early June to late Aug daily 10am–10pm; 35kr), just along from the tourist office. Run by the Red Cross, the museum documents the wartime German saturation bombing of the town, and the bitter and bloody sea and air battles in which hundreds of foreign servicemen died alongside a swathe of the local population. It was a complicated campaign, with the German invasion of April 1940 followed by an Allied counterattack spearheaded by the Royal Navy. The Allies actually recaptured Narvik, driving the Germans into the mountains, but were hurriedly evacuated when Hitler launched his invasion of France. The fight for Narvik lasted two months and the German commander wrote of the sea change amongst his Norwegian adversaries, who toughened up to become much more determined soldiers, and skilled ones at that: many were crack shots from their hunting days and all could ski. In the short term, this change of attitude prefigured the formation of the Resistance; in the long term it pretty much put paid to Norway's traditional isolationism. The museum gives a thoroughly moving and thoughtfully presented account of the battle for Narvik and then follows the German occupation of Norway until liberation in 1945.

The town's only other attraction is its **guided tours** of the LKAB mining company's ore-terminal complex (mid-June to mid-Aug 1 daily; 30kr), interesting if only for the opportunity to spend ninety minutes amid such giant, ore-stained contraptions. After its arrival by train, the ore is carried on the various conveyor belts to the quayside, from where some thirty million tons of it are shipped out a year. Sign up for the tours at the tourist office.

Fagernesfjellet

The best way to explore Narvik's mountainous environs is by **cable car** (mid-June to July noon–1am, Aug 1–9pm; 85kr return), which whisks passengers up the first 650m of the mighty **Fagernesfjellet**: its terminus is a stiff fifteen-minute walk above the town behind the train station. There's a restaurant and viewing point at the top of the cable car and from here, on a clear day, you can see the Lofoten islands and experience the midnight sun (end of May to mid-July). In addition, **hiking trails** delve further into the mountains, and there's a designated take-off point for **hang– and paragliders**, a few metres from the restaurant: check conditions first with the Hang og Paragliderklubb (℡906 18 115). The cable car also provides a shuttle service for **skiers and snowboarders** during the season (late November to early June). The network of skiing slopes and trails includes five ski lifts, 7km of prepared courses and unlimited off-piste skiing, with some floodlit areas; for further details contact Narvik ski centre, (℡76 96 04 94, ℇskinarvik@narviknett.no). Finally, the cable car stops running in windy conditions, so check with the tourist office before setting out.

Eating

Narvik is very short of decent **cafés** and **restaurants**. Probably the best option is the *Astrupkjelleren*, Kinobakken 1, where the mostly meaty main courses start at 150kr. Alternatively, there's the rather more formal restaurant of the *Grand Royal Hotel*, which specializes in Norwegian dishes using local ingredients, and is a member of the Arctic Menu scheme (see p.276). A third choice – though it will hardly set your taste buds rattling – is the *Fu Lam* Chinese restaurant, at Droningens gate 58.

Moving on from Narvik

There's a choice of several routes on from Narvik. The Nord-Norgeekspressen **bus** (North Norway Express bus; 1–2 daily) makes the four-hour hop north to Tromsø (see p.320), or you can take a direct bus from Narvik to Alta (1 daily except Sat; 10hr). Both trips give views of some wonderfully wild and diverse scenery, from craggy mountains and blue-black fjords to gentle, forested valleys – though it's not perhaps quite as scenic a journey as the E6 from Fauske to

The Ofotbanen

One of the real treats of a visit to Narvik is the **train ride** into the mountains that back the town and spread east across the Swedish border. Called the **Ofotbanen**, the line passes through some wonderful scenery, slipping between hostile peaks before reaching the rocky, barren and lakelet-studded plateau beyond. A remarkable achievement, the line was completed in 1903 and the navvies endured astounding hardships in the process. Trains from Narvik, run by Tågkompaniet (℡0046/690 69 10 17; ⊛www.tagkompaniet.se), cross the border – take your passport – and arrive (2–3 daily; 50min one way; 130kr return) at the Swedish settlement of **RIKSGRÄNSEN**, a hiking and skiing centre on the plateau. There's a large and surprisingly plush **hotel** here, the *Riksgränsen* (℡0046/98 04 00 80, ℻0046/98 04 31 25; ❹), where you can buy hiking maps and sports gear as well as renting mountain bikes. You can nose around the place for an hour or three before returning by train to Narvik, or you can hike at least a part of the way back on the **Rallarveien**, the old and recently refurbished trail built for the railway construction workers in the last century. This extends west for 15km to Rombaksbotn, a deep and narrow inlet where the navvies once started their haul up the mountains; it also heads deeper into Sweden, to Abisko and Kiruna. A favourite option is to walk from Riksgränsen back towards the coast, picking up the return train at one of the Norwegian stations on the way. The area isn't nearly as remote now that the **E10** crosses the mountains to the north of the railway, but the terrain is difficult and weather unpredictable, so hikers will need to be well equipped. There is, in fact, a network of **trails and cabins** strung out in the mountains surrounding the railroad: you'll need to contact DNT affiliate Narvik og Omegn Turistforening (℡76 94 37 90; ℯjonhi@online.no) in advance if you want to use the cabins. Hiking **maps** are available from the Narvik Libris bookshop, Kongens gate 44, just up from Narvik tourist office.

Narvik. A third bus service, the Narvik-Lofoten Ekspressen (1–2 daily) runs west from Narvik to Sortland, Stokmarknes and Svolvær in the Lofoten islands (see p.303). On all these buses, plus the bus trips south from Narvik to Fauske (for connecting trains to Trondheim) and Bodø, rail-pass holders get a fifty percent discount.

Narvik's **Hurtigbåt** passenger express boat service to Svolvær operates all year (1 daily except Sat; 3–4hr; 290kr one-way). Rail-pass holders get a fifty percent discount. Finally, travellers on the **Ofotbanen** (see box above) can stay on the train beyond Riksgränsen for Kiruna and Stockholm – the ride to Stockholm takes around 18 hours.

The Vesterålen islands

A raggle-taggle archipelago in the Norwegian Sea, the **VESTERÅLEN ISLANDS**, and their southerly neighbours the Lofoten islands (see p.300), are like western Norway in miniature: the terrain is hard and unyielding, the sea boisterous and fretful, and the main – often the only – industry is fishing. The weather is temperate but wet, and the islanders' historic isolation has bred a distinctive culture based, in equal measure, on Protestantism, the extended family and respect for the ocean.

The archipelago was first settled by semi-nomadic hunter-agriculturalists some 6000 years ago, and it was they and their Iron-Age successors who chopped down the birch and pine forests that once covered the coasts. It was **boatbuilding** which brought prosperity to the islands: by the seventh century,

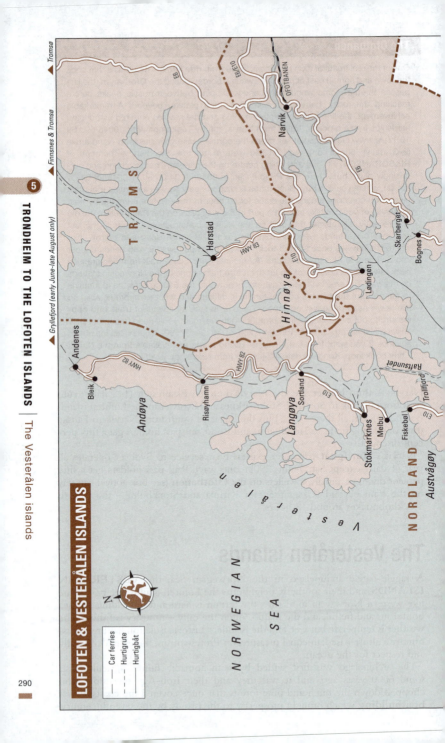

LOFOTEN & VESTERÅLEN ISLANDS

Car ferries
Hurtigrute
Hurtigbåt

N

NORWEGIAN SEA

Vesterålen

NORDLAND

Andøya

Bleik

Andenes

HWY 82

Risøyhamn

Langøya

Sortland

Melbu

Stokmarknes

Fiskebøl

Austvågøy

E10

Trollfjord

Raftsundet

HWY 82

Hinnøya

E10

Lødingen

Harstad

HWY 83

TROMS

E10

E6

Narvik

OFOTBANEN

E6/E10

E6

Skarberget

Bognes

▲ Tromsø

▲ Finnsnes & Tromsø

▲ Gryllefjord (early June–late August only)

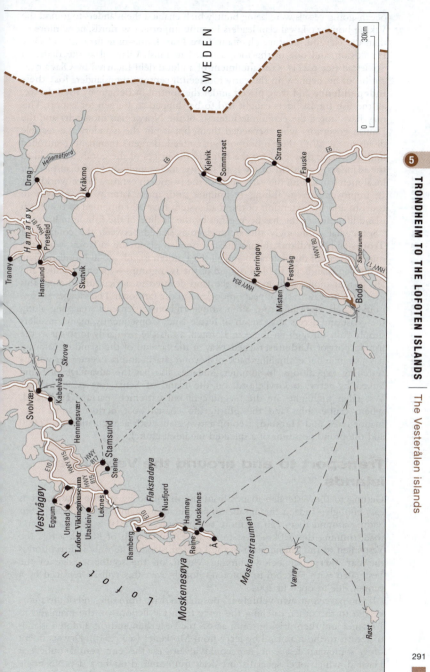

SWEDEN

30km

0

Hellemofjord

Drag

Kråkmo

E6

Kjelvik

Sommarset

Straumen

Fauske

E6

Tranøy

H a m a r ø y

Prestøid

HWY 81

Hamsund

Skutvik

Kjerringøy

HWY 834

Mister

Festvåg

HWY '80'

Saltstraumen

HWY '17'

Bodø

Skrova

Kabelvåg

Svolvær

Henningsvær

HWY 816

E10

Stamsund

HWY 817

Steine

Flakstadøya

Vestvågøy

Eggum

Unstad

Lofotr Vikingmuseum

Utakleiv

HWY 815

Leknes

HWY

Nusfjord

Hamnøy

Moskenes

E10

Ramberg

Reine

Å

Moskenesøya

Moskenstraumen

Værøy

L o f o t e n

Røst

ocean-going vessels were being built, which enabled the islanders to join in the Viking bonanza. Local clan leaders became important warlords, none more so than the eleventh-century chieftain **Tore Hund**, one-time liegeman of Olav Haraldsson, and one of the men selected to finish Olav off at the Battle of Stiklestad (see p.271) – the fulfilment of a blood debt incurred by Olav's execution of his nephew. In the early fourteenth century, the islanders **lost their independence** and were placed under the control of Bergen: by royal decree, all the fish the islanders caught had to be shipped to Bergen for export. This may have suited the economic interests of the Norwegian monarchy and the Danish governors who succeeded them, but it put the islanders at a terrible disadvantage. With their monopoly guaranteed, Bergen's merchants controlled both the price they paid for the fish and the prices of the goods they sold to the islanders – a system that was to survive, increasingly under the auspices of local merchants, until the early years of the twentieth century. Since World War II, improvements in fishing techniques and, more latterly, the growth in tourism and the extension of the road system have all combined to transform island life, though this has been offset by the decline of the fishing industry.

Somewhat confusingly, the archipelago is shared between the counties of **Troms** and **Nordland**: the northern Vesterålen islands are in Troms, while the southern half of the Vesterålen and all the Lofoten islands are in Nordland. The Vesterålen islands are the less rugged of the two groups – greener, gentler and less mountainous, with more of the land devoted to agriculture, though this gives way to vast tracts of peaty moorland in the far north. The villages are less immediately appealing too, often simple ribbon-settlements straggling along the coast and across any stretch of fertile land. Consequently, many travellers simply rush through en route to Lofoten, a mistake primarily in so far as the fishing port of **Andenes**, tucked away at the far end of the island of Andøya, has a strange but enthralling back-of-beyond charm and is a centre for whale-watching expeditions. In summer, Andenes also has the advantage of being linked by ferry to Gryllefjord, on the island of Senja (see p.293). Other Vesterålen highlights are the magnificent but extremely narrow **Trollfjord**, where cruise ships and the Hurtigrute coastal boat perform some nifty manoeuvres, and **Harstad**, a comparative giant with a population of 22,000 and the proud possessor of a splendid medieval church.

Transport to and around the Vesterålen islands

Getting to the Vesterålen islands from the mainland by **public transport** is easy enough – indeed, the number of permutations is almost bewildering – but getting around them can be more troublesome. The **E10** is the main island road, running the 370km west from the E6 just north of Narvik across the Vesterålen to the southern tip of the Lofoten islands. The only interruption is the **car ferry** (see below) linking Melbu, on the southern edge of the Vesterålen with Fiskebøl in Lofoten, though even this will be replaced by a tunnel, due to open in 2004.

If you have your own **vehicle** it's possible to drive from one end of the archipelago to the other, catching the ferry from Gryllefjord on the mainland to Andenes and then driving south across the Vesterålen and the Lofoten islands to return to the mainland by ferry from Moskenes (see p.310). Drivers intent on a somewhat less epic trip could investigate the **car rental** outlets at Harstad, which offer special short deals from around 600kr a day. No single itinerary stands out, but the E6 and E10 in from Narvik has the advantage of simplicity – with Harstad, Sortland and then Andenes being an obvious approach, plus Stokmarknes if you're heading on to Lofoten. Andenes has most to offer as a base thanks to its whale- and bird-watching trips and choice of accommodation.

Car ferries

The principal **car ferry** from the mainland to the Vesterålen islands departs from the jetty at **Bognes**, on the E6 between Fauske and Narvik, and sails to **Lødingen** (early June to mid-Aug 12 daily; mid-Aug to early June 5 daily; 1hr; passengers 39kr; car and driver 122kr; ☏177). It's first-come, first-served, so in summer it's a good idea to arrive a couple of hours early. From Lødingen, it's just 4km to the E10 at a point midway between Harstad and Sortland. A second, but this time seasonal, car ferry runs from remote **Gryllefjord**, 110km west of the E6 well to the north of Narvik, to **Andenes** at the northern tip of the Vesterålen (early to late June & mid-to late Aug 2 daily, late June to early Aug 3 daily; 1hr 40min; passengers 100kr; car and driver 275kr). Reservations are strongly advised: phone, fax or email Andøy Reiseliv in Andenes (☏76 14 18 10, ⓕ76 14 76 20, ⓔa-turist@online.no). A third car ferry links the Lofoten islands with Vesterålen about halfway along the E10: the **Melbu**-**Fiskebøl** ferry makes the twenty-five minute journey across the Hadselfjord every ninety minutes or so (passengers 24kr; car and driver 68kr; ☏177).

Boats: the Hurtigrute and Hurtigbåt

Heading north from Bodø, the **Hurtigrute** coastal boat threads a scenic route up through Lofoten to the Vesterålen islands, where it calls at four places: **Stokmarknes** and **Sortland** in the south, **Risøyhamn** in the north and **Harstad** in the east. None of the four is an especially appealing destination, but workaday Risøyhamn is well on the way to Andenes, while Harstad is a regional centre and transport hub with a fine old church. Cruising southwards from Tromsø, the Hurtigrute follows the same itinerary, but in reverse. Scenically, the highlight is the **Raftsundet**, a narrow sound between Svolvær and Stokmarknes, off which branches the magnificent Trollfjord. Unfortunately, the Hurtigrute leaves Svolvær northbound at 10pm and so the Raftsundset is only visible during the period of the midnight sun (late May to mid–July); in the opposite direction, however, boats leave Stokmarknes at a much more convenient 3.15pm. This stretch of the journey takes three hours and in summer costs around 200kr for passengers and 297kr for cars.

The northbound Hurtigrute leaves Bodø for the Lofoten and Vesterålen islands at 3pm, and departs Tromsø heading south at 1.30am daily. Passenger tickets are reasonably priced, with the sixteen-hour journey from Bodø to Harstad costing around 700kr, Tromsø to Harstad (6hr 30min) 470kr in summer, with significant off-season discounts. The fare for transporting a car plus passenger is 1080kr from Bodø to Harstad, and 790kr from Tromsø to Harstad. Advance reservations are essential, but can be made just a few hours beforehand by phoning the captain – ask down at the harbour or at the port's tourist office for assistance. Special deals, which can reduce costs dramatically, are advertised at local tourist offices.

The main **Hurtigbåt** passenger express boat services are **Tromsø to Harstad** (2 daily; 2hr 45min; 365kr); **Narvik to Svolvær** in Lofoten (Mon–Fri & Sun 1 daily; 4hr; 286kr); and **Bodø to Svolvær** (Mon–Fri & Sun 1 daily; 3hr 30min; 250kr). In all cases, advance booking – most easily done via the local tourist office – is recommended.

Buses

A long-distance **bus** leaves **Narvik** once or twice daily to run along the E6 and then the E10 as far as Sortland. Here, you can usually change, after an hour or two's wait, for the onward bus to **Stokmarknes**, the Melbu-Fiskebøl ferry and then **Svolvær**. Once daily, another long-distance bus runs up the E6 from **Bodø** and **Fauske** to meet the **Bognes-Lødingen** car ferry. At Lødingen, there's a choice of two onward connecting buses: one service continues north to **Harstad**, the other heads west for **Stokmarknes**, the Melbu-Fiskebøl ferry and **Svolvær**. As examples of journey times, Narvik-Sortland takes three hours, Bodø-Sortland seven hours, and Bodø-Svolvær ten.

Most of the **local buses** across Vesterålen are operated by Nordtrafikk (☎177 in Nordland, otherwise ☎75 77 24 10). They tend to be adequate in the summer and very patchy out of season. One of the most useful services links Sortland with Andenes (1–3 daily; 2hr).

Harstad

Readily reached by car, bus and the Hurtigrute, **HARSTAD**, just 130km from Narvik, is easily the largest town on the Vesterålen islands. It's home to much of northern Norway's engineering industry, its sprawling docks a tangle of supply ships, repair yards and cold-storage plants spread out along the gentle slopes of the Vågsfjord. This may not sound too enticing, and it's true that Harstad wins few beauty contests, but the town does have the odd attraction, and if you're tired of sleepy Norwegian villages, it at least provides a bustling interlude.

The sights

The main item of interest, the **Trondenes kirke** (early June to mid-Aug guided tours on Mon at 10am, 2pm & 4pm; Tues, Wed & Sun at 2pm, 4pm & 6pm; Thurs & Fri 2pm & 4pm; 25kr), occupies a lovely leafy location beside the fjord 3km north of the town centre at the end of the slender Trondenes peninsula. To get there, take the local "Trondenes" **bus** (Mon–Sat 1 hourly; 10min), which leaves the station beside the tourist office and goes past the church, or take a taxi from the rank by the bus station. By car, follow Highway 83 north from the centre and watch for the signposted turning on the right. The original wooden church was built at the behest of King Øystein (of *rorbuer* fame; see box on p.301) at the beginning of the twelfth century and had the distinction of being the northernmost church in Christendom for several centuries. The present stone church was erected in the fourteenth century, its thick walls and the scant remains of its surrounding ramparts reflecting its dual function as a church and fortress, for these were troubled, violent times. After the exterior, stern of necessity, the warm and homely **interior** comes as a surprise. Here, the dainty arches of the rood screen lead into the choir, where each of the three altars is surmounted by a late medieval wooden triptych in bas-relief. Of the trio, the middle triptych is the most charming. Its main panel, depicting the holy family, is fairly predictable, but down below is a curiously cheerful sequence of biblical figures, each of whom wears a turban and sports a big, bushy and exquisitely carved beard.

Back outside, the **churchyard** is bordered by a dry-stone wall and contains a Soviet memorial to the eight hundred prisoners of war who died hereabouts in World War II at the hands of the Germans. There's another reminder of the war in the form of the **Adolfkanon** (Adolf Gun), a massive artillery piece stuck on a hilltop in the middle of the peninsula, to the north of the church. It's inside a military zone, and the obligatory **guided tour** (early June to mid-

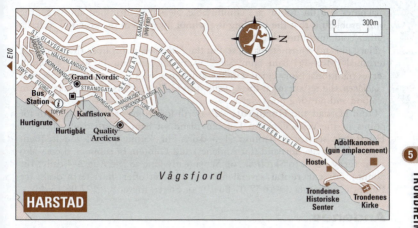

Aug daily at 11am, 1pm, 3pm & 5pm; 55kr), which begins at the gate of the compound, 1km from the gun, stipulates that you have to have your own vehicle to visit. Near the church, just south along the fjord, is the **Trondenes Historiske Senter** (Trondenes Historical Centre; mid-June to early Aug daily 10am–7pm; early Aug to mid-June Mon–Fri 10am–noon, Sun 10am–5pm, Sat closed; 65kr), a plush modern complex with exhibitions on the history of the locality – dioramas, mood music, incidental Viking artefacts and the like.

Frankly, downtown Harstad has little appeal, though the comings and goings of the ferry boats are a diversion. In late June, the ten-day **North Norway Arts Festival** (Festspillene i Nord-Norge; ⓦwww.festspillnn.no) provides a spark of interest with its concerts, drama and dance performances, though the town's hotels are full to bursting throughout the proceedings.

Practicalities

Although Harstad is easy to reach by bus or boat from Sortland, Tromsø and Narvik, it's actually something of a cul-de-sac for car drivers, who have to leave the E10 for the final thirty-kilometre drive north into town along Highway 83. Once you've arrived, however, you'll find almost everything you need in the immediate vicinity of the **bus station**: jetties for the **Hurtigbåt** passenger express and **Hurtigrute** coastal boat are just metres away, and next door is the **tourist office**, Torvet 8 (early June to mid-Aug Mon–Fri 7.30am–6pm, Sat & Sun 10am–3pm; mid-Aug to early June Mon–Fri 8am–4pm; ⓣ77 01 89 89, ⓦwww.destinationharstad.no, ⓔpost@destinationharstad.no), with a wide selection of tourist literature on Vesterålen.

As regards **accommodation**, the centre is dotted with modern chain hotels, among which the *Quality Arcticus Hotel* is a short walk from the Torvet at Havnegata 3 (ⓣ77 04 08 00, ⓕ77 04 08 01, ⓦwww.choicehotels.no; ❼, s/r ❹), in an attractive quayside location. A good alternative is the neat and trim *Grand Nordic Hotell*, a couple of minutes' walk from the Torvet at Strandgata 9 (ⓣ77 00 30 00, ⓕ77 00 30 01; ❻, s/r ❸). The HI **hostel** (June to late Aug; ⓣ77 07 28 00, ⓕ77 07 26 66; ⓔharstad.hostel@vandrerhjem.no; dorm beds 155k, doubles ❶; reception closed 4–6pm) has the advantage of a pleasant fjordside location, near the Trondenes kirke. It's easy to reach by the local "Trondenes" bus from the station (Mon–Sat 1 hourly; 10min), has self-catering facilities, washing machines and the rooms are comfortable, pleasantly furnished and large; the only problem is that the building is a school for most of the year and so has a rather cold, institutional feel.

Harstad is no gourmet's paradise, but the *Kaffistova*, across from the Hurtigbåt terminal (Mon–Fri 8am–6pm, Sat 9.30am–2.30pm, Sun 11.30am–4.30pm), serves traditional Norwegian standbys at inexpensive prices, and in the evening *Gallionen*, the restaurant at the *Quality Arcticus Hotel*, offers a reasonable line in seafood and pleasing fjord views.

From Harstad, the **Hurtigrute** sails north for Tromsø at 8am and south for points in the Vesterålen and Lofoten islands at 8am. Alternatively, there's a **Hurtigbåt** service to Tromsø (1–3 daily; 2hr 45min; 365kr) and frequent **buses** to Narvik, Sortland (for Andenes) and Lofoten. In summer, there's also a **car ferry** north to Skrolsvik, on Senja (early June to late Aug 2–4 daily; 1hr 50min). For **car rental**, several firms in Harstad offer short-term deals: try Europcar, Samagata 33 (☎77 01 86 10), or Hertz, Torvet 8 (☎77 06 13 46).

Andenes

Back on the **E10** about 30km south of Harstad, it's 50km southwest along the fjord to the turning for the Lødingen ferry (see p.293) and 50km more to Sortland (see p.299). Just before you reach Sortland, **Highway 82** begins its one-hundred-kilometre trek north, snaking along the craggy edges of the island of Hinnøya before crossing the bridge over to humdrum **Risøyhamn**, the only Hurtigrute stop on **Andøya**, the most northerly of the Vesterålen islands. Beyond Risøyhamn, the scenery is much less dramatic, as the mountains give way to hills in the west and a vast, peaty moor in the east. Highway 82 strips across this moorland offering panoramic views of the mountains back on the mainland, and ends its uneventful journey at the old fishing port of **ANDENES**. Here, lines of low-slung buildings lead up to the clutter of wooden warehouses and mini-boat repair yards that edge the harbour and its prominent breakwaters. "It is the fish, and that alone, that draws people to Andenes. The place itself has no other temptations," said the writer Poul Alm when he visited in 1944, and although this is too harsh a judgement today, the main emphasis, indeed, remains firmly nautical.

Among Scandinavians at least, Andenes is famous for its **whale safaris** (late May to mid-Sept, daily departures at 10.30am, with additional departures at 8.30am, 3.30pm & 5.30pm, subject to demand). These four- to five-hour cruises have a marine biologist on board to point out sperm, killer and minke whales, and dolphins, and claim a ninety-percent chance of a sighting. Tickets are 650kr per person including lunch (children 8–16 years, 450kr; 5–8 years, 350kr), and warm clothes are advised. It's best to **book** (☎76 11 56 00, ℻76 11 56 10, ✉booking@whalesafari.no) at least a day in advance, as the trips are popular, and indeed some are booked up weeks beforehand. The safaris begin with a guided tour of the **Hvalsenter** (Whale Centre; late May to mid-June & mid-Aug to mid-Sept daily 8am–4pm; mid-June to mid-Aug daily 8am–7.30pm; 60kr), close to the harbour, and actually a rather disappointing way to start. The museum's incidental displays on the life and times of the animal hardly fire the imagination, and neither does the massive, and deliberately dark and gloomy, display of a whale munching its way though a herd of squid.

The other recommended boat trip hereabouts is a cruise round the **bird island of Bleiksøya** (June to late Aug daily at 3.30pm, additional departures subject to demand; 1hr 30min; 250kr; bookings through the tourist office or direct ☎95 25 29 98), a pyramid-shaped hunk of rock populated by thousands of puffins, kittiwakes, razorbills and, sometimes, white-tailed eagles. Cruises

△ Honningsvåg, Nordkapp

leave from the jetty at **Bleik** (see below), an old and picturesque fishing hamlet around 7km southwest of Andenes, with a clear view of the islet; a local bus often makes the trip from Andenes to coincide with sailings. The tours cease in late August when the birds migrate south.

The Hisnakul and Polarmuseet

Andenes' indoor attractions consist of a couple of noteworthy museums: the **Hisnakul/Northern Lights Centre** (mid-June to mid-Aug daily noon–6pm; 40kr), in a refurbished timber warehouse near the Whale Centre, is a well-conceived museum-cum-exhibition centre that explores various facets of Andøya life. The centre is short on historical artefacts, plumping instead for imaginative displays such as the two hundred facial casts of local people made in 1994 and an assortment of giant replica bird beaks. There's also a comprehensive explanation of the northern lights (see box, p.320) – Andenes is a particularly good spot to see them – illustrated by first-class photographs and a slide show. The other museum, the **Polarmuseet** (Polar Museum; mid-June to mid-Aug daily 10am–6pm; 25kr), is beside the harbour too, located inside a modest little building with a pretty wooden porch. The interior is mostly dedicated to the Arctic knick-knacks accumulated by a certain Hilmar Nøis, an Andøy man who wintered on Svalbard no less than 38 times. The museum also sells tickets for the guided tour of the neighbouring **lighthouse** (same times; 25kr), a forty-metre-high maroon structure built in the 1850s.

Practicalities

Bisecting the town, Andenes' main street, Storgata, is long and straight and ends abruptly at the seafront. The **bus station** is a few metres to the east of Storgata, just back from the seafront, while the **tourist office** is on Storgata itself, again just back from the seafront (June–Aug daily 8am–8pm, Sept–May Mon–Fri 8am–4pm; ☎76 14 18 10, ⓦwww.whalesafari.no). It has a comprehensive range of local information and can make reservations for bird-island boat trips, whale safaris and the car ferry to Gryllefjord (there's a booking fee for the car ferry). It also has details of local **bicycle rental** and of **hiking trails** in the surrounding district.

Andenes has a fair sprinkling of inexpensive **accommodation** and several households offer **private rooms** – look out for the signs – but, considering how isolated a spot this is, you'd be well advised to make a reservation in advance. One of the nicest places to stay is the *Sjøgata Gjestehus*, Sjøgata 4 (☎76 14 16 37, ⓕ76 14 14 53, ⓔtovekhan@online.no; May–Sept; ❷), which provides simple but inexpensive rooms in a pleasant old timber building just 200m east of the tourist office. Less appealing is the nearby *Norlandia Lankanholmen Sjøhus*, on the seafront (☎76 14 28 50, ⓕ76 14 28 55; ❸), an unenticing modern complex comprising chalet-style huts, apartments and a very small and spartan HI **hostel** (same number; dorm beds 125kr, ❶; June–Aug). Of the town's two hotels, first choice is the *Norlandia Andrikken*, about 900m from the harbour at Storgata 53 (☎76 14 12 22, ⓕ76 14 19 33, ⓦwww.norlandia.no, ⓔandrikken@norlandia.no; ❺, s/r ❹). Although its main building is a routine modern concrete block with rooms to match, its **restaurant** is easily the best place in town – the Arctic char is superb, and prices are reasonable. For day-time snacks, head for *Jul. Nilsens Bakeri* (Mon–Fri 9am–3pm, Sat 9am–1pm), close to the bus station at Kong Hansgata 1.

If you don't fancy staying in Andenes, there's a prettier alternative 7km southwest along the coast in **BLEIK**, a comely hamlet of picturesque clapboard houses and white picket fences huddling between craggy hills and a long sandy beach. Here, the *Norlandia Havhusene Bleik* (☎76 14 57 40, ⓕ76 14 55 51; ❹) has several modern rooms, as well as a handful of *rorbuer* (❸–❻; see box, p.301).

Leaving Andenes by **bus**, there are daily services south to Risøyhamn and Sortland, though the latter are few and far between at the weekend. **Driving** south, Highway 82 eventually brings you to Lofoten. In summer, a **car ferry,** run by Senja Ferries (early June to late Aug 2–3 daily; 1hr 40min; passengers 100kr, cars 275kr; ☎76 14 66 00; ⓦwww.senjafergene.no), crosses to Gryllefjord on the mainland. From here, the 230km journey to Tromso can be easily done within a day, via Highway 86 to Finnsnes, then the scenic Highway 861 to **Botnhamn**, where a second car ferry crosses over to **Brensholmen** (June to late Aug 4–7 daily; 35min; passengers 50kr, cars 130kr), a few kilometres from the *Sommarøy Kurs og Feriesenter* (see p.327).

Sortland to Melbu

An unappetizing modern sprawl along the shore, **Sortland** is – by virtue of its location near the bridge linking the islands of Hinnøya and Langøya – something of a **transport hub**, and bus passengers usually have to change here for the onward journey south to Stokmarknes and Lofoten, or to catch the local bus north to Andenes (see p.296), which originates here. The **tourist office** at Kjøpmannsgata 2 (mid-June to late Aug Mon–Fri 10am–6pm, Sat & Sun 11am–5pm; Sept to mid-June Mon–Fri 10am–5pm; ☎76 11 14 80 ⓔvesteraalen.reiseliv@online.no, ⓦwww.visitvesteralen.com), is in the centre of town, a couple of hundred metres from the Hurtigrute quay and a five- to ten-minute walk from the bus station.

Stokmarknes and the Trollfjord

The **E10** hugs the shoreline for 30km as it pushes southwest from Sortland, before encountering the two bridges that span the straits between Langøya and **STOKMARKNES**, on Hadseløya. The longer bridge is equipped with a high frequency sound device that is supposed to stop Langøya's foxes in their tracks, keeping Hadseløya fox-free. Pocket-sized Stokmarknes is itself unremarkable, though its shoreline setting is pleasant enough and you can sample the delights of the **Hurtigrutemuseet** (mid-May to mid-June & mid-Aug to mid-Sept daily noon–4pm; mid-June to mid-Aug daily 10am–6pm; mid-Sept to mid-May Mon–Fri 2.30–4pm, Sat & Sun noon–4pm; 80kr), a museum devoted entirely to the history of the Hurtigrute, with a genuine 1950s ferry, the M/S Finnmarken, on display. The museum is located in the town centre just back from the rangy quayside, where there's a **statue** of Richard With, the skipper responsible for dreaming up the coastal ferry in the 1890s. Indeed, the main reason to stop off in Stokmarknes is to catch the **Hurtigrute** coastal boat south to Svolvær via the Trollfjord. The boat leaves at 3.15pm, sailing down the narrow sound, the **Raftsundet**, which separates the harsh, rocky shanks of Hinnøya and Austvågøya. Towards the southern end of the sound, the ship usually makes a short detour to the **Trollfjord**, a majestic tear in the landscape just 2km long. Slowing to a gentle chug, the vessels inch up the narrow gorge, smooth stone towering high above and blocking out the light. At its head, the boats effect a nautical three-point turn and then crawls back to rejoin the main waterway. It's very atmospheric, and the effect is perhaps even more extraordinary when the weather is up. The Hurtigrute will not, however, enter the Trollfjord when there's danger of a rock fall, which is most likely in spring: check at Stokmarknes tourist office before embarkation. The cruise from Sortland to Svolvær takes three hours and costs 200kr per passenger, 300kr for cars.

Most facilities in Stokmarknes are conveniently close: **buses** pull in near the harbourfront **tourist office** (mid-June to late Aug Mon–Fri 10am–5pm; ☎76 15 00 00), which has details of what little local **accommodation** there is. The obvious choice is the *Hurtigrutens Hus* (☎76 15 29 99, ℉76 15 29 95, ⓦwww.hurtigrutenshus.com; ❺), a brassy, modern hotel-cum-conference centre plonked on the Børøya islet, about fifteen minutes' walk from the tourist office and at the end of the first of two bridges back to Langøya.

From Stokmarknes, it's 15km south along the E10 to **MELBU**, where there's a **car ferry** to Fiskebøl on Lofoten (every 90min; 25min; 24kr for passengers, 68kr for a driver and car; ☎177), though this is due to be replaced by a tunnel in 2004. Melbu is also on the main bus routes to Svolvær from Fauske, Narvik and Tromsø.

The Lofoten islands

A skeletal curve of mountainous rock stretched out across the Norwegian Sea and fretted by myriad seastacks and skerries, the **Lofoten** islands have been the focal point of northern Norway's winter fishing from time immemorial. At the turn of the year, cod migrate from the Barents Sea to spawn here, where the cold of the water is tempered by the Gulf Stream. The season only lasts from February to April, but fishing impinges on all aspects of island life year-round. At almost every harbour stand the massed ranks of wooden racks used for drying the cod, burgeoning and odiferous in winter, empty in summer like so many abandoned climbing frames.

Sharing the same history, but better known and more beautiful than their Vesterålen neighbours, the Lofoten islands have everything from sea-bird colonies in the south to beaches and fjords in the north. The traditional approach is by boat from Bodø bringing you face to face with the islands' most striking feature, the towering peaks of the **Lofotenveggen** (Lofoten Wall), a 160-kilometre stretch of mountains, whose jagged teeth bite into the skyline, trapping a string of tiny fishing villages tight against the shore. The mountains are set so close together that on first inspection there seems to be no way through, but in fact the islands are riddled with straights, sounds and fjords.

The Lofoten islands have their own relaxed pace, and are perfect for a simple, uncluttered few days. For somewhere so far north, the weather can be exceptionally mild: summer days can be spent sunbathing on the rocks or hiking and biking around the superb coastline; and when it rains, as it frequently does, life focuses on the *rorbuer*, where freshly caught fish are cooked over wood-burning stoves, stories are told and time gently wasted. If that sounds rather contrived, in a sense it is – the way of life here is to some extent preserved like this for tourists. That said, it's rare to find anyone who isn't less than completely enthralled by it all.

The **E10** weaves a scenic route across Lofoten, running the 168km from **Fiskebøl** in the north to **Å** in the south, linking island to island by bridge and causeway, and occasionally tunnelling through the mountains. The highway passes through or within a few kilometres of all the islands' main villages, amongst which **Henningsvær** and **Å** are breathtakingly beautiful, with **Stamsund** coming close behind. All three make great bases for further explorations on foot or by boat, with abundant island cruises, sea-rafting, fishing excursions and bird-watching trips on offer. In addition, scores of places rent out fishing **boats** and equipment, though, because of the strong currents loc-

Staying in Rorbu

Right across Lofoten, **rorbuer** (fishermen's shacks) are rented out to tourists for both overnight stays and longer periods. King Øystein ordered the first *rorbuer* to be built round the coastline of the island of Austvågøya, in the twelfth century, to provide shelter for visiting fishermen who had previously been obliged to sleep under their upturned boats. Traditionally, they were built on the shore, often on poles sticking out of the sea, and usually coloured with a red paint based on cod-liver oil. They consisted of two sections, a sleeping and eating room and a smaller storage area. The name *rorbu* is derived from *ror*, "to row" and *bu*, literally "dwelling". Older islanders still ask "Will you row this winter?", meaning "Will you go fishing this winter?"

At the peak of the fisheries in the 1930s, some 30,000 men were accommodated in *rorbuer*, but during the 1960s the fishing boats became more comfortable and many fishermen preferred to sleep aboard. Most of the original *rorbuer* disappeared years ago, and whereas before the 1960s visitors could expect a *rorbu* to be in use as a fisherman's shack, nowadays they are built by the dozen, with the tourist trade specifically in mind. At their best, they are comfortable and cosy seashore cabins, sometimes a well-planned conversion of an original rorbu with bunk beds and wood-fired stoves; at their worst, they are little better than prefabricated hutches or garages in the middle of nowhere. Most have space for between four and six guests and the charge for a hut averages around 600kr per night – though some cost as little as 400kr, while others rise to about 1000kr. Similar rates are charged for the islands' **Sjøhus** (literally sea-houses), originally the large quayside halls where the catch was processed and the workers slept. Some of the original *sjøhus* have been cleverly converted into attractive apartments with self-catering facilities, many more into dormitory-style accommodation – though again the quality varies enormously. A full list of *rorbuer* and *sjøhus* is given in the *Lofoten Info-Guide*, a free pamphlet that you can pick up at any local tourist office.

aly, you should always seek advice about the conditions and stay close to the shore. Back on land, the **hiking** is good, with quiet byroads delving into the heart of the landscape, and there's plenty of scope for **mountaineering**. Austvågøya has the finest climbing, with some of the best ascents in Norway, and there's a prestigious climbing school at Henningsvær. There's more walking and yet more solitude on mountainous **Værøy** and flatter, more agricultural **Røst**, a pair of inhabited islands to the south of Å, reachable by ferry from Moskenes and Bodø.

As regards accommodation, the Lofoten islands have a sprinkling of hotels, a handful of which are first-rate (though some are blandly modern), as well as four HI hostels and numerous campsites, along with the local speciality, the rorbuer (see box, above). For information, a tourist website covers the whole of Lofoten (ⓦwww.lofoten-tourist.no; Ⓔtourist@lofoten-tourist.no), while timetable enquiries for all public transport in Nordland is on ☏177 (ⓦwww.177nordland.com).

Transport to and around the Lofoten islands

The Lofoten islands can be reached by car ferry, Hurtigbåt passenger express boat and the Hurtigrute coastal boat, but once you've got there you'll find **public transport** thin on the ground. What local **bus** services there are stick almost exclusively to the **E10**, the islands' only main road, which covers the

168km from Fiskebøl to Å. Leave the main highway, however, and you'll most-ly have to **walk** – hardly an onerous task in such beautiful surroundings – or, if you're lucky, hitch a ride from one village to the next on a local **boat**. Alternatively, **bike rental** is available at the Svolvær tourist office, some hostels and at many other hotels and guest houses: the booklet *Cycling in Lofoten* gives details of bike routes around the islands, and is sold at all tourist offices.

If you have your own **vehicle**, village-hopping is easy and quick, but it's only when you leave the car and head off into the landscape that the real character of Lofoten begins to reveal itself; allow time for at least one walk or sea trip. Conversely, if you don't have a vehicle and want to reach the islands' remoter spots, it's worth considering renting a car, an inexpensive option if a few people share the cost. There are local **car rental** outlets at Svolvær, Stamsund and Svolvær and Leknes airports, where special short-term deals can bring costs down to around 600kr a day. Incidentally, speed checks are frequent, with on-the-spot fines kicking off at 1000kr.

Car ferries

From the mainland to the Lofoten islands, the principal car ferry service, oper-ated by *Ofotens og Vesteraalens Dampskibsselskab* (OVDS; ☎177; ⓦwww.ovds.no), connects tiny **Skutvik**, 40km west of the E6 midway between Fauske and Narvik, with **Svolvær** (June to mid-Aug 8 daily; mid-Aug to May 2–3 daily; 2hr; car & driver 200kr, passengers 60kr; ☎177). Queues are commonplace and, as it's a first-come first-served ferry, it's best to arrive about two hours before departure to make sure of a place.

A second car ferry service, also operated by OVDS, links **Bodø** with three destinations in the southern peripheries of Lofoten (typically 1 daily): the boat usually calls first at the tiny port of **Moskenes**, just a few kilometres from the end of the E10, before sailing on to one or both of the small islands of **Røst** and **Værøy**. The trip from Bodø to Moskenes takes about four hours; allow a further two hours to Værøy, and two more for Røst, and be prepared for a rough crossing. The fare from Bodø to Moskenes is 125kr for passengers, 440kr for a car and driver. Advance reservations can be made through Bodø tourist office for a fee of 100kr; otherwise drivers should arrive at least two hours before departure to make sure of a place.

If you're driving to the Lofoten islands on the **E10**, which branches off the E6 north of Narvik, you'll use a third car ferry linking **Melbu** on the Vesterålen islands with **Fiskebøl** on Lofoten (every 90min; 25min; 24kr for passengers, 68kr for a car and driver; ☎177), though a tunnel will replace this ferry in 2004.

Boats: the Hurtigrute and Hurtigbåt

The northbound **Hurtigrute** leaves Bodø daily at 3pm calling at two ports in the Lofoten islands – Stamsund and Svolvær – before nudging through the Raftsundet en route to Stokmarknes. In summer, the passenger fare for the four and a half hour cruise from Bodø to Stamsund is about 400kr (car and driver 690kr), and 430kr (car and driver 740kr) for the six-hour journey to Svolvær. Advance reservations for cars are essential, though these can be made up to a few hours before departure by phoning the captain – ask down at the harbour or at the port's tourist office for assistance. Special deals, which can reduce costs dramatically, are commonly advertised at local tourist offices.

Hurtigbåt passenger express boats operate from **Bodø to Svolvær** (Mon–Fri & Sun 1 daily; 3hr 30min; 250kr) and **Narvik to Svolvær** (Mon–Fri & Sun 1 daily; 4hr; 286kr). In both cases, advance booking (via the local tourist office) is recommended.

Buses

There are three long-distance **bus** services linking the mainland with Lofoten. One is from **Fauske** to **Svolvær** (1 daily; 8hr 30min; one-way 433kr) via the Bognes–Lødingen and Melbu-Fiskebøl ferries; you can also start the journey in **Bodø**. A second connects **Narvik** with Svolvær (1–2 daily; 7–9hr; 370kr) via the Melbu–Fiskebøl ferry, while a third plys between **Tromsø** and Svolvær (Mon–Fri 1 daily; 15hr), though you have to change onto a local bus and wait for three and a half hours, just north of Narvik at the Bjerkvik crossroads.

On Lofoten, there are at least a couple of **local buses** between most of the larger villages on weekdays, but often nothing at all on Sunday, and sometimes Saturday too. In summer, buses run more frequently and on more routes, with one particularly useful service travelling south from Svolvær to Leknes and Å (late June to mid-Aug 1 daily). To avoid getting stuck, pick up a bus and ferry timetable from any island tourist office or bus station.

Planes

Flights leave Bodø for the **Lofoten** airports – or rather airstrips – at Svolvær and Leknes four to seven times a day. In addition, there are one or two flights a day from Bodø and Leknes to Røst: Værøy does not have an airstrip. The flights are operated by Widerøe, an SAS subsidiary, and tickets can be purchased at any travel agent or SAS agent as well as the *Radisson SAS Hotel* in Bodø; return fares from Bodø to Svolvær cost around 1200kr.

Note also that whereas Svolvær airport is merely 5km from town, Leknes airport is miles from anywhere you might want to visit, and the onward taxi will cost a fortune. There is car rental at both Svolvær (Avis (℡76 07 11 40; Europcar ℡76 06 83 33; Hertz ℡76 07 07 20) and Leknes (Europcar ℡76 05 40 70; Hertz ℡76 08 18 44), with good-value short-term deals from around 600kr per day.

Svolvær

By and large, **SVOLVÆR**, on the east coast of Austvågøya, the largest of the islands, is a rather disappointing introduction to Lofoten. The region's administrative and transport centre, it has all the bustle but little of the charm of the other island towns, though it does have more accommodation and better restaurants than its neighbours. The only attraction of any real interest in the town itself is the **Lofoten Krigsminnemuseum**, close to the Hurtigrute quay (War Museum; mid-June to mid-Aug Mon–Fri 10am–4pm & 6.30–10pm, Sat 11am–2pm & 6.30–10pm, Sun noon–3pm & 6.30–10pm; 50kr), which chronicles the British commando raids on Lofoten in 1941 (see box overleaf) by means of photographs and original artefacts.

Otherwise, you're better off heading out of town to explore Svolvær's dramatic environs on one of two local **boat trips**. Every day several cruises (return trip 3hr; 300kr; buy tickets on board) leave Svolvær for the **Trollfjord**, an impossibly narrow, two-kilometre-long stretch of water (see p.299). Alternatively, consider a stroll on the pretty islet of **Skrova**, just offshore from Svolvær. Its only settlement trails along a slender rocky spit, attached by a causeway to the main body of island, which is dominated by the steep Mount Høgskrova (258m). The Svolvær–Skutvik ferry (see above for times) usually calls at Skova, taking just thirty minutes and costing 25kr each way; ferry times almost always make a day-trip feasible.

Svolvær also boasts one of the archipelago's most famous **climbs**, the haul up to the top of the **Svolværgeita** (the Svolvær goat), a twin-pronged peak that rises high above the E10 to the northeast of town. The lower slopes of the mountain are hard enough, but the last 40m – up the horns of the "goat" – require considerable expertise. Daring mountaineers complete the thrill by jumping from one pinnacle to the other.

Arrival and information

Ferries from Svolvær dock about 1km west of the town centre, whereas the Hurtigrute docks in the centre, a brief walk from the **bus station** and the busy **tourist office**, just off the main town square near the harbour (late May to mid-June Mon–Fri 9am–4pm & Sat 10am–2pm; mid- to late June Mon–Fri 9am–4pm & 5–7.30pm, Sat 10am–2pm, Sun 4–7pm; late June to mid-Aug Mon–Fri 9am–4pm & 5–9.30pm, Sat 9am–4pm & 5–8pm, Sun 10am–9.30pm; mid-Aug to late Aug Mon–Fri 9am–7pm, Sat 10am–2pm; Sept to mid-May Mon–Fri 9am–4pm; T76 06 98 00). It has maps, accommodation lists and public transport details, and can reserve accommodation anywhere in Lofoten for a 50kr booking fee, and ferry tickets for a 130kr fee.

Accommodation

Svolvær's smartest **accommodation** is the gleaming *Rica Hotel Svolvær* (T76 07 22 22, F76 07 20 01, Wwww.rica.no; ④), whose various buildings, in the style of the traditional *sjøhus*, occupy a prime location on a tiny islet at the end of a causeway in the middle of the harbour. At the east end of the harbour, a longer causeway leads out to the slender islet of Svinøya, where accommodation at *Svinøya Rorbuer* (T76 06 99 30, F76 07 48 98, Wwww.svinoya.no) ranges from plain and simple *rorbuer* (❸) through to deluxe en-suite cabins (❼). Back in town, you can find more modest rooms at the long-established *Svolvær Sjøhus*, by the seashore at the foot of Parkgata (T76 07 03 36, F76 07 64 63, Wwww.svolver-sjohuscamp.no; ❷): to get there from the square, turn right up the hill along Vestfjordgata and it's to the right, past the library. Svolvær also has a handful of **hotels**, for the most part surly modern blocks that hardly set the architectural pulse racing, though the *Norlandia Royal Hotel* (T76 07 12 00, F76 07 08 50, Wwww.norlandia.no; ④), has comfortable rooms and a convenient location, a few metres up from the main square at the end of Torggata.

Restaurants and bars

Svolvær has a reasonable selection of **bars** and **restaurants**, the best you'll find on Lofoten. The *Café Bacalao*, down on the quay, is a spacious café-restaurant with snappy service and a menu that mixes Mediterranean and Norwegian

The British commando raids of 1941

Although the Germans occupied Norway in April 1940, it wasn't until a year later that the British prepared their response: it took the form of a **commando raid** on Lofoten. The aims were threefold: firstly, it was thought that a successful attack would boost British morale; secondly, it was a way of tying German troops down to garrison duty along the Norwegian coast; and thirdly, the British wanted to destroy as much of Lofoten's plentiful supply of herring oil as they could, to prevent the Germans using it as a raw material in the manufacture of their explosives.

In April 1941, the first commando raid hit Svolvær, Stamsund and Henningsvær, whilst a second, a few months later, attacked Reine and nearby Sørvangen at the southern end of Lofoten. The first was the more successful, bagging 200 prisoners and destroying hundreds of barrels of oil, but the Germans extracted a bitter revenge by burning down the houses of all those Norwegians deemed to have been sympathetic to the invaders.

cuisine with flair and imagination: lunches, and main courses in the evening, hover around 80kr, while huge salads cost 125kr. It serves excellent coffee too, and at night turns into the town's liveliest **bar**, jam-packed at the weekend. In addition, the restaurants of the *Rica Hotel Svolvær* and the *Svinøya Rorbuer* are both highly competent, with seafood their forte. The classiest restaurant, however, is *Du Verden*, in the centre at JE Paulsens gate 12 (☎76 07 70 99), where a creative menu features the freshest of local ingredients. In the evening, prices are high, but not unreasonable, and at lunch time the place is a snip – try the mouthwatering fish soup.

Kabelvåg

With its pretty wooden centre draped around the shore of a narrow and knobbly inlet, **KABELVÅG** is immediately more appealing than Svolvær, 6km east along the coast. The most important village on Lofoten from Viking times until the early years of the twentieth century, Kabelvåg was once the centre of the fishery and home to the islands' first *rorbuer*, built in 1120, as well as the first inn, which dates from 1792. The late nineteenth-century **Vågan kirke**, a big and breezy timber church beside the E10 on the eastern edge of the village, is a reminder of those busier times, its hangar-like interior built to accommodate a congregation of over a thousand.

The village holds other attractions too, primarily the **Lofotmuseet**, located 1500m west of the centre by the seashore in the neighbourhood of Storvågan (Lofoten Museum; May Mon–Fri 9am–3pm, Sat & Sun 11am–3pm; June–Aug daily 9am–6pm; Sept Mon–Fri 9am–3pm & Sun 11am–3pm; Sept–April Mon–Fri 9am–3pm; 40kr, but with a Storvågan multi-ticket including the gallery and aquarium 110kr). It traces the history of the islands' fisheries and displays the definitive collection of fishing equipment and other cultural paraphernalia. Nearby, also in Storvågan, is the **Galleri Espolin** (early June & late Aug daily 10am–6pm; mid-June to mid-Aug daily 10am–7pm; Sept–April Mon–Fri & Sun 11am–3pm; May daily 11am–3pm; ⓦwww.galleri-espolin.no; 70kr), which features paintings and sketches by Kaare Espolin Johnson (1907–1994), a renowned Norwegian artist of romantic inclination, who specialized in Arctic images and imagery. Storvågan's third attraction is the **Lofotakvariet** (aquarium; same times as the Galleri; 70kr), displaying a wide variety of Atlantic species.

Kabelvåg also has a good range of **outdoor pursuits** on offer. The main operator is *Jan's Adventure*, Rødmyrveien 26 (☎76 07 89 10, ⓕ76 07 19 55, ⓔpost@lofoten-aktiv.no, ⓦwww.lofoten-aktiv.no), who can organize everything from sea-kayaking and trekking through to skiing, fishing and cycling trips. The sea-kayaking courses are especially good, with a two-day training course (1150kr all-inclusive), followed by a three-day paddle round Lofoten (4200kr for both). Divers should contact *Lofotdykk*, at Kaiveien 15, in the centre of Kabelvåg (☎941 86 432, ⓕ76 07 82 71, ⓦwww.lofotdykk.no), for all manner of marine activities, including sea-rafting, Orca-watching safaris (Oct–Dec) and, of course, diving.

Practicalities

On weekdays there's a regular hourly **bus** service from Svolvær to Kabelvåg, but only a couple of buses a day on Saturdays and Sundays. Buses drop you near the centre of the village, where the pleasant *Kabelvåg Hotel* (☎76 07 88 00, ⓕ76 07 80 03; ⓦwww.dvgl.no; ❺) occupies an old timber building near the harbour. A second appealing choice is *Nyvågar Rorbuhotell* in Storvågan (☎76 06 97 00, ⓕ76 06 97 01, ⓦwww.top.no; ❻ per *rorbu*), comprising a scattering of smart, seashore, four-bedded *rorbuer*. Kabelvåg also has a very basic HI **hostel** in the school building east of the centre, 500m from the E10 (☎76 06 98 98, ⓕ76 06 98 81, ⓔkabelvaag.hostel@vandrerhjem.no; dorm beds 210kr, doubles ❷; June to mid-Aug), but a better bet, perhaps, is the well-equipped house run by diving-specialists *Lofotdykk*, (see p.305 for details), which comes complete with a sauna and outdoor *badestamp*; basic quads here go for 120kr per person per night.

As regards **food,** the *Krambua Restaurant*, in the *Kabelvåg Hotel*, serves good seafood, but the most enjoyable spot in town is the *Artcafé Ara Ara*, Torggata 10 (daily 7.30am–2pm & 7pm–1am). Its kicks off the day with filling, tasty breakfasts and continues at lunch and in the evening with good quality Norwegian food before turning into a bar at night, where you can sample the local Nordlandspils beer; the well-known *Kabelvåg Kunstskole* (Kabelvåg Art School) exhibits a selection of its students' work on the café's walls.

Henningsvær

Heading southwest from Kabelvag, it's 11km on the E10 to the 8km-long turning for **HENNINGSVÆR**, the most beguiling of headland villages, a cobweb of cramped and twisting lanes lined with brightly painted wooden houses. These frame a tiny inlet that literally cuts the place in half, forming a sheltered, picture-postcard harbour. Despite the regular coach parties who brave the narrowness of the two high-arched bridges into the village and swamp the 500 or so locals, Henningsvær is well worth an overnight stay.

Easily the smartest **hotel** is the quayside *Henningsvær Bryggehotell* (☎76 07 47 50, ⓕ76 07 47 30, ⓦwww.dvgl.no; ❺), an attractive modern building in traditional style right on the waterfront, but the more economical choice is the frugal *Den siste Viking*, Misværveien 10 (☎76 07 49 11, ⓔpostmaster@ nordnorskklatreskole.no; ❶), which provides unadorned lodging also right in the centre. It doubles as the home of Lofoten's best **mountaineering school**, Nord Norsk Klatreskole (same number; ⓦwww.nordnorskklatreskole.no), which operates a range of all-inclusive climbing holidays in the mountains near Henningsvær, catering for various degrees of fitness and experience. Prices vary depending on the trip, but a three-day, one-climb-a-day package costs in the region of 4200kr per person, including equipment, food and accommodation. Their prospectus is only printed in Norwegian, but they'll gladly discuss the various options with you in English if you drop by, or check out their webpage.

For the less athletic, **fishing trips** can be booked down at the harbour (a morning or afternoon's excursion costs around 300kr), or you could visit the **Galleri Lofotens Hus**, on Hjellskjæret (daily: March noon–3pm, late May to early June & mid-Aug 10am–6pm, mid-June to early Aug daily 9am–9pm, late Aug 11am–4pm; 60kr), which exhibits (and sells) the work of contemporary artist Karl Erik Harr. Also on display is a competent selection of late nineteenth- and twentieth-century Lofoten paintings by artists such as Einar Berge, Adelsteen Normann, Gunnar Berg and Otto Sinding – you can't miss his whopping *Funeral in Lofoten* of 1886 – plus historic and contemporary photographs and slides mostly of the islands. Henningsvær's Arctic light and the might of the mountains has long attracted Norwegian painters, making it somewhat of an artistic centre and, indeed, there's more art for sale – plus ceramics and glassware – at the nearby **Engelskmannsbrygga**, Dreyersgate 1 (Jan to mid-June & mid-Aug to Dec Tues–Sun noon–4pm, mid-June to mid-Aug daily 10am–6pm; free).

For **food**, the *Klatrekafeen*, at *Den siste Viking*, serves up a good range of

Norwegian standbys from 80kr, plus soup and salads and some ethnic options, all washed down with first-rate coffee. Much classier, however, is the waterside *Fiskekrogen Restaurant*, Dreyersgate 19 (℡76 07 46 52), where the seafood in general, and the fish soup in particular, are simply superb; main courses from 160kr.

Vestvågøy: Stamsund and around

It's the next large island to the southwest of Austvågøya, **Vestvågøy**, that captivates many travellers to Lofoten. This is due in no small part to the laid-back charm of **STAMSUND**, whose older buildings string along the rocky, fretted seashore in an amiable jumble of crusty port buildings, wooden houses and *rorbuer*. It also boasts its own modern art gallery – *Galleri 2*, 100m from the Hurtigrute dock (mid-June to mid-Aug Tues–Sun noon–4pm & 7–9.30pm; 20kr) – and in winter the mountains that back the village attract hundreds of snowboarders.

Stamsund is the first port at which the **Hurtigrute** coastal boat docks on its way north from Bodø, and is much the best place to stay on the island. Getting there **by bus** from Austvågøya is reasonably easy too, with several buses making the trip daily, though you do have to change at **Leknes**, the rather dull administrative centre, 15km to the west and the site of the airport. **By car**, the quickest way to Stamsund from Svolvær is to turn south off the E10 down Highway 815, a scenic 40km-long coastal drive.

Stamsund's **tourist office** is situated just 200m from the ferry dock (mid-June to mid-Aug daily 6–9.30pm; ℡76 05 69 96), though you'll get as much advice at the friendly, if rather chaotic, HI **hostel** (℡76 08 93 34, ℉76 08 97 39; late Dec to mid-Oct; dorm beds 90kr, doubles ❶), about 1km down the road from the port. The hostel consists of several *rorbuer* and a *sjøhus* perched over a bonny, pin-sized bay, and has a washing machine and tumble-drier, and self-catering facilities. You can rent bikes here at 100kr a day, and the warden is very knowledgeable on everything about Vestvågøy, from cycling through to hiking and fishing. The **fishing** is, in fact, first-class: the hostel rents out rowing boats and lines to take out on the (usually still) water, or you can take an organized fishing trip for just 200kr. Afterwards you can cook your catch on the wood-burning stoves and eat alfresco on the verandah overlooking the bay. A more upmarket option is *Skjærbrygga* (℡76 05 46 00, ℉76 05 46 01, ✉firmapost@skjaerbrygga.no, ⓦwww.skjaerbrygga.no; ❺), a combined **hotel**, *sjøhus* and *rorbuer*, right in the centre of Stamsund by the harbour. Most of its nineteen *rorbuer* (❻) are tastefully revamped old cabins dating from the 1940s, some are more modern and all are comfortable. Formerly a warehouse, *Skjærbrygga* has been pleasantly renovated and contains a café and a very good **restaurant**, with main courses featuring local ingredients and costing around 150kr. Cheaper *rorbuer* can be found 3km west along the coast in the hamlet of **STEINE**, where the cosy if rather spartan *Steine Rorbuer & Hytter* (℡ & ℉76 08 92 83; ❶) snuggle up to the seashore.

The west coast of Vestvågøy

Admirers of wild scenery should consider heading out to Vestvågøy's blustery **west coast**, where a few hardy fishing villages hung on until the 1950s, when they finally abandoned the land to the birds, the wind and the sea plus a handful of summer residents. The coast is accessed by a series of turnings off the **E10** as it slices across Vestvågøy's drab central valley: you'll need your own car, however, as cyclists face stiff gradients and often strong winds and, although the bus service along the E10 itself is reasonable, there are no regular buses off it to the west coast.

Beginning in Stamsund, the first part of the excursion is the hilly 15km-trip to the E10 at Leknes (see p.303). Keep going north along the E10 for another 3km to the first signposted byroad, which leads the 10km over the hills, along the seashore and through a narrow tunnel to **UTAKLEIV**, perched on the edge of a wide and windy bay and surrounded by austere cliffs. There's more stern scenery at the end of the next turning off the E10, this time at **UNSTAD**, a huddle of houses in a diminutive river valley set beneath the mountains and with wide views out to sea. From here, a popular 9km-long **hiking trail** runs past mountains and lakes on one side and the surging ocean on the other, to **EGGUM**. This tiny hamlet is an especially pretty spot, its handful of houses clinging onto a precarious headland dwarfed by the mountains behind it and with a whopping pebble beach in front. Eggum can also be reached by road from the E10 – it's the next turning along from the Unstad road – but before you reach its turn-off, you'll pass the flashy **Lofotr Vikingmuseum,** 14km from Leknes (mid-May to Aug daily 10am–7pm, Sept to mid-May Fri 1–3pm; 80kr; Ⓦ www.lofotr.no). Inspired by the accidental discovery of the site of a Viking chieftain's house by a local farmer in 1981, the museum contains a reconstructed 83-metre Viking house, with flickering lights, wood tar smells and so forth adding to the atmosphere. There's also a permanent exhibition of Viking artefacts found in the vicinity, and the boathouse contains a full-size replica of the Gokstad ship displayed in Oslo (see p.93).

South to Nusfjord

By any standard the next two islands of the archipelago, **Flakstadøya** (known to the Vikings as "Vargfot" or wolf's paw, due to its shape), and **Moskenesøya**, are extraordinarily beautiful. As the Lofoten islands taper towards their southerly conclusion, the rearing peaks of the Lofotenveggen crimp the sea-shredded coastline providing a scenic backdrop to a necklace of tiny fishing villages. The E10 travels along almost all of this shoreline, leaving Leknes to tunnel west under the sound separating Vestvågøy from Flakstadøya (toll 80kr). About 20km from Leknes, an even more improbable byroad somehow wiggles the 6km through the mountains to **NUSFJORD**, an extravagantly picturesque fishing village in a tight and forbidding cove. Unlike many fishermen's huts elsewhere in Lofoten, which were erected in response to tourist demand rather than that of the fishing fleet, the ones here are the genuine nineteenth-century article, and the general store, with its wooden floors and antique appearance, fits in nicely too. Inevitably, it's tourism that keeps the local economy afloat, and the village is firmly on the day-trippers' itinerary, but it's still a beguiling place, with **accommodation** available in more than thirty comfortably refurbished *rorbuer*. The one-bedroom versions hold two to four people (❷), the two-bedroom ones have space for five (from 800kr): advance reservations are strongly advised with *Nusfjord Rorbuanlegg* (☎76 09 30 20, Ⓕ76 09 33 78, Ⓦwww.rica.no). There's also a **bar-restaurant**.

Onto Hamnøy and Reine

Back on the E10, it's 5km beyond the Nusfjord turn-off to the **Flakstad kirke**, a distinctive onion-domed, red timber church built of driftwood in 1780: its brightly painted pulpit is another fine example of Gottfried Ezechiel's work (see the Bodin kirke, p.281). The church announces the beginning of **RAMBERG**, the island's administrative centre – if that's what you can call the smattering of services (garage, supermarket and suchlike) straggling the sandy

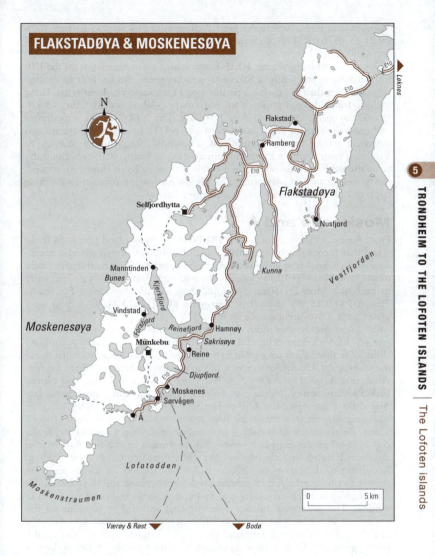

beach. Pressing on south, over the first of several narrow bridges, you're soon on **Moskenesøya**, where the road squirms across the mouth of the Reinefjord, hopping from islet to islet to link the fishing villages of Hamnøy, on the north side of the inlet, with Reine to the south. Both villages boast impossibly picturesque settings and **HAMNØY** also lays claim to an excellent restaurant, *Hamnøy Mat & Vinbu* (☎76 09 21 45; early March to Sept), whose short menu provides traditional Norwegian cuisine at its best: there's first-rate seafood, of course, not to mention cods' tongues – an island delicacy – and the rarely seen, but delicious, sago pudding. Hamnøy also possesses some very plain *rorbuer* – *Hamnøy Rorbuer* (☎76 09 23 20, ⊕76 09 21 54, ❷ – ❸) – though far more appealing are those on the tiny islet of **Sakrisøya**, midway between

Hamnøy and Reine, where the pretty yellow cabins of *Sakrisøy Rorbuer* (☎76 09 21 43, ⓕ76 09 24 88, ⓔsakrisøy@lofoten-info.no, Ⓦwww.rorbu.as; ➋ – ➌) are well kept and cosy.

Despite its stunning setting, **REINE**, stuck on a promontory just off the E10 immediately to the south of Sakrisøya, is rather seedy and has little to recommend it other than as a useful departure point for a variety of **boat trips**. These include midnight sun cruises (late May to mid-July 1 weekly; 5hr; 420kr), coastal voyages (June to mid-Aug 1 weekly; 4hr; 300kr), fishing expeditions and excursions to the Moskenstraumen (see p.311). In summer, there are also passenger ferries up the **Reinefjord**, a splendid, forty-minute journey to Vindstad, from where a handsome ninety-minute hiking trail leads along the steep shores of the Bunesfjord, then climbs a ridge to reach Bunes, an isolated, sandy west-coast cove. Ask around locally for further information about these trips, or call the Moskenes tourist office (see below).

Moskenes and Å

From Reine, it's about 5km to **MOSKENES**, the main island port from Bodø – not that there's much here, just a handful of houses dotted round a horse-shoe-shaped bay. There is, however, a helpful **tourist office** by the jetty (early to late June Mon–Fri 10am–5pm; late June to early Aug daily 10am–7pm; early to mid-Aug Mon–Fri 10am–5pm; mid-Aug to early June Mon–Fri 10am–2pm; ☎76 09 15 99), and a basic **campsite** (☎76 09 13 44; June–Aug), up a gravel track a five-minute walk away.

Five kilometres further south the road ends abruptly at the tersely named **Å**, one of Lofoten's most delightful villages, its huddle of old buildings rambling along a foreshore that's wedged in tight between the grey-green mountains and the surging sea. Unusually, so much of the nineteenth-century village has survived that a good portion of Å has been incorporated into the **Norsk Fiskevaersmuseum** (Norwegian Fishing Village Museum; late June to late Aug daily 11am–6pm; late Aug to late June Mon–Fri 11am–3pm; 40kr), an engaging attempt to recreate life here at the end of the nineteenth century. There are about fifteen buildings to examine, including a boat house, forge, cod-liver-oil processing plant, *rorbuer* and the houses of the two traders who dominated things hereabouts and the fishermen who did their bidding. According to the census of 1900, Å had 91 inhabitants, of whom ten were traders and their relatives, 18 servants, and 63 fishermen and their families. It was a rigidly hierarchical society underpinned by terms and conditions akin to serfdom. The fishermen did not own any land and had to pay rent for the ground on which their houses stood. Payment was made in the form of unpaid labour on the merchant's farmland during the summer harvest. No wonder Norwegians emigrated in their thousands. The museum has a series of displays which detail every aspect of village life – and very well presented it is too. Afterwards, you can extend your knowledge of all things fishy by visiting the **Tørrfiskmuseum** (Stockfish Museum; early to late June daily 11am–5pm; late June to late Aug daily 10am–5pm; 35kr) – stockfish being the air-dried fish that was the staple diet of most Norwegians well into the twentieth century.

Å doesn't offer much in the way of **hikes**, but there is one trail from the village which leads across the island and round the south shore of Lake Ågvatnet, before climbing over a steep ridge and then pushing on to the sea cliffs of the exposed west coast. The hike takes a whole day, and shouldn't be attempted in bad weather. Less energetic are the **boat trips** that leave from Å's jetty, including day-long fishing expeditions (Mon–Sat June–Aug 1 daily; 3hr; 280kr) and, weather and tides permitting, regular cruises (June to mid-Aug 1 weekly; 4hr; 400kr) to the **Moskenstraumen** – the dramatic maelstrom at the southern tip of Moskenesøya described by Edgar Allen Poe in his short story *A Descent into the Maelstrom*.

Even while I gazed, this current acquired a monstrous velocity. Each moment added to its speed - to its headlong impetuosity. In five minutes the whole sea...was lashed into ungovernable fury... Here the vast bed of the waters seamed and scarred into a thousand conflicting channels, burst suddenly into frenzied convulsion - heaving, boiling, hissing...

Practicalities

A local **bus** runs the length of the E10 from Leknes to Å at least once daily from late June to late August, less frequently the rest of the year. Times do not, however, usually coincide with ferry sailings to and from Moskenes. Consequently, if you're heading from the Moskenes ferry port to Å, you'll either have to walk – it's an easy 5km – or take a taxi.

All the **accommodation** in Å is run by one family, who own the year-round HI **hostel** (dorm beds 135kr, doubles ❶); an assortment of smart three- to ten-bedded *rorbuer* (550–1550kr per *rorbu*) surrounding the dock; and the adjacent *sjøhus*, which offers very comfortable and equally smart, hotel-standard rooms (❷). The same family also runs the cosy **bar** and the only **restaurant**, where the seafood is excellent. Bookings for all these can be made on ℡76 09 11 21 or ℡22 50 97 84, ℱ76 09 12 82 or ℱ22 50 97 06, ⓦwww.lofoten-rorbu.com.

Værøy & Røst

Værøy and Røst are the most southerly of the Lofoten islands, and the most time-consuming to reach: indeed, unless you're careful, the irregular ferry schedules can leave you stranded on either for a couple of days. The gist of the timetable is that **car ferries**, operated by OVDS (℡177; ⓦwww.ovds.no), either run from Bodø to Værøy and/or Røst once a day via Moskenes, or less frequently, sail direct to Værøy and/or Røst. The fare from Bodø to Værøy is 120kr per person, and 400kr for a car; Bodø to Røst is 140kr per person, and 490kr for a car; between Værøy and Røst it's 60kr per person, and 210kr for a car. From Bodø, Widerøe (℡91 00 12 00) operates one or two **flights** daily to Røst – but none to Værøy – with standby, summer and youth discount fares making a flight a reasonably economic proposition, especially if booked in advance.

Both Værøy and Røst are internationally famous for their **bird colonies**, hosting a multitude of puffins, eiders and gulls, as well as cormorants, terns, kittiwakes, guillemots, rare sea eagles and more recent immigrants like the fulmar and gannet. There are lots of **bird trips** to choose from, and for a three-hour excursion you can reckon on paying between 300kr and 400kr. The weather in the islands is uncommonly mild throughout the year, potential hiking routes are ubiquitous, and the occasional beach glorious and deserted.

Værøy

Of the two islands, **Værøy**, just 8km long, is the more visually appealing, comprising a slender, lightly populated, grassy-green coastal strip which ends suddenly in the steep, bare mountains that backbone the island. Værøy's few kilometres of roads primarily connect the farmsteads of the plain, but one squeezes round the mountains to wobble along a portion of the north coast. The island is, however, best explored on foot, either along the steep (and sometimes dangerous) footpaths of the mountains, or on the easier and clearer paths that lead out along the Nupsneset promontory. The most popular walk is the hiking trail that leads along the west coast from the end of the road to the isolated village of **Måstad**: Abandoned in the 1950s it's a tricky walk which takes two to three hours each way. The inhabitants of Måstad varied their fishy diet by catching puffins from the neighbouring sea cliffs, a hard and difficult task in which they were assisted by specially bred dogs known as puffin dogs, or Lundehund. These small – 32-38cm high – innocuous-looking dogs have three distinctive features: they have six toes; can close their ears against dust and moisture; and can bend their heads right round on to their backs.

Ferries dock at the southeast tip of the island, about 200m from the **tourist office** (mid-June to mid-Aug Mon–Fri 10am–2pm; ☎76 09 52 10), which can advise on boat tours and **accommodation** – though you would be foolhardy not to arrange this beforehand. The options are limited to a couple of places about 6km from the ferry dock: a **guesthouse** at the old vicarage, the *Gamle Prestegård* (☎76 09 54 11, ℻76 09 54 84; ⓦwww.prestegaarden.no; ❷), and a well-equipped HI **hostel** (mid-May to mid-Sept; ☎76 09 53 75, ℻76 09 57 01; dorm beds 100kr, doubles ❶), comprising some sensitively refurbished old *rorbuer*, some of which can be rented at other times of the year. The hostel also rents out boats and runs boat trips to the island's **bird cliffs**, which occupy the southwest corner of the island and are much too steep and slippery to approach on foot.

Røst

Even smaller than its neighbour, with a population of just 700, **RØST** is immediately different, its smattering of lonely farmsteads dotted over a flat, marshy landscape interrupted by dozens of tiny lakes. It was here in 1431 that the lifeboat of a shipwrecked Italian nobleman, Pietro Querini, was washed up after weeks at sea. Querini, and his fellow Venetians, stayed the winter and his written account is one of the few surviving records of everyday life in Nordland in the Middle Ages.

Røst **airport** is on the edge of the island, about 2km north of the main village, which is itself some 3km northeast of the **ferry port**. The **tourist office** (mid-June to mid-Aug Mon–Sat 10am–1.30pm and when the boat comes in; ☎76 09 64 11, ℻76 09 61 05) is close to the jetty. As for **accommodation**, there are plain and inexpensive lodgings at *Kårøy Rorbucamping* (☎76 09 62 38, ❶), and much more comfortable rooms at the new *Røst Bryggehotell og Rorbuer* complex (☎76 05 08 00, ℻76 09 60 40; ❸). The latter organizes **boat trips** to the jagged islets that rise high above the ocean to the southwest of Røst, their steep cliffs sheltering myriad seabird colonies.

Travel details

Trains

Narvik to: Riksgränsen (2–3 daily; 50min); Stockholm (1 daily; 18hr).
Trondheim to: Bodø (2–3 daily; 11hr); Dombås (3–4 daily; 2hr 30min); Fauske (2–3 daily; 10hr); Mo–i–Rana (2–3 daily; 7hr); Oslo (3–4 daily; 6hr); Otta (3 daily; 3hr); Røros (1–2 daily; 2hr 30min); Steinkjer (2–3 daily; 2hr); Stockholm (2 daily; 12hr).

Principal buses

Bodø to: Fauske (2–4 daily; 1hr 10min); Harstad (1 daily; 7hr 30min); Narvik (1–3 daily; 7hr 30min); Sortland (1–2 daily; 7hr); Svolvær (1 daily; 10hr 40min).

Fauske to: Bodø (2–5 daily; 1hr 10min); Harstad (1 daily; 6hr 30min); Narvik (1–3 daily; 5hr 30min); Sortland (1–2 daily; 6hr); Svolvær (1 daily; 9hr)
Harstad to: Fauske (1 daily; 6hr 30min).
Narvik to: Alta (1–3 daily except Sat; 9hr); Bodø (1–3 daily; 7hr); Fauske (1–3 daily; 5hr 30min); Sortland (1–2 daily; 4hr); Svolvær (1–2 daily; 6hr 40min); Tromsø (1–2 daily; 4hr 10min).
Sortland to: Andenes (1–3 daily; 2hr 15min).
Svolvær to: Å (Mon–Fri 1–2 daily; 3hr 20min).
Trondheim to: Bergen (2 daily; 14hr); Kristiansund (1–3 daily; 5hr); Otta (2 daily; 4hr); Stryn (2 daily; 7hr 20min); Ålesund (1–3 daily; 8hr).

Nord–Norgeekspressen

The Nord–Norgeekspressen (North Norway Express Bus) complements the railway system. It runs north from Bodø and Fauske to Alta in three segments: Bodø to Narvik via Fauske (1–3 daily; 7hr 30min); Narvik to Tromsø (1–2 daily; 4hr 20min); and Tromsø to Alta (2 daily; 6hr 30min). Alternatively, there's a direct bus from Narvik to Alta (Mon–Sat 1–2 daily; 9hr), where passengers can change for the connecting Nordkappekspressen bus onto Honningsvåg and Nordkapp (see p.354 for details).

Car ferries

Andenes to: Gryllefjord (early June to late Aug 2–3 daily; 1hr 40min).
Bodø to: Moskenes (June–Aug 2–4 daily;

Sept–May 1–2 daily except Sat; 4hr 15min); Røst (5 weekly; 8hr); Værøy (5 weekly; 6hr).
Bognes to: Lødingen (early June to mid-Aug 12 daily, mid-Aug to mid-June 5 daily; 1hr); Skarberget (15–21 daily; 25min)
Botnhamn to: Brensholmen (June to late Aug 4–7 daily; 35min).
Fiskebøl to: Melbu (every 90min; 25min).
Harstad to: Skrolsvik (early June to late Aug 2–4 daily; 1hr 50min).
Svolvær to: Skutvik (June to mid-Aug 8 daily; mid-Aug to May 2–3 daily; 2hr).

Hurtigbåt passenger express boats

Bodø to: Svolvær (Mon–Fri & Sun 1 daily; 5hr 30min).
Harstad to: Tromsø (1–2 daily; 2hr 45min).
Narvik to: Svolvær (Tues–Fri & Sun 1 daily; 3hr 30min).
Trondheim to: Kristiansund (1–3 daily; 3hr 30min).

Hurtigrute coastal boat

Northbound departures: daily from Trondheim at noon; Bodø at 3pm; Stamsund at 7.30pm; Svolvær at 10pm; Stokmarknes at 1am; Sortland at 3am & Harstad at 8am.
Southbound departures: daily from Harstad at 8am; Sortland at 1pm; Stokmarknes at 3.15pm; Svolvær at 7.30pm; Stamsund at 9.30pm; Bodø at 4am & Trondheim at 10am.
Journey time Trondheim–Harstad 43hr, Trondheim–Tromsø 51hr.

North Norway

CHAPTER 6 # Highlights

✳ **Sjømatrestauranten Arctandria** Arctic specialities, such as reindeer and seal, can be sampled at this excellent Tromso restaurant. **See p.326**

✳ **Alta's prehistoric rock carvings** Follow the trail round Northern Europe's most extensive collection of prehistoric rock carvings. **See p.328**

✳ **Juhl's Silver Gallery** The first and still the best of Finnmark's Sami-influenced jewellery-makers and designers. **See p.333**

✳ **The midnight sun at Nordkapp** Here, at the northern tip of Europe, continuous daylight lasts from early May to the end of July. **See p.339**

✳ **Repvåg** An old fishing station with traditional red-painted wooden buildings on stilts, framed by a picture-postcard setting. **See p.341**

✳ **The Hurtigrute** Sail around the northern tip of Norway and across the Barents Sea – the most spectacular section of this long-distance coastal boat trip. **See p.344**

✳ **Wildlife safaris on the Svalbard archipelago** More than a hundred species of migratory birds, as well as arctic foxes, polar bears, reindeer, seals, walruses and whales live in the icy wastes of this remote archipelago. **See p.351–352**

6

North Norway

Baedeker, writing a hundred years ago about Norway's remote **northern provinces** of Troms and Finnmark, observed that they "possess attractions for the scientific traveller and the sportsman, but can hardly be recommended for the ordinary tourist" – a comment which isn't too wide of the mark even today. These are enticing lands, no question, the natural environment they offer stunning in its extremes, with the midnight sun and polar night emphasizing the strangeness of the terrain, but the travelling can be hard, the specific sights widely separated and, when you reach them, subtle in their appeal.

Troms' intricate, fretted coastline has influenced its history since the days when powerful Viking lords operated a trading empire from its islands. Indeed, over half the population still lives offshore in dozens of tiny fishing villages, but the place to aim for is **Tromsø** the so-called "Capital of the North" and a lively university town where King Håkon and his government proclaimed a "Free Norway" in 1940, before fleeing into exile. Beyond Tromsø, the long trek north begins in earnest as you enter **Finnmark**, a vast wilderness covering 48,000 square kilometres, but home to just two percent of the Norwegian population. Much of the land was laid waste during World War II, the combined effect of the Russian advance and the retreating German army's scorched-earth policy, and it's now possible to drive for hours without coming across a building more than sixty years old. The first obvious target in Finnmark is **Alta**, a sprawling settlement and important crossroads that is famous for its prehistoric rock carvings. From here, most visitors head straight for the steely cliffs of **Nordkapp** (the North Cape), Europe's northernmost point, sometimes with a detour to the likeable port of **Hammerfest**, and leave it at that; but some doggedly press on to **Kirkenes**, the last town before the Russian border, where you feel as if you're about to drop off the end of the world. From Alta, the other main alternative is to travel inland across the eerily endless scrubland of the **Finnmarksvidda**, where winter temperatures plummet to –35°C. This high plateau is the last stronghold of the **Sami**, northern Norway's indigenous people, many of whom still live a semi-nomadic life tied to the movement of their reindeer herds. You'll spot Sami in their brightly coloured traditional gear all across the region, but especially in the remote towns of **Kautokeino** and **Karasjok**, strange, disconsolate places in the middle of the plain.

Finally, and even more adventurously, there is the **Svalbard** archipelago, whose icy mountains rise out of the Arctic Ocean 640km north of mainland Norway. Once the exclusive haunt of trappers, fishermen and coal miners, Svalbard now makes a tidy income from adventure tourism – everything from

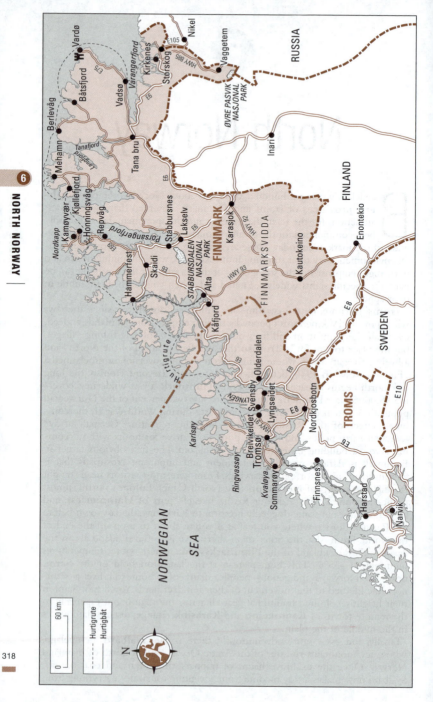

NORWEGIAN

SEA

Vardø

Berlevåg
Båtsfjord
Mehamn
Vadsø
Varangerfjord
Kirkenes
Storskog
Nikel

Vaggetem

RUSSIA

ØVRE PASVIK
NASJONAL
PARK

Tanafjord
Langfjord
Tana bru

Inari

FINLAND

Nordkapp
Kamøyvær
Kjøllefjord
Honningsvåg
Repvåg
Porsangerfjord
Stabbursnes
Lakselv
Karasjok
HWY 92

Enontekio

Hammerfest
Skaidi
STABBURSDALEN
NASJONAL
PARK
Alta
HWY 93
FINNMARKSVIDDA
Kautokeino

FINNMARK

Kåfjord

Olderdalen

Svensby
Lyngseidet
Nordkjosbotn

E8

SWEDEN

Karlsøy
Breivikeidet
Tromsø
Finnsnes

TROMS

E10

Ringvassøy
Kvaløya
Sommarøy
Harstad
Narvik

N

0   60 km

- - - - Hurtigrute
———— Hurtigbåt

318

guided glacier walks to snowmobile excursions and whale-watching. You can
fly there independently from most of Norway's larger towns, including Tromsø,
at bearable prices, though most people opt for a package tour.

Transport practicalities

Public transport in Troms and Finnmark is by **bus**, the **Hurtigrute** coastal
boat and **plane** – there are no trains. For all but the most truncated of tours,
the best idea is to pick and mix these different forms of transport – for example by flying from Tromsø to Kirkenes and then taking the Hurtigrute back,
or vice versa. What you should try to avoid is endless doubling-back on the **E6**,
which is often difficult as this is the only road to run right across the region.
To give an idea of the distances involved, from Tromsø it's 400km to Alta,
600km to Nordkapp and 950km to Kirkenes.

The principal long-distance bus is the **Nord-Norgeekspressen**, which links
Tromsø with Alta, from where there are onward services to Honningsvåg and
– from late June to mid-August – Nordkapp. Alta is also where you can pick
up buses to Karasjok and Kirkenes. North of Alta, almost all buses use the E6
and pass through Skaidi, where you change for the bus linking Hammerfest
with Karasjok and Kirkenes. Bus **timetables** are available at most tourist
offices and bus stations. On the longer rides, it's a good idea to buy **tickets** in
advance, or turn up early, as buses fill up fast in the summer.

The main **highways** are all well maintained, but **drivers** will find the going
a little slow as there's some pretty tough terrain to negotiate. You can cover
250–300km in a day without any problem, but much more and it all becomes
rather wearisome. Be warned also that in July and August the E6 north of Alta
can get congested with caravans and motorhomes on their way to Nordkapp.
You can avoid the crush by starting early or, for that matter, by driving
overnight – an eerie experience when it's bright sunlight in the wee hours of
the morning. In **winter**, driving conditions can be appalling and, although the
Norwegians make a spirited effort to keep the E6 open, they don't always succeed. If you're not used to driving in these sort of conditions, don't start here
– especially during the polar night. If you intend to use the region's minor,
often unpaved, roads, be prepared for the worst and certainly take food and
drink, warm clothes and, if possible, a mobile phone (which some car rental
firms can supply). Keep an eye on the fuel indicator too, as petrol stations are
confined to the larger settlements and they are often 100–200km apart. Car
repairs can take time since workshops are scarce and parts often have to be
ordered from the south.

Much more leisurely is the **Hurtigrute** coastal boat, which takes the best
part of two days to cross the huge fjords between Tromsø and Kirkenes. En
route, it calls at eleven ports, mostly remote fishing villages but also
Hammerfest and Honningsvåg, where it pauses for two or three hours so that
special buses can cart passengers off to Nordkapp and back. One especially
appealing option, though this has more to do with comfort than speed, is to
combine **car and boat** travel. Special deals on the Hurtigrute can make this
surprisingly affordable and tourist offices at the Hurtigrute's ports of call will
make bookings. Incidentally, you may well find that taking a rented car on the
Hutigrute works out cheaper than the cost of a one-way rental, with drop-off
charges reaching anything up to 3500kr.

With regard to **air travel**, the region has several **airports**, including those at
Alta, Hammerfest, Honningsvåg, Kirkenes, Tromsø and Longyearbyen, on
Svalbard. SAS and its many subsidiaries – including Widerøe, which flies in and
out of a string of small northern airstrips – offer summer discounts and passes,

Arctic phenomena

On and above the **Arctic Circle**, an imaginary line drawn round the earth at latitude 66.5 degrees north, there is a period around midsummer during which the sun never makes it below the horizon, even at midnight – hence the **midnight sun**. On the Arctic Circle itself, this only happens on one night of the year – at the summer solstice – but the further north you go, the greater the number of nights affected: in Bodø, it's from the first week of June to early July; in Alta, from the third week in May to the end of July; in Hammerfest, mid-May to late July; and in Nordkapp early May to the end of July. Obviously, the midnight sun is best experienced on a clear night, but fog or cloud can turn the sun into a glowing, red ball – a spectacle that can be wonderful but also strangely disconcerting. All the region's tourist offices have the exact dates of the midnight sun, though note that these are calculated at sea level; climb up a hill and you can extend the dates by a day or two. The converse of all this is the **polar night**, a period of constant darkness either side of the winter solstice; again the further north of the Arctic Circle you are, the longer this lasts.

The Arctic Circle also marks the typical southern limit of the **northern lights**, or Aurora Borealis, though this extraordinary phenomenon has been seen as far south as latitude 40 degrees north. Caused by the bombardment of the atmosphere by electrons, carried away from the sun by the solar wind, the northern lights take various forms and are highly mobile – either flickering in one spot or travelling across the sky. At relatively low latitudes hereabouts, the aurora is tilted at an angle and is often coloured red – the sagas tell of Vikings being half scared to death by them – but nearer the pole, they hang like gigantic luminous curtains, often tinted greenish blue. Naturally enough, there's no predicting when the northern lights will occur, but in wintertime they are not uncommon – and on a clear night they can be simply stunning.

which can make flying an economic possibility (see p.35 for further details).

As for **accommodation**, all the major settlements have at least a couple of hotels and the main roads are sprinkled with campsites. If you have a tent and a well-insulated sleeping bag, you can, in theory, bed down more or less where you like, but the hostility of the climate and the ferocity of the mosquitoes, which breed especially in the marshy areas of the Finnmarksvidda, make most people think (at least) twice. There are HI **hostels** at Tromsø, Alta and Lakselv and Karasjok.

Tromsø

TROMSØ has been called, rather preposterously, the "Paris of the North", and though even the tourist office doesn't make any pretence to such grandiose titles today, the city is without question the effective capital of northern Norway. Easily the region's most populous town, it has credentials that go back to the Middle Ages – there's been a church here since the thirteenth century, and seafarers were using its sheltered harbour long before. Tromsø received its municipal charter in 1794, when it was primarily a fishing port and trading station, and flourished in the middle of the nineteenth century when its seamen ventured north to Svalbard to reap rich rewards hunting Arctic foxes, polar bears and, most profitable of all, seals. Subsequently, Tromsø became famous as the jumping-off point for a string of Arctic expeditions, its celebrity status assured when the explorer Roald Amundsen flew from here to his death somewhere on the Arctic ice cap in 1928. Since those heady days, Tromsø has grown into an urbane and likeable small city with a population of 60,000 employed in a wide range of industries, and at the university and hospital. It's become an important port too, for although the city is some 360km north of the Arctic Circle, its climate is moderated by the Gulf Stream, which sweeps up the Norwegian coast and keeps its harbour ice-free. Give or take the odd museum, Tromsø is short on specific **sights**, but its amiable atmosphere, fine mountain-

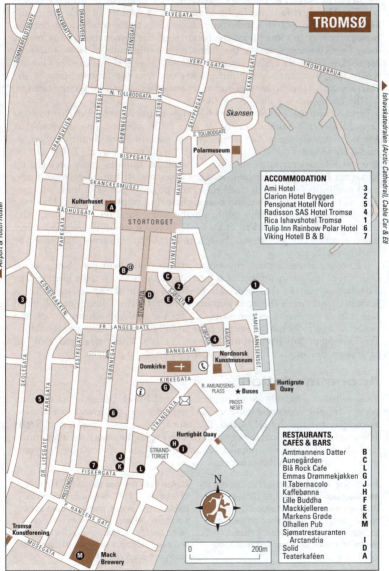

TROMSØ

ACCOMMODATION

Ami Hotel	3
Clarion Hotel Bryggen	2
Pensjonat Hotell Nord	5
Radisson SAS Hotel Tromsø	4
Rica Ishavshotel Tromsø	1
Tulip Inn Rainbow Polar Hotel	6
Viking Hotell B & B	7

RESTAURANTS, CAFÉS & BARS

Amtmannens Datter	B
Aunegården	C
Blå Rock Cafe	L
Emmas Drømmekjøkken	G
Il Tabernacolo	J
Kaffebønna	H
Lille Buddha	F
Mackkjelleren	E
Markens Grøde	K
Olhallen Pub	M
Sjømatrestauranten Arctandria	I
Solid	D
Teaterkaféen	A

▶ Ishavskatedralen (Arctic Cathedral), Cable Car & E8

◀ Airport & Youth Hostel

▼ Polaria (100m), Tromsø Museum (2.5km) & Art Museum

and-fjord setting, and a clutch of lively restaurants and bars more than compensate.

Arrival, information and orientation

At the northern end of the E8, 73km from the E6 and 250km north of Narvik (see p.286), Tromsø's compact centre slopes up from the waterfront on the hilly island of Tromsøya. The island is connected to the mainland by bridge and tunnel. The **Hurtigrute** docks in the town centre at the foot of Kirkegata, while **Hurtigbåt** services arrive at the quay about 150m to the south. Long-distance **buses** arrive at and leave from the parking lot-cum-bus station, a few metres away. Five kilometres west of the centre on the other side of Tromsøya, is the **airport**, from where fairly frequent Flybussen (Mon–Fri 7.30am–8pm hourly, Sat 6 daily, Sun 9am–8pm hourly; 40kr) run into the city, stopping at the *Radisson SAS Hotel* on Sjøgata and at several other central hotels; the taxi fare for the corresponding journey is 90kr.

Tromsø's **tourist office**, Storgata 61 (mid- to late May & mid-Aug to mid-Sept Mon–Fri 8.30am–4pm, Sat & Sun 10.30am–2pm; June to mid-Aug Mon–Fri 8.30am–6pm, Sat 10am–5pm & Sun 10.30am–5pm; mid-Sept to mid-May Mon–Fri 8.30am–4pm, Sat 10.30am–2pm; ☎77 61 00 00 ⓦwww.destinasjontromsoe.no), is a couple of minutes' walk straight up Kirkegata from where the long-distance buses stop. It issues free town maps, has a small supply of B&Bs (see below) and provides oodles of local information, including details of bus and boat **sightseeing trips** around neighbouring islands. Tickets for most trips can be purchased here and the tourist office also sells a one-day **tourist ticket** (60kr, valid 24hr from when it's first used) offering unlimited city bus travel, though most places of interest can easily be reached on foot.

The town centre is small enough to make **orientation** easy: Storgata, the main street and north–south axis, is interrupted by Stortorget, the main square. The busiest part of the town centre spreads south of the square as far as Kirkegata and east to the harbourfront. It only takes five minutes to walk from one side of the centre to the other, but for the outlying attractions you can either catch a local bus, or **rent a bike** from Sportshuset, Storgata 87 (Mon–Fri 9am–5pm, Sat 10am–4pm; ☎77 66 11 00). There is a **taxi** rank on Stortorget and another by the Domkirke (church).

Accommodation

Tromsø has a good supply of modern, central **hotels**, though the majority occupy chunky concrete high-rises. Less expensive are the town's **guesthouses** (*pensjonater*) and the HI **hostel**. The tourist office has a small list of **B&Bs** at around 300kr per double per night (200kr single), but most are stuck out in the suburbs. Tromsø is a popular destination, so advance booking is recommended, especially in the summer.

Hotels and guesthouses

Ami Hotel Skolegata 24 ☎77 68 22 08, ℗77 68 80 44, ⓦwww.amihotel.no. A pleasant guesthouse/ hotel on the hillside behind the town centre, with seventeen simple rooms. It's particularly popular for its wide views over the city, so book ahead in the summer. ❷

Clarion Hotel Bryggen Sjøgata 19-21 ☎77 78 11 00, ℗77 78 11 01, ⓦwww.choicehotels.no. Polished, super-modern chain hotel down on the waterfront, with small but tastefully furnished rooms. The fifth-floor jacuzzi offers fine sea (and sky) views. Substantial weekend and summer discounts on the rack rate. ❻, s/r ❸

Pensjonat Hotell Nord Parkgata 4 ☎ 77 66 83 00, ℱ 77 66 83 20, ⓦ www.hotellnord.no. Basic guesthouse, a good, stiff walk up the hill to the north of the centre. Both en-suite and shared facility rooms. ❷

Radisson SAS Hotel Tromsø Sjøgata 7 ☎ 77 60 00 00, ℱ 77 68 54 74, ⓦ www.radissonsas.com. This plush, downtown high-rise offers smart and comfortable modern rooms, and ultra efficient service. ❻, s/r ❹

Rica Ishavshotel Tromsø Fr. Langes gate 2 ☎ 77 66 64 00, ℱ 77 66 64 44, ⓦ www.rica.no. Perched on the harbourfront, this imaginatively designed hotel is partly built in the style of a ship, complete with a sort of crow's nest bar. Lovely rooms and unbeatable views of the waterfront. Best place in town. ❺, s/r ❸

Tulip Inn Rainbow Polar Hotel Grønnegata 45 ☎ 77 75 17 00, ℱ 77 75 17 10, ⓦ www.rainbow-hotels.no, ℯ polar@tr.telia.no. Small, modern rooms decorated in typical chain-hotel style, but summer and weekend discounts make this place a real bargain; central location too. ❹, s/r ❷

Viking Hotell Bed and Breakfast Grønnegata 18 ☎ 77 65 76 22, ℱ 77 65 55 10, ⓦ www.viking-hotell.no. Simple and straightforward guesthouse, centrally located, with spick and span, if rather frugal rooms. ❷

Hostels and campsites

Tromsdalen Camping Elvestrandvegen ☎ 77 63 80 37, ℱ 77 63 85 24. The nearest campsite to the city centre, 1800m east of the Ishavskatedralen, on the mainland side of the bridge, by a river and near a football field. Several city buses go near there – ask at the bus station. Open all year. Cabins also available ❶

Tromsø Vandrerhjem Åsgårdsveien 9, Elverhøy ☎ 77 65 76 28, ℯ tromso.hostel@vandrerhejm.no. About 2km west of the centre, this barracks-like HI hostel is a basic affair and can be noisy. No food is available, but there's a store close by and self-catering facilities. Reception closed 11am–5pm. A couple of city buses go near there – ask at the bus station – or else it's a stiff thirty-minute walk. Open late June to late Aug. Dorm beds 125kr, doubles ❶

The City

One of Tromsø's most distinctive buildings is its **Domkirke** (Tues–Sat 10am–4pm, Sun 10am–2pm; free). Erected on Storgata in 1861, the cathedral bears witness to the prosperity of the town's nineteenth-century merchants, who became rich on the back of the barter trade with Russia. They part-funded the church's construction, the result being the large and handsome structure of today, whose imposing spire pokes high into the sky.

Behind the church, at Sjøgata 1, stands the **Nordnorsk Kunstmuseum** (Art Museum of Northern Norway; Tues, Wed & Fri 10am–5pm, Thurs 10am–7pm, Sat & Sun noon–5pm; ⓦ www.museumsnett.no /nordnorsk-kunstmuseum; 30kr), a well-presented collection of fine art and northern handicrafts from the 1850s onwards. It's not a large ensemble, but it does contain the work of many Norwegian painters, from lesser-known figures such as Axel Revold and Christian Krohg, to a handful of works by Edvard Munch (for more on whom, see p.99). There are also several Romantic peasant scenes by Adolph Tidemand and a couple of ingenious landscapes by both the talented Thomas Fearnley and Johan Dahl. The permanent collection is enhanced by frequent loans from the National Gallery in Oslo (see p.82) and by a lively programme of temporary exhibitions.

Back in front of the Domkirke, it's a gentle five-minute stroll north past the shops of Storgata to the main square, **Stortorget**, site of a daily open-air **market** selling flowers and knick-knacks. The square nudges down to the waterfront, where fresh fish and prawns are sold direct from inshore fishing boats throughout the summer. Follow the harbour round to the north and you're in the heart of old Tromsø: the raised ground close to the water's edge was the centre of the medieval settlement and it was here that the locals built the first fortifications. Nothing now remains of the medieval town, but you can discern the shape of a later, eighteenth-century **fort** in the modest knoll at the end of Skansegata.

North of the centre: the Polarmuseum

In an old wooden waterfront warehouse, metres from the end of Skansegata, is the city's most enjoyable museum, the **Polarmuseum i Tromsø** (Polar Museum; daily: mid-May to mid-June & mid-Aug to mid-Sept 11am–5pm; mid-June to mid-Aug 10am–7pm; mid-Sept to mid-May 11am–3pm; Ⓦwww.polarmuseum.no, 40kr). The museum begins with a rather unappetizing series of displays on trapping in the Arctic, but beyond is an outstanding section on Svalbard, which includes archeological finds recently retrieved from an eighteenth-century **Russian trapping station** there. Most of the finds come from graves in which the artefacts were preserved by the permafrost. Among many items, there are combs, leather boots, parts of a sledge, slippers and even – just to prove illicit smoking is not a recent phenomenon – a clay pipe from a period when the Russian company in charge of affairs did not allow trappers to smoke. Two other sections on the first floor focus on **seal hunting**, an important part of the local economy until the 1950s.

Upstairs, on the second floor, a further section is devoted to the polar explorer **Roald Amundsen** (1872–1928), who spent thirty years searching out the secrets of the polar regions. In 1901, he purchased a sealer, the *Gjøa*, here in Tromsø and then spent three years sailing and charting the **Northwest Passage** between the Atlantic and the Pacific. The *Gjøa* (now on display in Olso: see p.93) was the first vessel to complete this extraordinary voyage, which tested Amundsen and his crew to the very limits. Long searched-for, the Passage had for centuries been something of a nautical Holy Grail and the progress of the voyage – and at times the lack of it - was headline news right across the world. In 1910, Amundsen set out in a new ship, the *Fram* (also exhibited in Oslo; see p.93) for the Antarctic, or more specifically the **South Pole**. On December 14, 1911, Amundsen and four of his crew became the first men to reach the South Pole, famously just ahead of their British rival Captain Scott. The museum exhibits all sorts of oddments used by Amundsen and his men – from long johns and pipes through to boots and ice picks – but it's the photos that steal the show, providing a fascinating insight into the way Amundsen's polar expeditions were organized and the hardships endured. Amundsen clearly liked having his picture taken judging from the heroic poses he struck, his derring-do emphasised by an amazing set of eyebrows.

Finally, there's another extensive section on Amundsen's contemporary **Fridtjof Nansen** (1861–1930), a polar explorer of similar renown who, in his later years, became a leading figure in international famine relief. In 1895, Nansen and his colleague Hjalmar Johansen made an abortive effort to reach the North Pole by dog sledge after their ship got packed in by the ice. It took them fifteen months to get back to safety, a journey of such epic proportions that tales of it captivated all of contemporary Norway.

South of the centre: Tromsø Kunstforening, Polaria and the Tromsø Museum

On the south side of the city centre, on the corner of Storgata and Musegata, lies the profitable **Mack brewery**, which claims to be the world's northernmost brewery. Nearby, just up Musegata, **Tromsø Kunstforening** (Art Institute; Tues–Sun noon–5pm; 30kr) occupies part of a large and attractive late nineteenth-century building that used to house the municipal museum. Today, the gallery showcases imaginative temporary exhibitions of Norwegian contemporary art with the emphasis on the work of Nordland artists.

Doubling back down Musegata, it's a couple of hundred metres south along Storgata to **Polaria** (daily: mid-May to mid-Aug 10am–7pm; mid-Aug to mid-May noon–5pm, Ⓦwww.polaria.com; 75kr), a lavish waterfront complex which deals with all things Arctic. There's an aquarium filled with Arctic species, a gripping 180-degree cinema showing a film on Svalbard and several exhibitions on polar research.

About 3km further south of the centre, near the southern tip of Tromsøya, is the **Tromsø Museum** (June–Aug daily 9am–8pm; Sept–May Mon–Fri 8.30am–3.30pm, Sat & Sun 11am–5pm; 30kr), whose varied collections feature nature and the sciences downstairs, and culture and history above. Pride of place goes to the **medieval religious carvings**, naive but evocative pieces retrieved from various Nordland churches. There's also an enjoyable section on the Sami which features displays on every aspect of Sami life – from dwellings, tools and equipment through to traditional costume and hunting techniques. To get to the museum, take bus #28 from the centre (Mon–Sat every 30min, Sun hourly).

East of the centre: the Ishavskatedralen and the cable car

East of the town centre, over the spindly Tromsø bridge in the suburb of Tromsdalen, stands the desperately modern **Ishavskatedralen**, completed in 1965 (Arctic Cathedral; mid-April to May daily 3pm–6pm; June to mid-Aug Mon–Sat 10am–8pm, Sun 1–8pm; mid-Aug to Sept daily 3–6pm; 20kr). The church's strikingly white, glacier-like appearance is achieved by means of eleven immense triangular concrete sections, representing the eleven Apostles left after the betrayal. The entire east wall is formed by a huge stained-glass window, one of the largest in Europe. The organ is highly unusual, built to represent a ship when viewed from beneath - recalling the tradition, still seen in many a Norwegian church, of suspending a ship from the roof as a good-luck talisman for local seafarers. Among several bus services, the #28 (Mon–Sat every 30min, Sun every hour) comes this way – but it's only a few minutes' walk over the bridge.

From the Ishavskatedralen, it's a fifteen-minute walk – or a short ride on bus #26 – to the *fjellheisen* or **cable car** (March Sat & Sun 10am–5pm, April to mid-May & mid-Aug to Sept daily 10am–5pm, mid-May to mid-Aug daily 10am–1am; 65kr), which whisks up Mt Storsteinen. From the top (421m), the views of the city and its surroundings are extensive, and you can treat yourself to a meal with a panoramic backdrop on the terrace of the *Fjellstua* restaurant (☎77 63 86 55; daily early May & late Aug 11am–5pm, mid-May to mid-Aug 11am–midnight). Note that cable car services are suspended during bad weather.

Eating, drinking and entertainment

Tromsø has a good range of places to eat and drink: it boasts some first-rate **restaurants,** several enjoyable **cafés,** and a decent supply of late-night **bars**. The best of the cafés and restaurants are clustered around the tourist office, on Storgata, while most of the livelier bars – many of which sell Mack, the local brew – are also pretty central.

The **Kulturhuset**, Grønnegata 87 (☎77 66 38 00; Ⓦwww.kulturhuset .tr.no), is the principal venue for cultural events of all kinds, while the main **cinema**, the odd-looking Fokus, is close by at Grønnegata 94 (☎77 75 30 80). The tourist office has details of performances.

Cafés

Aunegården Sjøgata 29. Large cafè/restaurant situated in the listed 1830s Aunegården building. Serves all the standard Norwegian dishes at moderate prices, but these are as nothing compared with the wonderful cakes made at its own bakery. The cheese cake, in particular, is to die for. Mon–Thurs 10.30am–11.30pm, Fri & Sat 10.30am–12.30am, Sun 3–11.30pm.

Kaffebønna Strandtorget 1. Smart, specialist coffee house serving the best coffee in town, plus tasty snacks straight from its own bakery. Daily 9am–6/7pm.

Solid Storgata 73. A brisk, modern café in the daytime, that turns into a busy bar at night. Tasty snacks and light meals are served at lunch time.

Restaurants

Cuisine Orientale Sjøgata 25 ☎77 65 65 66. Serves different kinds of Asian cuisine, including Chinese and Indian. Good food at affordable prices with main courses from 100kr. Daily 5pm–late.

Emmas Drømmekjøkken Kirkegata 8 ☎77 63 77 30. "Emma's dream kitchen" lives up to its name with an imaginative and wide-ranging menu. Much praised in the national press as a gourmet treat – but it is expensive. Smart too. Mon–Sat 6pm–midnight; closed Sun.

Il Tabernacolo Storgata 36 ☎77 61 10 50. Claims to be the world's northernmost and Tromsø's only authentic Italian restaurant – few would dispute either tag. Serves first-class pizza and pasta dishes plus all the other Italian classics in cosy, pastel-painted surroundings. Reasonable prices. Tues–Sat 6–11pm, Sun 4–11pm; closed Mon.

Markens Grøde Storgata 30 ☎77 68 25 50. Classy Norwegian cuisine featuring local fish and game innovatively prepared. Lots of seasonal specialities. Expensive. Tues–Sat 5.30–11pm; closed Mon.

Sjømatrestauranten Arctandria Strandtorget 1 ☎77 60 07 20. Some of the best food in town, either in the upstairs fish restaurant, where main courses start at around 170kr, or downstairs in the café-bar *Skarven* where prices are about twenty percent less. The range of fish in the restaurant is quite superb, with the emphasis on Arctic species, and there's also reindeer and seal. The café-bar has less variety, but the quality is just as good. Mon–Sat 5–10pm; closed Sun.

Bars

Amtmannens Datter Grønnegata 81. Café-bar with arty student clientele, newspapers, internet access and lots of different types of beer. Mon–Thurs noon–2am, Fri & Sat noon–3.30am, Sun 3pm–2am.

Blå Rock Café Strandgata 14. The place to go for loud rock music. Has occasional live acts too, and the best burgers in town. Mon–Thurs 11.30am–2am, Fri & Sat 11.30am–3.30am, Sun 1pm–2am.

Mackkjelleren Sjøgata 12, but entrance on Storgata. Popular beer haunt in a basement whose whitewashed walls are covered with old Tromsø aphorisms and proverbs: the locals are usually keen to translate. Some karaoke and live acts, plus DJ nights with the emphasis mostly on the 1980s. Mon 11am–midnight, Tues–Thurs 11am–2am, Fri–Sat 11am–3am, Sun 3pm–midnight.

Skipsbroen Fr. Langes gate 2. Inside the *Rica Ishavshotel* (see p.323), this smart little bar overlooks the waterfront from on high – it occupies the top of a slender tower with wide windows and sea views. Relaxed atmosphere, but lots of tourists. Mon–Thurs 6pm–1.30am, Fri & Sat 3pm–3am; closed Sun.

Teaterkaféen Grønnegata 87, on the corner of Stortorget. Inside the *Kulturhus*, this arts centre café-bar is long on conversation and student style. Daily 11am–1am.

Ølhallen Pub Storgata 4. Solid, some would say staid, brewery pub, adjoining the Mack brewery, whose various brews are its speciality. Mon–Thurs 9am–5pm, Fri 9am–6pm & Sat 9am–3pm.

Listings

Airlines Braathens, Tromsø airport ☎815 20 000; SAS, Tromsø airport ☎810 03 300; Widerøes Flyveselskap, Tromsø airport ☎ 810 01 200

Banks Gjensidige NOR Sparebank, Storgata 92; Nordea, Grønnegata 80.

Car rental Europcar, Alkeiveien 5 and at the airport (☎77 67 56 00); Hertz, Richard Withsplass 4 (☎77 62 44 00).

Diving and Sea rafting Dykkersenteret AS, Stakkevollveien 72 (☎77 69 66 00, ⓦwww.dykkersenteret.no), organizes guided diving tours to local wrecks in the surrounding fjords. Also runs fishing and midnight sun excursions plus equipment rental.

DNT Troms Turlag, Grønnegata 32 (Tues, Wed & Fri 10am–2pm, Thurs 10am–6pm, ☎77 68 51 75, ⓔtromstur@online.no), has information on local hiking trails and DNT huts.

Hiking See DNT (above) and Outdoor Pursuits (below).

Internet Access at the Amtmannens Datter café-bar, Grønnegata 81 (Mon–Thurs noon–2am, Fri & Sat noon–3.30am, Sun 3pm–2am).

Left luggage Coin-operated lockers inside the *Venteromskafé*, beside the Hurtigbåt quay (mid-July to Aug Mon–Fri 6.30am–midnight, Sat 9am–midnight, Sun noon–midnight; Sept to mid-July Mon–Fri 6.30am–midnight, Sat 9am–3pm, Sun noon–midnight); and at the bus station (Mon–Fri 8.15am–4.30pm).

Maps Bokhuset AS, Storgata 86.

Newspapers Jacobs, Storgata 55, has a good selection of international newspapers and magazines.

Off-licence *Vinmonopolet* at Storgata 33.

Outdoor pursuits Tromsø Villmarksenter, Kvaløysletta (☏77 69 60 02, ℻77 69 60 39, ⓦwww.villmarksenter.no), offers a wide range of activities from guided glacier walks, kayak paddling and mountain climbing in summer, to ski trips and dog-sled rides in winter. Overnight trips staying in a *lavvo* (a Sami tent) can also be arrranged.

Pharmacy Svaneapoteket, Fr. Langes gate 9 (☏ 77 60 14 80).

Post office Main office at Strandgata 41 (Mon–Fri 8.30am–5pm, Sat 10am–2pm).

Ski rentals Sportshust, Storgata 87 (☏77 66 11 00).

Taxi ☏77 60 30 00 (24hr).

Travel agents Bennett Reisebyrå, Roald Amundsensplass 1 (☏77 62 15 00).

Around Tromsø: Sommarøy and the route to Andenes

Driving west from Tromsø past the airport, Highway 862 crosses the Sandnessundet straits to reach the mountainous island of **Kvaløya**, whose three distinct parts are joined by a couple of narrow isthmuses. On the far side of the straits, Highway 862 meanders south along the coast, offering lovely fjord and mountain views as it runs past a series of old wooden farmhouses. After about 60km, you reach **Brensholmen**, where a ferry (June to late Aug 4–7 daily; 35min; passengers 50kr, car & driver 130kr) crosses over to **Botnhamn**. From here, it's a further 160km to Gryllefjord where another ferry (early June to late Aug 2–3 daily; 1hr 40min; passengers 100kr, car & driver 275kr) takes you across to Andenes on Vesterålen (see p.296).

This coastal journey to Andenes is a popular tourist route, but if you ignore the Brensholmen ferry and stay on the road, it's just 10km or so to **Sommarøy**, a flat, treeless but grassy islet that lies just offshore from Kvaløya. Here, the relaxing *Sommarøy Kurs og Feriesenter* (☏77 66 40 00, ℻77 66 40 01, ⓦwww.sommaroy.no) offers basic hotel accommodaton (❹, s/r ❸) and high quality, well-equipped cabins for up to ten people for around 1200kr per day. The restaurant is excellent too, particularly for Arctic specialities, and there are two traditional *badestamp* – wooden hot-tubs seating up to ten people – one inside and one outdoors, next to the sea.

Into Finnmark: from Tromsø to Alta

Beyond Tromsø, the vast sweep of the northern landscape slowly unfolds, with silent fjords cutting deep into the coastline beneath ice-tipped peaks which themselves fade into the high plateau of the interior. This forbidding, elemental terrain is interrupted by the occasional valley, where those few souls hardy enough to make a living in these parts struggle on – often by dairy farming. A particular problem for the farmers is the abundance of Siberian garlic (*Allium sibiricum*): the cows love the stuff, but if they eat a lot of it, the milk tastes of onions. In summer, cut grass dries everywhere, stretched over wooden poles that form long lines on the hillsides, like so much washing hung out to dry.

Slipping along the valleys and traversing the mountains in between, the **E8** and then the **E6** follow the coast pretty much all the way from Tromsø to Alta, some 420km and about nine hours' drive to the north. Drivers can save around 120km (although not necessarily time and certainly not money) by turning off the E8 25km south of Tromsø onto **Highway 91** – a quieter, more scenic route, offering yet more extravagant fjord and mountain views. This cuts across a peninsula and then uses two **car ferries** to rejoin the E6 at Olderdalen, some 220km south of Alta. The first ferry is from **Breivikeidet to Svendsby** (Mon–Thurs 6am–8pm, Fri 6am–9pm, Sat 8am–8pm, Sun 10am–9pm; every 1–2hr; 25min; 60kr car and driver; ☎77 71 14 00); the second, a 22km-drive beyond Svensby, is from **Lyngseidet to Olderdalen** (Mon–Thurs 7am–7pm, Fri 7am–9pm, Sat 9am–7pm, Sun 11am–9pm; every 1–2hr; 40min; 80kr car and driver). This is the route used by most long-distance buses, and is at its most spectacular between Svensby and Lyngseidet, as it nudges along a narrow channel flanked by the imposing peaks of the Lyngsalpene, or Lyngen Alps.

Whichever route you chose you'll enter **Finnmark** some 60km short of the tiny village of **KÅFJORD**, whose recently restored nineteenth-century church was built by an English company who operated the area's copper mines until they were abandoned as uneconomic in the 1870s. The Kåfjord itself is a narrow arm of the Altafjord, and, sheltered by mountains, it was used as an Arctic hideaway for the *Tirpitz* and other German battleships during World War II to protect them from the British. From here, it's just 20km further to Alta.

From April to late October, the twice-daily Nord-Norgeekspressen **bus,** operated by Nor-Way Bussekspress, leaves Tromsø for Alta (seven hours); from late June to mid-August, one bus daily continues from Alta onto Nordkapp (fourteen hours). In addition, FFR buses (☎78 43 36 77; Ⓦwww.ffr.no) link Alta with Hammerfest (1–2 daily except Sat; 2hr 30min) and Kirkenes (late June to mid-Aug 1–2 daily; mid-Aug to late June 1–2 daily except Thurs & Sat; 10hr). There are no boats between Tromsø and Alta; northbound, the **Hurtigrute** leaves Tromsø at 6.30pm, taking eleven hours to reach Hammerfest (see p.336), its next major port of call.

Alta

Despite the long haul to get here, first impressions of **ALTA** are not encouraging. With a population of just 16,000, the town strings along the E6 for several kilometres, comprising a series of unenticing settlements. The ugliest part is **Alta Sentrum**, now muddled by a platoon of soulless concrete blocks. Alta was interesting once – for a couple of centuries not Norwegian at all but Finnish and Sami, and host to an ancient and much-visited Sami fair. World War II polished off the fair and destroyed all the old wooden buildings that once clustered together in Alta's **Bossekop** district, where Dutch whalers settled in the seventeenth century.

For all that, Alta does have one remarkable feature, the most extensive area of **prehistoric rock carvings** in northern Europe. This UNESCO World Heritage site, the **Helleristningene i Hjemmeluft** (Rock Carvings in Hjemmeluft), is located beside the E6 as you approach Alta from the southwest, some 2.5km before the Bossekop district, and forms part of the **Alta Museum** (May daily 9am–6pm; early June and late Aug daily 8am–8pm; mid-June to mid-Aug daily 8am–11pm; Sept daily 9am–6pm; Oct–April Mon–Fri 9am–3pm, Sat & Sun 11am–4pm; Ⓦwww.alta.museum.no; May–Sept 70kr, Oct–April 35kr). On entering, you'll pass through the museum building,

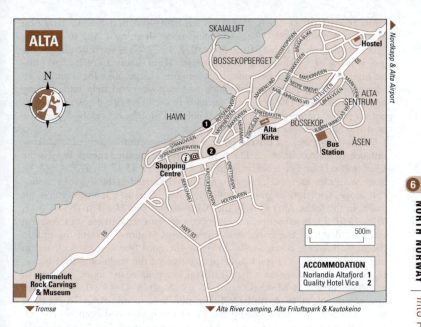

ACCOMMODATION
Norlandia Altafjord 1
Quality Hotel Vica 2

▼ Tromsø   ▼ Alta River camping, Alta Friluftspark & Kautokeino

which provides a wealth of background information on the carvings, as well as on prehistoric Finnmark in general. It also offers a potted history of the Alta area, with exhibitions on the salmon-fishing industry, copper mining and so forth. The **rock carvings** themselves extend down the hill from the museum to the fjordside. A clear and easy-to-follow footpath and boardwalk circum-navigate the site, taking in all the carvings in about an hour. On the trail, there are **thirteen vantage points** offering close-up views of the carvings, recog-nizable though highly stylized representations of boats, animals and people picked out in red pigment (the colours have been retouched by researchers). They make up an extraordinarily complex tableau, whose minor variations – there are **four identifiable bands** – in subject matter and design indicate suc-cessive historical periods. The carvings were executed, it's estimated, between 6000 and 2500 years ago, and are indisputably impressive: clear, stylish, and touching in their simplicity. They provide an insight into a prehistoric culture that was essentially settled and largely reliant on the hunting of land animals, who were killed with flint and bone implements; sealing and fishing were of lesser importance. Many experts think it unlikely that these peoples would have expended so much effort on the carvings unless they had spiritual significance, but this is the stuff of conjecture.

Practicalities

Long-distance **buses** make two stops in Alta, one at the **bus station** in Alta Sentrum, the other at Alta airport, 4km north along the E6 in the Elvebakken district. Get off at Alta Sentrum for the rock carvings – it's a 4.5km walk back along the E6, or catch a **local bus** (*bybussen*; Mon–Fri 6am–8pm, Sat 10am–3pm; every thirty minutes) from the bus station to Bossekop and walk the 2.5km from there. Alternatively, a taxi from the centre will cost around 60kr: try Alta Taxi on ☏78 43 53 53.

Alta **tourist office** (early June Mon–Fri 8am–4pm; mid-June to early Aug Mon–Fri 8am–6pm, Sat 10am–4pm, Sun noon–4pm; early Aug to end Aug Mon–Fri 8am–4pm & Sat 10am–3pm; ☎78 45 77 77; Ⓦwww.destinasjonalta .no) is at Bossekop's shopping centre, near the Rimi supermarket. It offers public internet access (1kr per minute, minimum charge 30kr for 30min), can advise on hiking the Finnmarksvidda (see opposite) and help with finding **accommodation**. The latter is a particularly useful service if you're dependent on public transport – the town's hotels and motels are widely dispersed – or if you're here at the height of the season.

Alta has two excellent **hotels**, both in Bossekop within comfortable walking distance of the tourist office. The first, a couple of hundred metres away, is the *Quality Hotel Vica,* Fogdebakken 6 in Bossekop (☎78 43 47 11, Ⓕ78 43 42 99; Ⓦwww.vica.no; ❺, s/r ❹), a small, cosy hotel decorated in the style of a mountain lodge, with lots of pine panelling. It also offers free internet access for guests in the lobby. Alternatively, the *Norlandia Altafjord Hotell* (☎78 43 70 11, Ⓕ78 43 70 13, Ⓦwww.norlandia.no; ❹), a five- to ten-minute walk away to the west, down by the fjord, offers three sorts of rooms – run-of-the-mill in the main building, cottage-style down by the fjord (the best choice), and in turf-roofed buildings, a spick-and-span version of the traditional-style house. By far the cheapest option is the HI **hostel**, in a plain chalet about 700m north of Alta Sentrum at Midtbakkveien 52 (☎ & Ⓕ78 43 44 09, Ⓔalta.hostel @vandrerhjem.no; ❶, dorm beds 125kr; mid-June to mid-Aug). To get there from Alta Sentrum, walk east up the E6 to the next roundabout, where you turn left and then first left again – a fifteen-minute stroll. Food isn't available, but there are self-catering facilities. There are also several **campsites** in the vicinity of Alta. The largest is *Kronstad Camping* (☎78 43 03 06, Ⓕ78 43 11 55), a year-round site with cabins, beside the E6 at the east end of town, some 5km from Alta Sentrum, but this is a thoroughly unappetising place and you're much better off using the well-equipped, four-star *Alta River Camping* (☎78 43 43 53, Ⓕ78 43 69 02, Ⓔannjenss@online.no), by the river about 4km out of town along Highway 93.

Easily the best **restaurant** in town is at the *Quality Hotel Vica*, which specializes in regional delicacies – cloudberries, reindeer and the like. Prices are very reasonable and traditional Sami dishes are often on the menu, too.

Alta Friluftspark

Aside from the rock carvings, the only other reason to linger in Alta is for the **Alta Friluftspark** (☎78 43 33 78, Ⓕ78 43 34 65, Ⓦwww.alta-friluftspark.no), 15km to the south off Highway 93, beside the river in Storelvdalen. Here, all manner of Finnmark experiences are on offer, from snowmobile tours, ice-fishing and reindeer racing in winter, to summer boat trips along the 400m-deep Sautso canyon, Scandinavia's largest. At the Friluftspark, Canyon Huskies (☎78 43 33 06, Ⓦwww.canyonhuskies.no) can organize half-day sled dog tours, while Fjord Halibut (☎78 43 13 67, Ⓔbjkvernm@online.no) arranges fishing trips on the Altafjord.

The Friluftspark's other attraction is its **Nordlysiglooen** (Northern Lights Igloo; late Jan to March/April; ☎78 43 33 78, Ⓕ78 43 34 65, Ⓦwww .alta-friluftspark.no), a 1100sqm hotel built entirely out of ice and snow, including the beds and the glasses in the bar. Unfortunately, the igloo only offers accommodation to groups of ten or more – at around 1100kr per person – but you can just visit the place and have a look around (80kr).

The Finnmarksvidda

Venture far inland from Alta and you enter the **Finnmarksvidda**, a vast mountain plateau which spreads southeast beyond the Finnish border. Rivers, lakes and marshes lattice the region, but there's barely a tree, let alone a mountain, to break the contours of a landscape whose wide skies and faraway horizons are eerily beautiful. Distances are hard to gauge – a dot of a storm can soon be upon you, breaking with alarming ferocity – and the air is crystal-clear, giving a whitish lustre to the sunshine. A couple of roads cross this expanse, but for the most part it remains the preserve of the few thousand semi-nomadic **Sami** who make up the majority of the local population. Many still wear traditional dress, a brightly coloured affair of red bonnets and blue jerkins or dresses, all trimmed with red, white and yellow embroidery. You'll see permutations on this traditional costume all over Finnmark, but especially at roadside souvenir stalls and, on Sundays, outside Sami churches.

Setting aside the slow encroachments of the tourist industry, lifestyles on the Finnmarksvidda have remained remarkably constant for centuries. The main occupation is **reindeer-herding**, supplemented by hunting and fishing, and the pattern of Sami life is mostly still dictated by the animals. During the winter, the reindeer graze the flat plains and shallow valleys of the interior, migrating towards the coast in early May as the snow begins to melt, and temperatures inland begin to climb as high as 30°C. By October, both people and reindeer are journeying back from their temporary summer quarters. The long, dark winter is spent in preparation for the great **Easter festivals**, when weddings and baptisms are celebrated in the region's two principal settlements, **Karasjok** and – more especially – **Kautokeino**. As neither place is particularly appealing in itself, this is without question the best time to be here, when the inhabitants celebrate the end of the polar night and the arrival of spring. There are folk-music concerts, church services and traditional sports, including the famed reindeer races, with the animals pulling passenger-laden sleighs. Details of the Easter festivals are available at any Finnmark tourist office, or on the Kautokeino festival website (ⓦwww .saami-easterfestival.org). Summer visits, on the other hand, can be disappointing, since many families and their reindeer are at coastal pastures and there is precious little activity.

From Alta, the only direct route into the Finnmarksvidda is south along Highway 93 to Kautokeino, a distance of 130km. From here, Highway 93 continues south into Finland, while, 30km north back along the Alta road, Highway 92 branches off northeast to Karasjok, where it rejoins the E6 (but well beyond the turning to Nordkapp). **Bus** services across the Finnmarksvidda, operated by FFR (ⓣ78 43 36 77; ⓦwww.ffr.no), are little more than adequate: there are one or two buses a day from Alta to Kautokeino except on Saturdays, while a limited service runs the 250km along the E6 from Alta to Karasjok (late June to mid-Aug 2 daily except on Sat; late Aug to early June 1–2 daily 4 times a week). A further service links Karasjok with Hammerfest once or twice daily except on Saturdays, but there are no buses running the 130km between Karasjok and Kautokeino.

The best time to **hike** in the Finnmarksvidda is in August and early September – after the peak mosquito season and before the weather turns cold. For the most part the plateau vegetation is scrub and open birch forest, which makes the going fairly easy, though the many marshes, rivers and lakes often

The Sami

The northernmost reaches of Norway, Sweden and Finland, and the Kola peninsula of northwest Russia, are collectively known as **Lapland**. Traditionally, the indigenous population were called "Lapps", but in recent years this name has fallen out of favour and been replaced by the term **Sami**, although the change is by no means universal. The new name comes from the Sami word *sámpi* meaning both the land and its people, who now number around 70,000 scattered across the region. Among the oldest peoples in Europe, the Sami are probably descended from prehistoric clans who migrated here from the east by way of the Baltic. There are three distinct versions of the Sami **language**, each closely related to Finnish and Estonian, and each broken down into a number of markedly different regional dialects. They all have, however, many common features, including a superabundance of words and phrases to express variations in snow and ice conditions. In this chapter, we've given some of the more common Sami names in brackets after the Norweigan versions.

Originally, the Sami were a semi-nomadic people, living in small communities (*siidas*), each of which had a degree of control over the surrounding hunting grounds. They mixed hunting, fishing and trapping, preying on all the edible creatures of the north, but it was the wild reindeer that supplied most of their needs. This changed in the sixteenth century when the Sami switched over to **reindeer herding**, with communities following the seasonal movements of the animals. What little contact the early Sami had with other Scandinavians was almost always to their disadvantage – as early as the ninth century, a Norse chieftain by the name of Ottar boasted to the English king Alfred the Great of his success in imposing a fur, feather and hide tax on his Sami neighbours.

These early depredations were, however, nothing compared with the **dislocation of Sami culture** that followed the efforts of Sweden, Russia and Norway to control and colonize Sami land from the seventeenth century onwards. It took the best part of two hundred years for the competing nations to finally agree their northern frontiers – the last treaty, between Norway and Russia, was signed in 1826 – and meanwhile hundreds of farmers had settled in "Lapland", to the consternation of its indigenous population. At the same time, in the manner of many colonized peoples, Norway's Sami had accepted the **religion** of their colonizers, succumbing to the missionary endeavours of Pietist Protestants in the early eighteenth century. Predictably, the missionaries frowned upon the Sami's traditional shamanism, although the more progressive among them did support the use of Sami languages and even translated hundreds of works. Things got even worse for the Norwegian

---

impede progress. There are a handful of clearly demarcated **hiking trails** and a smattering of appropriately sited but unstaffed huts; for detailed information, ask at Alta tourist office.

Kautokeino

It's a two-and-a-half-hour bus ride from Alta across the Finnmarksvidda to **KAUTOKEINO** (*Guovdageaidnu*), the principal winter camp of the Norwegian Sami and the site of a huge reindeer market in spring and autumn. The Sami are not, however, easy town dwellers and whilst Kautokeino is useful to them as a supply centre, it's a desultory, desolate-looking place that straggles along Highway 93 on either side of the Kautokeinoelva River. Nevertheless, the settlement has become something of a tourist draw on account of the jewellers who have moved here from the south. Every summer, these jewellers line the long main street with souvenir booths, attracting Finnish day-trippers like flies. Their wares are not tourist tat, however, which a

Sami towards the end of the nineteenth century, when the government, influenced by the Social Darwinism of the day, embarked on an aggressive policy of "**Norwegianization**". New laws banned the use of indigenous languages in schools, and only allowed Sami to buy land if they could speak Norwegian. It was only in the 1950s that these policies were abandoned and slowly replaced by a more considerate, progressive approach.

More recently, the Sami were dealt yet another grievous blow by the **Chernobyl nuclear disaster** of 1986. This contaminated not only the lichen that feeds the reindeer in winter, but also the game, fish, berries and fungi that supplement the Sami diet. Contamination of the reindeer meat meant the collapse of the export market, and promises of compensation by the various national governments only appeared late in the day. Furthermore, the cash failed to address the fact that this wasn't just an economic disaster for the Sami, but a threat to their traditional way of life, based around reindeer herding. Partly because of the necessarily reduced role of reindeer – reindeer-herding is now the main occupation of just one-fifth of the Sami population – other expressions of Sami **culture** have expanded. Traditional arts and crafts are now widely available in all of Scandinavia's major cities and the first of several Sami films, *Veiviseren* (*The Pathfinder*), was released to critical acclaim in 1987. Sami music (*joik*) has also been given a hearing by world-music and jazz buffs. Although their provenance is uncertain, the rhythmic song-poems that constitute *joik* were probably devised to soothe anxious reindeer; the words are subordinated to the unaccompanied singing and at times are replaced altogether by meaningless, sung syllables.

Since the international anti-colonial struggles of the 1960s, the Norwegians have been obliged to re-evaluate their relationship with the Sami. In 1988, the country's constitution was amended by the addition of an article that read: "It is the responsibility of the authorities of the state to create conditions enabling the Sami people to preserve and develop its language, culture and way of life". The following year a Sami Parliament, the **Sameting**, was opened in Karasjok. Certain deep-seated problems do remain and, as with other aboriginal peoples marooned in industrialized countries, there have been heated debates about land and mineral rights and the future of the Sami as a people, above and beyond one country's international borders. Neither is it clear quite how the Norwegian Sami will adjust to having something akin to dual status – as an indigenous, partly autonomous people of the region and citizens of a particular country – but at least Oslo is asking the right questions.

visit to **Juhl's Silver Gallery** (June to early Aug daily 9am–7pm; mid-Aug to May daily 9am–6pm, but ring to confirm in winter; ☎78 48 61 89, Ⓦwww.juhls.no) will confirm. Here, Kautokeino's pioneer jewellers (see box on p.334) still make – and sell – exquisitely beautiful, high-quality silver work, as well as a broader range of high-quality craftwork. Not only that, but the interior of the workshop (regular free guided tours; 20min) is intriguing in its own right, with some rooms decorated in crisp, modern Scandinavian style, others done out in an elaborate version of Sami design and decorated with nomadic handicrafts from all over the world. The gallery, well sign-posted, is located on a ridge above the west bank of the Kautokeinoelva, 2.5km south of the town centre.

Back in the town centre, near the north bank of the river, the small **Kautokeino Bygdetun og Museum** (*Guovdageaidnu Gilisillju* or Kautokeino Parish Museum; mid-June to mid-Aug Mon–Sat 9am–7pm, Sun noon–7pm, mid-Aug to mid-June Mon–Fri 9am–3pm; 25kr) features a history of the town

The jewellers of Kaoutokeino

The first southern jewellers to move to Kautokeino were **Frank and Regine Juhls**, pioneers of a sort, who braved all sorts of difficulties – there were no roads across the Finnmarksvidda then – to set up their workshop here in 1959. It was a bold move at a time when the Sami were very much a neglected minority, but the Juhls had a keen interest in nomadic cultures and, although the Sami had no tradition of jewellery-making, they did adorn themselves with all sorts of unusual items traded with the outside world. Much influenced by the Sami style of self-adornment, the Juhls repeated and developed their various motifs, and their business prospered. The Juhls still set the artistic pace hereabouts and, although they now have shops in Oslo and Bergen, their workshop remains in Kautokeino. Today, however, the original plain and simple building has been replaced by an extensive complex of showrooms and workshops, whose pagoda-like roofs exhibit Sami influences.

inside and a number of draughty-looking Sami dwellings outside. You'll spot the same little turf huts and skin tents (known as *lavvo*) all over Finnmark – often housing souvenir stalls. Not far away, across the river to the south of the tourist office and along the main drag, stands the modern **Kautokeino kirke** (June to mid-Aug daily 9am–9pm; free), a delightful wooden building whose interior is decorated in bright, typically Sami colours, and looks particularly appealing when the Sami turn up here in their Sunday best. Also worth a quick look is the signposted **Kautokeino Kulturhuset** (*Guovdageaidnu Kulturviessu* or Cultural Centre), on the north side of town. Winner of various architectural awards, the building houses the only state-sponsored Sami theatre in Norway.

Practicalities

Doubling as Highway 93, Kautokeino's main street is 1500m long, with most of the town's facilities clustered on the north side of the river, near the **tourist office** (daily: June & Aug 9am–4pm, July 9am–7pm; ☎78 48 65 00; Ⓔe-mail@kautokeino.kommune.no), which marks what is effectively the town centre: the **bus stop** lies 350m to the north. The tourist office provides town maps and has details of local events and activities, from fishing and hiking through to "Sami adventures", which typically include a boat trip and a visit to a *lavvo* where you can sample traditional Sami food and listen to *joik*: prices start from around 300kr. The main local tour operator is Cavzo Safari (☎78 48 75 88, Ⓕ78 48 76 39, Ⓦwww.samitour.com/norsk/cavzo).

The only **hotel** as such is the modest and modern *Norlandia Kautokeino* (☎78 48 62 05, Ⓕ78 48 67 01; ❺, s/r ❹), on the north side of town just off Highway 93. There are also a couple of **campsites** near the river on the southern edge of town, primarily *Kautokeino Camping og Motell* (☎78 48 54 00, Ⓕ78 48 75 05), with cabins (❶) and a few frugal motel rooms (❷). The *Norlandia Kautokeino* has the town's only **restaurant**.

Karasjok

The only other settlement of any size on the Finnmarksvidda is **KARASJOK** (*Kárásjohka*), Norway's Sami capital, which straddles the E6 on the main route from Finland to Nordkapp and consequently sees plenty of tourists. Spread across a wooded river valley, it has none of the desolation of Kautokeino, yet it still conspires to be fairly mundane, despite the presence of the Sami parliament and the country's best Sami museum. The busiest place in town is the **tourist office** (*Karasjok Opplevelser;* early June & late Aug daily 9am–4pm; mid-June to mid-Aug daily 9am–7pm; Sept–May Mon–Fri 9am–4pm; ☎78 46 88 10, Ⓦwww.koas.no), on the north side of the river, beside the E6 and Highway 92 crossroads, in what amounts to the town centre. As well as issuing free town maps, booking accommodation and organizing Sami expeditions, the tourist office is also home to a miniature Sami theme park, **Sámpi** (same times; 90kr). Here, you can see traditional Sami dwellings, shops and a restaurant, a multimedia introduction to the Sami in the Magic Theatre (*Stálubákti*), and displays of ancient Sami skills, such as reindeer roping.

From the tourist office, it's a 200m-walk north along the Nordkapp road to Museumsgata, where you turn right for **De Samiske Samlinger** (*Sámi vourká dávvirat* or Sami Collection; mid-June to late Aug Mon–Sat 9am–6pm, Sun 10am–6pm; late Aug to Dec & April to mid-June Mon–Fri 9am–3pm, Sat & Sun 10am–3pm; 25kr). This attempts an overview of Sami culture and history, with the outdoor exhibits comprising an assortment of old dwellings that illustrate the frugality of Sami life. Inside, a large, clearly presented collection of incidental bygones includes a colourful sample of folkloric Sami costumes. You may also want to take a peek at the **Gamle kirke** (June–Aug daily 8am–9pm; free), just off Highway 92 on the south side of the river, which was the only building left standing in Karasjok at the end of World War II. Of simple design, it dates from 1807, making it easily the oldest surviving church in Finnmark.

Carry on from the Gamle kirke along Highway 92, and the next major turning on the right leads to the **Samisk Kunstnersenter** (*Sámi daiddaguovddás* or Sami Artists' Centre; mid-June to late Aug Mon–Sat 10am–3pm & Sun noon–5pm; late Aug to mid-June Mon–Fri 10am–3pm & Sun noon–5pm; free; ☎78 46 99 40). This unassuming gallery showcases the work of contemporary Sami artists, but don't expect folksy paintings – Sami artists are a diverse bunch and as likely to be influenced by post-modernism as reindeer-herding.

Hikes and tours into the Finnmarksvidda

However diverting Karasjok's sights may be, you'll only get a feel for the Finnmarksvidda if you venture out of town. The tourist office has the details of a wide range of local **guided tours**: options include dog-sledging, a visit to a Sami camp, a boat trip on the Karasjokka river, cross-country skiing and even gold-panning. The region's most popular long-distance **hike** is the five-day haul across the heart of the Finnmarksvidda, from Karasjok to Alta via a string of strategically located huts; ask at Alta's tourist office (see p.330) for details, but note that this is not for the faint-hearted or inexperienced. A more gentle walk is the 3.5km **Ássebákti nature trail**, which passes more than a hundred Sami cultural monuments – *lavvo* and so forth – en route. Clearly signed, the trail head is about 16km west of Karasjok along Highway 92 towards Kautokeino.

Practicalities

There is a limited **bus** service to Karasjok along the E6 from Alta and Kirkenes (late June to mid-Aug 2 daily except on Sat; late Aug to early June 1–2 daily 4 times a week), and another bus runs from Hammerfest to Karasjok (1–2 daily except on Sat), but there are no buses links with Kautokeino. Schedules mean that it's often possible to spend a couple of hours here before moving on, which is quite enough to see the sights, but not nearly long enough to get the real flavour of the place. Buses arrive at Karasjok's **bus station**, on Storgata, from where it's a signposted five- to ten-minute walk west to the **tourist office** (see above).

The best **hotel** in town is the *Rica Hotel Karasjok* (📞78 46 74 00, 📠78 46 68 02, 🌐www.rica.no; ❻, s/r ❹), a breezy modern establishment a short stroll north of the tourist office along the E6. More modest and less expensive accommodation is available at the unassuming *Annes Overnatting og Motell* (📞78 46 64 32; ❷), east of the tourist office along the E6 towards Kirkenes, and at the year-round *Karasjok Camping*, a ten-minute walk west from the tourist office on the Kautokeino road (📞78 46 61 35, 📠78 46 66 97; cabins ❷). There's also HI **hostel** accommodation some 7km out of town on the Kautokeino road in the cosy, home-made cabins of *Engholm Husky Vandrerhjem* (📞78 46 71 66, 🌐www.engholm.no). The hostel is open all year and has a sauna and self-catering facilities, as well as providing Arctic dinners, sitting on reindeer skins around an open fire. The owner, Sven, keeps about forty huskies which he uses for sledding tours, and can also organize fishing trips, guided wilderness hikes and horse riding; he will pick up guests from Karasjok by prior arrangement too. Dorm beds cost 150kr, while cabins cost 300kr per night plus 100kr per person.

For **food**, at the *Rica Hotel Karasjok*, the unusual *Gammen* restaurant serves Sami-style meals in a series of turf-covered huts. It's all good fun, provided you like reindeer meat, which is invariably the staple ingredient.

Hammerfest

HAMMERFEST, some 220km northwest of Karasjok and 150km north of Alta, is, as its tourist office takes great pains to point out, the world's northern-most town. It was also, they add, the first town in Europe to have electric street-lighting. Hardly fascinating facts perhaps, but both give a glimpse of the pride that the locals take in making the most of what is, indisputably, an inhos-pitable location. Indeed, it's a wonder the town has survived at all: a hurricane flattened the place in 1856; it was burnt to the ground in 1890; and the retreat-ing Germans mauled it at the end of World War II. Yet, instead of being aban-doned, Hammerfest was stubbornly rebuilt for a third time. Nor is it the grim industrial town you might expect from the proximity of the offshore oil wells, but a bright, cheerful port that drapes around a **horseshoe-shaped harbour** sheltered from the elements by a steep rocky hill. Hammerfest also benefits from the occasional dignified wooden building that recalls its nineteenth-cen-tury heyday as the centre of the *Pomor* trade in which Norwegian fish were traded for Russian flour by the boat-load. But don't get too carried away: Bill Bryson, in *Neither Here Nor There*, hit the nail on the head with his description of Hammerfest as "an agreeable enough town in a thank-you-God-for-not-making-me-live-here sort of way". Neither is the town's main employer, the harbourfront fish-processing plant, the stuff of Arctic romance.

The town

Running parallel to the waterfront, **Strandgata**, the town's principal street, is a busy, 500-metre-long run of supermarkets, clothes and souvenir shops, part-ly inspired by the town's role as a stop-off for cruise ships on the way to Nordkapp. However, most of the activity takes place on the main **town quay**, off Sjøgata, with tourists emerging from the liners to beetle around the har-bourfront, eating shellfish from the stalls along the wharf or buying souvenirs in the small, summertime Sami market. The Hurtigrute spends a couple of hours here too, arriving at an unsociable 5.15am on its way north, and at 11.45am heading south.

Beyond that, it's the general atmosphere of the place that appeals rather than any specific sight, though the tiny town centre does muster a couple of attractions, beginning with the **Isbjørnklubben** (The Royal and Ancient Polar Bear Society; Jan to mid–May & Sept–Dec Mon–Fri 11.30am–1.30pm; mid–May to late June & late Aug Mon–Fri 10am–3pm, Sat & Sun 11am–2pm; late June to early Aug daily 6am–5.30pm; 20kr), up from the quay in the basement of the town hall. The society's pint-sized museum – filled with stuffed polar bears and

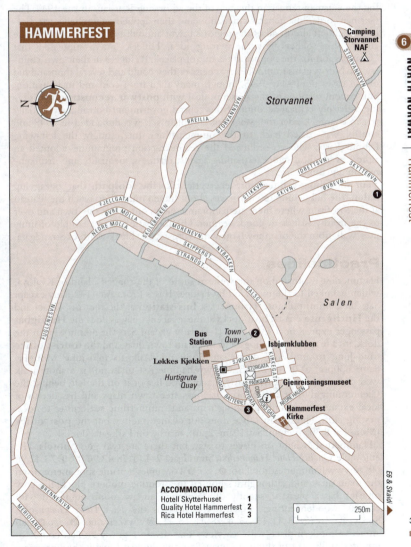

HAMMERFEST

Camping
Storvannet
NAF

Storvannet

STORVANNSVN

BREILIA

STORVANNSVN

IDRETTSVN.

SKYTTERVN

STIKKVN

SKIVN

ØVREVN

1

FJELLGATA

ØVRE MOLLA

NEDRE MOLLA

SKOLEBAKKEN

MORENEVN.

NYBAKKEN

SKIPPERGT

STRANDGT

SALSGT

FUGLENESVN

Salen

Bus
Station

Town
Quay

2

Isbjørnklubben

Løkkes Kjøkken

SJØGATA

KIRKEGATA

Hurtigrute
Quay

HAMNEGATA

PARKGATA

STORGATA

SJØGATA

STRANDGATA

Gjenreisningsmuseet

BATTERIET

NEDRE HAUEN

i

3

Hammerfest
Kirke

BRENNEBIVN

MERIDIANGT

E6 & Skaidi ▶

ACCOMMODATION
Hotell Skytterhuset — 1
Quality Hotel Hammerfest — 2
Rica Hotel Hammerfest — 3

0   250m

seal-skin-covered furniture – tells the story of Hammerfest as a trapping centre and also relates its own dubious history as an organization that hunted and trapped polar bears, eagles and arctic foxes. They'll try and cajole you into supporting the organization by becoming a member – honestly, you can live without forking out 150kr for the certificate. A good deal better is the purpose-built **Gjenreisningsmuseet** (Museum of Postwar Reconstruction; mid-June to Aug daily 10am–6pm, Sept to mid-June by appointment on ☏78 42 26 30; 40kr plus 20kr for English guide-book – the labelling is only in Norwegian), a five-minute walk west of the main quay up Kirkegata. This begins with a fascinating section on the hardships endured by the inhabitants of Finnmark during the German retreat, in the face of the advancing Russians in late 1944. The Germans ordered a general evacuation and then applied a scorched-earth policy, which left almost all of the region's towns and villages in ruins. Just in case any of his soldiers got the wrong idea, Hitler's orders stipulated that "Compassion for the population is out of place". Refugees in their own country, the Norwegians found shelter wherever they could and several thousand hid out in caves until May 1945, though many died from cold and malnutrition. Subsequent sections of the museum deal with **postwar reconstruction**, giving a sharply critical account of the central government bureaucracy initially put in charge. Under the weight of complaints, it was disbanded in 1948 and control was passed back to the municipalities. Interestingly, the left-wing Labour Party, who co-ordinated the reconstruction programme, adopted an almost evangelical stance, crusading against dirtiness, inequality and drunkenness in equal measure.

For something a little more energetic, take the **footpath** that zigzags up **Salen**, the hill behind town. It takes about fifteen minutes to reach the plateau at the top, from where there are panoramic views out across the town and over to the nearby islands in good weather. The footpath begins a couple of minutes' walk from the main town quay on Salsgata, one block south of Strandgata.

Practicalities

Hammerfest is situated on the western shore of the rugged island of Kvaløya, which is linked to the mainland by bridge. Buses (from Alta 1–2 daily except Sat; 2hr 30min) pull into Hammerfest **bus station** at the foot of Sjøgata and the **Hurtigrute** coastal boat docks at the adjacent quay, as does the **Hurtigbåt** passenger express boat from Alta (1–2 daily except Sat; 1hr 30min). From the dock, it's a brief walk up Sjøgata to the main town quay, and the **tourist office** (mid-June to mid-Aug daily 9am–5pm; mid-Aug to mid-June Mon–Fri 8am–3.30pm; ☏78 41 21 85, ⓦwww.hammerfest-turist.no) is a short walk west of here – head down Sørøygata and you'll spot it on the left, behind the Gjenreisningsmuseet (see above). It issues free town maps and has details of local excursions, including fishing trips and summertime sea cruises to local nesting cliffs. The tourist office does not change money, but the **post office** (Mon–Fri 8.30am–5pm, Sat 10am–2pm), nearby on Parkgata, does.

Hammerfest is light on places to stay, but there are two good **hotels**. The enjoyable *Quality Hotel Hammerfest*, Strandgata 2-4 (☏78 42 96 00, ℱ78 42 96 60, ⓦwww.hammerfesthotel.no; ❻, s/r ❺), occupies a prime spot, metres from the main quay, and, although it's housed in a routine modern block, the cosy interior has a pleasant, slightly old-fashioned air, its rooms equipped with chunky wooden fittings. Equally appealing is the *Rica Hotel Hammerfest*, Sørøygata 15 (☏78 41 13 33, ℱ78 41 13 11, ⓦwww.rica.no; ❺, s/r ❸), an attractive modern place with sea views that sits on a grassy knoll a couple of minutes' walk west of the main quay. The only budget hotel is the unprepossessing *Hotell Skytterhuset*, Skytterveien 24 (☎78 41 15 11, ℱ78 41 19 26; ❸), in a large prefabricated block on a hillside, some 3km from the town centre. To get there by car, head east from the main quay along Strandgata and, after about 400m, turn right along Skolebakken. This leads round a lake, Storvannet, at the bottom of a steep-sided valley, then climbs up the east side of Salen hill past the hotel. On the way, you'll pass the tiny lakeshore *Storvannet Camping NAF* (☎78 41 10 10; June to mid-Sept), with tent spaces and a few cabins (❶). Unless you're particularly energetic, you won't want to walk to either of these places from the centre – take a taxi.

For **food**, the *Rica Hotel Hammerfest* has the best **restaurant** in town, with sea views and delicious seafood; main courses start at around 190kr. More economical is *Løkkes Kjøkken*, across from the Hurtigrute quay at Storgata 2, a well-tended, family-run café providing tasty standard-issue Norwegian meals.

Moving on

From Hammerfest, FFR (Finnmark Fylkesrederi og Rutesselskap; ☎78 40 70 00, ⓦwww.ffr.no) **buses** run to Karasjok, Kirkenes and Alta (all 1–2 daily except Sat). All pass through Skaidi, on the E6, where you can change for either the Nordkappekspressen service to Honningsvåg and Nordkapp (late June to mid-Aug 1–2 daily), operated by Nor-Way Bussekspress (☎815 44 444, ⓦwww.nor-way.no), or the FFR bus to Honningsvåg (late June to mid-August 1–5 daily; mid-Aug to late June 1–2 daily 4 times a week). Note that not all the buses make the connection, so check at Hammerfest bus station before you set out.

The **Hurtigrute** coastal boat (ⓦwww.hurtigruten.com) heads south from Hammerfest at 1pm, taking ten-and-a-half hours to reach its next major port of call, Tromsø (passenger 690kr one-way, car 340kr). Sailing north, the Hurtigrute leaves at 6.45am and reaches Honningsvåg at 11.45am (360kr/318kr), where it stops for three and three quarter hours, giving enough time for connecting buses to make the return trip to Nordkapp.

Finally, Hammerfest has several **car rental** companies, which frequently offer attractive short-term deals from around 650kr a day. Try Hammerfest Bilsenter, Seilmakerveien 1 (☎78 40 78 20), or Hertz, Rossmollgate 48 (☎78 41 71 66).

Nordkapp

At the northern tip of Norway, the treeless and windswept island of **Magerøya** is mainly of interest to travellers as the location of the **Nordkapp** (North Cape), generally regarded as Europe's northernmost point – though in fact it isn't: that distinction belongs to the neighbouring headland of **Knivskjellodden**. Somehow, everyone seems to have conspired to ignore this simple latitudinal fact and now, while Nordkapp has become one of the most popular tourist destinations in the country, there isn't even a road to Knivskjellodden. Neither has the development of the Nordkapp as a tourist spot been without its critics, who argue that the large and lavish visitor centre – **Nordkapphallen** – is crass and grossly overpriced; their opponents simply point to the huge number of people who visit. Whatever, it's hard to imagine making the long trip to Magerøya without at least dropping by Nordkapp, and the island has other charms too, notably a bleak, rugged beauty that's readily seen from the **E69** as it threads across the mountainous interior from Honningsvåg, on the south coast, to Nordkapp, a distance of 34km.

The obvious base for a visit to Nordkapp is the island's main settlement, **Honningsvåg**, a middling fishing village with a clutch of chain hotels. More appealing, however, is the tiny hamlet of **Kamøyvaer**, nestling beside a narrow fjord just off the E69 between Honningsvåg and Nordkapp, and with a couple of family-run guesthouses. Bear in mind also that Nordkapp is within easy striking distance of other places back on the mainland – certainly the picturesque fishing-station-cum-hotel at **Repvåg**, and maybe even Hammerfest (see p.336) and Alta (see p.328), respectively 210km and 240km away.

Arriving **by bus** from Alta or Skaidi (for Hammerfest), Nor-Way Bussekspress's Nordkappekspressen stops at both Honningsvåg and Nordkapp (late June to mid-Aug Mon–Fri 2 daily, Sat & Sun 1 daily). The schedule is such that on weekdays you can take the first bus to Nordkapp, spend a couple of hours there and then catch the second bus back. If you catch the second bus, you'll have three hours at Nordkapp from 9pm to 12.15am – which means, of course, that you can view the midnight sun. If you take FFR's Alta to Honningsvåg bus (late June to mid-Aug 1–5 daily; mid-Aug to late June 1-2 daily 4 times a week), you'll need to either change onto the Nordkappekspressen bus for the fifty-minute journey (66kr each way) to Nordkapp, or **rent a car** in Honningsvåg: the tourist office there has details of local car rental companies – expect to pay around 650kr for a four-hour rental. Alternatively, the **taxi fare** from Honningsvåg to Nordkapp, including an hour's waiting time, is 700kr return, 900kr after 10pm, and 450kr one-way: contact Nordkapp Taxisentral (☏78 47 52 48).

Arriving **by car**, bear in mind that the last stretch of the Honningsvåg to Nordkapp road is closed by snow from about mid-October to mid-April – though the determined can still get there on a guided **snowmobile excursion** with Nordkapp Opplevelser (☏78 47 52 48, ✉tommen@ mobilpost.com). You can also reach Honningsvåg (but not Nordkapp) on the northbound **Hurtigrute** coastal boat, which arrives daily at 11.45am and departs at 3.30am: the boat is met by special buses, which take passengers off to Nordkapp and back.

North from Skaidi to Repvåg and Magerøya island

At the **Skaidi** crossroads, 60km from Hammerfest, the **E6** veers east to clip across a bleak plateau that brings it, in 23km, to the turning for Nordkapp. This road, the **E69**, scuttles north along the shore of the **Porsangerfjord**, a deep and wide inlet flanked by bare, low-lying hills whose stone has been fractured and made flaky by the biting cold of winter. Here and there, the shore is interrupted by massive monoliths, but for the most part the scenery is unusually tame and the shoreline accommodates a string of fishermens' houses – plus the wooden racks used to air-dry their catch. After 48km, the E69 zips past the byroad to **REPVÅG**, an old timber fishing station on a promontory just 2km off the main highway. A rare and particularly picturesque survivor from prewar days, the buildings here are painted red in the traditional manner and perch on stilts on the water's edge. The whole complex has been turned into the *Repvåg Fjordhotell og Rorbusenter* (☎78 47 54 40, ℱ78 47 27 51; April–Oct), with simple, unassuming rooms (❸) in the main building, as well as a cluster of *rorbuer*, or old fishermen's shacks (❷). It's a charming place to stay – solitary and scenic in equal proportions, the public areas of the hotel decked out with authentic nautical tackle and cosy furniture. Neither is tourism the only concern of the owners, as is evidenced by the split cod nailed to the outside walls to dry. Repvåg is an ideal base from which to reach the Nordkapp, though once you're ensconced here, you may settle instead for one of the hotel's boat and fishing trips out on the Porsangerfjord. Almost inevitably, the hotel **restaurant** specializes in seafood – and very good it is too.

Back on the E69, it's about 25km to the ambitious – and amazingly expensive – series of tunnels and bridges (125kr toll) that span the straits between the mainland and Honningsvåg, on the island of **Magerøya**, which you'll see long before you arrive there, a hunk of brown rock looking like an inverted blancmange.

Honningsvåg

HONNINGSVÅG, 180km from Hammerfest, is officially classified as a village, which robs it of the title of the world's northernmost town – hard luck considering it's barely any smaller nor less hardy in the face of adversity than its neighbour. The village, largely comprising a jumble of well-worn modern buildings that reflect its role as a minor fishing- and sea-port, straggles along the seashore, sheltered from the blizzards of winter by the surrounding crags. It has also accumulated several chain hotels, catering primarily for package tourists bound for the Nordkapp. Honningsvåg is at its prettiest at the **head of the harbour**, where an assortment of timber warehouses, dating back to the days when the village was entirely reliant on fish, make an attractive ensemble. Draped with fishing nets and tackle, these good-looking buildings perch on crusty timber stilts that jut out into the water. They have wide eaves to protect against the snow, and each has its own jetty where fishing smacks are roped in tight against the wind.

Practicalities

Honningsvåg is strung out along its main drag, Storgata, for about one kilometre. Buses from the mainland, including the long-distance Nord-Norgeekspressen, pull into the **bus station** at the west end of Storgata. The **Hurtigrute** coastal boat docks at the adjacent jetty and the northbound service is met by special Nordkapp excursion buses. The **tourist office** is here too (mid-June to mid-Aug Mon–Fri 8.30am–6pm, Sat & Sun noon–6pm; mid-Aug to mid-June Mon–Fri 8.30am–4pm; ☎78 47 25 99, ⓦwww.northcape .no).

All Honningsvåg's **hotels** are along or near Storgata. Walking east from the bus station, it's a few metres to the first, the *Rica Hotel Honningsvåg* (☎78 47 23

33, ⒻⒻ78 47 33 79, ⓌⓌwww.rica.no; mid–May to Aug; ❺), a routine modern block with nearly two hundred modern rooms. Its sister hotel, the year-round *Rica Bryggen* (Ⓣ78 47 28 88, Ⓕ78 47 27 24, Ⓦwww.rica.no; ❺), occupies a similar but slightly smarter concrete high-rise about 500m to the east, down at the head of the harbour. Again, the rooms are bright, modern and comfortable, but hardly inspiring. More appealing is the adjacent *Honningsvåg Brygge Hotel* (Ⓣ78 47 64 64, Ⓕ78 47 65 65, Ⓦwww.hvg.brygge.no; ❺), a tasteful and intelligent conversion of a set of wooden warehouses perched on one of the old jetties. The rooms here are smart and cosy – and advance reservations are strongly advised. Somewhat cheaper, but rather glum, rooms are also available at the *Arctic Hotell Nordkapp*, near the bus station at Storgata 12 (Ⓣ78 47 29 66, Ⓕ78 47 30 10; ❹). Alternatively, *NAF Nordkapp Camping* (Ⓣ78 47 33 77, Ⓕ78 47 11 77, Ⓔnordkapp.camping@nordkapp.com; late May to mid–Sept), comprising a **campsite** and cabins (❷), is located about 8km from Honningsvåg on the road to Nordkapp.

For **food**, the *Honningsvåg Brygge Hotel* boasts the best **restaurant** by far, the *Sjøhuset* (June to early Aug daily 2–11pm; mid–Aug to May Fri & Sat 6–11pm), where the seafood is delicious and main courses hover around 170kr; reservations are advised here, too.

North from Honningsvåg to Nordkapp

The E69 winds north out of Honningsvåg, clinging to the shore. After 9km, just beyond the conspicuous *Rica Hotel Nordkapp*, you'll see the turning for **KAMØYVÆR**, a pretty little village tucked in tight between the sea and the hills, just 2km from the main road. Here, right on the jetty, the old timber fishing station has been converted into the charming *Havstua* (Ⓣ78 47 51 50, Ⓕ78 47 51 91, Ⓦwww.havstua.no; ❸; May to mid–Sept), with twenty simple but smart and cosy rooms. It's a delightful spot and the food is also first-rate, but it's advisable to book dinner in advance. A few metres away, just back from the jetty, is the *Árran Nordkapp Gjestehus* (Ⓣ78 47 51 29, Ⓕ78 47 51 56, Ⓦwww.arranhotels.com; ❷; May to mid–Sept), not quite as appealing perhaps, but still a pleasant, family-run guesthouse in a brightly painted and well-tended home.

Beyond the Kamøyvær turning, the E69 twists a solitary course up through the hills to cross a high-tundra plateau, the mountains stretching away on either side. It's a fine run, with snow and ice lingering well into the summer and impressive views over the treeless and elemental Arctic terrain. From June to October this is pastureland for herds of reindeer, who graze right up to the road. The Sami, who bring them here by boat, combine herding with souvenir selling, setting up camp at the roadside in full costume to peddle clothes, jewellery and sets of antlers, which some motorists are daft enough to attach to the front of their vehicles. About 29km from Honningsvåg, the E69 passes the start of the well-marked **hiking trail** that leads to the actual tip of Europe, the headland of **Knivskjellodden**, stretching about 1500m further north than its famous neighbour. The 16km-long round-hike takes between two and three hours each way, but the terrain is too difficult and the climate too unpredictable for the inexperienced or poorly equipped hiker.

Nordkapp

Many visitors, when they finally reach the **Nordkapp**, feel desperately disappointed – it is, after all, only a cliff and, at 307m, it isn't even all that high. But for others there's something about this greyish-black hunk of slate, stuck at the end of a bare, wind-battered promontory, that exhilarates the senses. Some such feeling must have inspired the prehistoric Sami to establish a sacrificial site here, and the Nordkapp certainly stirred the romantic notions of earlier generations of tourists, often inspiring them to metaphysical ruminations. In 1802, the Italian naturalist Giuseppe Acerbi, author of *Travels through Sweden, Finland and Lapland*, exclaimed, "The northern sun, creeping at midnight along the horizon, and the immeasurable ocean in apparent contact with the skies, form the grand outlines in the sublime picture presented to the astonished spectator." Quite – though the seventeenth-century traveller Francesco Negri wasn't far behind: "Here, where the world comes to an end, my curiosity does as well, and now I can return home content."

Flights of fancy apart, North Cape was named by the English explorer **Richard Chancellor** in 1553, as he drifted along the Norwegian coast in an attempt to find the Northeast Passage from the Atlantic to the Pacific. He failed, but managed to reach the White Sea, from where he and his crew travelled overland to Moscow, thereby opening a new, northern trade route to Russia. Chancellor's account, published in the geographer Richard Hakluyt's *Navigations*, brought his exploits to the attention of seamen across Europe, but it was to be another three hundred years before the Northeast Passage was finally negotiated by the Swede Nils Nordenskjöld in 1879. In the meantime, just a trickle of visitors ventured to the Nordkapp. Among them, in 1795, was the exiled Louis Philippe of Orleans (subsequently king of France), but it was the visit of the Norwegian king **Oscar II** in 1873 that opened the tourist floodgates.

Nowadays the lavish **Nordkapphallen** (North Cape Hall; daily: April to late May & Sept to early Oct noon–5pm; late May to mid-June noon–1am; mid-June to early Aug 9am–2am; early Aug to end Aug noon–midnight; 185kr for 48hrs, including parking), hewn out of the rock of the Cape, entertains thousands of visitors. Fronted by a statue of King Oscar II, the main building contains a restaurant, café, a post office where you get your letters specially stamped, and a cinema showing – you guessed it – films about the cape. There's a viewing area too, but there's not much to see except the sea – and, weather permitting, the midnight sun from May 11 to July 31. Having made it here, you can join the Royal North Cape Club at the information desk for a 150kr lifetime membership fee. Gluttons for financial punishment can stay here too, from May to September, in **Suite 71° 10' 21"** (☎78 47 68 60) – as in Nordkapp's latitude. At the top of the building's one and only tower, the suite offers a 270-degree view through its enormous windows and is a favourite with honeymooners, though quite why this should be considered a romantic spot is hard to discern. If it's booked in advance, the suite costs 3700kr per night, but the price tumbles to around 2000kr if it's rented on spec.

A **tunnel** runs from the main building to the cliff face. It's flanked by a couple of little side-chambers, one of which is a chapel, where you can get married, and by a series of displays detailing past events and visitors, including the unlikely appearance of the King of Siam in 1907, who was so ill that he had to be carried up here on a stretcher. At the far end, the cavernous **Grotten Bar** offers caviar and champagne, long views out to sea through the massive glass wall and (of all things) a mock bird cliff. Alternatively, to escape the hurly-burly, you may decide to walk out onto the surrounding headland, though this is too bleak a spot to be much fun.

East to Kirkenes

East of Nordkapp the landscape is more of the same – a relentless expanse of barren plateaux, mountain and ocean. Occasionally the monotony is relieved by a determined village commanding sweeping views over the fjords that slice into the mainland, but generally there is little for the eyes of a tourist. Nor is there much to do in what are predominantly fishing and industrial settlements, and there are few tangible attractions beyond the sheer impossibility of the chill wilderness.

The **E6** weaves a circuitous course across this vast territory, travelling close to the Finnish border for much of its length before terminating, 600km from Nordkapp, at **Kirkenes**, a glum, remote town hard by the Russian border. En route, the only obvious target is the Sami centre of Karasjok (see p.334), 270km from Nordkapp, 220km from Hammerfest, and the region's most interesting town. Branching off the E6 at **Tana Bru**, 180km beyond Karasjok, **Highway 890** wiggles and worms its way to a string of north coast fishing villages, before arriving, after 140km, at its final destination, **Berlevåg**, on the northern coast. Back on the E6, just east of Tana Bru, the region's second main road, the coastal **E75**, branches off at **Varangerbotn**, 120km short of Kirkenes. This leads, after 125km, to the small port of **Vardø**, in a handsome island setting with some mildly interesting historical remains.

However, a quicker and far more pleasant way to reach the far east of the region is by the **Hurtigrute** coastal boat, which bobs along the spectacular shores of the Barents Sea, calling at a string of fishing villages and small ports, including Berlevåg and Vardø, before arriving at Kirkenes, where it turns around and begins the long journey back to Bergen. Quicker still, of course, is to **fly**. Most of the region's larger villages have an airstrip, with the main carriers being Widerøe (Ⓦ www.wideroe.no), which flies to Kirkenes and Berlevåg amongst others, and Arctic Air (Ⓦ www.arctic-air.no), which services Vardø.

Accommodation in this part of Norway is very thin on the ground, being confined to a handful of the larger communities. Reservations, therefore, are strongly advised. **Campsites** are more frequent and usually have cabins for rent, but they are mostly stuck in the middle of nowhere.

FFR (Ⓦ www.ffr.no) **buses** serve all the major settlements in the region, with one or two buses on at least four days a week, though rarely on Saturdays. The main long-distance bus follows the E6 from Alta to Kirkenes (11hr), via Skaidi, Karasjok, Tana Bru and Varangerbotn. It runs three times a week, and connects with other buses to the likes of Berlevåg and Vardø. Many of FFR's services operate all year, as the E6 and the E75 are kept open throughout the winter. This does not, however, imply that **drivers** will find conditions straightforward: ice and snow can make the roads treacherous, if not temporarily impassable, at any time, and driving through the long polar darkness (late Nov to late Jan) is extremely disorientating.

East from Nordkapp on the E6

Beyond its junction with the E69 Nordkapp road, the **E6** bangs along the western shore of the **Porsangerfjord**, a wide inlet that slowly shelves up into the sticky marshes and mud flats at its head. After about 45km, the road reaches the hamlet of **STABBURSNES**, which is home to the small but enjoyable **Stabbursnes Naturhus og Museum** (Stabbursnes Nature House and Museum; early June & mid- to late Aug daily 10am–5pm; mid-June to early

△ The Hurtigrute MS Finnmarken near Vesteralen

Aug daily 9am–8pm; Sept–May Tues & Thurs noon–3pm, Wed noon–6pm; 30kr), which provides an overview of the region's flora and fauna. There are diagrams of the elaborate heat-exchanger in the reindeer's nose that helps stop the animal from freezing to death in winter, and blow-ups of the warble fly which torments it in summer. There are also examples of traditional Sami handicrafts and a good section on Finnmark's topography, examining, for example, how and why some of the region's rivers are slow and sluggish, whilst others have cut deep gashes in the landscape. The museum is on the eastern periphery of – and acts as an information centre for – the **Stabbursdalen Nasjonalpark**, a wedge-edged chunk of land that contains the world's most northerly pine forest covering the slopes of the Stabbursdalen river valley, which runs down from the Finnmarksvidda plateau to the Porsangerfjord. The lower end of the valley is broad and marshy, but beyond lie precipitous canyons and chasms – challenging terrain, with a couple of marked hiking trails. If that sounds too much like hard work, opt instead for the easy 2.8-kilometre stroll east from the museum along the thick gravel banks of the Stabbursdalen river where it trickles into the Porsangerfjord. It's an eerily chill landscape and there's a good chance of spotting several species of wetland bird in spring and summer: ducks, geese and waders like the lapwing, the curlew and the arctic knot are common. Indeed, these salt marshes and mud flats are such an important resting and feeding area for migratory wetland birds that they have been protected as the Stabbursnes **nature reserve**.

From Stabbursnes, it's about 15km south to **LAKSELV**, an inconsequential fishing village at the head of the Porsangerfjord, and another 75km to Karasjok (see p.334), the best place to spend the night. Pushing on, the E6 weaves its way northeast along the Finnish border to reach **TANA BRU**, a Sami settlement clustered around a suspension bridge over the River Tana, which rattles down the Tanafjord to the Barents Sea. One of Europe's best salmon rivers, the Tana can be fished, though it needs to be booked months in advance and there are no end of restrictions: contact Tana Tourist Information, at the *Comfort Hotel Tana* (T78 92 53 98) for the full details. Tana Bru's best option for accommodation is the straightforward *Tana Turisthotell* (T78 92 81 98, F78 92 80 05, Wwww.tana-turisthotell.no; ❹), which also allows camping – its restaurant is very good, and a member of the Arctic Menu Scheme (see p.276).

Beyond the village, Highway 890 branches off north to Berlevåg (see below), while the E6/E75 pushes east for another 18km to **Varangerbotn**, where the highways diverge. Here the E75 heads off to Vadsø (see p.348) and Vardø (see p.347), while the E6 continues on to Kirkenes (see p.348), following the southern shores of the **Varangerfjord**, a bleak, weather-beaten run with all colour and vegetation being confined to the northern shore, with its scattered farms and painted fishing boats.

East from Nordkapp on the Hurtigrute

Beyond Nordkapp, the **Hurtigrute** steers a fine route round the top of the country, nudging its way between tiny islets and craggy bluffs, and stopping at a series of remote fishing villages. Amongst them the prettiest is **BERLEVÅG**, which sits amidst a landscape of eerie greenish-grey rock, splashes of colour in a land otherwise stripped by the elements. This tiny village, with a population of just 1200, was thrust into the limelight recently, when Knut Jensen's documentary *Heftig og Begeistret* (Cool & Crazy; 2001) deftly explored its cultural traditions and tight community spirit, focussing on the local men's choir, the **Berlevåg Mannsangforening**, founded in 1917. The film received rave reviews both in Norway and across Europe, giving a welcome boost to the choir, which still performs locally on occasion as well as touring extensively (℡ 48 24 97 49, ✉ arneli@organizer.net). Berlevåg also boasts some pretty testing scuba diving (contact Ishavets Dykkerklubb on ℡ 78 98 19 95). There are two places **to stay**, the best being the workaday *Ishavshotellet Berlevåg*, Storgata 30 (℡ 78 98 14 15, ℻ 78 98 16 63; ❸); the other is *Berlevåg Camping* on Havnegate (℡ 78 98 16 10, ℻ 78 98 08 11, ✉ berlevag.camping@ online.no), which also has cabins (❶).

FFR runs **buses** to Berlevåg from Tana Bru (1-2 daily except Sat; 2hr 30min).

Vardø

From Berlevåg, it's just over five hours on the Hurtigrute to **VARDØ**, Norway's most easterly town, built on an island a couple of kilometres from the mainland, to which it's connected by tunnel. Like everywhere else in Finnmark, Vardø was savaged in World War II and the modern town that grew up in the 1950s trails around the V-shaped harbour, that lies between two islands connected by a narrow causeway.

Vardø's main attraction is the **Vardøhus Festning** (Vardø fortress; daily: mid-June to mid-Sept 8am–9pm; mid-Sept to mid-June 8am–6pm; 20kr), a tiny star-shaped fortress, located a five- to ten-minute walk west of the Hurtigrute quay. The site was first fortified in 1300, but the present structure dates from the 1730s, built at the behest of King Christian VI. When this singularly unpre-possessing monarch toured Finnmark he was greeted, according to one of his courtiers, with "expressions of abject flattery in atrocious verse". Christian had the fortress built to guard the northeastern approaches to his kingdom, but it has never seen active service – hence its excellent state of preservation. A small **museum** in the complex of buildings that flank the fort's central courtyard, gives further details of the fortress's history.

The town's main museum, however, is the **Vardø Museum,** Pers Larssengate 32 (mid-June to mid-Aug daily 9am–6.30pm; mid-Aug to mid-June Mon–Fri 9am–3pm; 20kr), which occupies a sturdy stone building, Lushaugen, on the northwest edge of Vardø, about fifteen minutes' walk from the Hurtigrute quay. Spread over three floors, a series of well-presented displays explain Vardø's history, with sections devoted to explorers such as Willem Barents and Nansen Fridtjof; another dealing with the lucrative Pomor barter trade between north-ern Norway and Russia; and another examining local flora and fauna. Most interesting of all is the section on the witch-hunting fever that gripped Finnmark in the seventeeth century. Although the region had long been regarded by the church as the realm of the devil, witch-finding only took a hold in the 1620s – half a century or so later than the rest of Europe – when, it was alleged, a coven set up shop in a cave on the edge of town. Over the next sixty years more than eighty women were burned alive in Vardø, a huge number considering the size of the population.

Of Vardø's outdoor attractions, top of the list are the **boat trips** (April to mid-Oct daily; 160kr per person), which leave Vardø harbour to cruise round nearby **Hornøya**, a rocky islet and bird reserve where thousands of sea birds nest each summer. Advance bookings are essential (contact the tourist office; see p.348). Alternatively, a newly completed byroad threads its way northwest from Vardø along the coast, passing through a lunar-like landscape to reach, after 45km, the (largely) abandoned fishing village of **Hamningberg**. It's a pic-turesque spot and scores of locals walk here during Vardø's main festival – Pomordagene (Pomor Days), in early July.

The northbound **Hurtigrute** coastal boat reaches Vardø at 5am and leaves just thirty minutes later; southbound it docks at 4.45pm and leaves an hour later. FFR **buses** run the 50km from Varangerbotn to Vadsø (1–2 daily except Sat; 1hr 20min), where a second bus heads the 75km on to Vardø (1–2 daily; 1hr 30min); sometimes these services connect, sometimes they don't – check before you set out. Vardø's **tourist office** is metres from the Hurtigrute quay (June to late Aug Mon–Sat 9am–7pm, Sun noon–7pm; late Aug to May Mon–Fri 9am–5pm; ☎78 98 82 70, ⓦwww.hexeria.no), just up from the workaday *Vardo Hotell* at Kaigata 8 (☎78 98 77 61, ⒡78 98 83 97; ❹, s/r ❷), which is the best of the limited **accommodation** options.

Vadsø

VADSØ, a little under four hours by **Hurtigrute** from Vardø (northbound only), used to be largely Finnish-speaking, and even now half the population of 6000 claims Finnish origin. Its main claim to fame is as the administrative centre of Finnmark, which – to be blunt – isn't much to get excited about. Russian bombers and German soldiers between them destroyed almost all the old town during World War II; the result is the mundanely modern town centre of today. There's really no reason to get off the boat, but there are a couple of minor sights to see if you do, beginning with the **Innvandrermonumentet** (the Immigration Monument), bang in the centre of town, which commemorates the many Finns who migrated here in the eighteenth and nineteenth centuries. Nearby, the **Esbensengården**, an old patrician mansion dating from 1840, forms part of the municipal museum (late June to late Aug Mon–Fri 10am–6pm, Sat & Sun 10am–4pm; late Aug to late June Mon–Fri 10am–2pm; 20kr), which focuses on the Finnish immigrants, too. FFR **buses** from Varangerbotn and Vardø (see above), and a non-stop service from Kirkenes (1–2 daily except Sat; 3hr 30min), pull in at the bus station on Strandgate, on a stumpy promontory – 500m by 300m – at the southern end of town. It's about 1km from where the Hurtigrute docks on Vadsøya island, and connected to it by a bridge. The best **accommodation** in town is the comfortable chain hotel, the *Rica Hotel Vadsø*, right in the centre, at Oscars gate 4 (☎78 95 16 81, ⒡78 95 10 02, ⓦwww.rica.no; ❹).

After Vadsø, the **Hurtigrute** takes a couple of hours to cross the deep blue-black waters of the **Varangerfjord** on the last stage of its journey to Kirkenes. There's snow on the mainland here even in July, which makes for a picturesque chug across the fjord, the odd fishing boat the only sign of life.

Kirkenes and the Russian border

During World War II the mining town and ice-free port of **KIRKENES** suffered more bomb attacks than any other place in Europe apart from Malta. What was left was torched by the German army retreating in the face of liberating Soviet soldiers, who found 3500 local people hiding in the nearby iron-ore mines. The mines finally closed in 1996, threatening the future of the 6000-strong community, which is desperately trying to kindle trade with Russia to keep itself afloat.

Kirkenes is almost entirely modern, with long rows of uniform houses spreading out along the Bøkfjord, a narrow arm of the Barents Sea. If that sounds dull, it's not to slight the town, which makes the most of its inhospitable surroundings with some pleasant public gardens, lakes and residential areas – it's just that it seems an awful long way to come for not very much. That said, once you've finally got here it seems churlish to leave quickly, and it's certainly worth searching out the **Saviomuseet**, housed in the old library at

Kongensgate 10b, about 300m south of the tourist office (Savio Museum; late June to late Aug daily 10am–6pm; late Aug to late June Mon–Fri 10am–3pm; 25kr). This small museum displays the work of the local Sami artist **John Savio** (1902–38), whose life was brief and tragic. Orphaned at the age of three, Savio was ill from childhood onwards and died in poverty of tuberculosis at the age of 36. This lends poignancy to his woodcuts and paintings, with their lonely evocations of the Sami way of life and the overbearing power of nature. The museum also hosts some excellent travelling contemporary art exhibitions. Kirkenes' other museum of note, the **Grenselandmuseet** (Frontier Museum; mid-June to late Aug 10am–6pm; late Aug to mid-June Mon–Fri 10am–3.30pm; 40kr), is about 800m south of the tourist office, at the end of Solheimsveien beside one of the town's lakes. It deals mainly with the history of the region and its people, and includes a detailed account of the events of World War II, illustrated by some fascinating old photos. The part Kirkenes played in the war is also recalled by a couple of **monuments** – one dedicated to the town's wartime women in the main square, and a second to the Red Army on Roald Amundsens gate.

Practicalities

Kirkenes is the northern terminus of the **Hurtigrute** coastal boat, which arrives here at 10.30am and departs for Bergen at 1.30pm. It uses the quay just over 1km east of the town centre; a local bus shuttles between the two. Kirkenes **airport** is 14km southwest of town; regular flybussen (50kr) connect the airport with the centre. The **bus station** is at the end of Kirkegata on the west side of town, about 300m northwest of the central **tourist office** on Kjelland Torkildsens gate (early June to mid-Aug Mon–Fri 8.30am–6pm, Sat & Sun 11am–6pm; mid-Aug to early June Mon–Fri 8.30am–4pm; ⓣ78 99 25 44, ⓦwww.sor-varanger.kommune.no).

The town's best **hotel** is the *Rica Arctic*, whose eighty well-appointed rooms occupy a smart modern block next to the tourist office, at Kongensgate 1 (ⓣ78 99 29 29, ⓕ78 99 11 59, ⓦwww.rica.no; ❻). The similarly modern *Rica Hotel Kirkenes* is less enticing, in a glum-looking, three-storey block about 700m south of the tourist office at Pasvikveien 63 (ⓣ78 99 14 91, ⓕ78 99 13 56, ⓦwww.rica.no; ❻). More appealing – and affordable – is *Barbara's Bed & Breakfast*, Henrik Lunds gate 13 (ⓣ78 99 32 07, ⓦhome.trollnet.no/barbara; ❷), with just two cosy rooms at loft level in one of the town's older buildings, about 500m east of the tourist office. An alternative budget option is *Barents Frokost Hotell*, Presteveien 3 (ⓣ78 99 32 99, ⓕ78 99 30 96, ⓔgcelsius@ frisurf.no; ❷), with frugal rooms both en-suite and with shared facilities, to the east of the centre. As for **food**, the *Rica Arctic Hotel* has a very competent restaurant, but better still is *Vin og Vilt*, Kirkegata 5 (ⓣ78 99 38 11), which serves an excellent range of Arctic specialities including reindeer and char.

Around Kirkenes: Øvre Pasvik Nasjonalpark

Hidden away some 120km south of Kirkenes, where the borders of Norway, Finland and Russia intersect, is the ten-by-nine-kilometre parcel of wilderness that comprises the **Øvre Pasvik Nasjonalpark**, a western offshoot of the Siberian taiga. The park's sub-arctic pine forest covers a series of low-lying hills that make up about half the total area, and below lie swamps, marshes and lakes. Wolverines and bears live in the forest, and there are also traces of the prehistoric Komsa culture, notably the vague remains of pit-traps beside

Crossing into Russia

From Kirkenes, it's just 16km southeast along the **E105** to **Storskog**, Norway's only official border crossing-point with Russia. You can take photographs of the frontier, provided you don't snap any Russian personnel or military installations – which rather limits the options as there's little else to see. The crossing is busy for much of the year, but it's not open for casual day-trippers; in any case, the only convenient settlement nearby is the ugly Russian mining town of **Nikel**, around 40km to the south, from where you can – extraordinarily enough – travel by train all the way to Vladivostok. Several Kirkenes travel agents organize day and weekend tours into Russia, the most worthwhile being those to the Arctic port of **Murmansk**. The trips include a visa, which takes at least ten days to arrange, so advance booking is essential. Among the town's travel agents, Pasvikturist, in the centre at Dr. Wesselsgate 9 (T78 99 50 80, F78 99 50 57, Wwww.pasvikturist.no), and Bennett BTI, at the same address (T78 97 00 50, F78 97 00 60, Ekirkenes.btc@bennettbti .com), are as good as any. They have details of trips to Murmansk, both by **bus** (around 1800kr per person) and by **Hurtigbåt** express boat (1300kr). Incidentally, there is a Russian consulate in Kirkenes, at Arbeidergata 6 (T78 99 37 37), but they will not shortcut the visa process. If a Russian jaunt proves impossible, you'll have to be content with the reflection that if you have made it to Kirkenes and the border, you are further east than Istanbul and as far north as Alaska.

Lake Ødevatn. The Kirkenes tourist office has details of guided tours to the park, which are useful as you have to be an expert wilderness hiker-cum-survivalist to delve into the park under your own steam. The absence of natural landmarks makes it easy to get lost, especially as there are no marked footpaths, nor is there any map that can be relied upon. If you're undeterred, and have your own vehicle (there's no public transport), then drive south from Kirkenes for about 100km along Highway 885 through the pine forests of the Pasvik River valley as far as **Vaggatem**. Turn off the main road 1.5km or so further on and then follow the 9km-long, rough forest road south to a lake, **Sortbrysttjern**, from where a footpath takes you into the park at another lake, **Ellenvatn**. If you want to **stay** hereabouts, the only option is Vaggatem's *Øvre Pasvik Café and Camping* (T & F78 99 55 30, Wwww.pasvik-cafe.no), which also rents out ten simple wooden cabins (**1**).

Svalbard

The **Svalbard archipelago** is one of the most hostile places on earth. Six hundred and forty kilometres north of the Norwegian mainland (and just 1300km from the North Pole), two-thirds of its surface is covered by glaciers, the soil frozen to a depth of up to 500m. The archipelago was probably discovered in the twelfth century by Icelandic seamen, though it lay ignored until 1596 when the Dutch explorer Willem Barents named the main island, **Spitsbergen**, after its needle-like mountains. However, apart from a smattering of determined adventurers – from seventeenth-century whalers to eighteenth-century monks – few people ever lived here until, in 1899, rich coal deposits were discovered, the geological residue of a prehistoric tropical forest. The first **coal mine** was opened by an American seven years later and passed into Norwegian hands in 1916. Meanwhile, other countries, particularly Russia and Sweden, were getting into the coal-mining act, and when, in 1920, Norway's sovereignty over the archipelago was ratified by international treaty, it was on condition that those other countries who were operating mines could continue to do so. It was also agreed that the islands would be a demilitarized zone, which made them, incidentally, sitting ducks for a German squadron, which arrived here to bombard the Norwegian coal mines during World War II.

Despite the hardships, there are convincing reasons to make a trip to this oddly fertile land, covering around 63,000 square kilometres. Between late April and late August there's continuous daylight; the snow has virtually all melted by July, leaving the valleys covered in flowers; and there's an abundance of wildlife – over a hundred species of migratory birds, arctic foxes, polar bears and reindeer on land, and seals, walruses and whales offshore. In winter, it's a different story: the polar night, during which the sun never rises above the horizon, lasts from late October to mid-February; and the record low temperature is a staggering -46°C - not counting the wind-chill factor.

Practicalities

The simplest way to reach Svalbard is to **fly** to the archipelago's airport at Longyearbyen on Spitsbergen. Braathens operates services there from a variety of Norwegian cities, including Oslo, Bergen, Trondheim, Alta and Tromsø, on average four or five times weekly. SAS also flies to Longyearbyen, but only from

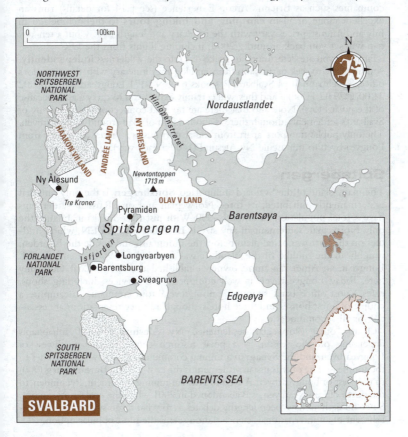

Oslo via Tromsø. The Tromsø-Longyearbyen flight takes an hour and thirty minutes and a standard fare with Braathens costs 5400kr return, though special deals are commonplace, reducing this to 1800–2000kr. However, before you book your flight, you'll need to reserve accommodation in Longyearbyen (see p.353) and – unless you're happy to be stuck in your lodgings – you'd be well-advised to book on **guided excursions** too. There's a wide range, from hiking and climbing through to kayaking, snowmobiling, glacier walking, helicopter rides, Zodiac boat trips, wildlife safaris and ice caving. Further information, including details of all the tour companies, is available from Info-Svalbard, Postboks 323, N-9171 Longyearbyen (℡79 02 55 50, ℱ79 02 55 51, ℮info@svalbard.net, ℠www.svalbard.net/eng), or try the excellent Spitsbergen Travel, Postboks 548, N-9171 Longyearbyen (℡79 02 61 00, ℠www.spitsbergentravel.no).You can take pot luck when you get there, but be warned that wilderness excursions are often fully booked weeks in advance.

Otherwise, there are **adventure cruises** around Svalbard, involving polar-bear spotting and the like. A four-day all-inclusive cruise with one night in a Longyearbyen hotel, for example, will cost from 6700kr to 15700kr (not including flights to Longyearbyen), depending on the standard of the boat: contact the Longyearbyen tourist office (see opposite) for details. In addition, companies such as Britain's Arctic Experience (see p.14 for details) runs an excellent range of all-in **camping and hiking tours** to the archipelago in July and August; prices vary with the itinerary and length of stay, but a ten-day trip will set you back around £2000, including flights from the UK.

Finally, if you are determined to strike out into the wilderness **independently**, you first have to seek permission from, and log your itinerary with, the governor's office, Sysselmannen på Svalbard, Postboks 633, N-9171 Longyearbyen (℡79 02 31 00, ℱ79 02 11 66) – and they will certainly expect you to carry a gun (because of the polar bears). Note also that there are no road connections between any of Svalbard's settlements, though there is about 45km of road around Longyearbyen. The only public transport, apart from the airport bus, is a pricey air service from Longyearbyen to minuscule Ny Ålesund (1400kr each way).

Spitsbergen

The main island of the Svalbard archipelago, **Spitsbergen**, is the only one that is permanently inhabited; its three Norwegian and one Russian settlements have a total population of around 3000. With just over 1500 inhabitants, the only Norwegian settlement of any size is **LONGYEARBYEN**, which huddles on the narrow coastal plain below the mountains and beside the Isfjorden, roughly in the middle of the island. It was founded in 1906, when John M. Longyear, an American mine owner, established the Arctic Coal Company here. Today, Longyearbyen is well equipped with services, including shops, cafés, a post office, bank, swimming pool, several tour companies, a campsite, a couple of guest houses and three hotels, though advance reservations are essential for all accommodation.

Of the other Norwegian settlements, **Ny Ålesund** (40–100 inhabitants depending on the season) is a polar research centre to the northwest of Longyearbyen, and the **Sveagruva** mining community (200 day-workers) lies to the southeast. The only Russian settlement is the coal-mining **Barentsburg** (900) to the west of Longyearbyen. A second Russian mining settlement, Pyramiden, to the north of Longyearbyen, was abandoned in 2001 when the coal seams ran out. Since then, there have been lengthy debates as to what to do with it – the establishment of an international science station seems the most popular option.

Longyearbyen practicalities

Longyearbyen **airport** is 5km west of the town, and both Braathens (☎815 20 000) and SAS (☎79 02 16 50) have offices there. An **airport bus**, the Flybussen (March–Sept; 45kr), runs from the airport into town, or you can take a **taxi** (80–100kr). The settlement trails inland from the Isfjorden for a couple of kilometres. The few buildings that pass for the town centre are located about 600m in from the fjord, and this is where you'll find the year-round **tourist office** (☎79 02 55 50; ⓦwww.svalbard.net), which has information on a wide range of trips, from dog-sledging and ice-caving to snowmobile excursions and glacier walks.

Longyearbyen's best **accommodation** is to be found at the plush *Radisson SAS Polar Hotel* (☎79 02 34 50, ⓕ79 02 34 51, ⓦwww.longyearbyen .radissonsas.com; ❼), just to the north of the tourist office, while more frugal lodgings are available in old miners' quarters to the west of the centre, across the river, at the *Mary-Ann Riggen* guesthouse (☎79 02 37 02, ⓕ79 02 10 97, Ⓔnggen@longyearbyen.net; ❸). Less agreeable, but worth a try if the others are full, is the *Spitsbergen Nybyen Gjestehus*, on the southern edge of town (☎79 02 63 00, ⓕ79 02 63 01, Ⓔnybyen@spitra.no; ❹). Finally, *Longyearbyen Camping* (☎79 02 10 68, ⓕ79 02 10 67, Ⓔinfo@terrapolaris.com; late June to early Sept), out near the airport, charges just 70kr per person per night. Surprisingly, they don't have any cabins, but there is a kitchen, laundry and heated toilets. Obviously, you must come fully equipped to survive what can be, at any time of the year, a cruel climate.

The *Polar Hotel's Restaurant Nansen* is the best place **to eat** in town, serving all manner of Arctic specialities from char to seal and (like it or not) whale. Other, less expensive options include the straightforward *Kafé Busen*, near the tourist office, or, across the river at the southern edge of town, the *Huset* (☎79 02 25 00), which also specializes in Arctic dishes and has a boisterous bar and the town cinema attached. For **drinking**, the liveliest hangout is the *Funken Bar*, in the *Funken Hotel,* to the south of the centre, while *Barents Pub* at the *Polar Hotel* is both smarter and more sedate.

Travel details

Buses

Alta to: Hammerfest (1–3 daily except Sat; 2hr 30min); Honningsvåg (late June to mid-Aug 1–2 daily; mid-Aug to late June 1–2 daily except Thurs & Sat; 4hr); Karasjok (late June to mid-Aug 1–2 daily; mid-Aug to late June 1–2 daily except Thurs & Sat; 5hr); Kautokeino (1–2 daily except Sat; 2hr 30min); Kirkenes (late June to mid-Aug 1–2 daily; mid-Aug to late June 1–2 daily except Thurs & Sat; 10hr); Skaidi (late June to mid-Aug 1–3 daily, mid-Aug to late June 1–3 daily except Tues, Thurs & Sat; 1hr 40min); Tromsø (April to late Oct 1–2 daily; 7hr).

Hammerfest to: Alta (1–3 daily except Sat; 2hr 30min); Karasjok (late June to mid-Aug 1–2 daily; mid-Aug to late June 1–2 daily except Thurs & Sat; 4hr 30min); Kirkenes (late June to mid-Aug 1–2

daily; mid-Aug to late June 1–2 daily except Thurs & Sat; 10hr 30min); Skaidi (late June to mid-Aug 1–2 daily; mid-Aug to late June 1–2 daily except Thurs & Sat; 1hr 30min).

Honningsvåg to: Alta (late June to mid-Aug 1–2 daily; mid-Aug to late June 1–2 daily except Thurs & Sat; 4hr); Nordkapp (late June to mid-Aug 1–2 daily; 50min).

Karasjok to: Hammerfest (late June to mid-Aug 1–2 daily; mid-Aug to late June 1–2 daily except Thurs & Sat; 4hr 30min); Kirkenes (late June to mid-Aug 1–2 daily; mid-Aug to late June 1–2 daily except Thurs & Sat; 5hr 15min).

Kautokeino to: Alta (1–2 daily except Sat; 2hr 30min).

Kirkenes to: Alta (late June to mid-Aug 1–2 daily; mid-Aug to late June 1–2 daily except Thurs & Sat; 10hr); Hammerfest (late June to mid-Aug 1–2 daily; mid-Aug to late June 1–2 daily except Thurs & Sat; 10hr 30min); Karasjok (late June to mid-Aug 1–2 daily; mid-Aug to late June 1–2 daily except Thurs & Sat; 5hr 15min); Vadsø (1–2 daily except Sat; 3hr 30min).

Skaidi to: Alta (late June to mid-Aug 1–3 daily, mid-Aug to late June 1–3 daily except Tues, Thurs & Sat; 1hr 40min); Hammerfest (late June to mid-Aug 1–2 daily; mid-Aug to late June 1–2 daily except Thurs & Sat; 1hr 30min).

Tromsø to: Alta (April to late Oct 1–2 daily; 7hr); Narvik (2 daily; 7hr); Nordkapp (late June to mid-Aug 1–2 daily; 13hr); Skaidi (late June to mid-Aug 1–2 daily; 9hr).

Vadsø to: Kirkenes (1–2 daily except Sat; 3hr 30min); Vardø (1–2 daily; 1hr 30min).

The Nord–Norgeekspressen and Nordkappekspressen

The Nord–Norgeekspressen (North Norway Express Bus) runs north from Bodø to Narvik and Tromsø, where you change buses – and stay overnight – before embarking on the next leg of the journey up to Alta. In Alta, one bus a day continues north; passengers on the other buses change again for the connecting Nordkappekspressen bus onto Honningsvåg and Nordkapp. The Nord–Norgeekspressen operates all year, the Nordkappekspressen from late June to mid-August. At other times of the year, FFR, the local transport company, operates a bus from Alta to Honningsvåg, but not Nordkapp.

Car ferries

Breivikeidet to: Svendsby (every 1–2hr; 25min).
Brensholmen to: Botnhamn (June to late Aug 4–7 daily; 35min).
Gryllefjord to: Andenes (early June to late Aug 2–3 daily; 1hr 40min).
Lyngseidet to: Olderdalen (every 1–2hr; 40min).
Hurtigbåt passenger express boats
Alta to: Hammerfest (1–2 daily except Sat; 1hr 30min).
Tromsø to: Harstad (1–3 daily; 2hr 45min).
Hurtigrute coastal boat (year-round; daily)
Northbound from: Tromsø at 6.30pm; Hammerfest at 6.45am; Honningsvåg at 3.30pm; Berlevåg at 11pm; Vardø at 5am; Vadsø at 8.45am; terminates at Kirkenes at 10.30am.
Southbound from: Kirkenes at 1.30pm; Vardø at 5.45pm; (no southbound stop at Vadsø); Berlevåg at 11.15pm; Honningsvåg at 7am; Hammerfest at 1pm; Tromsø at 1.30am.
The Tromsø–Kirkenes journey time is 42hrs.

contexts

contexts

History

Despite its low contemporary profile, Norway has a fascinating past. As early as the tenth century its people had explored – and conquered – much of northern Europe, and roamed the Atlantic as far as the North American mainland. Though initially an independent state, from the fourteenth century Norway came under the sway of first Denmark and then Sweden. Independent again from 1905, Norway was propelled into World War II by the German invasion of 1940, an act of aggression that transformed the Norwegians' attitude to the outside world. Gone was the old insular neutrality, replaced by a liberal internationalism exemplified by Norway's leading role in the environmental movement.

Early civilizations

The earliest signs of human habitation in Norway date from the end of the last Ice Age, around 10,000 BC. In the Finnmark region of north Norway, the **Komsa** culture was reliant upon seal-fishing, whereas the peoples of the **Fosna** culture, further south near present-day Kristiansund, hunted seals and reindeer. Both these societies were essentially static, dependent upon flint and bone implements. At Alta, the Komsa people left behind hundreds of **rock carvings and drawings**, naturalistic representations of their way of life dating from the seventh to the third millennia BC.

As the edges of the ice cap retreated from the western coastline, so new migrants slowly filtered north. These new peoples, of the **Nøstvet-økser** culture, were also hunters and fishers, but they were able to manufacture stone axes, examples of which were first unearthed at Nøstvet, near Oslo. Beginning around 2700 BC, immigrants from the east, principally the semi-nomadic **Boat Axe** and **Battle-Axe peoples** – so named because of the distinctive shape of their stone weapons/tools – introduced animal husbandry and agriculture. The new arrivals did not, however, overwhelm their predecessors; the two groups coexisted, each picking up hints from the other – a reflection of the harsh infertility of the land.

These late Stone Age cultures flourished at a time when other, more southerly countries were already using metal. Norway was poor and had little to trade, but the Danes and Swedes exchanged amber for copper and tin from the bronze-making countries of central Europe. A fraction of the imported bronze subsequently passed into Norway, mostly to the Battle-Axe people, who appear to have had a comparatively prosperous aristocracy. This was the beginning of the Norwegian **Bronze Age** (1500–500 BC), which also saw a change in burial customs. In the Stone Age, the Battle-Axe peoples had dug shallow earth graves, but these were now supplanted by **burial mounds** enclosing coffins in which supplies were placed in readiness for the afterlife. Building the mounds must have involved a substantial amount of effort, suggesting the existence of powerful chieftains who could organize the work, and who may also have been priests. Rock carvings became prevalent in southern Norway during this period too – workaday images of men ploughing with oxen, riding horses, carrying arms and using boats to navigate the coastal water passages that were supplemented by drawings of religious or symbolic significance. In general terms, however, the Bronze Age was characterized more by the development of agriculture than by the use of metal, and stone implements remained the norm.

Around 500 BC Norway was affected by two adverse changes: the climate deteriorated, and trade relations with the Mediterranean were disrupted by the westward movement of the Celts across central Europe. The former encouraged the development of settled, communal farming in an attempt to improve winter shelter and storage, with each clan resident in a large stone, turf and timber dwelling; the latter cut the supply of tin and copper and subsequently isolated Norway from the early **Iron Age**. The country's isolation continued through much of the **Classical period**. The Greek geographer Pytheas of Marseilles, who went far enough north to note the short summer nights, probably visited southern Norway, but the regions beyond remained the subject of vague speculation. Pliny the Elder mentions "Nerigon" as the great island south of the legendary "Ultima Thule", the outermost region of the earth, while Tacitus, in his *Germania*, demonstrated knowledge only of the Danes and Swedes.

The expansion of the **Roman Empire** in the first and second centuries AD revived Norway's trading links with the Mediterranean. Evidence of these renewed contacts is provided across Scandinavia by **runes**, carved inscriptions dating from around 200 AD, whose 24-letter alphabet – the *futhark* – was clearly influenced by Greek and Latin capitals. Initially, runes were seen as having magical powers – to gain their knowledge, the god Odin hung for nine nights on *Yggdrasill*, the tree of life, with a spear in his side (see p.378) – but gradually their usage became more prosaic. Of the eight hundred or so runic inscriptions extant across southern Norway, most commemorate events and individuals: mothers and fathers, sons and slain comrades.

The renewal of trade with the Mediterranean also spread the use of **iron**. Norway's agriculture was transformed by the use of iron tools, and the pace of change accelerated in the fifth century AD, when the Norwegians learnt how to smelt the brown iron ore, limonite, that lay in their bogs and lakes – hence its common name, **bog-iron**. Clearing the forests with iron axes was relatively easy and, with more land available, the pattern of settlement became less concentrated. Family homesteads leapfrogged up the valleys, and a class of wealthy farmers emerged, their prosperity based on fields and flocks. Above them in the pecking order were local **chieftains**, the nature of whose authority varied considerably. Inland, the chieftains' power was based on landed wealth and constrained by feudal responsibilities, whereas the coastal lords, who had often accumulated influence from trade, piracy, and military prowess, were less encumbered. Like the farmers, these seafarers had also benefited from the iron axe, which made boat-building much easier. An early seventh-century ship found at Kvalsund, near Hammerfest, was eighteen metres long, its skilfully crafted oak hull equipped with a high prow and stern, prefiguring the vessels of the Vikings.

By the middle of the eighth century, Norway had become a country of small, independent **kingships**, its geography impeding the development of any central authority. In the event, it was the **Yngling** chieftains of southeast Norway who attempted to assert some sort of wider control. Their first leaders are listed in the **Ynglinga Tal,** a paean compiled by the Norwegian *skald* (court poet) Thjodolf in the ninth century. According to Thjodolf, early royal life had its ups and downs: king Domaldi was sacrificed to ensure the fertility of his land; Dag was killed by an accidental blow from a pitchfork; and Fjolnir got up in the night to take a leak, fell into a vat of mead and drowned.

The Vikings

Overpopulation, clan discord and the lure of commerce all contributed to the sudden explosion that launched the **Vikings** (from the Norse word *vik*, meaning creek, and *-ing*, frequenter of), upon an unsuspecting Europe in the ninth century. The patterns of attack and eventual settlement were dictated by the geographical position of the various Scandinavian countries. The Swedish Vikings turned eastwards, the Danes headed south and southwest, while the Norwegians sailed west, their longships landing on the Hebrides, Shetland, Orkney, the Scottish mainland and western Ireland. The Pictish population was unable to muster much resistance and the islands were quickly overrun, becoming, together with the Isle of Man, the nucleus of a new Norse kingdom which provided a base for further attacks on Scotland and Ireland.

The Norwegians founded Dublin in 836, and from Ireland turned their attention eastward to northern Britain. Elsewhere, Norwegian Vikings settled the Faroe Islands and Iceland, and even raided as far south as Moorish Spain, attacking Seville in 844. The raiders soon became settlers, sometimes colonizing the entire country – as in Iceland and the Faroes – but mostly intermingling with the local population. The speed of their assimilation is, in fact, one of the Vikings' most striking features: **William the Conqueror** (1027–87) was the epitome of the Norman baron, yet he was also the descendant of Rollo, the Viking warrior whose army had overrun Normandy just a century before.

The whole of Norway felt the stimulating effects of the Viking expeditions. The economy was boosted by the spoils of war, the standard of living rose, and the population grew in physical stature as health and nutrition improved. Farmland was no longer in such short supply; cereal and dairy farming were extended into new areas in eastern Norway; new vegetables, such as cabbages and turnips, were introduced from Britain; and farming methods were improved by overseas contact – the Celts, for instance, taught the Norwegians how to thresh grain with flails.

The Vikings also rigorously exploited the hunting and fishing peoples who roamed the far north of Norway. Detailed information on Finnmark in the late ninth century comes from a surprising source, the court of **Alfred the Great**, which was visited by a Norwegian chieftain named **Ottar** in about 890. Ottar dwelt, so he claimed, "northernmost of all Norsemen", and he regaled Alfred with tales of his native land, which the king promptly incorporated within his translation of a fifth-century Latin text, the *History of the World* by Paulus Orosius. Ottar, who boasted that he owed political allegiance to no one, had a few cows, sheep and pigs and a tiny slice of arable land, which he ploughed with horses, but his real wealth came from other sources. Fishing, whaling and walrus hunting provided both food for his retinue and exportable commodities. He also possessed a herd of six hundred tame reindeer – plus six decoy animals used to snare wild reindeer – and extracted a heavy tribute from the Sami (see p.332), payable in furs and hides.

The Vikings' brand of **paganism** (see p.378), with its wayward, unscrupulous deities, underpinned their inclination to vendettas and clan warfare. Nevertheless, institutions slowly developed which helped regulate the bloodletting. Western Norway adopted the Germanic *wergeld* system of cash-for-injury compensation; every free man was entitled to attend the local *Thing (Ting)* or parliament, while a regional *Allthing* made laws and settled disputes. Justice was class-based, however, with society divided into three main categories: the lord, the freeman, and the thrall or slave, who was worth about eight cows. The Vikings were industrious slavers, opening slave markets wherever they went, sending thousands to work on their land back home and supplying the needs of other buyers.

Viking **decorative art** was also pan-Scandinavian, with the most distinguished work being the elaborate and often grotesque animal motifs that adorned their ships, sledges, buildings and furniture. This craftsmanship is seen at its best in the **ship burials** of Oseberg and Gokstad, both on display in Oslo's Viking Ships Museum (p.92). The Oseberg ship is thought to be the burial ship of Åse, wife of the early ninth-century Yngling king, Gudrød Storlatnes. She was also the mother of Halfdan the Black, whose body had a very different fate from her own – it was chopped up, and the bits were buried across his kingdom to ensure the fertility of the land.

Norway's first kings

It was from the Ynglings of Vestfold that Norway's first widely recognized king, **Harald Hårfagri** (Fair-Hair), claimed descent. Shortly before 900 (the exact date is unclear), Harald won a decisive victory at Hafrsfjord (near modern Stavanger), which gave him control of the coastal region as far north as Trøndelag. It sparked an exodus of minor rulers, most of whom left to settle in Iceland. The thirteenth-century *Laxdaela Saga* records the departure of one such family, the Ketils of Romsdal, who would not be "forced to become Harald's vassals or be denied compensation for fallen kinsmen". Harald's long rule was based on personal pledges of fealty; with the notable exception of the regional *Allthings*, there were no institutions to sustain it, and when he died his kingdom broke up into its component parts. Harald did, however, leave a less tangible but extremely important legacy: from now on every ambitious chieftain was not content to be a local lord, but strove to be ruler of a kingdom stretching from the Trøndelag to Vestfold.

Harald's son, **Erik Bloodaxe**, struggled to hold his father's kingdom together, but was out-manoeuvred by his youngest brother, **Håkon the Good**, who secured the allegiance of the major chieftains before returning home from England where he had been raised (and Christianized) at the court of King Athelstan of Wessex. Erik fled to Northumbria to become king of Viking York. Initially, Håkon was well-received and, although his attempts to introduce Christianity failed, he did carry out a number of far-ranging reforms. He established a common legal code for the whole of Vestfold and Trøndelag, and also introduced the system of *Leidangr*, the division of the coastal districts into areas, each of which was responsible for maintaining and manning a warship.

However, Håkon's rule was punctuated by struggles against Erik's heirs. With the backing of the Danish king Harald Bluetooth, they defeated and killed Håkon in battle in 960. Håkon's kingdom then passed to one of Erik's sons, **Harald Greycloak Eriksson**. This forceful man set about extending his territories with gusto. Indeed, he was, in Bluetooth's opinion, much too successful; keen to keep Norway within his sphere of influence, the Dane slaughtered Greycloak on the battlefield in 970 and replaced him with a Danish appointee, **Håkon Sigurdsson**, the last genuine heathen to rule Norway. But again Bluetooth seems to have got more than he bargained for. Sigurdsson based himself in Trøndelag, a decent distance from his overlord, and it's believed he soon refused to recognize Danish suzerainty: certainly the Christian Bluetooth would not have sanctioned Sigurdsson's restitution of pagan sacred sites.

In 995 **Olav Tryggvason**, another Viking chieftain who had been baptized in England, sailed to Norway to challenge Sigurdsson, who was conveniently dispatched by one of his own servants before the fighting started. Olav quickly asserted control over the Trøndelag and parts of southern and western Norway. He founded Nidaros (now Trondheim), from where he launched a sustained and brutal campaign against the pagan Tronds, which secured him the adulation of later saga writers. Despite his evangelical zeal, Olav's religious beliefs are something of an enigma: he had pagan magicians in his personal retinue, and was so good at predicting the future from bird bones that he was called *Craccaben* (Crowbone). Olav's real problem remained the enmity of the Danish-controlled southeastern regions of Norway, and of Bluetooth's son Svein Forkbeard, who regarded Norway as his rightful inheritance. In alliance with the Swedish king, Svein defeated Olav at a sea battle in the Skagerrak in 1000, and Norway was divided up among the victors.

Meanwhile, Norwegian settlers were laying the foundations of independent Norse communities in the Faroes and Iceland, where they established a parliament, the *Allthing*, in 930. The Norwegian Vikings went on to make further discoveries: Erik the Red, exiled from Norway and then banished from Iceland for three years for murder, set out in 985 with 25 ships, fourteen of which arrived in **Greenland.** The new colony prospered, and by the start of the eleventh century there were about three thousand settlers. This created a shortage of good farmland, making another push west inevitable. The two **Vinland sagas** (see p.393) provide the only surviving account of these further explorations, recounting the exploits of Leif Eriksson the Lucky, who founded a colony he called Vinland on the shores of **North America** around 1000 AD.

Norse settlers continued to secure resources from the Vinland region for the next few decades, until the native population drove them out. The Viking site discovered at L'Anse aux Meadows in Newfoundland may have been either Vinland itself or the result of one of the further foragings. The Greenland colonists carried on collecting timber from Labrador up until the fourteenth century, when the climate is known to have cooled and deteriorated, making the sea trip too dangerous. Attacks by the Inuit and the difficulties of maintaining trading links with Norway then took their toll on the main Greenland colonies. All contact with the outside world was lost in around 1410, and the last of the half-starved, disease-ridden survivors died out towards the end of the fifteenth century, just as Christopher Columbus was eyeing up his "New World".

The arrival of Christianity

In 1015, a prominent Viking chieftain, **Olav Haraldsson** sailed for Norway from England, intent upon conquering his homeland. Significantly, he arrived by merchant ship with just 100 men, rather than with a fleet of longships and an army, a clear sign of the passing of the Viking heyday. He gained the support of the yeoman farmers of the interior – a new force in Norway that was rapidly supplanting the old warrior aristocracy – and with Svein Forkbeard's son and successor Knut (King Canute of England) otherwise engaged, Haraldsson soon assumed the mantle of king of much of the country.

For twelve years Olav ruled in peace, founding Norway's first national government. His authority was based on the regional *Things* – consultative and broadly democratic bodies which administered local law – and on his willingness to deliver justice without fear or favour. The king's most enduring achievement, however, was to make Norway **Christian**. Olav had been converted during his days as a Viking, and vigorously imposed his new faith on his countrymen. Wherever necessary he executed persistent heathens and destroyed their sacred places. The dominant position of the new religion was ensured by the foundation of the Norwegian church, whose first priests were consecrated in Bremen.

It was foreign policy rather than pagan enmity that brought about Olav's downfall. By scheming with the Swedish king against Knut, who had now consolidated his position as king of Denmark and England, Olav provoked a Danish invasion, whose course was smoothed by massive bribes. The Norwegian chieftains, who had suffered at the hands of Olav, could be expected to help Knut, but even the yeomen failed to rally to Olav's cause, possibly alienated by his imperious ways. In 1028, Olav was forced to flee, first to Sweden and then to Russia, while Knut's young son Svein and his mother, the English Queen Aelfgifu, took the Norwegian crown. Two years later, Olav made a sensational return at the head of a scratch army, only to be defeated and killed by an alliance of wealthy landowners and chieftains at **Stiklestad**, the first major Norwegian land battle.

The petty chieftains and yeomen-farmers who had opposed Olav soon fell out with their new king: Svein had no intention of relaxing the royal grip and his rule was at least as arbitrary as that of his predecessor. The rebellion that ensued seems also to have had nationalistic undertones – many Norwegians had no wish to be ruled by a Dane. Svein fled the country, and Olav's old enemies popped over to Sweden to bring back Olav's young son, **Magnus**, who became king in 1035.

The chastening experience of Svein's short rule transformed the popular memory of Olav. With surprising speed, he came to be regarded as a heroic champion, and there was talk of miracles brought about by the dead king's body. The Norwegian church, looking for a local saint to enhance its position, fostered the legends and had Olav canonized. The remains of **St Olav** were then re-interred ceremoniously at Nidaros, today's Trondheim, where the miracles increased in scope, hastening the conversion of what remained of heathen Norway.

Harald Hardrada

On Magnus' death in 1047, **Harald Hardrada** (Olav's half-brother) became king, and soon consolidated his grip on the whole of Norway from the Trøndelag to the Oslofjord. The last of the Viking heroes, Hardrada was a giant of a man, reputedly almost seven feet tall with a sweeping moustache and eccentric eyebrows, and a warrior who had fought alongside Olav at Stiklestad. After the battle, he and his men had fled east, fighting as mercenaries in Russia and ultimately Byzantium, where Hardrada was appointed the commander of the Varangians, the Norse bodyguard of the Byzantine Emperor.

Back in Norway, Harald dominated the country by force of arms for over twenty years, earning the soubriquet "Hardrada" (the Hard) for his ruthless treatment of his enemies, many of whom he made "kiss the thin lips of the axe" as the saga writers put it. Neither was Hardrada satisfied with being king of just Norway. At first he tried to batter Denmark into submission through regular raiding, but the stratagem failed and he finally made peace with the Danish king, Svein, in 1064.

In 1066, the death of Edward the Confessor presented Harald with an opportunity to press his claim to the English throne. The Norwegian promptly sailed on England, landing near York with a massive fleet, but just outside the city, at Stamford Bridge, his army was surprised and trounced by Harold Godwinson, the new Saxon king of England. It was a battle of crucial importance, and one that gave rise to all sorts of legends, penned by both Norse and English writers. The two kings are supposed to have eyed each other up like prize-fighters, with Hardrada proclaiming his rival "a small king, but one that stood well in his stirrups", and Harold promising the Norwegian "seven feet of English ground, or as much more as he is taller than other men". Hardrada was defeated and killed, and the threat of a Norwegian conquest of England had – though no one realized it at the time – gone forever. Not that the victory did much good for Godwinson, whose weakened army trudged back south to be defeated by William of Normandy at the Battle of Hastings.

Medieval consolidation

Harald's son, **Olav Kyrre** (the Peaceful) – whose life had been spared after Stamford Bridge on the promise never to attack England again – went on to reign as king of Norway for the next 25 years. Peace engendered economic prosperity, and treaties with Denmark ensured Norwegian independence. Three native bishoprics were established, and cathedrals built at Nidaros, Bergen and Oslo. It's from this period, too, that Norway's surviving **stave churches** date: wooden structures resembling an upturned keel, they were lavishly decorated with dragon heads and scenes from Norse mythology, proof that the traditions of the pagan world were slow to disappear. (For more on stave churches, see p.174).

The first decades of the twelfth century witnessed the further consolidation of Norway's position as an independent power, despite internal disorder as the descendants of Olav Kyrre competed for influence. Civil war ceased only when **Håkon IV** took the throne in 1240, ushering in what is often called "The Period of Greatness". Secure at home, Håkon strengthened the Norwegian hold on the Faroe and Shetland islands, and in 1262 both Iceland and Greenland accepted Norwegian sovereignty. A year later, however, the king died in the Orkneys during a campaign to assert his control over the Hebrides, and three years later the Hebrides and the Isle of Man (always the weakest links in the Norwegian empire) were sold to the Scottish crown by Håkon's successor, **Magnus the Lawmender** (1238–80).

Under Magnus, Norway prospered. Law and order were maintained, trade flourished and, in striking contrast to the rough-and-ready ways of Hardrada, the king's court even followed a code of etiquette compiled in what became known as the *Konungs skuggsja* or "King's Mirror". Neither was the power of the monarchy threatened by feudal barons as elsewhere in thirteenth-century Europe. Norway's scattered farms were not susceptible to feudal tutelage and, as a consequence, the nobility lacked local autonomy. Castles remained few and far between and instead the energies of the nobility were drawn into the centralized administration of the state, a process that only happened several centuries later in the rest of western Europe. Norwegian **Gothic art** reached its full maturity in this period, as construction began on the nave at Nidaros Cathedral and on Håkon's Hall in Bergen.

Magnus was succeeded by his sons, first the undistinguished Erik and then **Håkon V** (1270–1319), the last of medieval Norway's talented kings. Håkon continued the policy of his predecessors, making further improvements to central government and asserting royal control of Finnmark through the construction of a fortress at Vardø. His achievements, however, were soon to be swept away along with the independence of Norway itself.

Loss of sovereignty

Norway's independence was threatened from two quarters. With strongholds in Bergen and Oslo, the **Hanseatic League** and its merchants had steadily increased their influence, exerting a monopoly on imports and controlling inland trade. The power of their international trading links was felt in Norway as the royal household grew increasingly dependent on the taxes the merchants paid. The second threat was **dynastic**. When Håkon died in 1319 he left no male heir and was succeeded by his grandson, the three-year-old son of a Swedish duke. The boy, Magnus Eriksson, was elected Swedish king two months later, marking the virtual end of Norway as an independent country until 1905.

Magnus assumed full power over both countries in 1332, but his reign was a difficult one. When the Norwegian nobility rebelled he agreed that the monarchy should again be split: his three-year-old son, Håkon, would become Norwegian king when he came of age, while the Swedes agreed to elect his eldest son Erik to the Swedish throne. It was then, in 1349, that the **Black Death** struck, spreading quickly along the coast and up the valleys, killing almost two-thirds of the Norwegian population. It was a catastrophe of unimaginable proportions, its effects compounded by the way the country's agriculture was structured. Animal husbandry was easily the most important part of Norwegian farming, and harvesting and drying winter fodder was labour-intensive. Without the labourers, the animals died in their hundreds and famine conditions prevailed for several generations.

Many farms were abandoned and, deprived of their rents, the petty chieftains who had once dominated rural Norway were, as a class, almost entirely swept away. The vacuum was filled by royal officials, the *syslemenn*, each of whom exercised control over a large chunk of territory on behalf of a Royal Council. The collapse of local governance was compounded by dynastic to-ing and fro-ing at the top of the social ladder. In 1380, Håkon died and Norway passed into Danish control with **Olav**, the son of Håkon and the Danish princess Margaret, becoming ruler of the two kingdoms.

The Kalmar Union

Despite Olav's early death in 1387, the resourceful Margaret persevered with the union. Proclaimed regent by both the Danish and (what remained of the) Norwegian nobility, she engineered a treaty with the Swedish nobles that not only recognized her as regent of Sweden but also agreed to accept any king she should nominate. Her chosen heir, **Erik of Pomerania**, was foisted on the Norwegians in 1389. When he reached the age of majority in 1397, Margaret organized a grand coronation with Erik crowned king of all three countries at Kalmar in Sweden – hence the **Kalmar Union**.

After Margaret's death in 1412, all power was concentrated in Denmark. In Norway, foreigners were preferred in both state and church, and the country became impoverished through paying for Erik's various wars. Incompetent and brutal in equal measure, Erik managed to get himself deposed in all three countries at the same time, ending his days as a Baltic pirate.

Union with Denmark

In 1439, Sweden left the union, and in 1450, a Danish count, Christian of Oldenburg, was crowned king of Norway and Denmark. Thereafter, Norway simply ceased to take any meaningful part in Scandinavian affairs. Successive monarchs continued to appoint foreigners to important positions, appropriating Norwegian funds for Danish purposes and even mortgaging Orkney and Shetland in 1469 to the Scots. Danish became the official tongue, replacing **Old Norse**, which came to be regarded as the language of the ignorant and inconsequential. Only the Norwegian church retained any power, though this was soon to be quashed by the Reformation.

Only once did it look as if Norway might break the Danish stranglehold, when a Swedish-Norwegian nobleman, **Knut Alvsson**, crossed the border and overran southern Norway in 1501–2, but the Danes soon fought back and Alvsson was treacherously murdered as he sued for peace.

The Danish victor, King **Christian II** imposed a crash programme of "Danicization" on the Norwegians and mercilessly hunted down his opponents, but his attempts to dominate the Swedes led to his forced abdication in 1523. The leaders of the Norwegian opposition rallied under the archbishop of Nidaros, Olav Engelbrektsson, but their attempt to gain terms from the new king Frederik I failed. The Danish civil war that followed the death of Frederik resulted in the victory of the **Protestant Christian III** and the loss of Norway's last independent national institution, the Catholic Church. In 1536 Christian declared that Norway should cease to be a separate country and that the Lutheran faith should be established there. Christian even carted the silver casket that had contained the bones of St Olav back to Copenhagen, where he melted it down into coins.

Thereafter, in many respects, Norway became simply a source of raw materials – fish, timber and iron ore – whose proceeds lined the Danish royal purse. Naturally enough, the Swedes coveted these materials too, the upshot being a long and inconclusive war (1563–70) which saw much of Norway ravaged by competing bands of mercenaries. Ironically, the Swedish attempt to capture Norway induced a change of attitude in Copenhagen: keen to keep their subjects happy, a degree of decentralization became the order of the day, and the Danes appointed a Governor–General (*Stattholder*) to administer justice in accordance with traditional Norwegian law.

Though slow to take root among the Norwegian peasantry, **Lutheranism** served as a powerful instrument in establishing Danish control. The Bible, catechism and hymnal were all in Danish and the bishops were all Danes too. Thus, the Norwegian **Reformation** was very much an instrument of Danish colonization rather than a reflection of widespread intellectual ferment: the urban apprentices and craftsmen who fired the movement elsewhere in Europe simply didn't exist in significant numbers here in rustic Norway. Neither had the **Renaissance** made much impact here: the first printing press wasn't established in Norway until 1643, and the reading public remained minuscule, though the country did produce a surprising number of humanist writers. Nonetheless, something of the Renaissance spirit did arrive in the form of

Christian IV (1588–1648). Among the Danish kings of the period, he proved the most sympathetic to Norway. He visited the country often, improving the quality of its administration and founding new towns – including Kongsberg, Kristiansand and Christiania (later Oslo) – whose buildings were laid out on a spacious gridiron plan.

At last the Norwegian economy began to pick up. The population grew, trade increased and, benefiting from the decline of the Hanseatic League, a native bourgeoisie began to take control of certain parts of the economy, most notably the herring industry. But Norwegian cultural self-esteem remained at a low ebb: the country's merchants spoke Danish, mimicked Danish manners and read Danish literature. What's more, Norway was a constant bone of contention between Sweden and Denmark, the result being a long series of wars in which its more easterly provinces were regularly overrun by the competing armies.

The year 1660 marked a turning point in the constitutional arrangements governing Norway. For centuries, the Danish Council of State had had the power to elect the monarch and impose limitations on his or her rule. Now, a powerful alliance of merchants and clergy swept these powers away to make **Frederik III** absolute ruler. This was, however, not a reactionary coup, but an attempt to limit the power of the conservative-minded nobility. In addition, the development of a centralized state machine would, many calculated, provide all sorts of job opportunities to the low-born but adept. As a result, Norway was incorporated into the administrative structure of Denmark with royal authority delegated to the *Stattholder*, who governed through what soon became a veritable army of professional bureaucrats.

In the event, there were indeed positive advantages for Norway: the country acquired better defences, simpler taxes, a separate High Court and further doses of Norwegian law, but once again power was exercised almost exclusively by Danes. The functionaries were allowed to charge for their services, and there was no fixed tariff – a swindler's charter for which the peasantry paid heavily. So much so, in fact, that one of the *Stattholders*, **Ulrik Gyldenløve**, launched a vigorous campaign against corruption, his efforts rewarded by a far-reaching series of reforming edicts promulgated in 1684.

The eighteenth and early nineteenth centuries

The **absolute monarchy** established by Frederik III soon came to concern itself with every aspect of Norwegian life. The ranks and duties of a host of minor officials were carefully delineated, religious observances tightly regulated and restrictions were imposed on everything from begging and dress through to the food and drink that could be consumed at weddings and funerals. This extraordinary superstructure placed a leaden hand on imagination and invention. Neither was it impartial: there were some benefits for the country's farmers and fishermen, but by and large the system worked in favour of the middle class. The merchants of every small town were allocated exclusive rights to trade in a particular area and competition between towns was forbidden. These local monopolies placed the peasantry at a dreadful disadvantage, nowhere more iniquitously than in the Lofoten islands, where fishermen not only had to buy supplies and equipment at the price set by the merchant, but had to sell their fish at the price set by him too.

The Dano-Norwegian functionaries who controlled Norway also set the **cultural** agenda, patronizing an insipid and imitative art and literature. The writings of **Petter Dass** stand out from the dross, however – heartfelt verses and descriptions of life in the Nordland where he worked as a pastor. There were liberal, vaguely nationalist stirrings too, in the foundation of the Norwegian Society in Copenhagen twelve years later.

More adventurously, there was renewed missionary interest in Norway's old colony of **Greenland**. Part of it was down to an eccentric ethnic obsession – the clergyman concerned, a certain Hans Egede, was looking for Inuit with Viking features – but Bergen's merchants footed the bill, on condition that Egede build them a fur-trading station there. In the event, it was a poor investment, as the trading monopoly was given to a Dane. There was also missionary work in Finnmark, where a determined effort was made to convert the Sami (see p.332). This was a very different undertaking from Egede's, and one that reflected the changing temperament of the Lutheran church of Norway, which had been reinvigorated by **pietist** clergymen. One of their number, Thomas von Westen, learnt the Sami language and led an extraordinarily successful mission to the far north. He was certainly a good deal more popular than many of his fellow pietists down south who persuaded Christian VI (1730–46) to impose draconian penalties for such crimes as not observing the Sabbath or not going to church regularly.

In the meantime, there were more wars between Denmark and Sweden. In 1700, **Frederik IV** (1699–1730) made the rash decision to attack the Swedes at the time when their king, Karl XII, was generally reckoned to be one of Europe's most brilliant military strategists. Predictably, the Danes were defeated and only the intervention of the British saved Copenhagen from falling into Swedish hands. Undeterred, Frederik tried again, and this time Karl retaliated by launching a full-scale invasion of Norway. The Swedes rapidly occupied southern Norway, but then, much to everyone's amazement, things began to go wrong. The Norwegians successfully held out in the Akershus fortress in Christiania (Oslo) and added injury to insult by holding on to Halden too. A naval commander, **Peter Tordenskiold**, became a national hero in Norway when he caught the Swedish fleet napping and ripped it to pieces off Strømstad. Karl was forced to retreat, but returned with a new army two years later. He promptly besieged the fortress at Halden for a second time, but while he was inspecting his troops someone shot him in the head – whether it was one of his own soldiers or a Norwegian has been the subject of heated debate ever since. Whatever the truth, Karl's death enabled the protagonists to agree the **Peace of Frederiksborg** (1720), which ended hostilities for the rest of the eighteenth century.

Peace favoured the growth of trade, but although Norway's economy prospered it was hampered by the increasing **centralization** of the Dano-Norwegian state. Regulations pushed more and more trade through Copenhagen, to the irritation of the majority of Norwegian merchants who were accustomed to trading direct with their customers. Increasingly, they wanted the same privileges as the Danes, and especially, given the chronic shortage of capital and credit, their own national bank. In the 1760s, Copenhagen did a dramatic U-turn, abolishing monopolies, removing trade barriers and even permitting a free press – and the Norwegian economy boomed. Nonetheless, the bulk of the population remained impoverished and prey to famine whenever the harvest was poor. The number of landless agricultural labourers rose dramatically, partly because more prosperous farmers were buying up large slices of land, and for the first time Norway had something akin to a proletariat.

Despite this, Norway was one of the few European countries little affected by the French Revolution. Instead of political action, there was a **religious revival**, with Hans Nielson Hauge emerging as an evangelical leader. The movement's characteristic hostility to officialdom caused concern, and Hauge was imprisoned, but in reality it posed little threat to the status quo. The end result was rather the foundation of a fundamentalist movement that is still a force to be reckoned with in parts of west Norway.

The end of union with Denmark

Denmark-Norway had remained neutral throughout the Seven Years' War (1756–63) between England and France, and renewed that neutrality in 1792, during the period leading up to the **Napoleonic Wars**. The prewar years were good for Norway: overseas trade, especially with England, flourished, and demand for Norwegian timber, iron and cargo-space heralded a period of unparalleled prosperity. However, when Napoleon implemented a trade blockade – the Continental System – against Britain, he roped in the Danes. As a result, the British fleet bombarded Copenhagen in 1807 and forced the surrender of the entire Dano-Norwegian fleet. Denmark, in retaliation, declared war on England and Sweden. The move was disastrous for the Norwegian economy, which had suffered bad harvests in 1807 and 1808, and the English blockade of its seaports ruined trade.

By 1811 it was obvious that the Danes had backed the wrong side in the war, and the idea of an equal union with Sweden, which had supported Britain, became increasingly attractive to many Norwegians. By attaching their coat-tails to the victors, they hoped to restore the commercially vital trade with England. They also thought that the new Swedish king would be able to deal with the Danes if it came to a fight – just as the Swedes had themselves calculated when they appointed him in 1810. The man concerned, **Karl XIV Johan**, was, curiously enough, none other than Jean-Baptiste Bernadotte, formerly one of Napoleon's marshals. With perfect timing, he had helped the British defeat Napoleon at Leipzig in 1813. His reward came in the **Treaty of Kiel** the following year, when the great powers instructed the Danes to cede to Sweden all rights in Norway (although they did keep the dependencies of Iceland, Greenland and the Faroes). Four hundred years of union had ended.

Union with Sweden 1814–1905

The high-handed transfer of Norway from Denmark to Sweden did nothing to assuage the growing demands for greater independence. Furthermore, the Danish Crown Prince Christian Frederik roamed Norway stirring up fears of Swedish intentions. The prince and his supporters convened a Constituent Assembly, which met in a country house outside Eidsvoll (see p.154) in April 1814 and produced a **constitution**. Issued on May 17, 1814 (still a national holiday), this declared Norway to be a "free, independent and indivisible realm" with Christian Frederik as its king. Not surprisingly, Karl Johan would have none of this and, with the support of the great powers, he invaded Norway. Completely outgunned, Christian Frederik barely mounted any resistance. In exchange for Swedish promises to recognize the Norwegian constitution and the *Storting* (parliament), he abdicated as soon as he had signed a peace treaty – the so-called **Convention of Moss** – in August 1814.

The ensuing period was marred by struggles between the *Storting* and **Karl XIV Johan** over the nature of the union. Although the constitution emphasized Norway's independence, Johan had a suspensive veto over the *Storting*'s actions, the post of *Stattholder* in Norway could only be held by a Swede, and foreign and diplomatic matters concerning Norway remained entirely in Swedish hands. Despite this, Karl Johan proved popular in Norway, and during his reign the country enjoyed a degree of independence. The Swedes allowed all the highest offices in Norway to be filled exclusively by Norwegians and democratic local councils were established, in part due to the rise of the peasant farmers as a political force.

Under both Oscar I (1844–59) and Karl XV (1859–72), however, it was **pan-Scandinavianism** that ruled the intellectual roost. This belief in the natural solidarity of Denmark, Norway and Sweden was espoused by the leading artists of the period, but died a toothless death in 1864 when the Norwegians and the Swedes refused to help Denmark when it was attacked by Austria and Prussia; some of the loudest cries of treachery came from a young writer by the name of Henrik Ibsen, whose poetic drama, *Brand*, was a spirited indictment of Norwegian perfidy.

Domestic politics were changing too, with the rise to power in the 1850s of **Johan Sverdrup**, who started a long and ultimately successful campaign to wrest executive power from the king and transfer it to the *Storting*. By the mid-1880s, Sverdrup and his political allies had pretty much won the day, though a further bout of sabre-rattling between the supporters of Norwegian independence and the Swedish king, **Oscar II** (1872–1907), was necessary before both sides would accept a plebiscite. This took place in August 1905, when there was an overwhelming vote in favour of the **dissolution of the union**, which was duly confirmed by the Treaty of Karlstad. A second plebiscite determined that independent Norway should be a monarchy rather than a republic and, in November 1905, Prince Karl of Denmark (Edward VII of England's son-in-law) was elected to the throne as **Håkon VII**.

Meanwhile, the gradual increase in prosperity had been having important **social implications**. The layout and buildings of modern Oslo – the Royal Palace, Karl Johans gate, the university – date from this period, whilst Johan Christian Dahl, the most distinguished Scandinavian landscape painter of his day, was instrumental in the foundation of the National Gallery in Oslo in 1836. Furthermore, other prominent members of the bourgeoisie were championing things Norwegian, in particular a massive six-volume topographical survey of the country prepared by Jens Kraft. In addition, the poet, prose writer and propagandist Henrik Wergeland proclaimed the ideals of the Romantic movement, decrying the civil servant culture that had dominated Norway for so long in favour of the more sincere qualities of the peasant farmer. By these means, sections of the middle class attempted to endow the Norwegian peasantry with all sorts of previously unidentified qualities, while the **temperance movement** sought to bring them up to these lofty ideals, by promoting laws to prohibit the use of small stills, once found on every farm. This policy was adopted by the government in 1844, and by the mid-nineteenth century, consumption of spirits had dropped drastically and coffee rivalled beer as the national drink.

Culturally, the late nineteenth century was a fruitful time for Norway, beginning with the rediscovery of the **Norwegian language** and its folklore by a number of academics. They formed the nucleus of the National Romantic movement, which did much to restore the country's cultural self-respect. Following on were authors like Alexander Kielland, who wrote most of his works between 1880 and 1891, and Knut Hamsun, whose most characteristic novel, *Hunger*, was published in 1890. In music, **Edvard Grieg** (1843–1907) was inspired by old Norwegian folk melodies, composing some of his most famous music for Ibsen's *Peer Gynt*, whilst the artist **Edvard Munch** completed many of his major works in the 1880s and 1890s. Finally, the internationally acclaimed dramatist **Henrik Ibsen** returned to Oslo in 1891 after a prolonged self-imposed exile.

Early Independence: 1905–39

Norway's **Independence** came at a time of further economic advance, engendered by the introduction of hydro-electric power and underpinned by a burgeoning merchant navy, the third-largest after the USA and Britain. Social reforms also saw funds being made available for unemployment relief, accident insurance schemes and a Factory Act (1909), governing safety in the workplace. An extension to the franchise gave the vote to all men over 25 and, in 1913, to women too. The education system was reorganized, and substantial sums were spent on new arms and defence. This prewar period also saw the emergence of a strong trade union movement and of a Labour Party committed to revolutionary change.

Since 1814 Norway had had little to do with European affairs, and at the outbreak of **World War I** it declared itself strictly neutral. Its sympathy, though, lay largely with the Western Allies, and the Norwegian economy boomed as its ships and timber were in great demand. By 1916, however, Norway had begun to feel the pinch as German submarine action hit both enemy and neutral shipping, and by the end of the war Norway had lost half its chartered tonnage and 2000 crew. The Norwegian economy also suffered after the USA entered the war because the Americans imposed strict trade restrictions in their attempt to prevent supplies getting to Germany, and rationing had to be introduced across Norway. Indeed, the price of neutrality was high: there was a rise in state expenditure, a soaring cost of living and, at the end of the war, no seat at the conference table. In spite of its losses, Norway got no share of confiscated German shipping, although it was partly compensated by gaining sovereignty of Spitsbergen and its coal deposits – the first extension of the Norwegian frontiers for 500 years. In 1920 Norway also entered the new League of Nations.

Later in the 1920s, the decline in world trade led to decreased demand for Norway's shipping. Bank failures and currency fluctuation were rife, and, as unemployment and industrial strife increased, a strengthening Norwegian **Labour Party** took advantage. With the franchise extended and the introduction of larger constituencies, it had a chance to win seats outside the large towns for the first time. At the 1927 election the Labour Party, together with the Social Democrats from whom they'd split, were the biggest grouping in the *Storting*. However they had no overall majority and because many feared their revolutionary rhetoric, they were manoeuvred out of office after only fourteen days. Trade disputes and lockouts continued and troops had to be used to protect scabs.

During the war, **Prohibition** had been introduced as a temporary measure and a referendum of 1919 showed a clear majority in favour of its continuation. But the ban did little to quell – and even exacerbated – drunkenness, and it was abandoned in 1932, replaced by the government monopoly on the sale of wines and spirits that remains in force today. The **1933 election** gave the Labour Party more seats than ever. Having shed its revolutionary image, a campaigning, reformist Labour Party benefited from the growing popular conviction that state control and a centrally planned economy were the only answer to Norway's economic problems. In 1935 the Labour Party, in alliance with the Agrarian Party, took power – an unlikely combination since the Agrarians were profoundly nationalist in outlook, so much so that their defence spokesman had been the rabid anti-Semite **Vidkun Quisling**. Frustrated by the democratic process, Quisling had left the Agrarians in 1933 to found **Nasjonal Samling** (National Unification), a fascist movement which proposed, among other things, that both Hitler and Mussolini should be nominated for the Nobel Peace Prize. Quisling had good contacts with Nazi Germany but little support in Norway – local elections in 1937 reduced his local representation to a mere seven, and party membership fell to 1500.

The Labour government under **Johan Nygaardsvold** presided over an improving economy. By 1938 industrial production was 75 percent higher than it had been in 1914 and unemployment dropped as expenditure on roads, railways and public works increased. Social welfare reforms were implemented and trade union membership increased. When war broke out in 1939, Norway was lacking only one thing – adequate defence. A vigorous member of the League of Nations, the country had pursued disarmament- and peace-oriented policies since the end of World War I and was determined to remain neutral.

World War II

In early 1940, despite the threat posed by Hitler, the Norwegians were preoccupied with Allied mine-laying off the Norwegian coast – part of their attempt to prevent Swedish iron ore being shipped from Narvik to Germany. Indeed, such was Norwegian naivety that they made a formal protest to Britain on the day of the **German invasion**. Caught napping, the Norwegian army offered little initial resistance and the south and central regions of the country were quickly overrun. King Håkon and the *Storting* were forced into a hasty evacuation of Oslo and headed north to Elverum, evading capture by just a couple of hours. Here, at the government's temporary headquarters, the executive was granted full powers to take whatever decisions were necessary in the interests of Norway – a mandate which later formed the basis of the Norwegian government-in-exile in Britain.

The Germans contacted the king and his government in Elverum, demanding, amongst other things, that Quisling be accepted as prime minister as a condition of surrender. Though their situation was desperate, the Norwegians rejected this outright and instead chose resistance. The ensuing campaign lasted for two months and, although the Norwegians fought determinedly with the help of a few British regulars, they were no match for the German army. In June both king and government fled to Britain from Tromsø in northern Norway. The country was rapidly brought under Nazi control, Hitler sending **Josef Terboven** to take full charge of Norwegian affairs.

The fascist **Nasjonal Samling** was declared the only legal party and the media, civil servants and teachers were brought under its control. As **civil resistance** grew, a state of emergency was declared: two trade union leaders were shot, arrests increased and a concentration camp was set up outside Oslo. In February 1942 Quisling was installed as "Minister President" of Norway, but it soon became clear that his government didn't have the support of the

Norwegian people. The church refused to co-operate, schoolteachers protested and trade union members and officials resigned en masse. In response, deportations increased, death sentences were announced and a compulsory labour scheme was introduced.

Military resistance escalated. A military organization (MILORG) was established as a branch of the armed forces under the control of the High Command in London. By May 1941 it had enlisted 20,000 men (32,000 by 1944) in clandestine groups all over the country. Arms and instructors came from Britain, radio stations were set up and a continuous flow of intelligence about Nazi movements sent back. Sabotage operations were legion, the most notable being the destruction of the heavy-water plant at **Rjukan**, foiling a German attempt to produce an atomic bomb. Reprisals against the resistance were severe, but only a comparative handful of Norwegians actively collaborated with the enemy.

The **government-in-exile** in London continued to represent free Norway to the world, mobilizing support on behalf of the Allies. Most of the Norwegian merchant fleet was abroad when the Nazis invaded, and by 1943 the Norwegian navy had seventy ships helping the Allied convoys. With the German position deteriorating, neutral Sweden adopted a more sympathetic policy to its Norwegian neighbours, allowing the creation of thinly-disguised training grounds for resistance fighters. These camps also served to produce the police detachments that were to secure law and order after liberation.

When the Allies landed in Normandy in June 1944, overt action against the occupying Germans was temporarily discouraged, since the Allies could not safeguard against reprisals. Help was at hand, however, in the form of the **Soviets** who crossed into the far north of Norway in late October, and drove back the Germans. Unfortunately, the Germans burned everything in their path as they retreated, forcing the local population into hiding. To prevent the Germans reinforcing their beleaguered Finnmark battalions, the resistance planned a campaign of mass railway sabotage, stopping three-quarters of the troop movements overnight. As their control of Norway crumbled, the Germans finally **surrendered** on May 7, 1945. King Håkon returned to Norway on June 7, five years to the day since he'd left for exile.

Terboven committed suicide and the NS collaborators were rounded up. A caretaker government took office, staffed by resistance leaders, and was replaced in October 1945 by a majority **Labour government**. The Communists won eleven seats, reflecting the efforts of Communist saboteurs in the war and the prestige that the Soviet Union enjoyed in Norway after the liberation. Quisling was shot, along with 24 other high-ranking traitors, and thousands of collaborators were punished.

Postwar reconstruction

At the end of the war, Norway was on its knees: the far north – Finnmark – had been laid waste, half the mercantile fleet lost, and production was at a standstill. Recovery, though, fostered by a sense of national unity, was quick; it took only three years for GNP to return to its prewar level. Norway's part in the war had increased her prestige in the world. The country became one of the founding members of the **United Nations** in 1945, and the first UN Secretary-General, Tryggve Lie, was Norwegian Foreign Minister. With the failure of discussions to promote a Scandinavian defence union, the *Storting* also voted to enter **NATO** in 1949.

Domestically, there was general agreement about the form that social reconstruction should take. In 1948, the *Storting* passed the laws that introduced the Welfare State almost unanimously. The 1949 election saw the government returned with a larger majority and Labour governments continued to be elected throughout the following decade with the dominant political figure being **Einar Gerhardsen**. As national prosperity increased, society became ever more egalitarian, levelling up rather than down. Subsidies were paid to the agricultural and fishing industries, wages increased, and a comprehensive social security system helped to eradicate poverty. The state ran the important mining industry, was the largest shareholder in the hydroelectric company and built an enormous steel works at Mo-i-Rana to help develop the economy of the devastated northern counties. Rationing ended in 1952 and, as the demand for higher-level education grew, new universities were created for Bergen, Trondheim and Tromsø.

Beyond consensus: modern Norway

The political consensus began to fragment in the early 1960s. Following the restructuring of rural constituencies in the 1950s, there was a realignment in centre politics, the outmoded Agrarian Party becoming the **Centre Party**. There was change on the left too, where defence squabbles within the Labour Party led to the formation of the **Socialist People's Party** (SF), which wanted Norway out of NATO and sought a renunciation of nuclear weapons. The Labour Party's 1961 declaration that no nuclear weapons would be stationed in Norway except under an immediate threat of war did not placate the SF, who unexpectedly took two seats at the election that year. Holding the balance of power, the SF voted with the Labour Party until 1963, when it helped bring down the government over mismanagement of state industries. A replacement coalition collapsed after only one month, but the writing was on the wall. Rising prices, dissatisfaction with high taxation and a continuing housing shortage meant that the 1965 election put a **non-socialist coalition** in power for the first time in twenty years.

Under the leadership of **Per Borten** of the Centre Party, the coalition's programme was unambitious. Nonetheless, living standards continued to rise and although the 1969 election saw a marked increase in Labour Party support, the coalition hung on to power. Also that year, **oil and gas** were discovered beneath the North Sea and, as the vast extent of the reserves became obvious, it became clear that the Norwegians were to enjoy a magnificent bonanza – one which was destined to pay about 25 percent of the government's annual bills.

Meanwhile, Norway's politicians, who had applied twice previously for membership of the **European Economic Community** (EEC) – in 1962 and 1967 – believed that de Gaulle's fall in France presented a good opportunity for a third application, which was made in 1970. There was great concern, though, about the effect of membership on Norwegian agriculture and fisheries, and in 1971 Per Borten was forced to resign following his indiscreet handling of the negotiations. The Labour Party, the majority of its representatives in favour of EEC membership, formed a minority administration, but when the **1972 referendum** narrowly voted "No" to joining the EEC, the government resigned.

With the 1973 election producing another minority Labour government, the uncertain pattern of the previous ten years continued. Even the postwar consensus on **Norwegian security policy** broke down on various issues – the question of a northern European nuclear-free zone, the stocking of Allied material in Norway – although there remained strong agreement for continued NATO membership.

In 1983, the Christian Democrats and the Centre Party joined together in a non-socialist coalition, which lasted only two years. It was replaced in 1986 by a minority Labour administration, led by **Dr Gro Harlem Brundtland**, Norway's first woman prime minister. She made sweeping changes to the way the country was run, introducing seven women into her eighteen-member cabinet, but her government was beset by problems for the three years of its life: tumbling oil prices led to a recession, unemployment rose (though only to four percent) and there was widespread dissatisfaction with Labour's high taxation policies.

At the **general election** in September 1989, Labour lost eight seats and was forced out of office – the worst result that the party had suffered since 1930. More surprising was the success of the extremist parties on both political wings – the anti-NATO Left Socialist Party and the right-wing, anti-immigrant Progress Party both scored spectacular results, winning almost a quarter of the votes cast, and increasing their representation in the *Storting* many times over. This deprived the Conservative Party (one of whose leaders, bizarrely, was Gro Harlem Brundtland's husband) of the majority it might have expected, the result being yet another shaky minority administration – this time a **centre-right coalition** between the Conservatives, the Centre Party and the Christian Democrats, led by Jan Syse.

The new government immediately faced problems familiar to the last Labour administration. In particular, there was continuing conflict over joining the **European Community**, a policy still supported by many in the Norwegian establishment but flatly rejected by the Centre Party. It was this, in part, that signalled the end of the coalition, for after just over a year in office, the Centre Party withdrew its support and forced the downfall of Syse. In October 1990, Gro Harlem Brundtland was put back in power at the head of a **minority Labour administration**, remaining in office till her re-election for a fourth minority term in 1993. The 1993 elections saw a revival in Labour Party fortunes and, to the relief of the majority, the collapse of the Progress Party vote. However, it was also an untidy, confusing affair where the main issue, membership of the EU, cut across the traditional left-versus-right divide.

Present-day Norway

Following the 1993 election, the country tumbled into a long and fiercely conducted campaign over **membership of the EU**. Brundtland and her main political opponents wanted in, but despite the near-unanimity of the political class, the Norwegians narrowly rejected the EU in a **1994 referendum**. It was a close call (52.5 percent versus 47.5 percent), but in the end farmers and fishermen, afraid of the economic results of joining, combined with women's groups and environmentalists, keen to protect Norway's high social care and "green" standards, and managed to swing opinion against the EU. Unlike the Labour government of 1972, the Brundtland administration soldiered on afterwards, wisely soothing ruffled feathers by promising to shelve the whole EU membership issue until at least 2000. Nonetheless, the 1997 election saw a move to the right, the main beneficiaries being the Christian Democratic Party and the ultra-conservative Progress Party. In itself, this was not enough to remove the Labour-led coalition from office – indeed Labour remained comfortably the largest party – but the right was dealt a trump card by the new Labour leader, **Thorbjørn Jagland**. During the campaign he had promised that the Labour Party would step down from office if it failed to elicit less than the 36.9 percent of the vote it had secured in 1993. Much to the chagrin of his colleagues, Jagland's political chickens came home to roost when Labour only received 35 percent of the vote – and the old coalition had to go, leaving power in the hands of an unwieldy right-of-centre, minority coalition. Bargaining with its rivals from a position of parliamentary weakness, the new government found it difficult to cut a clear path – or at least one very different from its predecessor – apart from managing to antagonize the women's movement by some reactionary social legislation whose none-too-hidden subtext seemed to read "A woman's place is in the home". In the Spring of 2000, the government resigned and the Labour Party resumed command – but not for long: in elections the following year, they took a drubbing and the right prospered, paving the way for the current ungainly centre-right administrative coalition.

Environmental issues have attracted much heated debate too, and Norway plays an active role in the campaign to raise their profile worldwide, backing it up domestically with increasingly stringent anti-pollution laws. **Road building** is also becoming very controversial. The long-standing rural isolation of parts of the country led to the postwar aspiration to connect all of the country's villages to the road system. Give or take the occasional hamlet, this has now been achieved and a second phase is underway, involving the upgrading of roads. Wherever this makes conditions safer, the popular consensus for it survives, but there is increasing opposition to the prestige projects so favoured by status-seeking politicians. In part, this change in attitude has been influenced by events abroad, especially the anti-road campaigns in the UK.

Norwegians, however, will not be shifted when it comes to **whaling and sealing**, continuing to stand firmly by industries that they've pursued for decades. This is inexplicable to many Western Europeans, who point to Norway's eminently liberal approach to most other matters, but the Norwegians see things very differently: why, many of them ask, is the culling of seals and mink seen in a different light from the mass slaughter of farmed animals?

In the long term, quite what Norway will make of its **splendid isolation** from the EU is unclear, though the situation is mitigated by Norway's membership of the European Economic Agreement (EEA), a free-trade deal of January 1994 to which the EU is also party. Whatever happens, and whether or not there is another EU referendum, it's hard to imagine that the Norwegians will suffer any permanent economic harm. They have, after all, a superabundance of natural resources and one of the most educated workforces in the world. Which isn't to say the country doesn't collectively fret – a modest increase in the amount of drug addiction and street crime has produced much soul-searching, the theory being that an advanced and progressive social policy should be able to eliminate such barbarisms. This thoughtful approach, so typical of Norway, is very much to the country's credit as is the refusal to accept a residual level of unemployment (of about 6–7 percent) that is the envy of many other Western governments.

Legends and folklore

Norway has an exceptionally rich body of historical legend and folk tradition, and one that plays an important part in the national conscious-
ness. Most famous are the **sagas**, mainly written in Iceland between the
twelfth and fourteenth centuries, and which constitute a vast collection
of part-historical, part-fictionalized stories covering several centuries of Norse
history. Thanks to the survival of one of these sagas, the *Poetic Edda* (see opposite), our knowledge of **Norse mythology** is far from conjectural. Much that
was not recorded there survived in the oral tradition, to be revived from the
1830s onwards by the artists and writers of the National Romantic movement.
Some members of this movement also set about collecting the **folk tales** and
legends of the rural regions. The difficulties they experienced in rendering the
Norwegian dialects into written form – there was no written Norwegian language per se – fuelled the language movement, and sent the academic Ivar
Aasen roaming the countryside to assemble the material from which he for-
mulated *Landsmål* (see p.419).

Sagas

The Norwegian Vikings settled in Iceland in the ninth century, and throughout the medieval period the Icelanders had a deep attachment to, and interest
in, their original homeland. The result was a body of work that remains one of
the richest sources of European medieval literature. That so much of it has survived is due to Iceland's isolation; most Norwegian sources disappeared centuries ago.

All the **sagas** feature real people and tell of events which are usually known
to have happened, though the plots are embroidered to suit the tales' heroic
style. They reveal much about a Norse culture in which arguments between
individuals might spring from comparatively trivial disputes over horses or
sheep, but where a strict code of honour and revenge meant that every insult,
whether real or imagined, had to be avenged. Thus personal disputes soon
turned into clan vendettas. Plots are complex, the dialogue laconic, and the
pared-down prose omits unnecessary detail. New characters are often introduced by means of tedious genealogies, necessary to explain the motivation
behind their later actions (though the more adept translations render these
explanations as footnotes). Personality is only revealed through speech, facial
expressions and general demeanour, or the comments and gossip of others.

The earliest Icelandic work, the **Elder** or **Poetic Edda** (various English editions are available), comprises 34 lays dating from as early as the eighth century, and gives insights into early Norse culture and pagan cosmogony and belief.
It's not to be confused with the **Younger** or **Prose Edda**, written centuries
later by Snorri Sturluson, the most distinguished of the saga writers.

Also noteworthy are *The Vinland Saga*, *Njal's Saga* and the *Laxdaela Saga*, tales
of ninth- and tenth-century Icelandic derring-do; and *Harald's Saga*, a rattling
good yarn celebrating the life and times of King Harald Hardrada. English
translations of all the above, by Magnus Magnusson and Hermann Palsson, are
published by Penguin.

Norse mythology

The Vikings shared a common **pagan faith,** whose polytheistic tenets were upheld across all of Scandinavia. The deities were worshipped at a thousand village shrines, usually by means of sacrifices in which animals, weapons, boats and other artefacts, even humans, were given to the gods. There was very little theology to sanctify these rituals; instead the principal gods – Odin, Thor and Frey – were surrounded by mythical tales attributing to them a bewildering variety of strengths, weaknesses and powers.

Odin and Frigga

The god of war, wisdom, poetry and magic, **Odin** was untrustworthy, violent and wise in equal measure. The most powerful of the twelve Viking deities, the Aesir, who lived at Asgard, he was also lord of the **Valkyries**, women warrior-servants who tended his needs while he held court at **Valhalla**, the hall of dead heroes. As with many of the other pagan gods, he had the power to change into any form he desired. Odin's wife, **Frigga**, was the goddess protecting the home and the family.

At the beginning of time, it was Odin who made heaven and earth from the body of the giant Ymir, and created man from an ash tree, woman from an alder. However, **Yggdrasil**, the tree of life which supported the whole universe, was beyond his control; the Vikings believed that eventually the tree would die and both gods and mortals would perish in the **Ragnarok**, the twilight of the gods. Among the Anglo-Saxons, the equivalent of Odin was Woden, hence the origin of the word "Wednesday".

Thor

One of Odin's sons, **Thor** appears to have been the most worshipped of the Norse gods. A giant with superhuman strength, he was the short-tempered god of thunder, fire and lightning. He regularly fought with the evil Frost Giants in Jotunheimen (see p.166), his favourite weapon being the hammer, Mjolnir, which the trolls (see p.380) had fashioned for him. His chariot was drawn by two goats – Cracktooth and Gaptooth – who could be killed and eaten at night, but would be fully recovered the next morning, providing none of their bones were broken. It's from Thor that we get "Thursday".

Loki

A negative force, **Loki** personified cunning and trickery. His treachery turned the other deities against him, and he was chained up beneath a serpent that dripped venom onto his face. His wife, **Sigyn**, remained loyal and held a bowl over his head to catch the venom, but when the bowl was full she had to turn away to empty it, and in those moments his squirmings would cause earthquakes.

Frey

The god of fertility, **Frey**'s pride and joy was Skidbladnir, a ship that was large enough to carry all the gods, but could still be folded up and put into his bag. He often lived with the elves (see p.380) in Elfheim.

Freya

Freya was the goddess of love, healing and fertility. "Friday" was named after her.

Hel

The goddess of the dead, **Hel** lived on brains and bone marrow. She presided over "Hel", where those who died of illness or old age went, living a miserable existence under the roots of Yggdrasil, the tree of life.

The Norns

Representing the past, the present and the future, the **Norns** were the three goddesses of fate, casting lots over the cradle of every new-born child.

Folk tales and legends

Norway's extensive oral folklore was first written down in the early nineteenth century, most famously by **Peter Christen Asbjørnsen** and **Jørgen Moe**, the first of whose compilations appeared to great popular acclaim in 1842. Despite all the nationalist kerfuffle regarding the Norwegianness of the tales, many of them were in fact far from unique to Norway. But while they shared many characteristics – and had the same roots – as folk tales across the whole of northern Europe, they were populated by stock characters who were recognizably Norwegian – the king, for example, was always pictured as a wealthy Norwegian farmer.

There are three types of Norwegian **folk tale**: **comical tales**; **animal yarns**, in which the beasts concerned – most frequently the wolf, fox and bear – talk and behave like human beings; and most common of all, **magical stories** populated by a host of supernatural creatures. The folk tale is always written matter-of-factly, no matter how fantastic the events it retells. In this respect it has much in common with the **folk legend**, though the latter purports to be factual. Norwegian legends "explain" scores of unusual natural phenomenon – the location of boulders, holes in cliffs etc – and are populated by a cast of supernatural beings, again broadly familiar across northern Europe.

The assorted **supernatural creatures** of folk tale and legend hark back to the pagan myths of the pre-Christian era, but whereas the Vikings held them of secondary importance to their gods, in Norwegian folk tales they take centre stage. In post-Christian Norwegian folk tradition, these creatures were regarded as the descendants of children that Eve hid from God. When they were discovered by him, they were assigned particular realms in which to dwell, but their illicit wanderings were legion. Towards the end of the nineteenth century, book illustrations by **Erik Werenskiold** and **Theodor Kittelsen** effectively defined what the various supernatural creatures looked like in the Norwegian public's imagination.

As mythologized in Norway, the creatures of the folk tales possess a confusing range of virtues and vices. Here's a brief guide to some of the more important.

Giants

Enormous in size and strength, the **giants** of Norwegian folklore were reputed to be rather stupid and capable both of kindly actions and great cruelty towards humans. They usually had a human appearance, but some were monsters with many heads. They were fond of carrying parts of the landscape from one place to another, dropping boulders and even islands as they went. According to the Eddic cosmogony, the first giant, Ymir, was killed by Odin and the world made from his body – his blood formed the sea, his bones the mountains and so on. Ymir was the ancestor of the evil Frost Giants, who lived in Jotunheim, and who regularly fought with Thor.

Trolls

Spirits of the underground, **trolls** were ambivalent figures, able both to hinder and help humans – and were arguably a folkloric expression of the id. The first trolls were depicted as giants, but later versions were small, strong, misshapen and of pale countenance from living in darkness; sunlight would turn them into stone. They worked in metals and wood and were fabulous craftsmen. They made Odin's spear and Thor's hammer, though Thor's inclination to throw the weapon at them made them hate noise; as late as the eighteenth century, Norwegian villagers would ring church bells for hours on end to drive them away. If the trolls were forced to make something for a human, they would put a secret curse on it; this would render it dangerous to the owner. Some trolls had a penchant for stealing children and others carried off women to be their wives.

Elves

Akin to fairies, **elves** were usually divided between good-hearted but mischievous white elves, and nasty black elves, who brought injury and sickness. Both lived underground in a world, Elfheim, that echoed that of humans – with farms, animals and the like – but made excursions into the glades and groves of the forests. At night, the white elves liked singing and dancing to the accompaniment of the harp. They were normally invisible, though you could spot their dancing places wherever the grass grew more luxuriantly in circular patterns than elsewhere. The black elves were also invisible, a good job considering they were extremely ugly and had long, filthy noses. If struck by a sunbeam, they would turn to stone. Both types of elf were prone to entice humans into their kingdom, usually for a short period – but sometimes forever.

Wights

In pre-Christian times, the Vikings believed their lands populated with invisible guardian spirits, the **wights** (*vetter*), who needed to be treated with respect. One result was that when a longship was approaching the shore, the fearsome figurehead at its prow was removed so as not to frighten the *vetter* away. Bad luck would follow if a *vetter* left the locality.

Draugen

Personifying all those who have died at sea, the **draugen** was a ghostly apparition who appeared as a headless fisherman in oilskins. He sailed the seas in half a boat and wailed when someone was about to drown. Other water spirits included the malicious river sprite, the **nixie**, who could assume different forms to lure the unsuspecting to a watery grave. There were also the shy and benign **mermaids** and **mermen**, half-fish and half-human, who dived into the water whenever they spied a human. However they also liked to dress up as humans to go to market.

Witches

As with **witches** across the rest of Europe, the Scandinavian version was an old woman who had made a pact with the Devil, swapping her soul in return for special powers. The witch could inflict injury and illness especially if she had something that the victim had touched or owned – anything from a lock of hair to an item of clothing. She could disguise herself as an animal, and had familiars – usually insects or cats – which assisted her in foul deeds. Most witched travelled through the air on broomsticks, but some rode on wolves bridled with snakes.

Viking customs and rituals

T he **Vikings** have long been the subject of historical myth and legend, but accurate and unbiased contemporary accounts are few and far between. A remarkable exception is the annals of **Ibn Fadlan**, a member of a diplomatic delegation sent from the Baghdad Caliphate to Bulgar on the Volga in 921–922AD. In the following extracts Fadlan details the habits and rituals of a tribe of Swedish Vikings, the **Rus**, who dealt in furs and slaves. The first piece notes with disgust the finer points of Viking personal hygiene, the second provides a sober eyewitness account of the rituals of a Viking ship burial.

Habits and rituals

I saw the **Rus** when they arrived on their trading mission and anchored at the River Atul (Volga). Never had I seen people of more perfect physique; they are tall as date-palms, and reddish in colour. They wear neither mantle nor coat, but each man carries a cape which covers one half of his body, leaving one hand free. Their swords are Frankish in pattern, broad, flat and fluted. Each man has (tattooed upon him) trees, figures and the like from the finger-nails to the neck. Each woman carries on her bosom a container made of iron, silver, copper or gold – its size and substance depending on her man's wealth. Attached to the container is a ring carrying her knife, which is also tied to her bosom. Round her neck she wears gold or silver rings; when a man amasses 10,000 *dirhems* he makes his wife one gold ring; when he has 20,000 he makes two; and so the woman gets a new ring for every 10,000 *dirhems* her husband acquires, and often a woman has many of these rings. Their finest ornaments are green beads made from clay. They will go to any length to get hold of these; for one *dirhem* they procure one such bead and they string these into necklaces for their women.

They are the filthiest of god's creatures. They do not wash after discharging their natural functions, neither do they wash their hands after meals. They are as stray donkeys. They arrive from their distant lands and lay their ships alongside the banks of the Atul, which is a great river, and there they build big wooden houses on its shores. Ten or twenty of them may live together in one house, and each of them has a couch of his own where he sits and diverts himself with the pretty slave-girls whom he has brought along to offer for sale. He will make love with one of them in the presence of his comrades, sometimes this develops into a communal orgy and, if a customer should turn up to buy a girl, the Rus will not let her go till he has finished with her.

Every day they wash their faces and heads, all using the same water which is as filthy as can be imagined. This is how it is done. Every morning a girl brings her master a large bowl of water in which he washes his face and hands and hair, combing it also over the bowl, then blows his nose and spits into the water. No dirt is left on him which doesn't go into the water. When he has finished the girl takes the same bowl to his neighbour – who repeats the performance – until the bowl has gone round to the entire household. All have blown their noses, spat and washed their faces and hair in the water.

On anchoring their vessels, each man goes ashore carrying bread, meat, onions, milk, and *nabid* (probably a Scandinavian kind of beer), and these he takes to a large wooden stake with a face like that of a human being, surrounded by smaller figures, and behind them tall poles in the ground. Each man prostrates himself before the large post and recites: "O Lord, I have come from distant parts with so many girls, so many furs (and whatever other commodities he is carrying). I now bring you this offering". He then presents his gift and continues "Please send me a merchant who has many dinars and *dirhems*, and who will trade favourably with me without too much bartering". Then he retires. If, after this, business does not pick up quickly and go well, he returns to the statue to present further gifts. If results continue slow, he then presents gifts to the minor figures and begs their intercession, saying, "These are our Lord's wives, daughters and sons". Then he pleads before each figure in turn, begging them to intercede for him and humbling himself before them. Often trade picks up, and he says "My Lord has required my needs, and now it is my duty to repay him". Whereupon he sacrifices goats or cattle, some of which he distributes as alms. The rest he lays before the statues, large and small, and the heads of the beasts he plants upon the poles. After dark, of course, the dogs come and devour the lot – and the successful trader says, "My Lord is pleased with me, and has eaten my offerings".

If one of the Rus falls sick they put him in a tent by himself and leave bread and water for him. They do not visit him, however, or speak to him, especially if he is a serf. Should he recover he rejoins the others; if he dies they burn him. If he happens to be a serf, however, they leave him for the dogs and vultures to devour. If they catch a robber they hang him in a tree until he is torn to shreds by wind and weather…

The burial

…I had been told that when their chieftains died cremation was the least part of their whole **funeral procedure**, and I was, therefore, very much interested to find out more about this. One day I heard that one of their leaders had died. They laid him forthwith in a grave, which they covered up for ten days till they had finished cutting-out and sewing his costume. If the dead man is poor they make a little ship, put him in it, and burn it. If he is wealthy, however, they divide his property and goods into three parts: one for his family, one to pay for his costume, and one to make *nabid*. This they drink on the day when the slave woman of the dead man is killed and burnt together with her master. They are deeply addicted to *nabid*, drinking it day and night; and often one of them has been found dead with a beaker in his hand. When a chieftain among them has died, his family demands of his slave women and servants: "Which of you wishes to die with him?" Then one of them says "I do" – and having said that the person concerned is forced to do so, and no backing out is possible. Those who are willing are mostly the slave women.

So when this man died they said to his slave women "Which of you wants to die with him?" One of them answered "I do". From that moment she was put in the constant care of two other women servants who took care of her to the extent of washing her feet with their own hands. They began to get things ready for the dead man, to cut his costume and so on, while every day the doomed woman drank and sang as though in anticipation of a joyous event.

When the day arrived on which the chieftain and his slave woman were going to be burnt, I went to the river where his ship was moored. It had been hauled ashore and four posts were made for it of birch and other wood. Further there was arranged around it what looked like a big store of wood. Then the ship was hauled near and placed on the wood. People now began to walk about talking in a language I could not understand, and the corpse still lay in the grave; they had not taken it out. They then produced a wooden bench, placed it on the ship, and covered it with carpets of Byzantine *dibag* (painted silk) and with cushions of Byzantine *dibag*. Then came an old woman whom they called "the Angel of Death", and she spread these cushions out over the bench. She was in charge of the whole affair from dressing the corpse to the killing of the slave woman. I noticed that she was an old giant-woman, a massive and grim figure. When they came to his grave they removed the earth from the wooden frame and they also took the frame away. They then divested the corpse of the clothes in which he had died. The body, I noticed, had turned black because of the intense frost. When they first put him in the grave, they had also given him beer, fruit, and a lute, all of which they now removed. Strangely enough the corpse did not smell, nor had anything about him changed save the colour of his flesh. They now proceeded to dress him in hose, and trousers, boots, coat, and a mantle of *dibag* adorned with gold buttons; put on his head a cap of *dibag* and sable fur; and carried him to the tent on the ship, where they put him on the blanket and supported him with cushions. They then produced *nabid*, fruit, and aromatic plants, and put these round his body; and they also brought bread, meat, and onions which they flung before him. Next they took a dog, cut it in half, and flung the pieces into the ship, and after this they took all his weapons and placed them beside him.

Next they brought two horses and ran them about until they were in a sweat, after which they cut them to pieces with swords and flung their meat into the ship; this also happened to two cows. Then they produced a cock and a hen, killed them, and threw them in. Meanwhile the slave woman who wished to be killed walked up and down, going into one tent after the other, and the owner of each tent had sexual intercourse with her, saying "Tell your master I did this out of love for him".

It was now Friday afternoon and they took the slave woman away to something which they had made resembling a doorframe. Then she placed her legs on the palms of the men and reached high enough to look over the frame, and she said something in a foreign language, after which they took her down. And they lifted her again and she did the same as the first time. Then they took her down and lifted her a third time and she did the same as the first and second times. Then they gave her a chicken and she cut its head off and threw it away; they took the hen and threw it into the ship. Then I asked the interpreter what she had done. He answered: "The first time they lifted her she said: "Look! I see my mother and father". The second time she said: "Look! I see all my dead relatives sitting around". The third time she said: "Look! I see my master in Paradise, and Paradise is beautiful and green and together with him are men and young boys. He calls me. Let me join him then!"

They now led her towards the ship. Then she took off two bracelets she was wearing and gave them to the old woman, "the Angel of Death", the one who was going to kill her. She next took off two anklets she was wearing and gave them to the daughters of that same woman. They then led her to the ship but did not allow her inside the tent. Then a number of men carrying wooden shield and sticks arrived, and gave her a beaker with *nabid*. She sang over it and emptied it. The interpreter then said to me, "Now with that she is bidding farewell to all her women friends". Then she was given another beaker. She took it and sang a lengthy song; but the old woman told her to hurry and drink up and enter the tent where her master was. When I looked at her she seemed completely bewildered. She wanted to enter the tent and she put her head between it and the ship. Then the woman took her head and managed to get it inside the tent, and the woman herself followed. Then the men began to beat the shields with the wooden sticks, to deaden her shouts so that the other girls would not become afraid and shrink from dying with their masters. Six men entered the tent and all of them had intercourse with her. Thereafter they laid her by the side of her dead master. Two held her hands and two her feet, and the woman called "the Angel of Death" put a cord round the girl's neck, doubled with an end at each side, and gave it to two men to pull. Then she advanced holding a small dagger with a broad blade and began to plunge it between the girl's ribs to and fro while the two men choked her with the cord till she died.

The dead man's nearest kinsman now appeared. He took a piece of wood and ignited it. Then he walked backwards, his back towards the ship and his face towards the crowd, holding the piece of wood in one hand and the other hand on his buttock; and he was naked. In this way the wood was ignited which they had placed under the ship after they had laid the slave woman, whom they had killed, beside her master. Then people came with branches and wood; each brought a burning brand and threw it on the pyre, so that the fire took hold of the wood, then the ship, then the tent and the man and the slave woman and all. Thereafter a strong and terrible wind rose so that the flame stirred and the fire blazed still more.

I heard one of the Rus folk, standing by, say something to my interpreter, and when I inquired what he had said, my interpreter answered: "He said: 'You Arabs are foolish'." "Why?" I asked. "Well, because you throw those you love and honour to the ground where the earth and the maggots and fields devour them, whereas we, on the other hand, burn them up quickly and they go to Paradise that very moment". The man burst out laughing, and on being asked why, he said: "His Lord, out of love for him, has sent this wind to take him away within the hour!" And so it proved, for within that time the ship and the pyre, the girl and the corpse had all become ashes and then dust. On the spot where the ship stood after having been hauled ashore, they built something like a round mould. In the middle of it they raised a large post of birch-wood on which they wrote the names of the dead man and the king of the Rus, and then the crowd dispersed.

The above extract, translated by Karre Stov, was taken from *The Vikings* by Johanes Brøndsted, and is reprinted by permission of Penguin Books.

Flora and fauna

There are significant differences in **climate** between the west coast of Norway, warmed by the Gulf Stream, and the interior, but these variations are of much less significance for the country's **flora** than altitude and latitude. With regard to its **fauna**, wild animals survive in significant numbers in the more inaccessible regions, but have been hunted extensively elsewhere, whilst Norway's west coast is home to dozens of enormous seabird colonies.

Flora

Much of the Norwegian landscape is dominated by vast **forests of spruce**, though these are, in fact, a relatively recent feature: the original forest cover was mainly of pine, birch and oak, and only in the last two thousand years has spruce spread across the whole of southeast and central Norway. That said, a rich variety of **deciduous trees** – notably oak, ash, lime, hazel, rowan, elm and maple – still flourish in a wide belt along the south coast, up through the fjord country and as far north as Trondheim, but only at relatively low altitudes. For their part, **conifers** thin out at around 900m above sea level in the south, 450m in Finnmark, to be replaced by a birch zone where there are also aspen and mountain ash. These deciduous trees contrive to ripen their seeds despite a short, cool summer, and can consequently be found almost as far north as the Nordkapp (North Cape) – as can the most robust of the conifers, the pine. Some 200m higher up, the birch fizzle out to be replaced by willow and dwarf birch, while above the timber line are bare mountain peaks and huge plateaux, the latter usually dotted with hundreds of lakes.

Norway accommodates in the region of 2000 plant species, but few of them are native. The most sought-after are the **berrying** species that grow wild all over Norway, mainly cranberries, blueberries and yellow **cloudberries**. Common in the country's peat bogs, and now also extensively cultivated, the cloudberry is a small herbaceous bramble whose fruits have a tangy flavour that is much prized in Norway. In drier situations and on the mountain plateaux, **lichens** – the favourite food of the reindeer – predominate, while in all but the thickest of spruce forests, the ground is thickly carpeted with **mosses** and **heathers**.

Everywhere, spring brings vivid **wild flowers**, splashes of brilliant colour at their most intense on the west coast where a wide range of mountain plants are nourished by the wet conditions and a geology that varies from limestone to acidic granites. Most of these species can also be found in the Alps, but there are several rarities, notably the **alpine clematis** (*Clematis alpina*) found in the Gudbrandsdal valley, hundreds of miles from its normal homes in eastern Finland and the Carpathian Mountains. Another, larger group comprises about thirty **Canadian mountain plants**, found in Europe only in the Dovre and Jotunheim mountains; quite how they come to be there has long baffled botanists.

The mildness of the west coast winter has allowed certain species to prosper beyond their usual northerly latitudes. Among species that can tolerate very little frost or snow are the star hyacinth (*Scilla verna*) and the purple heather (*Erica purpurea*), while a short distance inland come varieties that can withstand only short icy spells, including the foxglove (*Digitalis purpurea*) and the holly (*Ilex aquifolium*). In the southeastern part of the country, where the winters are harder and the summers hotter, the conditions support species that can lie dormant under the snow for several months a year – for example the blue anemone (*Anemone hepatica*) and the aconite (*Aconitum septentrionale*).

In the far north, certain Siberian species have migrated west down the rivers and along the coasts to the fjords of Finnmark and Troms. The most significant is the **Siberian garlic** (*Allium sibiricum*), which grows in such abundance that farmers have to make sure their cows don't eat too much of it or else the milk becomes onion-flavoured. Other Siberian species to look out for are the fringed pink (*Dianthus superbus*) and a large, lily-like plant, the sneezewort (*Veratrum album*).

Fauna

The larger Arctic **predators** of Norway, principally the lynx, wolf, wolverine and bear, are virtually extinct, and where they have survived they are mainly confined to the more inaccessible regions of the north. To a degree this has been caused by the timber industry, which has logged out great chunks of forest. The smaller predators – the fox, the Arctic fox, the otter, the badger and the marten – have fared rather better and remain comparatively common.

In the 1930s, the **beaver** had been reduced to just 500 animals in southern Norway. A total ban on hunting has, however, led to a dramatic increase in their numbers, and the beaver has begun to recolonize its old hunting grounds right across Scandinavia. The **elk** has benefited from the rolling back of the forests, grazing the newly treeless areas and breeding in sufficient numbers to allow an annual cull of around 40,000 animals; the red deer of the west coast are flourishing too. Otherwise, the Norwegians own about two million sheep and around 200,000 domesticated **reindeer**, most of whom are herded by the Sami. The last wild reindeer in Europe, some 15,000 beasts, wander the Hardangervidda and its adjacent mountain areas.

Among Norway's rodents, the most interesting is the **lemming**, whose numbers vary over a four-year cycle. In the first three to four years there is a gradual increase, which is followed, in the course of a few months, by a sudden fall. The cause of these variations is not known, though theories are plentiful. In addition to this four-year fluctuation, the lemming population goes through a violent explosion every eleven to twelve years. Competition for food is so ferocious that many animals start to range over wide areas. In these so-called **lemming years** the mountains and surrounding areas teem with countless thousands of lemmings, and hundreds swarm to their deaths by falling off cliff edges and the like. In lemming years, predators and birds of prey have an abundant source of food and frequently give birth to twice as many young as normal – not surprising considering the lemmings are extremely easy to catch. More inexplicably, the snowy owl leaves its polar habitat in lemming years, flying south to join in the feast: quite how they know when to turn up is a mystery. The Vikings were particularly fascinated by lemmings, believing that they dropped from the sky during thunderstorms.

With the exception of the raven, the partridge and the grouse, all the **mountain birds** of Norway are **migratory**, reflecting the harshness of winter conditions. Most fly back and forth from the Mediterranean and Africa, but some winter down on the coast. Woodland species include the wood grouse, the black grouse, several different sorts of owl, woodpeckers and birds of prey, while the country's lakes and marshes are inhabited by cranes, swans, grebes, geese, ducks and many waders. Most dramatic of all are the coastal nesting cliffs, where millions of **seabirds**, such as kittiwakes, guillemots, puffins, cormorants and gulls, congregate. What you won't see is the great auk, a flightless, 50cm-high bird resembling a penguin that once nested in its millions along the Atlantic seaboard but is now extinct: the last Norwegian great auk was killed in the eighteenth century and the last one of all was shot near Iceland a century later.

The waters off Norway once teemed with **seals** and **whales**, but indiscriminate hunting has drastically reduced their numbers, prompting several late-in-the-day conservation measures. The commonest species of **fish** – cod, haddock, coalfish and halibut – have been over-exploited too, and whereas there were once gigantic shoals of them right along the coast up to the Arctic Sea, they are now much less common. The cod, like several other species, live far out in the Barents Sea, only coming to the coast to spawn, a favourite destination being the waters round the Lofoten islands.

The only fish along Norway's coast that can survive in both salt and fresh water is the **salmon**, which grows to maturity in the sea and only swims upriver to spawn and later to die. In the following spring the young salmon return to the sea on the spring flood. Trout and char populate the rivers and lakes of western Norway, living on a diet of crustacea which tints their meat pink, like the salmon. Eastern Norway and Finnmark are the domain of **whitefish**, so called because they feed on plant remains, insects and animals, which keep their flesh white. In prehistoric times, these species migrated here from the east via what was then the freshwater Baltic; the most important of them are the perch, powan, pike and grayling.

Cinema

Overshadowed by its Nordic neighbours, **Norwegian cinema** has long struggled to make an impact on the international scene. In the last decade or so, however, a group of talented young film makers has emerged, who are responsible for a string of stylish, honest and refreshingly lucid films. Norway in general and northern Norway in particular has also developed a niche as a film location, most famously as the ice planet Hoth at the start of George Lucas' *The Empire Strikes Back* (1980).

Early Norwegian cinematic successes were few and far between, an exception being *Kon-Tiki*, a 1951 Oscar-winning documentary recording Thor Heyerdahl's journey across the Pacific on a balsa raft (see p.93), though the producer (and Oscar recipient) was a Swede, Olle Nordemar. In 1957, *Nine Lives* (*Ni Liv*), produced and directed by the Norwegian **Arne Skouen**, was widely acclaimed for its tale of a betrayed Resistance fighter, who managed to drag himself across northern Norway in winter to safety in neutral Sweden. Two years later **Erik Løchen**'s *The Hunt* (*Jakten*) was much influenced by the French New Wave in its mixture of time and space, dream and reality, as was the early work of **Anja Breien**, whose *Growing Up* (*Jostedalsrypa*) relates the story of a young girl who is the sole survivor from the Black Death in a remote fjordland village. Breien followed this up in 1975 with a successful improvised comedy *Wives* (*Hustruer*) in which three former classmates meet at a school reunion and subsequently share their life experiences. Breien developed this into a trilogy with *Wives Ten Years Later* (*Hustruer ti år efter*) in 1985 and *Wives III* in 1996. She also garnered critical success at Cannes with *Next of Kin* (*Arven*; 1979), and won prizes at the Venice film festival with *Witch Hunt* (*Forfølgelsen*; 1982), an exploration of the persecution of women in the Middle ages.

Liv Ullman (b. 1939) is easily the most famous Norwegian actor, but in Scandinavia she has worked mostly with Swedish and Danish producers and directors, most notably Ingmar Bergman (with whom she also had a daughter). In 1995, Ullmann brought the popular Norwegian writer Sigrid Undset's medieval epic *Kristin Lavransdatter* to the screen in a three-hour film that attracted mixed reviews. Another Norwegian writer to have had his work made into films is Knut Hamsun (see p.285 & p.396): in 1966, the Dane Henning Carlson filmed Hamsun's *Hunger* (*Sult*) and in the mid-1990s, the Swedish director Jan Troell filmed the superb biographical *Trial against Hamsun* (*Prosessen mot Hamsun*). In 1993, Oslo's **Erik Gustavson** directed *The Telegraphist* (*Telegrafisten*), based on a Hamsun story and its success landed him the task of bringing Jostein Gaarder's extraordinarily popular novel *Sophie's World* (*Sofies Verden*; 1999) to the screen, though this expensive and well-regarded film has yet to be released in the UK or US.

Nils Gaup is widely regarded as the most talented of Norway's current film directors. His debut film *The Pathfinder* (*Veiviseren*; 1987), an epic adventure based on a medieval Sami (see p.332) legend, was widely acclaimed both in Norway and abroad, not least because the dialogue was in the Sami language. Gaup followed it up with a nautical adventure, *Shipwrecked* (*Håkon Håkonsen*; 1990) and then a thriller *Head Above Water* (*Hodet over vannet;* 1993), which had a pretty woeful Hollywood remake starring Cameron Diaz and Harvey Keitel. Amongst other Norwegian successes in the 1990s, was **Pål Sletaune**'s *Junk Mail* (*Budbringeren*; 1997), a darkly humorous tale of an Oslo postman who opens the mail himself, and **Erik Skjoldbjaerg**'s *Insomnia* (1997), a film noir set in the permanent summer daylight of northern Norway. Stylish and compelling, it impressed Hollywood so much that it was remade in 2002 starring Al Pacino: inevitably, though, the newer version was a big glossy film, which lacked the grittiness of the original.

Much praised, too, are **Berit Nesheim**'s *The Other Side of Sunday* (*Søndagsengler*; 1996), the story of a vicar's daughter desperate to escape from her father's oppressive control, and **Eva Isaksen**'s *Death at Oslo Central* (*Døden på Oslo S*; 1990), a moving story of drug abuse and family conflict amongst the capital's young down-and-outs. Last, but certainly not least, is **Knut Erik Jensen**'s surprise hit, *Cool and Crazy* (*Heftig og Begeistret*; 2001), a gentle, lyrical documentary about the male voice choir of Berlevåg (see p.346), a remote community in the far north of the country. Much to Jensen's surprise, his film was picked up abroad and became a major hit on the art house cinema circuit.

By Emma Rose Rees

Books

Books in English on Norway, and for that matter on Scandinavia as a whole, are surprisingly scant: few travellers have written well (or indeed at all) about the region, and historical works tend to concentrate almost exclusively on the Vikings. That said, Norwegian literature is increasingly appearing in translation – notably the Icelandic sagas and selected modern novelists – and it's always worth looking out for a turn-of-the-century *Baedeker's Norway and Sweden*, if only for the phrasebook, from which you can learn the Norwegian for "Do you want to cheat me?", "When does the washerwoman come?" and "We must tie ourselves together with rope to cross this glacier."

The UK's Norvik Press, University of East Anglia, Norwich NR4 7TJ (☏01603/593 356, ☏01603/250 599; ⊛www.uea.ac.uk/llt/norvik_press) is one of the best publishers for seminal nineteenth-century and contemporary Scandinavian writing. It also has an American partner, Dufour Editions, PO Box 7, Chester Springs, Pennsylvania 19425, USA (☏610/458 5005 or ☏1-800 869 5677; ☏610 458 7103; ⊛www.dufoureditions.com). Several Scandinavian publishing houses also carry a reasonable range of English titles, principally Scandinavian University Press (*Universitetsforlaget*), Sehesteds gate 3, Postboks 508 sentrum, 0150 Oslo (☏24 14 75 00, ⊛www.universitetsforlaget.no).

Most of the books listed below should be readily available, though some are currently out of print (denoted o/p) or likely to be available only in certain countries (in which case we've indicated where the book remains in print). Titles marked with the ✸ symbol are particularly recommended.

Travel and general

Ranulph Fiennes *Ice Fall in Norway.* A jaunt on the Jostedalsbreen glacier with Fiennes and his pals in 1970, long before he got famous. A quick and enjoyable read, though the occasional sexist comment may make you wince.

Thor Heyerdahl *The Kon-Tiki Expedition.* You may want to read this before visiting Oslo's Kon-Tiki Museum (p.93). The intrepid Heyerdahl's accounts of his expeditions aroused huge interest when they were first published, and remain ripping yarns though surprisingly few people read them today. Also worth tracking down are Heyerdahl's *The Ra Expeditions* and *The Tigris Expedition*.

Roland Huntford *The Last Place on Earth.* There are dozens of books on the polar explorers Scott, Amundsen and Nansen, but this is one of the most recent, describing with flair and panache the race to the South Pole between Scott and Amundsen. Also worth a read is the same author's *Nansen: The Explorer as Hero*, a 750-page biography of the noble explorer, academic and statesman Fridtjof Nansen.

Lucy Jago *The Northern Lights: How One Man Sacrificed Love, Happiness and Sanity to Unlock the Secrets of Space.* Intriguing biography of Kristian Birkeland, who spent years ferreting around northern Norway bent on understanding the northern lights. As the title of the book implies, he paid a heavy personal price.

Mark Kurlansky *Cod: A Biography of the Fish that Changed the World*. This wonderful book tracks the life and times of the cod and the generations of fishermen who have lived off it. There are sections on over-fishing and the fish's breeding habits, and recipes are provided too. Norwegians figure frequently – cod was their staple diet for centuries.

Alison Raju *The Pilgrim Road to Nidaros*. The old medieval pilgrims' route from Oslo to Trondheim cathedral has recently been way-marked, and this unusual and exactingly researched book explores its every nook and cranny. Lots of helpful practical information as well as brief descriptions of every significant sight.

Christoph Ransmayr *The Terrors of Ice and Darkness*. Clever mingling of fact and fiction as the book's main character follows the route of the Austro-Hungarian Arctic expedition in 1873. A story of obsession and, ultimately, insanity.

Constance Roos *Walking in Norway*. This well-researched and informative guide outlines hiking routes in almost every part of Norway, with useful sections on conditions in the mountains and equipment. It's easily the best of its type on the market, though the descriptions of some of the hiking routes lack detail.

Elizabeth Su-Dale *Culture Shock, Norway: A Guide to Customs & Etiquette*. Everything you ever want to know about the Norwegians and their way of life. It's extremely useful if you're planning a long stay, though the book is a tad conventional in outlook. First published in 1995, an up-dated version came out in 2002.

Mary Wollstonecraft *Letters written during a Short Residence in Sweden, Norway and Denmark*. For reasons that have never been entirely clear, Wollstonecraft, the author of *A Vindication of the Rights of Women*, and mother of Mary Shelley, travelled Scandinavia for several months in 1795. Her letters home represent a real historical curiosity, though her trenchant comments on Norway often get sidelined by her intense melancholia.

History, sagas and mythology

Jack Adams *The Doomed Expedition*. Thorough and well-researched account of the 1940 Allied campaign in Norway in all its incompetent detail.

Peter Christen Asbjørnsen and Jørgen Moe *Norwegian Folk Tales*. Of all the many books on Norwegian folk tales, this is the one you want – the illustrations by Erik Werenskiold and Theodor Kittelsen are superb. In the Pantheon Fairy Tale and Folklore Library.

Johannes Brøndsted *The Vikings* (o/p). Extremely readable account with fascinating sections on social and cultural life, art, religious beliefs and customs: see p.382 for an extract from this book.

Martin Conway *No Man's Land*. Superb and vastly entertaining account of the history of Spitsbergen (Svalbard) from 1596 to modern times. Full of intriguing detail, such as Admiral Nelson's near-death experience (aged 14), when he set out on the ice at night to kill a polar bear. Published in Oslo by Damms Antikvariat (☎22 44 51 40; ⓦwww.damms.no), but not usually available elsewhere.

Hans Fredrik Dahl *Quisling: A Study in Treachery*. A comprehensive biography of Norway's infamous traitor, Vidkun Quisling – the man presented in all his unpleasant fullness. Published in hardback only – by Cambridge University Press – so it's expensive.

★ **H.R. Ellis Davidson** *The Gods and Myths of Northern Europe*. A handy, first-rate companion to the sagas, this "who's who" of Norse mythology includes some useful reviews of the more obscure gods. Importantly, it also displaces the classical deities and their world as the most relevant mythological framework for northern and western European.

Thomas Kingston Derry *A History of Scandinavia* (o/p). This is the most lucid and scholarly history of Scandinavia, including Iceland and Finland as part of its remit – a thorough account of the region from prehistoric times onwards. It's rather better as a reference source than as a read, however, and having been originally published in 1980, parts are out of date.

Paddy Griffith *The Viking Art of War*. Published in 1998, this detailed text examines its chosen subject well. Excellently researched with considered if sometimes surprising conclusions.

John Haywood *The Penguin Historical Atlas of the Vikings*. Accessible and attractive sequence of maps charting the development and expansion of the Vikings as explorers, settlers, traders and mercenaries. Also the *Encyclopaedia of The Viking Age*, an easy-to-use who's who and what's what of the Viking era.

★ **David Howarth** *Shetland Bus*. Entertaining and fascinating in equal measure, this excellent book, written by one of the British naval officers involved, details the clandestine wartime missions that shuttled between the Shetlands and occupied Norway.

★ **Gwyn Jones** *A History of the Vikings*. Superbly crafted, erudite account of the Vikings with excellent sections on every aspect of their history and culture. The same author wrote *Scandinavian Legends and Folk Tales*, an excellent and enjoyable analysis of its subject.

★ **Magnus Magnusson and Hermann Palsson** (translators) *The Vinland Sagas: The Norse Discovery of America*. These two sagas tell of the Vikings' settlement of Greenland and of the "discovery" of North America in the tenth century. The introduction is a particularly interesting and acute analysis of these two colonial outposts. See also Snorri Sturluson (below).

Alan Palmer *Bernadotte*. Biography of Napoleon's marshal, later King Karl Johan of Norway and Sweden, a fascinating if enigmatic figure whom this lively and comprehensive book presents to good effect.

Else Roesdahl *The Vikings*. A clearly presented, 350-page exploration of Viking history and culture, including sections on art, burial customs, class divisions, jewellery, kingship, kinship and poetry. An excellent introduction to its subject.

Alexander Rumble (et al) *The Reign of Cnut*. Often overlooked, King Cnut (aka Canute) ruled a vast swathe of northern Europe – including England and Norway – at the beginning of the eleventh century.

This academic book has several interesting chapters on aspects of his reign – for example military developments and his influence on the names of people and places in England.

Peter Sawyer *Kings and Vikings: Scandinavia and Europe AD 700–1100.* Traces the origins of Viking activity, assesses its effects on the rest of Europe and on Scandinavia itself, and follows the Vikings' gradual transformation from bands of pagan raiders into Christian farmers and merchants. Concise and to the point.

Peter Sawyer (ed) *The Oxford Illustrated History of the Vikings.* Published in 2001, this book brings together the latest historical research on the Vikings in a series of well-considered essays by leading experts. Includes sections on religion, ship-building and diet.

Kathleen Stokker *Folklore Fights the Nazis: Humor in Occupied Norway 1940–1945.* A book that can't help but make you laugh, and one that also provides a real insight into Norwegian society and its subtle mores. The only problem is that Stokker adopts an encyclopedic approach, which means you have to plough through the poor jokes to get to the good ones. Published by the University of Wisconsin Press, it's rarely available in ordinary bookshops.

Raymond Strait *Queen of Ice, Queen of Shadows: The Unsuspected*

Life of Sonja Henie (UK: o/p; US: Scarborough House). In-depth biography of the ice-skating gold medallist, film star and conspicuous consumer, whose art collection was bequeathed to the Oslo museum that bears her name (see p.94).

Snorri Sturluson *Egil's Saga, Laxdaela Saga, Njal's Saga,* and *King Harald's Saga.* These Icelandic sagas (for more on which, see p.377) were written in the early years of the thirteenth century, but relate tales of ninth- and tenth-century derring-do. There's clan warfare in the Laxdaela and Njal sagas, more bloodthirstiness in Egil's, and a bit more biography in King Harald's, penned to celebrate one of the last and most ferocious Viking chieftains – Harald Hardrada (see p.362). Amongst those who worked on these English translations was the former UK TV celebrity Magnus Magnusson, who has long been a leading light in the effort to popularize the sagas: see also the *Vinland Sagas,* above.

Eilert Sundt *Sexual Customs in Rural Norway: A Nineteenth-Century Study.* First published in 1857, the product of a research trip by a pioneer sociologist, this book doesn't have much sex, but does have lots about rural life – a hard existence if ever there was one. Interesting sections on diet, clothes and associated manners and mores.

Architecture and the visual arts

Marie Bang *Johan Christian Dahl* (Scandinavian University Press, currently o/p). Authoritative and lavishly illustrated book on Norway's leading nineteenth-century landscape painter.

Einar Haugen and Camilla Cai, *Ole Bull: Norway's Romantic Musician and Cosmopolitan Patriot.* A neglected figure, Ole Bull (see p.200), the nineteenth-century virtuoso violinist and utopian socialist, deserves a better historical fate. This biography attempts to rectify matters by delving into every facet of his life, but it's ponderously written and over-detailed. For Bull lovers only. Hardback, published by the University of Wisconsin Press.

★ **J.P. Hodin** *Edvard Munch*. The best available general introduction to Munch's life and work, with much interesting historical detail. Beautifully illustrated, as you would expect from a Thames & Hudson publication.

★ **Neil Kent** *The Triumph of Light and Nature: Nordic Art 1740–1940*. Immaculately illustrated, erudite chronicle of Scandinavian art during its most influential periods.

Highly recommended; another superb book from Thames & Hudson.

Robert Layton *Grieg*. Clear, concise and attractively illustrated book on Norway's greatest composer. Essential reading if you want to get to grips with the man and his times.

Marion Nelson (ed) *Norwegian Folk Art: The Migration of a Tradition* (UK o/p: US Abbeville). Lavishly illustrated book discussing the whole range of folk art, from wood carvings through to bedspreads and traditional dress. It's particularly strong on the influence of Norwegian folk art in the US, but the text sometimes lacks focus.

Literature and literary biography

Kjell Askildsen *A Sudden Liberating Thought*. Short stories, in the Kafkaesque tradition, from one of Norway's most uncompromisingly modernist writers: see p.408 for the title story.

Jens Bjørneboe *The Sharks*. Set at the end of the last century, this is a thrilling tale of shipwreck and mutiny by a well-known Norwegian writer, who had an enviable reputation for challenging authoritarianism of any description. Also recommended is his darker trilogy – *Moment of Freedom*, *The Powderhouse* and *The Silence* – exploring the nature of cruelty and injustice.

Johan Bojer *The Emigrants*. One of the leading Norwegian novelists of his day, Bojer (1872–1959) wrote extensively about the hardships of rural life. *The Emigrants*, perhaps his most finely crafted work, deals with

a group of young Norwegians who emigrate to North Dakota in the 1880s – and the difficulties they experience. In Norway, Bojer is better known for *Last of the Vikings* (o/p), a heart-rending tale of fishermen from the tiny village of Rissa in Nordland, who are forced to row out to the Lofoten winter fishery no matter what the conditions to stop from starving. It was first published in 1921.

Camilla Collett *The District Governor's Daughters*. Published in 1854, this heartfelt demand for the emotional and intellectual emancipation of women is set within a bourgeois Norwegian milieu. The central character, Sophie, struggles against her conditioning and the expectations of those around her. An important early feminist novel published by the enterprising Norvik Press (see p.391).

Per Olov Enquist *The visit of the Royal Physician*. Wonderfully entertaining, and beautifully written novel, set in the Danish court in Copenhagen when Denmark governed Norway.

Knut Faldbakken *Adam's Diary*. Three former lovers describe their relationships with the same woman – an absorbing and spirited novel by one of Norway's better writers; o/p in US.

Robert Ferguson *Enigma: the Life of Knut Hamsun* (o/p). Detailed and well-considered biography of Norway's most controversial writer. The same author also wrote *Ibsen*, an in-depth biography of the playwright (also o/p).

★ **Jostein Gaarder** *Sophie's World*. Hugely popular novel that deserves all the critical praise it has received. Beautifully and gently written, with puffs of whimsy all the way through, it bears comparison with Hawking's *A Brief History of Time*, though the subject matter here is philosophy, and there's an engaging mystery story tucked in too. Also try Gaarder's *Through A Glass Darkly*.

Janet Garton (ed) & Henning Sehmsdorf (trans) *New Norwegian Plays*. Four plays written between 1979 and 1983, including work by the feminist writer Bjørg Vik and a Brechtian analysis of Europe in the nuclear age by Edvard Hoem. Currently o/p, but contact Norvik Press or Dufour direct (see p.391) and they should be able to rustle up a copy.

Knut Hamsun *Hunger*. Norway's leading literary light in the 1920s and early 1930s, Knut Hamsun (1859–1952) was a writer of international acclaim until he disgraced himself by supporting Hitler – for which many Norwegians never forgave him. Of Hamsun's many novels, it was *Hunger* (1890) that made his

name, a trip into the psyche of an alienated and angst-ridden young writer, which shocked contemporary readers. The book was to have a seminal influence on the development of the modern novel. In the latter part of his career, Hamsun advocated a return to the soil and basic rural values. He won the Nobel Prize for Literature for one of his works from this period, *Growth of the Soil*, but you have to be pretty determined to plough through its metaphysical claptrap. In recent years, Hamsun has been tentatively accepted back into the Norwegian literary fold and there has been some resurgence of interest in his works; there's also been a biographical film, *Hamsun*, starring Max von Sydow.

William Heinesen *The Black Cauldron*. It would be churlish to omit the Faroe islander William Heinesen, whose evocative novels delve into the subtleties of Faroese life – and thereby shed light on the related culture of western Norway. This particular book, arguably his best, is rigorously modernistic in approach and style – an intriguing, challenging read, with the circling forces of Faroese society set against the British occupation of the Faroes in World War II.

Sigbjørn Holmebakk *The Carriage Stone*. (UK o/p: US Dufour). Evil and innocence, suffering and redemption, with death lurking in the background, make this a serious and powerful novel. These themes are explored through the character of Eilif Grotteland, a Lutheran priest who loses his faith and resigns his ministry.

Henrik Ibsen *Four Major Plays*. The key international figure of Norwegian literature, Ibsen (see p.133) was a social dramatist with a keen eye for hypocrisy, repression and alienation. His most popular plays, primarily *A*

Doll's House and *Hedda Gabler*, pop up in all sorts of editions, but other works can be harder to get hold of. This particular collection, in the Oxford World Classics series, contains both these favourites as well as *Ghosts* and *The Master Builder*. What's more, it's inexpensive and translated by one of the leading Ibsen experts James McFarlane.

Björn Larsson *Long John Silver*. Larsson, a veteran Swedish sailor with an extensive knowledge of eighteenth-century British sea lore, uses his specialist knowledge to great effect in this chunky but charming novel that provides an extra twist – or two – to Stevenson's original.

Jonas Lie *The Seer & Other Norwegian Stories* (UK o/p: US Dufour). Part of the Norwegian literary and cultural revival of the late nineteenth-century, Jonas Lie is largely forgotten today, but this collection of mystical folk tales makes for intriguing reading. It is printed alongside his first great success, the novella *The Seer*, in which a teacher is saved from insanity, born of ancient (pagan) superstitions, by the power of Christianity. Also *Weird Tales from Northern Seas: Norwegian Legends* (UK o/p: US Penfield), a collection much enjoyed by no less than Roald Dahl.

Sigbjørn Obstfelder *A Priest's Diary*. The last, uncompleted work of a highly regarded Norwegian poet who died of consumption in 1900, aged 33. A moody, intense piece of prose-poetry, it is just a segment of an ambitious project that Obstfelder intended to be his life's major undertaking.

Cora Sandel *Alberta and Freedom, Alberta Alone, & Alberta and Jacob*. Set in a small town in early twentieth-century Norway, the *Alberta* trilogy follows the attempts of a young woman to establish an independent life/identity. Characterized by sharp insights and a wealth of contemporary detail.

Amalie Skram *Under Observation* and *Lucie*. Bergen's Amalie Skram (1846–1905) married young and went through the marital mangle before turning her experiences into several novels and a commitment to women's emancipation. For the period, the novels are extraordinarily progressive, and are an enjoyable read too: see p.398 for an extract of *Lucie*.

Sigrid Undset *Kristin Lavransdatter: The Cross, The Bridal Wreath, The Garland & The Mistress of Husaby*. The prolific Undset, one of the country's leading literary lights, can certainly churn it out. This historical series – arguably encapsulating her best work – is set in medieval Norway and has all the excitement of a pulp thriller, along with subtle plots and deft characterizations. Undset's best selling books at present – *The Axe* and *The Son Avenger* – are in the Master of Hestviken series, more tales of medieval derring-do.

Herbjørg Wassmo *Dina's Book: A Novel*. Set in rural northern Norway in the middle of the nineteenth century, this strange but engaging tale has a plot centred on a powerful but tormented heroine: see p.404 for an extract. Also *Dina's Son*, again with a nineteenth-century setting, but with intriguing sections focused on the protagonist's move from rural Norway to the city.

Literature

I t was **Jostein Gaarder**'s *Sophie's World* that brought Norwegian literature to a worldwide audience in the 1990s, though in fact the Norwegians have been mining a deep, if somewhat idiosyncratic, literary seam since the middle of the nineteenth century. From Ibsen onwards, the country's authors and playwrights have been deeply influenced by Norway's unyielding geography and stern pietism, their preoccupations often focused on anxiety and alienation. **Amalie Skram**, a contemporary of Ibsen, is largely forgotten today, but her *Lucie* is a sharply observed novel and a pioneering feminist work to boot. *Lucie* provides the first of the three extracts we have included; the others are by **Herbjørg Wassmo** and **Kjell Askildsen**, two of Norway's finest contemporary writers.

Amalie Skram

Born in Bergen in 1846, **Amalie Skram** was the daughter of a shopkeeper, who went bankrupt when she was seventeen – a riches to rags story reminiscent of Ibsen's early life (see p.133). She married out of poverty, but the marriage – to a sea captain – went wrong and her husband's refusal to grant a divorce brought on a nervous breakdown in 1877. Recovered, Amalie moved to Christiania (Oslo) in 1881 and here she became involved in both the political movement for an independent Norway and a number of progressive social issues, primarily attempts to regulate prostitution. Amalie also became a familiar figure on the Oslo literary scene and was well known for her controversial or, rather, progressive views. Published in 1888, *Lucie* was a coruscating attack on bourgeois morality in general, and male sexual hypocrisy in particular, with the eponymous heroine gradually ground down into submission. Inevitably, the novel created a huge furore. The extract below describes one key episode in the increasingly oppressive relationship between Lucie and her husband, Gerner.

Lucie

At the Mørks'

Dinner was over, and the women were seated around a table in the sitting room drinking coffee.

Mrs Mørk was talking about the difficulties she was having with her maids. The nursery maid had got up in the middle of the night to go to a dance, and the baby had screamed until he was blue in the face before they heard it in their bedroom.

'Oh these maids, these maids! And of course they break everything. If your purse was as deep as the ocean it still wouldn't be enough.' Mrs Lunde was speaking. The wife of a sea captain, she had eight children and struggled mightily to get along on her monthly allowance.

And then they launched into stories about their housemaids' wastefulness and profligacy. When one flagged, the other started in.

Lucie listened with a stiff smile. None of the women turned to address her, but almost unconsciously left her out of the conversation. To remedy this painful situation, she feigned interest, shook her head frequently, and said at the right times, 'No, you don't say. How dreadful!'

The men strolled in from the smoking room; with glowing faces and smiling eyes, they seated themselves among the women.

A young fellow with red hands and flaxen hair combed into a stiff point over his forehead struck up a conversation with Lucie.

'Has madam gone to many balls this winter?' he asked.

'No, I'm afraid not. My husband doesn't care to dance, unfortunately.' Lucie smiled invitingly.

'Is that right?' the gentleman said, exposing all of his large, ugly teeth. 'He really should be obliged to, when he has such a young wife, don't you think? I suppose you weren't at the carnival either?'

'An outstanding likeness of Mrs. Mørk, don't you think?' Gerner [her husband] came over to Lucie and handed her a photograph, while turning his back on the man with the teeth.

A slight shock went through Lucie. She had not seen Gerner come in with the others and thought he was still in the smoking room.

'Yes, it's a good likeness,' she said, eagerly looking at the photograph.

Gerner pulled a chair over to the table and sat down.

'Don't you think so, too?' In her confusion, Lucie reached behind her husband and handed the photograph to the gentleman, who stood there smiling like an idiot.

'Can't you leave that dolt alone?' Gerner whispered. 'Next you'll be asking him how many balls *he's* been to.'

'What do you say, Mrs. Gerner,' said Mrs. Mørk. 'Do you want to play cards or sit and talk?'

'My wife likes to play whist,' Gerner hurriedly replied.

'Have I done something wrong again?' Lucie muttered, looking anxiously at Theodor. 'He's Mrs. Mørk's brother, you know.'

'That shopkeeper,' Gerner answered savagely. 'Mrs. Mørk's brother, is *that* what you consider refined company? Yes, I'm coming now.' Mørk had called out that the table for ombre was ready in the smoking room.

'They're dancing at Mrs. Reinertson's,' Lucie said as she shuffled the cards, glancing up at the ceiling, which was actually shaking.

'Now, *there's* a widow who loves to entertain,' said Mrs. Mørk. 'It hasn't been a week since we were at a big party up there.'

'But we didn't dance then,' Lucie said with a sigh.

'No, but only the young people were invited tonight. There are loads of cousins in the family.'

'It seems a bit unusual for a widow to do that kind of thing,' opined Mrs. Lunde.

'Her brother, the pastor in Arendal, is very worldly too,' lisped a pregnant little assistant pastor's wife with heavy blue rings under her eyes. 'He's always scandalising the congregation, Jensen says.'

'And she defends *Albertine* [a controversial novel of the period],' Mrs Lund went on. 'Well as I always say, if you don't have any children….I'm so pleased with my eight. I'd rather have 16 than none. Your lead, Mrs. Gerner.'

There was much more talking and gossiping than playing. Lucie tried to get into the conversation a couple of times, but wasn't successful. Feeling uncomfortable and out of place, she pretended to be intent on the cards. When it was finally time to eat supper she breathed a sigh of relief.

'I think that was the doorbell,' Mørk said. They had finished supper and were just getting up from the table.

'It must have been the street door,' his wife answered. 'But what in the world is that?'

They all paused, hands on their chairs, as they were moving them back from the table. Drifting in from the next room came an intermittent muffled clamour and the tones of a violin playing a march. Mrs. Mørk went over and opened the door. The others turned around quickly with a buzz of astonishment.

The sitting room was jammed with people wearing carnival costumes and masks on their faces. It was a gaudy mixture of knights and their ladies, peasants and Italian fishermen, gypsies and dancing girls. In front of them stood a fiddler dressed as a peasant and Mrs. Reinertson in a pale grey silk dress, a gold comb in her shiny brown hair.

'Well, what do you think?' Mrs. Reinertson said laughingly to Mrs. Mørk, who had stopped in the doorway. She clapped her hands. 'My guests couldn't be restrained, they're simply wild tonight. First they scared the life out of me by coming in carnival costumes, and then they absolutely insisted on coming down here. You mustn't take offence.'

'How could you think that – what a fun idea they had. Come in, do come in.'

'Oh now you're shy,' Mrs. Reinertson laughed at her guests, who were clustered together with their arms linked, giggling in embarrassment and whispering behind their masks. 'What did I say?'

'How marvellous of you to come and liven us up.' With a bray of laughter Mørk walked around shaking hands with the masked guests, who bowed and curtsied and made somewhat fruitless attempts to be amusing.

'Now make yourselves at home and *act* your parts to your heart's content. By heaven, we'll have champagne! Here Lina.' He handed a ring of keys through the dining room door.

'Now really Aksel,' said his wife angrily, snatching the keys away from him. 'The maids in the wine cellar….'

'Look, Mrs. Lund!' Lucie was so excited that she impulsively took Mrs. Lund's arm and pointed at a harlequin who was walking on his hands among the armchairs. 'Oh Lord. Oh Lord, the lamp!' she cried, clinging tightly to her arm. The harlequin's feet were close to a porcelain lamp on a little marble table.

With a strained expression, Mrs. Lund moved away from Lucie. 'A bit common, don't you think,' she said to the assistant pastor's wife, taking her by the arm.

Champagne corks were going off explosively in the dining room and Mørk poured. 'If you please, ladies and gentlemen!' he called. 'People who want champagne must come in here!'

'But first take off your masks!' said Mrs. Reinertson with a clap of her hands, after which they all took off their masks and let them dangle from their arms. Then they began to laugh and talk, recognise and introduce themselves, as they all crowded around the table in the dining room to drink champagne.

There were speeches and toasts, and gradually the somewhat forced animation that had covered embarrassment gave way to a rush of good cheer.

Lucie was looking through narrowed eyes at a good-looking young man, tall and broad-shouldered, with a black moustache, red lips, and gleaming healthy teeth. He was wearing sandals on his feet and a monk's cowl over his lieutenant's uniform.

'Your health, madam,' he said clinking his glass against Lucie's. 'Long live celibacy!'

'Long live what?' Lucie asked, laughing heartily. 'I don't know what you mean.'

'You are adorable, madam!' The lieutenant threw back his head and gazed at her rapturously with brown, laughing eyes. 'Should I explain it to you? Oh no, I would rather explain what celibacy is *not*. We'll take our glasses with us.' He offered her his arm.

'Don't be such a flirt, Knut,' Mrs. Reinertson whispered in his ear, as he and Lucie walked by. 'Her husband is so jealous.'

'Then we'd better cure him,' Knut replied. 'She's so sweet and amusing, Aunt.'

'Let's sit over here.' The lieutenant led Lucie to a little sofa in a corner of the sitting room beneath a tall arrangement of leafy plants, and sat down beside her. He began to chat with her in a soft, confiding tone.

Gerner observed them from the dining room, where he was talking to a knight's lady dressed in black velvet with a tall mother of pearl comb in her hair. He watched Lucie laugh and drink champagne. Occasionally she would lean back and lift her feet off the floor. Once she turned away, as if her admirer had been too forward, and the lieutenant gave her a surprised look and became earnest and intense. Gerner's half-shut eyes were narrowed more than usual and his nostrils twitched nervously.

'What are you staring at?' the knight's lady asked, turning around.

'That monk over there is amusing.' – Gerner forced his mouth into a smile. – 'That fop of a lieutenant in the monk's cowl.'

'Oh Knut Reinertson. Knut Lionheart.'

'Oh yes? Why do they call him that,' Gerner interrupted.

'I don't know really, but I suppose it's because he's a heartbreaker. – Who is the lady he's talking to?'

'It's my wife,' answered Gerner, looking at the knight's lady with his eyes wide open.

'Oh I see – well I'm sure we were introduced but I didn't hear the name. She is really very charming. – If only he doesn't hypnotise her.'

'Hypnotise?'

'Yes, didn't you hear about that? It's quite dreadful the things he gets people to do and say. At a party the other night – papa wouldn't give me permission to try it. – What! Go up to Mrs. Reinertson's and dance? – Oh yes, let's do that!' She clapped her hands.

'What do our guests say?' cried Mrs. Mørk looking over at her husband.

'Let's go up, go up,' they all answered.

'Let me lead the way,' Mrs. Reinertson said, taking the fiddler by the arm.

'That's what I call hospitable,' Mørk exclaimed, offering Mrs. Lund his arm.

Gerner wanted to reach Lucie to tell her they should go home, but he couldn't get past all the people and furniture. He stretched sideways over the others' shoulders in order to catch her glance, but she pretended not to notice.

'Devil take it,' Gerner mumbled, when he saw her follow the others out of the door, flushed and laughing on the lieutenant's arm.

'Tonight I intend to enjoy myself,' Lucie said to her escort, lifting her knees in a little dance. 'It's certainly been a long time. – Imagine, I haven't gone dancing one single time since I got married.'

I don't care if he kills me, I'm having a good time tonight, she thought. There'll be a scene anyway, might as well get some fun out of it.

'Do you not have a partner, Gerner?' asked Mrs. Mørk. 'Then you'll have to be content with me.'

He bowed silently and they left the room.

From the entryway he saw Lucie and the lieutenant turning into the bend of the staircase that led to Mrs. Reinertson's apartment. They were close together. His head was bent toward Lucie's and she was looking up at his face as he spoke.

Mrs. Mørk chattered on and on, but Gerner heard nothing; he just stared up the stairs with a white face and clenched lips.

'I wish I had a sixth sense,' said the lieutenant.

'Oh, and why is that?' Lucie asked.

'So I could look into your soul and read my fate.' His face was mirthful but his voice was solemn.

'Oh you,' Lucie laughed, poking him in the side with her elbow.

'Every young woman's heart is an unresolved riddle, a boundless deep – an ocean of – in a word – riches and possibilities – oh, a bottomless...' he paused for a moment. 'It's a sin to keep such a treasure locked away.'

Lord, he's sweet, and it's so poetic, the way he talks, Lucie thought, her face alight with rapture. And he's such a gentleman.

'Oh I think you'd soon have your fill of that treasure, I do, Lieutenant Reinertson.' Her voice was trembling with delight and agitation.

'Try me, madam,' he begged earnestly. 'Tell me what you are thinking, feeling, what delights you, makes you suffer' – he softly squeezed her arm – 'especially suffer, for is there any human being who doesn't suffer?' – They had now come upstairs into rooms lit by candelabras and lamps, where the musician struck up a waltz.

And then the dancing couples whirled down the large, rectangular dining room.

Reinertson clasped Lucie firmly to his chest and danced off. She closed her eyes and leaned back against his arm. Never before had dancing felt so delicious. She felt like she was flying through the air and that her body was almost dissolving in a wonderful, tingling sensation. The furniture, the people, and everything else drifted away. She was conscious only of him and herself, and, from far away, the sound of the music. If only it never, never had to end.

'I'd surrender my soul to the pains of Hell for the key to her rooms,' the lieutenant whispered after the dance, when they were sitting in an alcove off the dining room.

Blood pounded in Lucie's ears. She leaned back, fanning herself with her handkerchief. A soft smile trembled at the corners of her mouth, and her breast rose and fell. 'Oh, if only I had met you before, Reinertson,' she whispered back, and squeezed his hand.

This is getting amusing. She thinks I'm in love with her, thought the lieutenant.

'We can still get to know each other, of course,' he said softly, squeezing her hand in return. Rubbish, I can't be bothered with this, he thought a second later, just as Lucie was about to answer. He released her hand and said. 'Come, let's dance the gallop together.'

They stood up and Lucie took his arm.

In the doorway, they met Gerner.

'Well here you are, finally,' he said. 'It's time to go home.'

Lucie could tell from his voice how much it was costing him to control himself. But she didn't feel the slightest trace of fear, only a boundless joy that she was going to dance with *him* again.

'Just a couple of times around, counsellor,' said Reinertson, 'then I'll return her to you.'

He danced off with her. Gerner watched them.

'Now I'll take my leave and surrender your wife to the hands of her natural guardian, as they say.' The lieutenant had brought Lucie back to Gerner. 'Goodnight, madam. Thank you for this evening. Goodnight, counsellor.' He bowed and left.

Lucie's eyes followed him through the room with a longing expression. She seemed to have completely forgotten that Gerner was standing beside her.

'Do you hear, we're leaving.' He grabbed her firmly by the wrist and walked her towards the door.

'I should say goodbye first, don't you think?' Lucie tried to free her hand.

He tightened his grip and actually pulled her past the dancing couples. 'You're coming now!'

'Leave without thanking them?' Lucie said sharply, out in the front hall.

'Don't try to prolong the scandal.' Gerner opened the door and pushed Lucie out through it. He could barely get his words out and his hands were shaking.

I don't care if he's in a good mood or a rotten mood, Lucie thought, as they were walking down the stairs. As long as I can see that darling Reinertson again soon.

But when they were putting on their coats in the Mørks' well-lit front hall, the sight of Theodor's pallid cheeks and clenched lips sent a chill through Lucie.

Striding down the street. Theodor took such long steps that Lucie had to trot to keep up with him. Finally she slowed and trailed along behind.

'Is is your intention to play the part of a streetwalker tonight?' Gerner had stopped by the university to wait for Lucie.

'How can anybody keep up when you run like that,' Lucie answered angrily and walked past him.

'You are to conduct yourself properly.' In a couple of steps Gerner was beside her. 'Reminding everybody of what a trollop I married.' His voice was distorted with rage.

'You're really so crude,' Lucie said indifferently, walking hurriedly, almost running.

'If a man so much as looks at you, your whole body starts to tremble,' Gerner went on, getting more and more agitated. 'You make me look ridiculous.'

'Well, that's not difficult, is it,' she said with a scornful breath.

Gerner could have hit her.

'You be careful,' he snarled. 'You're a tart, and you'll never get that out of your blood.'

'A tart! I really have to laugh. You should hear what Mrs. Reinertson has to say. I suppose you were lily-white when you married me.'

'Now you start with impertinences – you've wisely refrained from that until now.'

'But I won't stand for you treating me this way any more.' She spoke breathlessly because of their quick pace on the slippery snow. 'I won't stand for it any longer, just so you know. I suppose you think being married to you is so glorious!'

'Be quiet!' He grabbed her shoulders and shook her so violently that her little fur hat flew off her head. They had turned onto Drammensveien, and he gave her a shove that propelled her a few steps along the street.

Without uttering a sound, Lucie bent over to retrieve her hat, then took off down Drammensveien with her hat in her hand, as if she were running for her life.

Herbjørg Wassmo

Two volumes of poetry marked **Herbjørg Wassmo**'s writing debut in 1976, at the age of 34. Shortly afterwards she switched to prose, subsequently writing two series of popular novels about contrasting women. **Dina**, the female protagonist of *Dina's bok* (Dina's Book, 1989) and *Lykkens sønn* (The Son of Fortune, 1992), is wilful to the point of ruthlessness: she eliminates her husband and takes a new lover, while the funeral is in progress elsewhere. Yet beneath her toughness is a deep sense of betrayal: rejected as a child by her father after she accidentally caused her mother's death, Dina has grown up expecting betrayal. Set in the mid-nineteenth century, the Dina stories have as their backdrop a rural community in Wassmo's native northern Norway. The extract below comes from the beginning of *Dina's Book*.

Dina's Book

The eyes of the Lord preserve knowledge, and he overthroweth the words of the transgressor.

Proverbs 22:12

Dina had to take her husband, Jacob, who had gangrene in one foot, to the doctor on the other side of the mountain. November. She was the only one who could handle the wild yearling, which was the fastest horse. And they needed to drive fast. On a rough, icy road.

Jacob's foot already stank. The smell had filled the house for a long time. The cook smelled it even in the pantry. An uneasy atmosphere pervaded every room. A feeling of anxiety.

No one at Reinsnes said anything about the smell of Jacob's foot before he left. Nor did they mention it after Blackie returned to the estate with empty shafts.

But aside from that, people talked. With disbelief and horror. On the neighbouring farms. In the parlours at Strandsted and along the sound. At the pastor's home. Quietly and confidentially.

About Dina, the young wife at Reinsnes, the only daughter of Sheriff Holm. She was like a horse-crazy boy. Even after she got married. Now she had suffered such a sad fate.

They told the story again and again. She had driven so fast that the snow crackled and spurted under the runners. Like a witch. Nevertheless, Jacob Gronelv did not get to the doctor's. Now he no longer existed. Friendly, generous Jacob, who never refused a request for help. Mother Karen's son, who came to Reinsnes when he was quite young.

Dead! No one could understand how such a terrible thing could have happened. That boats capsized, or people disappeared at sea, had to be accepted. But this was the devil's work. First getting gangrene in a fractured leg. Then dying on a sleigh that plunged into the rapids!

Dina had lost the power of speech, and old Mother Karen wept. Jacob's son from his first marriage wandered, fatherless, around Copenhagen, and Blackie could not stand the sight of sleighs.

The authorities came to the estate to conduct an inquiry into the events that had occurred up to the moment of death. Everything must be stated specifically and nothing hidden, they said.

Dina's father, the sheriff, brought two witnesses and a book for recording the proceedings. He said emphatically that he was there as one of the authorities, not as a father.

Mother Karen found it difficult to see a difference. But she did not say so.

No one brought Dina down from the second floor. Since she was so big and strong, they took no chance that she might resist and make a painful scene. They did not try to force her to come downstairs. Instead it was decided the authorities would go up to her large bedroom.

Extra chairs had been placed in the room. And the curtains on the canopy bed were thoroughly dusted. Heavy gold fabric patterned with rows of rich red flowers. Bought in Hamburg. Sewn for Dina and Jacob's wedding.

Oline and Mother Karen had tried to take the young wife in hand so she would not look completely unpresentable. Oline gave her herb tea with thick cream and plenty of sugar. It was her cure for all ills, from the scurvy to childlessness. Mother Karen assisted with praise, hair brushing, and cautious concern.

The servant girls did as they were told, while looking around with frightened glances.

The words stuck. Dina opened her mouth and formed them. But their sound was in another world. The authorities tried many different approaches.

The sheriff tried using a deep, dispassionate voice, peering into Dina's light-grey eyes. He could just as well have looked through a glass of water.

The witnesses also tried. Seated and standing. With both compassionate and commanding voices.

Finally, Dina laid her head of black, unruly hair on her arms. And she let out sounds that could have come from a half-strangled dog.

Feeling ashamed, the authorities withdrew to the downstairs rooms. In order to reach agreement about what had happened. How things had looked at the place in question. How the young woman had acted.

They decided that the whole matter was a tragedy for the community and the entire district. That Dina Grønelv was beside herself with grief. That she was not culpable and had lost her speech from the shock.

They decided that she had been racing to take her husband to the doctor. That she had taken the curve near the bridge too fast, or that the wild horse had bolted at the edge of the cliff and the shaft fastenings had pulled loose. Both of them.

This was neatly recorded in the official documents.

They did not find the body, at first. People said it had washed out to sea. But did not understand how. For the sea was nearly seven miles away through a rough, shallow riverbed. The rocks there would stop a dead body, which could do nothing itself to reach the sea.

To Mother Karen's despair, they gradually gave up the search.

A month later, an old pauper came to the estate and insisted that the body lay in Veslekulpen, a small backwater some distance below the rapids. Jacob lay crooked around a rock. Stiff as a rod. Battered and bloated, the old fellow said.

He proved to be right.

The water level had evidently subsided when the autumn rains ended. And one clear day in early December, the unfortunate body of Jacob Grønelv appeared. Right before the eyes of the old pauper, who was on his way across the mountain.

Afterward, people said the pauper was clairvoyant. And, in fact, always had been. This is why he had a quiet old age. Nobody wanted to quarrel with a clairvoyant. Even if he was a pauper.

Dina sat in her bedroom, the largest room on the second floor. With the curtains drawn. At first she did not even go to the stable to see her horse.

They left her in peace.

Mother Karen stopped crying, simply because she no longer had time for that. She had assumed the duties that the master and his wife had neglected. Both were dead, each in his or her own way.

Dina sat at the walnut table, staring. No one knew what else she did. Because she confided in no one. The sheets of music that had been piled around the bed were now stuffed away in the clothes closet. Her long dresses swept over them in the draught when she opened the door.

The shadows were deep in the bedroom. A cello stood in one corner, gathering dust. It had remained untouched since the day Jacob was carried from the house and laid on the sleigh.

The solid canopy bed with sumptuous bed curtains occupied much of the room. It was so high that one could lie on the pillows and look out through the windows at the sound. Or one could look at oneself in the large mirror with a black lacquered frame that could be tilted to different angles.

The big round stove roared all day. Behind a triple-panelled folding screen with an embroidered motif of beautiful Leda and the swan in an erotic embrace. Wings and arms. And Leda's long, blond hair spread virtuously over her lap.

A servant girl, Thea, brought wood four times a day. Even so, the supply barely lasted through the night.

No one knew when Dina slept, or if she slept. She paced back and forth in heavy shoes with metal-tipped heels, day and night. From wall to wall. Keeping the whole house awake.

Thea could report that the large family Bible, which Dina had inherited from her mother, always lay open.

Now and then the young wife laughed softly. It was an unpleasant sound. Thea did not know whether her mistress was laughing about the holy text or if she was thinking about something else.

Sometimes she angrily slammed together the thin-as-silk pages and threw the book away like the entrails from a dead fish.

Jacob was not buried until seven days after he was found. In the middle of December. There were so many arrangements to be made. So many people had to be notified. Relatives, friends, and prominent people had to be invited to the funeral. The weather stayed cold, so the battered and swollen corpse could easily remain in the barn during that time. Digging the grave, however, required the use of sledge-hammers and pickaxes.

The moon peered through the barn's tiny windows and observed Jacob's fate with its golden eye. Made no distinction between living and dead. Decorated the barn floor in silver and white. And nearby lay the hay, offering warmth and nourishment, smelling fragrantly of summer and splendour.

One morning before dawn, they dressed for the funeral. The boats were ready. Silence lay over the house like a strange piety. The moon was shining. No one waited for daylight at that time of year.

Dina leaned against the windowsill, as if steeling herself, when they entered her room to help her dress in the black clothes that had been sewn for the funeral. She had refused to try them on.

She seemed to be standing there sensing each muscle and each thought. The sombre, teary-eyed women did not see a single movement in her body.

Still, they did not give up at once. She had to change her clothes. She had to be part of the funeral procession. Anything else was unthinkable. But finally, they did think that thought. For with her guttural, animal-like sounds, she convinced everyone that she was not ready to be the widow at a funeral. At least not this particular day.

Terrified, the women fled the room. One after another. Mother Karen was the last to leave. She gave excuses and soothing explanations. To the aunts, the wives, the other women, and, not least of all, to Dina's father, the sheriff.

He was the hardest to convince. Bellowing loudly, he burst into Dina's room without knocking. Shook her and commanded her, slapped her cheeks with fatherly firmness while his words swarmed around her like angry bees.

Mother Karen had to intervene. The few who stood by kept their eyes lowered.

Then Dina let out the bestial sounds again. While she flailed her arms and tore her hair. The room was charged with something they did not understand. There was an aura of madness and power surrounding the young, half-dressed woman with dishevelled hair and crazed eyes.

Her screams reminded the sheriff of an event he carried with him always. Day and night. In his dreams and in his daily tasks. An event that still, after thirteen years, could make him wander restlessly around the estate. Looking for someone, or something, that could unburden him of his thoughts and feelings.

The people in the room thought Dina Grønelv had a harsh father. But on the other hand, it was not right that such a young woman refused to do what was expected of her.

She tired them out. People decided she was too sick to attend her husband's funeral. Mother Karen explained, loudly and clearly, to everyone she met:

'Dina is so distraught and ill she can't stand on her feet. She does nothing but weep. And the terrible thing is, she's not able to speak.'

First came the muffled shouts from the people who were going in the boats. Then came the scraping of wood against iron as the coffin was loaded onto the longboat with its juniper decorations and its weeping, black-clad women. Then the sounds and voices stiffened over the water like a thin crusting of beach ice. And disappeared between the sea and the mountains. Afterward, silence settled over the estate as though this were the true funeral procession. The house held its breath. Merely let out a small sigh among the rafters now and then. A sad, pitiful final honour to Jacob.

The pink waxed-paper carnations fluttered amid the pine and juniper boughs across the sound in a light breeze. There was no point in travelling quickly with such a burden. Death and its detached supporting cast took their time. It was not Blackie who pulled them. And it was not Dina who set the pace. The coffin was heavy. Those who bore it felt the weight. This was the only way to the church with such a burden.

Now five pairs of oars creaked in the oarlocks. The sail flapped idly against the mast, refusing to unfurl. There was no sun. Grey clouds drifted across the sky. The raw air gradually became still.

The boats followed one another. A triumphal procession for Jacob Grønelv. Masts and oars pointed toward ocean and heaven. The ribbons on the wreaths fluttered restlessly. They had only a short time to be seen.

Mother Karen was a yellowed rag. Edged with lace, it is true.

The servant girls were wet balls of wool in the wind.

The men rowed, sweating behind their beards and moustaches. Rowing in rhythm.

At Reinsnes everything was prepared. The sandwiches were arranged on large platters. On the cellar floor and on shelves in the large entry were pewter plates filled with cakes and covered by cloths.

Under Oline's exacting supervision, the glasses had been rubbed to a glistening shine. Now the cups and glasses were arranged neatly in rows on the tables and in the pantry, protected by white linen towels bearing the monograms of Ingeborg Grønelv and Dina Grønelv. They had to use the linen belonging to both of Jacob's wives today.

Many guests were expected after the burial.

Dina stoked the fire like a madwoman, although there was not even frost on the windows. Her face, which had been grey that morning, began slowly to regain its colour.

She paced restlessly back and forth across the floor with a little smile on her lips. When the clock struck, she raised her head like an animal listening for enemies.

Translated by Nadia Christensen; reprinted by permission of Norvik Press.

Kjell Askildsen

Born in Mandal in southern Norway in 1929, **Kjell Askildsen** came to literary prominence in the 1950s with his Kafkaesque accounts of alienated individuals. Subsequent stories adopted a more political tone and although his output has been far from prolific he is widely regarded as one of Scandinavia's finest writers. In recent years, Askildsen has chosen to express himself through the **monologues** of old men, whose ordinary, everyday struggles hold loneliness and despair at bay, though these are themselves just manifestations of the abyss – the metaphysical nothingness of existence. These are not, however, dreary, self-indulgent monologues, for each is underpinned by a steel-like spirit of endurance and illuminated with sharp flashes of dry humour. Nor are they devoid of human values, such as the desire for justice, human dignity, and common decency, upheld in spite of the cool knowledge of life's futility and the quirky frailty of old age. *A Sudden Liberating Thought* was published in 1987.

A Sudden Liberating Thought

I live in a basement; it's due to the fact that my life has been going downhill, in every sense of the word.

My room has only one window, and only its upper portion is above the sidewalk; this causes me to see the outside world from below. It's not a very big world, but it often feels big enough.

I can only see the legs and the lower part of the body of those who walk by on the sidewalk on my side of the street, but after living here for four years I mostly know to whom they belong. This is because there's little traffic; I live far up a dead end street.

I am a taciturn person, but sometimes I talk to myself. The things I say then have to be said, it seems to me.

One day, having just seen the lower part of the landlord's wife pass by as I stood by the window, I felt suddenly so lonely that I decided to go out.

I put on my shoes and coat and stuck my reading glasses in my coat pocket, just in case. Then I left. The advantage of living in a basement is that you walk up when you are rested and down when you come home tired. That's the only advantage, I guess.

It was a warm summer day. I went to the park beside the abandoned fire-house, where I can usually sit undisturbed. But I had scarcely sat down when some old fellow my own age came along and sat down beside me, though there were plenty of vacant benches. I had gone out because I felt lonely, to be sure, but not to talk; just for a change. I was becoming more and more nervous that he would say something, and I even thought of getting up and leaving, but where was I to go, this being the place I'd set my mind on. But he remained silent, and that struck me as being so sympathetic that I felt quite well-disposed toward him. I even tried to look at him, without attracting his attention, of course. But he noticed it, because he said, 'You will excuse me for saying so, but I sat down here because I thought I wouldn't be disturbed. I can move if you wish, no trouble.'

'Sit,' I said, somewhat bewildered. Naturally, I didn't make any further attempt to observe him, he had my deepest respect. Naturally too, even more so, I did not speak to him. I felt something strange inside me, something not-lonely, simply a kind of well-being.

He sat there for about half an hour; then he got up, with a bit of difficulty, turned to me and said, 'Thanks. Goodbye.'

'Goodbye.'

He left, taking remarkably long steps and flailing his arms, as though sleep-walking.

The following day at the same time, or a little earlier, I went again to the park. After all the thoughts and speculations he had evoked in me, it seemed some-how the natural thing to do; it was hardly a free choice, whatever that may be.

He came. I saw him from afar and recognized him by his gait. That day too there were vacant benches, and I was curious to know whether he would choose to sit with me. I looked in another direction naturally, pretending I hadn't even seen him, and when he sat down I made as though I didn't notice him. He didn't seem to take any notice of me either; it was a somewhat unusu-al situation – a sort of unplanned non-meeting. I must admit I felt uncertain whether or not I wanted him to say something, and after half an hour or so I felt just as uncertain whether to leave first or wait till he had gone. Actually, it wasn't an unpleasant uncertainty – I could go on sitting there in any case. But suddenly it occurred to me for some reason or other that he had gotten an edge on me, and then my decision came easily. I stood up, looked at him for the first time and said, 'Goodbye.'

'Goodbye,' he answered, looking me straight in the eye. One couldn't find fault with his glance in any way.

I left. As I was walking away, I couldn't help wondering how he would char-acterize my gait, and suddenly I felt my body jam up and my steps turn stiff and awkward. I was annoyed, no use denying it.

That evening as I stood beneath the window looking out – there wasn't very much to see – I thought that if he came the following day I would say some-thing. I even figured out what I was going to say, how I would introduce what might turn out to be a conversation. I would wait a quarter of an hour and then I would say, without looking at him, 'It's about time we start talking.' No more, just that. Then he could answer or not answer, and if he didn't answer I would get up and say, 'In the future I would prefer that you sit on another bench.'

I also came up with many other things that evening, things I would say if a conversation should develop, but I rejected most of them as uninteresting and too commonplace.

The following morning I was excited and uncertain, even wondering whether I shouldn't stay home. I resolutely pushed aside the decision of the evening before; if I did go, I certainly wouldn't say anything.

I went, and he came. I didn't look his way. Suddenly it occurred to me how odd it was that he always came less than five minutes after I myself had turned up – as if he had been standing somewhere nearby and seen me coming. Sure, I thought, of course he lives in one of those buildings beside the firehouse, he can see me from one of the windows.

There was no time to speculate any further on this, for he suddenly began talking. I have to admit that what he said made me feel pretty uneasy.

'Excuse me,' he said, 'but if you don't mind, perhaps it's about time we start talking.'

I didn't answer right away; then I said, 'Perhaps. If there's something to say.'

'You aren't sure there's anything to say?'

'I'm probably older than you.'

'That's not impossible.'

I didn't say any more. I felt a disagreeable uneasiness, on account of the peculiar exchange of roles that had taken place. He was the one who had started the conversation, and very nearly with my own words, and it fell to me to answer as I had imagined he might answer. It was as if I could just as well be him and he just as well be me. It was disagreeable. I wanted to leave. But having, so to speak, been forced to identify with him, I found it difficult to hurt or even offend him.

A minute may have gone by before he said, 'I'm eighty-three.'

'Then I was right.'

Another minute passed.

'Do you play chess?' he asked.

'A long time ago.'

'Almost nobody plays chess any more. All those I've played chess with have died.'

'It's been at least fifteen years,' I said.

'The most recent one died last winter. No great loss actually, he didn't have his wits about him any more. I would always beat him after less than twenty moves. But he did get a certain pleasure from it, presumably the last pleasure that remained to him. Maybe you knew him.'

'No,' I said quickly, 'I didn't know him.'

'How can you be so... Well, that's your business.'

He was certainly right about that and I felt like saying so, but gave him credit for not completing his question.

Then I saw him turn his face to look at me. He sat like this for quite a while. It was anything but pleasant, so I got my eyeglasses from my coat pocket and put them on. Everything in front of me – trees, houses, benches – disappeared in a fog.

'You're nearsighted?' he said after a while.

'No,' I said, 'quite the contrary.'

'I mean – you need glasses to see what's far away.'

'No, quite the contrary. It's the things nearby I have problems with.'

'I see.'

I didn't say any more. When I noticed that he turned his face away again, I removed my glasses and put them back in my pocket. He said nothing more either, so when I thought a suitable amount of time had passed, I got up and said courteously, 'Thanks for the chat. So long.'

'So long.'

I walked away with firmer steps that day, but when I got home and had calmed down, I started again making hasty plans for my next meeting with him. Pacing the floor, I came up with many absurdities, a subtlety or two as well; I wasn't above triumphing over him a bit, but that was simply because I looked upon him as my equal, in spite of everything.

I didn't sleep well that night. When I was still young enough to believe that the future could offer surprises, it often happened that I slept poorly, but that was long ago, before it became clear to me, I mean absolutely clear, that the day you die it doesn't matter whether you've had a good or a miserable life. So the fact that I slept poorly that night both surprised and upset me. Nor had I eaten anything that could've caused it, only a couple of boiled potatoes and a tin of sardines; I had slept soundly on that many times before.

The following day he didn't come until almost a quarter of an hour had gone by. I had started giving up hope – it was an unaccustomed feeling: having a hope to give up. But then he came.

'Good morning,' he said.

'Good morning.'

Then we said nothing more for a while. I knew very well what I would say if the pause grew too long, but I preferred that he talk first, and he did.

'Your wife ... is she still alive?'

'No, she isn't, it's been a long time, I've mostly forgotten her. And yours?'

'Two years ago. Today.'

'Oh. Then it is a day of mourning of sorts.'

'Well, yes. You can't help feeling the loss, of course. But I don't celebrate it by visiting her grave, if that's what you mean. Graves are a damn nuisance. Beg pardon. I didn't choose my words very well.'

I didn't answer.

'Beg pardon,' he said, 'if I've hurt your feelings, I didn't mean it that way.'

'You haven't.'

'Good. For all I knew you might even be religious. I had a sister who believed in eternal life. What conceit!'

I was again struck by the fact that he actually sat there speaking my lines, and for a moment I was foolish enough to think that it was nothing but my imagination, that he didn't even exist, that in reality I sat there talking to myself. And it was probably this piece of folly that made me ask a completely unpremeditated question, 'Who are you really?'

Fortunately he didn't answer immediately, so I managed to edge away somewhat from a rather awkward situation.

'Don't misunderstand me. I wasn't really speaking to you. It was simply that I came to think of something.'

I noticed how he turned his face to look at me, but this time I didn't take out my glasses. I said, 'Besides, I would rather not leave the impression that I am in the habit of asking about things to which there are no answers.'

Afterward we sat in silence. It wasn't a restful silence; I would have preferred to leave. In a couple of minutes, I thought – if he hasn't said anything in two minutes I'll leave. And I began to count the seconds in my mind. He didn't say anything, and I got up, to the second. He also got up, the very same moment.

'Thanks for the chat,' I said.

'The same to you. Too bad you won't play chess.'

'I don't think you would enjoy it very much. Besides, your partners seem to be in the habit of dying.'

'Yes indeed,' he said, suddenly seeming absent-minded.

'So long,' I said.

'So long.'

That day I was more tired than usual when I got home; I had to lie down a few moments. After a while I said aloud, 'I'm old. And life is very long.'

When I woke up the next morning it was raining. To say I was disappointed would be putting it mildly. But as the day wore on and the rain didn't let up, I realized I would go to the park no matter what. I wouldn't be able not to. It wasn't important to me that he should show up as well, that wasn't the point. It was only that, if he came, I wanted to – had to – be there. As I found myself sitting on that wet bench in the rain, I even hoped he wouldn't come. There was an element of exposure, of indecency, in sitting so completely alone in a rain-soaked park.

But he came all right – didn't I know it! By contrast with me, he wore a black raincoat that reached almost to the ground. He sat down.

'You defy the weather,' he said.

It was obviously meant just as an observation, but because of what I had been thinking immediately before he turned up, it seemed to me somewhat tactless, so I didn't answer. I noticed I had become ill-humoured and that I regretted having come. Besides, I was starting to get wet and my coat felt heavy, it seemed almost ludicrous to go on sitting there, so I said, 'I just went out for some fresh air, but then I got tired. I'm an old man.'

And to forestall any speculations on his part, I added, 'Old habit, you know.'

He didn't say anything, which struck me, quite absurdly, as being provocative. And what he said finally, after a long pause, didn't make me feel any more well-disposed toward him.

'You don't like people very much, do you, or am I mistaken?'

'Like people?' I answered. 'What do you mean?'

'Well, you know, it's only the sort of thing one says. I didn't mean to be intrusive.'

'Of course I don't like people. And of course I like people. If you asked me if I liked cats or goats, or butterflies for that matter, but people. Besides, I hardly know anybody.'

I regretted my last remark at once, but luckily that was not what he latched on to.

'That was quite something,' he said. 'Goats and butterflies!'

I could hear him smiling. I had to admit I had been unduly dismissive, so I said, 'If you want a general answer to a general question, I do like both goats and butterflies more unconditionally than I like people.'

'Thanks, I got the point long ago. I'll remember to be more precise the next time I presume to ask you something.'

He said this in a friendly way, and it is no exaggeration to say that I felt sorry, even though my being difficult was simply due to my low spirits. And because I felt sorry, I said something I at once felt sorry having said, 'Beg pardon, but words are almost the only things still left to me. Beg pardon.'

'By all means. It was my fault. I ought to have considered who you are.'

My heart sank – did he know who I was? Did he come here every day because he knew who I was? I couldn't help feeling both uneasy and insecure, so much so that I acted almost automatically, sticking my hand into my coat pocket in search of my glasses.

'What do you mean?' I said. 'Do you know me?'

'Yes. If that's the right word. We have met before. I didn't realize it when I first sat down on this bench. It gradually dawned on me that I'd seen you before, I just wasn't able to place you, not till yesterday. It was something you said, and suddenly I knew what my connection with you was. You don't remember me, do you?'

I stood up.

'No.'

I looked straight at him. I was quite unaware of ever having seen him.

'I am... I was your judge.'

'You, you —'

I couldn't think of anything more to say.

'Sit down, please.'

'I'm wet. Indeed! You were... so it was you. Indeed! Well, goodbye, I have to go.'

I left. It wasn't a dignified exit, but I was upset, and I walked faster than I'd done in many years. When I got home I had barely the strength to rid myself of my soaked overcoat before tumbling into bed. I had violent palpitations, and I was firmly determined never to set foot in the park again.

But after a few moments, when my pulse functioned normally again, my thoughts began to do so as well. I accepted my reaction: something hidden had emerged into the light again and I'd been caught off guard, that was all. There was no mystery about it.

I got up from the bed. It gives me a certain satisfaction to state that I was my old self once more, completely. I planted myself underneath the window and said aloud, 'He shall see me again.'

The following day the nice weather was back, which was a relief, and my coat was practically dry. I went to the park at the usual time; he wasn't going to notice anything irregular about me, or imagine he'd got an edge on me.

But when I approached the bench he was already there, so he was the one who was behaving irregularly.

'Good morning,' he said.

'Good morning,' I answered, taking my seat, and so as to take the bull by the horns I added at once, 'I thought you might not show up today.'

'Bravo,' he said. 'Zero for you.'

That was an answer I couldn't find fault with. He was, indeed my equal.

'Did you often feel guilty?' I asked.

'I don't understand.'

'As a judge, did you often feel guilty? After all, it was your profession to assign to others the required amount of guilt.'

'It was my profession to define the law on the basis of other people's assessment of guilt.'

'Are you trying to excuse yourself? It isn't necessary.'

'I didn't feel guilty. On the other hand, I often felt at the mercy of the law's rigidity. As in your own case.'

'Yes. Because you're not superstitious, after all.'

He gave me a quick glance.

'What do you mean by that?' he said.

'It is only superstitious people who think it is a doctor's business to prolong the suffering of those who are doomed.'

'Aha, I understand. But aren't you afraid that legalization of euthanasia could be misused?'

'Of course it couldn't be misused. For then euthanasia would no longer be euthanasia but murder.'

He didn't answer; I cast a sidelong glance at him: he had a sullen, impassive expression. That was okay by me, though I didn't know whether his sullenness was due to what I had said, or whether he simply looked like that habitually; it was hard to tell, since I had practically never looked at him. Now I felt like making up for lost time and inspecting him thoroughly, and so I did, openly, turning my face and staring at his profile. It was the least I could permit myself in the presence of the man who had sentenced me to prison for several years. I even fished out my glasses and placed them on my nose. It wasn't at all necessary, I could see him clearly without, but I felt a sudden desire to provoke him. It was so unlike me to stare directly at a person that I felt alien to myself for a moment; it was a strange and not at all disagreeable sensation. And the fact that I committed this one breach of my usual behaviour turned out to be surprisingly infectious. For the first time in many years, I laughed; it must have sounded quite ugly. Anyway, without looking at me, he said in a brusque tone, 'I don't care what you're laughing at, but it doesn't sound like you're enjoying yourself. And that's a pity. For in other respects you are a sensible person.'

I immediately felt mollified, as well as a little ashamed, and I withdrew my eyes from his angry profile, saying, 'You're right. It wasn't much of a laugh.'

More than that I didn't want to give him.

We sat in silence. I thought about my wretched life and grew melancholy. I visualized the judge's home, with good chairs and big bookshelves.

'You probably have a housekeeper?' I said.

'Yes. Why do you ask about that?'

'I'm merely trying to imagine the existence of a retired judge.'

'Oh, it's nothing to brag about. You know, the inactivity, all those idle days.'

'Yes, time refuses to pass.'

'And it's the only thing that's left.'

'Time that gets to feel too slow, full of illness to boot perhaps, which slows it even more – then it's over. And when the moment finally comes, we think: what a meaningless life.'

'Well, meaningless – '

'Meaningless.'

He didn't answer. Neither of us said another word. After a while I got up; however lonely I felt, I didn't want to share my depression with him.

'Goodbye,' I said.

'Goodbye, doctor.'

Depression breeds sentimentality, and the word 'doctor,' spoken without a tinge of irony, sent a warm wave through me. I turned abruptly and hurried off. And right there and then, before I was out of the park, I knew I wanted to die. I wasn't surprised; at most I was surprised that I wasn't. All at once both my depression and my sentimentality seemed to have vanished. I slowed my pace, feeling an inward calm that called for slowness.

When I got home, still feeling a lucid calm inside me, I took out writing paper and an envelope. On the envelope I wrote: 'To the judge who sentenced me.' Then I sat down at the little table where I usually eat and began to write this story.

Today I went to the park for the last time. I was in a strange, almost audacious mood, due perhaps to the unaccustomed joy I had felt in putting my previous meetings with the judge into words or, more likely, to the fact that I hadn't wavered in my decision, not for a moment.

Today, too, he was sitting there when I came. I thought he looked troubled. I greeted him more amicably than usual, it came quite naturally to me. He gave me a quick glance, as if to ascertain whether I really meant it.

'Well,' he said, 'you're having one of your better days today?'

'I'm having my good day, yes. And you?'

'Reasonably good, thanks. So you don't believe any more that life is meaningless?'

'Oh yes, completely.'

'Hmm. I wouldn't be able to live with such a realization.'

'You're forgetting the instinct of self-preservation, aren't you? It's very tenacious and has been the bane of many a rational decision.'

He didn't answer. I hadn't intended to sit there long, so after a brief pause I said, 'We won't be seeing each other any more. Today I've come to say goodbye.'

'Is that so? What a pity. Are you going away?'

'Yes.'

'And you won't be back?'

'No.'

'Hmm. Really. I hope you won't think me too familiar when I tell you I'll miss our meetings.'

'Nice of you to say so.'

'Time will drag even more.'

'There are lonely men sitting on many other benches.'

'Oh, you don't understand what I mean. May I ask where you're going?'

Some have maintained that he who knows he's going to die within twenty-four hours feels free to do whatever he wants. It isn't true; one is, even then, incapable of acting contrary to one's nature, one's self. To be sure, giving him an open and honest answer wouldn't have been to behave contrary to my nature, but I had decided in advance not to reveal my destination to him, seeing no reason why I should upset him – he was, in spite of everything, the only person who would be bereaved by my passing, if I may say so. But what should I answer?

'You will be informed,' I said at last.

I noticed he was taken aback, but he didn't say anything. Instead he put his hand in his inside pocket and took out his wallet. After looking around in it for a moment, he held out his card to me.

'Thanks,' I said, putting it in my coat pocket. I felt I should go. I got up. He too got up. He held out his hand. I took it.

'Take care,' he said.

'Thanks, you too. Goodbye.'

'Goodbye.'

I left. I had a feeling he didn't sit down again, but I didn't turn around to check. I walked calmly homeward, thinking about nothing in particular. Something inside me was smiling. After reaching the basement I stood awhile underneath the window and looked out at the empty street, before sitting down at the table to finish this story. I'm going to put the judge's card on top of the envelope.

It's done. In a moment I'll fold the sheets and place them in the envelope. And now, just before it's going to happen, as I am about to undertake the only definitive act a human being is capable of executing, there is one thought that overshadows all the others: Why didn't I do this long ago?

Translated by Sverre Lyngstad; reprinted by permission of Norvik Press.

Language

Language

Language

T here are two official Norwegian languages: **Riksmål** or **Bokmål** (book language), a modification of the old Dano–Norwegian tongue left over from the days of Danish dominance; and **Landsmål** or **Nynorsk**, which was codified during the nineteenth-century upsurge of Norwegian nationalism and is based on rural dialects of Old Norse provenance. Roughly eighty percent of schoolchildren have *Bokmål* as their primary language, and the remaining twenty percent are *Nynorsk* speakers, concentrated in the fjord country of the west coast and the mountain districts of central Norway. Despite the best efforts of the government, *Nynorsk* is in decline – in 1944 fully one-third of the population used it. As the more common of the two languages, *Bokmål* is what we use here.

You don't really need to know any Norwegian to get by in Norway. Almost everyone speaks some English, and in any case many words are not too far removed from their English equivalents; there's also plenty of English (or American) on billboards, the TV and at the cinema. Mastering "hello" or "thank you" will, however, be greatly appreciated, while if you speak either Danish or Swedish you should have few problems being understood. Incidentally, Norwegians find Danish easier to read than Swedish, but orally it's the other way round.

Phrasebooks are fairly thin on the ground, but Berlitz's Norwegian–English version has a mini-dictionary, a useful grammar section and a menu reader, as does Dorling Kindersley's Norwegian–English phrase book. There are several **dictionaries** to choose from, all of which include pronunciation tips and so forth. The best is generally considered to be the Collins *English-Norwegian Dictionary*, though at over 1000 pages, it's not exactly lightweight. As for learning the language, the *Teach Yourself Norwegian* course, by Margaretha Danbolt Simons, is recommended and comprises tapes and books.

Pronunciation

Pronunciation can be tricky. A **vowel** is usually long when it's the final syllable or followed by only one consonant; followed by two it's generally short. Unfamiliar ones are:

ae before an r, as in b**a**d; otherwise as in s**ay**

ø as in f**u**r but without pronouncing the r

å usually as in s**aw**

øy between the ø sound and b**oy**

ei as in s**ay**

Consonants are pronounced as in English except:

c, **q**, **w**, **z** found only in foreign words and

pronounced as in the original language

g before i, y or ei, as in **y**et; otherwise hard

hv as in **v**iew

j, **gj**, **hj**, **lj** as in **y**et

rs almost always as in **sh**ut

k before i, y or j, like the Scottish lo**ch**; otherwise hard

sj, **sk** before i, y, ø or øy, as in **sh**ut

Words and phrases

Basic phrases

do you speak English? – **snakker du engelsk?**

yes – **ja**

no – **nei**

do you understand? – **forstår du?**

I don't understand – **jeg forstår ikke**

I understand – **jeg forstår**

please – **vær så god** (is near enough, though there's no direct equivalent).

thank you (very much) – **takk (tusen takk)**

you're welcome – **vær så god**

excuse me – **unnskyld**

good morning – **god morgen**

good afternoon – **god dag**

good night – **god natt**

goodbye – **adjø**

today – **i dag**

tomorrow – **i morgen**

day after tomorrow – **i overmorgen**

in the morning – **om morgenen**

in the afternoon – **om ettermiddagen**

in the evening – **om kvelden**

Some signs

entrance – **inngang**

exit – **utgang**

gentlemen – **herrer/menn**

ladies – **damer/kvinner**

open – **åpen**

closed – **stengt**

arrival – **ankomst**

police – **politi**

hospital – **sykehus**

cycle path – **sykkelsti**

no smoking – **røyking forbudt**

no camping – **camping forbudt**

no trespassing – **uvedkommende forbudt**

no entry – **ingen adgang**

pull/push – **trekk/trykk**

departure – **avgang**

parking fees – **avgift**

Questions and directions

where? (where is/are?) – **hvor? (hvor er?)**

when? – **når?**

what? – **hva?**

how much/many? – **hvor mye/hvor mange?**

why? – **hvorfor?**

which? – **hvilket?**

what's that called in Norwegian? – **hva kaller man det på norsk?**

can you direct me to ...? – **kan de vise meg veien til ...?**

it is/there is (is it/is there) – **det er (er det?)**

what time is it? – **hvor mange er klokken?**

big/small – **stor/liten**

cheap/expensive – **billig/dyrt**

early/late – **tidlig/sent**

hot/cold – **varm/kald**

near/far – **i nærheten/langt borte**

good/bad – **god/dårlig**

vacant/occupied – **ledig/opptatt**

a little/a lot – **litt/mye**

more/less – **mer/mindre**

can we camp here? – **kan vi campe her?**

is there a youth hostel near here? – **er det et vandrerhjem i nærheten?**

how do I get to ...? – **hvordan kommer jeg til ...?**

how far is it to ...? – **hvor langt er det til ...?**

ticket – **billett**

single/return – **en vei/tur-retur**

can you give me a lift to ...? – **kan jeg få sitte på til ...?**

left/right – **venstre/høyre**

go straight ahead – **kjør rett frem**

Numbers

0 – **null**	17 – **sytten**
1 – **en**	18 – **atten**
2 – **to**	19 – **nitten**
3 – **tre**	20 – **tjue**
4 – **fire**	21 – **tjueen**
5 – **fem**	22 – **tjueto**
6 – **seks**	30 – **tretti**
7 – **sju**	40 – **førti**
8 – **åtte**	50 – **femti**
9 – **ni**	60 – **seksti**
10 – **ti**	70 – **sytti**
11 – **elleve**	80 – **åtti**
12 – **tolv**	90 – **nitti**
13 – **tretten**	100 – **hundre**
14 – **fjorten**	101 – **hundreogen**
15 – **femten**	200 – **to hundre**
16 – **seksten**	1000 – **tusen**

Days and months

Sunday – **søndag**	April – **april**
Monday – **mandag**	May – **mai**
Tuesday – **tirsdag**	June – **juni**
Wednesday – **onsdag**	July – **juli**
Thursday – **torsdag**	August – **august**
Friday – **fredag**	September – **september**
Saturday – **lørdag**	October – **oktober**
January – **januar**	November – **november**
February – **februar**	December – **desember**
March – **mars**	(Note: days and months are never capitalized)

Food and drink terms

Basics and snacks

appelsin, marmelade – marmalade	**melk** – milk
brød – bread	**mineralvann** – mineral water
eddik – vinegar	**nøtter** – nuts
egg – egg	**olje** – oil
eggerøre – scrambled eggs	**omelett** – omelette
flatbrød – crispbread	**ost** – cheese
fløte – cream	**pannekake** – pancakes
grøt – porridge	**pepper** – pepper
iskrem – ice cream	**potetchips** – crisps (potato chips)
kaffefløte – single cream for coffee	**pommes-frites** – chips (French fries)
kake – cake	**ris** – rice
kaviar – caviar	**rundstykker** – bread roll
kjeks – biscuits	**salat** – salad
krem – whipped cream	**salt** – salt

sennep – mustard
smør – butter
smørbrød – open sandwich
sukker – sugar

suppe – soup
syltetøy – jam
varm pølse – hot dog
yoghurt – yoghurt

Meat (kjøtt) and game (vilt)

dyrestek – venison
elg – elk
kalkun – turkey
kjøttboller – meatballs
kjøttkaker – rissoles
kylling – chicken
lammekjøtt – lamb
lever – liver
oksekjøtt – beef

postei – pâté
pølser – sausages
reinsdyr – reindeer
ribbe – pork rib
skinke – ham
spekemat – dried meat
stek – steak
svinekjøtt – pork
varm pølse – frankfurter/hot-dog

Fish (fisk) and shellfish (skalldyr)

ansjos – anchovies (brisling)
blåskjell – mussels
brisling – sprats
hummer – lobster
hvitting – whiting
kaviar – caviar
krabbe – crab
kreps – crayfish
laks – salmon
makrell – mackerel
piggvar – turbot
reker – shrimps

rødspette – plaice
røkelaks – smoked salmon
sardiner – sardines (brisling)
sei – coalfish
sild – herring
sjøtunge – sole
småfisk – whitebait
steinbit – catfish
torsk – cod
tunfisk – tuna
ørret – trout
ål – eel

Vegetables (grønsaker)

agurk – cucumber/gherkin/pickle
blomkål – cauliflower
bønner – beans
erter – peas
gulrøtter – carrots
hodesalat – lettuce
hvitløk – garlic
kål – cabbage
linser – lentils
løk – onion

mais – sweetcorn
nepe – turnip
paprika – peppers
poteter – potatoes
rosenkål – Brussels sprouts
selleri – celery
sopp – mushrooms
spinat – spinach
tomater – tomatoes

Fruit (frukt)

ananas – pineapple
appelsin – orange
aprikos – apricot
banan – banana
blåbær – blueberries

druer – grapes
eple – apple
fersken – peach
fruktsalat – fruit salad
grapefrukt – grapefruit

jordbær – strawberries
multer – cloudberries
plommer – plums
pærer – pears

sitron – lemon
solbær – blackcurrants
tyttbær – cranberries

Cooking terms

blodig – rare, underdone
godt stekt – well done
grillet – grilled
grytestekt – braised
kokt – boiled
marinert – marinated
ovnstekt – baked/roasted

røkt – smoked
stekt – fried
stuet – stewed
sur – sour, pickled
syltet – pickled
saltet – cured

Norwegian specialities

brun saus – gravy served with most meats, rissoles, fishcakes and sausages
fenalår – marinated mutton, smoked, sliced, salted, dried and served with crispbread, scrambled egg and beer
fiskeboller – fish balls, served under a white sauce or on open sandwiches
fiskekabaret – shrimps, fish and vegetables in aspic
fiskesuppe – fish soup
flatbrød – a flat unleavened cracker, half barley, half wheat
gammelost – a hard, strong smelling, yellow-brown cheese with veins
geitost/gjetost – goat's cheese, slightly sweet and fudge-coloured. Similar cheeses have different ratios of goat's milk to cow's milk
gravetlaks – salmon marinated in salt, sugar, dill and brandy
juleskinke – marinated boiled ham, served at Christmas
kjøttkaker med surkål – homemade burgers with cabbage and a sweet and sour sauce
koldtbord – a midday buffet with cold meats, herrings, salads, bread and perhaps soup, eggs or hot meats

lapskaus – pork, venison (or other meats) and vegetable stew, common in the south and east, using salted or fresh meat, or left-overs, in a thick brown gravy
lutefisk – fish (usually cod) preserved in an alkali solution and seasoned; an acquired taste
multer – cloudberries – wild berries (med krem) mostly found north of the Arctic Circle and served with cream
mysost – brown whey cheese, made from cow's milk
nedlagtsild – marinated herring
pinnekjøtt – western Norwegian Christmas dish of smoked mutton steamed over shredded birch bark, served with cabbage; or accompanied by boiled potatoes and mashed swedes (kålrabistappe)
reinsdyrstek – reindeer steak, usually served with boiled potatoes and cranberry sauce
rekesalat – shrimp salad in mayonnaise
ribbe, julepølse – eastern Norwegian Christmas medisterkake dish of pork ribs, sausage and dumplings
spekemat – various types of smoked, dried meat
Trondhjemsuppea – kind of milk broth with raisins, rice, cinnamon and sugar

Bread, cake and desserts

bløtkake – cream cake with fruit
fløtelapper – pancakes made with cream, served with sugar and jam
havrekjeks – oatmeal biscuits, eaten with

goat's cheese
knekkebrød – crispbread
kransekake – cake made from almonds, sugar and eggs, served at celebrations

lomper – potato scones-cum-tortillas

riskrem – rice pudding with whipped cream and sugar, usually served with *frukt saus*, a slighly thickened fruit sauce

tilsløtbondepiker - stewed apples and

bread-crumbs, served with cream

trollkrem – beaten egg whites (or whipped cream) and sugar mixed with cloudberries (or cranberries)

vafle - waffles

Drinks

akevitt – aquavit
appelsin – orange squash
saft/juice – juice
brus – fizzy soft drink
eplesider – cider
fruktsaft – sweetened fruit juice
kaffe – coffee
melk – milk
mineralvann – mineral water
øl – beer
sitronbrus – lemonade

te med melk/sitron – tea with milk/lemon
vann – water
varm sjokolade – hot chocolate
vin – wine
søt – sweet
tørr – dry
rød – red
hvit – white
rosé – rosé
skål – cheers

Glossary

Apotek Chemist.
Bakke Hill.
Bokhandel Bookshop.
Bre Glacier.
Bro/bru Bridge.
Brygge Quay or wharf.
Dal Valley/dale.
DNT (Den Norske Turistforening) Nationwide hiking organization whose local affiliates maintain hiking paths across almost all the country.
Domkirke Cathedral.
Drosje Taxi.
E.kr AD.
Elv/bekk River/stream.
Ferje/ferge Ferry.
Fjell/berg Mountain.
Flybussen Airport bus (literally "plane bus").
F.kr BC.
Foss Waterfall.
Gågate Urban pedestrianized area.
Gate (gt.) Street.
Gamle byen Literally "Old Town"; used wherever the old part of town has remained distinct from the rest (eg Fredrikstad, p.117). Also spelt as one word.
Hav Ocean.
Havn Harbour.

Hurtigbåt Passenger express boat; usually a catamaran.
Hurtigrute Literally "quick route", but familiar as the name of the boat service along the west coast from Bergen to Kirkenes.
Hytte Cottage, cabin.
Innsjø Lake.
Jernbanestasjon Railway station.
Kirke/kjerke Church.
Kfum/kfuk Norwegian YMCA/YWCA.
Klokken/kl. O'clock.
Klippfisk Salted whitefish, usually cod.
Moderasjon Discount or price reduction.
Moms or mva Sales tax – applied to almost all consumables.
Museet Museum.
NAF Nationwide Norwegian automobile association. Membership covers rescue and repair.
NORTRA Government agency, partly privatized, responsible for producing much tourist literature and a series of books on various aspects of Norway – from fishing through to motoring.
Rabatt Discount or price reduction.
Rådhus Town hall.
Rorbu Originally a simple wooden cabin built near the fishing grounds for incoming (ie

non-local) fishermen. Many cabins are now used as tourist accommodation.

Sami Formerly called Lapps, the Sami inhabit the northern reaches of Norway, Finland and Sweden – Lapland.

Sentrum City or town centre.

Sjø Sea.

Sjøhus Harbourside building where the catch was sorted, salted, filleted and iced. Many are now redundant and some have been turned into tourist accommodation.

Skog Forest.

Slott Castle, palace.

Stavkirke Stave church.

Storting Parliament.

Tilbud Special offer.

Torget Main town square, often home to an outdoor market; sometimes spelt Torvet.

Vandrerhjem Youth hostel.

Vann/vatn Water or lake.

Vei/veg/vn. Road.

Øy/øya Islet.

Art and architectural terms

Ambulatory Covered passage around the outer edge of the choir in the chancel of a church.

Art Deco Geometrical style of art and architecture popular in the 1930s.

Art Nouveau Style of art, architecture and design based on highly stylized vegetal forms. Popular in the early part of the twentieth century.

Baroque The art and architecture of the Counter-Reformation, dating from around 1600 onwards, and distinguished by extreme ornateness, exuberance and complex but harmonious spatial arrangement of interiors.

Classical Architectural style incorporating Greek and Roman elements – pillars, domes, colonnades, etc – at its height in the seventeenth century and revived, as Neoclassical, in the nineteenth century.

Fresco Wall painting – made durable through applying paint to wet plaster.

Gothic Architectural style of the thirteenth to sixteenth centuries, characterized by pointed arches, rib vaulting, flying buttresses and a general emphasis on vertical lines.

Misericord Ledge on choir stall on which occupant can be supported while standing;

often carved with secular subjects (bottoms were not thought worthy of religious ones).

Nave Main body of a church.

Neoclassical Architectural style derived from Greek and Roman elements – pillars, domes, colonnades, etc – popular in Norway throughout the nineteenth century.

Renaissance Movement in art and architecture developed in fifteenth-century Italy.

Rococo Highly florid, light and graceful eighteenth-century style of architecture, painting and interior design, forming the last phase of Baroque.

Rood screen Decorative screen separating the nave from the chancel.

Romanesque Early medieval architecture distinguished by squat forms, rounded arches and naive sculpture.

Stucco Marble-based plaster used to embellish ceilings, etc.

Transept Arms of a cross-shaped church, placed at ninety degrees to nave and chancel.

Triptych Carved or painted work on three panels. Often used as an altarpiece.

Vault An arched ceiling or roof.

Index

and small print

Index

Maps entries are in **colour**

INDEX

Twenty Years of Rough Guides

In the summer of 1981, Mark Ellingham, Rough Guides' founder, knocked out the first guide on a typewriter, with a group of friends. Mark had been travelling in Greece after university, and couldn't find a guidebook that really answered his needs.There were heavyweight cultural guides on the one hand – good on museums and classical sites but not on beaches and tavernas – and on the other hand student manuals that were so caught up with how to save money that they lost sight of the country's significance beyond its role as a place for a cool vacation. None of the guides began to address Greece as a country, with its natural and human environment, its politics and its contemporary life.

Having no urgent reason to return home, Mark decided to write his own guide. It was a guide to Greece that tried to combine some erudition and insight with a thoroughly practical approach to travellers' needs. Scrupulously researched listings of places to stay, eat and drink were matched by careful attention to detail on everything from Homer to Greek music, from classical sites to national parks and from nude beaches to monasteries. Back in London, Mark and his friends got their Rough Guide accepted by a farsighted commissioning editor at the publisher Routledge and it came out in 1982.

The Rough Guide to Greece was a student scheme that became a publishing phenomenon. The immediate success of the book – shortlisted for the Thomas Cook award – spawned a series that rapidly covered dozens of countries. The Rough Guides found a ready market among backpackers and budget travellers, but soon acquired a much broader readership that included older and less impecunious visitors. Readers relished the guides' wit and inquisitiveness as much as the enthusiastic, critical approach that acknowledges everyone wants value for money – but not at any price.

Rough Guides soon began supplementing the "rougher" information – the hostel and low-budget listings – with the kind of detail that independent-minded travellers on any budget might expect. These days, the guides – distributed worldwide by the Penguin group – include recommendations spanning the range from shoestring to luxury, and cover more than 200 destinations around the globe. Our growing team of authors, many of whom come to Rough Guides initially as outstandingly good letter-writers telling us about their travels, are spread all over the world, particularly in Europe, the USA and Australia. As well as the travel guides, Rough Guides publishes a series of dictionary phrasebooks covering two dozen major languages, an acclaimed series of music guides running the gamut from Classical to World Music, a series of music CDs in association with World Music Network, and a range of reference books on topics as diverse as the Internet, Pregnancy and Unexplained Phenomena. Visit **www.roughguides.com** to see what's cooking.

Rough Guide credits

Text editor: Amanda Tomlin
Series editor: Mark Ellingham
Editorial: Martin Dunford, Jonathan Buckley, Kate Berens, Ann-Marie Shaw, Helena Smith, Olivia Swift, Ruth Blackmore, Geoff Howard, Claire Saunders, Gavin Thomas, Alexander Mark Rogers, Polly Thomas, Joe Staines, Richard Lim, Duncan Clark, Peter Buckley, Lucy Ratcliffe, Clifton Wilkinson, Alison Murchie, Matthew Teller, Andrew Dickson, Fran Sandham, Sally Schafer, Matthew Milton, Karoline Densley (UK); Andrew Rosenberg, Yuki Takagaki, Richard Koss, Hunter Slaton (US)
Production: Link Hall, Helen Prior, Julia Bovis, Katie Pringle, Rachel Holmes, Andy Turner, Dan May, Tanya Hall, John McKay,

Sophie Hewat
Cartography: Maxine Repath, Melissa Baker, Ed Wright, Katie Lloyd-Jones
Cover art direction: Louise Boulton
Picture research: Sharon Martins, Mark Thomas
Online: Kelly Martinez, Anja Mutic-Blessing, Jennifer Gold, Audra Epstein, Suzanne Welles, Cree Lawson (US)
Finance: Gary Singh
Marketing & Publicity: Richard Trillo, Niki Smith, David Wearn, Chloë Roberts, Demelza Dallow, Claire Southern (UK); Simon Carloss, David Wechsler, Megan Kennedy (US)
Administration: Julie Sanderson

Publishing information

This third edition published May 2003 by
Rough Guides Ltd,
80 Strand, London WC2R 0RL.
345 Hudson St, 4th Floor,
New York, NY 10014, USA.
Distributed by the Penguin Group
Penguin Books Ltd,
80 Strand, London WC2R 0RL
Penguin Putnam, Inc.
375 Hudson Street, NY 10014, USA
Penguin Books Australia Ltd,
487 Maroondah Highway, PO Box 257,
Ringwood, Victoria 3134, Australia
Penguin Books Canada Ltd,
10 Alcorn Avenue, Toronto, Ontario,
Canada M4V 1E4
Penguin Books (NZ) Ltd,
182–190 Wairau Road, Auckland 10,
New Zealand
Typeset in Bembo and Helvetica to an
original design by Henry Iles.

Printed in China

© Phil Lee 2003

472pp includes index
A catalogue record for this book is available from the British Library

ISBN 1-84353-054-6

3 5 7 9 8 6 4

Help us update

We've gone to a lot of effort to ensure that the third edition of **The Rough Guide to Norway** is accurate and up-to-date. However, things change – places get "discovered", opening hours are notoriously fickle, restaurants and rooms raise prices or lower standards. If you feel we've got it wrong or left something out, we'd like to know, and if you can remember the address, the price, the time, the phone number, so much the better.

We'll credit all contributions, and send a copy of the next edition (or any other Rough Guide if you prefer) for the best letters. Everyone who writes to us and isn't already a subscriber will receive a copy of our full-colour thrice-yearly newsletter. Please mark letters: "**Rough Guide Norway Update**" and send to: Rough Guides, 80 Strand, London WC2R 0RL, or Rough Guides, 4th Floor, 345 Hudson St, New York, NY 10014. Or send an email to **mail@roughguides.com**

Have your questions answered and tell others about your trip at **www.roughguides.atinfopop.com**

Acknowledgements

The author's thanks go to the Norwegian Tourist Board in London for their efficient assistance, and to Norvik Press for permission to print three literary extracts from their publication list. Special thanks also to my patient and persevering editor, Amanda Tomlin, and to Jayne Varnam for helping me out in emergencies.

Readers' letters

Thanks to all the following for their letters and emails: John Brandham; Fiona Brooks-Wood; Robert Brown; Chris Burin; T Chadwick; Chanin Changtor; Christian Clough; Lawrence Cotter; Daphne Cronin; Trond Deetjen; Fabian Dollbaum; Jeff Eastmead; Jenni Ellis; Chris & Florence Ewels; Lawrence Flowers; Claudia Froldi; Nicky Griffin; Stuart Hicks; Andrew Hickson; Jason Hsu; Vince Hunt; Joachim Larsen; Marcus Lodwick & Sarah Simnett; Jeffrey Mahn; Marlies Morsink; Peter Ogunremi; PL Pounds; Gareth Rees; John Reeves; C Roberts; Ann Robinson & Andrew Wintersgill; Helena Romao; Errol Russell; Nikolaj Sorensen; Andrew Straw; Jill Truman; Esther Vollebregt; Dave Walden; Jennie Want; and David Watson.

Photo credits

Cover

Main front picture Bergen ©Imagestate
Front small top picture Vigeland Sculpture ©Park Robert Harding
Front small lower picture ©Getty
Back top cover picture Lyngenfjord ©Pictor
Back lower picture Geiranger ©Getty

Colour introduction

The Midnight Sun, Finnmark/Lappland ©Greg Evans
Glacier climbing tour, Briksdalsbreen Glacier, Western Fjords ©Gavin Hellier/Robert Harding
Moccasins, Finnmark/Lappland ©Greg Evans
Cross country skiing, Geilo Ski Resort ©H.Elton/Axiom
Puffin with fish in beak ©Per Eide/NTR
Norwegian National Day, Oslo ©Gavin Hellier/Robert Harding
Roald Amundsen ©Corbis
Shellfish, Bergen Fish Market, Bergen ©Sophie Molins/Hutchison Library
Sami Easter festival ©Tiziani & Gianni Baldizzone/Corbis
Bartender serving Aquavit ©Bo Zaunders/Corbis
Aurlandsfjord, Western Fjords ©Gavin Hellier/Robert Harding
Traditional fishing trawler, Tysfjord ©Dominic Harcourt-Webster/Robert Harding
Air-dried fish ©Phil Lee
Near Harstad ©Leslie Garland/Travel Ink
Aurora Borealis, Narvik, Arctic Norway ©Dominic Harcourt-Webster/Robert Harding
Reflections in the fjord, Nystolen, Jostedalsbreen ©Chris Coe/Axiom

Things not to miss

01 Bearded seal on ice, Svalbard, Arctic ©L. Murray/Robert Harding
02 Flåm mountain railway, west coast Norway ©Chris Coe/Axiom
03 *The Scream* by Edvard Munch ©Burstien Collection/Corbis/DACS
04 The Oseberg Ship, Viking Ships Museum, Oslo ©Greg Evans
05 View over the city from Mount Ulkriken, Bergen ©Robert Harding/Digital Vision
06 Mandal, Norway's best beach, Sjøsanden ©Phil Lee
07 Landscape reflection, Svalbard ©N. Price/Trip
08 Kjerringøy trading station with boat ©Espen Mortensen/Destinations Bodø
09 Art Nouveau in Alesund ©Phil Lee
10 Henningsvær ©Terje Rakke/NTR
11 Hjørundfjord ©Phil Lee
12 *Union Hotel*, Øye ©Phil Lee
13 Swimming in the Oslofjord ©Paul A. Souders/Corbis
14 The Vigeland sculpture park, Oslo ©Greg Evans
15 The Norwegian Fishing Village Museum at Å in winter ©Stig Einarsen/Lofoten Fotogalleri
16 View of the Geirangerfjord ©E. Simanor/Robert Harding
17 View over the Jotunheimen region ©A.Tovy/Trip
18 Whale-watching ©Staffan Widstrand/Corbis
19 Nidaros Cathedral, Trondheim, Sor Trondelag ©Greg Evans
20 Jostedalsbreen glacier flowing into fjord, Norway ©Chris Coe/Axiom
21 Viking carving, Urnes Stave Church ©Phil Lee
22 Edvard Greig's house, Troldhaugen,

Bergen ©Robert Harding Picture Library
23 Rock carvings, Alta ©Phil Lee
24 Midnight Sun at Nordkapp ©Trym Ivar
Bergsmo/Samfoto/NTR
25 The seabird colony on Værøy in the
Lofotens ©Stig Einarsen/Lofoten Fotogalleri

Black and white photos

Vigeland's sculpture of mother and son
©Michael Jenner
Constitution Day, Royal Palace, Oslo, ©Gavin
Hellier/Robert Harding
Preikestolen near Stavanger, views over the
Lysefjord ©Frithjof Fure/NTR
Gamle Stavanger ©D. Saunders/Trip

Stave church, Borgund ©Gavin Hellier/Robert
Harding
Fish market, Bergen ©Robert Harding Picture
Library
View over Alesund ©John G. Egan/Hutchison
Library
Performance at the Stiklestad National
Cultural Centre ©Ted Spiegel/Corbis
Whale watching ©Pagani Flavio/Corbis
Sygma
Honningsvåg, Nordkapp ©Gavin
Hellier/Robert Harding
Reindeer on a hillside ©Greg Evans
The Hurtigrute MS Finnmarken near
Vesteralen ©Ove Aalo/OVDS

stay in touch

roughnews

Rough Guides' FREE full-colour newsletter

News, travel issues, music reviews, readers' letters and the latest dispatches from authors on the road

If you would like to receive roughnews, please send us your name and address:

Rough Guides, 80 Strand,
London WC2R 0RL, UK

Rough Guides, 4th Floor, 345 Hudson St,
New York NY10014, USA

newslettersubs@roughguides.co.uk

• TRAVEL • MUSIC • REFERENCE • PHRASEBOOKS •

Rough Guides travel

Rough Guides publishes new books every month.

Music

Acoustic Guitar
Blues: 100 Essential CDs
Cello
Clarinet
Classical Music
Classical Music: 100 Essential CDs
Country Music
Country: 100 Essential CDs
Cuban Music
Drum'n'bass
Drums
Electric Guitar & Bass Guitar
Flute
Hip-Hop
House
Irish Music
Jazz
Jazz: 100 Essential CDs
Keyboards & Digital Piano
Latin: 100 Essential CDs
Music USA: a Coast-To-Coast Tour
Opera
Opera: 100 Essential CDs
Piano
Reading Music
Reggae
Reggae: 100 Essential CDs
Rock
Rock: 100 Essential CDs
Saxophone
Soul: 100 Essential CDs
Techno
Trumpet & Trombone
Violin & Viola
World Music: 100 Essential CDs

World Music Vol1
World Music Vol2

Reference

Children's Books, 0–5
Children's Books, 5–11
China Chronicle
Cult Movies
Cult TV
Elvis
England Chronicle
France Chronicle
India Chronicle
The Internet
Internet Radio
James Bond
Liverpool FC
Man Utd
Money Online
Personal Computers
Pregnancy & Birth
Shopping Online
Travel Health
Travel Online
Unexplained Phenomena
Videogaming
Weather
Website Directory
Women Travel

Music CDs

Africa
Afrocuba
Afro-Peru
Ali Hussan Kuban
The Alps
Americana
The Andes
The Appalachians
Arabesque
Asian Underground
Australian Aboriginal Music
Bellydance
Bhangra
Bluegrass

Bollywood
Boogaloo
Brazil
Cajun
Cajun and Zydeco
Calypso and Soca
Cape Verde
Central America
Classic Jazz
Congolese Soukous
Cuba
Cuban Music Story
Cuban Son
Cumbia
Delta Blues
Eastern Europe
English Roots Music
Flamenco
Franco
Gospel
Global Dance
Greece
The Gypsies
Haiti
Hawaii
The Himalayas
Hip Hop
Hungary
India
India and Pakistan
Indian Ocean
Indonesia
Irish Folk
Irish Music
Italy
Jamaica
Japan
Kenya and Tanzania
Klezmer
Louisiana
Lucky Dube
Mali and Guinea
Marrabenta Mozambique
Merengue & Bachata
Mexico
Native American Music
Nigeria and Ghana
North Africa

Nusrat Fateh Ali Khan
Okinawa
Paris Café Music
Portugal
Rai
Reggae
Salsa
Salsa Dance
Samba
Scandinavia
Scottish Folk
Scottish Music
Senegal & The Gambia
Ska
Soul Brothers
South Africa
South African Gospel
South African Jazz
Spain
Sufi Music
Tango
Thailand
Tex-Mex
Wales
West African Music
World Music Vol 1: Africa, Europe and the Middle East
World Music Vol 2: Latin & North America, Caribbean, India, Asia and Pacific
World Roots
Youssou N'Dour & Etoile de Dakar
Zimbabwe

Rough Guides music, reference & CDs

Rough Guide Reference

cultmovies
THE ROUGH GUIDE TO
THE GOOD, THE BAD AND THE VERY WEIRD INDEED

Man Utd
2001–02 SEASON
Jim White & Andy Mitten
An UNOFFICIAL GUIDE in association with 'UNITED WE STAND'

Videogaming
THE ROUGH GUIDE TO

the soundest,
sanest, wittiest
advice you'll
ever get

THE ROUGH GUIDE TO
Pregnancy
and birth
KAZ COOKE

Unexplained
Phenomena
A ROUGH GUIDE SPECIAL
Mysteries and Curiosities of Science, Folklore and Superstition
Bob Rickard and John Michell

Children's Books 0–5 years
THE ROUGH GUIDE TO
Nicholas Tucker

Children's Books 5–11 years
THE ROUGH GUIDE TO
Nicholas Tucker

Elvis
THE ROUGH GUIDE TO
THE MAN • THE MUSIC • THE MOVIES • THE MYTH Paul Simpson

Pocket History Series

England
The Rough Guide Chronicle

China
The Rough Guide Chronicle
JUSTIN WINTLE

India
The Rough Guide Chronicle

France
The Rough Guide Chronicle
IAN LITTLEWOOD

"Solidly written, immaculately researched, Rough Guides
are as near as modern guides get to essential"
Sunday Times, London

www.roughguides.com

Music Reference Guides

CD Guides

Mini Guides

"The Rough Guides are near-perfect reference works"
Philadelphia Inquirer

www.roughguides.com

Rough Guide Music Guides

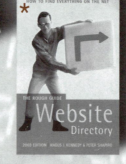

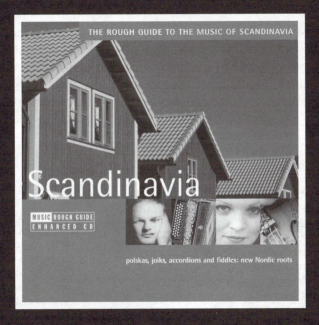

The ideas expressed in this code were developed by and for independent travellers.

Learn About The Country You're Visiting

Start enjoying your travels before you leave by tapping into as many sources of information as you can.

The Cost Of Your Holiday

Think about where your money goes - be fair and realistic about how cheaply you travel. Try and put money into local peoples' hands; drink local beer or fruit juice rather than imported brands and stay in locally owned accommodation. Haggle with humour and not aggressively. Pay what something is worth to you and remember how wealthy you are compared to local people.

Embrace The Local Culture

Open your mind to new cultures and traditions - it will transform your experience. Think carefully about what's appropriate in terms of your clothes and the way you behave. You'll earn respect and be more readily welcomed by local people. Respect local laws and attitudes towards drugs and alcohol that vary in different countries and communities. Think about the impact you could have on them.

Exploring The World – The Travellers' Code

Being sensitive to these ideas means getting more out of your travels - and giving more back to the people you meet and the places you visit.

Minimise Your Environmental Impact

Think about what happens to your rubbish - take biodegradable products and a water filter bottle. Be sensitive to limited resources like water, fuel and electricity. Help preserve local wildlife and habitats by respecting local rules and regulations, such as sticking to footpaths and not standing on coral.

Don't Rely On Guidebooks

Use your guidebook as a starting point, not the only source of information. Talk to local people, then discover your own adventure!

Be Discreet With Photography

Don't treat people as part of the landscape, they may not want their picture taken. Ask first and respect their wishes.

We work with people the world over to promote tourism that benefits their communities, but we can only carry on our work with the support of people like you. For membership details or to find out how to make your travels work for local people and the environment, visit our website.

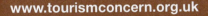
www.tourismconcern.org.uk

Tourism Concern
Campaigning for Ethical and Fairly Traded Tourism